VORWORT

Focus on Success – 5th edition: Ausgabe Wirtschaft ist konzipiert für Lernende an Fachoberschulen und Berufskollegs. Es setzt Englischkenntnisse auf dem Niveau des mittleren Abschlusses voraus und bereitet auf die neuesten Prüfungen zur Erlangung der Fachhochschulreife vor. Das Lehrwerk führt zur Stufe B2 des Gemeinsamen europäischen Referenzrahmens.

Focus on Success – 5th edition: Ausgabe Wirtschaft ist ein komplett neu erarbeitetes Lehrwerk und bietet neue, interessante Texte, aktuelle Themen und einen auf den Lehrplan und Prüfungen abgestimmten Aufgabenapparat.

Das Lehrwerk beinhaltet alles, was Sie für einen erfolgreichen Englischunterricht benötigen:

- 4 *Foundation Course*-Units, in denen Grundkenntnisse, inklusive Grammatik, Wortschatz und Methodenkompetenzen, aufgefrischt werden können.
- 8 *Main Course*-Units, die einheitlich aufgebaut sind:
  - *Focus*: Der Einstieg ins Thema – bildgesteuert, anregend und motivierend.
  - *Text A und Text B*: zwei lange Abschnitte, in denen das Thema der Unit von verschiedenen Blickwinkeln beleuchtet wird.
  - *Business options*: Zusatzmaterialien zur Erweiterung und individuellen Schwerpunktsetzung aus einem wirtschaftlichen Blickwinkel.
- 4 *Exam preparation*-Units, die jeweils 3 Themenbereiche mit längeren Texten beinhalten.
- 4 *Job skills*-Units, die auf das Berufsleben vorbereiten und relevante Fertigkeiten und Sprache einführen und üben.
- 12 *Business topics*, die unterschiedliche Themen aus der Wirtschaft betrachten. Dabei spielen abwechslungsreiche Textsorten und praxisrelevante Themen eine wichtige Rolle.

Die Übungen, die auf die Texte folgen, schulen eine Vielzahl von *Skills* (mit Hilfe von *Building skills*-Kästen, die die Fertigkeiten einführen und aufbauen, und *Skills checklists*, die die Kenntnisse immer wieder auffrischen) sowie Wortschatz (*Working with words*) und Grammatikkenntnisse (*Getting it right*). Sie trainieren darüber hinaus gezielt alle Aufgabentypen, die in der Abschlussprüfung vorkommen.

Jede Unit enthält auch differenzierte Übungen, die die unterschiedlichen Lernniveaus ansprechen. ⊙ kennzeichnet eine einfachere Übung und ● eine Übung mit mehr Herausforderung.

Außerdem enthält der Anhang eine Fülle an Referenz- und Übungsmaterial:

- Die *Skills files* bieten einen Leitfaden zu Strategien, um das Lernen effektiver zu gestalten, plus Übungsmaterialien dazu, und fördern somit das selbstständige Lernen. Anhand der Webcodes (auf www.cornelsen.de/webcodes zu finden) kann man die Hörtexte der *Skills files* unabhängig von der Audio-CD hören und die Lösungen selbst kontrollieren.
- Die *Grammar files* enthalten neben ausführlichen Grammatikerklärungen auch zusätzliches Übungsmaterial zur Vertiefung der neu gewonnenen Kenntnisse.
- Die Wörterverzeichnisse umfassen eine *Unit word list* mit allen neuen Wörtern in chronologischer Reihenfolge und eine *A–Z word list* mit allen neuen Wörtern in alphabetischer Reihenfolge. Eine thematisch geordnete *Basic word list* steht darüber hinaus zum kostenlosen Download zur Verfügung.

Wir hoffen, dass Ihnen die Arbeit mit **Focus on Success – 5th edition: Ausgabe Wirtschaft** Freude bereitet und das Lehrwerk zu einem gelungenen und erfolgreichen Unterricht beiträgt.

Die Autoren und der Verlag

CONTENTS

FOUNDATION COURSE

Page	Unit	Title/Themes	Grammar	Skills
6	1	The cult of celebrity	Position of adverbs of time ▪ Simple present ▪ Present progressive	Predicting what the text will be about ▪ Preparing to listen
12	2	The world of sport	Simple past ▪ Present perfect ▪ Pronouns ▪ Possessive adjectives	Taking notes while reading ▪ Taking notes while listening
18	3	Fashion and brand power	Adjectives ▪ Adverbs of manner ▪ Comparison of adjectives and adverbs	Learning phrases for discussion ▪ Preparing for group discussions
25	4	Leisure and free time	*Will* future ▪ *Going to* future ▪ Countable and uncountable nouns ▪ Quantifiers	Describing cartoons ▪ Written mediation
31		**Job skills 1:** Emails ▪ telephoning		

MAIN COURSE

Page	Unit	Title/Themes	Grammar	Skills	Business options
35	5	The virtual world A: Using social media B: Unwanted guests	Simple past ▪ Present perfect	Skimming a text ▪ Dealing with unknown words	Shopping from the couch
45	6	Advertising A: New ideas in advertising B: Creating a brand	*Will* future ▪ *Going to* future	Giving a presentation ▪ Scanning a text for specific information ▪ Describing graphs and bar charts	Products have lives too!
55	7	Family and beyond A: Living in a family B: Leaving home	Relative clauses ▪ Simple past ▪ Past progressive	Taking notes while reading ▪ Taking notes while listening	Companies just want to get to know *you*
65	8	Entering the world of work A: Three job advertisements B: New trends at the workplace	*if* sentences type 1 ▪ *if* sentences type 2	Written mediation ▪ Writing a comment	Female to male ratio in education and management
75		**Job skills 2:** CVs and cover letters ▪ interviews			
79	9	Multiculturalism A: Life as a refugee B: The question of integration	Past perfect ▪ Simple past ▪ *if* sentences type 3	Reading for understanding ▪ Describing and analysing statistics	Intercultural business contexts
89	10	Helping others A: Different ways to help B: A charity in action	Present perfect ▪ Present perfect progressive	Comparing figures in charts	The power of microloans
99	11	Global reach A: Four globalization case studies B: Where to manufacture products?	The passive	Analysing cartoons ▪ Describing change in charts	If the world were one hundred people
109	12	Changing society A: Making room for the young B: Towards a new social harmony	Modal verbs ▪ The passive	Using a dictionary ▪ Writing a comment	Internships: exploitation or opportunity?
119		**Job skills 3:** Giving directions ▪ bookings and reservations			

EXAM PREPARATION

Page	Unit	Title/Themes	Grammar	Business options
123	13	**The challenges of the modern state** A: Terrorism B: The dangers of digital life C: The surveillance society	Verb + infinitive Verb + gerund	Corporate burnout: how to avoid it
135	14	**Energy and the environment** A: The real cost of energy B: How do we keep the lights on? C: The problem of waste	Indirect speech	Is bigger always better?
147	15	**Feeding the world** A: How can we feed so many? B: Big problems – new solutions C: A case study	Participles	Refugees: who is fleeing to Europe?
159	16	**Technology** A: The spread of digital communication B: Artificial Intelligence C: The future of robotics?	Grammar revision	In offices of the future, sensors may track your every move
171		**Job skills 4:** Meetings ■ small talk ■ presentations		

BUSINESS TOPICS

Page	Unit	Title	Page	Unit	Title
175	1	Personalized advertising	193	7	Population, wealth and refugees
178	2	Built-in obsolescence	196	8	The future job market
181	3	Saturation from advertising	199	9	Technological advances and cybercrime
184	4	Styles of business leadership	202	10	Crops, chemicals and genetic mutation
187	5	Global workplaces and mergers	205	11	Sustainable agriculture
190	6	Corporate social responsibility	208	12	Industrial Revolution 4.0

APPENDIX

212	Files	275	Unit word list	348	Irregular verbs
214	Skills files (plus extra exercises)	319	A–Z word list	349	Quellenverzeichnis
249	Grammar files (plus extra exercises)	346	Geographical names		

1 The cult of celebrity

FOUNDATION COURSE

1 TALKING ABOUT CELEBRITY

A Choose one photo which expresses 'the cult of celebrity' best. Tell your neighbour why you have chosen it.

B Think: Make a list of four or five people who are famous in your country.

Pair: Show your list to a partner and decide which of them are celebrities. Sort the names into 'A celebrities' and 'B celebrities'. (Rank them in order of popularity.)

Share: Using your lists, decide what makes a celebrity. What do they do to deserve their celebrity status? Define 'celebrity'.

Useful phrases
- fans/paparazzi/cameras
- to wait for sb / to take photos
- to earn money / to sell photos

- How do you feel about … ?
- The paparazzi always/often …
- When a celebrity dies, …
- The newspapers sometimes …
- The fans usually …

C Study the headlines. What do they say about the advantages/disadvantages of being a celebrity? Make up some headlines of your own.

> Luxury store opens at midnight for celebrity shoppers

> ROCK LEGEND MICKEY HAS THIRD FACE-LIFT

> STALKER ENTERS STAR'S VILLA!

> DESIGNER CLOTHES AND JEWELLERY AT CELEBRITY BALL

D Would you like to be a celebrity? Why? / Why not?

2 GETTING IT RIGHT

→ Position of adverbs of time, S. 273; Simple present, S. 249

A Put the words in the correct order to make simple present statements.

1. always / a fan magazine / buy / on Fridays / I
2. at the weekend / go / to gigs / usually / we
3. I / never / talent shows / watch
4. for hours / queue / sometimes / to see our favourite stars / we
5. charity concerts / gives / the group / regularly
6. often / in the summer / they / tour

B Two fans are talking about their favourite celebrities. Put the verbs in brackets into the correct form of the simple present to complete the dialogues.

Ann My sister and I (love) ▬¹ rock music. We (be) ▬² fans of Willi Roberts. We (spend) ▬³ all our money on gigs.
Bob (you/go) ▬⁴ to every gig he (have) ▬⁵?
Ann My sister usually (do) ▬⁶. She (not miss) ▬⁷ a gig but I (not have) ▬⁸ enough time. Sometimes she (bring) ▬⁹ home T-shirts and CDs from the gigs. I always (read) ▬¹⁰ about the concerts in the fan magazine. What about you? (you/have) ▬¹¹ a favourite celebrity?
Bob My friends and I (watch) ▬¹² every film that Jim Razor (make) ▬¹³.
Ann (he/be) ▬¹⁴ the actor who (appear) ▬¹⁵ on TV with a different girlfriend every week?
Bob Yes. That (be) ▬¹⁶ part of his image. He (break up) ▬¹⁷ hotel rooms, too. I (not follow) ▬¹⁸ him on Twitter or Facebook but Jim (hit) ▬¹⁹ the headlines every week.
Ann Yes. Celebrity stories always (sell) ▬²⁰ well.

C Now listen and check your answers.

3 SPEAKING

→ Interaktion, S. 246

A Work with a partner. Ask and answer questions about celebrities.

- Who is your favourite celebrity?
- Where do you see them? How often?
- How much money do you spend on tickets, fan articles, etc.?
- How much time do you spend following them on Twitter or other social media?

Make up some of your own questions.

Useful phrases

- to go to a film/gig
- to spend money on tickets / fan articles
- to follow sb / a star on social media
- What do you think/like about … ?
- Where / How often do you … ?
- How much money do you spend on … ?
- I (don't) like …
- I never spend any money/time on …
- I spend a lot of / some money/time on …

B Tell the class what you found out.

Mia loves Rory Storm. She collects everything. She spends a fortune on fan articles. She goes to all his concerts and gets his autograph every time.

Tom is a fan of Formula 1. His favourite driver is Glen Gold. He watches every race on TV. The tickets are too expensive. Glen often appears at celebrity charity events.

1 The cult of celebrity

4 READING

→ Vorbereitung auf das Lesen, S. 214

> **BUILDING SKILLS: Predicting what the text will be about**
>
> If you have an idea what a text is about before you start reading it, you will find it easier to understand. Make use of all the clues on the page to help you.
> - Study the headline: this will give you the first clue to what the text is about.
> - Look at any photos or illustrations that go with the text: who or what do they show?
> - The captions under the photos also give further information about the text.

What do you think the article is going to tell you about talent shows? Make some notes, then read and check.

EVERYBODY'S GOT TALENT

Most of the people who appear on talent shows like *American Idol* and *Britain's Got Talent* are young and good looking. Some of them are also very talented.

Everyone is scared when they walk onto a stage in front of a huge audience and the judges. When the audience laughs at you because of the way you look, you need to know you have mega-talent. Jonathan Antoine and Charlotte Jaconelli are great singers. They want to share their talent with the world.

Imagine this: Jonathan and Charlotte are coming onto the *Britain's Got Talent* stage. Some members of the audience are laughing. Others are clearly feeling uncomfortable. One of the judges says, 'Just when you think things couldn't get any worse,' as the singers take their spot on stage.

Imagine the change taking place as they start to perform. Some members of the audience are crying, others are standing on their chairs and waving their arms in the air.

There is something magical about the moment. The singers are listening to the cheers. Hopes for the life they dream about are washing over their faces. They are experiencing a life-changing moment.

Jonathan Antoine and Charlotte Jaconelli at the Classical Brit Awards 2013

Jonathan has a great voice. Charlotte's voice is young and more pop. One of the judges said he was afraid that Charlotte would hold back Jonathan, who is the real talent of the group. In the end, the same judge voted for the pair to move on together to the next level of the competition.

That was in 2012. Charlotte and Jonathan finished second in that season and signed a good contract with a record company. Their first album, 'Together', was released in the same year and their follow-up, 'Perhaps Love', came out a year later. Jonathan and Charlotte are now following solo careers.

(298 words)

FOUNDATION COURSE 1

5 LOOKING AT THE TEXT
→ Produktion: Wh-Fragen beantworten, S. 228

A Work with a partner and answer the following questions in full sentences.

1. Who is the article about?
2. Where are they?
3. Why are they there?
4. What happened first?
5. What happened in the end? Why?
6. When did this take place?

B Now compare your answers with your notes from exercise 4.

6 WORKING WITH WORDS
→ Ein Wörterbuch benutzen, S. 217

A Copy and complete the table using your dictionary. The given words are all from the text.

Noun	Verb	Adjective
	to appear	
competition		
	to dream	
	to experience	
idol		
judge		
/	to perform	

B Use some of the words you have found to complete the sentences. Change the form of the verbs if necessary.

1. People ▄ in a talent show because they want to be famous.
2. The singer was nervous. He was shaking all through the ▄ .
3. The star always looks dirty. He's really not interested in his ▄ .
4. When they received their prize, one of the winners said, 'This is a great ▄ for us.'
5. The judge often criticizes people before they begin. He is very ▄ .
6. He's a real celebrity, audiences ▄ him.
7. Women often have a ▄ look in their eyes when he sings.
8. She takes part in a lot of shows. She's a really ▄ judge.

7 GETTING IT RIGHT
→ Simple present ▪ Present progressive, S. 249

A Imagine you are at the *Britain's Got Talent* show right now. Put the verbs into the correct form of the present progressive.

1. The performers (get) ▄ made up at the moment.
2. The judge (study) ▄ his script.
3. Jonathan (practise) ▄ his song.
4. You (speak) ▄ to your friend on your mobile phone.
5. Your friend asks: 'What (you/do) ▄ ¹ at the moment?'
   You answer: 'I (wait) ▄ ² for the show to start.'
6. Your friend asks: 'What (the members of the audience / do) ▄ ¹?'
   You answer: 'They (talk) ▄ ² to each other. They (look forward to) ▄ ³ a good show.'

1 The cult of celebrity

B Write complete sentences with the correct form of the verbs in brackets.

1. I ▬ *Britain's Got Talent* every week. (watch / am watching)
2. When the show ▬¹ at 10.45, I always ▬² to bed. (finish / is finishing ▪ go / am going)
3. Charlotte and Jonathan ▬¹ to become stars. They ▬² to win *Britain's Got Talent*. (want / are wanting ▪ try / are trying)
4. They usually ▬ their song in the morning. (practise / are practising)
5. Jonathan ▬ on his own at the moment. (sings / is singing)
6. The judge ▬¹ near the TV studio. This evening he ▬² home after the show. (lives / is living ▪ walks / is walking)

C Work with a partner and write six sentences about Jonathan, Charlotte and the judge using verbs in the simple present and in the present progressive. Remember to use signal words.

8 DISCUSSION
→ Interaktion: An Diskussionen teilnehmen, S. 246

In small groups, discuss talent shows. Say what you (don't) find good about them. Would you like to take part in one? Explain why / why not. Make notes and tell the class.

9 LISTENING
→ Vor dem Hören, S. 225

BUILDING SKILLS: Preparing to listen

Preparing yourself for the listening task will help you to understand listening texts more easily. Make use of everything on the page that can help you before you start listening.
- Study any photos or illustrations on the page for clues about the listening topic.
- Read the questions carefully and look at any other background information.
- Think about any words related to the topic that you might hear.

THE PRICE OF FAME
Kelly and childhood sweetheart Sam to split

10.30 Good morning, fans!

Gerry Davis interviews today's celebrities

In today's interview, Kelly Green, current £100,000 prize winner of Miss Model talks about her greatest achievement, who inspires her and her biggest challenge. She also talks to Gerry about her relationship with long-time lover, Sam. (She believes that the tabloid press love it when a celebrity has problems.)

A Before you listen, study the photos and the texts. Then answer these questions.

1. Who is Gerry's interview partner?
2. Why is she in the news?
3. What are the four main topics of the interview?
4. What is her relationship with the press?

FOUNDATION COURSE   1

B With a partner, match these German expressions to the English expressions you might hear.

1	größte Leistung	a	an international career as a fashion model
2	größter Erfolg	b	biggest success
3	eine internationale Karriere als Model	c	greatest achievement
4	einen Traum erfüllen	d	problems in the headlines
5	die Presse wird zu aufdringlich	e	stars crying their eyes out
6	Probleme in den Schlagzeilen	f	the press comes too close
7	Stars am Heulen	g	to fulfil a dream
8	einen Vertrag haben	h	to have a contract

C Listen to the interview and say whether these statements are true or false. Correct the wrong statements.

1 Kelly's dream is to have her own fashion label.
2 Veronica Vernon is Kelly's manager.
3 Giselle Goodrich is a top fashion model.
4 Kelly does not admire Giselle.
5 Kelly always enjoys media attention.
6 She understands why the press focuses on celebrities' problems.
7 Sam understands Kelly's problems.
8 Kelly is looking forward to living in Milan.

10 ROLE-PLAY

→ Interaktion: Ein Rollenspiel gestalten, S. 247

Work with a partner. You are going to role-play an interview with a celebrity.

Partner A: You are the interviewer, Gerry Davis (see exercise 9).
Partner B: You are the celebrity. Choose a name for yourself, or use your own name. Decide which area you work in, e.g. sport, film, modelling, reality TV.

Before you start, read through what you are going to say and make notes.
Partner B, tell Partner A your name. Partner A begins.

Gerry Davis	Celebrity
→ Welcome the guest and thank him/her for coming. Say that you know he/she is always busy.	→ Say that you are happy to be here. Say that you are never too busy for your fans.
→ Ask the celebrity to describe his/her greatest achievement or biggest success.	→ Describe an achievement or your biggest success, e.g. your latest album is top of the charts, you are footballer of the year.
→ Congratulate the celebrity and ask who inspires him/her.	→ Say who inspires you. (This can be a real person.)
→ Say that you find that interesting. Then ask what the star's biggest challenge is.	→ Sometimes you get tired. Sometimes the work is hard, but you love what you do. Explain that your fans give you a lot of support, so you can face any challenges that appear.
→ Say that the fans always love to hear the star say things like that. Ask what the star is doing now.	→ Say what you are doing at the moment, e.g. you are working on your next album, training for the next big match.
→ Thank the celebrity for talking to you and wish him/her all the best.	→ Thank Gerry for interviewing you. Say goodbye to him and to your fans.

11

2 The world of sport

FOUNDATION COURSE

1 TALKING ABOUT SPORT

A Think: What sports do you enjoy? Are you a participant or a spectator? What sports do not interest you?

Pair: Tell a partner and explain why you enjoy / do not enjoy sports.

Share: Do a class survey and rank the sports according to the numbers of classmates who do and watch them.

B Copy and complete the mind map with all the sports you know.

Useful phrases
■ to (not) be interested in running/ cycling/…
■ to (not) be keen on football/…
■ to (not) enjoy/like/love tennis/…
■ to (not) support a team
■ to (not) be a fan of sb / a team
■ How often do you do … ?
■ When do you go … ?
■ Who do you play … with?

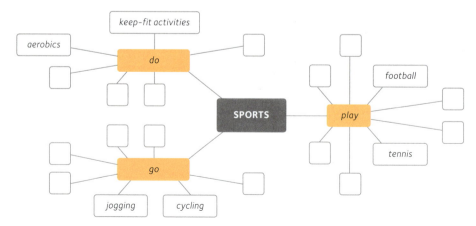

12

2

2 GETTING IT RIGHT
→ Simple past, S. 251; Present perfect, S. 253

A Put the verbs in brackets in the correct form of the simple past to complete the dialogues.

1. **A** Mary (play) ▬¹ hockey for the Austrian team before she (move) ▬² to Germany.
   B Oh, that's interesting. I (not know) ▬³ that.
2. **A** What sports (you/do) ▬¹ when you (be) ▬² younger?
   B I (go) ▬³ riding when I (be) ▬⁴ at school.
3. **A** I (ring) ▬¹ your doorbell last night but you (be) ▬² out. Where (you/go) ▬³ ?
   B I (not go) ▬⁴ anywhere. I (be) ▬⁵ tired after jogging so I (go) ▬⁶ to bed early.
4. **A** (you/queue) ▬¹ at the stadium for your tickets?
   B No, I (buy) ▬² them online.

B Use the words to make sentences. Use the present perfect form of the verb.

1. I / just / buy / a chess set.
2. My sister / just / learn / how to ride a bicycle.
3. Martin and Fred / already / go / to the swimming pool.
4. you / ever / drive a racing car?
5. Martha / read / the rules of the game / yet?

C Complete the sentences with *for* or *since*.

1. I haven't seen Tom at the gym ▬ Christmas.
2. Why doesn't he come out? He has been in the changing rooms ▬ three hours.
3. Today is the big day. I have had my tickets ▬ two weeks.
4. Malcolm isn't playing today. He has had a cold ▬ last Tuesday.
5. It's World Cup time again. My national team hasn't taken part ▬ 1998.
6. Kevin has played tennis at this club ▬ over ten years.

3 SPEAKING

A Work in groups. Ask and answer questions about sports personalities you like and admire.

- Who is your favourite sports personality? Say which sport they are involved in.
- Why do you admire them? Explain what they do that makes you look up to them.
- Have you ever lost interest in a sports personality you really liked? Explain why.

Useful phrases

- to play for a club/team
- to admire / look up to sb
- to be a champion/hero

- Why do you follow/support … ?
- How long have you … ?
- What made you decide not to … ?
- How long did you … ?

B Tell the class what you found out.

> Connie has been a fan of the sprinter Jo Myles since she won gold at the Paralympics. Connie admires her because she has overcome her disabilities.

> Jason admired the swimmer Ian Jones for a long time, but he lost interest in him when he stopped winning medals.

2 The world of sport

4 PREDICTING

→ Vorbereitung auf das Lesen, S. 214

Look quickly at the text – don't read it! – then choose the best ending to complete the sentence below.

The text is about …
a   deaths in early bicycle races.
b   taking illegal substances to improve performance.
c   some very bad injuries that have occurred during races.

SKILLS CHECKLIST: Predicting

☑ Have I read the title?
☑ Have I looked at the photo?
☑ Have I read the caption under the photo?

WHEN HEROES FALL

Professional cycling has a long history of doping problems.

Professional cycling has a long history. The first recorded bicycle races began in the early 1800s and, throughout the decades, improvements in materials used for bikes have led to faster races. There have been heroes in every race but some of them have fallen.

Lance Armstrong was born in Texas on 18 September 1971. He started his sports career at the age of 12 when he came fourth in a swimming competition. From 1984 to 1990, he competed in junior triathlon competitions and became national triathlon champion in 1989 and 1990. In 1992, Armstrong began his career as a professional road racing cyclist. He won the Tour de France seven times between 1999 and 2005. In 2011, he announced his retirement from competitive cycling. A few months later, the United States Anti-Doping Agency (USADA) looked at samples and charged Armstrong with doping. After that, the organization took away his seven Tour de France titles.

Reports about doping in professional cycling are not new. According to the 1997 International Olympic Committee study on the Historical Evolution of Doping Phenomenon in the late 19th century, doping during a competition was not illegal. The study referred to a Welsh cyclist in 1886 who drank a mixture of cocaine, caffeine and strychnine and died during a race. Ten years later, cyclists who used nitroglycerine to stimulate their hearts and improve their breathing suffered hallucinations. During a race in New York, the American champion Marshall Taylor refused to continue as he believed he was being chased by a man with a knife.

Today, an insider said: 'Nobody bats an eyelid when people are doping. I know some cyclists who have doped ever since they started to enter competitions. They win a lot of races but, in the end, these guys are really losers. When you fall, you fall alone. The corrupt system cycles on without you.'

(311 words)

FOUNDATION COURSE 2

5 UNDERSTANDING THE TEXT
→ Sich während des Lesens Notizen machen, S. 223

BUILDING SKILLS: Taking notes while reading

Taking notes while reading makes it easier to remember the information in a text. It is also a useful skill if you have to answer questions on, or summarize, a text. Use these tips to organize your notes:
- Read the text all the way through to make sure you understand what it is about.
- Prepare a page in your notebook with the text heading, a reference to where to find the text, a note on what the text is about and today's date.
- Use the most important aspects of the text as sub-headings and write your notes under these headings.
- Scan the text for key words, dates and other signals, such as repetition, that will tell you what the author considers important. Include these aspects in your notes.

A First read the text on page 14 quickly and put the headings below into the correct order 1–4.

> doping in professional cycling not new ▪ doping today ▪ fallen hero ▪
> history of professional cycling

B Now read the text carefully and make notes in your notebook. Use the headings from exercise 5A to organize your notes.

C Answer these questions on the text.

1. When were bicycle races first recorded?
2. What helped cyclists to race faster?
3. What is Lance Armstrong's connection to professional cycling?
4. Why did the USADA take his titles away from him?
5. According to a study, was doping in cycling legal or illegal in the 19th century?
6. What happened to a Welsh cyclist in 1886 as a result of doping?
7. What does an insider think about cyclists who dope?
8. What does the insider think about cycling competitions?

When heroes fall
(Focus on Success, p. 14)
Text is about: …
Date: …
1 …
2 …
3 …
4 …

6 WRITING
→ Produktion: Einen Text zusammenfassen, S. 229

Use your answers to the questions in exercise 5C to write a short summary of the text. These phrases will help you to structure your summary.

Useful phrases

- The article is about …
- According to the text, the first …
- It seems that better bikes …
- One of the most famous modern cyclists was …
- It appears that he was …
- In general, doping in cycling …
- As someone who knows the business says, …
- According to him/her, …
- To sum up, …

15

2 The world of sport

7 GETTING IT RIGHT
→ Pronouns, S. 268

Replace the highlighted expressions with a subject pronoun.
1. John doesn't go to the gym regularly.
2. Molly and Pam have joined a dance class.
3. Cilla doesn't do any exercise at all.
4. The dog always runs beside me.

Now replace the highlighted expressions with an object pronoun.
5. I called John from the gym last week.
6. The instructor was happy to see Molly and Pam.
7. Molly and Pam would like Cilla to join the class.
8. I tripped and fell over the dog yesterday.

Complete these dialogues with subject and object pronouns.
1. A Do ▭¹ know the woman who takes the dance class, Kate?
   B No, ▭² don't. Can ▭³ introduce ▭⁴ to ▭⁵ ?
2. A Paul and I would like to go to the class but ▭¹ don't know where ▭² is.
   B Molly and Pam said ▭³ and Paul can go to the class with ▭⁴.
3. A These jazz pants are nice. If ▭¹ fit ▭², ▭³ will take ▭⁴.
   B Yes, ▭⁵ fit perfectly. This T-shirt is nice, too. Why don't ▭⁶ buy ▭⁷, too?

8 GETTING IT RIGHT
→ Possessive adjectives, S. 268

Add possessive adjectives to complete the dialogue.

A How did you enjoy ▭¹ keep-fit class last night?
B I loved it but ▭² muscles are aching this morning. Alan was full of energy at the end but, of course, it's ▭³ job.
A Alan's the trainer, right? Did your sister enjoy ▭⁴ session with him?
B Sure. She suggested we should take ▭⁵ parents along, too.
A What's ▭⁶ opinion of keep-fit? Would they go?
B I think my mum would. When she was a teacher, it was ▭⁷ job to organize school sports.

9 PREPARING TO LISTEN
→ Rezeption: Hörverstehen, S. 225

You are going to hear an interview with a Zumba instructor.

A Before you listen, read this short introduction and answer the following questions.

1. What is Zumba?
2. Where and when did it start?
3. Who invented it?

What is Zumba?

You've probably heard of the fitness craze Zumba, a workout known as a dance fitness party. It started in the 1990s, in the slums of Cali, Columbia, when an aerobics instructor called Beto Perez forgot his tape of aerobics music for the class he was teaching. Instead of cancelling the class, he went to his car and took his tape of the traditional salsa and merengue music he listened to while he was driving and improvised his aerobics class using the music. In 1999, Beto Perez took his new aerobic dance programme to Miami, Florida. He named the new-style aerobics Zumba. It wasn't long before Zumba became a worldwide craze. Zumba is a cardio-dance workout – a fitness workout which is good for the heart.

FOUNDATION COURSE 2

B Complete the sentences on the left with the correct definition on the right.

1. Salsa, merengue, cha-cha-cha, samba and tango are …
2. Reggae, jazz, African beats, country, hip-hop and pop are …
3. Someone who is overweight is …
4. A person who is slim is …
5. Cardio (cardiovascular) means …
6. Metabolism is …
7. A calorie is …
8. Someone who is tired of life …

a. a unit used for measuring how much energy food will produce.
b. connected with the heart and the blood vessels.
c. cannot feel joy and excitement any longer.
d. Latin American dances.
e. musical styles.
f. the chemical processes in living things that change food into materials for growth.
g. thin in a way that is attractive.
h. too heavy for the size of their body.

10 LISTENING

→ Rezeption: Hörverstehen – Notizen machen, S. 227

BUILDING SKILLS: Taking notes while listening

It can sometimes be difficult to take notes while listening because the speakers don't stop to wait while you are writing. Because of this, you may miss important points. Don't panic! If you practise taking notes every time you listen, you will soon get the hang of it.
- Read the task carefully and look at any other information on the page before you listen.
- Prepare and structure your notes the same way as for a reading task (see page 15).
- Keep focused on the task and note down relevant key words and expressions.

A Now listen to the interview and take notes.

B Look at your notes and say if the following statements are true or false. Correct the incorrect statements.

1. Zumba only uses Latin American music.
2. Only young and beautiful people go to Zumba classes.
3. Zumba is good for your health.
4. Almost everyone feels tired after a Zumba session.
5. Zumba can help people who feel unhappy.
6. The interviewer does not want to try Zumba.

Zumba (Focus on Success, p. 17)
Listening is about: …
Date: …
Gerry Davis: …
Candy Wilson: …

11 WRITING

→ Produktion: Schreiben S. 228

A friend who feels overweight is unhealthy and unhappy. Use your notes and the phrases below to write an email describing Zumba and suggest how this could help him/her.

Useful phrases

- Hello (*first name*)
- I've just heard an interview with … . She is a …
- Zumba is a … but you don't have to be able to …
- It's lots of fun and has … health benefits.
- It's good for … / increases … / reduces … / helps people … / boosts … / burns …
- … if you're feeling low, …
- The atmosphere is …
- I would like to … / Would you like to … ?
- Hope to hear from you …
- All the best (*your name*)

3 Fashion and brand power

FOUNDATION COURSE

Times Square, New York

Piccadilly Circus, London

1 TALKING ABOUT BRANDS

A Think: You see brand names and slogans wherever you go. Write down three brand names and their slogans.

B Pair: Compare your list of slogans with a partner.

C Share: Which, if any, of these brands do you buy regularly? Which of them would you never buy?

> **Useful phrases**
> - I love/like … . I shop there regularly.
> - I prefer … . Their clothes are more fashionable than the clothes at …
> - I never drink/eat/wear/buy …
> - Which is better … ?
> - What do/don't you like about … ?

2 CLASS SURVEY

Ask other people in the class about their favourite brands. Do a class survey and find the top ten brands that people spend their money on.

3 READING

→ Rezeption: Leseverstehen, S. 214

Match the following statements and questions to the gaps (A to D) in the text on page 19.

1. Basically, it all comes down to emotional thinking.
2. Last but not least, brands let us show the world who we are.
3. What might make 'our' brand attractive to us?
4. Why do shoppers always go for a specific brand?

3

WHY DOES IT HAVE TO BE A BRAND NAME?

— A — A lot of consumer choices are made according to the price or the availability of the product. If it is affordable, we'll buy it. If it's easy to find, we'll take it. What do we do, though, when we go into a shop and see two similar products which cost more or less the same, one made by company X and one by company Y? We buy the brand we prefer.

— B — Does it simply come down to quality, packaging and price? Perhaps personality affects the type of brands we choose? Or could it be education or family background? All of these things play a part of course but why do we buy one brand and not another?

— C — Some sportswear companies use sports celebrities to advertise their goods. The clothes they wear won't make you run faster or play better but the advertising suggests that wearing the same brand will make you a better athlete. It tells the buyer: 'Like your hero, you are an over-achiever. You never give up. You want more.' People who choose brands that are advertised like this are looking for a challenge. By buying these brand-name products, they feel they are on the road to achieving more.

— D — Using the right brand can help us display our values and beliefs. Brands can show that you belong to the same group. We can use brands to show that we are different from other people or to show that we are the same as others.   (246 words)

4 LOOKING AT THE TEXT

→ Rezeption: Leseverstehen, S. 214

Use information from the text to complete the sentence beginnings (1–6) by adding a sentence part from the first box (a–f) and an ending from the second box (g–l).

EXAMPLE: *A lot of shoppers choose goods depending on whether they have enough money to buy them and if they can get the products easily.*

1 ~~A lot of shoppers choose goods depending on~~ …
2 If two products made by two different companies are available, …
3 A lot of things can persuade us to buy a product, …
4 Who we are affects our choices, for example, …
5 Some companies use a famous person to advertise their goods hoping that …
6 If you follow a fashion or have certain ideas, …

a and both cost more or less the same, …
b our character and education …
c including how the product is packed …
d shoppers who identify with the famous person …
e the brands you choose can show other people …
f ~~whether they have enough money to buy them~~ …

g and how much it costs.
h ~~and if they can get the products easily.~~
i or how we grew up.
j we buy the brand we like better.
k who you are and what you think.
l will buy the product.

19

3 Fashion and brand power

5 GETTING IT RIGHT
→ Adjectives ■ Adverbs of manner, S. 270

A Complete the dialogues with the adjective or adverb form of the words in brackets.

1. **A** I wish I had some money. I'd like to buy a new computer but they're so ▬¹. (expensive)
   B Don't worry. Even good computers are ▬² nowadays. (cheap)
2. **A** That dress is ▬¹. It must have cost a lot of money. (beautiful)
   B No, it didn't. You can buy brand-name clothing ▬² at outlet stores. (cheap)
3. **A** Are these the shoes you told me about? They look ▬¹. (great)
   B Yes. I bought them on the Internet and they fit me ▬². (perfect)
4. **A** A ▬¹ model of my phone comes out tomorrow. (new)
   B If you want one, you'll have to be ▬². They get sold out very ▬³. (quick ■ quick)

B Rewrite these sentences with the adverbs in the best position.
→ Position of adverbs of time, S. 273

1. I'll buy myself a pair of designer jeans. (tomorrow)
2. Pete has bought a tablet. (just)
3. Mary chooses her children's clothes. (always)
4. **A** I have spent all my allowance. (already ■ again)
   B Then you won't be able to do any more shopping. (this month)
5. **A** There you are. Shall we get something to eat? (at last ■ now)
   B No, I'm not hungry. I've eaten two burgers. (today ■ already)

6 WORKING WITH WORDS
→ Ein Wörterbuch benutzen, S. 217

Copy and complete the table using your dictionary. The given words are in the text.

Noun	Verb	Adjective	Adverb
▬		similar	▬
▬	to prefer	▬	▬
▬	▬	▬	simply
celebrity / ▬	▬	▬	
athlete		▬	▬
challenge / ▬	▬	▬	
▬ / ▬	to achieve	▬	

Complete the sentences with words from the same word family as the words in brackets.

1. There is not much (similar) ▬ between these designer jeans and the ones from the discount label.
2. Which smartphone do you want to buy? Do you have a (prefer) ▬?
3. I love these hand-made sweaters. They are (simply) ▬ but high-quality clothes.
4. The company had a party to (celebrity) ▬ the success of the new brand.
5. I'm sure my new running shoes help me to run faster. I feel really (athlete) ▬ now.
6. The course was very (challenge) ▬. It was like running a half-marathon.
7. It was a great (achieve) ▬ to get a sports celebrity to advertise the brand.

20

FOUNDATION COURSE 3

7 GETTING IT RIGHT
→ Comparison of adjectives and adverbs, S. 271

A Make adjective or adverb comparisons with the words in brackets.

1. It's much (cheap) ▬¹ to buy no-name goods than designer brands. Designer clothes are (expensive) ▬² than 'normal' clothes.
2. The green T-shirt is (fashionable) ▬¹ than the blue one, but the yellow T-shirt is the (fashionable) ▬² of them all.
3. You can buy goods (easy) ▬ on the Internet than from crowded stores.
4. Usain Bolt is the (fast) ▬¹ man in the world, but he will run even (fast) ▬² in our running shoes.
5. People buy products from a company (regular) ▬ if they identify with the brand.

B Make comparison sentences with the words in brackets.

⊕ = … than ▪ ⊜ = as … as ▪ ⊖ = not as … as

1. A lot of people say brand names are (⊕ good) *better than* no-name products but I don't agree. I think a no-name product can be just (⊜ good) *as good as* a brand name.
2. This drink tastes (⊕ sweet) ▬¹ the other one but it is (⊖ tasty) ▬² yours.
3. We know you're a fast runner but our shoes will make you run (⊕ fast) ▬ ever before.
4. My new tablet PC was (⊖ expensive) ▬¹ my old laptop and I can download things just (⊖ quick) ▬² before.
5. Their products are (⊖ good) ▬¹ ours. Their prices are (⊜ competitive) ▬² ours but their quality is (⊕ bad) ▬³ ever.

8 LISTENING
→ Rezeption: Hörverstehen, S. 225

🄾 8 Anne, Bella, Colin and David go running together as often as they can. When Anne collects a T-shirt for Bella to wear at a sponsored women's run, it's not long before a discussion about running clothes starts.

Listen to the discussion and answer the following questions.

1. What does Anne have for Bella?
2. What does Colin think about people who spend a lot of money on sportswear?
3. Why is it good that sports gear firms sponsor events?
4. What is Anne's opinion on the best clothes for running?
5. Where does Anne's gear come from?
6. According to Anne, who makes the clothes she wears?
7. According to Colin, where is sportswear made?
8. How does Bella stop her friends arguing?

3 Fashion and brand power

9 PHRASES FOR DISCUSSION

→ Interaktion: An Diskussionen teilnehmen, S. 246

> **BUILDING SKILLS: Learning phrases for discussion**
>
> Learning phrases for discussion (see the flap on the back cover) and how to use them will help you express yourself clearly and logically in a debate or a role-play.
> - Before you begin a discussion, make sure you know as many phrases for discussion as possible and when to use them correctly.
> - Whenever you have the chance to listen to a discussion, pay attention to the phrases people use and remember how these expressions help to structure the discussion.

A Copy this table into your notebook and write the expressions from the list below under the right heading.

Language for discussion				
Giving an opinion	Giving reasons	Agreeing with an opinion	Disagreeing with an opinion	Interrupting

a Actually, I think …
b Yes, that's just how I see it.
c If you ask me, …
d (Sorry), … I don't agree.
e It seems to me that …
f Just a moment, I'd like to say something.
g The thing is, you see …
h Sorry to interrupt, but …
i That's quite right.
j The main reason is (that) …

Keep your table safe. You can add more expressions as you work through the book.

B Listen to the discussion in exercise 8 again and listen for the expressions from exercise 9A. Were they used in the way you decided above?

C Have a short discussion about running clothes with three other people.

- On the one hand, … , but on the other hand …
- I agree with … because …
- In fact, I think that …
- Taking everything into account, …
- I see what you mean, but …
- On the whole, …

22

FOUNDATION COURSE 3

10 READING
→ Rezeption: Leseverstehen, S. 214

Read the following blog and the comments below. Match the comments to the paragraphs in the blog.

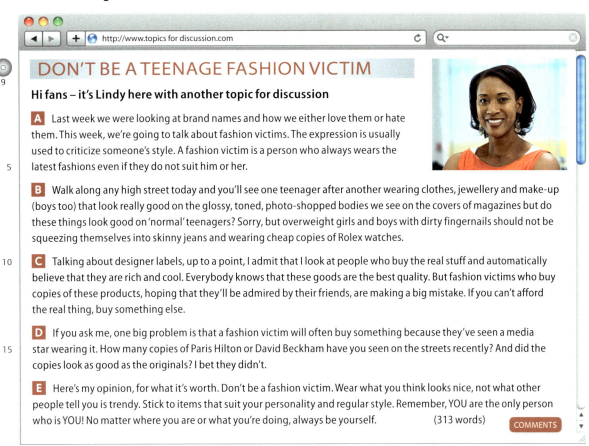

DON'T BE A TEENAGE FASHION VICTIM

Hi fans – it's Lindy here with another topic for discussion

A Last week we were looking at brand names and how we either love them or hate them. This week, we're going to talk about fashion victims. The expression is usually used to criticize someone's style. A fashion victim is a person who always wears the latest fashions even if they do not suit him or her.

B Walk along any high street today and you'll see one teenager after another wearing clothes, jewellery and make-up (boys too) that look really good on the glossy, toned, photo-shopped bodies we see on the covers of magazines but do these things look good on 'normal' teenagers? Sorry, but overweight girls and boys with dirty fingernails should not be squeezing themselves into skinny jeans and wearing cheap copies of Rolex watches.

C Talking about designer labels, up to a point, I admit that I look at people who buy the real stuff and automatically believe that they are rich and cool. Everybody knows that these goods are the best quality. But fashion victims who buy copies of these products, hoping that they'll be admired by their friends, are making a big mistake. If you can't afford the real thing, buy something else.

D If you ask me, one big problem is that a fashion victim will often buy something because they've seen a media star wearing it. How many copies of Paris Hilton or David Beckham have you seen on the streets recently? And did the copies look as good as the originals? I bet they didn't.

E Here's my opinion, for what it's worth. Don't be a fashion victim. Wear what you think looks nice, not what other people tell you is trendy. Stick to items that suit your personality and regular style. Remember, YOU are the only person who is YOU! No matter where you are or what you're doing, always be yourself. (313 words)

COMMENTS

JANE I agree with Lindy on this point. Some people should not draw attention to themselves. I've seen boys with acne wearing purple shirts. Yuck! As far as I'm concerned, I'm a bit overweight, so I never wear tight clothes. I don't feel comfortable in them and I don't want people staring at me.

KATY I have to agree with you completely on that point. My own view of the matter is that a lot of teenagers simply don't know who they really are. I don't want to pretend I'm someone else. I'm happy to be me. Everyone is unique. Right?

LIAM Lindy, I see what you mean about copying stars but don't you think that's part of growing up? Young people should be free to experiment with who they are and how they look. If you like a particular star, why not copy the way they dress?

MARK Sorry, Lindy. I don't agree. Some people who buy the latest styles can look really great. I think the secret is not overdoing it. I mean, you don't have to wear every trendy item you own all at once.

NELE I'm afraid I can't accept your criticism of people who buy fakes. I want to look good but I don't have much money. I'm happy that I have a great collection of bags and shoes that look just like the originals (YSL, Prada, Versace, Gucci) and they were all affordable. (240 words)

3 Fashion and brand power

11 WORKING WITH WORDS

A Match words from box A to words from box B to make collocations from the text on page 23. There is only one match for each word.

A		B	
best	fashion	copies	names
brand	high	fashions	quality
cheap	latest	jeans	street
designer	skinny	labels	victims

B Write replies to two of the comments giving your own opinion. Use some of the collocations from exercise 11A.

12 DISCUSSION

→ Interaktion: An Diskussionen teilnehmen, S. 246

BUILDING SKILLS: Preparing for group discussions

Preparing yourself for the particular situation will help you take part in a discussion successfully.
- Before you start, always think about your opinion and what you want to say.
- Prepare some bullet points related to the aspects of the topic.
- Write down key words and phrases in English.

A Preparation: Work with a partner. You and your partner are going to discuss fashion with another pair. Before you start, read the ideas below with your partner and share your opinions. Decide what you want to say and make some notes.

B Discussion: Now find another pair and talk about fashion. Try to use as much language for discussion as you can.

C Tell the class the results of your discussion.

SKILLS CHECKLIST: Group discussions

- ✓ Have I thought about what I want to say?
- ✓ Have I prepared some bullet points?
- ✓ Have I written down key phrases in English?

4 Leisure and free time

FOUNDATION COURSE

1 TALKING ABOUT FREE-TIME ACTIVITIES

A Use your own ideas and ideas from the photos to ask and answer questions about what you like or don't like doing in your free time.

> I enjoy playing music.

> I love surfing the Internet.

> I don't mind shopping, but I prefer to hang out with friends.

B What activities would you like to do which you can't? Use ideas from the box to explain why you don't do these activities.

> cost of activity ▪ don't have the transport to get there ▪ lack of time ▪
> no one to go with me ▪ not available in my area ▪ parents don't let me

C Imagine you have the chance to do one of the activities you spoke about above. Describe what you are going to do or say what you think you will do.

> I'm going to take riding lessons at the local riding school. I'm going to go there twice a week.

> I think I'll take a photography course. I'll need to save up for a good camera first.

25

4 Leisure and free time

2 GETTING IT RIGHT

→ *Will* future ▪ *Going to* future, S. 257

Put the verbs into the correct form of the *will* or *going to* future.

1 I've decided to spend less time in front of the computer. I (play) ▇ football instead.
2 I think the weather (be) ▇¹ nice this afternoon so we (be able to) ▇² go for a run.
3 I (go) ▇¹ shopping now but I promise I (be) ▇² back later.
4 Lucy's parents gave her some money for her birthday. She (spend) ▇ it on driving lessons.
5 Martin needs a new hobby so he (join) ▇¹ the chess club. I hope he (like) ▇² it.
6 I have got a free weekend so I (help) ▇ my dad in the garden.
7 Tim (study) ▇¹ in Bristol. He hopes he (find) ▇² some interesting clubs to join there.
8 Mike and I (watch) ▇¹ TV this evening. (you/watch) ▇² with us?

3 ANALYSING A CARTOON

→ Produktion: Cartoons beschreiben und analysieren, S. 236

> **BUILDING SKILLS: Describing cartoons**
>
> Before you begin to describe or analyse a cartoon, always read the instructions carefully so that you know what you have to do.
> ■ Read the caption under the drawing or any speech bubbles in the cartoon and think about how they relate to the picture.
> ■ Look at everything in the picture and describe it carefully, using the present progressive to say what people are doing.
> → Present progressive, S. 213
> ■ If you don't get the joke, just concentrate on describing the cartoon. Do not waste time trying to figure it out.

A Study the cartoon, then use the words from the box to complete the description below.

> behind ▪ cartoonist ▪ face ▪ under ▪
> home ▪ in front of ▪ probably ▪
> emoticon ▪ worried

"We know it makes you happy, but your father and I think you're spending too much time on the computer."

The cartoon shows a boy sitting ▇¹ a computer at ▇². He is ▇³ in his bedroom. His parents are standing ▇⁴ him. The boy's father looks ▇⁵. His mother appears to be saying the words written ▇⁶ the cartoon. The boy's ▇⁷ does not have the usual eyes, nose and mouth. The ▇⁸ has drawn it as an ▇⁹ instead.

B Choose the best sentence ending to complete the interpretation of the cartoon.

The cartoonist seems to be making the point that …
 a parents of teenagers are often worried about their children.
 b spending all your time online will change you from a human being into a computer.
 c teenagers are happiest when they're chatting.

FOUNDATION COURSE 4

4 READING

→ Rezeption: Leseverstehen, S. 214

A survey among teenagers in the USA showed that many of them spend their free time hanging out in shopping malls.

A Before you read the text, match the words and phrases below to the correct German translation. (The alphabetical wordlist at the back of the book will help you.)

1	curfew	5	adequately	a	angemessen	e	Aktion
2	legal guardian	6	measures	b	Befreiungen	f	Sperrstunde
3	retailer	7	initiative	c	Einzelhändler/in	g	Vormund
4	incident	8	exemptions	d	Maßnahmen	h	Zwischenfall

LIFE'S SO UNFAIR! Shopping mall sets 6 pm curfew for teenagers – unless they bring their parents

Teenagers have been hanging out in shopping malls with their friends for decades but one mall is putting an end to the tradition – at least after 6 pm. North Park Center in Dallas has set a 6 pm curfew after which time any person aged 17 or under must be accompanied by a parent or legal guardian. After the curfew any young teens without an adult will be approached and asked to provide ID and if they don't have any, a parent will either need to come join them or pick them up.

Although young teens and some of their parents may object to the curfew, North Park spokesman Mark Annick argued that all the center's retailers backed the new rules.

'I really do respect that there are parents who may not agree with us completely,' Annick told CBS news.

He went on to say that the rules were not brought in after any particular incidents or complaints but in a bid to maintain a family atmosphere for the estimated 26 million visitors who come to the mall each year. The new rules also state that visitors must dress 'appropriately for a family-oriented shopping center. Clothes must adequately cover the body. Visible undergarments are not permitted.'

The measures have divided opinions with some parents backing the curfew, others saying it should be later and some saying it is not needed at all.

'If the intent is to stop the loitering and just mall walking and things like that, I think it's a great idea,' one parent said. Another parent disagreed with the mall's initiative, saying, 'These kids are old enough to have drivers licenses, so I don't see why they need to be escorted around the mall.'

Teens who work at the mall and those who are just there to watch a movie are the only exemptions to the curfew.

North Park is the largest shopping center in North Texas boasting more than 235 stores and restaurants. (328 words)

Abridged and adapted from: www.dailymail.co.uk

B Now read the text carefully and make notes.

C Explain in 3–4 sentences what the text is about.

SKILLS CHECKLIST: Taking notes

☑ Have I read the whole text?
☑ Have I scanned the text for key words?
☑ Have I noted down the key words?

27

4 Leisure and free time

5 MEDIATION
→ Schriftliche Mediation, S. 240

> **BUILDING SKILLS: Written mediation**
>
> Written mediation means communicating the general sense of a text in another language to someone who does not understand the original.
> - Before you start to write, read the instructions carefully and make sure you understand the *situation*, *who the mediation is aimed at* and *what form your text should be*, e.g. an email, a list, etc.
> - Remember that you should only give the information that the person you are mediating for needs. Leave out any details that are not relevant.
> - You should not translate the text word for word, so you can paraphrase 'difficult' expressions.

A Read the German instructions below and describe the situation in your own words. Say who the mediation is aimed at and what sort of text you have to write.

> Sie arbeiten in einer kleinen Boutique in einem Einkaufszentrum in Ihrer Stadt. Ihr Chef / Ihre Chefin und andere Ladenbesitzer beklagen sich über die Gruppen von Jugendlichen, die sich nach der Schule im Einkaufszentrum treffen, um dort herumzuhängen. Sie stören die normalen Kunden und die Läden machen weniger Umsatz. Ihr Chef / Ihre Chefin gibt Ihnen den Text (Seite 27) und bittet Sie, die Details auf Deutsch auf einem Handzettel festzuhalten, den er/sie für seine/ihre Kollegen kopieren kann.

B Re-read the text on page 27 and decide which points your boss and his/her colleagues need to know and make a note of them.

C Now put those points into German in a structured text. Make sure your text is in the form your boss wants.

D When you have finished, read your German text and check that it is correct. Ask yourself this question: Have I given the sense of the text in a way that my boss and his/her colleagues will easily understand?

6 GETTING IT RIGHT
→ Countable and uncountable nouns, S. 274

Complete the sentences with the English translations of the German words in brackets.

1. Some kids were messing around in the shop and caused a lot of ▬¹ to some of the electronic ▬² on sale. (*Schaden* ▪ *Geräte*)
2. Some teachers like to give out ▬¹ at the weekend but I am always busy helping my mum with the ▬². (*Hausaufgaben* ▪ *Hausarbeiten*)
3. We moved house last weekend. Lifting ▬¹, for example, is really heavy ▬². (*Möbel* ▪ *Arbeit*)
4. I have found a lot of ▬¹ for my project online. I also got ▬² from my sister. (*Informationen* ▪ *Hilfe*)
5. If you are worried about you son's ▬¹ at school, you can ask his teacher for ▬². (*Fortschritte* ▪ *Rat*)
6. Every generation of parents complain about the ▬¹ of their children. When my parents were young, their parents said their ▬² was too long. (*Verhalten* ▪ *Haare*)
7. There is no ▬ that shopping centres are safer places if teenagers have to leave after 6 pm. (*Beweise*)

FOUNDATION COURSE 4

IT'S ALL RIGHT, MUM, I'M ONLY PRACTISING MY SOCIAL SKILLS

What do teenagers do in their free time? Some of them hang out in chat rooms exchanging moans about school or talking about the opposite sex. Others text, tweet or post their activities as they happen. Most teenagers today use social media to stay connected to their peers.

5 Many parents complain that their children prefer computers to 'real' people but they don't seem to realize that most of the kids are actually working actively to interact with other people. It used to be the shopping centre but today the places to meet are online. Social network sites are often the only 'public' spaces in which teens can get
10 together with their friends in today's busy world.

Kids today don't really have much free time. Apart from homework, a lot of them have organized after-school activities or jobs. Some parents do not allow their children to go out after school; they have to help in the house or look after younger siblings.

A generation ago, it was usual for teens to visit each other at home after school. Today's teens often
15 don't know any people of their age who live nearby. Social media gives teenagers the opportunity to socialize and relax with people of their own age after school. Instead of complaining, parents should be pleased when they see their kids texting or chatting online. These teens are simply using today's technology to learn social skills and have fun with friends.

(239 words)

7 LOOKING AT THE TEXT

→ Rezeption: Leseverstehen, S. 214

A Read the text. Say in two sentences what it is about.

B Say if the following statements are true or false according to the text. Give reasons for all of your answers.

1. Teenagers use all types of social media to keep in touch with their friends.
2. Parents would prefer their children to meet their friends face-to-face.
3. Teens like to meet their friends in shopping centres.
4. Kids have a lot to do after school.
5. Parents are happy when their children do outdoor activities.
6. A lot of teenagers meet in each other's homes after school.
7. Social media is often the only way kids can have contact with each other after school.
8. Teenagers can strengthen their relationships using social media.

8 WORKING WITH WORDS

A All of the words in the box appear in the text. Match six of them with their definitions, 1–6.

a generation ▪ activities ▪ moans ▪ peers ▪ siblings ▪ social skills ▪ to interact ▪ to prefer

1. brothers and sisters
2. complaints about something
3. people who are the same age or have the same social status as you
4. the ability to talk easily to other people and do things in a group
5. to communicate with somebody, especially while you work, play or spend time with them
6. to like one thing or a person better than another

B Write your own definitions for the two extra words as they appear in the text.

29

4 Leisure and free time

9 GETTING IT RIGHT
→ Quantifiers, S. 274

Choose the correct word or phrase from the box to complete the dialogues.

> any ▪ some ▪ many ▪ much

1. **A** Do you have ___¹ time this evening? I need ___² help with my homework.
   B Sorry, I have too ___³ homework myself at the moment. I don't need ___⁴ more.
2. **A** How ___¹ social media sites are you on?
   B I was on four, but my dad said I was spending too ___² time online so I only use one now.
3. **A** Have you got ___¹ friends on Facebook that you have never met before?
   B I don't have ___² Facebook friends at all. I don't have ___³ time for social networks.

> a few ▪ a little ▪ few ▪ little

4. **A** I can't come round till later. I have ___¹ more things to do at home.
   B That's all right by me. I need ___² more time to organize things before you arrive.
5. **A** There's ___¹ point in explaining what you're doing to your parents.
   B I know. Very ___² parents remember how things were when they were young.
6. **A** My friends have ___¹ interest in Facebook. They are all on WhatsApp.
   B I only know ___² people who still use Facebook.

10 MEDIATION
→ Schriftliche Mediation, S. 240

Sie hören zufällig, wie Ihre Mutter und Ihre Tante sich über Ihre zwei Cousins unterhalten. Sie sind beide Teenager und verbringen viel Zeit in ihren sozialen Netzwerken im Internet. Ihre Tante ist besorgt und möchte wissen, warum die junge Leute sich nicht mehr mit ihren Freunden nach der Schule treffen, so wie sie und Ihre Mutter es gemacht haben, als sie Teenager waren.

Sie beschließen, Ihrer Tante eine E-Mail zu schreiben, in der Sie die wichtigsten Punkte des Textes *It's all right, Mum, I'm only practising my social skills* auf Deutsch erklären.

> **SKILLS CHECKLIST: Written mediation**
> ☑ Have I read the situation?
> ☑ Have I understood who the mediation is for?
> ☑ Have I written the right sort of text?

11 DESCRIBING A PICTURE
→ Produktion: Bilder beschreiben und analysieren, S. 236

Your aunt shows you this picture of your cousins.

A Describe the photo. Explain how it relates to the text *It's all right, Mum, I'm only practising my social skills.*

B Describe the photo. Compare the children's behaviour with your own use of social media.

Job skills 1
Emails ▪ telephoning

Eric Jung is studying at a vocational college and is looking for work experience during the summer. Earlier this morning he received two emails.

1 LOOKING AT THE EMAILS

A Read the emails and answer these questions.

Email 1
1. How does the writer of the first email know Eric?
2. Why does he think Eric might be interested in his suggestion?
3. How will Eric get more information?

Email 2
4. Who has written the second email?
5. Where is she writing from?
6. What does Eric have to do next, and when?

1
Von: leon.dubois@deglado.com
Betreff: Work experience for you?
An: Eric Jung < ejung@gmx.com>

Hi Eric

How's it going? Listen, I had a great idea. You know that I'm just finishing work experience in an import/export company in Bristol, England, and I know you're looking, so why don't you apply for my job? The boss is always looking for trainees who can speak another language (not English) as their native language. I think your German's pretty good, eh? ;-)

I've asked the secretary to send you some info. I know it's not London (your dream city!), but Bristol's cool and the work is interesting. Like that crazy American girl said that night at the backpackers' hostel: DON'T TALK ABOUT IT, JUST DO IT!!

So, what about it, my friend? I'll be gone by the time you get here but maybe cu in Paris sometime?

Cheers!
Léon

2
Von: sarah.brown@delgado.com
Betreff: Work placement
An: Eric Jung < ejung@gmx.com>
▶ 📎 1 Anhang: OnlineAdWorkExperience.docx

Work Experience at Delgado Import/Export

If you are just about to complete your education, a placement in our company will give you an insight into how a small business is run. You will work in a small team and find out at first hand all about business.

Minimum of GCSE or equivalent.

Dear Mr Jung

I have your contact details from Léon Dubois. Léon has mentioned that you might be interested in applying for a work placement in our company, Delgado Import/Export, in Bristol.

Attached is a copy of the job advertisement that will be posted online next week.

Please let me know if you are interested in applying for the position by Thursday, 9 March at the latest.

Yours sincerely

Sarah Brown
Secretary
Delgado Import/Export

Job skills 1

B Work with a partner and compare and contrast the two emails.

Look at language, style of writing, use of slang and abbreviations.

> Leon's language shows that he and Eric are friends. His email is quite chatty.

> Yes, that's right. And the secretary's language is very formal. She's written a business email.

TIP	Email etiquette
1	Make sure that the subject line of your email is as clear as possible.
2	Include your name and contact details at the end of your email.
3	Attach documents when you say you will, and make sure they are correct. (Get into the habit of attaching documents before you write your email, then you won't forget them.)
4	Until you know somebody well, keep your emails formal and don't use slang or short forms like CU.
5	Never TYPE IN CAPITAL LETTERS as it looks like you are shouting and could seem rude.
6	Before you send your email, check the spelling.

2 LOOKING AT EMAIL ETIQUETTE

A Not long after he sent his application to Delgado Import/Export, Eric receives the following email. Look at the body of the email and choose the best option for a business email from the brackets.

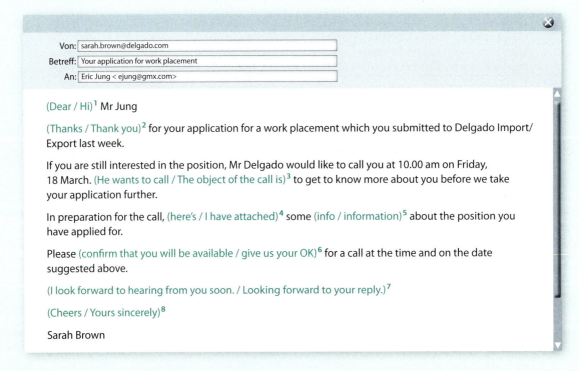

Von: sarah.brown@delgado.com
Betreff: Your application for work placement
An: Eric Jung < ejung@gmx.com>

(Dear / Hi)[1] Mr Jung

(Thanks / Thank you)[2] for your application for a work placement which you submitted to Delgado Import/Export last week.

If you are still interested in the position, Mr Delgado would like to call you at 10.00 am on Friday, 18 March. (He wants to call / The object of the call is)[3] to get to know more about you before we take your application further.

In preparation for the call, (here's / I have attached)[4] some (info / information)[5] about the position you have applied for.

Please (confirm that you will be available / give us your OK)[6] for a call at the time and on the date suggested above.

(I look forward to hearing from you soon. / Looking forward to your reply.)[7]

(Cheers / Yours sincerely)[8]

Sarah Brown

B Now study the set-up of the corrected email with a partner. Refer to the tip box. Has the writer followed all of the rules of email etiquette? Explain your answer.

Emails • telephoning

3 WRITING AN EMAIL

Schreiben Sie die E-Mail für Eric und verwenden Sie dabei die unten stehenden Punkte.

- Danken Sie Sarah für ihre E-Mail.
- Bestätigen Sie das Datum und die Uhrzeit des Telefongesprächs.
- Sagen Sie, dass Sie zum Zeitpunkt des Gesprächs keinen ausreichenden mobilen Netzempfang haben werden. Erklären Sie, dass Sie Zugang zu einem Telefon haben werden, sich aber nicht sicher sind, wie die Telefonnummer lautet. Schlagen Sie vor, dass Sie die Firma selbst zu der vorgeschlagenen Uhrzeit anrufen.
- Beenden Sie die E-Mail mit einer passenden Schlussformel.

4 PREPARING FOR A TELEPHONE CALL

Eric looks at some material about telephoning in English which he has from college. Unfortunately, some parts of the material have become separated from the rest.

A Read the tips for telephoning in English (1–6) and match them to the headlines (a–f).

- a During the call
- b Preparation
- c Making small talk
- d Softening bad news
- e Starting the call
- f Telephone numbers

Telephoning in English

1 Think about what you want to say before you start and note down some phrases.
2 Say your first name and your surname and the name of your company clearly.
3 Make sure you note down all proper names correctly. If you do not understand something, ask the other person to repeat the information. Ask the person on the other end of the line to speak more slowly if necessary.
4 English speakers often chat about a general topic, such as the weather, at the start of a call.
5 English speakers usually begin bad news with phrases such as *I'm afraid (that) …* or *I'm sorry, but …*
6 When you give telephone numbers, say each digit separately, except for double digits, e.g. 012334799 = *oh (AE: zero) one two double-three four seven double-nine*.

B Read the phrases on the fronts of the flash cards Eric made for learning English phrases for telephoning and match them to the German on the back of the cards. → Vokabeln lernen, S. 220

1 Can I speak to … (*name*), please?
2 Could you repeat that, please?
3 Could you spell your name, please?
4 Good morning, … (*name*) speaking.
5 I'll put you through.
6 It was nice talking to you.
7 Who's calling, please?
8 Would you like to leave a message?

a Guten Morgen, … (*Name*) am Apparat.
b Ich stelle Sie durch.
c Bitte wiederholen Sie.
d Buchstabieren Sie bitte Ihren Namen.
e Ich würde gerne … (*Name*) sprechen.
f Möchten Sie eine Nachricht hinterlassen?
g Es war schön, mit Ihnen zu reden.
h Wie ist Ihr Name, bitte?

Job skills 1

5 LISTENING
→ Rezeption: Hörverstehen, S. 225

It is 10 o'clock on Friday morning and Eric is ready to call Mr Delgado. As things turn out, Eric has to make two calls.

A Listen to Eric's first call to Bristol. What went wrong? Which phrases from exercise 4B do you hear?

B Listen to Eric's second call to Bristol and answer the questions.

1. Who answers the phone?
2. Why can't Mr Delgado speak to Eric at the moment?
3. Why is it likely that Delgado Import/Export is a nice company to work for?
4. Why has Eric not read the information leaflet?
5. How does Eric make the other person feel better about her mistake?
6. What is the rule about using first names at the company?

6 ROLE-PLAY
→ Interaktion: Ein Rollenspiel gestalten, S. 247

Work with a partner. Read through what you are going to say below and make notes. Then carry out the telephone conversation.

Partner A	Partner B
→ Start the call by giving your name and the name of your company.	→ Greet your partner and say who you are. Make some small talk.
→ Greet the caller by name and respond to the small talk. Ask how you can help.	→ Ask to speak to someone in the office.
→ Explain that the person is not available. Offer to take a message.	→ Leave a message.
→ Make a note of the message and read it back to the caller.	→ Thank your partner and say goodbye.

Useful phrases: Telephoning

Making a call
- Good morning. My name's …
- Good afternoon. This is … from XYZ.
- I'm calling about …
- I'm enquiring about …
- I'd like some information on …
- Could you tell me about …?
- I'd like to speak to Mr/Ms …
- Could you put me through to the … department, please?
- Can I leave a message?
- Can you ask him/her to call me back?
- I'll call again later.

Taking a call
- ABC Company. Jane Smith speaking.
- Accounts Department. John here. How can I help you?
- Could you hold on a moment?
- I'll try to connect you.
- Hold the line, please.
- I'm sorry. Mr/Ms … is unavailable at the moment.
- I'm afraid the line is engaged.
- Would you like to leave a message?
- Can I help at all?
- I'll make sure he/she gets your message.

5 The virtual world

MAIN COURSE

FOCUS

A On your own, look at the photos above and make notes about the role of social media in society today. Discuss your notes with a partner and then in class.

B In groups of three or four, draw a poster showing how you use social media. Include the points below and your own ideas.

- when you use social media
- when you don't use social media
- which social media you use
- why you use social media
- how much money/time you spend on social media

C Gallery walk: Put your posters up on the walls of your classroom and look at them all. As you walk round the class, make notes on the following points:

- which social media your class uses most
- why most people use social media
- how much the class spends on social media per month

D In class, talk about how important social media is to you and why.

5 The virtual world

TEXT A Using social media

BEFORE YOU READ

→ Rezeption: Leseverstehen – Grobverständnis, S. 214

A Describe the picture in a few sentences.

B Skim the text below and decide if it is about …

a the problems of young people today.
b how lonely people use the Internet.
c social media habits in the UK.
d Facebook and Twitter.

> **BUILDING SKILLS: Skimming a text**
>
> Skimming means moving your eyes over a text very quickly in order to get the main ideas.
> - Read the title carefully because it summarizes the article. Use a dictionary for unknown words.
> - Read all of the first paragraph and any more sub-headings.
> - Read the first sentence of all the other paragraphs. The most important ideas are normally here.
> - Scan the text for clues to meaning, e.g. words which are underlined, in **bold type** or *italics*.
> - Read all of the final paragraph. This usually summarizes the text.

BRITONS SPEND 62M HOURS A DAY ON SOCIAL MEDIA

That's an average of one hour for EVERY adult and child

Britons spend an estimated 62 million hours each day on Facebook and Twitter, according to a new survey on social media habits.

The poll suggests that around 34 million hours
5 are spent on Facebook each day, with a further 28 million hours on Twitter. And almost a third (30%) of the UK's 33 million Facebook users are on the network for at least an hour a day, with 13% spending at least two hours on Facebook
10 each day.

More than a quarter (26%) of UK women on Facebook check their pages at least 10 times a day, compared to less than one in five (18%) of men. Of the UK's estimated 26 million Twitter users, almost a third (31%) spend more than an hour a day on the network, while 14% – more than 3.6
15 million people – say their daily usage exceeds two hours. The results are based on a survey of 1,500 adults carried out by OnePoll for online bank, first direct*.

The survey also found Facebook was named as the primary social media platform by 59% of people. Only 9% named Twitter as their first-choice network, while 7% chose LinkedIn. And 11% of Twitter users say it is important for them to have more 'followers' on their feed than their friends, compared
20 to just 4% of Facebook users who say it is important to appear more 'popular' than their friends.

Dr David Giles, a reader in media psychology at Winchester University, said: 'People's social media habits tend to be largely dependent on the number of friends who are on the social network with them. If all your friends are on Facebook or Twitter all the time, you risk cutting yourself off from a social life by not doing the same. So you spend several hours every day online simply to avoid feeling left out of
25 conversations, or being isolated from your friends.'

* company name

MAIN COURSE 5

> Rebecca Dye, social media manager at first direct, said: 'The survey shows just how central Facebook and Twitter are to people's lives at the moment, often at the expense of other communications and **regardless** of how often they're actually posting updates or tweeting.
>
> 30 'It's important we **engage** with our customers in ways that best suit their lives, so the more people are using social media channels to have conversations, or just to "listen in", the more we need to develop our presence in social media,' she added. (422 words)

From: www.independent.co.uk

1 WORKING WITH WORDS

Match the highlighted words in the text with the following definitions. There are three more highlighted words than you need.

1 asking a small, representative number of people questions to find out what most people do or think
2 cut off
3 to interact with, to get involved with
4 is more or greater than
5 not worrying about
6 to seem
7 the number you get when you add amounts together and divide the sum by the number of amounts
8 the things people do every day
9 to not let sth happen
10 two or more

2 LOOKING AT THE TEXT

→ Rezeption: Leseverstehen, S. 214

Use words from the text to complete the sentences.

1 Facebook and Twitter are popular ▬ sites.
2 Twitter is less popular than ▬.
3 26% of women check their Facebook accounts ▬.
4 Every day 14% of UK Twitter users are online for more than ▬.
5 First direct is a(n) ▬.
6 Someone who is interested in what you post on Twitter is called a ▬.
7 Dr Giles works at a ▬.
8 Dr Giles says some people spend a lot of time on Facebook and Twitter to make sure they are not ▬.

3 DISCUSSION

→ Interaktion: An Diskussionen teilnehmen, S. 246

Read the following complaints made by teachers about their students.

> Young people today use social media much too much and have no time for homework, sport, hobbies or even their own families. They are up all night on the Internet and are so tired the next day that they can't concentrate at school.

> They are unfit, can't spell and have poor handwriting (they only use their thumbs to text).

> They are wasting their childhood and their money. Parents should take away their children's phones at night and switch off the Internet. Students should hand in their phones when they enter the school building.

A Look at the teachers' criticisms and suggestions and write down if you agree or disagree.

B Use your notes to have a class discussion.

C At the end of your discussion take a vote in class on whether you agree or disagree with the following statement: 'If we use social media less, our school work will become better.'

5 The virtual world

4 WRITING
→ Produktion: Schreiben, S. 228

**Use your poster (Focus) and your own ideas to write a blog entry about the importance of social media. Use the *Language for writing* expressions on the back cover flap.
Structure your answer like this:**
- Give your blog a title (e.g. 'A day offline?' or 'Last night a smartphone saved my life', etc.).
- Tell a very short anecdote about how social media helped or caused a problem for you or a friend (e.g. *Last Saturday night I posted a call for help on my Facebook wall and then …*).
- Next write two paragraphs about the advantage(s) and disadvantages of social media.
  – If you like social media, first write about the disadvantages.
  – If you dislike social media, first write about the advantages.
- Write a conclusion to show what you think about social media.

Write a blog entry to explain why smartphones should or shouldn't be allowed in lessons at school. Use the *Language for writing* expressions on the back cover flap.

5 LISTENING
→ Rezeption: Hörverstehen, S. 225

You are going to hear a call to the telephone helpline of *cyberbullying.online*, an organization that helps people suffering from online bullying.

Listen and complete the sentences.

1. Sarah is unhappy because ▪ .
2. People are sending her ▪ .
3. The counsellor asks Sarah if ▪ .
4. The counsellor says she can get help from ▪ .
5. Sarah went to ▪ and drank ▪ .
6. The counsellor tells Sarah she can make an appointment over ▪ .
7. Sarah doesn't want to ▪ .
8. The counsellor is going to send Sarah ▪ .

6 GETTING IT RIGHT
→ Simple past, S. 251

Use the key words to summarize Sarah's conversation with the counsellor using the simple past. Start like this:
Sarah phoned a cyberbullying helpline and talked to Frank about …

(Sarah) horrible pictures ▪ Internet ▪ everyone ▪ school ▪ can see them ▪ Facebook ▪ desperate
(Frank) need ▪ support ▪ parents
dad ▪ live ▪ girlfriend ▪ mother ▪ work all day ▪ brother ▪ young ▪ other family members ▪ too far away
advise ▪ contact ▪ school counsellors ▪ understand ▪ help ▪ students
not want ▪ go back to school ever again
possible ▪ make ▪ appointment ▪ counsellor ▪ phone
still unhappy ▪ messages ▪ Facebook ▪ not want ▪ delete
not necessary ▪ delete ▪ account ▪ promise ▪ send ▪ email ▪ practical help

7 MEDIATION

→ Schriftliche Mediation, S. 240

Cyberbullying.online schickt Sarah eine E-Mail. In dieser wird erklärt, welche Schritte sie unternehmen kann, um nicht mehr gemobbt zu werden. Ein Freund/eine Freundin von Ihnen wird auf einem sozialen Netzwerk gemobbt und bittet Sie um Hilfe. Er/Sie möchte für eine Zeit lang nicht mehr erreichbar sein, will aber nichts Endgültiges machen, denn seine/ihre Daten sind ihm/ihr wichtig.

Lesen Sie die folgende E-Mail durch und entnehmen Sie ihr die Informationen, die Ihrem Freund / Ihrer Freundin helfen könnten. Schreiben Sie ihm/ihr eine E-Mail.

> **SKILLS CHECKLIST: Written mediation**
> ☑ Have I read the situation?
> ☑ Have I written the right sort of text?
> ☑ Have I left out unnecessary details?

Hi

Thank you for contacting *cyberbullying.online*. To stop getting messages on Facebook (or any other social media account) you can *block people*, *deactivate* or *delete* the account and also *take legal action*.

How to block (unfriend) people
– Log into *General Account – Settings*.
– Click on the Security icon – *How do I stop someone from bothering me?*
– Follow the instructions carefully.

How to deactivate your Facebook account
– Press *More* in the bottom right-hand corner of the Facebook start screen.
– Scroll down to and click on *Settings – General – Account – Deactivate*.
– Follow the instructions carefully.
You can reactivate your account later at any time.

How to delete your Facebook account
It's best to do this on a computer. Before you delete your account, remember it takes at least 90 days; if you delete an account and then log in again before the 90 days are up, you reactivate the account; when you delete your Facebook account, you lose all your data.

– First go to *Settings* and download a copy of all the data Facebook has on you.
– Log out of or delete phone and tablet apps, including Facebook Home.
– Write an Account Deletion Epitaph, so people know you have closed your account, e.g.

> *I am no longer available on Facebook because I have deleted my account.*

– Go to the Facebook account deletion page and follow the instructions carefully.

Legal action
– Report cyberbullying to your school, institution and/or the police.
– Hire a specialist lawyer and take legal action. Your lawyer will contact web service providers and ask them to delete your data. In 80% of the cases they agree.

Remember – there is <u>always</u> a solution to any problem. Thousands of young people suffer from cyberbullying and when they get help, it stops!

Cyberbullying Help Team

5 The virtual world

TEXT B **Unwanted guests**

→ Rezeption: Leseverstehen, S. 214

BEFORE YOU READ

Why do you think the mother is angry with her son? Skim the text and write down what they could be saying to each other.

SKILLS CHECKLIST: Skimming

☑ Have I studied the headline?
☑ Have I read the sub-heading?
☑ Have I read the first paragraph?

'Don't have any parties'

Last words of mother leaving for holiday to her schoolboy son, 17, days before drunken Facebook crashers trashed her £1m house

Drunken revellers have trashed a £1.1million house after gatecrashing a schoolboy's Facebook event – days after his mother went on holiday and told him: 'Don't have any parties'.

The group caused an estimated £15,000 of damage and left vomit all over the terraced property in Highgate, north London, while riot police were called to break up 600 people in the street outside.

Now mother-of-four Catherine Seale, 54, who had gone to France on holiday with her husband when the trouble began, has warned of the dangers of putting personal details online.

Her son, Christopher, 17, had invited 60 friends round to his house on September 21 for his birthday, but a friend who put the event on Facebook did not realise the invitation could be seen by anyone.

Mrs Seale, whose 53-year-old husband Adam is a company director, said: 'All parents should be warned that this could happen if you go away and leave your 17-year-old alone. I think if anyone is going to throw a party, they need to look at their privacy settings on Facebook. It's absolutely essential that children are made aware of this.' […]

One girl at the party was taken to hospital with alcohol poisoning. Laughing gas canisters were tossed across Mrs Seale's living room carpet. Christopher and his aunt worked round the clock

to clean up, but the house smelled of vomit and alcohol for days. Mrs Seale added: 'The last thing I told him before I went away was "don't have any parties". The carpet was trashed and they damaged a skylight because somebody fell on it. […]

Chris paid a bouncer £60, telling him to only let in the 60 invited guests but the bouncer, who was paid in advance, was unable to cope and ran away when hundreds more party goers turned up. […] Mrs Seale heard about the trouble when a shocked mother who had dropped off her son at the party phoned to tell her that children aged between 14 and 18 were wrecking her home and got the first flight back after hearing of the chaos. […]

Mrs Seale added: 'It doesn't seem to have done him any harm at school. Apparently, he has even got a girlfriend out of it. I think his reputation has shot up because of it, which isn't very good for us parents.'

(417 words)

Abridged from: *www.dailymail.co.uk*

MAIN COURSE

5

1 LOOKING AT THE TEXT
→ Rezeption: Leseverstehen, S. 214

A Put the following statements about the text in the right order starting with *f*.

a A mother brought her son to the party by car.
b Christopher Seale decided to have a birthday party.
c Everybody saw the message.
d He invited 60 friends.
e Hundreds of people came to the party.
f Mr and Mrs Seale went to France on holiday.
g Mrs Seale flew home immediately.
h Somebody posted a message about the party on Facebook.
i The bouncer couldn't stop people from entering the house.
j The mother saw the chaos and phoned Mrs Seale in France.
k They got drunk and broke things.
l They told their son not to have any parties while they were away.

> **BUILDING SKILLS: Dealing with unknown words**
>
> There's no need to panic when you read a word you haven't seen before in a text. Think about these questions before you look the word up in a dictionary:
> - Is the word similar to a German word you know, e.g. *democracy/Demokratie*?
> - Is the word from the same word family as an English word you already know, e.g. *prefer – preference – preferable*?
> - Can you guess the meaning of the word from the context, i.e. the general sense of the sentence or the paragraph?

→ Mit unbekannten Wörtern umgehen, S. 216

B Say what it means: With a partner, talk about what the following words mean by looking at the way they are used in the text.

1 drunken (line 1)   4 essential (line 25)   7 to cope (line 39)
2 revellers (line 1)   5 trashed (line 34)   8 shot up (line 49)
3 vomit (line 6)   6 bouncer (line 37)

2 WORKING WITH WORDS

A Find words in the text that go with the following words (= collocations).

terraced ▪ riot ▪ personal ▪ throw ▪ privacy ▪ alcohol ▪ laughing

EXAMPLE: *terraced property*

B Use some of the collocations from exercise 2A to complete this text.

Before you ▬¹ and post the details on Facebook, you should check your ▬² because you don't want hundreds of people to come uninvited. If there's too much noise, your next-door neighbours will call the ▬³, especially if you live in a small ▬⁴ with houses on either side. If a party gets out of control, people sometimes drink too much and end up in hospital with ▬⁵, so remember: small is beautiful.

5 The virtual world

3 GETTING IT RIGHT

→ Simple past ■ Present perfect, S. 254

A Copy the table and put the following time expressions in the correct list.

> 2 years ago ■ at 7 o'clock this morning ■ at Christmas ■ ever ■ in 2000 ■ never ■
> in February ■ in the spring ■ just ■ last month ■ on Friday ■ on my birthday ■
> since 2005 ■ this morning ■ this week ■ today ■ yesterday ■ yet

Simple past (finished time / time in the past)	Present perfect (unfinished time / time up to now)
2 years ago, …	ever, …

B Complete the sentences with the simple past or the present perfect.

Simple past	Present perfect
1 Last week Sarah *received* a hundred Facebook messages.	This week she *hasn't received* any messages.
2 Yesterday she ▬ fifteen text messages.	Since 7 am this morning she has written eight text messages.
3 A few days ago she drank six cocktails at a party.	Since then she ▬ water.
4 Last week she ▬ to a counsellor five times.	In the last three days she has talked to a counsellor three times.
5 Six friends phoned her yesterday.	Three friends ▬ her today.
6 She ▬ Facebook last week.	She hasn't used Facebook this week.
7 She didn't speak to her counsellor yesterday.	She ▬ to her counsellor today.
8 She ▬ any photos last week.	She hasn't uploaded any photos this week.

C Complete the radio interview with a counsellor using the simple past or present perfect.

Reporter	Thanks for coming to the studio, Frank.
Frank	My pleasure.
Reporter	How long (you/be) ▬¹ a counsellor now?
Frank	I (start) ▬² about ten years ago.
Reporter	And can you tell us about your work?
Frank	Yes, certainly. At the beginning I only (do) ▬³ telephone counselling but since last year we (have) ▬⁴ so many cases of cyberbullying that I now give face-to-face counselling, too.
Reporter	Could you explain the difference?
Frank	Telephone counselling is often just the beginning. If someone (lose) ▬⁵ a loved one for example, they can phone our hotline to get help and support. Yesterday I (speak) ▬⁶ to a young man with that problem. We (talk) ▬⁷ for an hour and now he (make) ▬⁸ an appointment to see me next week.
Reporter	I see. How many people (you/help) ▬⁹ over the years up to now?
Frank	I really don't know. I (take) ▬¹⁰ about 30 calls last week alone, so it must be thousands …

| MAIN COURSE | 5 |

4 ROLE-PLAY

→ Interaktion: Ein Rollenspiel gestalten, S. 247

Last Saturday night while your parents were away for the weekend, you had a party at your house/flat. You invited 20 friends on Facebook and bought food and drinks, including beer and wine for them. Suddenly, in the early hours of Sunday morning your flat/house was full of gatecrashers. They drank all the beer and wine and turned up the music so loud that the neighbours called the police. When your parents returned, they found the house/flat a complete mess.

Work in groups of three. Expand the notes to act out a role-play.

Parents (two students taking turns to speak)	You
→ (*angry/horrified/shocked*) arrive ▪ find ▪ house ▪ mess	→ sorry ▪ mess ▪ gatecrashers ▪ not my friends
→ how ▪ gatecrashers ▪ hear about ▪ party?	→ probably ▪ see ▪ invitation ▪ Facebook
→ not ▪ click on ▪ 'Invite only'?	→ forget
→ how many ▪ guests ▪ you ▪ invite?	→ 20
→ how many ▪ gatecrashers ▪ come?	→ about 100
→ you ▪ know ▪ gatecrashers?	→ not know any of them
→ cost ▪ at least £2,000 (€2,500) ▪ clean up ▪ house!	→ (*shock*)
→ holiday ▪ Mallorca ▪ cancelled!	→ (*horror*) clean carpet ▪ wash walls ▪ myself?
→ also ▪ apologize ▪ neighbours ▪ in person!	→ write ▪ letter?
→ expect ▪ perfect behaviour ▪ next three months ▪ talk about ▪ Mallorca ▪ again	→ your own answer
→ no more ▪ parties ▪ at home	→ your own answer

5 USING THE INTERNET

Cancer fundraiser Stephen Sutton dies aged 19

[…] The 19-year-old, from Burntwood in Staffordshire, raised more than £3.2m ($5.36m) for charity after news of his plight spread on social media. […]

Stephen was diagnosed with terminal cancer aged 15. Rather than dwell on his misfortune, the teenager drew up a "bucket list" of things he wanted to achieve before he died. This led to him completing a skydive and playing drums in front of 90,000 people before the Uefa Champions League final at Wembley last May. […] He had initially set out to raise just £10,000 ($16,800) for charity, but his fundraising campaign attracted huge attention last month after he posted a selfie online. […]

From: *www.bbc.com*

A **Mediation:** Erzählen Sie Ihrem/Ihrer Partner/in auf Deutsch den Inhalt des Artikels.

B **Project:** Do you know of further examples of inspirational behaviour which have used Internet technology to benefit society? Research the details online with a partner and report your findings to the class.

5 The virtual world — BUSINESS OPTIONS

BEFORE YOU READ

Do you prefer shopping in a physical store or online? Give reasons.

SHOPPING FROM THE COUCH

Times and consumers' habits are changing. People are living increasingly stressful lives and prefer to spend their free time on the couch rather than in a store. That's where ecommerce stores are stepping in. Customers now do their browsing through a search engine until they end up where they want to be.

Once inside a virtual store, information is collected about you: what kind of products you are looking at, indicating what age and social group you most likely fall into, and perhaps even your purchasing power. This information is useful for companies, but it also helps the customer save time. Online stores can predict what kind of product you may need next and they help you find it straight away. This approach saves you the frustration of roaming through the aisles of big physical stores only to discover that the item you wanted to purchase is currently not in stock.

Competing with the large players on the ecommerce market has become increasingly difficult for traditional stationary stores. Physical stores don't have the capacity to reach the same client base or offer the same range of products. The challenge now is to increase efficiency to compete with online stores and to find a way to capitalize on the value of being there – physically close to the customer.

(221 words)

1 LOOKING AT THE TEXT

→ Rezeption: Leseverstehen, S. 214

What are the advantages of ecommerce compared to stationary trade? Summarize the main points.

2 THINK – PAIR – SHARE

→ Interaktion, S. 246

In a survey of 1,011 people in 2014, participants were asked to name three advantages of ecommerce.

1. Rate the reasons displayed in the graph according to your priorities.
2. Agree on the three reasons that you and your partner consider most important.
3. Present your reasons to the class. Use the results to draw a similar graph for your class.

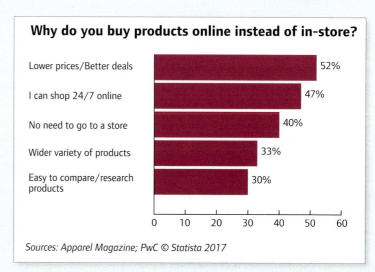

Why do you buy products online instead of in-store?

- Lower prices/Better deals — 52%
- I can shop 24/7 online — 47%
- No need to go to a store — 40%
- Wider variety of products — 33%
- Easy to compare/research products — 30%

Sources: Apparel Magazine; PwC © Statista 2017

3 DISCUSSION

→ Interaktion, S. 246

What are the strengths of physical stores compared to online stores? Discuss in class.

6 | Advertising

MAIN COURSE

FOCUS

A Advertising can be found everywhere. With a partner make a list of all the places (real and virtual) where you can find advertisements and report your findings to the class.

billboard ▪ digital signage ▪ viral ad ▪ virtual billboard ▪ …

B Experts say good adverts must have at least one of the elements below. With a partner look for these elements in photos 1–4. Write one or two sentences about each photo and then discuss your ideas in class.

ambition ▪ emotion ▪ entertainment ▪ excitement ▪
horror ▪ human interest (e.g. love, tragedy) ▪
humour ▪ identification ▪ inspiration ▪ mystery ▪
provocation ▪ sex ▪ shock ▪ surprise

C Find some interesting examples of advertising and bring them to your next English lesson. Explain to the class which of the elements they contain.

6 Advertising

TEXT A New ideas in advertising

WHILE YOU READ

Take notes on how each idea in the three following texts benefits society.

SKILLS CHECKLIST: Taking notes
- ☑ Have I read the whole text?
- ☑ Have I scanned the text for key words?
- ☑ Have I noted down the key words?

THE FUN THEORY IN ADVERTISING

A Volkswagen brings the fun
Giant piano stairs and other 'Fun Theory' marketing

If stairs played musical notes when you walked on them, would you be more likely to take them?

The video of people skipping the escalator in favor of composing music on the piano stairs of Odenplan subway station in Stockholm, Sweden, has been viewed more than 2.5 million times on YouTube.

The video is part of a new viral marketing campaign called "The Fun Theory." The concept, created by Volkswagen Sweden and ad agency DDB Stockholm, is based on the idea that "fun is the easiest way to change people's behavior for the better." [...]

The goal with these fun, do-good videos is to promote VW's new environmentally friendly BlueMotionTechnologies brand in an increasingly more competitive eco-car market.

"As traditional advertising is becoming less effective, and the competition in the market for environmentally sound cars is becoming fiercer, we believed we needed a more innovative approach to draw attention to BlueMotion," DDB Stockholm deputy manager Lars Axelsson said in an e-mail.

The video of the giant piano stairs reports that the number of commuters who chose the stairs over the escalator increased by 66% when the stairs were musical black-and-white piano keys.

The first of the campaign's three phases started with the release of the three viral videos, which aim to inspire the public to enter the campaign's contest, the second phase, by submitting their best video experiment of "The Fun Theory" to the website.

The winner gets a prize of €2,500 (about $3,700), and once the competition finishes "The Fun Theory" is "proven" by the video submissions, linking to VW and its new thoughtful technology: Its cars are good for the environment and fun for the driver. [...]

Next on the campaign: a glass recycling game machine, says DDB Stockholm. "By making driving and the world more fun, we turn the VW brand into a hero," Axelsson said. "Our experiments and our Fun Theory films make the world a better and more fun place to live." (343 words)

From: www.latimes.com

B The glass recycling game machine

In Sweden many people recycle their plastic bottles and cans but fewer recycle their glass. To encourage people to do so Volkswagen and DDB Stockholm have invented a bottle bank arcade which gives you points each time you throw a bottle into it like the machines in an amusement arcade. It makes a funny noise to attract the attention of passers-by and explains to them on its display how to play. The idea is so successful that in one evening over 100 people used the bottle bank arcade but only two used a nearby conventional bottle bank. (102 words)

MAIN COURSE 6

C The world's deepest bin

VW and DDB have also invented a very special rubbish bin which encourages people to use it. When you throw something in, it sounds as if the object is falling into a hole hundreds of metres deep. After five seconds the sound of falling stops and is followed by a loud crash. In one day people threw 72 kg of rubbish into the bin but only 31 kg of rubbish into a nearby conventional bin over the same period of time. (85 words)

1 LOOKING AT THE TEXTS

→ Rezeption: Leseverstehen, S. 214

Choose the correct statement (a, b or c) to complete the sentences about the texts.

1 When you step on the stairs at this station …
   a you hear a song.
   b you play a note.
   c you stop the escalator.

2 VW and DDB believe that …
   a people will do something new if it's fun.
   b everything people do must be fun.
   c more people will have fun if they take a subway train.

3 Lars Axelsson believes that today the best way to advertise a car is with …
   a traditional advertising.
   b environmental arguments.
   c new ideas.

4 DDB's Lars Axelsson says that "The Fun Theory" will make people think that …
   a VW thinks carefully about technology and does its best to protect the environment.
   b VW drivers are heroes.
   c VW makes the best viral videos.

5 The Swedes …
   a only drink out of plastic bottles and metal cans.
   b never recycle glass.
   c recycle less glass than metal or plastic.

6 The world's deepest rubbish bin …
   a is built over a hole hundreds of metres deep.
   b sounds like it is built over a deep hole.
   c is much bigger than a conventional rubbish bin.

2 WORKING WITH WORDS

A Match the verbs with a noun to make collocations. They are all in text A.

Verbs		
to take	to promote	to draw
to compose	to release	to enter

Nouns		
a brand	a video	music
a contest	attention to	the stairs

B Use words from texts B and C to complete the following paragraph.

The government ▪¹ people to recycle ▪² bottles but bottle banks aren't much fun to use. That's why the ad agency's idea of making a bottle bank seem like a machine in an ▪▪³ is so clever. ▪⁴ notice it because it attracts their ▪⁵ by making a ▪▪⁶. They then get ▪⁷ for each bottle they throw in.
The very special ▪⁸ bin is just as clever because each time you throw an ▪⁹ in it, you think it has fallen into a ▪¹⁰ hole in the ground. You even hear the ▪¹¹ as it hits the bottom. This effect makes it far more attractive than a ▪¹² bin.

47

6 Advertising

3 WRITING
→ Produktion: Schreiben, S. 228

Explain in a few sentences which of the three fun ideas you prefer and why.

Useful phrases
■ In my opinion / In my view, … ■ In addition, … ■ For this reason, …   ■ First / First of all, … ■ Because of this, … ■ All in all, …

4 PRESENTATION
→ Präsentieren, S. 243

BUILDING SKILLS: Giving a presentation

A presentation, using an overhead projector (OHP) or PowerPoint slides, is an effective way to show a new product or idea or give information. It can be given by one person or two people taking turns to speak.
1. Make sure your slides have clear illustrations, your spelling is correct and the vocabulary has been checked.
2. Number your slides and print them out together with your notes on hand-held cards for quick reference.
3. Practise what you are going to say with the other presenter or a partner before giving the presentation.

Your class decides to enter the next *Fun Theory* competition to invent something from everyday life that will benefit society. Form groups of 3–4 students and present a new idea to your class.

◉ **Choose one of the three invention ideas on page 212 and present it to your class.**

◉ **Use your own idea for a *Fun Theory* invention and present it to your class.**

SKILLS CHECKLIST: Presentations
- ☑ Have I checked the slides?
- ☑ Have I looked at the *Useful phrases*?
- ☑ Have I practised the presentation in my team?

Use PowerPoint slides, a video, OHP transparencies, (a) poster(s), or other visuals. Practise the presentation in your team first.

Useful phrases: Presentations

Introductions
- Hello / Good morning/afternoon/evening.
- My name's … and this is my colleague …

Starting
- Today we're going to look at … (*topic*)
- Let's begin by looking at / talking about …

Describing
- As you can see from this diagram/slide/illustration, …
- In this slide/diagram you can see how …

Handing over
- … is now going to talk to you about …

Finishing
- All in all / In conclusion / To sum up, …
- Thank you / Thanks for coming to this presentation.
- If you have any questions, we'll be pleased to answer them.

→ Job skills 4, S. 174

	MAIN COURSE	**6**

5 LISTENING
→ Rezeption: Hörverstehen, S. 225

Jim Tarrant, who owns an advertising agency in New York, is the guest on a radio programme.

A Listen and say if the statements are true or false. Correct the false statements.

1. Jim's first advertising slogan was for washing powder.
2. Jim says that advertising is legalized lying.
3. Jim doesn't think the 4 Ps are out of date.
4. Niche marketing means one advertisement is designed to reach a maximum number of people.
5. Product placement has been around for a long time.
6. Guerilla marketing is only used to shock people in Third World countries.

B Complete the sentences from the dialogue with the words you hear.

1. I heard they were looking for a ▪▪ for their new soap.
2. After a few years as the ad manager at the soap factory you ▪▪ ▪▪ your own agency.
3. An ad agency has to make a product ▪▪ ▪▪ somehow.
4. We ▪▪ ▪▪ ▪▪ the slogan 'It lets me be me'.
5. The 4 Ps are: p▪▪ , p▪▪ , p▪▪ , and p▪▪ .
6. Nobody drank any but people bought the bottles for a dollar each and ▪▪ a lot of money.

6 MEDIATION
→ Schriftliche Mediation, S. 240

A Hören Sie sich das Gespräch noch einmal an und machen Sie sich Notizen zu diesen Stichwörtern:

- Jugend
- Eigene Firma
- Wichtige Einsichten
- Trends

SKILLS CHECKLIST: Taking notes

☑ Have I structured my notes?
☑ Have I focused on the task?
☑ Have I noted the key information?

B Verfassen Sie mithilfe der Stichworte einen kurzen deutschen Text über das Leben des Jim Tarrant für die Homepage Ihrer Schule. Überschrift: „Erfolgreiche Menschen unserer Zeit".

7 CREATING A MARKETING MIX

A First, match the four Ps from exercise 5B with the following definitions.

a. This is what a company does to increase the sales of a product or service.
b. This means where a customer needs to go to get a product or service. Internet and telephone sales are making this factor less and less important.
c. How much will a customer pay? Customers expect this factor to be low for some things and high for others.
d. This can be an object or a service. It has a life-cycle, meaning that sales start low, grow to a maximum, fall and stop.

B Form groups of 3–4 students and decide what the best marketing mix is for the goods and services below. Write down your results and present them to the class.

a car wash ▪ a hairdressing salon ▪ a laptop ▪ a local electrician ▪ a new perfume ▪ a new sports car ▪ fruit and vegetables ▪ washing powder

49

6 Advertising

8 GETTING IT RIGHT

→ *Will* future ▪ *Going to* future, S. 257

A Tom Slater at Ad-Agency-Plus in Edinburgh is talking about a meeting the next day. Use the notes to make sentences with the *will* future (predicted actions), the *going to* future (intended actions) or the present progressive (fixed arrangements).

1. our / European salesmen / come / 3 pm / tomorrow afternoon (fixed arrangement)
2. our / American partners / join / us / on Skype / 3.30 (fixed arrangement)
3. I / think / it / be / good meeting (predicted action)
4. we / talk / about guerrilla marketing (intended action)
5. I / suggest / flash mob / Victoria Station (intended action)
6. I / believe / our client / get / a lot of attention / this way (predicted action)

B Tom phones a colleague to tell her about the meeting. Complete the sentences using the present progressive (fixed arrangements) or the *will* future (predicted actions).

Tom	Hi Gillian, it's me, Tom.
Gillian	Hi Tom. How did the meeting go?
Tom	Very well. The Americans (fly) ▬¹ over next month to sign the contract. I think this deal (make) ▬² a big profit for the company.
Gillian	That's great, Tom, and I'm sure it (help) ▬³ you get a job at Head Office.
Tom	Let's hope so. I (see) ▬⁴ the Human Resources Director at 10 am next Tuesday and I expect he (want) ▬⁵ to talk about the deal. I've just booked my ticket to London.
Gillian	Oh, I see. How (you/travel) ▬⁶ to London? (you/fly) ▬⁷?
Tom	I (take) ▬⁸ the train. A long train trip (give) ▬⁹ me time to prepare for the meeting.
Gillian	Well good luck! I'm sure you (get) ▬¹⁰ the job.

C Marilyn Marshall and Jim Tarrant are chatting before the radio show. Choose the right future form to complete the text.

Jim	I'm afraid I only have limited time because I (meet) ▬¹ my publisher to discuss my new book straight after the show tonight.
Marilyn	No problem, Jim. I predict that a lot of people (phone) ▬² in and ask you questions but we can stop after 30 minutes. You work all day and night! When (you/take) ▬³ a vacation?
Jim	Funny you should ask that but my wife has booked me a month in Hawaii. I (take) ▬⁴ the first flight to Honolulu tomorrow morning.
Marilyn	That sounds great! What (you/do) ▬⁵ in Hawaii?
Jim	Well, first of all I (relax) ▬⁶ for a few days. I (play) ▬⁷ golf and get some sun.
Marilyn	I understand, but I'm sure that someone as active as you (get) ▬⁸ bored quickly!
Jim	I don't think so. My wife and children and their families (come) ▬⁹ to join me next Wednesday and I think we (have) ▬¹⁰ a lot of fun together.

Make sentences of your own using the three forms of the future. Write three or four sentences for each form, for example:

- Apple is launching a new tablet on … (*date*).
- I think it'll be a great success.
- I'm going to buy one as soon as I get a job.

MAIN COURSE 6

TEXT B Creating a brand

BEFORE YOU READ → Scannen nach Einzelinformationen im Text, S. 221

With a partner, see who is quicker to find the following details in the text on Steve Jobs:

1 the year when Steve Jobs returned to Apple
2 what GUI stands for
3 what the slogan in Apple's famous TV commercial was
4 what the Tokyo Tsoshiu Kogyo company is now called

Steve Jobs (1955–2011), Apple co-founder and CEO, in 2004

BUILDING SKILLS: Scanning a text for specific information

Scanning means picking out specific facts or information from a text without reading it closely.
- Read the questions carefully, so that you know exactly what you need to find.
- Scan the text line for line, focusing on *one* type of information *only*, for example, numbers, names, places, dates, capital letters or specific words.
- Don't stop if you come across a word you don't understand. You can always check the meaning later if you need to understand that particular word to answer a question.

STEVE JOBS: VISIONARY AND GENIUS

Steve Jobs was not only a technical genius. He was also a visionary and even as a young man of 25 he admired how companies branded their products to make them into household names, such as Polaroid, Hoover, Nylon and Kleenex. He also realized how clever the 'Tokyo Tsoshiu Kogyo' company was when it changed its name to Sony (which sounds a bit like sunny). He understood that the technology he was developing was new, threatening and scary, so he needed to come up with a name which would make it sound non-threatening and likeable. That's why he thought Apple was exactly right. He felt that this simple, safe brand name would help people trust the new technology he was about to introduce to the world. He decided to target young people for his products because they were the customers of the future and his strategy was always to sell exciting, high-end products at a high price and profit.

   Steve Jobs saw clearly that brands are part of our culture and everyday lives and that everything a brand does is an ad – positive or negative – for that brand. He understood that every way a brand touches you is a message. Today, Apple's customers are in a constant dialogue with Apple's products. They discover more and more clever functions as they use them. They can tell Apple about any problems they are having and get regular updates to fix them.

Steve Jobs also understood the importance of packaging and presentation. When you open the high-quality packaging of an Apple product it's as powerful as any ad. Steve Jobs also didn't want the Macintosh manuals to be written in technical jargon, so he made sure they were written in easy English that people could understand. As a young entrepreneur he looked far into the future and knew he had to make this technology accessible to anybody and everybody. The Apple Store is also probably the best ad Apple ever did. You can actually walk into the brand and touch it, feel it and get its energy back from the young people who work there. He launched the Macintosh in 1984 and introduced the graphical user interface (GUI) and the mouse, which touched things on the screen which we now touch with our fingers.

   Steve Jobs left Apple in 1985 to make films and returned in 1997 when the company was fighting to survive. He rebuilt the brand and introduced a series of new products – the iPhone, the iPod and the iPad. To prepare the public for his new ideas he brought out the famous TV commercial ending with the slogan 'Think different'. The commercial was called 'Here's to the Crazy Ones' and shows the famous people of our time who thought differently and changed the world.

(541 words)

6 Advertising

1 WORKING WITH WORDS

Find the following words or expressions in the text *Steve Jobs: visionary and genius*.

1. the opposite of threatening (paragraph 1)
2. the opposite of cheap and low quality (paragraph 1)
3. to repair (paragraph 2)
4. the box in which a product is sold (paragraph 3)
5. someone who risks their money by starting a business, company or firm (paragraph 3)
6. to continue to live (paragraph 4)

2 LOOKING AT THE TEXT

→ Rezeption: Leseverstehen, S. 214

Read the text and do the following tasks.

Paragraph 1 Explain how Sony made it easier for their company to become a household name; say why Apple is a good brand name.

Paragraph 2 'Today people are in a constant dialogue with Apple's products'. List the ways in which people are in a dialogue with Apple's products.

Paragraph 3 Summarize what Steve Jobs did to make Apple's products attractive and accessible.

Paragraph 4 Discuss Steve Jobs' reasons for choosing a TV commercial about the 'Crazy Ones' to advertise Apple's new products.

3 ANALYSING A GRAPH

→ Produktion: Schaubilder beschreiben und analysieren, S. 238

Look at the chart below, then do the tasks on page 53.

> **BUILDING SKILLS: Describing graphs and bar charts**
>
> Graphs and bar charts are ways of presenting figures and statistics in a clear visual form. If you have to describe a chart, make sure you understand exactly what the graph shows and the units that are used.
> - Use the simple present (→ page 213) to describe what the graph shows: *The chart/graph **shows** the change in media ad spending between 2011 and 2017.*
> - Use the simple past (→ page 215) to describe situations in the past or changes that are finished: *In 2011 media spending **was** $158.6 billion.*
> - Use the present perfect (→ page 217) to describe situations or changes that are unfinished: *Spending **has increased** by about 3.5% since 2011.*

US Total Media Ad Spending, 2011–2017
billions and % change

Source: www.eMarketer.com

MAIN COURSE

6

Useful phrases

- The bar chart shows the total media ad spending in the USA for the years 2011 to 2017.
- The years are shown on the x-axis. The figures are given in billions of dollars.
- The line (graph) also shows the change each year in per cent.

- In 2011 media ad spending was / came to $158.6bn.
- It rose by $6.75 billion in 2014. / It fell by 0.7% to 3.6% in 2013.
- Ad spending has increased by about 3–4% per year since 2011.
- Spending has grown by $13.6 billion over the last two years.

- The chart/graph shows us that … / We can see by the figures for … that …
- All in all, the trend is upwards/downwards. / There has been little change since …

1 With a partner, practise reading out the figures for media ad spending in the US from 2011 to 2014.
2 Explain what happened to the percentage change in media spending (red line) in 2012 and in 2013.
3 When was the biggest percentage change in media ad spending? When was the smallest?
4 How has media ad spending changed since 2011?
5 Write 4–5 sentences to describe the bar chart.

Saying numbers

1,000,000 = a/one million
1,000,000,000 = a/one billion
$171.01bn = a hundred and seventy-one point nought (zero) one billion dollars
$190.86bn = a hundred and ninety point eight six billion dollars

4 MIND MAP

In groups of 3–4 make a mind map about advertising. Include the following aspects:

- the different forms of advertising
- the target groups
- the benefits
- the dangers
- your own ideas

Mind map: ADVERTISING — FORMS, DANGERS, BENEFITS

5 DISCUSSION

→ Interaktion: An Diskussionen teilnehmen, S. 246

A **Write a few sentences explaining why you agree or disagree with the statement on the right.**

B **Use your list in a class discussion about branded goods and vote on whether the statement is right or wrong.**

> Advertising makes us spend money on things we don't need, especially branded goods.

6 WRITING

→ Produktion: Eine Stellungnahme schreiben, S. 234

Use the ideas on your mind map to write a comment about what H.G. Wells (a famous English writer) said about advertising.

> **"ADVERTISING IS LEGALIZED LYING."**
> H.G. WELLS

6 Advertising — BUSINESS OPTIONS

PRODUCTS HAVE LIVES TOO!

The lifecycle of a product can be divided into five stages, according to sales and profits during its 'lifetime': from the **initial creation and development stage** to its decline. Not all products go through all stages; some will fail after a certain stage and others will continually return to the growth stage.

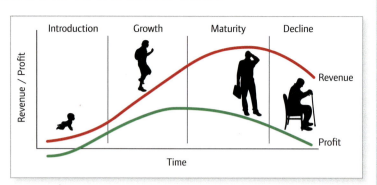

Once the creation and development process of a product has been completed, it reaches the **introductory stage** of its lifecycle. The new product is launched and brought onto the market, and potential consumers and suppliers are made aware of its availability. This is an expensive stage for the company as costs for distribution and promotion are high and sales are low.

At the **growth stage**, the product has been accepted onto the market, and sales and profits increase. This stage is also one at which the product faces competition, and the company has to ensure it stays relevant to consumers and the industry.

At the **maturity stage**, a product has reached its peak level of sales and profits and from this point on both will start to decline. If the product has been a success so far, companies will generally try to adapt to the changing market by modifying the product, its target market or the way it is marketed.

The final step in a product's lifecycle is the **decline stage**. Due to a decrease in sales of the product, profits gradually decline. This stage may be initiated by factors such as technological advancement in the industry, an increase in competition and changes in consumer tastes. As a result, the company is faced with the decision whether to drop, maintain or harvest the product. If the company decides to drop the product, it will either sell it or eliminate it entirely. Maintaining the product will involve trying to launch it back into the growth stage. Harvesting the product will require cost reductions. (319 words)

1 DESCRIBING GRAPHS
→ Produktion: Statistiken beschreiben und analysieren, S. 238

A Study the graph, illustrations and title above. What is a standard 'product lifecycle'?

B Describe the graph and explain the difference between revenue and profit.

2 LOOKING AT THE TEXT
→ Rezeption: Leseverstehen, S. 214

Take out your mobile phones and work in small groups to answer the questions.

- What models are your phones and how old are they? Are there any older or newer versions?
- What stages of the product lifecycle are your phones in currently?

3 DISCUSSION
→ Interaktion, S. 246

Due to the fast pace of technological innovations, product lifecycles are becoming shorter. What are the economic and environmental consequences of this development? Give examples.

7 Family and beyond

MAIN COURSE

FOCUS

People around me

Ideas and information around me

A Think about the influences that make people who they are.

1 Match the captions (a–h) to the pictures (1–8) above.

   a education   b extended family   c government   d immediate family
   e peer group   f religion   g role models   h the media

2 Note the three or four most important influences, in your opinion.
3 Work with a partner. Present your ideas to each other and discuss any differences.

B Work with a partner. Ask and answer questions about your backgrounds.

1 Change seats. Sit with someone that you do not know well.
2 Answer some of the questions below about yourself and make notes.
3 Try to answer the same questions about your partner. Ask if you do not know the answers.
4 Work in a small group. Take turns to introduce your partner's background to the others.

- Where do you come from?
- How do you live – with your family, with others, or alone?
- What household chores do you have to do?
- What do you do in your free time?
- How often are you able to go out with friends?
- When do you see your 'extended' family?

7 Family and beyond

TEXT A Living in a family

BEFORE YOU READ

→ Vorbereitung auf das Lesen, S. 214

Look at the text quickly and answer these questions:
What sort of thing does the writer always write about?
What age group does she write for?
What topic is she focusing on today?

SKILLS CHECKLIST: Predicting

☑ Have I read the title and the other headings?
☑ Have I read the introduction?

Teen Times May 15, 20..

22

PROBLEMS – PROBLEMS – PROBLEMS
by Pippa Parker

THIS WEEK: THE RIGHT SORT OF FAMILY

Just what sort of family is the right sort of family?

Should it be like reader Rajeev's family? … Or should it be more like reader Lisa's?

Well, read these letters from Rajeev and Lisa and see what you think.

Dear Pippa

I'm Asian-British, and my grandparents came over from India in the 1960s. We live together – three generations – and three of my aunts and
5   uncles and their families all live in the same street, too. I think you can safely say I'm from an extended family!
　　My twin sister and I used to love our close family life because there were always lots of people
10   around, and perhaps we were spoilt as we were the first grandchildren. When Mum and Dad were busy, our grandparents were the ones that we turned to. They and our cousins' families were also always there to offer day-to-day help, a meal or just a friendly chat. Then there was the time when our
15   parents' newspaper shop nearly went under, and everyone gave us financial and emotional support. It was the family that got us through, and I'll never forget that.
　　These days, things aren't quite so happy though. As we get older, we often want more freedom to do things our own way – go out with our friends at the weekend, dress the way that we want, say what we think about things – but it's getting more and more difficult, especially for Sita as she's a girl. Even when
20   Mum and Dad agree to something like going to a party, the rest of the family still seem to think they can criticize us because we're not traditional enough. They say we're forgetting our roots and our values. What's more, our grandparents keep saying we're the oldest, so we're the ones who have to set a good example for our younger cousins.
　　It's hard for Mum and Dad, too. In fact, they're probably the ones who are having the hardest time of
25   all: they're caught between my grandparents and us.
　　Does anyone else have these problems? I could really use some advice!

Rajeev Gupta

56

	MAIN COURSE	**7**

Dear Pippa

We moved over to England from Dublin a year ago and it's been a huge change. Back home, we were part of an extended family. Mum's parents lived with us and we had family all around, so there was always someone who was visiting to gossip or to borrow something or to play. Over here though, we're on our own – just Mum, Dad, my brother and me. Mum and Dad both have jobs now. Fine. But we've gone from being part of a big, noisy family to a lonely little nuclear family. As a long-distance commuter, Dad has to leave before 7.00 am, and we don't see him till after 7.00 at night. Then the rest of us go at 8.00. I catch the bus to school, and Mum takes Sam to his school on her way to the office.

School is OK, and there are various after-school sports and other activities that I'm involved in – drama, for example. I'm free to do whatever I want, and I've made two or three friends, too. So all that's good. But at the end of the day, it's back home alone to an empty house, and there's no one there with a cheerful hello in the old way. Instead, I do some chores to help Mum because I know she'll get home tired. I'm the one who makes Sam his tea now, and there isn't much time to relax and talk. There's dinner to help make and homework to do, and so life at home goes on from day to lonely day.

Big families can be a pain, I know. People don't just mind their own business: they keep minding everyone else's, and there's not much privacy. So that can produce tensions, especially between generations, but there are lots of laughs, too, and I miss that a lot.

It's Christmas next month, and I can tell you we can't wait to go home for that!

Lisa Doyle

So what's the answer? Whichever side of the hill we're on, it seems the grass is always greener on the other side. Perhaps the truth is that we really need a bit of both sorts of family life. We sometimes need the support of a wider family, and we sometimes also need the space to be free and independent. Actually, though, isn't that how things really are in many families today? Write in with your experiences. (764 words)

1 LOOKING AT THE TEXT

→ Sich während des Lesens Notizen machen, S. 223

BUILDING SKILLS: Taking notes while reading

- When you take notes while reading, always organize them in lists under sub-headings (see below) or using dates.
- You can leave out unnecessary words, such as pronouns and articles.
- It is quicker to use abbreviations and symbols, such as *e.g.*, &, +, –, =, etc.

A Work with a partner. Read one letter each and make notes on it.

Rajeev & Sita
Family type:
Feelings about situation in past:
Situation now & problems:
Needs:

Lisa
Family type a) present: ; b) past:
Feelings about situation in past:
Situation now & problems:
Looking forward to:

Now use your notes to explain the key points of your letter to your partner.

7 Family and beyond

B With your partner, do the following activities. → Rezeption: Leseverstehen, S. 214

1. Decide which letter writer seems less happy with life in a big family.
2. Consider who has more life experience to speak from.
3. Say what Pippa thinks about the need for a) support and b) freedom in family life.

C Say what it means: Explain the underlined words from the context of the text.

1. … when our parents' newspaper shop nearly <u>went under</u>, … (line 15)
2. It was the family that <u>got us through</u>, … (line 16)
3. As <u>a long-distance commuter</u>, Dad has to leave … (line 34)
4. Big families can be <u>a pain</u>, I know. (line 45)
5. <u>Whichever side of the hill we're on, it seems the grass is always greener on the other side.</u> (line 49)

2 WORKING WITH WORDS

A Say what *as* means in the following sentences: *because*, *in the position of* or *when*.

1. *As* we get older, we often want more freedom … (line 17)
2. … but it's getting more and more difficult, especially for Sita *as* she's a girl. (line 19)
3. *As* a long-distance commuter, Dad has to leave before 7.00 am. (line 34)
4. Rajeev wrote to Pippa *as* he really felt he needed some advice.
5. *As* someone from an extended family, Lisa does not like her new lifestyle.
6. She will probably find her new life in England easier *as* time goes by.

B Complete the text with *make* or *do*. Change the forms as necessary.

When Lisa gets home from school, she *does*¹ chores to help around the house, but first, she *makes*² coffee and relaxes for a few minutes. Then she ___³ a start on her jobs. First, she goes to her room to tidy up and ___⁴ her bed as she never has time for this in the morning. Next, she goes downstairs to see what other housework there is to ___⁵. She often ___⁶ some ironing, for example, or she sometimes needs to go out and ___⁷ some shopping at the supermarket. Then when mum and Sam get home, she ___⁸ her mum a cup of tea, and she ___⁹ her brother something to eat. That gives mum time to check her emails and ___¹⁰ her paperwork. Mum starts ___¹¹ dinner at 7 pm, ready for when dad returns from work, and that is when Lisa finally sits down at her desk and starts ___¹² her homework.

3 GETTING IT RIGHT

→ Relative clauses, S. 269

A Complete these sentences using *who*, *which* or *that*.

1. Rajeev was the one ___ wrote the first letter to Problems – Problems – Problems.
2. Lisa was the reader ___ provided the other letter for Pippa Parker's article.
3. Tension between Rajeev and others in his extended family is the thing ___ is worrying him.
4. However, Lisa is a girl ___ would clearly like to be back with her own large family again.
5. Problems – Problems – Problems is a page ___ appears every week in *Teen Times*.
6. *Teen Times* is a magazine ___ offers its readers lots of human interest stories.
7. It also has features like Pippa's – a page ___ helps readers with their problems and dilemmas.
8. Pippa is someone ___ has a real talent for helping young people with their problems.

MAIN COURSE **7**

B **Complete the story, adding *who*, *which* or *that* only where necessary.**

Teen Times is a magazine —¹ several other people in Lisa's year at school also read. It happened that a girl *who/that*² belonged to the drama club, like Lisa, was the one —³ saw it first. Her name was Gina, and although she did not know Lisa well, she thought, 'Wow! The letter —⁴ I'm looking at here might be from Lisa!' She read the letter again and compared it with the things —⁵ she knew about Lisa. 'Yes,' she thought, 'it was about a year ago when she arrived, and the place —⁶ she comes from is somewhere in Ireland. Another thing: the brother —⁷ she told us about is called Sam, too.'

She was not quite sure though. 'It's strange,' she thought. 'The Lisa —⁸ I know always seems happy and cheerful, but the Lisa —⁹ wrote this letter seems quite sad! Can they really be the same person?'

The next day, Gina saw Lisa at drama after school, showed her the article and asked, 'Are you really the one —¹⁰ wrote this letter?'

'Oh, that, er, yes,' Lisa said. 'Yes, that's the letter —¹¹ I wrote. I suppose I was stupid to use my real name.' She suddenly felt very embarrassed.

'Listen,' Gina said, 'I'm having a party on Saturday, so please come. There'll be lots of people —¹² will love to meet you!'

4 WRITING

→ Produktion: Schreiben, S. 228

Write Pippa's reply to Rajeev. Use this letter structure.

Paragraph 1: Thank him for his letter and for raising some interesting points.
Paragraph 2: Respond sympathetically.
Paragraph 3: Point out good things about his type of family situation.
Paragraph 4: Suggest how he can improve the situation.
Paragraph 5: Finish in a positive way.

Useful phrases

- Thank you very much for … and for raising …
- I was very sorry to read that … . It must be hard for you when …
- However, there are certainly some good things about your situation. As you yourself say, … . Then again, …
- Let me make one or two suggestions that may … . In my experience, it often helps to … . It might be useful to …
- I'm sure that if you … , you'll be able to …

TIP

Your reply is friendly and informal, so feel free to use contracted forms like *you're* instead of full forms like *you are*. (But remember to use full forms in more formal writing.)

Write to Pippa about someone that you know (or can imagine) – who has a family problem but who is too shy to ask for help.

Then write Pippa's reply. (You can use the same letter structure as above.)

5 DISCUSSION

→ Interaktion: An Diskussionen teilnehmen, S. 246

Pippa refers to the saying: 'The grass is always greener on the other side of the hill.'
How true do you think this is?

7 Family and beyond

TEXT B Leaving home

BEFORE YOU READ

Talk about the pros and cons of living away from your family.

Carrie — Moving out

I'm now 22, and I moved out five years ago. I was a grade A student, and I gave everything to my studies. But I was living with my dad over 20 miles from school, and things weren't going well. I had to get up ridiculously early to get the one and only bus out of our village to make it to school in the morning, and there were just two buses back after school. When I had to stay for extra studies, I didn't get home until after 7 pm! I had to make my own meals and eat alone as everyone else always ate before I got home from school. My dad and I also argued about everything. He always started on me for not hoovering the house before I left for school and not putting on a load of washing! What's more, he expected me to do that every day of the week. I was happy to do it at weekends but who hoovers every single day – and at 6.30 in the morning? Plus my dad was getting very nosey. He was going through the bin in my bedroom to find receipts to see what I was spending money on – my own money, by the way, as I had a part-time job at a supermarket. And on Saturdays, when I wanted to meet my friends in town, my dad banned me from getting the only morning bus! I had to get the only other bus – in the afternoon – and that left me just two hours with my friends. They always had lunch without me, and I felt left out.

My dad was turning into a real control freak, and I couldn't take it anymore. Maybe it was the same thing that had driven Mum away years before. Anyway, to cut a long story short, I moved out. I spoke to the *benefits people and explained my situation. Because I was moving away from home I was also moving away from my job, so I needed some help financially for a few months. My teacher helped me a lot, and she explained to the benefits office that my grades were dropping because of stress at home, so I needed the chance to complete school properly in order to move on to college. She also found me a small flat. It wasn't easy though. In fact, it was the hardest thing I've ever done – to go home alone every day instead of to a family. But I'm a better person now because of it, and I'm happy I did it.   (434 words)

*Department for Work and Pensions (DWP): manages most areas of welfare in the UK.

1 LOOKING AT THE TEXT

→ Rezeption: Leseverstehen, S. 214

A Put the pictures in the order (1–6) that Carrie describes her problems. Then do one of the tasks below.

- Briefly say what the problems were.
- Explain why you think Carrie found each of these things a problem.

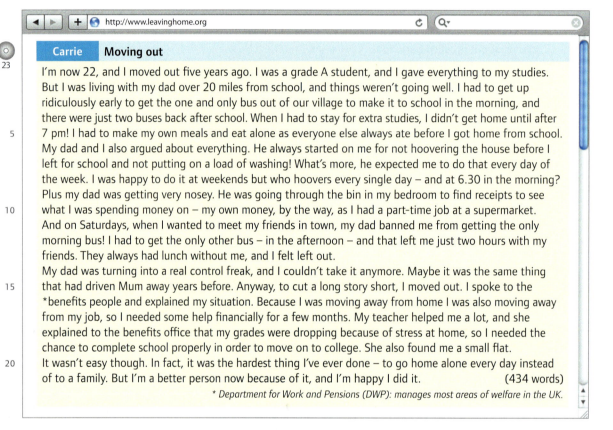

MAIN COURSE   7

B Say whether these statements about the text are true or false. Correct the false statements.

1. Carrie is writing about her recent situation at home.
2. She was probably the oldest of the young family.
3. The situation at home was getting worse.
4. The benefits office helped her financially and also gave her a flat.
5. She was very happy when she first moved away from home.

C Say what it means: Explain the underlined words and phrases in your own words.

1. … to make it to school in the morning, … (line 3)
2. He always started on me for not hovering … (line 6)
3. Plus my dad was getting very nosey. (line 9)
4. My dad was turning into a real control freak. (line 14)
5. … and I couldn't take it anymore. (line 14)

2 WORKING WITH WORDS

A Complete the story of Carrie's past life. Choose from these prepositions of time.

> at ▪ during ▪ from ▪ in ▪ on ▪ to

Carrie always got up ___¹ 6 o'clock ___² the morning ___³ weekdays in order to catch the 7 o'clock bus to town. She had school ___⁴ 9 am ___⁵ 3.30 pm, and then she often stayed for extra lessons. This meant that she had to catch the second bus home and only got there ___⁶ about 7 pm ___⁷ the evening. That was hard enough ___⁸ the summer, but ___⁹ the winter months she had to leave home and get home in the dark, and she hated it.

___¹⁰ the weekend, she had to do a lot of housework ___¹¹ Saturday morning and ___¹² Sunday, so she was only able to see her friends ___¹³ the afternoon ___¹⁴ Saturday.

Finally, ___¹⁵ her last year at school, it all got too much for her. ___¹⁶ a cold, wet evening ___¹⁷ November, she decided to leave home and start a new life.

B Complete the following with suitable phrasal verbs. Change the forms as necessary.

> **Paragraph 1:** move in ▪ move on ▪ move out
> **Paragraph 2:** get on ▪ get over ▪ get up
> **Paragraph 3:** turn back ▪ turn into ▪ turn out

When Mark and Karen had their first child, their tiny two-room flat was just too small, and it was time to ___¹ to the next stage of their lives – a bigger home. They ___ ___² on November 30th, and on December 1st, the next person ___ ___³. It was Carrie!

For Carrie, the little flat was perfect. It was in town, so she did not need to ___ ___⁴ at 6 am anymore, and she soon started to ___ ___⁵ much better at school. However, she was lonely, and it took her a long time to ___ ___⁶ the shock of leaving home.

However, Carrie did not even think of ___ the clock ___⁷ and returning to her old life. Instead, she got a few pieces of furniture, and she slowly ___ the little flat ___⁸ a home. After a few months, she was much happier, and she knew that her move was ___ ___⁹ very well.

7 Family and beyond

3 GETTING IT RIGHT
→ Simple past ■ Past progressive, S. 251

Complete the text about the day that Carrie left home. Put the verbs in the simple past or past progressive.

Carrie remembers very clearly the evening when she finally (decide) ▬¹ to leave home. While she (travel) ▬² home on the bus from school, she (open) ▬³ a book to try and study, but her mind (keep) ▬⁴ returning to her problems. Things (go) ▬⁵ from bad to worse at home, and she (not look forward to) ▬⁶ the evening ahead. Outside, it (get) ▬⁷ dark and it (start) ▬⁸ to rain, too. 'It looks like the way I feel,' she (think) ▬⁹.
As she (step) ▬¹⁰ off the bus, a cold autumn wind (blow) ▬¹¹ and it (rain) ▬¹² steadily. She (pull) ▬¹³ her coat tight, and she (turn) ▬¹⁴ down the dark lane towards the house. When she (enter) ▬¹⁵ the living room, her younger brother Ben (play) ▬¹⁶ a video game and her little sister Lucy (draw) ▬¹⁷ pictures. They (look) ▬¹⁸ up cheerfully to say 'hi!' before returning to their activities. In the next room, her dad (do) ▬¹⁹ some work on his laptop and he (not seem) ▬²⁰ to notice her. He just (say) ▬²¹: 'You (not do) ▬²² the washing this morning, so please make sure you do it tonight.'
That (be) ▬²³ the start of a very bad night.

4 LISTENING
→ Rezeption: Hörverstehen, S. 225

You are going to listen to a radio interview with Emma Schumann, a youth counsellor. She is talking about the things young people need to do when they look for their own place to live.

> **BUILDING SKILLS: Taking notes from listening**
> - Don't panic if you fall behind while you listen. Speakers often make false starts and repeat themselves. (Listen again for examples of this.)
> - Leave out unnecessary words such as pronouns and articles while taking notes.
> - You can also use abbreviations and symbols such as: *e.g., &, +, –, =, etc.*

🎧 24 **Copy the notes below, then listen to the interview to complete them.**

How to find right place	Dealing with money	Living with others
1 Look on ▬	1 ▬ your monthly ▬ for food, etc.	1 Set ▬
2 –//– in ▬	2 Always ▬	2 Do ▬
3 ▬ place	Looking after yourself	3 Talk ▬
4 ▬ people you will share with	1 Don't ▬	4 Respect ▬
	2 Cook ▬	

5 MEDIATION

Sie wohnen in einer WG mit anderen jungen Menschen zusammen. In der WG ist gerade ein Zimmer frei geworden.

Anhand Ihrer Notizen aus Übung 4 erklären Sie einem Freund / einer Freundin, worauf er/sie achten sollte, wenn er/sie das erste Mal von zu Hause auszieht und bei Ihnen einziehen möchte.

MAIN COURSE

7

6 DISCUSSION
→ Interaktion: An Diskussionen teilnehmen, S. 246

A Discuss in groups. Put the following tips in order of usefulness.

Advice for teenagers who are leaving home
- Washing-up is like saying sorry. It gets harder the longer you leave it.
- Just because you've got money in your bank account doesn't mean you have to spend it.
- Work first, play later.
- If you have to sniff your duvet cover to see if it needs washing, it probably does.
- Eat green vegetables. Raw, if necessary. Chips don't contain all the nutrients necessary to maintain good health.
- Inform your parents about what you're up to on a need-to-know basis. They need to know you're alive.

B Describe the picture. Then discuss what needs to happen in this student house.

Useful phrases

- The picture/cartoon shows a very …
- On the (left/right), there's a … (*room*), and in it we can see someone who is …
- In the corner / On the floor / By the sink, we can also see that …
- These students clearly have to …
- Just in the … (*room*), someone needs to … (*list of tasks*)
- Then in the … (*room*), someone should … (*list of tasks*)

C Read Emma Schumann's last words of advice and discuss these questions.

1. What might turn a home leaver into a boomerang kid?
2. What might turn a parent into a helicopter mum (or dad)?
3. How might people – a boomerang kid and a helicopter mum – feel in these situations?

Don't be a 'boomerang kid', who leaves home, and then finds it too difficult, and then gives up and goes back to the family home again. And don't turn your mum into a 'helicopter mum' who has to come and rescue you because you're doing things badly in your new home.

63

7 Family and beyond

BUSINESS OPTIONS

BEFORE YOU READ

You are about to buy a car. Which factors (e.g. price, brand, etc.) are most important to you?

COMPANIES JUST WANT TO GET TO KNOW *YOU*

Two common tools to categorize markets are segmentation and the use of 'personas'. These are used at different stages of the marketing process. Initially, marketers carry out research and interview real people in order to find out about their life goals, beliefs and attitudes towards certain services, products and experiences. Companies will use this data to create different personas to represent people who share similar
5 characteristics. This tool helps companies understand potential consumers and their motivations on a personal level. Examples of simple persona profiles are:

> **Jasmine** is a 17-year-old girl who goes to college and works part-time. When she finishes college, she wants to go to university and become a nurse. She likes helping people and believes in making the world a better place. In her free time
> 10 she meets friends and volunteers at a club to help disadvantaged children with their homework.

> **Mike** is in his early 20s and works for a supermarket chain. He is ambitious and wants to train to become a manager. He and his girlfriend, who also works, have got a young child. Mike doesn't have time for a social life because he is usually
> 15 too busy with work and looking after his child. He wants his daughter to have a good life and education.

At a later stage in the marketing process, companies think about markets in broader terms. Based on extensive data collections, marketers divide consumers into different groups, according to factors such as region, demographics (age, gender, race, education, occupation, etc.), social class and lifestyle. This
20 segmentation of the market makes it easier to reach target consumers.   (275 words)

DESCRIBING PERSONAS

You work in the marketing department of a company that produces breakfast cereals. Your newest type of cereal is 80 per cent whole grain, sugar free and organically produced. Whom will you market it to?

1 Work in pairs to design a persona for your product. Choose a name and think of character traits, interests and values. Brainstorm as much information as possible to write a detailed profile of your persona.

2 What market segment(s) does your persona belong to? Think in terms of region, demographics, social class and lifestyle.

3 Put up your profiles in class. Walk around to read the information on each persona. Make notes on the differences and similarities between them.

4 How many market segments are represented altogether? Use your notes to think about how to market your product to attract as many target consumers as possible. Discuss your ideas in class.

64

8 Entering the world of work

MAIN COURSE

FOCUS

Athletic abilities;
Mechanical abilities;
Working with objects, machines, tools, plants or animals;
Working outdoors;
→ mechanics, carpenters, engineers, police officers

REALISTIC The 'Doers'

INVESTIGATIVE The 'Thinkers'

Observing, learning, investigating, analysing, evaluating or solving problems;
→ psychologists, doctors, management consultants, computer programmers

Working with data;
Clerical, numerical ability;
Carrying out tasks in detail;
Following other people's instructions;
→ accountants, administrators, computer operators

CONVENTIONAL The 'Organizers'

ARTISTIC The 'Creators'

Artistic, innovative, intuitional abilities;
Unstructured work using imagination and creativity;
→ journalists, architects, designers, lawyers, dancers

Influencing, persuading, performing;
Leading or managing for organizational goals or economic gain;
→ managers, politicians, barkeepers

ENTERPRISING The 'Persuaders'

SOCIAL The 'Helpers'

Working with people;
Enlightening, helping, training, caring;
Skilled with words;
→ teachers, social workers, nurses, priests, counsellors

A Finding the right career is a big step in life, so it is important to think about what you want from a job before you start looking. List the following factors and your own ideas according to how important they are for you. Compare your results with a partner.

> a challenge ▪ a quiet life ▪ being your own boss ▪ company car ▪ excitement ▪ flexible working hours ▪ good pay ▪ good promotion prospects ▪ good working conditions ▪ helping people ▪ job security ▪ meeting people ▪ private medical insurance ▪ regular working hours ▪ travel

What are the most/least important factors? Discuss your findings in class.

B With a partner study the diagram above and decide which category is closest to your personality. (You may find that you have the characteristics of more than one category.)

C Choose one of the jobs in the category you have chosen, or a similar job, and write 4–5 sentences about it to describe the sort of work involved. Use ideas from the Internet and your own knowledge.

Useful phrases

- Working as (an architect) involves (designing buildings and dealing with construction workers).
- If you like (helping people), you'll enjoy the job of a (nurse) because …
- If you want to (work creatively) the job of a (designer) is ideal/attractive because it involves … (+ -ing form)
- On the one hand, (administrators) have … but on the other hand, …
- If you work as a/an … , you have to …
- (Bakers) have to … , but they don't need …
- The job of a/an … is very (satisfying/rewarding).

65

8 Entering the world of work

TEXT A Three job advertisements

BEFORE YOU READ

What sort of work experience would you like to do? Where would you look to find a suitable temporary job?

1 WONDERFUL WORLD ONLINE RECRUITMENT

COMPANY:	Sunseeker Entertainment Ltd
JOB TITLE:	Work placement as a hotel entertainer in Ibiza, Spain
TASKS:	Planning and carrying out suitable holiday activities for adults and children
WORKING HOURS:	Full-time, 40 hours per week; 3 months minimum
REQUIREMENTS:	Student status, good spoken English and/or German, basic Spanish
BENEFITS:	Free board and lodging + allowance of €200 (£160) per month Return airfare from home country to Ibiza (max. €250 or £200)
HOW TO APPLY:	Use the button below to email us your CV and cover letter.

2 UNITED KINGDOM
INTERNSHIP AT YOUTH CHARITY

YOUTH-CHANCE is a charity which sets up creative, artistic projects for youth communities in areas of high crime with no programmes for young people. It is staffed by highly motivated professionals, young people and interns, who all want to help local communities by offering exciting events and projects. Interns at YOUTH-CHANCE volunteer to work for 2–12 months, learn skills in the fields of management and administration and get useful work experience.

Interns will work at our modern, fully equipped youth centre in Hammersmith, South West London and/or at schools, theatres and other locations nearby. All interns are fully insured and receive a monthly allowance of £120 (€150) and free board and lodging (e.g. in homestay accommodation nearby). Travel expenses from and to the intern's home country are also paid.

Would you like to help? Send your CV and cover letter to Sylvester Page at sylvester@youth-chance.net or phone us on 0044 207 5499783.

YOUTH-CHANCE, 42 Vanston Square, London SW6 1QR, UK. Registered charity no. 52866320.

TOPTECH ONLINE RECRUITMENT – WE'LL GET YOU THAT JOB!

Post advertised:	Work placement as a theatre technician at Lloyd Theatre, Bath, UK
Allowance:	£1,000 per month
Working hours:	40 hours per week
Starting date:	ASAP
Duration:	6 months

The work placement student will …
- be part of a small team responsible for the set, lighting, sound and props for all productions
- carry out maintenance and repair work on theatre equipment

The successful candidate is …
- able to carry out basic electrical maintenance and DIY tasks
- friendly, helpful and flexible
- prepared to work evening and weekend shifts

Help will be given to find suitable local accommodation. Email your CV and cover letter to Tracy Winter in HR at tracy@lloyd-theatre.org or call 0117 315 7185.
The Lloyd Theatre is an equal opportunities employer.

3

MAIN COURSE

8

1 WORKING WITH WORDS

A Find the English equivalent of the following German expressions in the three job adverts.

1 Praktikum
2 Kost und Logis
3 Taschengeld
4 Unterkunft
5 Fahrtkosten
6 zuständig für
7 ein Arbeitgeber im Sinne der Chancengleichheit

B With a partner complete the word families using forms from the three job ads.

Verb	Noun	Noun (person)	Adjective
		intern	
	art	artist	
		volunteer	voluntary
to administer		administrator	administrative
to accommodate			
	technology		technological
to maintain			
	equality		

2 LOOKING AT THE TEXTS

→ Rezeption: Leseverstehen, S. 214

A With a partner study the three job ads again and draw up a table with the headings below showing the terms offered by the three employers.

- length of contract
- allowance
- accommodation
- food
- insurance
- travel expenses

B Which of the three jobs would you apply for? Which skills could you use to do the job?

3 DESCRIBING JOBS

Who says what? Match the sentences (a–d) with the photographs (1–4).

1 salesman
2 boutique owner
3 medical secretary
4 bank clerk

a If I don't give the customers what they want, they'll go elsewhere.
b We always give our customers the best financial advice.
c My company's product supplies energy from a sustainable source.
d It's nice to think you're helping people to get the treatment they need.

67

8 Entering the world of work

4 LISTENING

→ Rezeption: Hörverstehen, S. 225

You are going to hear two people being interviewed about their jobs. Listen and make notes under the following headings for each job:

- skills and qualifications
- type of work
- working hours
- pay
- promotion prospects
- job security
- job satisfaction

SKILLS CHECKLIST: Taking notes

- ✓ Have I used headings?
- ✓ Have I left out unnecessary words?
- ✓ Have I used abbreviations?

5 WRITING

→ Produktion: Schreiben, S. 228

Use your notes from exercise 4 to write a description of one of the two jobs. Use the *Useful phrases* on page 65.

Choose a job you know about and describe it in English using the headings in exercise 4 above and the *Useful phrases* on page 65.

6 GETTING IT RIGHT

→ *If* sentences, S. 264

A Complete the dialogue between a student and a careers advisor using the right form of the verbs in brackets in *if* sentences type 1.

Student: Now I'd like to ask some questions about pay. If I (work) ¹ as a bank clerk, how much (I/earn) ²?

Advisor: At entry level you (get) ³ about £1,160 per month if you (be) ⁴ at one of the big banks. If you (get) ⁵ promotion, you (earn) ⁶ a lot more. However, let me give you a word of warning. You (not get) ⁷ promotion if you (not be) ⁸ ambitious. If you (not apply) ⁹ for a better position after some time, no one (offer) ¹⁰ you one on a plate.

B Expand the notes to make more *if* sentences type 1.

EXAMPLE
you / get job / medical secretary / earn / £1,600 / month
If you get a job as a medical secretary, you'll earn £1,600 a month.

1. you / work / volunteer / get / £150 / month
2. you / only get / allowance / £40 / week / work / intern
3. you / get a job / bank clerk / earn / £14,000 / year
4. you / have better job security / be / fully qualified
5. you / love clothes / not find it hard / work / boutique
6. your yearly income / be irregular / be / boutique owner
7. you / want / make enough money / have to work / long hours / boutique owner
8. you / not be able / stay in a small shop / business / become successful
9. a good salesperson / earn / £1,000 / week / work hard
10. a salesperson / not sell enough / lose / job

| MAIN COURSE | 8 |

TEXT B New trends at the workplace

BEFORE YOU READ

Look at the photos on this page and on page 70. What do you think about this way of working?

MIND HOW YOU MOVE THAT CHAIR – IT'S HOT
HOT-DESKING IS A GROWING TREND, BRINGING A NEW CULTURE

MOST people dislike not having a desk of their own. They do not like the idea of arriving at the office, grabbing their "wheely" filing cabinet and making for the nearest free desk available.

Yet like it or not, this way of working is on the increase, bringing a changing office culture. The driving force behind this is to reduce property costs and it is made possible by ever-improving electronics.

Three years ago 95% of employees at ICL, the computer services company, had their own desks. Today, about 25% of the 20,000 workforce have no desk of their own. "A 40% increase predicted over the next two years has caused us to totally rethink our building requirements," says Richard Reed, director of corporate infrastructure.

"We opened a building in Staines which has 320 desks but supports 600 people. We see this building as a model for the future."

ICL has changed its culture from manufacturing to services, which requires a more mobile workforce. "We have three categories of employees," says Mr Reed. First, the pad-owners: they sit at their desk not less than three days a week. Second, the home-workers: they work a minimum of three days a week at home.

"Third, those who fall in neither of these and are, by default, mobile workers and therefore automatically hot-desk workers."

Mr Reed hot-desks, sometimes in one of the meeting rooms or going to the staff restaurant to plug into a computer; his secretary, who works for six bosses, is a home-worker but drives up the M4 once or twice a week to counteract loneliness.

"I'm afraid I do not have that homing instinct which I acknowledge others do – for example, those people who even though they do not have an allotted space in a car park will always tend to park in the same spot," says Mr Reed. "This has to be a gradual development programme, which addresses any concerns that employees might have about being able to do their job properly."

At the British Airways business centre near Heathrow, about 25% of the 3,500 employees hot-desk, and the figure has been rising. A wide-ranging training programme, cultural as well as electronic, helped to prepare employees for the changes in working practices.

"We wanted to make informality the norm," says Alison Hartigan, senior property manager. While she acknowledges some departments such as legal, finance and some strategy teams, are not so suitable for hot-desking, the majority are – sales, marketing, property, human resources, computers, and so on.

"Of course people are very territorial about space and in open-plan offices they personalise their space. With hot-desking they can't do that, it's the big barrier to cross."

Christopher Middleton, who joined IBM recently as a manager for smaller businesses, found hot-desking a culture shock, but a positive one. "You're judged purely on results, not on whether you're sitting at your desk all the time," he says.

"I have been coming into the office two days a week and the challenge is to book a desk in time

8 Entering the world of work

although there are drop-in areas where you can plug into a computer for a couple of hours."

Like many others who hot-desk, he finds he gravitates to the same desk when he comes into the office.

"It gives me a kind of continuity and feeling of belonging. Maybe I'll shake this off in time. I totally accept it might be difficult to change for some people. In my last firm, some people still wore suits and ties on dress-down Friday." […]

One sector which has had its fingers burned with hot-desking is the advertising industry. Large advertising agencies working globally who thought they could downsize their expensive prestigious buildings around the world found that this led rapidly to employees not identifying with the agencies any longer and leaving to set up their own businesses. It was an expensive disaster. […]

(662 words)

From: *www.telegraph.co.uk*

1 LOOKING AT THE TEXT

→ Rezeption: Leseverstehen, S. 214

Complete the sentences with the most suitable answer, a, b or c.

1 'Hot-desking' means …
   a you always have the best desk.
   b you always work at a different desk.
   c your desk is centrally heated.

2 Companies use hot-desking because …
   a they can use their office space better.
   b employees like moving around.
   c moveable desks last longer than fixed desks.

3 At ICL hot-desk workers are the employees who …
   a work in the office at least three days a week.
   b work at home at least three days a week.
   c have no fixed working routine.

4 Mr Reed's secretary …
   a never hot-desks.   b sometimes hot-desks.   c always hot-desks.

5 Mr Reed …
   a likes to park his car in the same space in the company car park.
   b prefers to work at the same desk when he's in the office.
   c has nothing against working in a different place all the time.

6 According to Alison Hartigan at British Airways, … departments are suitable for hot-desking.
   a a few   b most   c all

7 Christopher Middleton thinks that …
   a some people find it hard to change how they work.
   b male employees should always wear suits and ties.
   c Friday is the best day for hot-desking.

8 When advertising agencies introduced hot-desking …
   a they saved a lot of money.
   b they were able to open many more new offices.
   c their employees left.

MAIN COURSE

8

2 WORKING WITH WORDS

Find words or expressions in the text on pages 69–70 to match these definitions.

1. a piece of office furniture for storing files, documents, papers, etc. (paragraph 1)
2. buildings, e.g. office blocks (paragraph 2)
3. all the people who work at a company (paragraph 3)
4. needs (paragraph 5)
5. automatically (paragraph 6)
6. slow, not sudden (paragraph 8)
7. the department of a company that employs and trains people (paragraph 10)
8. the hard thing to do (paragraph 13)
9. casual, informal (paragraph 15)
10. make smaller (paragraph 16)

3 MEDIATION

→ Schriftliche Mediation, S. 240

BUILDING SKILLS: Written mediation

A mediated text should provide the person who reads it with the information he/she needs: it is not a word-for-word translation. When mediating a text use the following techniques:
- Read the whole text through for gist. Don't stop to look up unknown words while doing this.
- Go back and note down all the relevant facts for your 'reader'. Use a dictionary if necessary.
- Use your notes to present the relevant information in a German text in your own words.

Sie arbeiten für eine Firma, deren Mitarbeiter/innen oft im Außendienst unterwegs sind. Deswegen erwägt Ihre Firma Einsparungen bei den Büromieten.

Schreiben Sie eine E-Mail an die Leiterin der Personalabteilung, in der Sie die Vorteile von *hot-desking* erklären.

4 LISTENING

→ Rezeption: Hörverstehen, S. 225

Jenny Parker is a project manager at Green Energy Services. Today she is talking to Geoff Hall, the human resources director, about her new workplace.

A Listen to the dialogue and answer the questions.

29

1. What was the email about?
2. What does Jenny want to do?
3. How often are project managers in the office?
4. What solution does Geoff suggest?

B Complete the sentences with words from the dialogue. There is one word for each gap.

1. We would have more problems if we ▬ back to the old system, Jenny.
2. If we were in a bigger building, there ▬¹ ▬² enough room for everyone.
3. I'd change back to the old system if I ▬ .
4. If you ▬¹ a project manager spending two or three days a week on the road, you ▬² ▬³ a permanent place in the office.
5. If we ▬ you your own desk, you'd only use it two or three days a week.
6. You ▬¹ certainly ▬² a fixed desk if you did that.

71

8 Entering the world of work

5 GETTING IT RIGHT

→ *If* sentences, S. 264

A Two colleagues are discussing hot-desking. Complete these *if* sentences type 2.

Emma If I (get) ▬¹ a job at a big company with hot-desking, I would try to sit in the same place every day. How about you?

Frank I understand what you mean, Emma but if they asked me, I (be) ▬² quite happy to move around. If I (do) ▬³ that, I'd meet new people every day.

Emma But (you/get to know) ▬⁴ them if you only saw them once in a while? I (try) ▬⁵ to sit in the same place automatically if I (have) ▬⁶ to hot-desk. It's human nature.

Frank Hot-desking saves money. Companies (not want) ▬⁷ to do it if they (not think) ▬⁸ it was a good idea.

The finance director of a manufacturing company is telling his colleagues why hot-desking is necessary. Describe the following 'chain reactions' using *if* sentences type 2.

> we / buy a new office block → we / spend over £2,000,000 → we / have no money for new products → our company / lose its market share → many employees / lose their jobs → they / work for our competitors → our competitors / discover our company's secrets → this company / have to close

If we bought a new office block, we would spend over £2,000,000.
If we spent over £2,000,000, ...

Invent two more 'chain reactions' of your own.

If the computer system in a company using hot-desking broke down, ...
If we all went on strike, ...

B Ella Brown, the managing director of Green Energy Services, is talking to Geoff Hall, the human resources director, about how to save office space. Complete the sentences with suitable forms of the verbs in brackets (= *if* sentences types 1 and 2). Sometimes there is more than one word in a gap.

Ella If we (not do) ▬¹ something soon, we'll have no more room at all! If I were you, I (tell) ▬² the staff to have home office days.

Geoff Yes, that's one possibility but I think we (have) ▬³ a problem if we asked everybody to do that. If we (ask) ▬⁴ the project managers, I'm sure most of them will agree but I don't think we should ask the permanent office staff. We (find) ▬⁵ it difficult if some of them spent one day a week at home. For example, who will look after visitors if the receptionist (not be) ▬⁶ in the office?

Ella Yes, I see your point but (it/be) ▬⁷ better if we had job rotation? If we (do) ▬⁸ that, everybody will be able to stand in for everybody else.

Geoff But think of the costs of retraining them all, Ella! I don't think our finance director (agree) ▬⁹ if we suggested that. I think we should hot-desk. If we (buy) ▬¹⁰ some really modern-looking, hi-tech, plug-in wheely desks, I'm sure everyone will want one!

MAIN COURSE **8**

6 CLASSROOM SIMULATION

Try the following experiment with your class in your next English lesson:

Number the individual places at the desks in your classroom (not just each double desk) and put the numbers in a hat. Each student draws a number and sits at that place. If it is the student's regular place, the student must draw again to make sure it's a new place. <u>You must accept the new place without question to make this simulation work.</u> Spend the whole lesson at the new place.

After the lesson:
- Write lists of what you liked and disliked about having a new place.
- Compare your lists with those of two or three other students in your class.
- Have a class discussion about the advantages and disadvantages of sitting at a new place
  a) every lesson, b) every month, c) after the Christmas and Easter holidays.

7 DEBATE
→ Interaktion: An Diskussionen teilnehmen, S. 246

After the simulation, form groups of four or more and debate the pros and cons of sitting at a new place every lesson, every month or after the holidays. Half of your group must be for and the others against this idea. Split into 'pro' and 'con' groups and sit at separate desks.

Prepare for the debate like this:
1 Discuss in your 'pro' or 'con' group what you liked/disliked about sitting at a new place, e.g. different faces around you, getting to know people better, easier/harder to concentrate, more/less help from neighbours, etc.
2 Write down all your arguments in note form.
3 Use the *Language for discussion* expressions on the back cover flap of this book to make your notes into whole sentences.
4 Practise talking about your notes with the other member(s) of your group.

Conduct the debate like this:
5 The 'pro' group members present all their arguments. The 'con' group members take notes.
6 The 'con' group members present all their arguments. The 'pro' group members take notes.
7 The 'pro' and 'con' groups now ask and answer questions about the arguments they have heard.

8 WRITING
→ Produktion: Eine Stellungnahme schreiben, S. 234

> **BUILDING SKILLS: Writing a comment**
>
> A comment expresses your own opinion about a particular topic or question. To ensure that your comment is well structured follow these steps:
> - Study the instructions carefully to make sure you know exactly what to write about.
> - Structure your arguments logically, e.g. under headings or in a mind map. Include arguments for and against.
> - Refer to the question in your first sentence then present your arguments in separate paragraphs.
> - Conclude your comment with a final sentence clearly stating your opinion.

Use your notes from exercise 3 and your own ideas to write a short comment about hot-desking. Title: *Why I would or wouldn't like to hot-desk*.

8 Entering the world of work

BUSINESS OPTIONS

1 BRAINSTORMING

You have one minute to list as many famous business leaders and company founders as you can think of. Compare your lists in class. How many names are female and how many are male?

2 ANALYSING A GRAPH

→ Produktion: Statistiken beschreiben und analysieren, S. 238

Describe and analyse the graph. What conclusion can you draw from it?

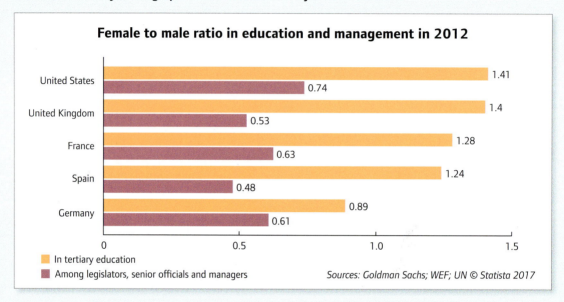

EXAMPLE In 2012, for every 100 men there were 141 women enrolled in tertiary education in the United States. At the same time, for every 100 male legislators, senior officials and managers there were 74 females.

3 DISCUSSION

→ Interaktion, S. 246

The female or gender quota means that organizations have to employ a certain percentage of females. The aim is to ensure that females have the same opportunities in their professional lives as men.

> "We need a female quota to assure equal pay and equal employment opportunities for women. The business world is dominated by middle-aged, white men. Without regulation from the outside, the corporate world won't change."

A Do you agree or disagree with the statement above? Make notes.

B Use your notes to discuss the female quota in class. At the end of the discussion, vote on whether governments should introduce a female quota.

Job skills 2
CVs and cover letters ▪ interviews

Eric Jung is looking for work in the UK. He applies for a post in London.

1 LOOKING AT THE CV

Compare the information on Eric's CV with the job advertisement. Say why he believes he is a suitable candidate for the position.

TRAINEE OFFICE ASSISTANT – General office duties

- We are a manufacturing company located in London.
- We are looking for a trainee to work in our export office.
- You are a careful and accurate worker, flexible and willing to learn.
- You speak good German and at least one other foreign language.
- Computer skills are a must.

Apply with CV and cover letter to Joan Shaw, Magnus & Klein plc, 1004 Thames Road, London SE7 2XY quoting reference FTD/0204.

Eric Jung
Klarastr. 430 · 79106 Freiburg · Germany
Phone (+49) 0761 234589 · Mobile (+49) 0176 28948610
Email ejung@gmx.com

Personal statement
Highly-motivated student of business studies seeking practical experience in the UK.

Work experience
June – August 20..	Delgado Import/Export, Bristol, England. Duties: general office work (answering telephone; writing emails) and updating spreadsheets.

Education and training
August 20.. – present	Berufskolleg, Freiburg (equivalent to British vocational college) Main subjects: Business Studies, English, German, Spanish Fachhochschulreife (German higher education entrance qualifications): Expected July 20..
August 20.. – July 20..	Realschule, Freiburg (equivalent to British secondary school) Mittlere Reife (Final exams similar to GCSE)

Skills
German (native speaker), English (fluent, oral and written), Spanish (intermediate)
Computer: MS Office
Good at working under pressure, friendly, flexible

Interests
Sport, travel

References
Names of referees available on request

Job skills 2

2 LOOKING AT THE COVER LETTER

A Read Eric's cover letter to Magnus & Klein plc and label the parts 1–10.

> body of the letter ▪ complimentary close ▪ date ▪ enclosure ▪ inside address ▪
> reference ▪ salutation ▪ signature ▪ subject line ▪ writer's address

Klarastr. 430
79106 Freiburg
Germany   **1**
Phone (+49) 0761 234589
Mobile (+49) 0176 28948610
Email ejung@gmx.com

Magnus & Klein plc
Attn: Ms Joan Shaw
1004 Thames Road   **2**
London
SE7 2XY
UK

5 April 20..   **3**

Your ref: FTD/0204   **4**

Dear Ms Shaw   **5**

Trainee Office Assistant   **6**

I would like to apply for the position of Trainee Office Assistant as advertised in today's copy of the *Financial Times Deutschland*.   **7**

As you can see from my CV, I am currently doing business studies at a German vocational college. During my work placement in a British import/export company, I had the opportunity to learn business practices and I am keen to add to my experience of international business by working further in an English-speaking country.

In addition to German, which is my native language, I speak fluent English and I have recently added Spanish to my list of foreign languages. I am sure that my language abilities will make me an asset to your team.

I would appreciate it if you considered my application and hope that you will grant me an interview.

I look forward to hearing from you soon.

Yours sincerely   **8**
Eric Jung
Eric Jung   **9**

Encl: CV   **10**

CVs and cover letters • interviews

B Find the following sections in the body of the letter. Write out the key phrases in your notebook.

1 asking to be considered for an interview
2 reference to details on CV
3 reference to the position
4 saying why the writer is applying for the position
5 stating why the applicant is the best person for the job

3 WRITING A COVER LETTER

You are going to work with a partner, compile your CV and write a cover letter.

1 Study the job advertisement on page 75 or choose one from page 66 and answer the following questions.
- What is the job title?
- Who is advertising the job?
- Where will the job applicant work?
- What educational background and skills does the job applicant need?
- How do you apply?

2 You and your partner are both going to apply for the job. Compile your own CV in English and write a cover letter. Use any items from Eric's CV and cover letter that are appropriate for you. When you have finished, exchange your CVs and cover letters and do peer correction.

1 With your partner, talk about what you would like to do in the future. Talk about where you would like to work and what type of work you would like to do. Make some notes and use them to write a short job advertisement. Pin it on the wall.

2 Choose one of the job advertisements from the wall and discuss it with your partner. You and your partner are both going to apply for the job. Compile your own CV in English and write a cover letter. Use any items from Eric's CV and cover letter that are appropriate for you. When you have finished, exchange your CVs and cover letters and do peer correction.

German school types and qualifications

Grundschule	primary school
Realschule	secondary school
Gymnasium	secondary/grammar school (GB), high school (USA)
Berufsschule	vocational school
Berufskolleg, Fachoberschule	vocational college
Fachhochschule	university of applied sciences
Mittlere Reife	GCSE (General Certificate of Secondary Education)
Abitur	A levels (GB), high school diploma (USA)
Fachhochschulreife	German higher education entrance qualifications
Noten 1–6	Grades A–F

Job skills 2

4 PREPARING FOR AN INTERVIEW

The HR office at Magnus & Klein has informed Eric that Ms Shaw will interview him on the phone next week. He prepares himself by making a list of questions Ms Shaw might ask him. He also thinks about what he would like to know from Ms Shaw.

A With a partner, study the list of typical interview questions and sort them under the correct heading. Then add one more question under each heading.

- About yourself
- About your motivation
- About your education, work experience and skills

1. Can you tell me something about yourself?
2. Why do you want to work for this company?
3. What are your strengths and weaknesses?
4. Why are you training at vocational college?
5. Why do you think you would be a good candidate for the job?
6. What have you learned that might help you in the position you're applying for here?

B Now study Eric's list of questions. With your partner, add two more questions.

- Who will I report to?
- When will I hear if I have the job or not?
- What kind of training will I be given?

> **TIP Using first names**
>
> Don't be surprised if a superior calls you by your first name when doing business in Anglo-American countries. It is best if you use *Ms* or *Mr* when speaking to superiors until they invite you to use their first name.

5 LISTENING

→ Rezeption: Hörverstehen, S. 225

30

A Listen to the main part of the interview. Which questions does Ms Shaw ask? How does Eric answer the questions? Make notes.

B Listen to the conclusion of the interview. What does Eric want to know? What is the next step in the application process?

6 ROLE-PLAY

→ Interaktion: Ein Rollenspiel gestalten, S. 247

Work with a partner. Use the role cards below to practise an interview for a job.

Partner A: you are the interviewer

You are going to interview your partner as if he/she is a candidate for a job. Start the interview by introducing yourself then ask the following questions.
- How would you describe yourself?
- What are your strengths and weaknesses?
- Why did you decide to study business management?
- Do you have any questions for me?

Partner B: you are the candidate

Your partner is going to interview you for a job. Think about the questions the interviewer might ask you. Make notes. When the interviewer asks you if you have any questions, choose two or three from this list.
- Who will I work with?
- What training will you give me?
- What will my responsibilities be?
- When will I hear if my application has been successful or not?

9 Multiculturalism

MAIN COURSE

FOCUS

A The photos above show festivals in Vancouver, Canada. Describe the people and what they are doing. What cultural backgrounds might these people have?

to carry ▪ to dance ▪ to light ▪ to march ▪ to perform
balloon ▪ candle ▪ dragon ▪ headdress ▪ lantern ▪ pipe band ▪ samba ▪ sari
Chinese ▪ Indian ▪ Hindu ▪ Irish ▪ Latin American

B Match photos 1–4 with the festivals in the cultural programme on the right. Make statements to a visitor.

If you visit Vancouver in early February, you can go to the Chinese New Year and (see) ...

February	Chinese New Year (lion dance, Tai Chi, dragon boat display)
March	St Patrick's Day Parade (march, music, ceilidhs)
Mid-summer	Carnaval Del Sol (Latin American dancing, cuisine, crafts)
Mid-autumn	Diwali (dancing, lanterns, traditional music, cuisine)

C Work with a partner. Think of local festivals that a visitor to your part of the world might enjoy. Create a calendar of events and then make statements to a visitor.

If you visit ... (place) in ... (time of year), you can ...

D Work with your partner again. List some of the different cultures in Germany today. Discuss any way that you get to know, or learn about, people from other cultures.

Say what changes you think these cultures bring to the traditional German way of life.

9 Multiculturalism

TEXT A Life as a refugee

BEFORE YOU READ → Vorbereitung auf das Lesen, S. 214

A Look at a map. What parts of the world would you probably cross on a flight from Germany to Eritrea?

B Look at the information about Eritrea and about the boy in the picture. Why might he be a refugee?

Eritrea:
Independent East African state on the Red Sea coast. Separated from Ethiopia after violent fighting in 1999–2000.

Family name: Kelo
Given name: Alem
Father's nationality: Ethiopian
Mother's nationality: Eritrean

31

refugee boy
Benjamin Zephaniah

Ethiopia
As the family lay sleeping, soldiers kicked down the door of the house and entered, waving their rifles around and shouting. Alem ran into the room where his parents were, to find that they had been dragged out of bed and forced to stand facing the wall.
5   The soldier who was in command went and stood so that his mouth was six inches away from Alem's father's ear and shouted, 'What kind of man are you?'
    Alem's father shuddered with fear; his voice trembled as he replied, 'I am an African.'
    Alem looked on terrified as the soldier shot a number of bullets into the floor around the feet of his father and mother.
10 His mother screamed with fear. 'Please leave us! We only want peace.'
    The soldier continued shouting. 'Are you Ethiopian or Eritrean? Tell us, we want to know.'
    'I am an African,' Alem's father replied.
15 The soldier raised his rifle and pointed it at Alem's father. 'You are a traitor.' He turned and pointed the rifle at Alem's mother. 'And she is the enemy.' Then he turned and pointed the rifle at Alem's forehead. 'And he is a mongrel.'
    Turning back to Alem's father he dropped his voice and
20 said, 'Leave Ethiopia or die.'

Background to the next part of Alem's life
The Kelo family moved to Eritrea, but equally bad things happened to them there. That was when Alem's parents decided that they must get him to safety in the UK. His father took him there and left him, knowing that because his son was without a parent, the system would look after him well. His plan succeeded: the authorities found Alem a welcoming family to live with – the Fitzpatricks – and soon he was beginning a new life, complete with a new school and new friends.

MAIN COURSE

9

Then came terrible news. While Alem and his father had been gone, 'very evil people' had killed Alem's mother and left her dead near the border. After his return to Eritrea, Alem's father had finally found her body and wrote that he must now get to Britain to be with him.

The law was not so kind to Mr Kelo. When he arrived, the authorities arrested him and sent him first to a detention centre and then to a cheap hotel that was used for refugees and homeless families. It was an unpleasant, unhappy place in a poor part of London.

And then the rules for Alem suddenly changed – for he had a parent to look after him now. The courts said that he had to leave his new family and move into his father's small hotel room. Soon, he was learning the life of normal refugees – shopping, for example.

Britain
They didn't spend very long at the supermarket; all they put in their basket was a small amount of vegetables, some tinned meat and a packet of biscuits. As they were queuing for the cashier, Alem noticed that other checkouts were less busy.

5 'Father, look at those other counters! Why are we waiting in this long queue? Let's go to one of them.'
Mr Kelo's eyes dropped as he realized that Alem hadn't understood the deal. 'We can't,' he said, 'we don't have any money.'
'So what are you paying with?'
Mr Kelo took out his wallet and pulled out what
10 looked like tickets. 'These, I have to pay with these. These are vouchers; look up there.'
He pointed to a sign above the counter where they were waiting. It read, 'Food vouchers only.'
'What is this all about?' Alem asked.
15 'These vouchers are for asylum seekers. We cannot buy clothes with them, we cannot get any change from our shopping with them, and we cannot use them at any other counter.'

The queue was long and full of exactly the same kind of people Alem had seen outside the court-
20 rooms, Asians, Africans, Romanians and Kosovans, all waiting with their heads hanging down, looking humiliated. Meanwhile, many other cashiers were sitting filing their nails or combing their hair, waiting for customers. Other shoppers just seemed to be a lot happier and some looked over to the 'Vouchers only' queue as if the customers there were exhibition pieces.
Alem could also see the humiliation on his father's face but as for himself he felt angry; he didn't
25 want to show it but he felt really angry. His father was a qualified person who had been in a good job and always proud to have earned every penny he had, but now he had been reduced to what amounted to living off aid. Alem looked up and down the queue, he wondered how many people there were in the same position. Which of the men and women were doctors, lawyers, nurses or mathematicians? Could he be standing next to one of Bosnia's most promising architects, or an Iranian airline pilot? His father saw
30 him silently shake his head in disgust as they shuffled down the line. (813 words)

From: Benjamin Zephaniah, *refugee boy*, Bloomsbury, London, 2001

---

1 LOOKING AT THE TEXTS

→ Rezeption: Leseverstehen, S. 214

A Put these events from Alem's life in the correct order.

a Alem's move to England
b his mother's death
c the move to Eritrea
d living in England with his father
e living in Ethiopia with his parents
f living in England with the Fitzpatricks
g his father's move to England

9 Multiculturalism

B Answer the questions below on the extracts from *refugee boy*. → Gründliches Lesen, S. 223

> **BUILDING SKILLS: Reading for understanding**
>
> In order to answer questions on the text, you usually have to read the text closely for understanding.
> - First, read the questions carefully so that you know exactly what you have to find out.
> - Look for key words in the questions that will help you to find the relevant areas of the text.
> - Read these pieces of the text sentence by sentence to find the answers.
> - Finally, check your answers. Read them carefully and compare them to the questions and the text to make sure that you have given the details requested.

1. What does Alem's father call himself, and what point is he trying to make to the soldier?
2. What name does the soldier call each member of Alem's family, and why?
3. What three things happen to Alem after his father leaves him in Britain on his own?
4. What three things happen to Alem when his father comes back to Britain to be with him?
5. When they join the checkout queue, why does Alem suggest joining a different queue?
6. Why is this impossible?
7. How does the situation make everyone in the queue feel?
8. Why does it affect people like Alem's father especially badly?

C Say what you think.

1. If you were in the same dangerous situation as Alem's parents, what would you do? Would you keep your young son with you and try to protect him yourself – or would you send him far away to somewhere safe, but unknown?
2. If you were in Alem's position, which decision would you prefer?

2 WORKING WITH WORDS

A Match words in box A to similar words from the texts in box B.

A	average ▪ line ▪ opposite ▪ place ▪ recognize	B	facing ▪ normal ▪ position ▪ queue ▪ realize

B Now choose the correct word to complete each sentence.

1. **a** The trees stand in a long ▬¹ beside the road. (line/queue)
   b I'm sorry, but you can't jump the ▬². Go to the back and wait for your turn. (line/queue)
2. **a** We hadn't met for five years, but I ▬¹ her immediately. (realized/recognized)
   b I was half-way to the airport when I ▬² that I'd forgotten my passport. (realized/recognized)
3. **a** Jim spoke after Carol at the meeting, and he presented the ▬¹ argument. (facing/opposite)
   b The task ▬² us today will be the hardest one of all. (facing/opposite)
4. **a** I always play in goal. What ▬¹ do you play? (place/position)
   b My home town is a lovely old ▬². You should come and see it. (place/position)
5. **a** Why does that child always behave so badly? It isn't ▬¹! (average/normal)
   b Statistics show that ▬² pay has risen by 2.5% in the last year. (average/normal)

MAIN COURSE 9

C Copy and complete the tables. Find the words in the texts.

Verb	Noun
to live	
	decision
	success
	earnings
	reduction

Noun	Adjective
	safe
	humiliated
qualification	
pride	
promise	

D Now use the pairs of words to complete the following. Make any necessary changes.

1. **A** Your sister hasn't had much ▬¹ with her new business yet, has she?
   B No, but things are slowly getting better, and I know she'll ▬² in the end.
2. All those books that you've put on top of that cupboard don't look ▬¹! I'm sure you're breaking the company's health and ▬² rules.
3. **A** We're spending too much money, so we'll have to make some ▬¹.
   B Well, let's ▬² what we spend on going out.
4. I have never felt so ▬¹ before. The ▬² of having to buy food with vouchers was more than I could take!
5. **A** Is Joe ▬¹ as a doctor yet?
   B Yes, he got his basic ▬² last year.
6. We can't yet make any ▬¹ about how successful this new cure for malaria will be, but our latest test results are ▬².
7. Things are so expensive! We all need to ▬¹ more money. The cost of living is going up faster than people's ▬².
8. **A** What have you ▬¹ to do with the old TV?
   B We've made a ▬² to sell it on eBay.
9. My great-grandfather had a very long ▬¹. He ▬² from 1911 to 2010.
10. Helen takes real ▬¹ in her school work. She should be especially ▬² of her excellent Maths and Science results this year.

3 GETTING IT RIGHT → Past perfect ▪ Simple past, S. 256

Put the verbs in brackets into the simple past or the past perfect.

Alem's father (choose) ▬¹ to take him to Britain even though they (never / be) ▬² there before. Once the two of them (land) ▬³ in London, they (take) ▬⁴ a taxi from the airport. They (go) ▬⁵ to a small hotel outside London which Mr Kelo (book) ▬⁶ the week before. Alem (love) ▬⁷ their visit to London the next day: he (never / see) ▬⁸ a city like it before. However, when he (wake up) ▬⁹ the next morning back at the hotel, his father (disappear) ▬¹⁰.

At first, Alem (just / think) ▬¹¹ that his father (go) ▬¹² downstairs to arrange breakfast. But then, after he (wait) ▬¹³ for a long time, the manager (come) ▬¹⁴ to the room with a letter from his father. The manager (tell) ▬¹⁵ Alem that his father (pay) ▬¹⁶ and (leave) ▬¹⁷ the hotel early that morning. Alem (learn) ▬¹⁸ from the letter that his father (go) ▬¹⁹ in order to return to Ethiopia. He slowly (understand) ▬²⁰ that his father (bring) ▬²¹ him to England for one reason only – because he would be safe there.

9 Multiculturalism

TEXT B The question of integration

BEFORE YOU READ

A What seems to be the purpose of the *Say it how you see it* website?

B Would you ever join an online discussion like this? What sort of subjects would you be interested in discussing?

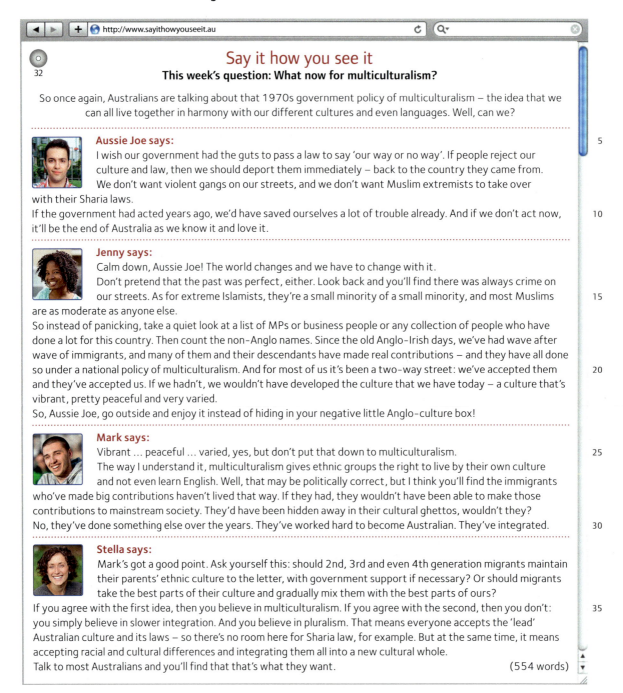

32

Say it how you see it
This week's question: What now for multiculturalism?

So once again, Australians are talking about that 1970s government policy of multiculturalism – the idea that we can all live together in harmony with our different cultures and even languages. Well, can we?

Aussie Joe says:
I wish our government had the guts to pass a law to say 'our way or no way'. If people reject our culture and law, then we should deport them immediately – back to the country they came from. We don't want violent gangs on our streets, and we don't want Muslim extremists to take over with their Sharia laws.
If the government had acted years ago, we'd have saved ourselves a lot of trouble already. And if we don't act now, it'll be the end of Australia as we know it and love it.

Jenny says:
Calm down, Aussie Joe! The world changes and we have to change with it.
Don't pretend that the past was perfect, either. Look back and you'll find there was always crime on our streets. As for extreme Islamists, they're a small minority of a small minority, and most Muslims are as moderate as anyone else.
So instead of panicking, take a quiet look at a list of MPs or business people or any collection of people who have done a lot for this country. Then count the non-Anglo names. Since the old Anglo-Irish days, we've had wave after wave of immigrants, and many of them and their descendants have made real contributions – and they have all done so under a national policy of multiculturalism. And for most of us it's been a two-way street: we've accepted them and they've accepted us. If we hadn't, we wouldn't have developed the culture that we have today – a culture that's vibrant, pretty peaceful and very varied.
So, Aussie Joe, go outside and enjoy it instead of hiding in your negative little Anglo-culture box!

Mark says:
Vibrant … peaceful … varied, yes, but don't put that down to multiculturalism.
The way I understand it, multiculturalism gives ethnic groups the right to live by their own culture and not even learn English. Well, that may be politically correct, but I think you'll find the immigrants who've made big contributions haven't lived that way. If they had, they wouldn't have been able to make those contributions to mainstream society. They'd have been hidden away in their cultural ghettos, wouldn't they?
No, they've done something else over the years. They've worked hard to become Australian. They've integrated.

Stella says:
Mark's got a good point. Ask yourself this: should 2nd, 3rd and even 4th generation migrants maintain their parents' ethnic culture to the letter, with government support if necessary? Or should migrants take the best parts of their culture and gradually mix them with the best parts of ours?
If you agree with the first idea, then you believe in multiculturalism. If you agree with the second, then you don't: you simply believe in slower integration. And you believe in pluralism. That means everyone accepts the 'lead' Australian culture and its laws – so there's no room here for Sharia law, for example. But at the same time, it means accepting racial and cultural differences and integrating them all into a new cultural whole.
Talk to most Australians and you'll find that that's what they want.

(554 words)

| MAIN COURSE | 9 |

1 LOOKING AT THE TEXT

→ Rezeption: Leseverstehen, S. 214

A Say which person (or people) expresses each idea. Explain your answers.

1 I believe that the government's programme of multiculturalism has worked well.
2 I believe that gradual cultural integration is the right way for Australia.
3 I am against the idea that immigration means more crime.
4 I am against mixing new cultures with the traditional national culture.
5 I support cultural 'give and take' between the old and the new.
6 I support throwing out any immigrants who do not accept the Australian way of life or who break the law.

B Say whether the following are true or false. Correct the false statements.

1 Aussie Joe seems to believe that all the members of violent street gangs are immigrants.
2 He says that a law against all immigration was needed a long time ago.
3 Jenny argues that non-Anglo-Irish immigrants have done most for today's Australia.
4 She feels that the many waves of immigration have led to a varied and lively culture.
5 Mark says that multiculturalism forces immigrants to integrate into mainstream society.
6 Stella agrees with the government's policy towards immigrants.
7 She points out that most Australians believe in accepting cultural differences and adding the best of them to the traditional Australian way of life.

C Say what it means: Explain the underlined expressions in your own words.

1 … pass a law to say <u>'our way or no way'</u>. (line 6)
2 And for most of us it's been <u>a two-way street</u> … (line 20)
3 … maintain their parents' ethnic culture <u>to the letter</u> … (line 33)
4 … everyone accepts <u>the 'lead'</u> Australian culture … (line 36)
5 … <u>there's no room here</u> for Sharia law … (line 37)

2 WORKING WITH WORDS

A Find words in the text that are the opposite of the following:

accept ▪ peaceful ▪ moderate ▪ majority ▪ similarity

B Now complete the following with pairs of words from exercise 2A.

1 The black ▬[1] in South Africa forms 70% of the population while at 17%, white South Africans form the largest single ▬[2].
2 We've ▬[1] Plans A and C mainly because they're too expensive, but we've ▬[2] Plan B because it offers a very good way forward and also because the price is right.
3 The struggles in Northern Ireland were very ▬[1] for many years, and many died. However, life there is much more ▬[2] today, thank goodness.
4 There are lots of ▬[1] between the old GR70 and the new GR71, and they look almost the same. The most important ▬[2] is the new car's much more powerful engine.
5 During the French Revolution, people with ▬[1] ideas took control. For them, anyone who was not with them was against them, and they did not listen to more ▬[2] views.

9 Multiculturalism

3 GETTING IT RIGHT

→ *If* sentences, S. 264

Form type 3 *if* sentences. Start each sentence with *if*.

1 Franz and Ana Beckman were very poor. They moved from their country village to Hamburg to find work.
If Franz and Ana Beckman had not been very poor, they would not have moved from ...
2 They moved to Hamburg. Franz found a good job in the shipyards there.
3 He found a good job. They were able to save a lot of money.
4 They had money in the bank. They were able to have a long holiday in Australia.
5 They travelled round Australia. They fell in love with the country.
6 They decided to emigrate to Australia. They had the chance to take over a small boat building company in Sydney.
7 Franz had the skills to build up the business. The company became a big success.
8 The Beckmans moved away from their poor home village many years before.
This immigrant success story happened.

Rewrite the underlined information in the following statements as type 3 *if* sentences.

1 The trouble is that <u>the Australian government refused to deport criminal immigrants in the past</u>. I think deportation was the right way for us to <u>avoid most of our problems with immigration</u>.
If the Australian government had not refused to deport ...
2 It was a very good thing that <u>Australia opened its doors to immigration from many more countries</u>. When that happened, <u>we were able to escape from our tired old Anglo culture</u>.
3 <u>Vancouver has become a great city of ethnic festivals</u>. It has happened because <u>immigrants from around the world have made it their home</u>.
4 <u>Vancouver attracted a large Chinese population in the 19th century</u>. As a result of that, <u>the city became Canada's only important port on the Pacific coast</u>.
5 <u>His parents</u> made sure that <u>Alem was safe from the fighting</u> by <u>sending him away</u>.
6 It was very sad that <u>Alem's mother did not go with her husband and son to England</u>. Because of that, <u>she died in the fighting while they were away</u>.

4 LISTENING

→ Rezeption: Hörverstehen, S. 225

You are going to listen to a discussion between Joan Carr, a Member of Parliament, and Tom Baker, an author, about immigration to the UK.

A Copy the list and listen to the first part of the discussion. Note the figures that Tom Baker gives.

Immigrant % of total population:
· UK: ▇   · Germany: ▇   · Austria: ▇   · Switzerland: ▇
Jobs:
· New jobs in future: ▇   · People retiring 2010–2020: ▇
Welfare:
· Immigrant unemployment since 2010: ▇
· Immigrants claiming unemployment benefits: ▇
Housing:
· New households per year: approx. ▇
· New immigrant households per year: approx. ▇

86

| | | MAIN COURSE | 9 |

B Now listen to the second part of the discussion and make notes on what Tom Baker and Joan Carr say about social tensions.

Social tensions
Possible course of action 1: ▬
· Likely effects – 1: ▬ ; *2:* ▬
Possible course of action 2: ▬
· Likely effects – 1: ▬ ; *2:*

5 ANALYSING FIGURES

→ Produktion: Statistiken beschreiben und analysieren, S. 238

BUILDING SKILLS: Describing and analysing statistics

To analyse statistics, you have to know exactly what sort of figures you are dealing with.
- Read the heading, labels and any other form of explanation carefully.
- Check that you understand the units (e.g. thousands, millions, etc.) that the figures are presented in.
- Make sure you know which figures are in these units (e.g. 80.5 million) and which figures are percentages (e.g. 14.7%) of a total.

A Copy the table and complete it with the figures from your notes in exercise 4A.

Populations of selected European countries (millions)			
Country	**Total**	**Immigrants**	**Percentage**
Germany	80.5	9.8	▬
Britain	64.1	7.8	▬
Austria	8.5	1.3	▬
Switzerland	8.1	2.3	▬

1 Explain what the numbers in columns 2 and 3 mean.
2 Contrast the types of information in columns 3 and 4.

B Use statistics from the table in 5A to complete this paragraph.

Nearly all European countries, big and small, have taken in many immigrants – especially in recent years. For example, Germany, with its very large population of over ▬¹ million, is also home to a little under ▬² million immigrants, or more than ▬³ % of the total. Again, Switzerland, with its much smaller population of just over ▬⁴ million, is host to more than ▬⁵ million immigrants, which is well over ▬⁶ % of the total population.

C Now interpret the figures for Britain and Austria in the same way. Use approximate numbers, e.g. *64.1 million → over 64 million*.

Start like this:
Similarly, the United Kingdom, with its large population of ... . At the same time, Austria, with its much smaller population of around eight and a half ...

6 WRITING

→ Produktion: Eine Stellungnahme schreiben, S. 234

Use your notes from exercise 4 and the figures from exercise 5 to write a short comment on the immigration situation in Britain.

9 Multiculturalism

BUSINESS OPTIONS

BEFORE YOU LISTEN

Gestures, rules of behaviour and rules of communication are different across cultures. The gesture on the right is used in Italy, France, Greece and Egypt with a different meaning in each country.

A Can you guess which meaning belongs to which culture?

- "This will take some time. Be patient, please."
- "I don't understand. What are you saying?"
- "Oh dear, that's scary!"
- "I'm happy to hear that. That's good!"

B Form groups of four to check your answers. Pick one country each and do a quick internet search on gestures in that culture.

LISTENING

→ Rezeption: Hörverstehen, S. 225

A Listen and underline the topics discussed.

Communication and etiquette:
ways of addressing people ■ making jokes ■ ways of greeting people ■ touching ■ personal space ■ etiquette in restaurants ■ eye contact ■ expressing criticism

Potential marketing pitfalls:
words and their meaning ■ designing slogans ■ offensive images ■ problems with packaging ■ colour associations ■ music in advertising ■ ethical standards

B Listen again and do the following tasks. You don't need to write full sentences.

1 Give three reasons why companies work with Alison.
2 Name an example of a cultural 'code'.
3 Briefly outline the issue of 'personal space' between different cultures.

C Answer the following questions briefly.

1 In what ways can eye contact be interpreted differently?
2 What is different about German and British ways of expressing criticism?
3 What advice does Alison give to people who will be working in intercultural settings?

D Are the following sentences true or false? Correct the false statements.

1 Car manufacturers should adapt their advertising to the side of the road people drive on in different countries.
2 It's important to give your brand different names in different countries.
3 Companies should be aware of what different colours mean in other cultures.

10 Helping others

MAIN COURSE

FOCUS

A Discuss the photos with a partner. Would you help or donate something in each case? Give reasons and report your decisions to the class.

B In class, discuss whether people should give money to beggars or not. Before you start, note arguments for and against.

C Look at the illustrations below with a partner and think about the different ways of giving help. Think about who gets the help and who gives the help.

D Now do these tasks:
- When did you last help someone? Write a sentence or two to describe what you did.
- When did someone last help you? Describe what happened in a few sentences.
- Exchange stories with your partner.

Useful phrases

- I would give some money/food to homeless people because …
- I wouldn't give any … because …
- to beg (for) …
- to donate (money/clothes/food)
- to make a donation (of …)
- to charity
- to collect for (people in need)
- a clothing container / collection box

89

10 Helping others

TEXT A Different ways to help

WHILE YOU READ

Match the headings below with the paragraphs (1–5).

> Donate ▪ Help people help themselves ▪ Use your fame to help others ▪
> Volunteer to be a counsellor ▪ Sponsor a poor child's education

1 George Clooney is famous for making blockbuster Hollywood movies but he also uses his fame to fight poverty. He and his Ocean's 11 co-stars Don Cheadle, Matt Damon and Brad Pitt, together with producer Jerry Weintraub, have set up a charity called Not On Our Watch, and its mission is to help stop human rights atrocities, such as in the Darfur region of Sudan. The charity invites people to find out about the crises, donate money, lobby politicians and write letters of complaint to companies benefiting from the conflict.

2 World Vision: When Priscilla was a child, a donor many thousands of miles from her Ghanaian village helped pay for her schooling. For years she exchanged letters with her British benefactor. Now she is 20, the charity has stopped the sponsorship and the relationship. 'Last year I wrote to them saying goodbye and thanked them for taking care of me up to this day,' says Priscilla, an accountancy student. 'When I was writing, I was full of tears. Tears were coming from my eyes.'

From: www.bbc.com

3 MicroLoan Foundation helps some of the poorest women in the world feed their families, send their children to school and pay for life saving medicines. We are a very different kind of charity, offering hope, not handouts. By providing small loans (average £60) and ongoing business training and support, MicroLoan empowers women in rural Malawi and Zambia to set up self-sustainable businesses. The profits from these businesses enable the women to work themselves and their families out of poverty.

From: www.microloanfoundation.org.uk

4 You can make an amazing difference at Samaritans. Our volunteers are changing lives every day, and developing valuable skills and friendships along the way. Volunteers are the heart of Samaritans. We welcome and value every volunteer, from all walks of life. Whatever your interests, experience or skills, we have a role for you.
We currently have over 20,000 volunteers giving up a few hours of their time every few weeks to help support people around the UK find their way, through whatever is troubling them.

From: www.samaritans.org

5 The Salvation Army
£26 could pay for two weekly parent-and-toddler groups where disadvantaged children can play in safety.
£52 could pay to keep a day centre for older people open for a day – providing hot meals and the promise of companionship.
£90 could pay for a bed for a month for a homeless person at one of our Lifehouses – which is often the first step towards rebuilding their lives. (401 words)

From: www.salvationarmyappeals.org.uk

MAIN COURSE   10

1 LOOKING AT THE TEXTS

→ Rezeption: Leseverstehen, S. 214

A Read the texts and match the charities with the issues they deal with. Note that some charities deal with more than one issue.

Charities	Issues
Not On Our Watch	poverty
World Vision	loneliness
MicroLoan Foundation	homelessness
Samaritans	psychological support
The Salvation Army	armed conflict
	education
	work

SKILLS CHECKLIST:
Reading for understanding

☑ Have I looked for key words in the questions?
☑ Have I found the key words in the text?
☑ Have I compared my answers with the questions and the text?

B Decide which of the charities provide help …

- in their home country
- in foreign countries
- in the long term
- in the short term
- by giving people money
- by giving people non-financial help

C Choose two of the charities described and explain how they fight poverty.

2 WORKING WITH WORDS

A Match six of the words in the box with their definitions below.

accountancy ▪ atrocities ▪ benefactor ▪ companionship ▪ conflict ▪ education ▪ disadvantaged ▪ foundation ▪ handouts ▪ loan ▪ poverty ▪ volunteer

1. the situation you are in when you have no money
2. someone who donates money to help others
3. keeping a list of a person's or company's financial data
4. an organization which has been set up to finance activities for the good of society
5. not having the money and opportunities that other people have
6. what you get when you have friends

Write definitions for the six words not needed above.

Do not write the word. Give your definitions to a partner. Can he or she find the correct words? (If your partner can find the words, your definitions were good!)

B Complete the text with six of the words in exercise 2A. Make any necessary changes.

In the USA many successful people 'give back' to society and become ▬¹ by setting up a ▬². Bill and Melinda Gates did so in 2000 in order to help ▬³ people all over the world. Their organization's focus is on two things: reducing extreme ▬⁴ and poor health in developing countries where the poorest people in the world live and improving the American ▬⁵ system in order to give youngsters a better start in life. If you want to work as a ▬⁶, you can find links on the organization's website.

91

10 Helping others

3 ANALYSING FIGURES

→ Produktion: Schaubilder beschreiben und analysieren, S. 238

Individual giving levels as percentage of gross domestic product (GDP)

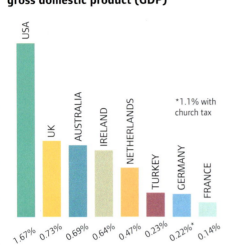

USA 1.67% | UK 0.73% | AUSTRALIA 0.69% | IRELAND 0.64% | NETHERLANDS 0.47% | TURKEY 0.23% | GERMANY 0.22%* | FRANCE 0.14%

*1.1% with church tax

A Here in the States we don't wait for the government to solve our problems. We solve them ourselves! We give to charity, help in the community and raise money for good causes. Last year the parents and students at our local school collected $10,000 to pay for a disabled child to have surgery. That child can now walk without help. Anyone can help. Just do it!

B I'm a volunteer for the church charity you see at many stations all over Germany. We help anyone in need, regardless of their religious beliefs. The help we give is sometimes just a train time but it can also be a hot meal and a bed for the night for a homeless person. Most of our funding comes from the church, which is financed by church tax.

C I work very hard in my restaurant but I pay a lot of money in tax to the government here in Turkey, so I'm not rich! Unfortunately, there are many poor  people everywhere, even children as young as four or five begging in the streets, so I give what I can when I see people in need. Sometimes I give them food or money, but when business is bad I have nothing to give.

D In France more than 50% of our income goes on tax! I feel sorry for people in need, both at home and abroad but I believe that helping is the responsibility of the  government, not mine. That's why my vote goes to the politicians who promise to spend more money on fighting poverty.

A Read the four statements and do the following tasks:

1. Describe how many Americans believe it is best to help people in need.
2. Explain how the church charity at German train stations is mainly staffed and funded.
3. List the factors which influence how much and when the Turkish restaurant owner gives to people in need.
4. Contrast the French and American attitude to charitable giving.

BUILDING SKILLS: Comparing figures in charts

When describing charts, it is important to be able to compare and contrast the different figures.
- Always name the factors which a bar chart or line graph compares ('x' and 'y' axis): *The chart above is about percentages and countries.*
- Look for and point out the most striking features: *We can clearly see a progression from France at 0.14% to the USA at 1.67%.*
- Contrast the categories with each other: *The UK is in second place while Turkey only ranks 6th.*
- Describe the relationships between the categories: *The value for Australia is three times as high as for Turkey.*

MAIN COURSE **10**

B Look at the bar chart on page 92 and say …

1 where individual giving is highest and lowest.
2 where Germany stands in the list.
3 how high individual giving is in Germany with and without church tax.
4 which two countries have almost the same level of personal giving.
5 what the bar chart shows very clearly.

C Describe the chart and say what it tells us about the different attitudes to individual giving in the different countries.

> **Useful phrases**
>
> - There is a clear progression from … to …
> - We can clearly see the difference/similarity between … and …
> - The value in the first column is far greater/less than …
> - twice / three times / four times as big as …
> - half the size of …
> - the highest/lowest
> - in first/last place / in the last place but one / in the middle

4 CLASS PROJECT

Your class decides to support a charity offering help to people with one of the problems listed in exercise 1A (poverty, loneliness, homelessness, psychological support, armed conflict, education, work), or your own idea.

Follow these steps to carry out the project:
1 Make a list of all the charities, people or projects you could support and choose one.
2 Decide how you will give support, for example by …
   - raising money with a sponsored walk or by selling food/cakes at an event.
   - giving practical help, such as going shopping, doing gardening.
   - donating or collecting clothes, giving or selling food.
   Or think of some ideas of your own.
3 Divide the class into smaller groups of three or four students and give each group a job.
4 Agree a target, for example €100 by the end of the month or (school) year, and start work.
5 If your class decides not to support a project, summarize your reasons in a few sentences.

5 WRITING → Produktion: Schreiben, S. 228

> Write a blog entry about your class project for your school's website. Include these points:
>
> - why your class chose this project
> - how you helped
> - feedback from the people you helped
>
> For more advice, read the notes for exercise 4 on page 38.

> Think of your own example of a charity event and describe it in an email to an English-speaking pen friend.

10 Helping others

TEXT B A charity in action

BEFORE YOU READ
→ Scannen nach Einzelinformationen im Text, S. 221

Scan the texts to find …
- the meaning of *orphans* and *orphanage*.
- the link between *flip-flops* and *Gandys*.

Orphans for Orphans

On Boxing Day in 2004, when the tsunami struck the little fishing village of Weligama on the southern coast of Sri Lanka, Rob (17) and Paul (15) Forkan were asleep in their hotel room. Their parents, Kevin and Sandra, and their two other siblings, Matty (12) and Rosie (8) were next door. Suddenly, Rob heard screams and saw water coming in under the door. Seconds later the first huge wave hit their hotel room smashing everything in its path. The two boys managed to climb onto the roof and they found their little brother, Matty, in a tree nearby. Later that day, they found their sister, Rosie, but their parents had been swept away whilst saving their two younger children. Despite this terrible blow and narrowly escaping death themselves, the four orphans managed to hitch-hike 200 km to the British Embassy in Colombo and then flew home to rejoin their two older sisters in the UK, one of whom adopted the younger children and gave them a home.

Many other children would have lost their way in life after such a terrible tragedy but Kevin and Sandra Forkan had always brought their children up to think of the needs of others first, which ultimately gave them the strength to survive themselves. They took their four youngest children out of school when Paul and Rob were 11 and 13 and moved to Goa in India to work on humanitarian projects. They did a great deal of voluntary work, such as helping in orphanages by teaching the children there, playing sports with them, helping them with cooking, handing out food and organizing sports days, whilst at the same time fund-raising for local charities. These activities gave them the confidence to feel that they could do anything and that nothing was hard to achieve. Paul says: 'Our parents gave us the attitude that if you get knocked off your bike, just get back on it. There are always people worse off than you.'

In 2011, after travelling around the world separately, Rob and Paul lived together again in Brixton, South London, and decided to set up a business together. Their inspiration came from Mahatma Gandhi, the father of India's independence movement, who always wore flip-flops. They decided to sell flip-flops called Gandys and use some of the profits to fund social projects in India and Sri Lanka. A description of their company's mission can be found on its website.

(419 words)

Paul Forkan with some of the orphans, 2013

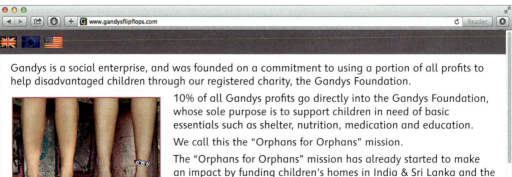

www.gandysflipflops.com

Gandys is a social enterprise, and was founded on a commitment to using a portion of all profits to help disadvantaged children through our registered charity, the Gandys Foundation.

10% of all Gandys profits go directly into the Gandys Foundation, whose sole purpose is to support children in need of basic essentials such as shelter, nutrition, medication and education.

We call this the "Orphans for Orphans" mission.

The "Orphans for Orphans" mission has already started to make an impact by funding children's homes in India & Sri Lanka and the vision is to open them all around the world. The opening of the first children's home will be built in memory of Rob and Paul's parents, Kevin and Sandra Forkan, and will mark the 10th anniversary of the tsunami.

(131 words)

From: *www.gandysflipflops.com*

MAIN COURSE

10

1 LOOKING AT THE TEXTS
→ Rezeption: Leseverstehen, S. 214

A Complete the sentences with information from the texts.

1 The Forkans' hotel was destroyed by …
2 The younger children were adopted by …
3 In Goa, the Forkans did voluntary work for …
4 Helping orphans gave the Forkan children …
5 Before living together in London, Rob and Paul each went on a long trip …
6 Both brothers very much admire …
7 The Gandys Foundation helps children who do not have …
8 Rob and Paul Forkan intend to open …

B Explain to a partner how …

1 the four orphans travelled from Weligama to Colombo.
2 they got help in the UK after the tsunami.
3 their voluntary work gave them confidence.

C Describe the brothers' personal reasons for their choice of charity work.

2 WORKING WITH WORDS

A Use the texts to match the verbs with the nouns to make collocations.

Verb		Noun	
to escape	to set up	an anniversary	death
to do	to make	an impact	work
to raise	to mark	a business	funds

B Find words in the texts to match the definitions.

1 to happen suddenly and have a damaging effect on sb/sth
2 brothers and/or sisters
3 to move suddenly with great force
4 to travel by asking for free rides in other people's cars
5 in the end, finally
6 unpaid; in order to help
7 a way of thinking and behaving
8 to finance
9 a promise
10 intention
11 a strong effect
12 food necessary to be healthy

C Replace the underlined words with some of the answers to exercises 2A and 2B.

When Hurricane Katrina <u>hit</u> ▬¹ the southern coast of the USA on 29 August 2005 it <u>carried</u> ▬² away everything in its path. Its <u>effect</u> ▬³ on the southern states was huge and <u>in the end</u> ▬⁴, it became clear that New Orleans' flood-control system had not fulfilled its <u>function</u> ▬⁵ and had probably increased the number of <u>fatalities</u> ▬⁶, which was at least 1,833. Many NGOs (non-governmental organizations) and citizens put in months of <u>unpaid</u> ▬⁷ work to help the victims and <u>collected</u> ▬⁸ US$4.25 billion in donations.

95

10 Helping others

3 MEDIATION
→ Schriftliche Mediation, S. 240

Sie möchten *Orphans for Orphans* unterstützen und eine Sammelbestellung für Gandys Flipflops aufgeben. Lesen Sie die Webseite auf Seite 94 noch einmal, dann schreiben Sie einen Aufruf an Ihre Mitschüler/innen in dem Sie erklären, warum sie *Orphans for Orphans* mit einer Bestellung unterstützen sollen.

4 LISTENING
→ Rezeption: Hörverstehen, S. 225

A team of students are making a radio programme about giving to charities. Today, they are conducting a survey in London. They want to hear people's views about giving to charity.

A Listen to the dialogues and write down the following details for each person:

- occupation
- date of last contribution to charity
- what the contribution was for
- total contribution this year

B Fill in the gaps with words from the interviews.

Interview 1
It'll only ▬¹ two minutes to answer our questions.
I've ▬² £100 this year.

Interview 2
I've been ▬³ at our local church for many years now.
It ▬⁴ a lot of money to run a church.

Interview 3
My husband and I have ▬ ▬⁵ a child in Africa for a number of years now.
We've ▬ ▬⁶ regular payments for the last six years.

Interview 4
I've ▬ ▬⁷ out at a walk-in medical centre for the homeless in south London.
I've ▬⁸ in about 80 hours at the medical centre this year.

5 GETTING IT RIGHT
→ Present perfect ▪ Present perfect progressive, S. 253

Write down the present perfect and present perfect progressive forms of these verbs:

1 I/live (*I've … / I've been …*)
2 she/work
3 you/help
4 they/sponsor
5 we/support
6 you/donate
7 he/collect
8 they/contribute

Expand the notes to make sentences with the present perfect or the present perfect progressive.

1 he / donate more than €1,000 / this year
2 he / talk to her for five minutes
3 people / give her €112.95 since last Monday
4 she / ask for donations since 9 am
5 she / collect / €23.50 today
6 she / collect since early this morning
7 she / stand outside for three hours
8 he / just give her €10

96

MAIN COURSE

10

6 ROLE-PLAY

→ Interaktion: Ein Rollenspiel gestalten, S. 247

An interviewer for a youth magazine is asking people in the street about what they give to charity.

Work with a partner. Read the role-cards and role-play the interviews. Use the present perfect (progressive) where possible.

Partner A: Interviewer

- Explanation of survey
- Occupation of interviewee?
- Date of last contribution to charity?
- Reason(s)?
- How much?
- How much this year?
- How long / make contributions to charities?

Partner B: Businesswoman

- Car saleswoman
- Six months ago
- Hurricane in the Philippines
- £50
- About £100
- For the last 10 years

7 WRITING

→ Produktion: Eine Stellungnahme schreiben, S. 234

University professor Dr Max Kelly has set up a charity called *We can all give more*. It encourages people to donate at least 10% of their income in order to fight extreme poverty and disease in the Third World. Here the charity explains some common misunderstandings (myths) about giving aid to developing countries.

A Match the myths (1–4) with the explanations (a–d).

1 The small amount of money I can give will have little or no effect.
2 Charity begins at home: we should treat the sick in our own country first.
3 Most of the money we give in aid is stolen by corrupt officials before it reaches the people in need.
4 By giving aid to developing countries we make them dependent on handouts.

a Effective charities provide concrete help (e.g. medicines, mosquito nets) not cash.
b Effective charities help people to become independent by teaching them skills such as farming, health care and hygiene.
c Developed countries already know how to treat preventable diseases. They can now help developing countries to do the same.
d Just $3 is enough to buy one mosquito net which can save a person's life.

B Choose one of the following writing tasks:

⊙ **Explain why you would or would not donate 10% of your income to end poverty in developing countries. Include ideas from exercise 7A.**

SKILLS CHECKLIST: Writing a comment
✓ Have I structured my arguments logically?
✓ Have I given arguments for and against?
✓ Have I given my own opinion?

● **Comment on the following statement.**
Proverb: *"If you give a man a fish, you feed him for a day. If you teach him to fish, you feed him for a lifetime."*

10 Helping others

BUSINESS OPTIONS

BEFORE YOU READ

In small groups, discuss solutions to the following problem. Write down all your suggestions, then agree on the solution that you like best. Present the best suggestion to the class.

> **Sofia**, a single mother, worked in a bakery for five years until it closed down. She is a talented baker and plans to start her own business, selling sandwiches and pastries to office workers. She needs money for equipment and ingredients. Additionally, she has to learn how to run a business and keep accounts.

NICARAGUA TEACHES A LESSON IN THE POWER OF MICROLOANS

Driving through the streets of Managua, the realities of life for the citizens of the poorest country in Central America are starkly apparent. Housing in Nicaragua's capital is a slum.

Rupert Scofield is the founder and chief executive of FINCA (Foundation for International Community Assistance), one of the world's largest charitable banks. FINCA is a pioneer in microfinance – small loans, usually of a few hundred dollars, to people who would otherwise have no access to capital. According to FINCA, 81 per cent of the population do not have a proper bank account and 41 per cent live below the poverty line.

Evana borrowed $200 to buy and sell cosmetics door to door, using the profits to pay her way through law school. Doña Julia Lilliam Ramirez runs a grocery store. A client of FINCA for 19 years, she used her first loan to buy cleaning products in Managua to sell in the nearby villages. She now uses the proceeds of her business to feed poor children in the neighbourhood.

But microfinance has its critics. FINCA has been in Nicaragua since 1992, and although it is clearly making a difference to people's lives on a small scale, the underlying problems of poverty in the country are hardly being addressed. Academic studies in recent years have come to the conclusion that there is no evidence microfinance has had any impact on world poverty.

Most people are benefiting from microfinance in a personal way. But they're not having an impact on the economy of the country as a whole. An exception is Nelson Lopez, who runs a small citrus farm. He borrowed $10,000 and pays back around $3,700 every six months. Mr Lopez owns his land but has used the money to buy soil, fertiliser, labour and insecticide. Banks don't finance small producers like him; that's why it's a big opportunity for FINCA.

(320 words)

Abridged from: *www.independent.co.uk*

1 LOOKING AT THE TEXT
→ Rezeption: Leseverstehen, S. 214

Decide if the statements are true (T) or false (F). Correct the false statements.

1. The living conditions in Managua are poor.
2. Doña Julia Lilliam Ramirez's business wasn't successful.
3. Microfinance has significantly reduced poverty in Nicaragua.
4. Most banks refuse to lend money to ordinary farmers like Nelson Lopez.

2 RESEARCH AND PRESENTATION
→ Präsentieren, S. 243

In small groups, do research on KIVA – an international non-profit organization that arranges microloans for small entrepreneurs. Choose a business represented by KIVA that you want to support and make notes on what it involves. Pitch your choice to the class.

11 Global reach

MAIN COURSE

FOCUS

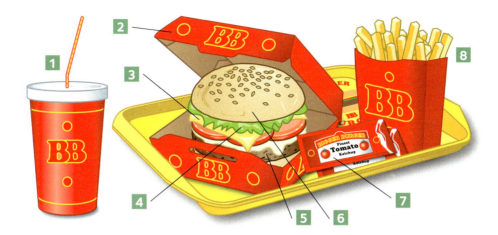

A In small groups, say where you like to go for a 'fast-food' meal and what you like to eat.

B Use the words below to describe the Bigger Burger meal above.

> bread roll ▪ burger ▪ cheese ▪ cold drink ▪ salad ▪ French fries ▪ cardboard packaging ▪ ketchup

C Make statements about the supply chain for items 1–8.

Useful phrases

- The … (*item*) is made/manufactured from … (*raw product*) that comes from … (*country*).
- … (*raw products*) originate from within/outside the EU.
- It is / They are grown in / imported from … (*country*).

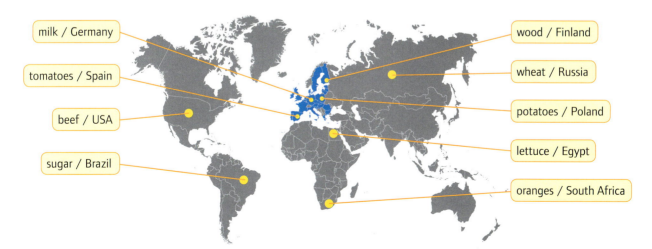

D Give your opinion. Say what you think about fast food.

99

11 Global reach

TEXT A Four globalization case studies

BEFORE YOU READ

Read the two definitions of the word *globalization*. Explain how a global fast-food company matches each definition.

globalization /ˌɡloʊbəlɪˈzeɪʃ(ə)n/ *noun* [U] **1** the growth of trade around the world, especially by large companies that produce and sell goods and services in many different countries **2** when similar goods and services, or cultural and social influences, spread around the world

40

Kintu Muwanga, Ugandan coffee farmer: In the old days, traders came to our village and bought from individual farmers. They paid terrible prices, and we were always poor. We couldn't afford to improve quality to get better prices: we couldn't afford anything. Then we started working with a Fairtrade company, Twin Trading, and we formed the Gumutindo Coffee Cooperative. Since then, our lives have been transformed. Experts helped to raise quality and switch to organic production. Buyers from Twin Trading agreed good prices and paid some of the money early. Facilities for processing and packing our coffee have been built, and the finished product now means even better prices. The result? Wonderful improvements, including safe water, a bigger clinic and a new secondary school.

Latifa Sattar, Bangladeshi textile worker: Millions of women like me work in clothing factories, and conditions are terrible. Meanwhile, the owners just think about getting rich on the backs of the workers. They simply don't care about health and safety, and workers are often injured. Recently, a whole factory collapsed and 1,000 people were killed.
And our hours are getting longer as deadlines keep getting tighter. We're often forced to work 14–16 hours a day, seven days a week. We're always told that if we don't fill the orders for the big western customers, the company will lose its contracts, the factory will close and we'll all lose our jobs. And the pay? It's just not enough for a family to live on.
Well, enough is enough. Someone from the national union made secret contact with us recently, and I say it's time to join and take action to fight for our rights!

Steve Race, American furniture factory worker: I lost my job a few years back when our factory closed and production went offshore to Indonesia. It was the main employer in town, so life was very hard for a lot of folks, and a lot moved away to find work. I stayed and set up my own carpentry business, but the local economy was depressed and business wasn't great. But then I went on a training programme and re-skilled in computer-aided manufacturing. That changed everything. I had to move, but I found work with a company which had just brought furniture production back from the Philippines. It's very automated, so there aren't a lot of jobs. But I've got one of them, and I'm very happy about that!

Li Ziyang, Chinese construction worker: I returned to Shanghai after spending the New Year holiday with my family in our small village, and I found that work had been stopped on the factory that we were building. The company had planned to use it to expand production of electronic components for export to America, but it turned out that their American customer had decided to manufacture the components themselves – in America.
Some of my co-workers want to stay and find work in Shanghai because there are still other projects. But a few of us want to go inland to find employment. The government is building new cities there, and I think that's the next big thing for China – developing the country for the people of China.

(528 words)

5

10

15

20

25

30

35

MAIN COURSE   11

1 LOOKING AT THE TEXTS

→ Rezeption: Leseverstehen, S. 214

A Read the texts and do the following tasks.

1 Contrast globalization's effects on the lives of the people mentioned in the texts. Say which have experienced positive changes and which have been affected negatively.
2 Describe what two of them have recently done to change their lives for the better.
3 Explain what the other two are probably going to do soon to improve their lives.

B Say what it means. Explain the underlined words and phrases in your own words.

1 … deadlines keep getting tighter. (line 14)
2 … if we don't fill the orders … (line 15)
3 Well, enough is enough. (line 18)
4 … production went offshore to Indonesia. (line 21)
5 Some of my co-workers want to stay … (line 35)
6 But a few of us want to go inland … (line 36)

SKILLS CHECKLIST:
Dealing with unknown words

☑ Have I thought about similar English words?
☑ Have I thought about the general meaning of the sentence?

C Say what you think.

1 Look at your answers to exercise 1A again. Which of these things do you think you may need to do to find or to stay in work in the future? Is there anything you would not like to do?
2 What has globalization done for you? (Think about, for example, media or shopping.)
3 Think about globalization and people in work in Germany. What pros and cons do you see from their point of view?

2 WORKING WITH WORDS

A Copy and complete the tables of verb-noun pairs. Find the words in the texts.

Verb	Noun	Verb	Noun	Verb	Noun
to farm			agreement		transformation
to own		to improve		to construct	
to employ		to govern			expansion
	manufacturer		development		decision

B Use pairs of words from exercise 2A to complete the following.

1 We ▬¹ bikes, and we're one of the biggest bike ▬² in Europe.
2 **A** When did you ▬¹ a date for the meeting?
   B I made the ▬² a week ago.
3 The company has made big ▬¹ to their product, and they've also ▬² the packaging.
4 **A** Who ▬¹ that old house? It looks a mess!
   B The ▬² hasn't been seen for three years.
5 The Internet is creating a huge social ▬¹. It's ▬² the way that humans live.
6 In a modern democracy, the people choose a ▬¹, and this then ▬² the country for several years – until it is time for the people to decide again.

101

11 Global reach

3 GETTING IT RIGHT

→ The passive, S. 261

Put these sentences into the passive. If you need to mention the subject, use 'by + agent'.

1 Karl Benz constructed the first successful petrol-driven car in 1885.
   The first successful petrol-driven car was constructed by Karl Benz in 1885.
2 By 1900, engineers had developed various other models across Europe and America.
3 Henry Ford introduced mass-production techniques in 1908.
4 As a result, workers had built over 15 million Ford Model Ts by 1928.
5 Since those early days, personal transport has transformed life around the world.
6 Family cars have given ordinary people the freedom to travel far and wide.
7 Today, companies make over 65 million cars a year in countries all over the world.
8 The Chinese alone produce nearly 20 million of them.
9 Companies export cars for sale in every part of the world.
10 Through exports and international supply chains, the world car industry has created many complex global links.

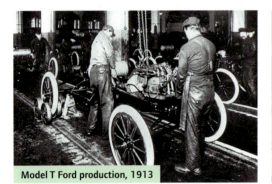

Model T Ford production, 1913

A380 final assembly line in the Jean-Luc Lagardère plant, Toulouse-Blagnac Airport.

Turn the following interview into a more formal news report, using the passive. You should also use more formal linking words/phrases.

So … → As a result, … ▪ But … → However, … ▪ Even so, … → Despite that, …

Start like this:
A number of excellent aircraft had been designed by … . However, …

A So, tell me, how did Airbus begin?
B Well, you see, European aircraft makers had designed a number of excellent aircraft in the 1950s and early 1960s. But they only sold them in small numbers because the American manufacturers were too powerful. So, in the late 1960s, several European governments and plane makers made plans for a shared European project – Airbus Industrie.
A I see. So what happened next?
B Well, after the organization had dealt with many political and technical problems, it finally tested the new A300 in 1972. The Airbus team then took it on a six-week sales tour of South and North America, and this created a lot of interest. Even so, only Lufthansa and Air France had actually bought the A300 by 1974. Then, in September of that year, Airbus finally sold the first four planes outside Europe – to Korean Airlines.

102

MAIN COURSE

11

A Wow! I expect everyone was very pleased about that!
B We certainly were! But Airbus only won the first really big prize – an order for 23 A300s – in 1978. That was from America's Eastern Airlines, six years after we had shown the plane to the US market back in 1972.
A Well, things have moved on a long way since then, haven't they?
B They certainly have. Today, Airbus builds the planes' components in factories across Germany, France, Britain, Spain and the Netherlands, and it brings all these parts together in Toulouse. It completes final assembly of all the planes there.
A And that's a lot of planes now, isn't it?
B Yes, since 1972, Airbus has taken over 14,000 orders, and it has delivered over 8,500. The world's airlines now accept these planes as some of the best in the world. So Airbus carries nearly half of all international travellers around the world today.

4 DESCRIBING A CARTOON

→ Produktion: Cartoons beschreiben und analysieren, S. 236

Describe the cartoon and analyse its message. (Look at the second text on page 100 again to help you with background information.)

BUILDING SKILLS: Analysing cartoons

Cartoons often contain cultural references, or references to events in the news.
- Don't panic if you don't understand the reference straight away.
- Particularly in an exam, the necessary information will usually be in a related text in the exam or in a topic that you have dealt with in class.
- Think about what you have read in class, or return to the exam text to check for references.

Useful phrases

- The cartoon consists of three pictures side by side, all under one heading: …
- The cartoon is an ironic comment on …
- First of all, it reminds us that huge numbers of …
- Secondly, it tells us that the employers make … because they spend so little on …
- This brings us to the third 'made in Bangladesh' picture – the collapse of a factory …
- This is a sharp attack on the owners' lack of care for anything except …

103

11 Global reach

TEXT B Where to manufacture products?

BEFORE YOU READ

Does a German brand name on a product always mean that it was made in Germany? Should it? Why / Why not?

Is it time to start re-shoring our manufacturing industries?

The World This Week reporter Mark Moro is talking to Tim Smith, head of the campaign group Make it in America.

Mark Moro: Is it time to start re-shoring our manufacturing industries – to bring back production that has been done abroad for many years? Tell us about the situation now, Tim.

5 **Tim Smith:** Well, let's just remember how bad things were a few years ago. Across the USA and the rest of the industrialized West, more and more jobs were being exported to China and other low-cost countries. It started when
10 cheap producers exported from there to the West and undercut western producers. Our own manufacturers were then forced to send their production offshore, too, just to stay in business. By around the year 2000, about
15 150,000 American manufacturing jobs were being lost every year. Whole sections of industrial cities like Pittsburgh were turning into wastelands, and unemployment just kept rising. It was the same in parts of Europe too, and it seemed impossible to do anything 20 about it.

Mark Moro: So what's changed?

Tim Smith: Jobs are being brought back from countries like China to the West.

Mark Moro: Why? 25

Tim Smith: The most important reason is cost. Countries like China aren't low-cost anymore. Wages are rising fast, and other costs are going up too – especially transport. Look. This bar chart shows the cost of making floor care 30 products for a US supermarket chain at home and in China. The chart shows a slight US cost advantage of three per cent. In other words, the job is now being done more cheaply in the USA. 35

Mark Moro: I see, so wages aren't very much cheaper in China than in America now. And importing all the way from China adds quite a lot to the total bill. 40

Tim Smith: Right, so production in America actually gives a small cost advantage now.

Mark Moro: And I suppose it's just easier to produce near where you're 45 going to sell.

Tim Smith: Yes, it's better in several ways. It's much faster, and that's important when markets change as quickly as they often do. If lots of 50

Cost advantage for floor care products

	USA (100)	CHINA (103)
Packaging	2	3
Import costs	–	13
Raw materials	27	27
Components	35	35
Labour	27	17
Other overheads (including rent, energy and maintenance costs)	9	8

Cost advantage: +3

Source: www.manufacturing.net

MAIN COURSE

11

customers suddenly want the red model instead of the blue one, the manufacturer needs to meet this demand quickly. But if production is in China, that's not possible.
55 What's more, there may be delays in a long supply chain, so it's necessary to hold extra stock in America – and that's expensive. Breakages and faulty goods just make that problem worse.
60 **Mark Moro:** Right, so 150,000 jobs a year were being lost before. What about now?

Tim Smith: Well, more recently about 40,000 jobs were still being exported each year, but about the same number were coming
65 back to this country. And the balance is changing further. In the coming years, some jobs will still go offshore, but many more will be re-shored.

Mark Moro: Can you be certain about that?

Tim Smith: Just look at some of the things that 70 are happening right now. For example, Apple are spending $100 million on new production facilities in the USA instead of offshore. Again, General Electric are bringing home water-heater production from China to Kentucky. 75 Then again, NCR are re-shoring production of cash machines from China, India and Brazil.

Mark Moro: Well, I'm sure that gives new hope to millions of people who are still looking for work, and also to many millions more 80 who want that *Made in America* label when they buy. (591 words)

1 LOOKING AT THE TEXT

→ Rezeption: Leseverstehen, S. 214

A Put these events in order from 1–7.

a The rate of western job losses slows.
b Many western jobs are lost every year.
c Cheap exports from e.g. China undercut western producers.
d More jobs return to the USA than go offshore.
e US producers move production offshore.
f The rate of US job losses balances the rate of jobs returned.
g Low-cost producers start to become more expensive.

B In your own words, say what the numbers from the text refer to.
1 150,000   2 three per cent   3 40,000   4 $100 million

Make up questions to produce answers that contain these numbers.
1 150,000   2 three per cent   3 40,000   4 $100 million

C Look at the bar chart on page 104 and do the following tasks:

1 Say what cost is completely avoided by production in the USA. How much of the cost of Chinese production is this?
2 Compare these costs of production in the US and in China:
   a raw materials   c other overheads
   b labour   d packaging
3 With a partner, think of some possible reasons for the differences.

Useful phrases
- exactly/roughly the same as …
- a little / (quite) a lot higher/lower than …

105

11 Global reach

2 WORKING WITH WORDS

A Match the words to form two-part nouns from the text.

> bar ■ campaign ■ cash ■ manufacturing ■ production ■ supply
>
> chain ■ chart ■ facility ■ group ■ industry ■ machine

B Use pairs of words from exercise 2A to complete the following. Make any changes necessary.

1 I need to get some money. Where's the nearest ▬?
2 A lot of people have joined our ▬ to stop development of a new airport in this area.
3 The ▬ shows the various costs of production in China and in the USA.
4 Food ▬ are sometimes very long. For example, bananas may come all the way from South America.
5 The company is closing its old factory in Dortmund and is opening a new ▬ near Dresden.
6 There has been a huge increase in production in the Chinese ▬ since 1980.

> **TIP**
>
> When two nouns (or an adjective and a noun) are often used together, they may become hyphenated or even one word, e.g. *low-cost* and *wasteland*. If you are not sure, check in your dictionary.

3 ANALYSING CHARTS

→ Produktion: Schaubilder beschreiben und analysieren, S. 238

> **BUILDING SKILLS: Describing change in charts**
>
> Line graphs usually show how figures change over a period of time.
> ■ You can describe changes with a verb + adverb, or with an adjective + noun (see below).
> ■ Remember to use the simple past to describe 'finished' changes:
> *Sales rose steadily from 2014 to 2016.*
> ■ Use the present perfect to describe changes that are 'unfinished':
> *Sales have risen steadily since 2014.*

Use pairs of words from the table to describe the lines 1–6 below.

Describing graphs and statistics that show changes through time					
verb + adverb		**adjective + noun**		**verb + adjective**	
to rise	rapidly	rapid	rise	to be	flat
to increase	sharply	sharp	increase	to remain	steady
to climb	steadily	steady	climb		
to fall	gradually	gradual	fall		
to decrease	slowly	slow	decrease		
to decline	slightly	slight	decline		

1 ↘	2 ↘	3 →	4 ↗	5 ↗	6 ↑

In chart 1, production fell sharply. / In chart 1, there was a sharp fall in production.

MAIN COURSE **11**

4 LISTENING
→ Rezeption: Hörverstehen, S. 225

42

A Look at the sales chart below and listen to part of the Sales Director's report. Say whether she is describing UK or EU export sales. Identify the six-year period.

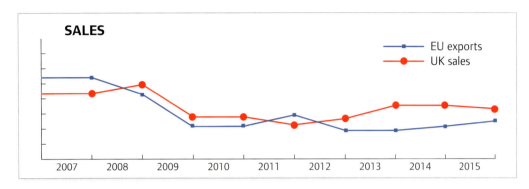

43

B Copy and expand the frame on the right for another chart. Listen to the Sales Director and draw the graph, giving it a title and writing the years.

5 DESCRIBING GRAPHS

A Work in pairs and look at the graph in exercise 4A again. Each of you describe a sales category and a five-year period for your partner to identify.

A In these five years, sales first fell rapidly for a year. But then they … . After that, …
B Ah, you're talking about … sales from … to … , aren't you?

B Work with a partner. Partner A look here. Partner B look at page 213.

Partner A: Describe the graph below to Partner B.

Useful phrases
- This graph shows sales from … (*year*) to … (*year*).
- In/During … (*year*), there was a slight/… rise/… in sales.
- From … (*year*) to … (*year*), sales rose/… slightly/… .

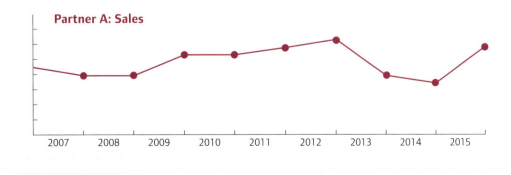

C Draw the graph that Partner B describes.

107

11 Global reach

BUSINESS OPTIONS

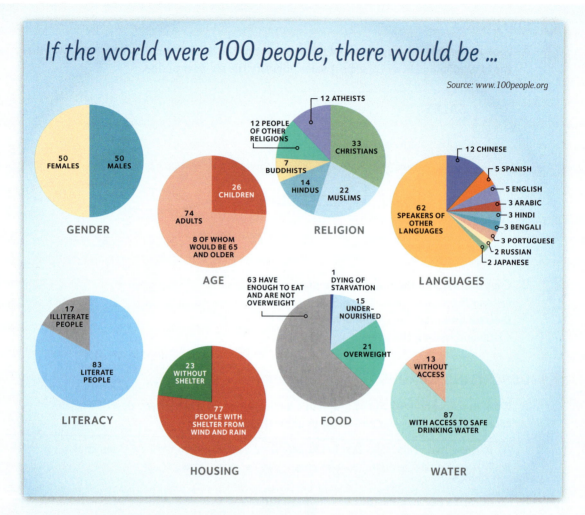

1 LOOKING AT THE INFOGRAPHIC
→ Interaktion, S. 246

A What does the infographic tell you about the world? Discuss in small groups.

B Which aspects of these statistics will change most in the next 20 years? Discuss how and why these changes will take place.

2 WRITING
→ Produktion: Schreiben, S. 228

You read this anonymous statement in an online forum. Choose one of the tasks below.

> "It's ok for refugees from countries at war to seek asylum in safe countries. But I don't agree with people fleeing to richer countries because of economic problems. They should actively try to improve the situation at home instead of becoming a burden on another state!"

A Do you agree or disagree? Write a short comment explaining your answer.

B Imagine you are an economic refugee from a poor country. Write a short answer to the statement.

12 Changing society

MAIN COURSE

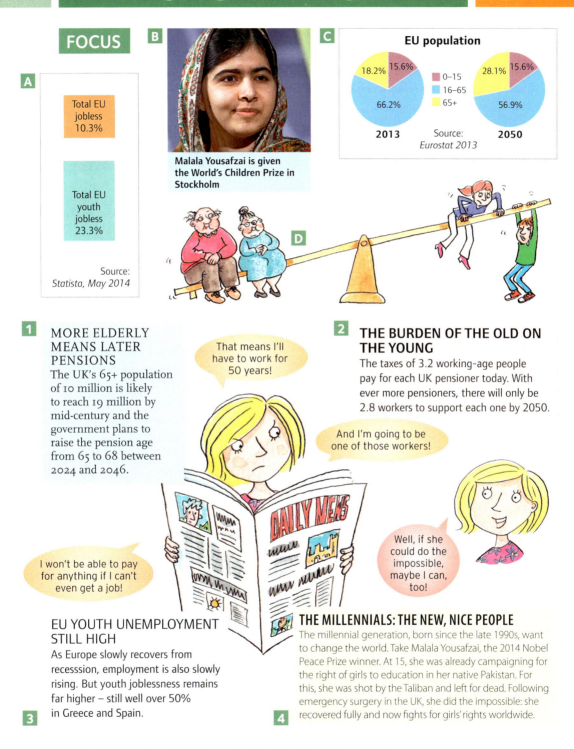

FOCUS

A Total EU jobless 10.3%
Total EU youth jobless 23.3%
Source: Statista, May 2014

B Malala Yousafzai is given the World's Children Prize in Stockholm

C EU population
2013: 0–15: 15.6%, 16–65: 66.2%, 65+: 18.2%
2050: 0–15: 15.6%, 16–65: 56.9%, 65+: 28.1%
Source: Eurostat 2013

1 MORE ELDERLY MEANS LATER PENSIONS
The UK's 65+ population of 10 million is likely to reach 19 million by mid-century and the government plans to raise the pension age from 65 to 68 between 2024 and 2046.

That means I'll have to work for 50 years!

2 THE BURDEN OF THE OLD ON THE YOUNG
The taxes of 3.2 working-age people pay for each UK pensioner today. With ever more pensioners, there will only be 2.8 workers to support each one by 2050.

And I'm going to be one of those workers!

I won't be able to pay for anything if I can't even get a job!

Well, if she could do the impossible, maybe I can, too!

3 EU YOUTH UNEMPLOYMENT STILL HIGH
As Europe slowly recovers from recesssion, employment is also slowly rising. But youth joblessness remains far higher – still well over 50% in Greece and Spain.

4 THE MILLENNIALS: THE NEW, NICE PEOPLE
The millennial generation, born since the late 1990s, want to change the world. Take Malala Yousafzai, the 2014 Nobel Peace Prize winner. At 15, she was already campaigning for the right of girls to education in her native Pakistan. For this, she was shot by the Taliban and left for dead. Following emergency surgery in the UK, she did the impossible: she recovered fully and now fights for girls' rights worldwide.

A Work with a partner. Take turns to describe the pictures A–D.

B Work together to match A–D to the newspaper headlines 1–4.

C Read the newspaper reader's comments. Discuss your own feelings about the future.

109

12 Changing society

TEXT A Making room for the young

BEFORE YOU READ

A What problems do many young people face today when they finish their education? Collect your ideas in a mind map.

B Look at the title of the article. What do you think the author wants, and what sort of people is she probably addressing?

PASS IT ON: give my generation more than a foot in the door

Georgia Leaker

I am one of the nearly one in five people under the age of 25 who are unemployed in Australia.

I'm 24 years old, have two university degrees and have been on Centrelink[1] payments for six months, and [...] I must now take a skills test that Centrelink believes may help me find employment.

While at university, I juggled three casual jobs, self-funded a university exchange to the US and worked for a congressman. After university, I continued my part-time retail job and also did several internships before I was able to get my first career job eight months later. I was hired as a journalist-production assistant at a small company. Eighty per cent of my job was being a personal assistant and doing office administration work. I was made redundant after 10 months, and I had to turn to Centrelink for help for the first time. I did two more internships (both of which I had to fight to get), hoping that my previous experience might land me a job.

During one internship someone in middle management wanted to hire me because I was skilled, and she was sick of endless interns. But she couldn't. The boss said no, because "interns are free and employees cost money". I terminated my internship immediately. [...]

I've applied for retail, administration and full-time nannying jobs, and I am qualified for all of them. (Although the retail industry won't hire me because I'm too "expensive".) I have also regularly applied for rural and out-of-state jobs.

In the past six months, despite the hundreds of job applications I've sent, I've had only four interviews. Two were retail and they chose younger, cheaper applicants. The other two offered pay packets under minimum wage. I didn't get any of them.

When Mia Freedman[2], who I've always admired, was my age, she was the editor of *Cosmopolitan* magazine. [...] Freedman was given lots of opportunities and during her internship, someone took a chance on her. She now runs a successful website, but she has publicly stated she doesn't pay, nor feel she ought to pay, most of her contributors. She's not alone; many successful people feel they needn't provide the next generation with the entry-level employment opportunities that they were given.

The system seems rigged against recent graduates and entry-level jobs are rare. Almost every media job wants someone with "at least five years experience". No one wants to spend the time training the next generation, and many companies would rather have an endless stream of interns to fill the gaps. This situation isn't unique to media jobs, either. Many of my friends, who have all sorts of qualifications, are also unemployed.

I'm sick of being told that I'm lazy and mooching off the system. I don't want to be thought of as a hopeless case by Centrelink. I don't want to spend my week alone, on the couch, watching daytime TV.

	MAIN COURSE	**12**

Around 17.7 per cent of people under the age of 25 are unemployed. Most of us are educated or skilled in some way and most don't want to be dole bludgers. We're just down on our luck and doing everything we can to get a door – any door – opened.

Take a chance on me and my generation. Help take the burden off the welfare system and help us to contribute to the future of the nation.

Our generation aren't useless, but we sure feel like we are.　(572 words)

From: *The Sydney Morning Herald*, July 9, 2013

Footnote:
Unexpectedly, Georgia received a lot of job offers after this article. Soon afterwards, she became Content Manager at an online business-to-business publication.

[1] **Centrelink:** Australian Government Department of Human Services

[2] **Mia Freedman:** Well-known Australian media person who, at 24, took over at the Australian edition of *Cosmopolitan* magazine – the youngest of all the editors of the 28 worldwide editions of *Cosmopolitan*.

1 LOOKING AT THE TEXT

→ Rezeption: Leseverstehen, S. 214

A Read the text and complete the following tasks.

1. Describe the youth unemployment situation in Australia.
2. Explain what the writer did to pay her way through university.
3. Compare her experience as an intern with that of Mia Freedman.
4. Outline how Georgia feels that Freedman's generation are being unfair to her own.
5. Describe what people in management are trying to avoid doing.
6. Explain what national benefits will follow if the writer's generation are given more help.

B Say what it means: Explain the underlined words and phrases in your own words.

1. … I juggled three casual jobs, … (line 7)
2. … self-funded a university exchange … (line 8)
3. … my previous experience might land me a job. (line 20)
4. … she was sick of endless interns. (line 23)
5. … someone took a chance on her. (line 42)
6. … We're just down on our luck … (line 67)

2 WRITING

→ Produktion: Eine Stellungnahme schreiben, S. 234

A Look at your answers to exercise 1A and add any further ideas about youth unemployment to your mind map from page 110.

B Now do one of the following tasks.

> Describe the job situation for young people in Germany. Give examples from your own experience or from the experience of your family and friends.

> Compare the job situation for young people in Germany with the situation that Georgia Leaker describes in Australia.

12 Changing society

3 WORKING WITH WORDS

A Copy and complete the tables with words from the text.

Noun (thing)	Noun (person)
journalism	
	producer
assistance	
	administrator
	manager

Noun (thing)	Noun (person)
	intern
	applicant
edition	
contribution	
graduation	

Noun (thing)	Noun (person 1)	Noun (person 2)
	employer	
	interviewer	interviewee

B Use pairs of words from exercise 3A to complete the sentences.

1 **A** I hear that there have been over 100 ▬¹ for the job?
   B Yes, and we've already asked several of the ▬² to come and talk to us.
2 I spend most of my time with customers now and that means I need ▬¹ with all the paperwork, so I'm advertising for an office ▬².
3 Joe was always interested in ▬¹, so he helped to run the school magazine. Now he's studying to be a ▬² at college.
4 Shipbuilding used to be a huge source of ▬¹ on the River Clyde near Glasgow, but now there's just one company left – with just 3,000 ▬².
5 The company is looking for new staff at the moment, and we're running nearly 30 ▬¹ today and tomorrow. Sue will be the main ▬², but Jack will see some of the applicants, too.
6 I've just started a six-month ▬¹ with TV South to get some experience working in media. There are three other ▬² there, too.
7 Sue has been a regular ▬¹ to the magazine for years. She's made a huge ▬² to its success.

4 GETTING IT RIGHT

→ Modal verbs, S. 259

A Complete the words of a young, unemployed person. Choose the correct modal verbs.

1 I know I (might not / shouldn't) ▬¹ hope for too much, but I think I (might / can't) ▬² still get one or two more replies to the applications I've already sent out.
2 But I (can't / couldn't) ▬¹ understand why people so often don't reply. They (shouldn't / may not) ▬² want to interview me, but it's very bad if they don't even write back.
3 Some days I feel very down, but I try to tell myself that I (mustn't / couldn't) ▬¹ give up, and that I (can't / have to) ▬² keep sending out more applications.
4 I really believe that I (could / must) ▬¹ do well in TV, so I really (should / can) ▬² apply to the local TV station one more time.
5 But this time, I think I'll phone. That way I (may / must) ▬¹ get through to someone who (should / can) ▬² help me.
6 Excuse me, but I (can't / must) ▬¹ run to catch the morning post. I (might not / can't) ▬² meet the deadline for this application if I don't go right now.

MAIN COURSE 12

B Replace the words in brackets with a pronoun + *must*, *mustn't*, *needn't* or *don't have to*.

1. **A** Someone's just phoned to offer Ben an interview. (Important for me to) ▬¹ call him now!
   B (Not necessary for you to) ▬² do that. I can see him just outside the front door.
2. **A** Quick! Where's my jacket? (Necessary for me to) ▬¹ go!
   B You're right. (Very important for you not to) ▬² be late on your first day at your new job.
3. **A** Tomorrow's a holiday, so (not essential for me to) ▬¹ get up early. In fact, (not important for me to) ▬² get up at all. I can sleep all day!
   B (Important for you not to) ▬³ talk like that. Even if (not necessary for you to) ▬⁴ go to work, there are plenty of jobs to do here at home.
4. **A** (Necessary for me to) ▬¹ go and have coffee with all those people?
   B Well, all right, (not essential for you to) ▬² go if you don't want to, but (really important for you not to) ▬³ miss the meeting afterwards.

C Complete the sentences with forms of *be able to*, *have to* or *could(n't)*.

1. I'm sorry, but I ▬ go now or I'll miss my train.
2. We've finished the job, so we ▬ go home soon. We just need to clean up.
3. It was too dark to see, but I ▬ hear someone outside.
4. I ▬ come tomorrow morning, but I'll be free after one o'clock.
5. Carrie ▬ play the piano very well when she was still only nine.
6. A child ran out in front of my bike, but I ▬ stop just in time.
7. The storm was so bad that we ▬ work hard to get the boat back into the harbour.
8. I'd lost my key, so I ▬¹ open the door. But I ▬² get in through an open window.

5 ROLE-PLAY

→ Interaktion: Ein Rollenspiel gestalten, S. 247

Jack Wade, Director of an online business publication called *BusinessAustralia.com*, read Georgia Leaker's article in *The Sydney Morning Herald* yesterday and liked the clear, direct way that she wrote it. He sent an email to the newspaper asking Georgia to call him back.

Work with a partner and create a role-play of the telephone call.

Student A

You are Georgia Leaker, and you have received an email from *The Sydney Morning Herald* asking you to call Jack Wade. He'd like to talk to you about a job. He wants you to call him after 2 pm. You are interested and decide to call back.
- Introduce yourself and refer to his email.
- Express interest in the job.
- Ask for a different date to the one he suggests for an interview.
- Ask where to meet and note down the details. Read them back to check.
- Close in a friendly way.

Student B

You are Jack Wade. You think Georgia Leaker may be the right person for the position of Content Manager at your company. This job requires someone who can edit articles from other contributors and who can also write original material. The address of your office is: 53 Gundaroo Street, Villawood.
- Explain the job briefly.
- Suggest a day and a time for a meeting.
- Offer a different date if necessary.
- Invite her to your office and give the address. Confirm the details.
- Close in a friendly way.

113

12 Changing society

TEXT B Towards a new social harmony

BEFORE YOU READ

Think of family members or family friends who have reached retirement age. What do they do? Do they relax at home or do they have active interests? Do they do volunteer work?

Today, The World This Week reporter Mark Moro is talking about our ageing society to two experts – Joan Blake, journalist and author for 55 years, and Tom West, founder of an online advice forum for young entrepreneurs.

Mark Moro: Let me put this question to you both. Are the new elderly a growing burden on the young or are they a growing resource? Joan, what's the senior citizen's point of view?

Joan Blake: Well, speaking as a pretty active 75-year-old, I have to say that I don't feel like a burden, and many other people my age are still going strong. We're much healthier than previous generations were, and we're also much better educated. So I think we've still got a lot to offer society.

Mark Moro: What do you think, Tom?

Tom West: I agree with Joan. If you look at the figures for Britain, the whole population is rising quite fast, but the population over 65 is rising much faster. In some countries like Germany and Italy, the situation is even more startling. While numbers of older people there are rising fast, too, total populations are falling – in Germany by over 10 million between now and 2050.

Mark Moro: OK. With statistics like that, the elderly simply can't be thrown onto the scrapheap: they have to be turned into a resource. But how can that be done?

Joan Blake: Several things need to change. First, older workers must be allowed to work for longer if they wish and if they can still do the job. Employers shouldn't be allowed to retire people just because they reach a certain age. That's already true in Britain, but it isn't in a lot of other countries.

Tom West: Yes, so some social engineering is required, but for that to work we really need to change social attitudes. Negative attitudes can be found everywhere and they simply must be changed. People are often felt to be past it either physically or mentally by a certain age. What's more, these negative attitudes ignore the positive sides of age – experience and know-how, social skills, reliability and care for quality work.

Mark Moro: And how do you change these attitudes?

Tom West: By giving older people a chance to show what they can do. It's happening a lot through our website now. Let me give just one example – Colin Ross. At 62, Colin was the director of his own company when he became very ill with cancer. He was lucky and he recovered, but he came out if it with a wish to do something different with the rest of his life. Now at the age of 66, he acts as adviser and mentor to young people who are just starting out in business for themselves. He has a lifetime of experience to offer the young, and he has already guided several start-up companies through the difficult early days.

Joan Blake: And here's another heart-warming example. CNA Language Schools in Brazil has teamed up with a home for the elderly in Chicago. Now, you see, most of CNA's students don't get the chance to practise their English with native speakers. At the same time, many of the elderly at Windsor Park Retirement Home are lonely and are only too happy to talk via regular Web chats and help the young Brazilians with their English. The conversations are then recorded and uploaded as private YouTube

videos for CNA teachers to study and work on later with their students.
There are big differences in age and cultural background, but these people have a lot to give each other, and their conversations are often very special. They soon start speaking from their hearts and become very close. I remember seeing one video where an elderly lady finishes by saying to her young friend, 'You are my new granddaughter!'

Mark Moro: What a great idea! That's a real win-win situation for both sides!

(658 words)

MAIN COURSE   12

1 LOOKING AT THE TEXT

→ Rezeption: Leseverstehen, S. 214

A Read the text and make notes under these headings:

- Topic of the interview
- Guests and their jobs
- Advantages of the elderly compared to the past
- Advantages of the elderly over the young
- Examples of the elderly helping the young

SKILLS CHECKLIST: Taking notes

☑ Have I read the whole text?
☑ Have I scanned the text for key words?
☑ Have I noted down the key words?

B Use your notes from exercise 1A to explain why the elderly should play a more important role in society in the future. Give some examples of how the elderly may help the young.

C Say what it means: Explain the underlined words and phrases in your own words.

1 … are still going strong. (line 7)
2 People are often felt to be past it … (line 34)
3 … experience and know-how, … (line 37)
4 … CNA … has teamed up with a home for the elderly … (line 54)
5 … and are only too happy to talk … (lines 58–59)
6 That's a real win-win situation for both sides! (lines 71–72)

D Think of your elderly family members or family friends and discuss these questions in class:

- In what ways do they stay in touch with younger people?
- How do you think this helps them – if at all?
- How might it help the younger people, too – if at all?

2 WORKING WITH WORDS

A Change the underlined words using *the* + adjective, e.g. *the elderly*.

1 In our ageing society, people who are elderly have a lot to offer those who are young.
2 In most ancient societies, people who were powerful often had total control of those who were weak.
3 In most modern societies, it is usually accepted that people who are rich should pay higher taxes than others to help those who are poor.

B Find three more partner words for *social* in the text.

social   climber / science / services / worker / ▬ / ▬ / ▬

C Now use word pairs from exercise 2B to complete the following sentences.

1 All children have to learn the ▬ they need to get on with other people.
2 Sue has gone on from school to study ▬ at university.
3 Rob is a terrible ▬ ! He spends all his time trying to make friends with rich people!
4 ▬ towards gay people have changed. Most people now accept them as normal.
5 With the help of ▬ and taxes, the UK created a more equal society after World War 2.
6 If parents can't look after their children properly, ▬ sometimes have to take over.
7 In that case, a ▬ will first visit the family to find out about the situation.

115

12 Changing society

3 USING A DICTIONARY
→ Ein Wörterbuch benutzen, S. 217

Read the dictionary definitions of *society* (1–5) below and match them to sentences a–e.

> **BUILDING SKILLS: Using a dictionary**
>
> When you find a word in a text that you think you know but that doesn't quite 'fit', always try to work out the meaning from the context first, or by thinking of similar words in German or English. If the meaning is still not clear, you may need to use a dictionary.
> - Don't just use the first definition that you come across!
> - Read through all the meanings carefully in order to find the right one. Meanings are often closely related, for example as in *society* 1–5 below.
> - Sometimes the meanings are quite different, e.g. *fire* as in *fire a gun* (= shoot), *fire an employee* (= end employment), and you have to choose the one that makes the most sense in the context.

society /səˈsaɪəti/ noun   **1** [U] people living together in organized communities, with laws and traditions that control the way they behave towards each other   **2** [C/U] a particular type of society, e.g. in a particular country or area, or at a particular time in history, or with a special characteristic
3 [U] the group of people in a country who are rich, powerful and/or from a high social class
4 [C] an organization or club for people who share a particular interest or take part in a particular activity
5 [U] *formal* the company or friendship of other people

a Ann does two after-school activities. She plays football and belongs to the drama society.
b It was the society wedding of the year, and the guest list was full of famous names.
c In western countries we expect society to help those who need help.
d James is a very private person: he always tries to avoid the society of other people.
e We live in an affluent, post-industrial society full of opportunities that earlier generations never dreamed of.

4 GETTING IT RIGHT
→ The passive, S. 261

You work for a construction company and you have to write a report on a management meeting about the new company policy on retirement.

**Read the statements below to continue the report.
Report the underlined sections with modal passive forms.**

At the meeting the following points were made.
· *Workers who are 65 must be …*
· *If they are …*

> **TIP**
>
> As a report is a formal written document, use full forms, e.g. *they are*, not *they're*.

A So we agree that we must allow workers who are 65 to continue in work if they want to.
B Yes, and if they're strong enough, we shouldn't stop them from staying in their old jobs.
A OK, but we'll have to consider workers who are less strong case by case.
B Yes, we can't expect people in that situation to carry on doing outdoor construction work. We'll need to offer them less physically tiring work.
A OK, but to do this, I think we should interview workers like these to find out what other skills they have.
B We might offer a few people jobs in the warehouse. We could retrain them as forklift drivers.
A But we needn't necessarily retrain older workers. We can use their life-long skills for training apprentices.

| | | MAIN COURSE | 12 |

5 LISTENING
→ Rezeption: Hörverstehen, S. 225

Mark Moro is now interviewing another expert on our ageing society – this time not to talk about the benefits, but instead to discuss the problems.

A Copy the notes. Then listen to the interview and complete them.

Population (millions)
- Germany – Now: ▩ – 2050: ▩
- UK – Now: ▩ – 2050: ▩

UK elderly (millions)
- Over 65 – Now: ▩ (= ▩ %) – 2050: ▩ (= ▩ %)
- Over 80 – Now: ▩ – 2050: ▩

Pensioner welfare (pensions, winter fuel, etc.)
- Cost per year: ▩ · % of total UK welfare: ▩

Health costs per household
- Retired: ▩ · Non-retired: ▩

B Use your notes to complete the following tasks.

1. Compare population change in Germany and in the UK.
2. Compare general UK population change and population change among the elderly.
3. Compare the cost of welfare for the UK elderly and the cost for everyone else.
4. Compare the average health care costs for retired and non-retired UK households.

6 WRITING
→ Produktion: Eine Stellungnahme schreiben, S. 234

Write a comment on *Our ageing society*. Explain the expression *our ageing society*. Then describe and evaluate some of the problems and point out any opportunities that it gives us.

BUILDING SKILLS: Writing a comment

Always make sure you understand the task before you start to write a comment. In the task above, you need to give basic information about *Our ageing society*, describe some of the pros and cons, and give your own opinion on the topic.
- Always collect ideas to help you first, either in the form of a mind map, a list or simple notes. You will usually find information from your reading and listening, in this case Text B (page 114) and exercise 5 (above).
- Organize your notes to help you structure the text. You need to give an introduction to the topic and a conclusion with your opinion. You also need to support your arguments with examples.
- Use linking words or connecting phrases to structure your text and make it easier for the reader to follow your arguments.

Useful phrases

Adding facts:	Listing ideas:	Giving examples:	Comparing and evaluating:
■ Moreover, …	■ First of all, …	■ For example, …	■ Although …
■ Furthermore, …	■ Secondly, …	■ For instance, …	■ Despite the fact that …
■ In addition, …	■ Then again, …		

117

12 Changing society — BUSINESS OPTIONS

BEFORE YOU READ

What is important to you, personally, in choosing an internship? Make notes and discuss in class.

Internships: exploitation or opportunity?

Business Expert spoke to Sahil Patel, CEO of a booming software company, and university student Catherine Monk about internships. Patel's company offers internships to graduate students. Monk has initiated a campaign for the rights of interns.

Business Expert: In your opinion, what should companies offer interns?

Patel: An internship is an opportunity to learn, grow, and make mistakes before you start a 'real' job. Companies should challenge interns and encourage them to show what they are capable of. Feedback is important. Interns need to know what they are doing well and what they could improve.

Monk: Interns shouldn't be treated as people who are there to do menial jobs all day. There needs to be an element of learning, opportunities to partake in, company training workshops, etc. There should be at least one employee to support and guide interns throughout their time at the company.

Business Expert: Do you think all internships should be paid?

Monk: Definitely! There should be a minimum internship wage so that interns can afford to pay rent and living costs, as well as transport to and from work, healthcare – in short, all necessary expenses.

Patel: In an ideal world, yes but an intern is not as productive as a regular employee. An internship is a great opportunity to show your potential, make mistakes that won't hurt your professional reputation and leave with tangible experience and skills for your CV. Companies will be more willing to give interns this opportunity if they are not forced to pay them.

Business Expert: What can be done to stop companies taking advantage of interns?

Patel: Extreme exploitation should be reported to the authorities. But again, even if the internship is unpaid, I wouldn't see it as exploitation, as long as there are plenty of opportunities for interns to network, meet people in the industry, learn and improve their skills.

Monk: My campaign's aim is to establish minimum standards for internships in terms of wages, educational value and legal rights. Interns shouldn't receive exactly the same pay and conditions as other employees because then the educational value gets lost. But they do have the right to a certain standard of living – and learning.

Business Expert: What advice would you give to young people thinking about doing an internship?

Monk: Research the company where you want to do your internship carefully. Check your contract and terms of payment and don't be afraid to ask questions. If, at any stage, you are unhappy with the conditions or feel that you are not learning enough, talk to somebody in charge.

Patel: Grab the opportunity with both hands! Try to get noticed: come up with original ideas and suggestions. Also, try to take something tangible with you when you leave, a project that you have managed, however small, is something that you can show to future employers. And, once you have left, stay in touch. Contacts could lead to a future position or a recommendation.

(495 words)

MEDIATION
→ Schriftliche Mediation, S. 240

Sie arbeiten in einem Berufsberatungszentrum für Jugendliche. Ihre Vorgesetzte möchte, dass Sie ein Informationsblatt für Schülerinnen und Schüler erstellen, welches grundlegende Fragen zur Auswahl und Durchführung erfolgreicher Praktika beantwortet. Fassen Sie zu diesem Zweck die zentralen Informationen des Artikels auf Deutsch zusammen.

Job skills 3
Giving directions ▪ bookings and reservations

Eric's application for a job in the UK was successful and he starts today at Magnus & Klein, a small manufacturing company in London. The company is located in the Four Lofts Business Park. Ms Shaw, the office manager, has sent him written instructions on how to get to the office.

1 UNDERSTANDING DIRECTIONS

A Follow the instructions and find the offices of Magnus & Klein on the plan of the business park.

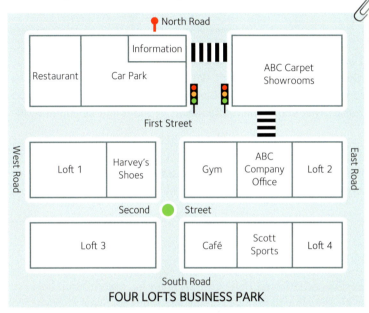

> When you get off the bus in North Road, walk back a few metres to the entrance to the park. Pass the information box and walk down to the traffic lights. Turn right into First Street and take the first left. You'll see a gym on your left. Keep going till you come to Second Street. Turn right into Second Street and walk past Harvey's Shoes on your right. Our office is in the same building, opposite Loft 3.

B Work with a partner and do one of the following tasks.

- Take turns to give each other directions to different companies or places in the park.

   Choose a company or a place in the park. Do not tell your partner the name of the company or place he/she is going to. Describe how to get there from the Magnus & Klein office. Can he/she find the way and name the company or the place?

   Remember to start at the Magnus & Klein office every time.

- With your partner, think of a company or a place within walking distance of your school. Write directions how to get there from the school. Do not write down the name of the company or the place. Give your directions to another pair. Can they find out where you are sending them?

Useful phrases: Giving directions

- Turn right/left.
- Go straight ahead/on.
- Keep to the right/left.
- It's on the right-hand side / on the left-hand side.

119

Job skills 3

2 LISTENING

→ Rezeption: Hörverstehen, S. 225

When Eric arrives at Magnus & Klein, Ms Shaw gives him a tour of the offices.

A Study the floor plan and the list of places below. Then listen and find the places on the floor plan.

1 Accounts
2 Human Resources
3 Ms Shaw's office
4 the kitchen
5 the men's toilet
6 the storeroom

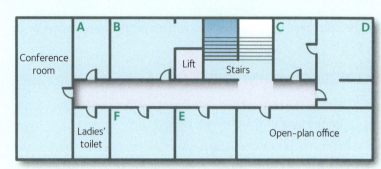

B Work with a partner and do one the following tasks.

- Draw a simple floor plan of a school. Name three or four of the rooms (e.g. classrooms, staff room, toilets). Leave the remaining rooms blank. Without showing your partner, make a list of the names of the rooms you have left blank. Give your floor plan to your partner and give him/her a tour. Your partner should fill in the names of the rooms as you describe them.

- With your partner, think about how you should leave your classroom if the fire alarm goes off. Write down the directions from memory, then check on the emergency exit plan in your classroom.

3 MAKING A HOTEL BOOKING

Magnus & Klein plc are going to exhibit at the Bristol Trade Fair. Ms Shaw has asked Eric to book accommodation for herself and a colleague. Eric has booked online and sends Ms Shaw an email giving details of the booking.

A Complete the email below using words from the box. There are two words more than you need.

> free ▪ from ▪ included ▪ near ▪ non-smoking ▪ not smoking ▪
> opposite ▪ single ▪ to ▪ within

Dear Ms Shaw

As requested, I have booked accommodation for you and Tony Browne in the Bristol Fair Hotel ▇▇ [1] Thursday, 17 October ▇▇ [2] Sunday, 20 October as follows:
Two ▇▇ [3] rooms, both of them ▇▇ [4]. The cost of the rooms is £84 per night, breakfast ▇▇ [5].
The hotel is located ▇▇ [6] to the fair area and there are several good restaurants ▇▇ [7] walking distance.
There is also a car park ▇▇ [8] the hotel.

Best wishes
Eric

120

Giving directions • bookings and reservations

A few days before the fair, Ms Shaw asks Eric to contact the hotel and give them some extra information.

B Listen to Eric's phone call to the hotel and make notes on the following:

1 the name of the person who takes the call
2 the booking number
3 the problem
4 why it is important that the hotel has the new information

4 WRITING AN EMAIL

→ Job Skills 1, Email etiquette, S. 32

Using the email and your notes from exercise 3, write Eric's email to Tony Browne confirming the booking. Add a suitable subject line.

From: Eric Jung <ericjung@magnusklein.co.uk>
Subject:
To: Tony Browne <tonybrowne@magnusklein.co.uk>
cc: Joan Shaw <joanshaw@magnusklein.co.uk>

Hello Tony

This is just to let you know that I have booked …

As you will be arriving after the check-in time of 10 pm, I have called the hotel …

I hope the hotel is OK and that you enjoy your trip.

Best
Eric

TIP Formal and informal business emails

When writing business emails to new contacts, superiors or people you don't know well (for example, colleagues at a new job), you should begin your email with *Dear …* and end with *Regards* or *Best wishes*. With business contacts or colleagues you know well, you can start emails with *Hello …* or *Hi …* and end with *Best*.

5 RESERVING A CONFERENCE ROOM

The Magnus & Klein team are having a meeting with some business partners during the trade fair. Ms Shaw asks Eric to reserve a conference room.

A Work in a group of four. Discuss Ms Shaw's wishes and rank them in order of importance (1 is most important). Give reasons for your rankings.

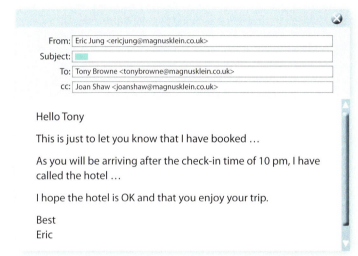

Eric
We are having a meeting with some business partners on Saturday, 19 October. Please book a conference room for the whole day and arrange lunch for 9 people.
We need a room with seating for 9 people including one person in a wheelchair; a projector, screen and a flip chart; Wi-fi; a selection of non-alcoholic drinks. Lunch should include vegetarian options.
Try to get a conference room at the fair or near to the fair area and please don't exceed £300, including lunch.
JS

121

Job skills 3

B In your group, split into two pairs: Partners A and B, and Partners C and D. Each pair is going to look at offers for conference rooms and then try to persuade the other pair to choose the room they have selected.

Partners A and B

Work together and compare the offers on the right with what Ms Shaw would like. Choose a room and develop arguments which will persuade Partners C and D to reserve this room for the meeting.

Bristol Trade Fair Area Conference Rooms
– Book by the hour, half day or full day –

Our conference centre on the top floor of the Fair Area is accessible by lift. There is wheelchair access throughout the building and disabled facilities on every floor.

We have three conference rooms to suit your needs.
Prices: £180 (69 m²), £155 (38 m²), £110 (22 m²)

All rooms are equipped with high-end audio-visual equipment and free wireless high-speed internet connection.

- Hot and cold drinks, fruit and snacks included in the price of the room
- Free national and local calls
- Free 'host' Internet connection
- Free stationery

A la carte lunch menu at prices starting from £18 per person.
Non-alcoholic drinks included in the price.
Special dietary requirements can be catered for.

Bristol Fair Hotel
MEETING ROOM FACILITIES

Our hotel is located next to the Bristol Fair Area. You can hold a meeting and stay overnight with us at reasonable prices.

Room	Size	Price
River	73 m²	£210
Mountain	50 m²	£175
Plain	26 m²	£120

All prices include modern technology. We can mix and match equipment (e.g. screen, projector, pinboard, flip charts with markers) according to your wishes.
Catering throughout the whole event, snacks and non-alcoholic drinks are included in the price of the room. Buffet lunch: £14 per person.

- Disabled facilities throughout the hotel.
- Wi-fi in the meeting rooms and in public areas.
- Private bar available for a relaxing end to your event.

If you are a guest of our hotel, the rental price for the conference room is reduced by £5 for each booked hotel room.

Partners C and D

Work together and compare the offers on the right with what Ms Shaw would like. Choose a room and develop arguments which will persuade Partners A and B to reserve this room for the meeting.

6 BOOKING A CONFERENCE ROOM BY EMAIL

Write an email to the company whose conference room you have chosen. Give the date and times when you would like the room. Describe what services you would like.

Useful phrases

- to book/reserve a conference room for … people
- to be equipped with …
- to confirm a reservation for …
- to send an invoice to …

13 The challenges of the modern state

FOCUS

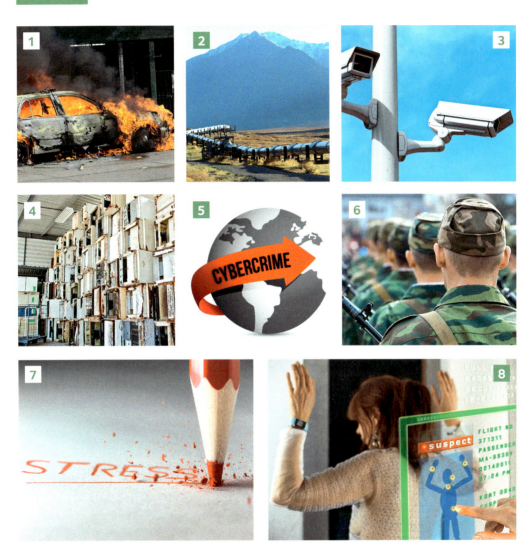

A **Think:** Rank the problems shown in the photos according to what you think is most important. Use the words in the box or your own descriptions.

> body scanners ▪ data protection ▪ electronic waste ▪ energy dependence ▪
> extremism ▪ human rights ▪ identity theft ▪ mental health ▪ online security ▪
> phishing ▪ radicalization ▪ stress ▪ surveillance cameras ▪ terrorist attacks ▪ war

Write two or three sentences about the problems you think are most important.

B **Pair:** Compare your list with a partner and discuss your choices.

C **Share:** Discuss your ideas in class.

123

13 The challenges of the modern state

TEXT A Terrorism

BEFORE YOU READ   → Rezeption: Leseverstehen, S. 214

A Skim the first text to find out what happened to the two brothers.

B Scan the second text to find another expression for *police work*.

50

THE BOSTON MARATHON

Two hours after the winners crossed the finishing line of the 117th Boston Marathon, two pressure cooker bombs exploded killing three people and injuring 264. Three days later, the FBI released photographs and a surveillance video of two suspects, who were brothers. They were found the same day and after a firefight with the police, the older brother died and the younger one escaped.

Four days later, thousands of police officers in Watertown, Massachusetts took part in a huge manhunt for the younger brother. Public transport, most private businesses and all public institutions were shut down and residents were told to stay indoors, making Watertown into an urban desert. At around 7 pm, a Watertown resident discovered the younger brother hiding in a boat in his back yard and

he was arrested. He later stated that he and his brother had also planned to bomb Times Square in New York. He claimed that they were self-radicalized and had learned to build bombs on the Internet.

(167 words)

THE NATURE OF MODERN TERRORISM

[…] Methods for engaging in political violence have changed, and multiple forms of terrorism will probably dominate the "battlefields" of the twenty-first century. […] Modern terrorism is a new phenomenon. It requires supporting systems from the technological world. First, to be effective, terrorism must be seen and heard. As one terrorist commander summarized, it is better to kill one person in front of a camera than to kill a hundred in a secret location. Terrorists need an audience.

The second aspect of modernity's impact on terrorism involves mobility. This can be done locally or globally. The goal is to get to the target and get away. An attack can originate in the hills of South Waziristan and be carried out in London […].

Finally, the modern world provides weapons or materials that can be turned into weapons.

These devices, in turn, are more powerful than instruments of the past. […]

These three factors – instant communication, mobility, and access to destructive technology – mean that terrorism will continue to plague the world. […] When not used as a tactic in guerrilla war, terrorism is essentially a problem for law enforcement and the criminal justice system. […] One of the best tools in the anti-terrorist arsenal is to develop law enforcement agencies that act as extensions of neighborhoods. These agencies can root out all types of problems before they happen, including terrorism. […] Finally, it would be helpful if the mass media, especially cable news, would spend time explaining the complex background of modern terrorism. This would be much more responsible than breathlessly awaiting the next stage in a terrorist drama. […]   (265 words)

From: Jonathan R. White, *The Huffington Post*

EXAM PREPARATION 13

1 LOOKING AT THE TEXTS
→ Rezeption: Leseverstehen, S. 214

A Read the first text and explain how …

1. the bombers made their explosive devices.
2. the police were able to get photographs of the suspects.
3. the brothers became extremists.

B Read the second text and match the sentence halves.

1. There will be many different forms of …
2. Modern technology enables terrorists to …
3. Terrorist attacks are often planned in places which …
4. Nowadays, it is easy to find materials …
5. Nobody expects terrorism …
6. In many cases, it is the job of the police …
7. The police can root out some terrorism …
8. Terrorism is often sensationalized …

a. which can be made into weapons.
b. to deal with terrorists.
c. by the mass media.
d. to stop in the near future.
e. by working closely with the local community.
f. reach large audiences all over the world.
g. terrorism in the twenty-first century.
h. are a long way away from the target.

2 WORKING WITH WORDS

A Study the texts to see how the verbs in box A are used with the nouns in box B.

A		B	
to release	to carry out	a manhunt	the problems
to take part in	to turn into	an attack	the world
to shut down	to plague	photographs	violence
to engage in	to root out	public transport	weapons

B Use some collocations from exercise 2A to complete the text. Make any necessary changes.

When four suicide bombers ___¹ on London Transport on 7 July 2005, there was no warning and 56 people died, including the terrorists. The attack was so devastating that the authorities had to ___² for the rest of the day, which meant there were no trains or buses in Central London. Some time later, the police ___³ of the attackers showing them carrying large rucksacks of home-made explosives at London's Kings Cross station. Attacks of this nature continue to ___⁴, and law enforcement agencies everywhere now have emergency plans to deal with such events. However, experts agree that it is best to ___⁵ which lead to terrorist attacks before extremists ___⁶ and kill innocent people.

C *Cross* can be a verb (*to cross*) or a noun (*a cross*). Use the definitions below to find more words in the two texts that have the same verb and noun form.

1. to make available for the public
2. to believe sb is guilty of sth
3. to take sb to a police station and hold them there
4. to make different
5. to give help
6. to have a strong effect on sth
7. to use weapons to hurt or kill sb

D Write 4–5 sentences containing your answers to exercise 2C as nouns or verbs.

13 The challenges of the modern state

3 MEDIATION
→ Schriftliche Mediation, S. 240

Ihre Schule nimmt an einem Projekt in Zusammenarbeit mit einer großen Regionalzeitung teil. Die Schüler und Schülerinnen sind aufgefordert, Artikel über aktuelle Themen zu schreiben, die dann in der Zeitung veröffentlicht werden.

Benutzen Sie die relevanten Inhalte der beiden Texte, um einen Zeitungsartikel über die Rolle der modernen Technik im Terrorismus des 21. Jahrhunderts zu verfassen.

4 LISTENING
→ Rezeption: Hörverstehen, S. 225

Tonight, the BBC's radio phone-in programme *World Have Your Say* is dealing with the question, 'Is the state really under threat from terrorism?'

A Before you listen, work with a partner and guess which person says each statement below.

Fatima, Turkish student

Joshua, Christian priest

Andrea, German student teacher

Reginald, ex-army officer

a In my experience talking with terrorists gets you nowhere. We need to find them and stop them.
b The West must stop sending weapons to conflict zones.
c Children must learn not to use violence to solve conflicts.
d I believe in focusing on the values and beliefs we all share, not on our differences.

B Listen and check your answers.

C Listen again and write down the missing words. Sometimes you need more than one word for each gap.

1 The government is responsible for ▬ its citizens.
2 If we want ▬ in a free world, spending on the police and the armed forces must be massively increased.
3 I believe in ▬ for the threat before it's too late.
4 Westerners enjoy ▬ in safety and comfort
5 They risk ▬[1] all this if they continue ▬[2] weapons to conflict zones.
6 I remember ▬ about the horrors of the Second World War at school.
7 I started ▬ about the reasons for violence.
8 A member of my church suggested ▬ a prayer vigil.
9 I agreed ▬ so immediately.
10 Joshua recommends ▬ for peace.

EXAM PREPARATION 13

5 ROLE-PLAY

→ Interaktion: Ein Rollenspiel gestalten, S. 247

With a partner, choose the speaker from exercise 4 whose opinions you disagree with most. Role-play a discussion between yourself and that person about how to prevent terrorism. Take turns with your partner to play both roles.

BUILDING SKILLS: Preparing for a discussion

You should always prepare thoroughly before you start any kind of speaking activity. If you have to take part in a discussion, you can prepare by making notes of the main arguments:
- Think of the ideas and arguments that your opponent might use and make a list of them.
- Make a list of your own ideas and arguments.
- Look at the points you disagree about most strongly and think of arguments you can use against your opponent.

Useful phrases

Partly agreeing with an opinion:
- I don't entirely/quite agree with you.
- I see what you mean, but …
- There's some truth in what you say. However, …

Saying something in another way:
- (Well,) What I mean is, …
- In other words, …
- Let me put it another way, …

6 GETTING IT RIGHT

→ Verb + infinitive ■ Verb + gerund, S. 262

A Choose the right verb form to complete these sentences.

The security services are responsible for (to protect / protecting) ▬¹ the citizens of a country from terrorist attacks. The security services also expect the citizens (to help / helping) ▬² them do their job and they encourage them (to give / giving) ▬³ them helpful information. However, communicating sensitive information to MI5, Britain's internal security service, is not so simple. Although the organization recommends (to use / using) ▬⁴ its secure Internet contact form, many people decide (to write / writing) ▬⁵ a letter instead because they prefer (to post / posting) ▬⁶ it anonymously. Some computer experts encourage people to stop (to use / using) ▬⁷ phones and computers for important messages and only use paper. They feel that using the Internet for sensitive material involves (to take / taking) ▬⁸ too many security risks.

B The verbs in the box are all followed by gerunds. Complete the sentences with a suitable verb from the box, making any necessary changes.

avoid ■ enjoy ■ hate ■ involve ■ mind ■ miss ■ recommend ■ risk

1. Police work often ▬ observing a suspect over a long period of time.
2. If you ▬ having a lot of free time, it's best not to join the police force.
3. The police ▬ taking extra safety precautions when there is a terrorist threat.
4. They say it's best to ▬ going out late at night.
5. When this happens, some people ▬ meeting their friends at the local pub.
6. Others don't ▬ staying at home in the evenings.
7. Some people even cancel their holidays because they don't want to ▬ travelling to a dangerous place.
8. Most people ▬ losing their freedom but are willing to do so for a short time.

13 The challenges of the modern state

TEXT B The dangers of digital life

BEFORE YOU READ → Rezeption: Leseverstehen – Grobverständnis, S. 214

Skim the text and explain which of the following statements is true and why the others are false:

1 Uwe Buse was unable to defend himself against any of the hackers' attacks.
2 Uwe Buse was able to defend himself against some of the hackers' attacks.
3 Uwe Buse was able to defend himself against most of the hackers' attacks.

When hackers take over your life

When *Spiegel* reporter Uwe Buse decided to try out a test on himself and invited hackers to take over his life, he had no idea what he was letting himself in for. He wanted them to find out as much as possible about his private and professional life without any help from him at all and then use this knowledge to harm him. He would then try to fight back as an exercise in digital self-defence.

He first contacted a specialist firm in Tübingen which hacks into company networks at the request of their owners and instructed them to hack into his mobile and laptop. In Tübingen, three young hackers, who had made their illegal hobby into their profession, installed undetectable spyware on his mobile and laptop. When the laptop was switched back on, the message from its virus scanner was: 'Your computer is safe.'

The spyware on Uwe Buse's mobile immediately started transmitting GPS data to the hackers every two seconds. That evening the hackers tracked him back to Bremen, noted his home address and took a look at his house using Street View. They logged his every movement and also found out he had a school-age daughter when she phoned him to tell him she had arrived safely at school. They recorded the phone call and intercepted the photo of herself she sent him. They knew what she looked like.

At 9 o'clock the same day, when Uwe Buse sat down at his laptop to start work, he thought he was alone. He was mistaken. The camera in his laptop started taking photos of him every five minutes and sending them to the hackers. In addition, every keystroke he made on his computer was recorded in a handy Excel table, which also showed the names of the programs he was using, which windows were open on his monitor, the data he was inputting and the time. The table was also sent to the hackers every five minutes.

When he logged into his Amazon and email accounts, they recorded the access codes and by scanning his Amazon account, quickly saw that he rode a motorbike and

128

had dry skin. They went on to find out his wife and children's names, his wife's email address, the number of her mobile, where she worked and what she looked like. They noted that the Buses didn't own a car and used car-sharing. Next the hackers sent a silent SMS to the reporter's mobile to switch on the microphone and record everything he said. This also went unnoticed.

On the second day of the experiment he logged into his bank account and the hackers recorded the access codes. They did the same with his Facebook, PayPal and iTunes accounts. They now had the data they needed and on the third day they switched to attack.

The driver of the delivery van which stopped outside Uwe Buse's house carried a large cardboard box to the front door. When asked what was in the box he replied: 'It's a lawnmower.' Buse refused delivery and sent the van away. The attack had begun.

The hackers used his email account to write an email in his name to the car-sharing firm and tell them he had knocked off the two outside mirrors of the car but had no time to stick them back on again.

The washing machine ordered in Buse's name was priced at €415.39 but when he got an email from Amazon confirming the purchase, he quickly phoned the hotline and cancelled it. Amazon advised him to change his password, which he did, but the spyware sent the new password straight to the hackers. After some more phone calls Amazon told him his account had been 'totally destroyed' and could no longer be saved. They advised him to report the matter to the police and be more careful when surfing the net in future.

The hackers' next target was his Facebook account. They posted an extremely embarrassing public message about his private life on his wall, prompting him to try to delete his account. However, as the hackers had changed all his personal details, he was unable to get into his account and could not contact anyone at Facebook because there is no hotline.

Next the hackers logged into his online bank account and withdrew all his money, placing it on untraceable prepaid cards. When he contacted his bank, they told him to report it to the police. They promised to try to get his money back and sent him a new access code for his account – by post.

Before he could go to the police, however, he was informed that he had sent his boss at *Spiegel* an email telling him that he was 'sick and tired' of him and was leaving the magazine straightaway to get a better paid job at the hackers' company in Tübingen.

Finally, his hackers contacted him to warn him that they were going to put some very nasty material on his laptop and then inform the police. He begged them not to do so and a few days later conceded utter defeat.

The spyware package used by the hackers is obtainable on the American market for as little as $33 per month. The software makers openly encourage worried parents, suspicious spouses and company bosses to spy on their children, partners and employees. The fact that using such programs is illegal in almost all countries is hidden in the small print.

When Uwe Buse asked his tormentors how to protect himself, they told him not to use Windows computers, online banking or mobile banking and not to install any unnecessary apps. They advised him to keep his virus scanner and software up-to-date, set up a firewall, use an encrypted mobile phone, go to the bank in person and use paper.

(970 words)

13 The challenges of the modern state

1 LOOKING AT THE TEXT
→ Rezeption: Leseverstehen, S. 214

A Read the text on pages 128–129 and do the following tasks.

1. Study the text and list the information the hackers found out about Uwe Buse's …
   a) house, b) family and c) preferred means of transport.
2. Describe how the hackers obtained the access codes to his online accounts.
3. The hackers launched six attacks against Uwe Buse. Outline each attack briefly.
4. How many attacks was he able to defend himself against?
5. Why was he able to defend himself against the Amazon but not the Facebook attack?
6. Explain how Uwe Buse stopped the seventh attack and discuss the possible consequences if it had taken place.
7. Analyse each of the attacks (including the cancelled seventh attack) and put the consequences it had or would have had into one of the following categories:
   a) criminal, b) financial, c) job-related and d) social.

B Say what you think.

1. Discuss the reasons why parents, spouses and company bosses might use a spyware program.
2. Evaluate each of the hackers' suggestions as to how to protect yourself from digital attack.

2 WORKING WITH WORDS

A Match the words or expressions with their meanings.

1	to let yourself in for sth	a	to take money out of a bank account
2	mistaken	b	horrible
3	to refuse	c	important information written in very small letters
4	purchase	d	to put into code
5	to withdraw	e	immediately
6	untraceable	f	to do sth unpleasant or difficult
7	straightaway	g	impossible to find
8	nasty	h	wrong
9	the small print	i	to say you will not do sth
10	to encrypt	j	sth you have bought

B Work in pairs. Write your own definitions of four or five words in the text, mix them up and show them to your partner. Can your partner match the words to the definitions?

C Complete the text with a suitable phrasal verb, by adding a particle to the verbs below.

verbs: try ▪ take ▪ find ▪ switch ▪ get ▪ set

particles: back ▪ on ▪ out (2×) ▪ over ▪ up

Thanks to cybercrime there are fewer bank robberies because it's easier to ___¹ a computer than rob a bank. Many people never ___² that their computer has been hijacked. They just ___ it ___³ as usual, ___⁴ a digital payment of some form and click on 'OK'. However, if their account has been hacked, there is a good chance they will never ___ their money ___⁵. When hackers steal credit card data, they make a copy of the card and ___ it ___⁶ it with a small sum of money first. If it works, they use it for bigger payments.

130

EXAM PREPARATION

13

TEXT C The surveillance society

In this section you are going to read two short extracts from a novel and a newspaper article about surveillance.

BEFORE YOU READ

What do you associate with the term 'surveillance society'?

In 1949 George Orwell published *Nineteen Eighty-Four*, a novel about a fictional totalitarian state called Oceania. The following extracts describe the posters of the leader, Big Brother, which are everywhere, and the use of telescreens by the Thought Police.

… the poster with the enormous face gazed from the wall. It was one of those pictures which are so contrived that the eyes follow you about when you move. BIG BROTHER IS WATCHING YOU, the caption beneath it ran.

… The telescreen received and transmitted simultaneously. Any sound that Winston made, above the level of a very low whisper, would be picked up by it, moreover, so long as he remained within the field of vision which the metal plaque commanded, he could be seen as well as heard. There was of
5 course no way of knowing whether you were being watched at any given moment. How often, or on what system, the Thought Police plugged in on any individual wire was guesswork. It was even conceivable that they watched everybody all the time. But at any rate they could plug in your wire whenever they wanted to. You had to live – did live, from habit that became instinct –
10 in the assumption that every sound you made was overheard, and, except in darkness, every movement scrutinized.   (176 words)

From: George Orwell, *Nineteen Eighty-Four*

to gaze – *starren, blicken*
to contrive – *bewerkstelligen*
telescreen – *Televisor*
simultaneously – *gleichzeitig*
to pick up – *registrieren*
field of vision – *Sichtfeld*
plaque – *Platte*
to command – *beherrschen*
to plug in on – *sich in etw einschalten*
guesswork – *Mutmaßung, Spekulation*
conceivable – *denkbar*
assumption – *Annahme*
to scrutinize – *genau ansehen, überprüfen*

1 LOOKING AT THE TEXT

→ Rezeption: Leseverstehen, S. 214

A Read the extracts from the novel and complete these tasks.

1 What is the most important characteristic of the poster? Write two or three sentences to describe its effect.
2 Explain in a few words how the poster is helpful to Big Brother.
3 Discuss the functions of the telescreen with a partner, then list them in order of importance.
4 Compare your order of importance with other students in your class and discuss any differences of opinion.

B Think: George Orwell's novel is seen as a warning against a totalitarian society. Can you think of any parallels today or in history?

C Pair: Discuss your ideas with a partner and them write them down in a few sentences.

D Share: Present your ideas in class.

13 The challenges of the modern state

2 READING

→ Rezeption: Leseverstehen, S. 214

A Before you read: Think about places you would expect to see CCTV cameras and places where you wouldn't expect (or want) to see CCTV cameras. Make a list.

B While you read: Note down the estimated numbers of CCTV cameras in Britain. Make a list of where they are located.

ONE SURVEILLANCE CAMERA FOR EVERY 11 PEOPLE IN BRITAIN, SAYS CCTV SURVEY

Britain has a CCTV camera for every 11 people, a security industry report disclosed, as privacy campaigners criticised the growth of the "surveillance state".

5 The British Security Industry Authority (BSIA) estimated there are up to 5.9 million closed-circuit television cameras in the country, including 750,000 in "sensitive locations" such as schools, hospitals and care homes. […]

Simon Adcock, of the BSIA, said: "[…] Effective CCTV schemes are an invaluable
10 source of crime detection and evidence for the police. For example in 2009, 95% of Scotland Yard murder cases used CCTV footage as evidence."

But Nick Pickles, director of the privacy campaign Big Brother Watch, said: "This report is another stark reminder of how out of control our surveillance culture has become.

15 "With potentially more than five million CCTV cameras across country, including more than 300,000 cameras in schools, we are being monitored in a way that few people would recognise as a part of a healthy democratic society." […]

It estimated there are between 291,000 and 373,000 cameras in public sector schools, plus a further 30,000 to 50,000 in independent schools.

20 Surgeries and health centres have an estimated 80,000 to 159,000, while there are believed to be between 53,000 and 159,000 cameras in restaurants, the report said.

(216 words)

From: www.telegraph.co.uk

C Work with a partner and do these tasks.

1 Compare your two lists. Are there any places mentioned that you didn't expect to see?
2 Which figures from the text do you find surprising? Explain why (not).

D Say what it means: Explain these phrases in your own words.

1 'sensitive locations' (line 7)
2 an invaluable source of crime detection (lines 9–10)
3 (another) stark reminder (line 13)
4 our surveillance culture (line 13)
5 a healthy democratic society (line 17)

E Discuss in class: Do you think there are too many CCTV cameras in Germany? Do you feel threatened by too many surveillance cameras?

EXAM PREPARATION 13

3 WORKING WITH WORDS

A Find words in the text on page 132 that go with the following words. There is sometimes more than one answer.

CCTV ▪ health ▪ independent ▪ privacy ▪ public ▪ security ▪ surveillance

B Complete the sentences with a suitable collocation from exercise 3A.

1 The ▬ has just released a report with new estimates on the use of CCTV in Britain.
2 Care homes and ▬ are just some of the 'sensitive locations' where CCTV schemes are used.
3 Many companies want to know more about their employees' behaviour, so they install ▬ .
4 Cameras have also been installed in at least 291,000 ▬[1] and 30,000 ▬[2].
5 Angry ▬[1] believe that society in Britain is on its way to becoming a ▬[2].

4 WRITING

→ Produktion: Eine Stellungnahme schreiben, S. 234

Two readers publish the following comments about the article in *The Telegraph*:

Terry Wilkins, Manchester

"I totally agree with Simon Adcock when he says 'that effective CCTV schemes are an invaluable source of crime detection and evidence for the police.'"

"Nick Pickles is 100% right to say that 'we are being monitored in a way that few people would recognize as a part of a healthy democratic society.'"

Alice Trent, Northern Ireland

⊙ **Choose one of the opinions above and write a comment to be published in *The Telegraph* online, explaining why you agree with it.**

● **Write your own comment on the following statement:**

'Surveillance, whether by camera, phone or Internet, makes the world a safer place. If you have nothing to hide, you have nothing to fear.'

SKILLS CHECKLIST:
Writing a comment

✓ Have I structured my arguments clearly?
✓ Have I given examples to support my arguments?
✓ Have I used linking words and phrases?

133

13 The challenges of the modern state — BUSINESS OPTIONS

BEFORE YOU READ

What is burnout and how does it differ from stress? Discuss in pairs.

CORPORATE BURNOUT: HOW TO AVOID IT

Burnout is not stress: it is a complete inability to get out of bed, an inability to function, an addictive, overwhelming exhaustion; a condition resulting in disillusionment and a dysfunctional attitude towards work, colleagues and family.
There are a number of steps organisations can take to reduce the possibility of leadership burnout. For a
5 start, is 24/7 contact really necessary? Simple cultural changes such as no e-mails after 7pm or before 7am can really make a difference.
Flexible, annual work patterns, lateral development to combat repetitive work, routine mentor meetings, shorter summer hours and study leave are just some of the other concepts currently being considered.
Promoting healthy eating and exercise can also be highly effective. Some organisations are already seeing a
10 difference by discounting gym membership, providing fresh fruit, insisting on regular breaks and stamping out the "sandwich at your desk" lunch culture.
While these are positive steps, nothing can replace the need for realism. The most important thing is to look at the workloads handled by employees and ask, is this a realistic expectation? (181 words)

Abridged from: www.theguardian.com

1 WORKING WITH WORDS

Match the highlighted words in the text to these definitions.

1 amount of work
2 disappointment
3 every year
4 to fight
5 negative behaviour
6 rhythm/schedule of work
7 sideways development
8 state of extreme tiredness
9 work that is done again and again

2 MEDIATION

→ Schriftliche Mediation, S. 240

Als Mitglied des Betriebsrates sind Sie über die zunehmende Belastung der Belegschaft in Ihrem Unternehmen besorgt. Auf der nächsten Betriebsversammlung möchten Sie erläutern, anhand welcher Symptome ein Burnout erkennbar ist und wodurch zur Prävention beigetragen werden kann. Fassen Sie hierzu die relevanten Informationen aus dem Text auf Deutsch zusammen.

3 THINK – PAIR – SHARE

At least 4.1 million German workers have experienced mental or emotional stress at work. Burnout doesn't just affect the individual, but comes with an economic price tag attached. It costs German workplaces 9 billion euros annually in lost productivity.

Study the text and infographic. In what ways can individuals deal with stress in the workplace? Make notes and discuss with a partner, then share your ideas with the class.

Germany: Burned-Out Workforce

14 Energy and the environment

EXAM PREPARATION

FOCUS

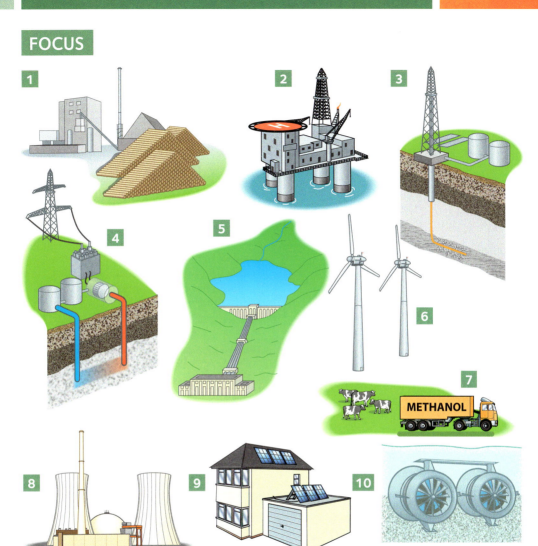

A Name the different forms of energy (1–10) above using the words in the box.

solar power ▪ geothermal power ▪ nuclear power ▪ biomass ▪ fracking ▪
tidal power ▪ hydro-electric power ▪ wind power ▪ methane ▪ fossil fuel

B Group the sources of energy in the diagram under these two headings:

Renewable energy sources	Non-renewable energy sources

C Work in a small group. Imagine a complete breakdown of conventional, non-renewable energy supplies in Germany. (They make up about 75% of the total energy sources.) Imagine this happening in winter. How do you think it would affect everyday life?

135

14 Energy and the environment

TEXT A The real cost of energy

BEFORE YOU READ

Read the title. Say what you know about climate change. What might 'the debate' be about?

CLIMATE CHANGE: IS THE DEBATE OVER?

A Is climate change really happening? If so, are humans responsible, and how bad could it be for the world – and us? The issues are complex, and the debate has been long and often angry.

B Republican Senator for Texas Ted Cruz wants the freedom to use all energy sources, especially fossil fuels, and he argues strongly that these are not causing climate change. 'The problem with climate change,' he said recently to CNN, 'is that there's never been a day in the history of the world when the climate wasn't changing.'

'So you don't believe there's a man-made cause of global warming or climate change?' he was asked.

'What I think is that the data is not supporting what the advocates are arguing,' he replied. In the last 15 years, there had been no recorded warming, he went on. It hadn't happened, and they didn't have an explanation for that.

C However, Professor James Hanson, one of the world's best-known climate scientists recently rejected the views of 'deniers' like Cruz that climate change had stopped and that the effect of rising carbon dioxide levels on climate was not as great as had been previously thought. Speaking on BBC's Radio 4, he accepted that warming had been slower since 1998, but 'that's just natural variability,' he said. 'If you look over a 30–40 year period, the expected warming is two-tenths of a degree per decade, but this doesn't mean each decade is going to warm two-tenths of a degree: there is too much variability.'

Professor Hanson has very strong views on the causes of this warming. He has said that 'CEOs of fossil fuel companies should be tried for high crimes against humanity and nature' and that 'coal-fired power plants are factories of death.'

What do other experts say? According to a new survey of scientific studies by NASA, 97% agreed that climate change is real and that humans are at least partly to blame. Quoting this figure, CNN news anchor Carol Costello said, 'Why are we still debating climate change? There is no debate. Climate change is real.'

D So let us look at some actual data. The Industrial Revolution brought large-scale use of fossil fuels, and this steadily put more carbon dioxide and other 'greenhouse gases' into the atmosphere. Before, much of Earth's energy from the sun had been reflected back into space: by the 20th century, more and more of that energy was being held back and no longer escaped. The result was gradual global warming. The chart below supports the connection.

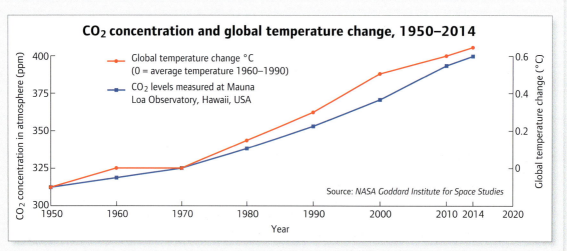

Source: NASA Goddard Institute for Space Studies

EXAM PREPARATION

14

E In 2014, atmospheric CO_2 passed 400 parts per million (ppm) at speed while scientists warned again that the level must not rise beyond 450ppm. If it does, they predict, major climate changes will start to follow. At 560ppm, twice the average level of 280ppm before the Industrial Revolution, these changes will become disastrous and unstoppable. In Europe, summers will get much hotter and winters much wetter with many more sudden, violent storms – and we will be the lucky ones. In other parts of the world, life will become difficult or impossible. Africa's deserts will expand fast, hurricanes will force people to leave Central America and the USA's south-eastern coasts. Wild cyclones will do the same in Asia, from China to India. At the same time, the warming oceans will expand while the Greenland and Antarctic ice sheets continue to melt, raising sea levels by a centimetre per year (far beyond today's 2.9 millimetres per year). Many low-lying islands and coasts, along with great coastal cities such as New York and Shanghai will be drowning.

Is this disastrous picture of the future realistic? The answer is worrying. If emissions continue to grow as they are, the International Panel on Climate Change (IPCC) tells us that CO_2 levels will reach *1,000ppm* by 2100.

F However, a recent report prepared for the UN offers fresh hope. It argued that the world could still act in time to prevent the worst effects of climate change and also enjoy continued economic growth. This would be possible as long as the global economy was transformed in the next 15 years. Co-author Lord Stern, a leading expert on climate economics, said that dealing with climate change urgently would be cheaper than trying to do so decades in the future. In fact, it could create better economic growth than the old high-carbon model, he said. He gave the example of cities that were expanding massively in the developing world. If global investment in existing high-carbon infrastructure continued, a great opportunity would be lost. If, however, cities were designed around public transport, they could have more efficient economies because people would not have to spend hours in their cars commuting and polluting. This would mean lower carbon emissions, he said, and this in turn would mean better health and a better quality of life.

The report concluded that both rich and poor countries needed to act strongly to limit CO_2 emissions and to reduce dependence on coal and other dirty fuels. At the same time, economic growth could be encouraged through investment in renewable energy, sustainable cities, modern farming techniques and better-designed transport.

G To return to our questions: yes, climate change is happening, and humans are almost certainly largely responsible. As for how bad it could be, it seems that we still have one more chance to decide.

(897 words)

1 LOOKING AT THE TEXT

→ Rezeption: Leseverstehen, S. 214

A Skim the text and match the headings (1–7) below to the sections (A–G) of the text.

1 A win-win plan for carbon control and economic growth
2 Carbon and warming: a short history
3 Climate change this century: a worst-case scenario
4 The big climate questions that we face today
5 The opinion of most climate scientists
6 Three answers to three questions
7 Views of a climate change sceptic

B Read the text carefully and do the following tasks.

→ Umgang mit Operatoren, S. 232

1 Contrast the views of Cruz and Hanson on recent climate data.
2 Say what two sorts of information the chart shows. Describe the relationship between them.
3 Contrast the effects of climate change in parts of Africa and the south-eastern USA.
4 Describe two causes of future coastal flooding.
5 Give an example of the transformation that the new UN report calls for.

137

14 Energy and the environment

C Say what it means: Explain the underlined phrases from the text in your own words.

1 ... 'coal-fired power plants are <u>factories of death</u>.' (line 36)
2 ... CNN <u>news anchor</u> Carol Costello said, ... (line 41)
3 ... tells us that CO_2 levels will reach <u>1,000ppm</u> by 2100. (line 78)
4 This would be possible <u>as long as</u> the global economy was transformed ... (line 83)
5 If global investment in existing <u>high-carbon infrastructure</u> continued, ... (line 92)
6 ... a better <u>quality of life</u>. (lines 99–100)

2 WORKING WITH WORDS

A Match words from box A to words in box B to make collocations related to the environment.

A	B
carbon ▪ climate ▪ fossil ▪ global ▪ greenhouse ▪ ice ▪ industrial ▪ power ▪ public ▪ sea	change ▪ emissions ▪ fuel ▪ gases ▪ levels ▪ plant ▪ revolution ▪ sheet ▪ transport ▪ warming

B Use collocations from exercise 2A to complete the following paragraph.

Oil, coal and natural gas are all ¹. At the start of the ▬², coal was used to power nearly all manufacturing, as well as all trains. However, these days coal is mostly used in coal-fired ▬³ to produce electricity. By contrast, most forms of ▬⁴, such as trains and buses, now use diesel. Carbon dioxide is one of a number of ▬⁵ in the atmosphere that are causing global temperatures to rise. The rise of temperatures all over the world is called ▬⁶. This is almost certainly leading to changes in weather conditions that are together known as ▬⁷. The results are becoming clear. For example, the Arctic ▬⁸ has been getting smaller for many years. ▬⁹ are rising, too, and many coastal cities are probably going to be flooded in the future. The only answer is to limit ▬¹⁰ by reducing our dependence on coal and other dirty fuels.

3 GETTING IT RIGHT

→ Indirect speech, S. 266

Rewrite these statements in indirect speech for a newspaper report. Change the contracted forms (e.g. *We're*) to full forms (*We are*) and make any other changes necessary.

During my trip to northern Canada last month, I spent time with a small Inuit community, and I had the chance to learn a little about the effects of climate change there.

1 'We're having big problems because the sea ice started melting two weeks ago,' community leader Jim Kupak told me.
Community leader Jim Kupak told me that they were ...
2 He said, 'It isn't safe any more for us to go out on the ice – the way we've always done.'
3 'We've had to end our hunting season very early because we can't risk falling through the ice and killing ourselves,' he explained.
4 'I'm worried we may find ourselves very short of food in the coming months,' he added.
5 He finished by saying, 'The ice is melting earlier every year, and we won't be able to continue our way of life much longer if it doesn't stop.'

EXAM PREPARATION   14

> **Write part of a school magazine report about a visit arranged by Mrs Bell, Head of Science. Use these reporting verbs and the underlined words in the conversation.**
>
> add ▪ promise ▪ remind ▪ say ▪ tell ▪ thank ▪ welcome

Mrs Bell is welcoming the guest speaker, Dr Ross:

Bell Dr Ross, we're very happy to see you here at Garston Sixth-Form College. It's very good of you to give Garston some time, and I'm <u>sure</u> we're all going to hear a fascinating talk.

Ross Well, let me just say that I'm very grateful to you all for the chance to speak to you, and I <u>hope</u> you'll hear at least a few things you'll find interesting.

Bell I'm <u>sure</u> we will. Remember, we specialize in science and technology at Garston, and so we're really looking forward to hearing about your new climate research.'

Ross Right, well, first of all, let me <u>admit</u> that climate change is a complex subject, which means I'll have to talk about some complex ideas, but I'll try and explain things in plain and simple English. Now, my team and I have just finished a report on our work in the Arctic that we started two years ago, and so I can say something about that. I also <u>think there may</u> be enough time to talk about our present project, in the Antarctic. By the way, next time we want to go somewhere warmer!

Mrs Bell, Head of Science, welcomed Dr Ross to our school. She said that it was ... , and she was sure that ...

4 WRITING → Produktion: Eine Stellungnahme schreiben, S. 234

A Read the following statement. Find points for and against it in the information box below.

> *'As a developing country, China should be allowed to produce carbon emissions freely unlike developed nations.'*

Background information
1 From 2005–11, China added roughly two large coal-fired power stations every week for seven years. It is still building many more.
2 The country now burns 4 billion tons of coal p.a., the USA 1 billion and the EU 0.6 billion.
3 Fossil fuels still provide 87% of the country's energy, including 70% from coal. (The fossil fuel figure for Germany is about 57%.)
4 China's emissions per person are slightly lower than the EU's and much lower than in the USA. (China's population is 1.356 billion, while the USA's is 319 million and the EU's is 504 million.)
5 Producing goods competitively for developed countries causes many of China's emissions (i.e. developed countries have exported their pollution).
6 China needs its cheap coal for a fast-growing economy to provide new jobs and a rising standard of living.
7 The country's heavy pollution is causing a falling quality of life and health – and rising anger – among ordinary Chinese people.
8 China is now developing renewable energy sources twice as fast as the USA.

B Now write a comment on the statement. Put together several pairs of points for and against it, and end with your own conclusion. Use suitable phrases to connect your arguments.

139

14 Energy and the environment

TEXT B How do we keep the lights on?

BEFORE YOU READ   → Vorbereitung auf das Lesen, S. 214

Read the headline and look at the diagram. Predict what the article is going to be about.

Does our energy security lie deep beneath our feet?

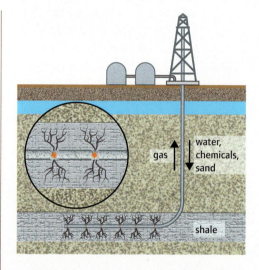

Julie Branson reports:
I was on my way by train from London to Brussels – to the latest conference on the environment. Opposite me sat Matt Radley,
5 CEO of Energistic UK, a small company with big plans for fracking in the UK. He had agreed to be interviewed on our journey and I wanted his take on this controversial new UK energy source.
10 First, I asked him to explain the word 'fracking'. 'It's short for hydraulic fracturing,' he told me.
 'It's the breaking of shale rocks deep underground to allow gas and oil to escape.'
15 I inquired how fracking was actually done. 'We drill down into shale formations, and then we pump down a mixture of water, chemicals and sand at high pressure. This pressure fractures the rock, and the sand
20 keeps the new cracks open. The gas or oil is then brought to the surface and collected there.'
 When I asked if this technology was new, he told me that it was new to Britain, but that
25 over two million wells had already been drilled, mainly in the USA, and that this cheap-to-produce oil and gas had greatly reduced prices over there. 'What's more,' he added enthusiastically, 'Fracking will soon
30 make America the world's biggest producer of oil and gas.'
 What about the UK? I wanted to know whether Britain, too, had useful amounts of shale gas and oil. 'Yes,' he replied. 'In fact,
35 Britain has huge quantities, and at Energistic UK, it's the gas we want. It's the cleanest of all the fossil fuels, and it's also the easiest to process and get to market. What's more, we really need it. The UK used to get all its gas
40 from the North Sea, but most of that has now gone, and we have to import 70% of our requirement. We need the energy security of our own gas again.'
 But I was wondering why fracking was such a good option when shale gas was still a 45
fossil fuel. I asked whether it would be better to leave the gas in the ground and rely on other energy sources instead, particularly renewables. Matt Radley's eyes lit up. 'No,' he said, 'and I'll tell you why.' 50
 'Please do,' I replied.
 'Right. Let's look at them one by one.' We had just come out of the tunnel near Sangatte, and he went on, 'There's a big nuclear power station very near here, so let's 55
start with nuclear. France has got lots of nuclear plants, and they may seem to produce cheap power, but they're very expensive to build and very expensive to close down at the end of their working lives. We also have to 60
wonder how safe they and their waste are.'
 'What about tidal power, like the barrage at the mouth of the River Rance in Brittany?'
 'Well, that was constructed half a century ago, and there aren't many others even now. 65

EXAM PREPARATION   14

It sounds like free energy, but without big government subsidies, they don't get built. Wave power is even more difficult. If you can make and install equipment that will survive the power of the sea and the salt corrosion, fine. But it isn't happening.'

I moved on and asked if geothermal might work better. 'Yes, but it's only cost-effective in places like Iceland, which have hot rock formations close to the surface.'

Then I turned to hydroelectric power, and Matt Radley was quite positive. 'It's cheap and reliable, and it provides about six per cent of world energy,' he said. The problem was that in Britain there was little possibility of much further expansion.

'Well, what about free heat directly from the sun?' I asked.

'Ah, yes, solar energy,' came the reply. 'It's good in sunny regions, and it's getting cheaper, but in Britain we need most power on dark winter evenings and we can't rely on solar power for that!'

Finally, we turned to wind power, and my interviewee became a little annoyed. Onshore wind farms had only been built because of big subsidies, he said, and we were all paying those through higher energy prices. Offshore wind farms were much more efficient, he went on, but they were also much more expensive to build and maintain. Again, more subsidies.

On the high cost of wind and solar power, he pointed out that the world had invested $600 billion in wind and $700 billion in solar during the last ten years – huge amounts – but together these two technologies were producing just two per cent of the world's energy.

'So,' he concluded, 'let's stop picking losers. Let's go for shale gas!'

(770 words)

1 LOOKING AT THE TEXT
→ Rezeption: Leseverstehen, S. 214

A Read the text and put these energy sources in the order that they are discussed.

a fracking   c hydroelectric   e solar   g wave
b geothermal   d nuclear   f tidal   h wind

B Say whether the following are true or false. Correct the false statements.

1 Julie Branson and Matt Radley met on the way to Brussels by chance.
2 Sand is needed during fracking in order to stop the cracks from closing.
3 Matt Radley said that fracking was new to the UK and to the rest of the world, too.
4 Shale gas is less polluting than oil or coal, but it is still not clean.
5 Nuclear power may not be safe, but at least it is cheap.
6 Tidal power is easier to use than wave power, but it still does not make much economic sense.
7 Of all the renewables that Matt Radley discussed, he was most positive about geothermal and hydroelectric.
8 Matt Radley said that offshore wind farms were much more cost-effective than wind farms that were built onshore.

C Say what it means: Explain the underlined phrases in your own words.

1 … and I wanted his take on this controversial source of energy. (line 8)
2 'It's short for hydraulic fracturing,' he said. (line 11)
3 I wanted to know whether Britain, too, had useful amounts of shale gas … (line 33)
4 'So,' he concluded, 'let's stop picking losers.' (lines 105–106)
5 'Let's go for shale gas!' (line 106)

14 Energy and the environment

2 WORKING WITH WORDS

A Copy and complete the tables with verbs and nouns from the text.

Verb	Noun	Verb	Noun	Verb	Noun
	production		explanation	to expand	
to opt		to form		to corrode	
	reduction		installation		conclusion

B Use words from the same family to complete these sentences. They are all in exercise 2A.

1. Industrial waste greatly ▬¹ the numbers of fish in many rivers, but the huge ▬² in pollution in recent years has brought new life back.
2. **A** We need to ▬¹ more of our own food in this country.
   B You're right, but the problem is that ▬² just isn't going up very much.
3. The Government's advisers have finally ▬¹ their study of new energy sources, and their ▬² is that wind, solar and fracking will all be necessary.
4. Auto Shanghai plan to ▬¹ production of electric vehicles from 50,000 per year to 200,000, and their ▬² programme starts next year.
5. **A** Can anyone ▬¹ why this machine isn't working?
   B The ▬² is actually quite simple: you haven't turned on the power!
6. ▬¹ is the big problem with this bridge. Parts of the structure have been very badly ▬², and they need to be replaced immediately.
7. The International Panel on Climate Change (IPCC) was ▬¹ in 1988, and its ▬² led to much clearer scientific studies of global climate change.
8. **A** How long will it take to ▬¹ all the solar panels on the roof?
   B The whole ▬² process should take just two days.
9. With the new houses being built over there, people will have two heating ▬¹: they can choose gas or they can ▬² for a mix of gas and solar.

3 GETTING IT RIGHT

→ Indirect speech, S. 266

A Rewrite the questions as indirect questions, using the reporting verbs in brackets. Make any other changes that are necessary.

Matt Radley faced these questions at a press conference as Energistic UK prepared to begin work.

1. *New York Times* journalist: 'Is Energistic an independent company?' (inquire)
   A journalist from the New York Times inquired if Energistic was ...
2. BBC's Economics Editor: 'How many staff does Energistic have?' (ask)
3. Reporter from Radio 4: 'Have you had any previous practical experience of fracking?' (want to know)
4. Financial journalist from Frankfurt: 'How much has the company had to spend in order to prepare for commercial production? (inquire)
5. Local newspaper editor: 'Why has Energistic chosen to begin operations in our part of the country?' (inquire)
6. Environmental scientist: 'Do you really think you can get planning permission to go ahead?' (query)

B Rewrite the requests, instructions and advice in indirect speech, using the reporting verbs in brackets. Make any other changes that are necessary.

Annie is living away from home for the first time. After just a month, she receives a huge electricity bill and needs help. She calls home.

1 'Could you call Mum or Dad to the phone please?' she said to her brother Ben. (want … to)
She wanted her brother Ben to call Mum or Dad to the phone.
2 'Wait a minute while I get Dad in from the garden,' Ben said. (tell … to)
3 'Dad, could you talk to Annie on the phone?' said Ben. (ask … to)
4 'Dad, can you please, please tell me what to do about my crazy electricity bill for £537?' Annie begged. (beg … to)
5 'You'd better tell the electricity company that there's been a mistake,' her father advised her. (advise … to)
6 'Why don't you come home at the weekend and tell us how you're getting on?' he added. (invite … to)

4 LISTENING

→ Rezeption: Hörverstehen, S. 225

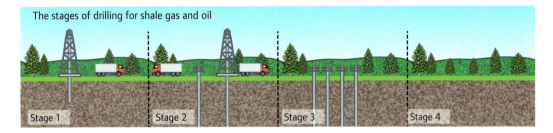

A Listen and complete these tasks.

1 Say what sort of event is starting.
2 Explain what the event is going to be about.
3 Say who has been invited to speak, and what you already know about his ideas.
4 Make notes about the four stages of fracking. Note a) the activity at each stage, and b) the time it takes.

B Now listen and note the worries that people have about fracking in the right order. Add details about each point.

earthquakes ▪ environmental damage ▪ gas ▪ traffic and noise

C Listen again and note what Matt Radley says to calm the worries.

5 DISCUSSION

→ Interaktion: An Diskussionen teilnehmen, S. 246

Work in a small group and discuss the following questions.

1 In principle, do you think fracking should be allowed or not?
2 Imagine you are now members of the local council. Should you accept or reject Matt Radley's particular project. (Consider the pros and cons from a local point of view.)

14 Energy and the environment

TEXT C The problem of waste

BEFORE YOU READ

What do you think happens to all the electrical appliances that we throw away?

WHERE DO OUR SCRAP TVS END UP?

Every year, Germany produces millions of tons of electrical waste. A large proportion of that doesn't end up in recycling but instead simply disappears. The German TV programme Panorama wanted to know where, so some broken TVs were fitted with tracking devices – and the trace led the reporters to Africa.

According to UN estimates, Germans produce two million tons of electrical waste every year. In all these TVs, computers, DVD players, stereos, loudspeakers, fridges and smartphones there are poisonous substances like arsenic, lead, cadmium and mercury. Because of this, the German Electrical and Electronic Appliances Law forbids the dumping of toxic waste in developing countries. Despite this, only 700,000 tons of electrical waste finds its way into the nationwide recycling system each year. No one really knows what happens to the remaining 1.3 million tons. It simply disappears – apparently most of it to Africa.

But why? It costs a lot of money to ship old TVs thousands of kilometers over the sea. Who profits from it? That is what the *Panorama* reporters wanted to find out, using an old TV and a tracking device. Together with a battery pack, the device was hidden in the TV's loudspeaker box. It transmitted its exact position at regular intervals and it also reacted to movement. Every time it was unloaded or moved, the transmitter sent an alarm to the reporters' mobile phones.

The TV was picked up by a man advertising free collection of broken electrical appliances on eBay. That was the start of a journey which shone some light on a shadowy but well-organized economic activity that customs and police are largely powerless to prevent.

The first stop on the journey was a dubious scrap dealer in Hamburg, where exporters select

Electrical waste dump in Agbogbloshie, Ghana

their goods. They collect old TVs and fridges in a warehouse, until they have enough to fill a ship with 40-foot containers.

A long wait

After six nights waiting in Ghana, the reporters finally received a signal early in the morning. The TV had moved. No longer at the harbour, it was now in Accra, Ghana's capital, on the corner of Abeka Road and George W. Bush Highway.

The signal was strong because the TV had been unloaded and was now out in the open. When they arrived at the street corner, hundreds of TVs were piled up in the mud. A policeman sat under an umbrella and watched the clearance sale. The reporters asked where the goods came from. 'England.' Wrong!

A few metres farther on, eight silver Sony TVs were sitting next to the wall of a house. They found the mark they had made on the back of one of them. They shook it to activate the movement sensor and a message soon appeared on their phone, showing that the appliance had been moved. They returned the

TV and replaced it: they wanted to find out how its journey would continue.

The end of the journey
Journey's end was Agbogbloshie in Ghana, the biggest electrical waste dump in Africa and one of the ten most toxic places in the world.

About 500 containers of electrical appliances reach Ghana every month. Around Christmas, when Europeans replace old appliances with new ones, up to 1,000 arrive. Not all the electrical waste stays in Ghana: much is transported across West Africa, to Burkina Faso, Niger, Mali or Benin. But Ghana is the hub, and key to profit there is Agbogbloshie.

Forwarding agencies, shipping and transport companies all make money from the waste, as do middlemen and repair shops in Accra. At the very bottom of the value chain are the boys of Agbogbloshie. They break TVs apart with hammers, and they set fire to the insulating foam in order to separate the cable coating from the copper. For this, they get just 50 cents per TV.

Just 15 years ago this district of Accra was still a breeding ground for European migratory birds, but today it is the graveyard of our rubbish. It is also a place that poisons the many children and young people who work there. They are the ones who would have gutted the reporters' TV by hand if they had not finally found it at a dealer and bought it back for 100 euros. Worthless to them, the TV made money for a total of 11 people or companies along its 77-day journey to the scrapyard.

(721 words)

1 LOOKING AT THE TEXT
→ Rezeption: Leseverstehen, S. 214

A Read the text and complete the following tasks.

1. Explain the mystery of Germany's electrical waste.
2. Outline the method that the reporters used to discover the truth.
3. Contrast the purpose of German law and the actual situation in Agbogbloshie.
4. Say what the writer means by 'Ghana is the hub' (lines 76–77).
5. Name the 'people or companies along the journey' (lines 96–97) that the article mentions.

B Think of the last electrical appliance that your family threw away. Describe how you got rid of it. Do you think it went (or did not go) into the national recycling system?

2 MEDIATION
→ Schriftliche Mediation, S. 240

Sie bekommen folgende E-Mail von Ihrer Tante:

Antworten Sie auf die E-Mail Ihrer Tante. Erklären Sie ihr, was möglicherweise mit dem alten Kühlschrank passieren könnte, wenn er nicht ordentlich entsorgt wird.

… Zu Weihnachten gönnen wir uns einen fantastischen amerikanischen Kühlschrank mit allem Drum und Dran. Wir schmeißen den alten sofort weg … er wird morgen abgeholt … ;-)

3 WRITING
→ Produktion: Eine Stellungnahme schreiben, S. 234

Write a comment on the following statement.

'I don't understand that German law against sending electrical waste here. All kinds of people make money out of it – even those kids at Agbogloshie. Without the scrap TVs, they wouldn't have anything.'

Electrical waste trader in Accra, Ghana

14 Energy and the environment — BUSINESS OPTIONS

BEFORE YOU READ

In an economic context, the term 'degrowth' refers to the reduction of goods, services and consumption after a long period of economic growth. In pairs, brainstorm what personal and economic actions 'degrowth' might involve. Share your ideas with the class.

Is bigger always better?

Mainstream economists consider economic growth the way forward for all countries, bringing progress, innovation and higher living standards. An economy which is growing supports itself by continuously increasing its capacity to produce goods and services. Jobs are created in order to increase production, and the money earned by workers in these jobs is itself spent on goods and services. But is this model really working for
5   humanity and the environment?

A large percentage of humanity does not have enough to live on, while consumption in rich countries is creating ecological overshoot. Natural environments cannot keep producing enough resources to support the people living in them. Fossil fuels such as coal and oil
10 will one day run out, we are eating too much meat and fish, cutting down too many forests, polluting environments and damaging the ecosystem.

Some governments are already encouraging people to save resources and to reduce their ecological footprint. Investments in renewable energy and green capitalism demonstrate attempts to reduce the human impact on
15 the environment which sustains us. And yet – none of it is enough.

Some economists have started to suggest degrowth as an alternative to increased consumption. If economies produce just as much as they consume, there is no excess. Degrowth is accomplished through small scale initiatives such as urban gardens in cities or local sharing
20 economies. In Berlin, people have started to lend and borrow possessions, from DIY tools to gardening equipment and wine glasses, at "libraries of things", removing the need to own any of these items.

Others are making and mending their own clothes and repairing home gadgets themselves in an attempt to make existing goods last longer and avoid buying new ones. Many of these initiatives have the added social
25 benefit of bringing people together.

A bigger challenge is perhaps to convince companies to produce less and governments to embrace the idea of sufficiency instead of gain. Companies would need to scale down the production of goods, employees would work fewer hours but have more time for producing and growing what they need and for leisure and social contact. A degrowth economy might even be more fun for everyone.

(360 words)

LOOKING AT THE TEXT

→ Rezeption: Leseverstehen, S. 214

A Work in small groups. You are volunteers in a community organization that promotes sustainable living. Write down tips on how consumers and organizations can reduce their ecological footprint and contribute to degrowth in your area. Present your ideas to the class.

B While listening to the presentations, write down all the ideas that were not on your list. At the end, take a minute to consider all the tips. Which of the suggestions would you be prepared to include in your own life? Discuss in class and give reasons.

15 Feeding the world

EXAM PREPARATION

FOCUS

One thing after another

A Work with a partner. Take turns to describe and analyse the cartoons.

cactus ▪ carbon emissions ▪ climate change ▪ deliver babies ▪ drought ▪
environmental pollution ▪ global warming ▪ greenhouse gases ▪ natural resources ▪
over-exploitation of resources ▪ rising population ▪ stork

B Now find links from cartoon to cartoon to explain the title 'One thing after another'.

C Discuss these questions with a partner.

1 Do you think the 'resources' stork has got weaker or stronger since you were born? Think of cases of drought and famine that have been in the news.
2 Do you think these problems are only found in developing countries – or are people ever short of food and other basics in rich countries such as Germany?

15 Feeding the world

TEXT A How can we feed so many?

BEFORE YOU READ

→ Scannen nach Einzelinformationen im Text, S. 221

Scan the text for the following information:

a the area equivalent to the worldwide land use for crops
b the area equivalent to the worldwide land use for pastureland
c the percentage of crops that are used to feed animals

THE PLANET REPORT   September 20..

A PLAN TO FEED THE PLANET

The world has a problem – people. The human population passed 7 billion in 2012 and will probably hit 9.5 billion by 2050. That is a 35% increase in less than 40 years.

Does this mean a 35% increase in crop production, too? No, it actually means a 100% increase, from 9.5 billion tons to 19 billion, and the reason is this: as people in developing countries like India and China get a little more money, they always demand a richer diet with much more meat. Providing this requires far more crop production just to feed animals.

But nearly a billion people are already hungry, so we cannot possibly feed billions more, can we? Well, yes we can, and we can do it without taking more from Nature than we already have. To succeed, though, we must do four vital things.

1 Stop clearing more land for farming.
Growing more food has always meant taking more land from its natural state, including whole regions such as the North American prairies and the huge forests of Europe, each with its ancient ecosystem. Today, we use a land area the size of South America to grow crops and another the size of Africa for animal pastureland. Over half the world's ice-free land has been turned to human uses, and by far the greatest of these uses is agriculture.

We are destroying forests along with many plant and animal species, and while doing this, we are creating an even greater crisis. We are reducing Earth's ability to store carbon emissions from human activities – emissions that are pushing the planet towards disastrous climate change.

It is time to stop driving down this road to catastrophe.

The World's Total Land Area: 57.7 million square miles, of which:

Ice-covered: 7.4m sq miles (12.8%)	Other undeveloped: 23.4m sq miles (40.6%)	Farmland: 19.4m sq miles (33.6%)	Other human uses: 7.5m sq miles (13.0%)

Greenland & Antarctic ice sheets	mountains, forest, desert, tundra	pastureland, cropland	cities, infrastructure e.g. roads & railways, planted forests, etc.

EXAM PREPARATION 15

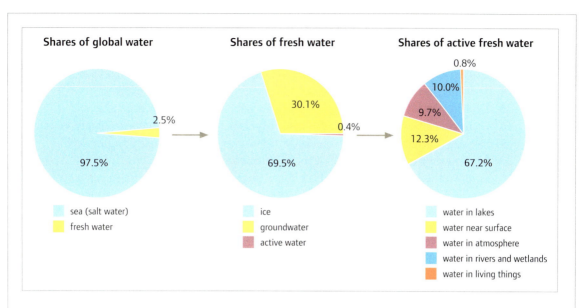

2 Produce more efficiently.
A typical American farmer produces three tons of crops per acre, whereas a farmer in sub-Saharan Africa may only produce half a ton. With better crop varieties and better techniques, that difference can be greatly reduced. Meanwhile, western agriculture can continue to become more efficient in other ways. Farm chemicals are expensive and polluting, so using less of them is very important. GPS and computer technology now help farmers decide what, when and where fertilizer is needed. This saves money and reduces pollution of precious water resources.

People have not always understood that water is so precious. Very little of our Blue Planet's water is fresh water that we can easily use, and after polluting and wasting much of it, we now find that clean supplies are declining. Farming takes 70% of all human water use and is at the centre of this crisis. Many farmers who draw their water from underground now have to go ever deeper to reach it.

Again, science is helping. New crop varieties that need less water are appearing. Better irrigation and new kinds of farming are also helping to reduce waste, making sure that the water we use is used well.

3 Change what we eat.
Feeding 9.5 billion people would be much easier if more crops actually fed people. In fact, just 55% of crop production is used that way, while a massive 36% feeds animals – mainly for meat production. (The rest is used in biofuel and other industrial production.)

Producing meat is not an efficient process: many kilos of grain are needed for every kilo of meat produced. Moreover, one kilo of grain takes 1,500 litres of water, but to produce one kilo of beef it takes 15,000.

Clearly, meat consumption must be reduced, starting perhaps with the rich, developed world. For many people in these countries, consuming less meat and more fruit and vegetables would also be a big step towards better health.

4 Cut waste.
Up to half of all food production is lost or wasted. In developed countries, a lot is thrown away because too much is prepared or because it has passed its use-by date. In poor countries, food is often wasted because it is stored badly or because transport to market takes too long. Just solving these problems alone would allow the planet to feed itself.

So yes, we can get through the coming food crisis, but only if we change the ways we produce, consume and think about food. Some changes will be huge and will need the cooperation of millions. Others will be small and individual – like the choices we make when doing the family food shopping at the supermarket.   (736 words)

15 Feeding the world

1 LOOKING AT THE TEXT
→ Umgang mit Operatoren, S. 232

A Read the text on pages 148–149 carefully and complete these tasks.

1. Explain why a population 35% larger will require a 100% increase in food production.
2. Say why the destruction of forest by humans is destructive for humans.
3. Explain why it is very important to use less water and to protect its quality.
4. Contrast the ways that science can help farmers in developing and in developed countries.
5. Say why it would be a) easier and b) better to start reducing meat consumption in developed countries instead of developing countries.
6. Contrast the ways in which food is often wasted in developed and in developing countries.

B Say what it means: Explain the underlined words and phrases in your own words.

1. … will probably hit 9.5 billion … (line 3)
2. We are destroying forests along with many plant and animal species, … (line 29)
3. … a farmer in sub-Saharan Africa … (line 39)
4. … now have to go ever deeper to reach it. (lines 57–58)
5. New crop varieties … are appearing. (line 60)
6. … because it has passed its use-by date. (line 85)
7. … the coming food crisis. (line 90)

2 WORKING WITH WORDS

Match meanings a–t to abbreviations and symbols 1–20.

1	am	5	m	9	wk	13	pw	17	=
2	e.g.	6	sq (miles)	10	yr	14	incl	18	+
3	etc.	7	approx	11	pa	15	&	19	–
4	i.e.	8	hr	12	pm	16	%	20	×

a and
b and so on
c approximately
d is, equals
e any time from midnight to midday
f any time from midday to midnight; per month
g hour
h in other words
i including
j metre; million
k minus
l per week
m per annum, per year
n per cent
o plus; over
p square (miles)
q such as, for example
r times, multiplied by
s week
t year

Expand these notes.

1. Job title: Junior Manager
Terms & conditions: Work 40 hrs pw; Starting: 9.00 am & finishing 5.00 pm; 3 wks paid holiday pa; salary £1,750.00 pm = £21,000.00 pa

Terms and conditions for the job of Junior Manager are as follows. You will work …

2. New Dawn Garment's new factory 8,300sq m & employs 650 workers. Produces 140,000+ garments pw = approx 7.3m garments pa, incl e.g. shirts, jeans, dresses, jackets, etc.

New Dawn Garment's new factory has an area of … It produces …

EXAM PREPARATION 15

3 ANALYSING CHARTS
→ Produktion: Schaubilder beschreiben und analysieren, S. 238

Analyse the graphics in the text, interpreting their abbreviations and symbols to do so.

1 Analyse the diagram on page 148 with statements like this.
Ice-covered land makes up 7.4 million square miles, or 12.8 percent of the world's total land area, and it consists largely of the … . Other undeveloped land makes up …

2 Analyse the pie charts on page 149 with statements like this.
Of all the water in the world, 97.5 percent is salt water, and just … . Of all the freshwater in the world, …

4 GETTING IT RIGHT
→ Participles, S. 268

Join the pairs of sentences. Turn the first sentence into a participle clause using the word in brackets.

1 Sue Dryden went through a painful divorce three years ago. She moved to Amarillo, Texas with her young son Craig. (after)
After going through a painful divorce three years ago, Sue Dryden moved to Amarillo, Texas with her young son Craig.

2 They got there. She quickly had to get a job because her ex-husband was sending very little money. (after)

3 Sue lost her job a year ago. She and Craig had lived well enough on her salary of $2,200 per month. (before)

4 She lost that job. She has only been able to find part-time work at $7.75 per hour. (since)

5 She goes food shopping. She always tries to work out how much she can spend and what she can buy with that. (before)

6 She pays her rent and utility bills. She often does not have enough left to buy everything they need. (after)

7 She fell on such hard times. She has often gone to the local church food pantry for help. (since)

8 She collects her food parcel there. She is sometimes embarrassed to see volunteer workers that she knows from her old workplace. (while)

5 WRITING
→ Produktion: Eine Stellungnahme schreiben, S. 234

Write a comment on the following statement.

'THERE IS PLENTY OF FOOD TO FEED THE WORLD. ALL WE HAVE TO DO IS TO STOP WASTING IT, THEN NOBODY WILL GO HUNGRY ANY MORE.'

Useful phrases: partly agreeing with sb/sth

- While I agree that … , I do not accept that …
- I take the point that … . However, I question whether …
- For one thing, … . For another, …
- Then again, …

151

15 Feeding the world

TEXT B Big problems – new solutions

BEFORE YOU READ
→ Scannen nach Einzelinformationen im Text, S. 221

Scan the text and say which is the main topic of the interview.

a the pros and cons of GM food
b how farmers can make more profit
c ways of providing more food for humans

The World This Week reporter Mark Moro is talking to scientist Dr Tanya Tate, an expert from the United Nations Development Programme.

Mark Moro: The big question facing us in the future is how is the planet going to feed itself? How can science help? First of all, let's talk about genetically modified food, or GM for short. As we all know, it's supported by some, but also feared by many. Dr Tate, could you tell us what GM is exactly?

Tanya Tate: To explain that, we need to look first at natural selection. Plant and animal species have always adapted to fit their particular environment on the planet. Members of a species with the best adaptations survive and pass their successful genes to the next generation. Others that are not so well adapted don't reproduce so successfully, and sooner or later, they become extinct.

Mark Moro: Haven't farmers used this natural process to breed better crops and better livestock since pre-historic times?

Tanya Tate: Yes, they take over the selection process in order to make more profit. This is selective breeding, and it works like this. They decide what physical features to aim at – more wool on a sheep, for example, or better resistance to disease. They then choose animals or plants to breed from – ones that are already nearer that ideal than others. After repeating the process for several generations, they then have an improved species.

Mark Moro: Improved because the herd or the crop is more productive and is therefore more valuable.

Tanya Tate: Right, and coming back to GM, we can see that this modern technology pushes the idea of species improvement much further. We can now modify the genetic code of a plant seed or an animal embryo by adding genes taken from other species. For example, adding a gene from a desert plant species can help a vegetable crop survive with much less water.

Mark Moro: This is species improvement by laboratory design, isn't it?

Tanya Tate: That's right.

Mark Moro: It sounds very useful.

Tanya Tate: It is, and this sort of GM technology will certainly help in parts of the world now suffering drier conditions – sub-Saharan Africa, for example.

Mark Moro: So what's the problem with GM food?

Tanya Tate: Well, let's think about a gene added to a crop that makes it resistant to herbicide – the sprays used to kill weeds. The weeds die, and the crop gets all the water and fertilizer provided by the farmer.

Mark Moro: So far, so good. That should produce the best crop possible.

Tanya Tate: But what if some of the pollen produced by the crop reaches weeds growing nearby? What if it fertilizes those weeds? In no time, we could have weeds that are resistant to herbicide. We could soon find ourselves with weeds resistant to all known chemical controls – weeds that might take over the world!

Mark Moro: That would be a big downside! So, are there other new ways to help produce the food we need?

Tanya Tate: Yes, in particular there's an exciting technology called hydroponics.

Mark Moro: 'Hydro'? That means it is connected with water?

Tanya Tate: Yes, hydroponic farming doesn't use soil. Instead, it uses water containing the
80 exact amount of nutrients required. This way, roots don't have to grow through thick soil, sometimes finding the necessary nutrients but often not. Instead, the nutrients are absorbed easily by the plant roots as they grow down
85 into the flow of water. That's much more efficient, and crops grow very fast. What's more, it's a closed system, so the same water is used again and again, and there's no pollution of rivers and groundwater.

90 **Mark Moro:** Wow! Is this something very new?

Tanya Tate: No, it was first used in the 1930s. American flights to Hawaii landed for fuel on a piece of rock called Wake Island. Thanks to hydroponics they also took off again with fresh
95 salad and vegetables for the passengers. Today, it's used a lot in Iceland, another place with very little soil, and at the Amundsen Scott South Pole Station, a place with no soil at all, of course!

100 **Mark Moro:** Fine, but is it being used more widely than that?

Tanya Tate: Yes, it's taking off in many parts of the world. Farmers can grow up to 20 high-quality crops a year, causing very little waste and pollution and making very good money. 105
It takes up much less space than ordinary farming, too.

Mark Moro: What's the next step?

Tanya Tate: Vertical farms. People are now creating city-centre farms in tall buildings to 110 grow food for the people right where the people are. That means another big saving: food miles. The environmental cost of taking food many miles from farm to supermarket almost disappears! (795 words) 115

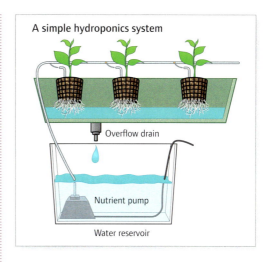

A simple hydroponics system

---

1 LOOKING AT THE TEXT

→ Rezeption: Leseverstehen, S. 214

A Read the text and make notes. Use your notes to do these tasks.

1 Outline briefly the three methods of improving farm productivity that the speakers discuss.
2 Contrast the effects of natural selection and selective breeding.
3 Explain why disease resistance can be just as important for productivity as sheep that produce more wool.
4 Explain the sort of benefit GM offers, and the sort of danger that it creates.
5 List the environmental advantages of hydroponics.
6 List the economic advantages of hydroponics.

B Say what it means: Explain the underlined words and phrases in your own words.

1 The big question <u>facing us</u> … (line 5)
2 … since <u>pre-historic times</u>? (line 23)
3 <u>So far, so good.</u> (line 61)
4 But <u>what if</u> some of the pollen produced by the crop reaches weeds growing nearby? (line 63)
5 <u>In no time</u>, we could have weeds … (line 66)
6 That would be <u>a big downside</u>! (line 71)

15 Feeding the world

2 WORKING WITH WORDS

→ Rezeption: Ein Wörterbuch benutzen, S. 217

take [Phrasal verbs]

take in 1 understand clearly the meaning or importance of something 2 trick someone into believing something that is not true   **take off** 1 remove something, especially clothes 2 leave the ground and start flying 3 suddenly start to be popular or successful   **take on** 1 accept a job or responsibility 2 give a job to someone 3 fight or compete against someone or something   **take over** 1 start doing something that someone else was doing 2 take control of something   **take up** 1 fill an amount of space or time 2 start doing a particular job or activity

Read the sentences with their examples of phrasal verbs formed from *take*. Then check the dictionary entry above and decide which meaning matches each example.

1 We could soon find ourselves with weeds that might **take over** the world! *meaning 2*
2 Thanks to hydroponics planes **took off** again with fresh salad vegetables.
3 Hydroponics is **taking off** in many parts of the world.
4 Hydroponics **takes up** much less space than ordinary farming.

Read these sentences to decide which phrasal verb and which meaning each requires.

1 I had to read her letter three times before I could ▬ the awful truth. *take in – meaning 1*
2 You'd better ▬ that wet jacket and warm yourself by the fire.
3 The company is moving to Stuttgart, and we're ▬ 20 new staff there.
4 Sally's ▬ too much, and she's making herself ill with all the stress.
5 Silke pretends that she's happy and she ▬ most people, but I know that she's really very sad.
6 I've ▬ the guitar recently, and I'm enjoying it a lot.
7 Would you mind ▬ the cooking while I get a few things from the shop?
8 Next Saturday, our team are ▬ the champions, and I really hope we'll win!

3 GETTING IT RIGHT

→ Participles, S. 268

Change the relative clauses (starting with *who*, *which*, *that*) to *-ing* or *-ed* clauses.

Fish are an important source of food <u>which has been hunted</u> for thousands of years and <u>which still provides</u> millions of people with much of their protein. However, the modern techniques which have been developed to make fishing more efficient are too successful. In many parts of the world, the huge numbers that are being caught leave too few fish to maintain stocks, and so wild fish populations are crashing.

One answer to the fish stock crisis which is developing worldwide is to reduce the amount of fishing, and this is something that is happening today in the North Sea, for example.

Another answer is fish farming, which has now developed along coasts and in rivers and lakes all over the world. However, such fish farms often have severe problems which include pollution and disease. Someone who is taking a different approach is Brian O'Hanlon with his huge diamond-shaped fish cages that have been built eight miles off the coast of Panama and which contain up to a million fish. Far out at sea, these cages, which are constantly washed by the open sea, remain unpolluted and disease-free.

Fish are an important source of food hunted for thousands of years and still providing ...

EXAM PREPARATION   15

4 LISTENING
→ Rezeption: Hörverstehen, S. 225

You are going to hear Tanya Tate talking about a commercial hydroponics system.

Lettuce is grown in a hydroponic culture in a dome greenhouse in Japan in July 2012.

A worker harvests fresh produce from a tower at Sky Greens vertical farm in Singapore in July 2014.

A Copy these notes, then listen and complete them. Which system is Tanya Tate describing?

> Name of system:
> Country designed:
> Used to grow:
> Basic shape:
> Movement (horizontal/vertical):
> Speed of turn:
> Size:
> Running cost per frame:

B Now listen to the second part of Tanya's talk and make notes. Then answer these questions.

1. What two advantages does this system have over traditional farming?
2. Why will food production need to be close to cities in the future?
3. What makes food farming in Singapore difficult?
4. Why is the government of Singapore unhappy about this situation?
5. What does the government want to do to change this?

5 PROJECT

Work in small groups and research hydroponics farming systems online. Choose one of the commercial systems currently in operation and present it to the class.

6 WRITING
→ Produktion: Schreiben, S. 228

> **PROPOSALS SOUGHT FOR CITY POWER STATION REDEVELOPMENT**
>
> After more than 80 years of service, the Old City Power Station has closed. With its splendid, high turbine hall and all-glass roof, it is a Grade 1 industrial building that cannot simply be pulled down. By law, it must be redeveloped in some way that will be useful to the city community. The Redevelopment Committee have already received several proposals but would welcome more.

You see this article in a local paper in the UK and think the power station could be redeveloped as a hydroponics farm. Write a letter to the chairperson of the Redevelopment Committee.

- Describe the basic concept of hydroponics and its advantages.
- Explain the particular advantages of redeveloping the power station as a hydroponics farm.
- Support your argument with an example of a successful project of the same sort.

15 Feeding the world

TEXT C A case study

BEFORE YOU READ

What are the alternatives to farming on an industrial scale in Germany?

IS GM THE BEST WAY FORWARD FOR AFRICA?

Millions of poor African farmers depend on one or two crops such as cassava both to sell and to feed their families. If disease strikes, they face disaster. Today, high-tech GM technology is
5 beginning to offer the possibility of new versions of such crops modified to resist pests, but so far only four African countries – Egypt, Sudan, South Africa and Burkina Faso – have allowed the commercial planting of GM crops. Fear is one
10 reason for this, but more importantly the basic fact is that most African farmers need a simpler, cheaper way forward.

In Tanzania there are no GM crops yet. But some farmers are learning that a simple low-tech
15 solution – planting a diversity of crops – is one of the best ways to deter pests. Tanzania now has the fourth largest number of certified organic farmers in the world. Part of the credit belongs to a young woman named Janet Maro.

20 Maro grew up on a farm near Kilimanjaro, the fifth of eight children. In 2009, while still an undergraduate at the Sokoine University of Agriculture in Morogoro, she helped to start a non-profit organization called Sustainable
25 Agriculture Tanzania (SAT). Since then she and her small staff have been training local farmers in organic practices. [...]

Morogoro lies about a hundred miles west of Dar es Salaam, at the base of the Uluguru Mountains,
30 and Maro takes me into the mountains to visit three of the first certified organic farms in Tanzania. We lurch up a steep, rutted road in a pickup. Greened by rains drifting in from the Indian Ocean, the slopes remain heavily forested.
35 But increasingly, they've been cleared for farming by the Luguru people. [...]

She stops at a one-room brick house with partially plastered walls and a corrugated metal roof. Habija Kibwana, a tall woman in a short-sleeved
40 white blouse and wraparound skirt, invites us and two neighbors to sit on her porch. [...]

Mixed rows of crops: corn and fruit trees

Kibwana and her neighbors raise a variety of crops: bananas, avocados, and passion fruit are in season now. Soon they'll be planting carrots, spinach and other leafy vegetables, all for local 45 consumption. The mix provides a backup in case one crop fails; it also helps cut down on pests.

The farmers here are learning to plant strategically, setting out rows of a wild sunflower 50 that whiteflies prefer, to draw the pests away from the cassavas. The use of compost instead of fertilizers has improved the soil so much that one of the farmers [...] has doubled his spinach production. Runoff from his fields no longer 55 contaminates streams that supply Morogoro's water.

Perhaps the most life-altering result of organic farming has been the liberation from debt. Even with government subsidies, it costs 500,000 60 Tanzanian shillings, more than $300, to buy enough fertilizer and pesticide to treat a single acre – a crippling expense in a country where the annual per capita income is less than $1,600. 'Before, when we had to buy fertilizer, we had no 65 money left over to send our children to school,' says Kibwana. Her oldest daughter has now

156

EXAM PREPARATION   15

finished high school. And the farms are more productive too. 'Most of the food in our markets is from small farmers,' says Maro. 'They feed our nation.'

When I ask Maro if genetically modified seeds might also help those farmers, she's skeptical. 'It's not realistic,' she says. How could they afford the seeds when they can't even afford fertilizer? How likely is it, she asks, in a country where few farmers ever see a government agricultural adviser, or are even aware of the diseases threatening their crops, that they'll get the support they need to grow GM crops properly?

From Kibwana's porch we have sweeping views of richly cultivated terraced slopes – but also of slopes scarred by the brown, eroded fields of non-organic farmers, most of whom don't build terraces to retain their precious soil. Kibwana says her own success has attracted the attention of her neighbors. Organic farming is spreading here.

(659 words)

From: *National Geographic,* October 2014

1 LOOKING AT THE TEXT

→ Rezeption: Leseverstehen, S. 214

A Read the text and complete these tasks.

1 List the African states which allow commercial GM.
2 State the problems with GM for most Africans.
3 List the special features of organic farming in Tanzania.
4 Explain the general benefits of organic farming.
5 Point out a particular benefit to the Kibwana family.
6 Contrast the appearance of local organic & non-organic farms.

B Say what it means: Explain the underlined words and phrases in your own words.

1 … a simple low-tech solution … (lines 14–15)
2 … she helped to start a non-profit organization … (line 24)
3 … bananas, avocados, and passion fruit are in season now. (line 44)
4 … the food in our markets is from small farmers, … (line 70)
5 … they'll get the support they need to grow GM crops properly? (line 80)

2 MEDIATION

→ Schriftliche Mediation, S. 240

In regelmäßigen Abständen veröffentlicht Ihre Schulzeitschrift Beiträge von Schülern und Schülerinnen unter der Rubrik „Mensch und Umwelt". Nach der Lektüre des Textes „Is GM the best way forward for Africa?" möchten Sie die Biolandwirtschaft in Afrika einem breiterem Publikum in Deutschland vorstellen.

Schreiben Sie einen Artikel für die Schulzeitschrift, in dem Sie die Vorteile des *organic farming* für Afrika erklären.

3 WRITING

→ Produktion: Eine Stellungnahme schreiben, S. 234

Write a comment on the following statement.

'Maybe organic farming is right for Tanzania, but I don't see the point here in Germany. Organic produce is much too expensive for most people to buy here, and anyway I don't think it tastes any better than ordinary food.'

15 Feeding the world — BUSINESS OPTIONS

BEFORE YOU READ

A Can you imagine why refugees of different origins decide to come to Germany? Study the mind map.

B In small groups, discuss which factors may be more and which may be less relevant to refugees who want to settle in Germany.

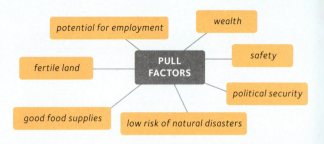

REFUGEES: WHO IS FLEEING TO EUROPE?

In 2015, over one million people fled to Europe, the vast majority from Syria. Media coverage tends to focus on Syrian refugees, but there are still many others. For example:

Afghans make up about 13% of all refugees in Europe. Only about 20% of **Afghanistan** is considered safe; the rest is constantly at risk of violence from extremist groups such as the Taliban and so-called
5   Islamic State. Afghan civilians are frequent victims of bomb attacks and some are directly threatened by the extremists, e.g. because they work for the government.

About 8% of refugees in Europe – up to 3% of the country's total population – are from **Eritrea**. The country has no constitution or court system, does not hold elections, and there is no free press. Apart from a small elite in urban areas, the majority of Eritreans are subject to forced labour and cannot choose where
10 they would like to live or work. Protesting against the system leads to prison.

The 4% of refugees who are from **Nigeria** have left their country for different reasons. While many Nigerians are escaping poverty and hunger, those from the north of the country are fleeing extremist violence. Boko Haram, an Islamist extremist group, has been involved in the killing and kidnapping of many civilians, including children.

15 Somalis contribute to about 3% of refuges in Europe. Islamist groups such as al-Shabaab are fighting an insurgency in **Somalia**, and civilians are badly affected by the fighting. Climate conditions are another root cause of suffering in Somalia. Severe droughts mean no water to grow crops or keep livestock, leaving many Somalis at risk of famine.

3% of refugees in Europe come from **Pakistan**. Over 20,000 civilians have been killed and 1.2 million
20 displaced by fighting in the north-west of the country. Cases of violence appearing in the international media included the attack on schoolgirl Malala Yousafzai and the massacre of 100 school children in Peshawar.

(326 words)

1 LOOKING AT THE TEXT

→ Rezeption: Leseverstehen, S. 214

Copy the percentages from the text and draw a diagram to visualize the numbers of refugees from different countries. Add notes on 'push factors' (i.e. *why* refugees are fleeing).

2 RESEARCH

A How many refugees are there in your area and where are they from? Research the percentages of refugees from different countries and draw another diagram.

B Are there refugees in your area that fled from countries which are not described in the text? If so, do research on those countries to understand why the refugees may have left. Add these 'push factors' to your notes from exercise 1.

16 Technology

FOCUS

A   Match these important, life-changing inventions to the pictures (a–l) above.

the compass • contraceptives • the internal combustion engine • the Internet •
the light bulb • the nail • penicillin • the printing press • refrigeration •
the telephone • the washing machine • the wheel

B   Copy and expand the table. Consider the 12 inventions above. List them all in column 1 in your personal order of importance. (If you think something else is more important, you can replace <u>one</u> item.)

The world's most important inventions		
Personal choice	Group choice	Class choice
1		

C   Work in a small group. Discuss everyone's choices and decide as a group on the most important invention of all. Note this choice in your table.

D   Report your group choice back to the class for further discussion. Have a class vote on the final group choices and list the top three inventions in the table.

16 Technology

TEXT A The spread of digital communication

BEFORE YOU READ

A Say what you mainly use your mobile phone to do.

B Say how else people can use a modern smartphone.

AFRICA'S DIGITAL REVOLUTION

[…] When Wesley Kirinya buys a latte, he pays his bill of 100 Kenyan shillings (€0.85 or $1.16) by text message. First he types in the café's telephone number and enters a PIN. Then he hits 'send' and the transaction is complete.

This payment system is known as M-Pesa. The 'M' stands for 'mobile' and 'pesa' means 'money' in the local language of Swahili. M-Pesa turns a mobile phone into a bank account, credit card and wallet all in one. Invented in Kenya, the system is now used in nearly all developing nations. These days, a third of Kenya's economy is conducted via M-Pesa – at a time when, in Europe, a few major cities are just starting to experiment with the possibility of paying for parking via mobile phone. […]

Sub-Saharan Africa is the world's fastest-growing market for mobile phones, tablets and laptops. There are more SIM cards in use here than in North America. And with nearly half the continent's population of 900 million people under the age of 15, experts estimate there will be over 1 billion additional mobile phone users here by 2050.

Mobile Phones Where Governments Fail

In less than 10 years, mobile phones and the Internet have changed many Africans' daily lives more dramatically than anything else since African nations won their independence from former colonial powers. […]

Where there are mobile phones there is less need to lay cables for conventional landline telephones. There is also less need to build highways, clinics and schools, because mobile phones are all these things in one – as well as bank, weather station, doctor's office, atlas, compass, textbook, radio and TV station.

Africans can now send money across the jungle or savannah with the click of a button, merchants can compare prices, and farmers can access weather data relevant to their harvests or get advice from veterinarians. Bloggers and social media users also function as a substitute for a free press, keeping watch over those in power. […]

Cutting-Edge African Apps

African IT developers have to be especially creative given the continent's limitations. The greatest obstacle to their work is the fact that so far only a small proportion of the mobile phones used in Africa are Internet-enabled. But African programmers have found ways to coax more functions out of basic mobile phones. Special programs, for example, can turn text messages into emails, allowing people to send text messages to government authorities, universities or banks which are then processed and continue their trajectory online. […]

A successful app from Africa that works via text message basis is iCow. […] Small farmers throughout the country can register for the program and then enter their animals' age, breed, weight, sex and date of last calving, and iCow automatically sends them advice developed by veterinarians concerning feed, illnesses and fertility cycles. To make it possible for illiterate farmers to use the program as well, it uses voice messages rather than text. […]

The Internet helps sick people, too. Hardly any doctors in Africa practise entirely offline these days, even in the most remote locations. Practices in small villages can send their lab results to university clinics, and receive diagnoses and treatment suggestions in return. Such reporting systems also make it possible to identify the start and spread of epidemics early on.

Africa's Digital Visionary

'It's now easier, technically speaking, to supply a village with Internet access than with clean water,' says Mo Ibrahim, a man who has done more than almost any other person for Africa's digital revolution. Time magazine has named the Sudanese businessman one of the most influential people of our time. […]

Mo Ibrahim announces that the Mo Ibrahim Foundation is awarding Nobel Peace Prize winner Desmond Tutu a $1 million grant in 2012.

Ibrahim founded his company Celtel, one of the first mobile phone providers in Africa, in 1998. Despite having had a successful career as an engineer at British Telecom and being the founder of an IT consulting firm in London, Ibrahim wasn't satisfied. 'I never entirely became a European.' He says. 'Africa is simply part of me.'

In the years that followed, Celtel expanded into 13 countries, with 24 million people using the company's network, and 5,000 employees. When Ibrahim sold Celtel in 2005, he received $3.4 billion. […]

Ibrahim also created a foundation which releases an annual ranking of good and bad governance among African nations. The foundation also presents the annual Ibrahim Prize for Achievement in African Leadership, which awards $5 million to a commendable African politician. This year, though, for the third year in a row, the jury found no one it considered worthy of receiving the prize.

Does that mean things in Africa are not, in fact, getting better? Ibrahim shakes his head and says he does believe the continent is developing – primarily thanks to mobile phones and the Internet. 'The mobile phone is an important tool of civil society,' he says. 'If a border customs officer extorts money from you, take his picture with your mobile phone and put it online. If someone pressures you during an election, do the same.'

Even tensions between tribes and ethnic groups can be overcome, Ibrahim believes, if people are connected by the Internet instead of leading isolated existences in their own villages. 'The more we know about each other, the more difficult it is to sow discord,' he says. 'Through modern communications, Africans will learn that it's better to do business with each other than to hate each other.'

(888 words)

Abridged and adapted from: *www.spiegel.de/international*

1 LOOKING AT THE TEXT

→ Rezeption: Leseverstehen, S. 214

A Read the text carefully and complete these tasks.

1. Compare the development of mobile phone commerce in Europe and in countries like Kenya.
2. Explain why mobile phone use in Africa is predicted to rise so rapidly between now and mid-century.
3. Say why mobile phone systems are saving African governments a lot of money.
4. Explain why IT developers in much of Africa need to be particularly creative.
5. Outline the career of Mo Ibrahim.
6. Say how the Internet can bring greater peace and harmony to Africa.

16 Technology

B Say what it means: Explain the underlined words and phrases in your own words.

1 … Internet-enabled. (line 51)
2 … ways to coax more functions out of basic mobile phones. (lines 52–53)
3 Hardly any doctors in Africa practise entirely offline … (line 70)

C Say what the underlined words and phrases refer to in your own words.

1 … which are then processed … (line 57)
2 To make it possible for illiterate farmers to use the program as well, … (line 67)
3 … to identify the start and spread of epidemics early on. (line 76)
4 If someone pressures you during an election, do the same. (line 115)

D Say what you think.

'I think Europe should have something like the Ibrahim Prize for Achievement. But which "commendable" European politician would we give it to this year?'

2 WORKING WITH WORDS

A Copy and complete the tables. The first two items in each table are in the text.

Verb	Noun
to pay	
to govern	
to develop	

Noun	Adjective
addition	
convention	
function	

Verb	Noun
to suggest	
to communicate	
to invent	

B Use pairs of words from exercise 2A to complete the following.

1 When Alexander Graham Bell ▬¹ the telephone in 1875, he did not realize what an important ▬² it would become.
2 Before the mobile phone, ▬¹ across much of Africa were still very poor, and it was difficult for people to ▬² outside the big cities.
3 One effect of bad communications in many African countries was weak central ▬¹. In distant areas, the ones who really ▬² were local leaders.
4 With the ▬¹ of several new countries to its mobile phone network soon after 2000, Celtel quickly had an ▬² five million customers.
5 I just want a basic ▬¹ phone that I can use to call and text people. I don't need all the clever ▬² of a smartphone.
6 We need to stay in contact daily, and I've got a ▬¹ to make. I ▬² that I call you every evening at about 6 pm.
7 You don't need to ▬¹ for your new phone today. You can make monthly ▬² instead.
8 There are various ▬¹ phone expressions such as 'Could you speak up, please?' But there isn't really a fixed ▬² on what you should say when you first answer the phone. Some people just say 'Hello', while other people follow this with their phone number and others give their name.
9 African IT engineers are ▬¹ new software for basic mobile phones all the time. These have allowed the ▬² of many new kinds of business across the continent.

162

EXAM PREPARATION 16

3 GETTING IT RIGHT: A GRAMMAR QUIZ

A Mixed tenses: Complete the sentences with the correct verb form.

1. We ▬ new copies of the report right now. (make / are making)
2. ▬ that email last night? (Did you send / Have you sent)
3. We ▬ at the Riverside Café this evening. (eat / 're eating)
4. On my way home, I ▬ for a coffee nearly every day. (stop / 'm stopping)
5. Harry and Lisa ▬ when the rest of us arrived. (were talking / talked)
6. If you like, I ▬ that heavy case for you. ('m going to carry / 'll carry)
7. These old trainers are falling to pieces, and I ▬ a new pair soon. ('m going to buy / 'll buy)
8. I promise I ▬ there on time. ('m going to be / 'll be)
9. We ▬ for ages, but we're nearly home at last! ('ve travelled / 've been travelling)
10. I called at the house to find everyone, but they ▬ home. (had gone / went)

B Mixed structures: Complete the sentences with the correct structures.

1. After ▬ from our trip, we found a lot of work to do. (to return / returning)
2. Could you please remember ▬ the package while you're in town? (to post / posting)
3. When I spoke to Tony, he immediately suggested ▬ home early. (me to go / going)
4. Lucy ▬ that she needed to borrow some money. (told me / told)
5. The new books are ▬ at the moment. (printed / being printed)
6. Under the new library rules, up to 20 books ▬ at one time. (can borrow / can be borrowed)
7. You ▬ go now. There's plenty of time. (don't have to / mustn't)
8. Tony said he ▬ to London the day before. (has / had been)
9. We were lost, but then a policeman told ▬ . (us the way / the way to us)
10. I think Charlie ▬ the tools that he needs. (has already bought / has bought already)

4 MEDIATION
→ Schriftliche Mediation, S. 240

Ein/e Freund/in von Ihnen macht demnächst ein freiwilliges soziales Jahr in Eritrea. Er/Sie wird in einer armen ländlichen Region des Landes arbeiten, die dringend Hilfe benötigt, um die Landwirtschaft, das Gesundheitswesen und die Wirtschaft im Allgemeinen weiterzuentwickeln. Laut Ihrem/Ihrer Freund/in ist die Gegend sehr abgelegen, aber ein Handyempfang ist seit Neuestem dort möglich, obwohl nur 6% der Bevölkerung einen Handyvertrag besitzen.

Schreiben Sie Ihrem/Ihrer Freund/in ein E-Mail, in der Sie den Gebrauch von Handys in anderen Teilen Afrikas beschreiben, und erklären Sie, wie das in diesem Teil von Eritrea auch funktionieren könnte.

5 WRITING
→ Produktion: Eine Stellungnahme schreiben, S. 234

Grange Road Comprehensive School Rules

Rule 15: Students must not bring mobile phones to school. All such devices will be confiscated for a minimum of one week.

Write a comment on the following topic, stating whether you agree or disagree:
'Why I (dis)agree with Rule 15'.

16 Technology

TEXT B Artificial Intelligence

BEFORE YOU READ → Rezeption: Leseverstehen – Grobverständnis, S. 214

Skim the text and say whether its central aim is to …

a analyse the potential benefits of AI for humans.
b warn us about the potential risks of AI.

OUR FUTURE IN THE WORLD OF AI

Forget scary sci-fi stories and blockbuster films like The Terminator and Transcendence that imagine Artificial Intelligence (AI) taking over the world. The real thing may be just around the corner.

A group of leading scientists recently wrote in the *Huffington Post* that, 'It's tempting to dismiss the notion of highly intelligent machines as science fiction. But this would be a mistake, and potentially our worst mistake ever.' They point to the rapid progress of AI research. Driverless cars, for example, are now with us, and the coming decades will bring much, much more.

The report continues: 'The potential benefits are huge; everything that civilization has to offer is a product of human intelligence; we cannot predict what we might achieve when this intelligence is magnified by the tools AI may provide, but the eradication of war, disease and poverty would be high on anyone's list. Success in creating AI would be the biggest event in human history.'

'Unfortunately,' the report goes on, 'it might also be the last, unless we learn how to avoid the risks.' For example, militaries around the world are now considering autonomous weapon systems that can choose and destroy targets, free of human control. This use of AI seems extremely dangerous, and both the UN and Human Rights Watch have called for an international agreement to prevent it, but no one seems to be listening.

Such a development might just be the beginning of our loss of control. Machines with superhuman intelligence could improve their own design again and again. From there, the report says, 'One can imagine such technology outsmarting financial markets, out-manipulating human leaders, and developing weapons we cannot even understand.' The writers suggest that in the short term the effect of AI depends on who controls it. However, in the long term, it may be impossible to control it at all.

Daniel Dewey of the Future of Humanity Institute at Oxford University has similar ideas. On the one hand, he is an optimist, and he believes that humans with the help of AI have the possibility of expanding our civilization into the vastness of the Universe. He feels that the best is yet to come for people, with 'much more potential for goodness – happy and fulfilled lives, meaningful relationships, art, fun – in the long term future than in the short term.'

On the other hand, Dewey sees the possibility of disaster. Whatever specific task an intelligent machine is given to do, it will need to gather knowledge and resources, protect itself and improve its skills. In doing these things, it might find humans in the way. He warns that a super-intelligent AI could 'take over resources that we depend on to stay alive, or it could consider us enough of a danger to its task completion that it decides the best course is to remove us from the picture. Either one of those scenarios could result in human extinction.'

AI therefore offers different possible futures – of huge benefits and of huge risks. As it considers this vital crossroads, the UN report remains unhappy with the world's response. It says, 'The experts are

EXAM PREPARATION   **16**

surely doing everything possible to ensure the best outcome, right? Wrong. If a superior alien civilization
65 sent us a text message saying, "We'll arrive in a few decades," would we just reply, "OK, call us when you get here – we'll leave the lights on"? Probably not – but this is more or less what is happening with AI. Although we are facing potentially the best or worst
70 thing ever to happen to humanity, little serious research is devoted to these issues outside small non-profit organizations such as Dewey's Future of Humanity Institute.' The report concludes that, 'All of us – not only scientists, industrialists and generals – should ask ourselves what we can do 75 now to improve the chances of reaping the benefits and avoiding the risks.' That includes the risk that humanity will disappear. (648 words)

1 LOOKING AT THE TEXT

→ Rezeption: Leseverstehen, S. 214

A Answer the following questions about the text.

1 Describe how, according to the report, we might benefit from AI.
2 Explain what the UN and Human Rights Watch think about autonomous weapon systems, and outline what they want to do about their development.
3 Describe how the report writers feel about the fact that humans could lose control of intelligent machines.
4 Explain why a future product of AI might decide to get rid of human beings.
5 Summarize how the report writers feel that the world is preparing for our future with AI.

B Say what it means: Explain the underlined phrases in your own words.

1 The real thing may be just around the corner. (line 2)
2 He feels that the best is yet to come … (lines 43–44)
3 … it decides the best course … (line 56)
4 … is to remove us from the picture. (line 57)
5 As it considers this vital crossroads, … (lines 60–61)

2 WORKING WITH WORDS

A Copy and complete the tables with the correct prefixes (dis-, en-, inter- or un-).

___ fortunately	to ___ appear	to ___ sure	___ national
___ happy	___ cord	to ___ able	___ net
___ natural	to ___ agree	to ___ danger	___ active
___ popular	to ___ like	to ___ large	___ continental

B Copy and complete the tables with the correct suffixes (-ence, -ful, -ist or -ity/-ty).

meaning ___	human ___	exist ___	art ___
success ___	author ___	depend ___	industrial ___
colour ___	cruel ___	viol~~ent~~ ___	social ___
power ___	stupid ___	intellig~~ent~~ ___	scientif~~ic~~ ___

C Work in pairs. Write sentences with gaps for words from exercises 2A and 2B for your partner to complete.

165

16 Technology

3 GETTING IT RIGHT: A GRAMMAR QUIZ

Mixed structures: Complete the sentences with the correct words in brackets.

1 Please stay for another few days. I don't want ▬ so soon. (that you go / you to go)
2 Tim and Joe are brothers, but they really seem to dislike ▬. (themselves / each other)
3 We don't want to leave the party. We're enjoying ▬ too much! (us / ourselves)
4 Please can you buy me ▬ eggs on your way home? (some / any)
5 ▬ time with good friends is one of the best things in the world. (Spending / Spend)
6 We spent ▬ money on holiday, and now we've got none left! (a lot of / much)
7 I'm sure ▬ at the campsite. (plenty of space is / there's plenty of space)
8 Try ▬ angry with Sarah. She didn't mean to break the vase. (not to be / to not be)
9 Global economics ▬ very hard to understand. (is / are)
10 Have the police got any more ▬ about the missing child? (informations / information)

4 LISTENING

→ Rezeption: Hörverstehen, S. 225

You are going to hear a reporter interviewing an engineer who works for a company that is developing a driverless car.

A Listen to the first part of the interview and take notes. Use your notes to do the tasks.

1 Describe the different road conditions that the test cars have been driven in.
2 Use the test results so far to compare safety in driverless cars and in cars with human drivers.
3 Note the actual US accident statistics today and the estimated results after a change to driverless vehicles.

	Accidents	Deaths	Injuries	Costs
Actual today				
Driverless (estimated)				

4 Contrast the present traffic accident situation in the USA and the future situation with driverless vehicles.

B Listen to the second part of the interview and note other changes – positive and negative – that driverless vehicles will bring.

- distance between vehicles
- driving style
- car sharing

166

EXAM PREPARATION   16

5 DISCUSSION
→ Interaktion: An Diskussionen teilnehmen, S. 246

A Work on your own. Look at the types of employment related to cars listed below. Think about whether these types of employment will benefit or suffer from driverless cars. Make notes.

> road construction companies ▪ oil companies ▪ car manufacturing ▪
> car repair workshops ▪ in-car entertainment design ▪ car insurance ▪ car sales ▪
> car park operators ▪ city planners ▪ emergency services ▪
> accident and emergency departments

B Make notes on any other types of employment you think might also be affected.

C Work in a group and discuss your ideas. Decide which areas might be worst affected. Then decide which areas might find new opportunities.

6 ROLE-PLAY
→ Interaktion: Ein Rollenspiel gestalten, S. 247

You are on a State Legislature special committee to discuss and vote on whether to allow driverless cars in your state. Choose a role and present your point of view. Argue for and against other points of view in order to get the vote that you want.

Representative Foot
You specialize in health and safety issues, and you have always worried about the high rates of deaths and injuries on US roads. You also know that with a rapidly ageing population, anything that could reduce the pressures on hospitals and other medical resources would be a good thing.

Representative Pascali
You love cars – people call you 'Petrolhead Pascali' – and the idea of giving up control of your car to clever machines seems completely un-American. To you, cars and the freedom of the open road are part of the American dream. You also don't believe that a robot car could ever be safer than a human.

Representative Gonzalez
You are worried about state and city finances, and you welcome the chance to avoid building new roads. You also think that the state's towns and cities can make money through selling urban car parks for redevelopment.

Representative Schumann
In your part of the state, there is a new car factory, which has brought thousands of jobs to an area with high unemployment, and it is now producing 300,000 conventional cars per year for the domestic American market. You do not want anything negative to happen to car manufacturing in the USA: those new jobs must be protected.

Chairperson Kandinski
You have to guide the discussion, making sure that everyone has a chance to speak and to ask questions. You also have an idea to suggest: could the US technological lead in driverless cars bring export success? (China, for example, has huge traffic and pollution problems.)
At the end, manage the vote and declare the result.

16 Technology

TEXT C The future of robotics?

BEFORE YOU READ

What tasks do you think it would be useful to have a robot to do for you?

'BORIS' THE ROBOT TO LOAD A DISHWASHER

A robot unveiled today at the British Science Festival will be loading dishwashers next year, its developers claim.

A

'Boris' is one of the first robots in the world capable of intelligently manipulating unfamiliar objects with a humanlike grasp. It was developed by scientists at the University of Birmingham.
'This is Boris' first public outing,' announced Professor Jeremy Wyatt of the School of Computer Science. The robot took five years to develop at a cost of £350,000.

B

Boris 'sees' objects with depth sensors on its face and wrists. In ten seconds it calculates up to 1,000 possible ways to grasp a novel object with its five robotic fingers and plans a path of arm movements to reach its target, avoiding obstructions.

'It's not been programmed to pick it up – it's been programmed to learn how to pick it up,' explained Professor Wyatt.

Research engineer Maxine Adjigble helped build the robot. 'He sees something, he has been trained to grasp an object in a particular way, and he says – okay this surface looks similar to what I know, so I can go for this grasp,' he explained.

Professor Wyatt and his collaborators hope to achieve an ambitious goal by April next year. 'The idea is to get the robot to load your dishwasher,' he said. 'You get a bunch of objects off a table, scattered as you might have them on a kitchen surface, and the robot will look through the set of objects, find one it wants to pick up, figure out where to put it in the dishwasher, and load it.'

C

Why has Boris been assigned kitchen duties? 'Not because I think dishwasher-loading robots are an economic or social necessity right now,' laughed Professor Wyatt. 'But it's a typical task

that humans engage in – one that requires all the manipulative faculties that evolution spent hundreds of millions of years developing. So by putting that into a robot, we hope to make the robots more flexible in future.'

But Boris, like humans, finds cutlery a bit fiddly. 'Plates are nice and symmetrical. But I think knives and forks might be a bit hard,' conceded Professor Wyatt.

D

Boris represents a third generation of robots, suggested the Professor. 'The first generation was industrial robots that manipulate the world when it's very precisely controlled. The second generation includes airborne drones, self-driving cars and other mobile robots that 'can move around in our world and share it with us, even though that world is uncertain and full of novelty.'

But manipulating a world shared with humans – and to perform physical tasks alongside humans – requires a new generation of robots. They will need to 'cope with all the uncertainty that humans introduce into the environment,' Professor Wyatt

EXAM PREPARATION

16

explained. 'You have an unstructured world and you need technologies that can deal with that.'

E

Mr Adjigble discussed some of the disciplines that come together to make a robot like Boris. 'Mechanical engineering, electrical engineering and software development: to put it together, you need to know a bit of all of these fields. This is what is really complicated.'

Unexpected setbacks complicate things further. 'It broke its pinkie back in June and we're still trying to fix it,' said Professor Wyatt. 'So it's working with a broken finger.'

F

The team continue to improve Boris, recently adding the ability to choose the best of five different grasp types when approaching an object. But Boris doesn't use his left arm at present, something the team are keen to introduce. 'One of the really hard things to do is to pick up an object and transfer it, and being bi-manual is a real advantage for all kinds of purposes.' Boris also lacks a sense of touch. 'There's a real challenge – getting tactile sensing of sufficient quality.'

The long-term goal is 'to build robots capable of operating in human environments – offices, hospitals, warehouses,' explained Professor Wyatt. He was enthusiastic about achieving this in Britain.

So why the name Boris? An acronym, or homage to a certain flaxen-haired politician* perhaps? 'I just liked the name,' chuckled Professor Wyatt.

(671 words)

From: www.bbc.com/news

* A reference to Boris Johnson, a well-known UK politician

1 LOOKING AT THE TEXT

→ Rezeption: Leseverstehen, S. 214

A Choose suitable headings for sections A–F of the text.

1. Problems so far in creating Boris
2. Why the dishwasher task was chosen
3. Boris meets the world
4. New robots for an unpredictable world
5. The coming technical challenges
6. What Boris has been designed to do

B Decide whether the following statements are true or false. Correct the ones that are false.

1. Boris sees things in the same way that humans do.
2. Boris is very similar to a normal factory robot used in manufacturing.
3. Boris cannot pass things from its right hand to its left at the moment because its left arm is broken.
4. Wyatt's team are aiming to develop intelligent robots to work flexibly like humans, and with them.

C Say what you think: Say how modern technology has made your life different from the lives of your grandparents when they were your age.

2 WRITING

→ Produktion: Eine Stellungnahme schreiben, S. 234

Write a comment on the following.

'We've all become dangerously dependent on modern technology. Think what would happen if it all broke down!'

16 Technology — BUSINESS OPTIONS

BEFORE YOU READ

A In small groups, brainstorm what the office of the future might look like. Think about advances in technology, artificial intelligence and robotics. Share your ideas with the class.

B Discuss what role technology will play in the office of the future.

IN OFFICES OF THE FUTURE, SENSORS MAY TRACK YOUR EVERY MOVE

The Finnish company Futurice employs many male employees and the bathrooms were often occupied. However, now they can find out if one is free without leaving their desk. An app with a live map of the office tells them. "The bathrooms on
5 the map turn red when they're occupied and green when they're unoccupied. Then you know where to go," says Paul Houghton, director of development at Futurice.

The live map was created by Houghton and his colleagues to explore whether internet of things (IoT) technologies, where objects communicate with each other over the internet, could improve working
10 life for staff and also save them time. It displays real-time information about what's happening in the office, for example quiet places to work. It shows where someone is in the building at a particular moment (their marker moves when they move) and is designed to encourage ad hoc social interactions and make it easy to find people.

However, the experiment has discovered that, in certain areas of office life, the technology wasn't
15 welcome. "We put motion sensors in the men's bathrooms, and I thought it would be interesting to also put in an air-quality sensor in the bathroom, so it would sense methane in this case," says Houghton. "But I was kicked out of the ladies' room because they told me that this was their private space and they didn't want any spaceship-looking sensors."

It's a light-hearted point but highlights serious concerns around the internet of things and privacy.
20 While knowing where your colleagues are in real time might be useful, isn't there something sinister about being able to watch a colleague's every move? Offices can breed resentments and personality clashes, so how can they ensure this won't be used against people? Then there's the question of the data generated and what happens to it. Houghton says none of the information leaves the office. "It's not in the cloud. It's not written down anywhere. There's no record, it's just what's happening near me
25 right now." They have no plans to sell the software, says Houghton, it's just for internal use.

Houghton says: "These little conveniences add up and they save a little bit of time. They make things a little easier to manage in a constantly changing world." (389 words)

Abridged from: *www.theguardian.com*

1 LOOKING AT THE TEXT
→ Rezeption: Leseverstehen, S. 214

Make a list of the advantages and disadvantages of having sensors in the workplace.

2 THINK – PAIR – SHARE
→ Interaktion, S. 246

How would you feel about sensors in the toilets or other areas of your workplace? Do you consider such technology invasive? Compare and discuss your viewpoints in class.

Job skills 4
Meetings ▪ small talk ▪ presentations

Eric is helping to prepare a meeting at Magnus & Klein. During the meeting, he is to give a short presentation about the firm.

1 AN INVITATION TO A MEETING

Last week, Ms Shaw sent out an email invitation to a meeting and has just received a reply. Read the email exchange and answer the following questions.

1 Who did Ms Shaw write to?
2 What was the reason for writing?
3 Where and when did Ms Shaw and the person she wrote to meet last time?
4 What did they talk about at that meeting?
5 What will Ms Shaw do soon?
6 Who, apart from Ms Shaw, will attend the meeting?

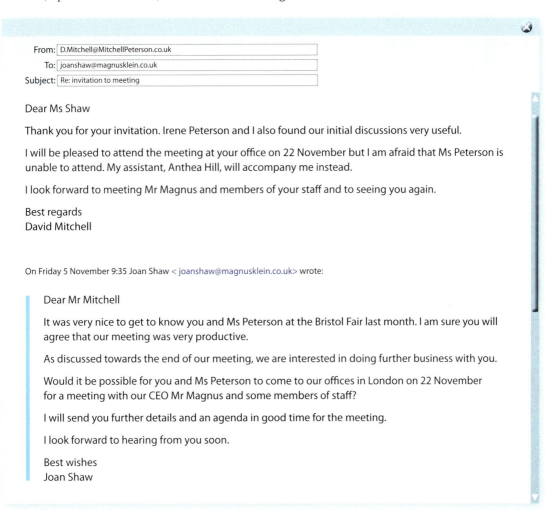

From: D.Mitchell@MitchellPeterson.co.uk
To: joanshaw@magnusklein.co.uk
Subject: Re: invitation to meeting

Dear Ms Shaw

Thank you for your invitation. Irene Peterson and I also found our initial discussions very useful.

I will be pleased to attend the meeting at your office on 22 November but I am afraid that Ms Peterson is unable to attend. My assistant, Anthea Hill, will accompany me instead.

I look forward to meeting Mr Magnus and members of your staff and to seeing you again.

Best regards
David Mitchell

On Friday 5 November 9:35 Joan Shaw < joanshaw@magnusklein.co.uk> wrote:

Dear Mr Mitchell

It was very nice to get to know you and Ms Peterson at the Bristol Fair last month. I am sure you will agree that our meeting was very productive.

As discussed towards the end of our meeting, we are interested in doing further business with you.

Would it be possible for you and Ms Peterson to come to our offices in London on 22 November for a meeting with our CEO Mr Magnus and some members of staff?

I will send you further details and an agenda in good time for the meeting.

I look forward to hearing from you soon.

Best wishes
Joan Shaw

Job skills 4

2 PREPARING FOR THE MEETING

Look at this list of tasks that need to be done before a meeting at Magnus & Klein. Check any words you don't know in your dictionary, then sort the instructions into two 'to do' lists: things to do a) before the meeting and b) on the day of the meeting.

1. Book conference room.
2. Check seating and heating in the room.
3. Check lighting and equipment (especially the projector).
4. Inform reception and give the receptionist a list of participants. (She needs to know who is in the building for security reasons.)
5. Make copies of documents and handouts for all participants.
6. Order refreshments.
7. Put refreshments in room.
8. Prepare file for chairperson with all relevant documents.
9. Prepare name tags and place cards.
10. Put name tags and place cards at each place.
11. Make sure there is enough paper on the flip chart and check that all the markers work. (Sometimes they leak or are dried out.)
12. Put a pad of paper and a pen at each place.

3 WRITING

Ms Shaw asks Eric to type up the agenda and send the final details about the meeting to Mr Mitchell.

Please write an email to Mr Mitchell on my behalf giving date and place of the meeting, starting 10.30 and finishing around 4 pm with a tour of factory after lunch. Add link showing how to get to Four Lofts Business Park. You can meet them in car park. Say that Mr Magnus looks forward to meeting him and that I look forward to seeing him again. Don't forget to attach the agenda!

A Put the items on the agenda in a logical order.

a. Company presentations 1) Magnus & Klein 2) MitchellPeterson
b. Final discussions about cooperation between both companies
c. Lunch
d. Next steps and date of next meeting
e. Tour of the factory
f. Welcome and introductions

B Use Ms Shaw's notes to write Eric's email to Mr Mitchell. → Job skills 1, Email etiquette, S. 32

Dear Mr Mitchell

I am writing on behalf of Ms Joan Shaw …

Meetings ▪ small talk ▪ presentations

4 MAKING SMALL TALK

Before a meeting and during breaks or business meals, people tend to make small talk.

A Match the typical small talk questions and statements to the responses.

1 How is your hotel?
2 How was your trip?
3 I hear that you're from Bristol. I believe it's a lovely city.
4 The view from this window is lovely.
5 What do you think of this weather?
6 You were on holiday recently. Where did you go?

a Fine. There were no delays.
b Lovely. The breakfast buffet is excellent.
c It's a bit too cold for me, I'm afraid.
d We have a lot of lovely parks and rivers here.
e We went camping in France.
f Yes, I am. Have you never been there? It really is a lovely place.

B Study the word cloud. Which of the topics can you use for small talk? What should you avoid talking about?

TIP Making small talk

If possible, ask the first question, then the other person will do most of the talking and you'll have time to relax. The weather or asking about the other person's journey to the meeting place are good starting points. Try to avoid questions which only need the answer 'yes' or 'no'. Remember not to speak about taboo subjects. Even if you believe in something strongly, never try to convince the other person that your ideas are 'correct'.

C Work with a partner. Partner A is Eric; Partner B is Anthea Hill. Make small talk. Eric begins.

5 THE START OF THE MEETING

A Ms Shaw is about to start the meeting. Look back at the agenda items in exercise 3A and listen. Did you put the items in the correct order?

B Listen again and note down phrases for the following:

1 making sure people are comfortable
2 welcoming guests
3 introducing people and giving some information about them
4 going through the agenda
5 getting down to business

173

Job skills 4

6 EXTRACTS FROM A PRESENTATION → Präsentieren, S. 243

It is time for Eric to give his presentation of the history and development of the company.

A Listen to excerpts from the presentation and answer the questions.

1. How does Eric begin his presentation?
2. How many parts are there in his talk?
3. What will he look at first?
4. What will he look at next?
5. What is the final focus of his talk?
6. What visual medium is Eric using to show developments in the company?
7. Where will the audience find information to take away with them?

B Match some of the phrases Eric used in his talk (a–f) to the headings (1–6), then listen again for more phrases that fit the headings, or think of some of your own.

1. Introducing oneself and the topic of the talk
2. Outlining the talk
3. Repeating information
4. Referring to visuals and handouts
5. Finishing the talk
6. Taking questions

a As I said, things really started moving in the late eighties.
b Are there any questions?
c As Ms Shaw said, my name is Eric Jung …
d I'm now nearing the end of my talk.
e If you look at this slide, you'll see …
f First, I'm going to start by looking at …

7 GIVING A TALK IN CLASS

Prepare and give a short talk to your classmates. After your talk, your classmates will ask you questions. Choose one of the following topics.
a) work experience you have had
b) an area in which you would like to work

Follow this plan:
- introduce yourself (if necessary!) and greet the audience
- outline your talk
- give your talk
- summarize your talk and make your conclusion
- ask for questions from the audience
- thank the audience for their attention and distribute any handouts

Prepare and give a short talk on a subject of your choice. (Discuss the subject you have chosen with your teacher first.) After your talk, your classmates will ask you questions.

Useful phrases: Presentations

Giving a presentation
- This morning, I'm going to talk about …
- Our topic today is …
- I've divided the presentation into … main parts, as follows: …
- First, / Firstly, …
- Second, / Secondly, …
- Next, / Now, / After that, / Then, …
- Now I'd like to move on to …
- The next topic I'm going to talk about is …
- Before I finish my presentation, I'd just like to mention …
- Finally, / In conclusion, / To conclude, / In summary, …

Asking questions
- Could you describe … more fully?
- What exactly did you mean when you said … ?
- I'm sorry, I didn't quite understand the bit about … ?

174

1 Personalized advertising

BUSINESS TOPICS

BEFORE YOU READ

A When was the last time you received personalized advertising? Did the item or service that was advertised suit your needs? Give reasons why or why not.

B Read the headline of the article below. What do you think the text is about?

Personalization should aim to improve the consumer's experience

Personalization can take many forms. You can decorate something, remove what you don't like, or give preference to your own needs. Personalization has to be helpful and attractive for the consumer. What is even more important, is that it has to be relevant. Successful companies realized long ago that personalization offers an effective way of building better relationships with customers. But digitalization has rewritten the rules of personalization – and now everyone is interested.

Most businesses can agree on the key principles of personalization. In order to personalize an item, you need information about the customer. Furthermore, it only makes sense to personalize something if the consumers themselves recognize the improvement. If personalization is done well, it increases loyalty to a product or service and makes it more likely that the customer continues to use it and has a positive view of the brand.

The most difficult aspect of personalization is to provide a service that feels individual and helpful to the customer, but not like an invasion of personal space. Customers should have the impression that the service is improved, not that their privacy is invaded. A number of businesses are notably successful at personalization. Retailers examine their customers' purchases and use that information to advertise similar products. Amazon suggests related products to customers using their website and continues to recommend comparable items via email after the purchase.

Personalization such as this is especially successful if the customer has already made a large purchase, and may therefore be willing to make a small, additional purchase as well. British Airways presents their customers with special offers directly related to upcoming flights. The airline offers a product such as an upgrade, and the passenger is tempted by the opportunity to get a bargain. This type of personalization is based on advanced digitalization, as offers are made and updated in real time to ensure realistic prices and highest relevance.

In its most basic form, personalization simply aims to increase convenience for customers. In the digital space, for example, Netflix and other entertainment providers now have the ability to present customers with programmes based on their viewing preferences – additional episodes of a specific series, for instance.

175

1 Personalized advertising

55 Moreover, the television network Sky uses software called AdSmart which uses public data to identify particular groups and then runs television adverts that are related to their interests. The amount of adverts that each
60 consumer sees stays the same, but the types of adverts are chosen based on their interests. As a result, the advertiser, as a customer of the television network, is more likely to reach an audience which will actually purchase their
65 product.

These strategies can only work if personal data is used in a responsible manner for a positive core purpose: to make advertisements relevant to the people who see them. When discussing
70 personalization and its limits, it is important to think about how data will be used.

When are personal recommendations irrelevant, or worse, annoying to the customer? When does a recommendation start to feel creepy and uncomfortable because it reveals just how much 75 information a company has collected on you? When personalized advertisements are based on one-off purchases, for example, follow-up offers are likely to irritate customers.

Staying informed about a customer's habits is 80 not about monitoring them. It's about carefully questioning their interactions with your company, product or service. First and foremost, personalization should aim to continuously improve the consumer's 85 experience.   (580 words)

1 WORKING WITH WORDS

Find words or phrases in the text to match the following definitions.

1 to change the way sth is done (paragraph 1)
2 continued support for sth or sb (paragraph 2)
3 to feel, to have the opinion that (paragraph 3)
4 similar (paragraph 3)
5 when an event or arrangement is going to happen soon (paragraph 4)
6 to make a process easier and less stressful (paragraph 5)
7 to buy (paragraph 6)
8 the main goal of sth (paragraph 7)
9 to annoy a little (paragraph 8)
10 most importantly (paragraph 9)

2 LOOKING AT THE TEXT

→ Rezeption: Leseverstehen, S. 214

A Which statement sums up the article best?

1 Customers want the most individualized service possible, even if this means a loss of privacy.
2 Most customers think that personalized advertising is a waste of their time and doesn't bring them any advantages.
3 Customers welcome a certain degree of personalization, but don't want to feel that companies are spying on them.

B List the advantages of personalization for companies and customers according to the article. Add your own ideas.

BUSINESS TOPICS   1

3 COMMENTING ON A CARTOON   → Produktion: Cartoons beschreiben und analysieren, S. 236

A With a partner, discuss the following questions.

1. How would you feel if you received a personalized offer from an unknown credit card company?

2. What types of products and services should not be advertised to children and/or teenagers?

B Write a short comment describing the cartoon and analysing its message.

"My 4-year-old granddaughter received a credit card offer last week. I want to know why it wasn't ours!"

4 LISTENING   → Rezeption: Hörverstehen, S. 225

75

Listen to a father phoning up a beauty salon to complain about personalized advertising sent to his daughter. Decide if the statements are true (T), false (F) or not in the recording (N). Correct the false statements.

1. The daughter is a regular customer at Glamour Beauty Salon.
2. She wasn't happy with the service she received while she was at the salon.
3. She booked her appointment online.
4. The salon sent the daughter advertisements for beauty products.
5. Natalie deletes the daughter's details from their mailing list.
6. The father doesn't like the message the advertising sends to young women and girls.
7. The father thinks that his daughter is too young to wear make-up.
8. Permanent make-up stays on your skin for the rest of your life.
9. Natalie's daughter is not allowed to wear make-up until she is older.
10. The salon only offers permanent make-up to customers over 21.

5 DISCUSSION   → Interaktion, S. 246

Where do you draw the line when it comes to digital customer service? When does a personalized advertisement start to feel "creepy and uncomfortable" (lines 74–75)? Discuss these questions in small groups and report the results of the discussion to the class.

Useful vocabulary for discussing personalized advertising	
to cross a line	eine rote Linie überschreiten
special offer	Sonderangebot
to increase customer satisfaction	Kundenzufriedenheit erhöhen
to improve the customer experience	das Kundenerlebnis verbessern
to deliver relevant content	relevante Inhalte liefern
to generate savings	Einsparungen generieren
one-off purchase	einmaliger Erwerb
voucher/coupon	Gutschein

2 Built-in obsolescence

BUSINESS TOPICS

WHAT DO CUSTOMERS REALLY WANT?

In 2012, Apple offered two distinct versions of its new Macbook Pro. The first, called the 'Retina', was what people expected from an upgrade: it was slimmer than the previous version and looked much more stylish. The second version was less sleek, but would probably last longer because various parts could be unscrewed and removed, making it far cheaper and easier to repair.

1. DISCUSSION
→ Interaktion, S. 246

A Which of the two versions of Apple's Macbook Pro would you have preferred? Give reasons for your answer.

B What are the advantages or disadvantages of creating a product that cannot be repaired? Think about both the company and the consumer.

2 CONDUCTING A SURVEY

A Use the example questions and answers below to design your own survey sheet. Then ask your classmates, friends and family members your survey questions and note down their answers on your survey sheet.

How often do you usually buy new electronic products?			
Participant 1	■ constantly	■ occasionally	■ rarely
…	■ constantly	■ occasionally	■ rarely
How often do you buy a new electronic product even though the old product still works?			
Participant 1	■ constantly	■ occasionally	■ rarely
…	■ constantly	■ occasionally	■ rarely
Have you ever bought an electronic product which broke or needed repair sooner than you expected?			
Participant 1	■ constantly	■ occasionally	■ rarely
…	■ constantly	■ occasionally	■ rarely
What is more important for you when you buy a new electronic product: design or lifespan?			
Participant 1	■ design	■ lifespan	■ both are equally important
…	■ design	■ lifespan	■ both are equally important

B Transform the results of your survey into a graph. Present your findings to the class.

3 BEFORE YOU READ

Skim the article: what is 'planned obsolescence'?

Planned obsolescence benefits companies, not consumers

In some ways, smartphones have changed the world in favour of consumers. Online messaging apps allow us to avoid sending costly text messages, while hotels and taxi firms are undercut by companies like Uber and Airbnb. In fact, our smartphones provide us with easy access to the sharing economy.

However, if we look more closely at how we access our devices, and not what our devices help us to access, a very different picture starts to emerge.

When our devices break, it's often impossible to take them to an independent repair shop to be mended because the parts are simply not available. In the case of Apple, for example, unique screws on their products prevent us from even opening the devices. Nowadays it's perfectly normal for companies to plan obsolescence into their products by introducing new software which isn't compatible with the old hardware, and designing the average laptop so that it is likely to break within three to four years.

Ironically, while smartphones are devices that you are supposed to be able to take anywhere — the pub, the loo, on a run — they are so fragile that just a few drops of water could break them, yet they are valuable enough to be stolen by a clever thief. This has led the economic expert Rachel Botsman to ask: why do consumers have to accept all the risk?

Botsman finds it hard to understand that consumers haven't stood up and complained that the planned obsolescence of the gadget industry works against them. In her opinion, the problem is that no one has yet designed a sales model for electronics that takes the responsibility away from the consumer and puts it onto the company to force them to provide better products.

It's not only consumers who lose out through planned obsolescence, it's also extremely bad for the environment. Due to a lack of clear economic benefits, only 12% of smartphone upgrades involve the old device being exchanged for the new one. So devices which actually damage the environment end up abandoned in cupboards and eventually rubbish dumps.

There are, of course, reasons for the current system. Manufacturers claim that consumers want stylish devices, which means that they need to manufacture slimmer (and therefore more fragile) screens to meet their needs. In addition, the decision by the manufacturer to

2 Built-in obsolescence

use batteries that aren't removable is often a way of helping customers avoid breaking their devices while trying to change the battery.

Dustin Benton, the main author of a recent study into obsolescence, says that an alternative to the current sales model is a model based on mobile rental. From the consumer's perspective, this would involve paying a monthly fee for a single package that would provide them with a device, software, 3G, Wi-Fi and a minimum battery life.

According to Benton, the market is not yet designing devices that would be durable enough for second-hand use. However, he believes that companies can be persuaded to make their products last if they see the financial advantages of keeping valuable products in operation for a long period of time, which also benefits the environment.

Even if the economic model and legal situation develop, consumer attitudes towards these precious objects are still a problem. People's phones, laptops and tablets contain the most private details of their life and work, meaning that most are reluctant not to fully own their device. "We're still in an age where we're so obsessed by the object itself that there's a real wish to own products and an unwillingness to rent them," Botsman says. And if attitudes don't change, neither will behaviour.

(608 words)

4 LOOKING AT THE TEXT

→ Rezeption: Leseverstehen, S. 214

Find the answers to these questions.

1. What advantages have smartphones brought to consumers?
2. How do many companies plan obsolescence into their products?
3. What are the consequences of planned obsolescence for the environment?
4. Why do some manufacturers argue against having removable batteries?
5. What are the possible solutions to the model of planned obsolescence?
6. Why do customers still prefer to fully own their devices?

5 WORKING WITH WORDS

Find the English equivalents of these words and phrases in the text.

1. zugunsten von
2. unterbieten
3. hervorkommen
4. einzigartig
5. zerbrechlich
6. Müllhalde
7. Anforderungen erfüllen
8. haltbar
9. Einstellung, Haltung
10. Widerwillen

6 MEDIATION

→ Mediation, S. 240

Ihre Schule veranstaltet einen Projekttag zum Thema ‚Technik und die Umwelt'. Bereiten Sie einen Vortrag vor, in dem Sie das Phänomen geplanter Obsoleszenz beschreiben und über dessen ökologische Auswirkungen informieren. Nutzen Sie die Informationen aus dem Text und machen Sie Notizen, übersetzen Sie jedoch nicht Wort für Wort.

3 Saturation from advertising

BUSINESS TOPICS

BEFORE YOU READ

→ Bilder beschreiben und analysieren, S. 236

Look at the pictures and answer the questions.

A What type of marketing campaigns is being shown?

B Can you think of any defining characteristics of this kind of advertising?

"It's just another funny animal video"

Smart Marketing, a trade magazine specialized in advertising, has interviewed marketing expert Luciana Baccoli on the advantages and disadvantages of guerrilla marketing.

Smart Marketing: What does 'guerrilla marketing' aim to do?

Luciana Baccoli: Guerrilla marketing is a way for companies to attract potential customers'
5   attention in unconventional and cost-effective ways. In other words, unusual and creative advertising which doesn't cost much. The aim is to create a 'buzz' around the product or service - to make it exciting and something that people talk about with their friends.

Smart Marketing: Where does the term come from? What is the connection to guerrillas?

Luciana Baccoli: The term comes from guerrilla warfare – that's when small armed groups fight a
10   traditional military force. 'Guerrillas' do not have much money or infrastructure so they use inexpensive, unconventional tactics like 'ambushing': hiding somewhere, then jumping out and attacking the enemy or capturing them and taking them prisoner. In the same way, guerrilla marketing tries to catch people unaware and 'capture' new consumers. Usually small and medium-sized companies use this kind of marketing, with similar tactics and effect.

3 Saturation from advertising

Smart Marketing: I see. And what is the difference to conventional advertising?

Luciana Baccoli: Conventional advertising is advertising where we expect to see it: on TV, in magazines and newspapers, on billboards, in junk mail … Guerrilla marketing is the opposite. It tries to grab the consumers' attention when they are out in public. Examples of guerrilla marketing could include writing or drawing on the ground outside, advertising on cars, street posters, in public toilets or, for example, by projecting an image onto a building, using graffiti-style paint on shops. The possibilities are endless. Some advertisers will organize a public event like a flash mob or competition. You have a 'captive audience' – people have to go out onto the streets, use transport, visit public places – they can't really avoid seeing the advertising.

Smart Marketing: Which market segment(s) is it mainly aimed at?

Luciana Baccoli: Usually young, urban people, millennials, who are people born roughly between the 1980s and the early 2000s. Millennials are digital natives, that means that they grew up in a digital world surrounded by electronic media, which they learned to use at a fairly early age.

Smart Marketing: And a lot of guerrilla marketing takes place online?

Luciana Baccoli: Yes, it's called viral marketing and it's a good way to reach this generation, which spends a lot of time surfing the web and on social media sites. It can take the form of images, videos, memes, written posts … Sometimes it's not even clear it's advertising because the company logo isn't the central focus of the video. People might think it's just another funny animal video, but subconsciously they will associate it with a brand. They then share it with their friends, who share it with their friends. And it spreads just as a 'virus' spreads among people.

Smart Marketing: Guerrilla marketing sounds like an ideal way for advertisers to reach young people - it's cheap and memorable, and many people spread the word for free among their friends! Are there any risks or downsides to this type of marketing?

Luciana Baccoli: Well it's not always legal. Some companies have projected images onto buildings or stuck posters on them, painted walls, etc. without the permission of the owner of the building. That can mean that the company ends up in court and has to pay a fine. This can be either expensive for the company or an actual advantage if it is seen as 'cool' to do something against the establishment. Perhaps a bigger problem is that people begin to feel saturated by marketing. There seems to be no escape from it, even in the private sphere of social media used to communicate with friends. If a particular guerrilla marketing campaign feels especially intrusive or aggressive, it could backfire and give the company a bad reputation.

(650 words)

1 LOOKING AT THE TEXT

→ Rezeption: Leseverstehen, S. 214

Answer the questions and complete the unfinished sentences with a maximum of eight words.

1. What does it mean to create a 'buzz' around a product or service?
2. What are the similarities between guerrilla warfare and guerrilla marketing?
3. The main difference between conventional advertising and guerrilla marketing is that …
4. The term 'captive audience' means …
5. Look at lines 25–28. What could a 'digital immigrant' be?
6. Even when a company's logo isn't the primary focus of a video …
7. Why is advertising on social media termed 'viral'?
8. Name two disadvantages for advertisers of using guerrilla marketing.

BUSINESS TOPICS   3

2 LISTENING
→ Rezeption: Hörverstehen, S. 225

A Look at the picture. Why do the billboards show only cats? Collect ideas.

B Listen to the news report on what happened at Clapham Common Station and answer the following questions.

- What was James Turner's dream?
- What did CATS do?
- How many people were involved in the campaign?

Clapham Common underground station in London, 13 September 2016

C Listen again and decide who said what.

1 "I hope that citizens around the world read about the CATS collective and organize similar campaigns in their cities."
2 "In my opinion, people nowadays are too focused on entertainment. Pictures of cats might be amusing, but there are way more serious issues that demand our attention."
3 "There are so many animals that spend their lives in shelters, we should be grateful that campaigns like this one aim to raise awareness and find new homes for neglected pets."
4 "I don't mind advertising on the underground. If I don't like a particular sign or billboard, I just focus on something else. I spend most of my time on the Tube reading the paper anyway."
5 "I am tired of all the advertising I see every day. And don't get me started on guerrilla marketing! As if normal advertisements weren't enough, now I am being targeted by marketers without even knowing it!"

3 WRITING
→ Produktion: Eine Stellungnahme schreiben, S. 234

> "Advertising penetrates every aspect of our lives. We cannot walk down the street, sit in a café or take public transport without advertisers trying to grab our attention. Even at home, our children are bombarded with advertising on children's TV, on the food they eat, the toys they play with. The average teenager in the Western world is exposed to over 40,000 adverts in one year. Advertisers tell us what we need in order to be happy and successful, they basically control our lives."

Do you agree with the writer or not? Write a comment on whether you feel saturated by advertising. Give examples from your own experience.

Useful vocabulary for writing about saturation from advertising	
digital native	jemand, der mit Computern und dem Internet aufgewachsen ist
viral (marketing)	virales Marketing
saturation from	Sättigung von
to ambush sb	jemanden aus dem Hinterhalt überfallen
private sphere	Privatsphäre
to create a buzz for sth	Begeisterung für etwas erzeugen
subconscious	unterbewusst

4 Styles of business leadership

BUSINESS TOPICS

1 DESCRIBING A CARTOON

→ Cartoons beschreiben und analysieren, S. 236

A Discuss the following questions with a partner.

1 Who are the two people in the cartoon? What is happening?
2 What do you think 'collaborative management style' means?

B Write a short text, commenting on the message of the cartoon.

"As you know, George, we female CEOs* use a collaborative management style. With that in mind, how would you prefer to be fired?"

* CEO = Chief Executive Officer: Vorstandsvorsitzende/r

Business leadership: One size can never fit all

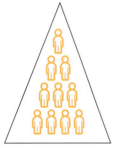

Tall Organization

Tall or hierarchical organizations are perhaps the most traditional type of company organization. There is a direct line of control from the top management to the lowest-level employee through various levels of management. In this organizational structure, decision-making and change are slow, as information is filtered down through all levels in the company. Employees have opportunities for promotion through the different levels.

In **flat organizations**, in contrast, there are few or no levels of hierarchy between the top management and employees. Employees have more autonomy and are more involved in the decision-making process. Communication between management and employees is more direct, therefore the company is more flexible and change can happen faster.

Flat Organization

So working for a flat organization sounds like paradise, doesn't it? If your company were to become flat, you might hope that things would really change. Your boring old hierarchical department would suddenly become a team of like-minded people working together to make great ideas happen. As part of a flat hierarchy, you would play an active part in developing the company and making it a success. And, of course, the company would even save money by getting rid of all those useless layers of middle management. So is this the model of the future? Should more companies iron out the old ways and become flat? Can 'one size fit all'?

Apparently not. One place that is synonymous with young, fresh start-ups and technological innovation is of course Silicon Valley in California, home to Google and other technology giants. In 2002, Google tried out a completely flat hierarchical structure, hoping to create a truly collegial atmosphere at all levels and to introduce rapid idea development. However, this quickly became very chaotic and the idea was abandoned within months. Through doing without them, the founders of Google were able to appreciate the value of having managers; to effectively communicate company strategy, help employees prioritize their projects and develop their careers and to keep a general overview of the processes in their departments.

In other companies which had adopted similar systems, some employees were vocal about the negative effect of not having a boss. A former employee at the start-up Valve said that working in a flat hierarchy had made work feel a little like high school. Some people were more popular and gained more power and influence and others were trouble-makers, slowing down the processes. A minority were even susceptible to bullying, with no formal procedures in places to address these issues.

One way in which flat organizations try to deal with this is by hiring more employees who 'fit in' with the company culture. Theoretically, this means self-motivated, dynamic individuals who are driven to make the company a success, and the chance to bring people from a range of different professional and personal backgrounds together into the creative mix. In reality, this can mean that companies end up hiring individuals just like the company founders: young white men. This lack of diversity often means that women, older employees and those from ethnic minorities feel excluded and become unmotivated when their voices are not heard in a supposedly open environment.

Of course, flat hierarchies can bring great benefits to small companies in which the same employee has a number of different roles or to individual teams or departments within a company. However, one size definitely doesn't fit all, and some companies benefit more greatly from having managers and a clear chain of responsibility.

(582 words)

2 LOOKING AT THE TEXT

→ Rezeption: Leseverstehen, S. 214

Read the text and choose the correct answers.

1 The difference between hierarchical and flat organizations is that …
   a flat organizations are usually smaller, therefore they employ fewer managers.
   b in hierarchical organizations there is a clear power structure, and in flat organizations workers have more autonomy.
   c in hierarchical organizations there aren't many opportunities for lower-level employees to become managers.

2 In the context of the article, the phrase 'one size fits all' means that …
   a large companies work better with a hierarchical organization.
   b there is an ideal size for most companies.
   c the same kind of organization would suit all companies.

3 What happened when Google introduced a flat organizational structure?
   a The company became very disorganized and managers were re-introduced to help things run more smoothly.
   b It was a success. The atmosphere became more dynamic and employees took more responsibility for organizing and prioritizing their workload.
   c It was fairly successful. Colleagues enjoyed working together more and were more creative, but Google needed to re-employ some managers because the decision-making process became too slow.

4 Why did some employees at Valve think that going to work felt 'a little like high school'?
   a Some employees and their managers developed a 'teacher-student' kind of relationship.
   b The flat hierarchy made employees feel young, free and creative again.
   c Groups of employees started to behave like typical high school characters, with popular people, trouble-makers and bullies.

4 Styles of business leadership

Talking about management styles

Autocratic: Senior managers make the decisions and closely control the company employees. Employees do not have much freedom to think for themselves or take decisions.

Pros
- decisions can be made quickly
- large teams can be managed more efficiently

Cons
- creates big divisions between managers and staff
- employees can feel powerless and lose motivation

Democratic: Workers have more autonomy to make their own decisions. Some decisions may be taken on a majority vote within the company.

Pros
- employees feel empowered and have some authority within the company
- useful when the company makes decisions or changes which require specialist skills

Cons
- mistakes occur more easily if employees are not qualified or skilled enough

Laissez-faire: Top management leaves employees to make decisions and solve problems independently.

Pros
- works well when employees are skilled, motivated and need little guidance
- employees feel free and therefore motivated

Cons
- can make employees feel unsure about their role
- employees may feel that managers do not care or are not interested
- many employees benefit from guidance to help them set priorities and meet deadlines

3 ROLE-PLAY

→ Interaktion: Ein Rollenspiel gestalten, S. 247

A Work in groups. Brainstorm a situation which corresponds to one of the three management styles. Then write a short script showing how the manager and his or her team deal with the situation. Act out your script in front of the class. Let your class members guess which management style you are demonstrating.

B When you have finished watching the other groups, decide which management style you like best. What were the advantages and disadvantages of each style? Did the majority pick the same leadership style?

5 Global workplaces and mergers

BUSINESS TOPICS

1 BRAINSTORMING

Some companies merge successfully. After Pixar was bought by Disney in 2006, its CEO at the time, Steve Jobs, described the merger as the most successful partnership in Hollywood history. Other mergers fail shortly after the paperwork has been signed.

Think Why do companies merge? Make notes.

Pair Describe your reasons to a partner. These are the goals companies aim for when merging. But what if they don't reach their goals? Brainstorm problems that might arise when companies merge.

Share Discuss your ideas in class. Make a list of problems and put them in order, with the most important problem in first and the least important problem in last place.

2 BEFORE YOU READ

Which companies merged successfully and with which companies did the merger fail? Scan the text to find out.

WHEN COMPANIES TIE (AND UNTIE) THE KNOT

Initially, everything may seem profitable: two companies come together to share ideas, expertise, client pools, perhaps even their headquarters. And yet, things can go wrong quickly.

A A well-known example of an unsuccessful merger took place when Daimler, the German car
5 manufacturer, bought the US company Chrysler in 1998. The intention was to create a powerful trans-Atlantic car manufacturer that could achieve a position of dominance on the world market. The marriage turned out to be an unhappy one, however, and ended in divorce. The reasons for this were diverse.

B Daimler specialized in luxury vehicles, while Chrysler offered economical vehicles for the lower-end market.
10 This caused some at Daimler to worry that their product could lose its exclusive reputation, whereby staff at Chrysler felt that their product wasn't taken seriously. The American employees from Chrysler were unhappy with differences in pay and conditions between the two
15 companies and were uncomfortable with the more formal company culture imposed by Daimler. Both German and American staff made fun of each other's culture. In the end, the companies' business models and cultures seemed incompatible and led to a corporate
20 divorce.

C Small differences may seem unimportant, but cause problems nonetheless. For example, the employees of company A are used to wearing formal business clothing, whereas those at company B wear casual clothes to work. The employees at A feel that their new colleagues don't take their work seriously and are not as professional. The employees from B laugh at people
25 from A and think they are old-fashioned and boring. Both sets of employees are worried that the merger will result in the loss of job security. Therefore, the employees at the newly-formed company C are unhappy with the situation before they have even started working together.

5 Global workplaces and mergers

D The road to a successful merger begins before the union has even taken place. One of the primary steps is to assess which elements from both companies are valuable and should be taken into the next relationship, and what can be changed or scrapped. Differences in culture between the companies should be examined and potential points of conflict recognized. For example, when the US companies Vocon and Conant Architects merged in 2013, the first hurdle was that Vocon saw itself as a 'fun' company and Conant's corporate identity was more traditional. One used paper cups for coffee, the other reusable mugs. While these may seem like insignificant details, they can affect how valuable employees feel in their working environment, and influence whether they decide to remain with the company.

E A second vital component is transparency: employees should be informed as soon as possible what the merged companies aim to achieve together and should be given the chance to ask questions throughout the process. Susan Austin, Chief Human Resources Officer at Vocon understood that employees would feel anxious about their job security and changes to their working environment. She took both organizations' company handbooks and noted key differences in order to explain to employees how things might change. The differences ranged from dress codes to systems of dealing with complaints, and other organizational issues. Austin realized that if people know what is going on, they are less likely to panic.

F The next part of the integration process is to bring employees of both companies together and to see each other as members of the same company. Most employees will not know each other beforehand and might feel insecure or suspicious of their new colleagues. Some companies instigate a 'buddy' programme to help people from both companies get to know each other on a personal level. Others organize company events or parties, or light-hearted interviews to help people bond.

G Once the integration stage is complete, Human Resources is responsible for a successful stabilization phase. Unsolved problems are addressed and employees from both former companies learn to work together as one team. For Vocon and Conant this has been a largely successful process and the two companies are still united. Daimler and Chrysler are still dealing with issues left behind from their divorce. As in love, not all corporate partnerships are successful, but putting time and effort into developing a carefully considered merger plan seems to pay off.

(718 words)

3 WORKING WITH WORDS

Find words or expressions in the text to match the following definitions.

1 Cheaper products aimed at people who are unable to or do not want to spend a lot of money.
2 The way in which employees and managers behave and interact with colleagues, clients and business partners.
3 The ways in which a company generates income and profit, and plans to grow in the future.
4 The knowledge that you are unlikely to lose your position in a company.
5 A big problem or difficulty which needs to be overcome.
6 The way a company portrays itself to the outside world, through factors such as building and office design, communication style, advertising, etc.

BUSINESS TOPICS 5

4 LOOKING AT THE TEXT
→ Rezeption: Leseverstehen, S. 214

A Match the questions to the paragraphs which contain the relevant information. There are two more questions than you need.

1. Why was the merger unsuccessful?
2. What can be done to reassure employees before and during a merger?
3. What can merging companies do to help things go more smoothly?
4. Who is to blame when mergers go wrong?
5. What happens during the final stage of a merger?
6. In what ways do the German and the American working cultures differ?
7. Why did the companies Daimler and Chrysler decide to merge?
8. How can new colleagues get to know each other better?
9. What can go wrong before companies merge?

B Answer the questions.

5 MEDIATION
→ Schriftliche Mediation, S. 240

Sie arbeiten für einen deutschen Zeitschriftenverlag, der im kommenden Jahr mit einem britischen Verlag fusioniert. Sie sind damit beauftragt, einen Leitfaden für die erfolgreiche Unternehmenszusammenführung zu konzipieren. Fassen Sie für die Einleitung des Leitfadens die wichtigen Informationen aus dem Text auf Deutsch zusammen. Übersetzen Sie dabei nicht Wort für Wort.

6 WRITING
→ Produktion: Schreiben, S. 228

Two managers from recently merged companies in Germany and Spain comment on the difficulties they have experienced. Choose one of the statements and write a brief response suggesting a solution to the problem.

"A high number of people in my department expressed concerns about cooperating with their new colleagues from Germany. Many of our employees felt that their German team members were standoffish and brushed off well-meaning attempts at small talk. There was a tangible sense of disappointment, and many were worried that the collegial atmosphere within our company would suffer."

Amalia Gómez Reina, Sevilla

"Some of my staff have pointed out that their new colleagues from Spain work less efficiently than expected. There have been occasions when Spanish co-workers have arrived late to meetings and then proceeded to initiate small talk rather than get down to business. Since time is money, my employees feel that such behaviour is disrespectful. It has also proven difficult to discuss problems, as the Spanish team members seem to be easily offended by criticism."

Dr. Jürgen Spitzmüller, Stuttgart

189

6 Corporate social responsibility

BUSINESS TOPICS

1 ANALYSING A CARTOON

→ Cartoons beschreiben und analysieren, S. 236

Individual people's understanding of what is ethical and what is not may differ. The same is true for different industries and businesses. In some companies employees make decisions based on their own sense of responsibility. Other companies develop codes of conduct as guidelines.

A What is your understanding of 'corporate social responsibility'? Is it the same as 'business ethics'? Study the cartoon and make notes.

B Write a short text describing the cartoon and commenting on its message.

2 BEFORE YOU READ

→ Rezeption: Leseverstehen - Grobverständnis, S. 214

Find a partner, then work on your own. Skim the text to answer the questions. Who is faster at spotting the information – you or your partner?

1. When was the concept of Corporate Social Responsibility first introduced?
2. How do companies look after their employees' health?
3. Who else do a company's CSR standards apply to?
4. What are examples of products that are bad for you?

Is corporate social responsibility good business?

The concept of Corporate Social Responsibility or CSR has existed since the 1960s and is becoming increasingly important. Consumers and shareholders have come to expect companies to show commitment to some form of social responsibility. Typical examples of CSR include supermarkets stocking locally sourced or fair trade products, clothing companies demonstrating that workers in
5 factories in the developing world are being treated fairly, or the use of sustainable materials in manufacturing. Some companies go one step further and become engaged in corporate philanthropy. This may take the form of making donations to local or international charities, supporting local youth,

or developing poverty-reduction or environmental
10 programmes. Both CSR and corporate philanthropy help companies to obtain social licence, i.e. informal public approval of the company and its actions; thus maintaining consumer and shareholder loyalty and profits.

Young people entering the job market are
15 increasingly demanding that employers demonstrate high ethical standards with respect not only to their employees but also to society as

a whole. This is mutually beneficial in the light of the concept of Creating Shared Value (CSV), by which companies look after their workers. CSV may include opportunities for exercise, providing nutritious food in the canteen, or contributing to employees' professional development through regular training and education. If done well, it improves the qualification, health and contentment of the staff. Additionally, CSV can manifest itself in the use of sustainable resources, ensuring the future supply of materials and economical value.

Through CSR, companies create their own standards of safety and environmental, social and ethical responsibility. These apply to entire logistics networks and require sustainable supply chain management at each stage of a product's life: from the factory floor to delivery companies taking goods to the end customer. If companies self-regulate, there is less need for governments to get involved. CSR helps companies to build good reputations and may discourage the authorities from looking more closely into the companies' less ethical behaviour. This is especially important for companies whose products are potentially 'harmful' to the public, such as alcohol, tobacco or junk food.

Companies that take CSR seriously also invest in risk management. Industrial accidents, environmental disasters and other corporate scandals can quickly damage the image of a company and undo any of the positive effects achieved through CSR and philanthropy. (386 words)

3 LOOKING AT THE TEXT

→ Rezeption: Leseverstehen, S. 214

A With a partner, talk about what the following words mean by looking at the way they are used in the text.

1 corporate philanthropy (line 6)
2 social licence (lines 10–11)
3 mutually beneficial (line 18)
4 Creating Shared Value (line 18)
5 supply chain management (lines 26–27)
6 to self-regulate (line 29)
7 risk management (line 36)

B Choose the correct statement (a, b or c) to complete the sentences about the text.

1 Consumers and shareholders increasingly expect companies to …
   a actively demonstrate that they care about society and the environment.
   b donate a share of their profits to charity.
   c offer the best price possible for their goods.

2 Through CSV, employers …
   a demonstrate that they really care about the people who work for them.
   b contribute to the community by improving the education and health of employees and their families.
   c keep their employees as happy and healthy as possible so that they retain or increase their value for the company.

3 An effective CSR campaign aims to …
   a discourage the government and other regulatory bodies from investigating the company's activities too closely.
   b encourage people to see companies as responsible members of society.
   c make a valuable and long-lasting contribution to the local and international community.

6 Corporate social responsibility

   4 CSR no longer protects a company's reputation if …
   - **a** they are not seen to be taking CSR seriously enough.
   - **b** the company is publically accused of unethical behaviour or damage to the environment.
   - **c** people get hurt while being involved in CSR-related social or environmental projects.

4 LOOKING AT THE INFOGRAPHIC

A Brainstorm one example of CSR for each of the areas shown in the infographic.

B Discuss your ideas with a partner. How many of your ideas are similar? How many are different? Choose the three ideas that you consider most important.

C Present your three most important ideas to the class. Do you know any companies that have such programmes?

5 RESEARCH AND PRESENTATION

Divide the class into six groups, one for each of the CSR areas shown in the infographic. In your group, research three examples of companies that invest in your area of CSR.

A Create a poster that includes the following information on each of the companies:

- **Key facts and figures:** area of business (sector, product(s), size and location(s))
- **Image:** slogans, buzz words and a representative picture
- **CSR:** What measures have been taken within your CSR area? Has there been any media or public response to these measures? Give brief details.
- **Criticism:** Have there been any scandals or industrial accidents? Have employees complained about unfair treatment? Give brief details.

B Hang the posters on the walls of your classroom. Which of the companies' CSR strategies do you find convincing? Which do not convince you? Make notes and discuss your impressions in class. Explain the reasons for your impression.

6 WRITING

→ Produktion: Eine Stellungnahme schreiben, S. 234

> "The only beneficiary of CSR is the company itself. It is a tool to attract idealistic employees and consumers who aim to spend money with a clear conscience. Meanwhile, the company's priorities remain the same: profits, profits, profits."

> "Society as a whole benefits from CSR. Combined with corporate philanthropy, it is helpful in addressing the negative effects of capitalism and cultivating sustainable business practices."

Choose the opinion that you find more convincing. Write a comment on why you agree with it.

7 Population, wealth and refugees

BUSINESS TOPICS

1 ACTIVITY

For this activity you need space to move around your classroom. Before starting, push all the tables to the walls. Line up the chairs at the sides of the room but keep them within reach.

A Take six sheets of paper and label them with the names of these continents: North America, Latin America/Caribbean, Europe, Africa, Asia and Australia/Oceania.

B Arrange the sheets on the floor of your classroom according to where the continents are located on the world map.

C Your class represents the population of the world. Form groups that correspond to the size of the different continents' populations. Stand on your continent's paper.

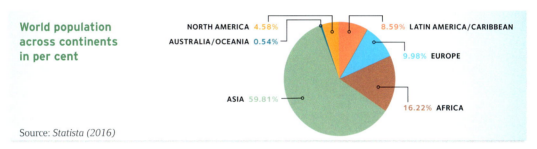

World population across continents in per cent

NORTH AMERICA 4.58%
AUSTRALIA/OCEANIA 0.54%
LATIN AMERICA/CARIBBEAN 8.59%
EUROPE 9.98%
AFRICA 16.22%
ASIA 59.81%

Source: *Statista (2016)*

D Use the chairs in your classroom as a representation of each continent's GDP*. Divide and distribute the chairs on your continents according to their GDPs.

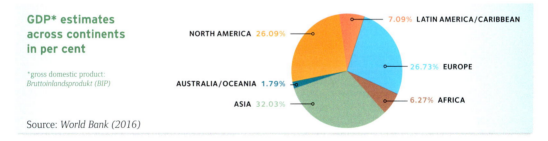

GDP* estimates across continents in per cent

*gross domestic product: Bruttoinlandsprodukt (BIP)

NORTH AMERICA 26.09%
LATIN AMERICA/CARIBBEAN 7.09%
EUROPE 26.73%
AFRICA 6.27%
ASIA 32.03%
AUSTRALIA/OCEANIA 1.79%

Source: *World Bank (2016)*

E Return to your continents and sit on the chairs. Make notes on the following aspects:
- Which continent(s) does not have enough chairs to seat its population?
- Which continent(s) has the exact number of chairs necessary?
- Which continent(s) has more chairs than necessary to seat its population?

F Form groups and distribute according to the number of refugees on each continent.

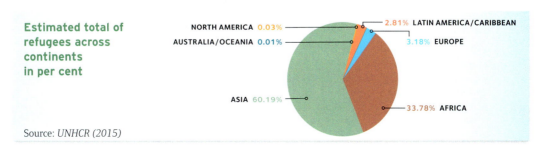

Estimated total of refugees across continents in per cent

NORTH AMERICA 0.03%
AUSTRALIA/OCEANIA 0.01%
LATIN AMERICA/CARIBBEAN 2.81%
EUROPE 3.18%
AFRICA 33.78%
ASIA 60.19%

Source: *UNHCR (2015)*

7 Population, wealth and refugees

2 THINK – PAIR – SHARE
→ Interaktion, S. 246

How did you feel throughout the activity? Discuss the questions below.

Think   What did you learn about the way in which population, wealth and refugees are spread around the world?
Pair   What are the reasons for the distribution of population, wealth and refugees?
Share   What could be done to improve the situation? Present your suggestions to the class.

Useful vocabulary for talking about population, wealth and refugees			
overpopulation	Überbevölkerung	hopelessness	Aussichtslosigkeit
depleting resources	schwindende Ressourcen	distribution of wealth/ resources	die Verteilung des Wohlstandes/der Ressourcen
famine	Hungersnot		
persecution	Verfolgung	capitalism	Kapitalismus
influx of refugees	der Zustrom von Flüchtlinge	divide between rich and poor	die Kluft zwischen Reich und Arm
asylum seekers	Asylbewerber	charity	Wohltätigkeits- organisation
shelter	Schutz, Obdach		
desperation	Verzweiflung	to flee	flüchten

3 BEFORE YOU READ
→ Rezeption: Leseverstehen – Grobverständnis, S. 214

In general, do refugees have a positive or negative effect on the economy of the countries taking them in? Skim the text to answer the question.

A prominent economist destroyed the argument against re-homing refugees across Europe

Refugees repay double the money countries spend taking them in, according to the former economic adviser to the president of the European Commission Philippe Legrain.

Europe is in the midst of the worst refugee crisis since World War II. Both politicians and the voting public are concerned that the cost of re-homing them will take a toll on the economy of the countries providing them with shelter. But Legrain said there are long-term economic benefits to the influx of refugees in the EU. Refugees can contribute economically in many ways: as workers of all skill levels, entrepreneurs, innovators, taxpayers, consumers and investors.

Their efforts can help create jobs, raise the productivity and wages of local workers, stimulate international trade and investment, and boost innovation, enterprise and growth. From a global perspective, enabling people to move to more technologically advanced, politically stable and secure countries boosts their economic opportunities and world output.

Some refugees do dirty, difficult, (relatively) dangerous and dull jobs that locals spurn, such as cleaning offices and caring for the elderly, which is the fastest area of employment growth in advanced economies. This enables locals to do higher-skilled and better-paid jobs that they prefer. The International Monetary Fund estimated that "additional spending in the EU on refugees will raise its GDP."

BUSINESS TOPICS 7

This is based on the assumption that all the refugees will join the workforce. Generally, countries with high birth rates or high immigration have higher economic growth, because those countries have a higher portion of younger workers receiving wages and paying taxes. Legrain said that "policymakers and practitioners should stop considering refugees as a 'burden' to be shared, but rather as an opportunity to be welcomed. With a suitable upfront investment and wise policies, welcoming refugees can yield substantial economic dividends." (305 words)

Abridged from: *www.businessinsider.de*

4 WORKING WITH WORDS

A Find equivalents of these phrases in the text.

1 to find alternative accommodation for
2 to return twice the amount of money you were given
3 to have a negative effect on
4 peaceful, unlikely to change dramatically
5 to get a job
6 spending money on a project before work begins
7 to bring significant financial benefits

B Match the words to their equivalents.

1 influx   a well-developed
2 to stimulate   b the arrival of a large amount of people
3 advanced   c to reject
4 to boost   d belief
5 to spurn   e salary
6 assumption   f to encourage the development of
7 wages   g to increase or improve

5 LOOKING AT THE TEXT → Rezeption: Leseverstehen, S. 214

Answer the following questions about the text in your own words.

1 How do refugees benefit workers in the countries they flee to?
2 In which field are employment opportunities growing the fastest in developed countries?
3 Why do economies grow more steadily in countries with a high influx of immigrants?
4 What is meant by the phrase "a 'burden' to be shared"? (line 30)

6 MEDIATION → Schriftliche Mediation, S. 240

Sie haben sich mit einem Freund unterhalten, der den Zustrom von Flüchtlingen nach Europa als bedenklich empfindet. Wenig später lesen Sie im Internet den obenstehenden Artikel und entschließen sich, Ihrem Freund eine E-Mail zu schreiben, in der Sie die wesentlichen Informationen des Textes auf Deutsch erklären. Übersetzen Sie nicht Wort für Wort.

8 | The future job market — BUSINESS TOPICS

BEFORE YOU READ

Think about the future job market. What sort of skills will be needed most in the next ten to twenty years? Which new jobs or fields of work might be created? Discuss with a partner.

JOBS FOR THE FUTURE

In less than ten years' time, people will be applying for jobs that don't exist today. There will be plenty of opportunities in new fields such as virtual reality and space travel. Robots will become increasingly important in the workplace and open up new career paths in areas which do not exist yet. Employees will need to develop a special range of skills and knowledge across different fields, to be ready for the
5 new demands of the future job market. Here are suggestions of what type of jobs you might be applying for in the future:

Space Tour Guide

Many people's childhood dream may soon come true when it becomes possible for ordinary people
10 to explore space. Companies are developing commercial spacecraft and are planning to offer space flights for tourists within the next ten years. A wide range of jobs will become available in this area, looking after the safety and comfort of
15 passengers. A guide would need the traditional skills of a tour guide: knowledge about the place they are in, the ability to lead groups of people and answer questions, as well as to handle complaints. A Space Tour Guide would have the added
20 challenge of issues such as weightlessness, and what to do in a medical or other emergency in space.

Human Body Designer

Advances in medical science and bio-engineering will make it possible to prolong human life. It will
25 become possible and affordable to replace human organs and other body parts. Human Body Designers will design customized body parts and make a big difference to the lives of people who, due to accident, injury or illness, used to have to live without certain body parts. There may also be a new market for people who want personalized body parts for fashion reasons.

Ethical Technology Advocate

Over the next decade, robots will begin to play a greater role in our lives. By 2018, there will already be over 55,000 new jobs in robotics. We will see robots working in a number of roles, doing office tasks, manual labour and working in customer services. An Ethical Technology Advocate will be responsible for creating moral and ethical rules for the use of robots in

196

companies. He or she will act as a kind of communicator or 'human interface' between humans, robots and artificial intelligence (AI). As robots and AI become increasingly sophisticated and can already decide, for example, whether or not to hurt a person, it is critically important to set strict international
40 guidelines for safety and ethical issues.

Personal Content Curator

There are a number of ways to store your personal electronic data, but what about your memories, thoughts and ideas? By the year 2020 software-brain interfaces, created by neuroscientists, may become mainstream. Ordinary people will be able to read and save thoughts, memories and dreams.
45 As with electronic data, the question arises of how best to store the information so that the most important data is available quickly, and particularly valuable memories are safely stored. A Personal Content Curator will help individuals and companies to create systems that organize this data, increase the storage capacity of their brains and give them instant access to important memories and thoughts.

(537 words)

1 WORKING WITH WORDS

Find the words or phrases in the text that match these definitions.

1 to offer different job opportunities (paragraph 1)
2 a vehicle used outside of the Earth's orbit (paragraph 2)
3 to modify something, especially to fit one person or task (paragraph 3)
4 working with your hands; physical work (paragraph 4)
5 a point at which different systems can meet and interact (paragraph 4)
6 general rules for doing something (paragraph 4)

2 LOOKING AT THE TEXT

→ Rezeption: Leseverstehen, S. 214

Which person is needed? Match the tasks to the jobs

1 My friend had an amazing dream last night and would like to experience it again.
2 An elderly piano player has painful hands and can't play the piano anymore.
3 A travel company wants to offer customized trips to people who have already been to most regions of the world.
4 A company plans to use robots to perform manual tasks, but has no experience with robotics.

3 PROJECT

→ Interaktion, S. 247

Divide your class into four groups, one for each job described in the text. You are Human Resources Managers looking for entry-level candidates and have arranged a meeting to design a suitable job advertisement for your company.

A Discuss and agree on the following:

- The name of your company and a brief description of what it does
- What skills, qualifications and personal qualities are expected of potential employees
- What your company has to offer potential employees in terms of salary, development opportunities and working environment

B Pin your adverts to the walls of your classroom. Walk around and read all the job offers.

8 The future job market

4 WRITING A COVER LETTER
→ Job skills 2: Cover letters, S. 76

Group one is now assigned the job advertisement created by group two – and vice versa. Group three is assigned the job advertisement written by group four – and vice versa. In your groups, consider the skills, qualifications and personal qualities requested in your job offer and write a cover letter for the advertised position. If there are more than three students in your group, split up into two smaller groups and write two different cover letters for the same position.

5 PREPARING FOR AN INTERVIEW
→ Job skills 2: Interviews, S. 78

You have been invited to an interview for the job opening that you applied for in exercise 4. In your groups, brainstorm the questions you might be asked during the interview. Prepare your answers and think of questions that you could ask the interviewers.

6 ROLE-PLAY
→ Job skills 2: Interview, S. 78   → Interaktion: Ein Rollenspiel gestalten, S. 247

A Read the cover letter(s) that you have received for your job advertisement from exercise 3. You are going to interview a candidate for the job. Brainstorm questions that you would like to ask.

B Group one will interview and be interviewed by group two. Group three will interview and be interviewed by group four. As interviewers, all members of your group participate in the role-play. As applicants, choose one group member who will play the candidate. The other member(s) take(s) the role of silent observer(s). In preparation for the interview, study your role-cards.

Role-card: Interviewers

The candidates may be nervous. Try to help them feel comfortable in the situation. Memorize the questions you would like to ask to avoid looking at your notes too often. Keep in mind the goal of the interview: to find out if the candidate is suitable.

Role-card: Applicants

Before the interview, re-read your cover letter and the job advert. Even if you feel nervous, try to look confident and to watch your body language. Make eye contact when answering questions. Ask questions at the end to show your interest in the company.

Role-card: Observers

During the interview, take notes on what is going well and what could be improved.
Are the interviewers' questions clear and relevant? Are the candidates' answers clear and relevant? Does their body language project confidence? Do they show interest in the company?

C Act out the interviews. At the end of each interview, the interviewers and applicant receive feedback from the observer(s). If your group has interviewed more than one applicant, decide which candidate is more suitable for the job. Give reasons for your choice.

7 EVALUATION

Share your experience of the job interviews with the class. What went well and what would you like to do differently next time?

9 Technological advances and cybercrime

BUSINESS TOPICS

BEFORE YOU READ

Take one minute to make notes on what you associate with Silicon Valley. Which companies are based there and what do you know about them? Share your associations with the class.

How Silicon Valley Shapes Our Future

Travis Kalanick, founder and CEO of Uber publicly insults the competition, mocks his own customers on Twitter and believes that politicians are incompetent. Uber is a good - no, a great - product. Essentially carpooling at the push of
5   a button, it is an extremely simple service and one whose implementation is technically brilliant and easy to use. But the company is a mirror image of its founder: aggressive, ruthless and overly ambitious.

After Portland, Oregon, banned the company from
10   operating in the city late last year, Kalanick launched the service there anyway. The head of the local bureau of transportation was furious. "They think they can just come in here and violate the law?" he asked. "Apparently they believe they're gods."

There has been similar resistance in many other cities around the world, including in Germany, where Uber ignored court orders. But Uber isn't the only company with ambitions of taking over the world.
15   That's how they all think: Google and Facebook, Apple and Airbnb – all the digital giants along with the myriad of smaller companies in their wake. Their goal is never a niche market; it's the entire world.

The technological advances made in the last decade have been breathtaking, but it is likely still just the beginning. Driverless cars were considered to be a crazy fantasy not
20   long ago, but today nobody is particularly amazed by them. All the world's knowledge condensed into a digital map and easily accessible? Normal. The fact that algorithms in the US control some 70 percent of all trading on the stock market? Crazy, to be sure. But normal craziness.

25   Dozens of companies are trying to figure out how to use drones for commercial use, be it for deliveries, data collection or other purposes. Huge armies of engineers are chasing after the holy grail of artificial intelligence. And the advances keep coming. Machines that can learn, intelligent robots: We have begun overtaking science fiction.

30   The phenomenon is still misunderstood, first and foremost by policymakers. It isn't about "the Internet" or "the social networks," nor is it about intelligence services and Edward Snowden or the question as to what Google is doing with our data. We are witnessing nothing less than a societal transformation that nobody will be able to avoid. The digital revolution isn't just altering specific sectors of the economy; it is changing the way we think and live.

35   The new global elite are no longer based on Wall Street. They have their headquarters in Silicon Valley, the 80-kilometer (50-mile) long valley south of San Francisco. They are founders and CEOs like Sergey Brin of Google, Tim Cook of Apple and Mark Zuckerberg of Facebook. They are more recent newcomers like Travis Kalanick of Uber and Joe Gebbia of Airbnb. And they are all supported by an army of programmers, computer experts and engineers who are constantly seeking to replace an old concept
40   with a new product.

199

9 Technological advances and cybercrime

They don't want to just determine what we consume, but how we consume it and how we live. They aren't trying to capture just one economic sector, but all of them. The religion of Wall Street is money. But the religion of Silicon Valley goes much deeper. The people from the valley believe that their high-tech solutions will create a better future for all of mankind. But they are not interested in external
45   interference. The Silicon Valley elite has little use for policymakers. Their message seems to be: If societal values such as privacy and data protection stand in the way, then we simply have to develop new values.

This much is certain: Over the coming years, we will have a global debate about what the framework for the digital future needs to look like. Those who wish to play a part in shaping the future
50   need to understand how Silicon Valley leaders view the world and what they want.   (654 words)

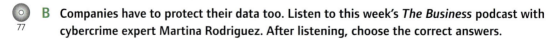

Abridged from: *www.spiegel.de*

1 WORKING WITH WORDS

Find English equivalents of these words and phrases.

1   jemanden verspotten
2   skrupellos
3   das Gesetz brechen
4   unzählige
5   komprimiert
6   etwas überholen
7   Entscheidungsträger/in
8   versuchen, etwas zu tun
9   Einmischung
10 So viel steht fest.

2 LOOKING AT THE TEXT
→ Rezeption: Leseverstehen, S. 214

Say whether the following statements are true (T), false (F) or not in the text (N). Correct the false sentences.

1   Uber was launched in Portland despite an official ban.
2   Uber wants to become the biggest private transport company in Germany.
3   The majority of the companies trading on the stock market produce algorithms.
4   It is becoming normal to use drones for deliveries and collecting data.
5   The digital revolution is making fundamental changes to the way governments rule countries.
6   The most powerful people in the world are based in the financial district of New York.
7   Privacy and data protection is the top priority for the Silicon Valley elite.

3 LISTENING
→ Rezeption: Hörverstehen, S. 225

A Do you do something to protect your personal data online? If so, what do you do? If not, what could you do? Discuss in class.

B Companies have to protect their data too. Listen to this week's *The Business* podcast with cybercrime expert Martina Rodriguez. After listening, choose the correct answers.

(77)

1   According to the presenter, who is particularly at risk from cybercrime?
    a   Large companies who employ a large number of people.
    b   Small companies which don't have enough resources to invest in sophisticated programs to protect electronic data.
    c   Self-employed people who use their computers both for work and privately.

200

BUSINESS TOPICS 9

2 Why should companies keep a record of who has access to which data?
   a If company data is stolen, it will make it easier to trace from where and how it was stolen.
   b To make sure that all passwords are changed once an employee leaves the company.
   c So that managers will know which employees they can talk to about which topics.

3 A 'need to know basis' means that …
   a a record should be kept of all employees' internet use at work.
   b certain data should only be accessible to employees who need it in order to do their job.
   c all company data can be available to all employees but there should be strict rules about not sharing information to people outside the company.

4 Why is it important for companies to have a secure wireless connection?
   a It prevents employees from using the internet at work for private purposes.
   b Companies often lose money when private people use their wireless networks.
   c It is not so easy for criminals to hack into the company system.

C Listen again and make a list of Martina's tips for companies.

4 DESCRIBING STATISTICS
→ Statistiken beschreiben, S. 238

In 2015, 1,074 German companies with ten or more employees took part in a survey that asked what types of computer crime they had already fallen victim to.

A How would you describe the chart? Practise with a partner.

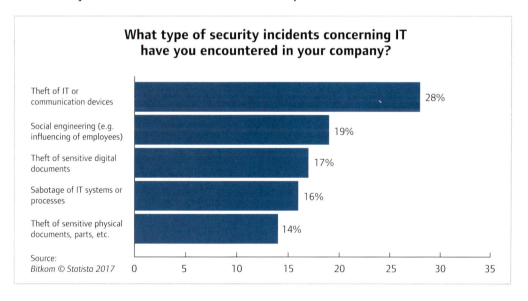

B What information surprises you the most? Discuss in class.

5 MEDIATION
→ Schriftliche Mediation, S. 240

Ihre Firma hat kürzlich einen neuen Mitarbeiter eingestellt. Als Teamleiter/in liegt es in Ihrer Verantwortung, Angestellte über Risiken und Vorschriften im Hinblick auf Datenschutz zu informieren. Bereiten Sie sich auf ein persönliches Gespräch vor, indem Sie die zentralen Informationen aus den Aufgaben 3 und 4 stichpunktartig ins Deutsche übertragen.

201

10 Crops, chemicals and genetic mutation

BUSINESS TOPICS

BEFORE YOU READ

A Study the word cloud. Can you guess what the text is about?

B Scan the text to check if you were right.

C What do you already know about the topic? Use words from the cloud to discuss in class.

A marriage of giants

In 2016, the German chemical and pharmaceutical company Bayer, which is best known for inventing aspirin, bid to take over the US agrochemical company Monsanto in a deal worth about $66 billion. Monsanto already has a monopoly over the seed and chemical market in the USA and, as a result, the deal would create the world's largest seeds and pesticides company. Due to two previous major deals in
5   the agriculture industry, the Bayer-Monsanto takeover would leave almost two-thirds of the world's seeds and pesticides production in the hand of only three companies.

Werner Bauman, chief executive of Bayer, believes that the merger has the potential to bring significant financial rewards for shareholders, and to benefit consumers and society as a whole. Amongst politicians, activists, regulators, scientists and farmers, however, the deal has encountered significant
10 opposition.

Bernie Sanders, the senator of Vermont who ran against Hillary Clinton in the race for the presidential nomination of the Democratic Party in 2016, has called for industry regulators to block the merger. Sanders has argued that takeovers of this type increase the profits of multinational corporations while raising prices for ordinary consumers. Many farmers in the USA, who are already seeing their farm
15 incomes decrease, are worried about the merger of their main agricultural suppliers, which could leave them relying on less than a handful of suppliers and vulnerable to price rises. Additionally, Monsanto's leaving the country may result in delays and complications in ordering vital farm supplies.

Monsanto has been subject to controversies over the years. A notable example was the company's development of 'Agent
20 Orange,' a potent herbicide used between 1961 and 1971 during the Vietnam War. The herbicide not only caused severe environmental effects, but provoked terrible illnesses and long-term health problems for the large number of Vietnamese men, women and children who came into contact with the
25 substance. Controversies similar to this have led to a widespread mistrust of the company.

Genetically modified (GM) seeds are currently banned in many EU countries and discouraged in Germany due to health and environmental concerns. Environmentalists are worried that
30 the merger of Bayer and Monsanto will force smaller seed suppliers off the market until farmers have little choice but to buy the corporation's GM seeds. The potential long-term health risks resulting from the consumption of genetically-modified food are still not known and there has been much public outcry over the sale of such products without clear labelling.

35 Hugh Grant, CEO of Monsanto, does not accept the criticism of his company. He defends GM crops as elementary to the necessary increase of food production in order to feed the rapidly growing world population. As global warming
40 decreases natural sources of water, Monsanto's seeds are modified to need less water to survive. Grant has criticized environmentalists for not considering these benefits and not recognizing the need for GM-based agriculture.   (478 words)

1 WORKING WITH WORDS

Match the underlined words in the text with these definitions.

1 Plants or animals whose genes have been manipulated to produce a certain characteristic.
2 Chemical or other substances used to destroy unwanted plants.
3 When two or more companies join together to become one business.
4 Exclusive control of a product or service on the market.
5 Chemical or other substances used to destroy insects which harm plants.
6 Organizations which check whether companies behave ethically and fairly.
7 Something produced by a plant so that more plants can grow.
8 People who have invested in a company and own (small) parts of it.
9 When one company takes control of another.
10 When an individual or a group of people are not protected.

2 LOOKING AT THE TEXT

→ Rezeption: Leseverstehen, S. 214
→ Produktion: Einen Text zusammenfassen, S. 229

A Make notes on the information provided about:

- the current seeds and pesticides market
- people who own shares in Bayer and/or Monsanto
- the current situation of many farmers in the USA
- GM seeds and the EU

B Compare your notes with a partner and add information that you may have overlooked. Use your notes to write a brief summary of the text.

3 RESEARCH

A Half of your class represents Bayer, the other half represents Monsanto. Research information online about your company including:

- When, where and by whom the company was founded
- The products offered by the company
- Major achievements of the company
- How the company is perceived by the general public
- Scandals the company has been involved in (if any)

B Share your information and collect it on a group poster. Present your poster to the class.

10 Crops, chemicals and genetic mutation

4 DEBATE

→ Interaktion: An Diskussionen teilnehmen, S. 246

You are preparing for a debate over the merger of Bayer and Monsanto. At the end of your debate, the Federal Trade Commission* has to come to a conclusion as to whether they recommend that the merger be prevented or not.

A Divide the class in half. Your teacher will choose two students from both groups to form a smaller, third group. The three groups represent:

Supporters of the merger	Opponents of the merger	Neutral participants
Your group consists of: - company representatives from Bayer and Monsanto - shareholders of the company - supportive consumers	**Your group consists of:** - environmentalists - farmers - opposing consumers	The four members in your group represent members of the Federal Trade Commission (FTC)* *(etwa: Bundeskartellamt in den USA)

B Within your groups, decide which members represent which interest group. Use the information researched on Bayer and Monsanto in exercise 3 to prepare your arguments for the debate. Also consider what arguments the opposite party may have and how you will react to them.
Members of the FTC decide on how to introduce and moderate the debate. Draft questions that you would like the other two parties to answer throughout the debate.

C The debate begins with an introduction by the members of the FTC. Supporters and opponents take turns to present their arguments and react to the points made by the opposite party. FTC members may ask questions and interrupt if members of either party go off topic. At the end of the debate, supporters and opponents both receive one minute to sum up their most important arguments and make a final statement.

D The FTC receives two minutes of discussion time to weigh up the arguments made by both parties and concludes the debate by giving a recommendation for or against the merger.

Useful vocabulary for discussing crops, chemicals and GM	
drought	Dürre
famine	Hungersnot
harvest	Ernte
livestock	Vieh
effect	Auswirkung
food security	Ernährungssicherung
genetic mutation	genetische Mutation
irreversible consequences	unumkehrbare Konsequenzen
to modify sth	etw modifizieren, verändern
medical research	medizinische Forschung
gene therapy	Gentherapie
overpopulation	Überbevölkerung

11 Sustainable agriculture

BUSINESS TOPICS

BEFORE YOU READ

Consider the following statement from the text below. Can you imagine in what ways food and agriculture will have to change? Discuss with a partner and share your ideas with the class.

> "Climate is changing. Food and agriculture must too."

Coming together to feed the world

By 2050, the world population is predicted to rise to almost 9 billion. The question of how to feed this increasing population in the light of diminishing natural resources presents a huge challenge. World Food Day, celebrated every year on the 16th October by organizations concerned with food security, such as the World Food Programme and International Fund for
5   Agricultural Development, aims to raise awareness of environmental and other issues creating and sustaining global poverty and hunger. Each year, World Food Day has a different theme. In 2016, the theme was 'Climate is changing. Food and agriculture must too', highlighting the effect of climate change on food production and the need to change the way countries think about and produce food.

10 Around 60% of people are predicted to live in cities within the next 15 years. As a result, sustainable urban agriculture will become just as important as small-scale rural farming in producing healthy and nutritious food for local populations. Urban farming
15 has to overcome challenges that differ from those surfacing in rural farming. Lack of space to grow crops and keep animals is a concern. Nonetheless, small-scale, sustainable urban farming is becoming more popular, and city dwellers around the world
20 are finding ways to grow crops and keep farm animals and bees in urban environments.

Food Field in Detroit is just one initiative which is making creative use of the urban environment to produce food. Noah Link and Alex Bryan wanted to offer residents an alternative to the corporate food system and turned the grounds of an abandoned school into
25 a farm. The farm is partly supplied by donated equipment and supported by local volunteers. Local people can choose what they want the farm to produce and have it delivered weekly to their homes. Produce from the farm is also sold at local markets and to restaurants. Food Field plans to expand the farm to include chicken coops for laying eggs, an aquaponics system and beekeeping.

30 The **Edible Garden Project**, based in the North Shore area near Vancouver, transforms urban spaces into edible landscapes. Rooftops, backyards, parks, school playgrounds and abandoned spaces in the area have all become gardens and places for the community to meet. The project also has a strong educational and social focus and teaches people of all ages and backgrounds to grow their own organic food. Local people are encouraged to use
35 extra space in their garden or backyard to produce food to share with people who are less well off. They also support people living in social housing and help them to create their own small gardens.

11 Sustainable agriculture

In the London district of Dalston, the **FARM:shop** includes aquaponic fish farming, an indoor allotment, a polytunnel, a rooftop chicken coop and a café. The aim is to show city dwellers that it is possible to produce food within limited space and to grow vegetables and raise fish in the most environmentally-friendly way possible. FARM:shop also contributes to the community, for example through participation in a six-month study into how indoor urban farming can help mental health patients. The study showed that patients' confidence and well-being significantly improved through being part of the project and caring for plants.

The popularity of sustainable gardening projects and urban farms is growing in various countries. Not only are people finding ways to provide sufficient nutrition for the future, but also learning about other benefits, such as improving mental health, bringing people together and teaching valuable skills.

(581 words)

1 LOOKING AT THE TEXT

→ Rezeption: Leseverstehen, S. 214

A Copy the table onto a sheet of paper. Complete it with information about the projects.

Name of project	Location	Urban space(s) used	Produce	Other projects
Food Field	…	…	…	…
…	…	Rooftops, backyards, schools, abandoned spaces	Organic food	…
…	…	…	…	Support for mental health patients

B Explain the underlined words and phrases in your own words. You can use a monolingual dictionary for help.

1 … in the light of <u>diminishing</u> natural resources (line 2)
2 … organizations concerned with <u>food security</u> … (lines 3–4)
3 … sustainable <u>urban</u> agriculture … (lines 11–12)
4 … small-scale <u>rural</u> farming … (line 13)
5 … and <u>city dwellers</u> around the world … (line 19)
6 <u>Produce</u> from the farm … (line 27)
7 … an <u>aquaponics</u> system and beekeeping. (lines 28–29)
8 … transforms urban spaces into <u>edible landscapes</u>. (lines 30–31)
9 … <u>abandoned</u> spaces in the area … (line 32)
10 … to share with people who are less <u>well off</u>. (lines 35–36)
11 … an indoor <u>allotment</u> … (lines 39–40)
12 … <u>mental health</u> patients (line 47)
13 … confidence and <u>well-being</u> … (line 48)

206

| | BUSINESS TOPICS | 11 |

2 LOOKING AT THE INFOGRAPHIC

Water is a limited natural resource and access to clean drinking water is not guaranteed for everyone, especially those living in desert areas in developing countries. Study the infographic, then do the tasks below.

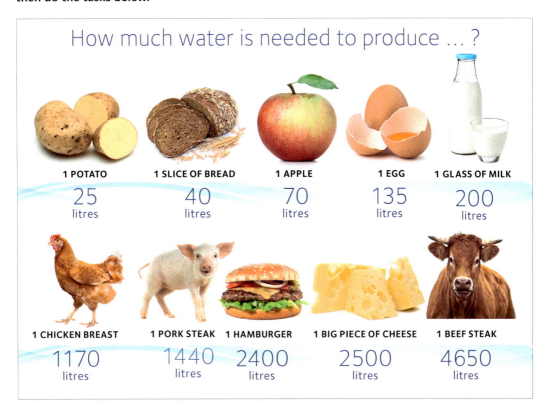

1. Calculate how much water you consume through food in one week.
2. Share the result with your class. Add up how much water your class consumes in one week.
3. How could you limit your consumption of water in everyday life? Share your ideas in class.
4. Which of these changes would you be willing to make? Adapt your calculation from Step 1 based on how you would change your eating habits.
5. Share the new result with your class. Add up how much water would be saved if all the students in your class changed their eating habits.

3 PROJECT

→ Interaktion, S. 246

Work in small groups to plan your own sustainable farming project. Discuss and agree on:

- The name and logo of your project
- The location of your project
- How your project will be financed
- What you will produce and how
- How you will advertise your project
- Which other local community projects or people you will help (if any)

Design a leaflet for your project and present it to the class.

12 Industrial Revolution 4.0

BUSINESS TOPICS

1 COMMENTING ON A CARTOON
→ Cartoons beschreiben und analysieren, S. 236

A Which statement refers to which cartoon?

1 "In time, smart technology will outsmart humans and turn into a threat."
2 "To trust smart gadgets over human knowledge and competence is naïve."
3 "Smart gadgets may be amusing, but the majority of them are useless."

"The patient handed me this 'wearable technology' and said 'all the answers are there'."

"And this wearable smartwatch sends a text to my wearable smartglasses to let me know when I'm not wearing any pants."

B Check your answers with a partner. Explain which of the viewpoints you agree with most.

2 BEFORE YOU READ
→ Rezeption: Leseverstehen – Grobverständnis, S. 214

The text names four industries which are expected to change dramatically due to technological advances. Can you guess which ones? Share your ideas with a partner, then skim the text to find out if you were right.

INDUSTRIAL REVOLUTION 4.0

Technology is evolving fast. Those of us who own a computer or a smartphone know that by the time we have bought a new device, it will already be out of date. And it is not just the IT world which is evolving rapidly, other industries are also radically changing the way we live, sleep, shop and travel.

5 The home automation or 'smart' home industry is expanding rapidly in the areas of security, safety and energy saving. Companies are investing billions in environmentally-friendly solutions designed to reduce dependence on energy and keep more money in consumers' pockets. Some of the latest developments
10 include wireless video surveillance devices, customized home lighting, smart locks and a range of energy-efficient home appliances. Much of the technological infrastructure in this industry already exists, the challenge is getting consumers to adopt the new technology, pick devices which best suit their needs,
15 and for companies to make sure that they work and interact with each other seamlessly.

Despite not sounding like a particularly young and energetic field, the sleep industry is developing fast. Much investment and innovation goes into making sure that people enjoy a good night's sleep. Technology is set to play an even larger role in 'sleep optimization' over the next ten years. Look out for a number of new gadgets coming onto the market, from mobile phone apps to personalized mattresses and trackers to monitor your sleep patterns.

E-commerce has become established in the retail industry, but companies continue to develop new ways of expanding the concept. 'Click and collect', in which customers place and order online and pick it up at the store has become popular among shoppers, especially at large retail stores. One company, Nordstrom, has taken this one step further and has invented a system in which customers don't even need to go into the store. The customer calls or texts Nordstrom when they are near the store and an employee brings their purchases to them when they arrive, eliminating the need to get out of the car.

Mobile phones are playing an increasingly important role in the travel industry. Many travellers are already used to searching for and booking flights on their phones, as well as using the device as a boarding pass, removing the need to print anything. In Australia research is being done into the possibility of producing biometric cloud passports, in which users swipe their finger across a scanner to identify themselves, making it unnecessary to travel with an actual physical document. The technology that would make such a process possible already exists, the hurdle is to convince passengers and authorities to take the technology on board and to implement a global system of paperless passports.

(460 words)

3 WORKING WITH WORDS

Match the words to their definitions.

1 to evolve
2 device
3 surveillance
4 to customize
5 home appliance
6 seamlessly
7 retail
8 to expand
9 to swipe
10 hurdle

a a machine used for household tasks
b to move your finger across a screen
c to become bigger, to increase in size or volume
d a piece of electronic equipment
e the sale of products to consumers
f close observation
g to adapt something to personal expectations
h a problem, difficulty
i to develop and change
j smoothly and continuously, without problems

4 LOOKING AT THE TEXT

→ Rezeption: Leseverstehen, S. 214

Decide if these statements are true (T), false (F) or not in the text (N). Correct the false statements.

1 Many new devices are already out of date when we buy them.
2 Companies are making devices that are not as damaging to the environment, but are costlier for consumers.
3 The technological infrastructure to manufacture necessary devices for a smart home already exists, but no products have been released onto the market yet.
4 The sleep industry is an important market for new, smart technological inventions.
5 Nordstrom staff bring goods from their store to customers' cars.
6 Paperless passports already exist in Australia.
7 To create a system of paperless passports, authorities from different countries would have to come together and agree on a plan of action.

12 Industrial Revolution 4.0

5 BRAINSTORMING AND PRESENTATION
→ Präsentieren, S. 243

Divide the class into four groups, one for each industry mentioned in the text. You are product designers and have been asked to come up with a new product (or a new design for an existing product) to present at a technology innovation trade fair. Think about the following aspects:

- Which target group your product is aimed at (families, teenagers, children, etc.)
- Why people will want your product and how they will use it
- The name and design of your product (if possible, make a sketch)
- How much your product will cost and where it will be sold

Present your product at the trade fair. During the other groups' presentations, take notes on what you like about their products. Afterwards, decide which of the products you would most like to own, and carry out a quick class vote. (Do not vote for your own group's product!)

6 MEDIATION
→ Schriftliche Mediation: Vorbereitung, S. 240

You are preparing for a discussion on 'smart schools'. You have found this German article online and want to present its arguments during the discussion. Mediate relevant pieces of information into English. Do not translate word for word.

Schule in Deutschland: smart aber unfair?

Fünf Wochen nach Ankündigung ihres Digitalpakts hat Bildungsministerin Wanka auf dem nationalen IT-Gipfel Taten folgen lassen. In Saarbrücken eröffnete sie Deutschlands erste „Smart School" mit digitalem Unterricht in allen Fächern - den Prototypen für den Wandel, der alle Schulen erfassen soll.

Fünf Wochen sollten auch lang genug gewesen sein, um nachzurechnen: Wankas fünf Milliarden schwerer Digitalpakt, verteilt auf 40 000 Schulen, das macht jeweils 125 000 Euro. Angesichts von Laptop- und Smartphone-Preisen ist das knauserig.

Es kommt also nicht von ungefähr, wenn Bayerns Bildungsminister Ludwig Spaenle nun fordert: „Bring your own device". Gemeint ist, dass Schüler im Unterricht ihre eigenen Geräte nutzen sollen - weil es sich kein Land leisten kann, alle mit der nötigen Technik zu versorgen. Nur, ist die Konfusion damit nicht programmiert? Wer soll das Wirrwarr von Hard- und Software beherrschen, wenn Schulen mit 800 Schülern gerade mal einen halben IT-Experten haben?

Schlimmer noch: Der Vorschlag bringt Ungleichheit in die Schule. Denn der Wetteifer unter Schülern, wenn es um Marken, Design und Kostspieligkeit geht, macht vor dem Smartphone nicht halt, im Gegenteil. Ja, pauschale Handyverbote in der Schule sind von gestern. Das pauschale Gegenteil aber auch. Für digitale Lernmedien sollte die digitale Schule sorgen. So viel Fairness muss sein.

(202 words)

Abridged from: *www.sueddeutsche.de*

7 DISCUSSION
→ Interaktion, S. 246

Take a moment to think about the questions and make notes. Discuss in small groups.

A Do you agree that asking students to bring their own devices to school is unfair?

B What role do you think digital learning media should have in school education?

APPENDIX

Page

212	Files
214	Skills files (plus extra exercises)
249	Grammar files (plus extra exercises)
275	Unit word list
319	A–Z word list
346	Geographical names
348	Irregular verbs
349	Quellenverzeichnis

Files

Unit 6, Text A, Exercise 4 → Page 48

1 Fun tram tickets

Problem: Lots of people don't pay for tickets when they travel on public transport.
Current solution: Spend a lot of money on ticket inspectors who fine people without tickets.
Fun solution: Make it fun to buy a ticket: when you stamp it, you could win an instant lottery!

2 The speed camera lottery

Problem: People break the speed limit.
Current solution: Fine people who break the speed limit.
Fun solution: Reward people for keeping to the speed limit. Use the money from the fines.

3 Wiki traffic lights

Problem: Motorists jump red lights.
Current solution: Fine motorists who do this or take away their driving licence, or both.
Fun solution: Make it interesting to wait at traffic lights by answering general knowledge questions.

4 Pinball exercise machine

Problem: Neither young nor old people exercise enough.
Current solution: No solution.
Fun solution: Combine a step machine and a pinball machine to make exercising at the bus stop fun.

Unit 11, Text B, Exercise 5B → Page 107

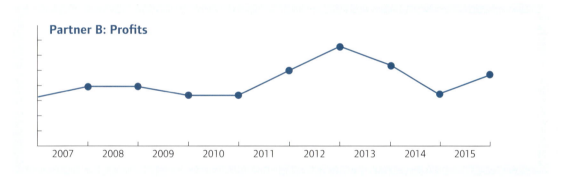

Skills files

Diese *Skills files* helfen Ihnen, Ihre Sprachfertigkeiten zu trainieren, damit Sie Erfolg in der Prüfung haben. Wenn Sie sich regelmäßig mit dem Lernprozess beschäftigen (mit den *Building skills boxes* und *Skills checklists* in den Units und den Materialien hier), fällt Ihnen der Umgang mit der englischen Sprache jeden Tag leichter. Hier gehen Sie Schritt für Schritt durch verschiedene Aufgabentypen und bekommen viele hilfreiche Tipps, wie Sie Ihre Fähigkeiten verbessern können. Um Ihre Kenntnisse zu festigen, gibt es auch Übungen zu den verschiedenen Strategien. Lösungen zu diesen Aufgaben finden Sie auf www.cornelsen.de/webcodes: Geben Sie einfach den Webcode FOSSKLO im Webcode-Suchfeld ein. Transkripte und Audio-Dateien finden Sie auch auf dieser Webseite durch Eingabe der Webcodes, die bei den entsprechenden Übungen stehen.

Lösungen → Webcode: FOSSKLO

1 REZEPTION: LESEVERSTEHEN

A Vorbereitung auf das Lesen (Vorhersage / *prediction*)

Eine Vorhersage bedeutet, dass Sie versuchen, den Inhalt des Textes zu erraten, bevor Sie ihn lesen. Wenn Sie sich hierzu Zeit nehmen, bevor Sie mit dem Lesen des Textes bzw. dem Beantworten der Fragen beginnen, können Sie den Text besser verstehen und Sie stellen sicher, die Aufgaben richtig zu lösen.

- Lesen Sie die Fragen und finden Sie heraus, was Sie tun sollen.
- Sehen Sie sich den Aufbau des Textes genau an und lesen Sie die Überschrift und Unterzeile bzw. die Einleitung, wenn es eine gibt. Das sollte Ihnen Hinweise liefern, worum es in dem Text geht.
- Sehen Sie sich die dazugehörigen Bilder bzw. Zeichnungen an und lesen Sie deren Unterschriften. Dies wird Ihnen helfen, sich vom Text „ein Bild zu machen".

B Grobverständnis (Sinn erfassen / *reading for gist / skimming*)

Lesen, um den Sinn zu erfassen oder einen Text überfliegen bedeutet, die wichtigsten Punkte schnell zu lesen. Nachdem Sie sich Gedanken dazu gemacht haben, wovon der Text handeln könnte (Vorhersage, s.o.):

- Lesen Sie den ersten Satz jeden Absatzes (und den letzten Satz, wenn der Absatz lang ist), denn dort können Sie häufig das Wesentliche des Textes entnehmen.
- Konzentrieren Sie sich auf die Schlüsselwörter, die Ihnen den Sinn des Textes vermitteln, z. B. Nomen, Verben und (häufig) die dazugehörigen Adjektive und Adverbien. Wörter, die unterstrichen bzw. fett gedruckt oder kursiv gestellt sind, sind i.d.R. wichtig.
- Überspringen Sie jene Wörter, die Sie nicht verstehen. Bleiben Sie ruhig! Meist wird die Bedeutung dieser Wörter aus dem Zusammenhang heraus klar, und manchmal taucht etwas später ein Synonym auf. Zum Schluss finden Sie wahrscheinlich heraus, dass Sie den Text verstehen, ohne diese Wörter zu kennen.
- Lesen Sie den ganzen letzten Absatz, da dieser häufig eine Zusammenfassung des Textes darstellt.

Üblicherweise folgen Prüfungstexte, die zum Überfliegen gedacht sind, einer klaren Struktur. Argumente und Beweise werden logisch präsentiert und wichtige Punkte werden häufig in der Zusammenfassung wiederholt.

Rezeption: Leseverstehen

Übung 1 (Fertigkeiten 1A und 1B)

A Bevor Sie die Fragen beantworten, sehen Sie sich den Textaufbau und das dazugehörige Foto genau an, und wählen Sie dann das beste Ende aus, um den folgenden Satz zu vervollständigen.

Prediction: The text is about …
- **a** cycling versus walking as a free-time activity.
- **b** accidents involving cyclists and walkers who are not paying attention.
- **c** what happens when people walk on the road instead of on the pavement.

B Überfliegen Sie den Text und wählen Sie die passendste Antwort zu den folgenden Fragen aus.

1. What is the biggest danger for people cycling in the city?
   - **a** busy traffic
   - **b** listening to music while cycling
   - **c** people listening to iPods while walking

2. What can happen as a result?
   - **a** people get hurt
   - **b** bicycles are destroyed
   - **c** walkers and cyclists have arguments

C Beantworten Sie die restlichen Fragen zum Text in Ihren eigenen Worten.

1. When did the problem start?
2. What happened last year?
3. What do cyclists and pedestrians needs to do to change things?

Pedestrians are the great menace to cyclists

What do you think would be the greatest menace to cyclists riding around the roads of a busy city? Lorries, motorbikes, bendy buses, perhaps? Not in my experience. For me, arguably the biggest danger – and without doubt, the biggest irritation –
5 are pedestrians, who, since the proliferation of the iPod, are more likely than any other moving object inadvertently to place themselves directly in my path while I'm cycling, forcing me either to brake suddenly or to swerve out into the traffic – both of which could end up in a nasty accident.

People wearing headphones do not take care when crossing roads

10 (…) Since the propagation of digital music players, an increasing number of people walk around in a complete daze – stepping into cycle lanes, walking out from behind stationary vehicles and crossing roads without so much as a turn of the head, to check if something is coming.

(…) Collisions between bikes and pedestrians can be fatal. Last year, for example, a teenager was
15 killed in Buckingham when a cyclist crashed into her. By all accounts, the cyclist was at fault, and should certainly have slowed down, rather than simply shouting at the girl to get out of his way. Nevertheless, it shows the damage a bike can do in a collision with a pedestrian.

I understand that many cyclists are not very considerate on the roads, and that many pedestrians feel intimidated by cyclists who badger them off a crossing even when they've got a green man.
20 My golden rule of the road is that everyone should give way to whoever has priority at the time.

(…) Pedestrians need to look where they're going and pay a little more respect to cyclists. I just hope it doesn't take more fatal collisions for this message to start getting through.   (289 words)

Abridged from: *www.independent.co.uk*

Skills files

C Mit unbekannten Wörtern umgehen → Vokabeln lernen, S. 220

Wenn Sie während des Lesens einem Wort begegnen, das Sie nicht kennen, sollten Sie sich fragen, ob es notwendig ist, das Wort zu verstehen, um den Text zu verstehen und die Fragen zu beantworten. Wenn Sie das Wort tatsächlich benötigen, versuchen Sie, bevor Sie nach dem Wörterbuch greifen (bzw. online nachschlagen), die Bedeutung des Wortes selbst herauszufinden. Manchmal verstehen Sie die Bedeutung eines Wortes, ohne es bewusst zu „kennen". Wenn dem nicht so ist, nutzen Sie folgende Strategien:

- Erarbeiten Sie es sich aus dem Zusammenhang heraus. Sehen Sie sich genau an, wie das Wort im Satz benutzt wird und wie es mit dem Inhalt dieser Textstelle zusammenhängt.
- Nutzen Sie Ihr Wissen über die deutsche Sprache. Viele englische Wörter haben ähnliche deutsche Entsprechungen bzw. stammen sie von derselben Wurzel ab, z. B.: *ten*/zehn, *light*/Licht, *night*/Nacht, *biology*/Biologie, *democracy*/Demokratie.
- Bringen Sie mehr über Wortbildung in Erfahrung (wie man Wörter aus anderen Wörtern bilden kann):

Vorsilben (*Prefixes*)
Vorsilben können die Bedeutung eines Wortes verändern.

anti-	'against'	clockwise → anticlockwise
co-	'together'	operate → co-operate
inter-	'between'	national → international
sub-	'under' / 'below'	standard → substandard
super-	'above' / 'over'	power → superpower
trans-	'across'	form → transform
dis-		agree → disagree
in-		correct → incorrect
im-	'not' / 'opposite'	possible → impossible
ir-		responsible → irresponsible
un-		friendly → unfriendly
mis-	'not correctly'	understand → misunderstand
re-	'again'	discover → rediscover

Nachsilben (*Suffixes*)
Nachsilben können die Wortart eines Wortes verändern.

Verbs → nouns

Verb	Suffix	Noun
organize	-ation	organization
express	-ion	expression
bake	-er	baker
begin	-ing	beginning
argue	-ment	argument

Nouns → adjectives

Noun	Suffix	Adjective
continent	-al	continental
beauty	-ful	beautiful
day	-ly	daily
hunger	-ry	hungry

Rezeption: Leseverstehen

Verbs → adjectives

Verb	Suffix	Adjective
advise	-able	advisable
rain	-y	rainy
care	-ing	caring

Adjectives → nouns

Adjective	Suffix	Noun
stupid	-ity	stupidity
happy	-ness	happiness

Adjectives → adverbs

Adjective	Suffix	Noun
awful	-ly	awfully
democratic	-ally	democratically

Übung 2 (Fertigkeit 1C)

Lesen Sie den ersten Absatz des Textes *Pedestrians are the great menace to cyclists* auf S. 215 noch einmal und suchen Sie die Wörter aus der u. s. Tabelle heraus. Schreiben Sie die Tabelle ab und notieren Sie, wie Sie die Wörter verstehen können, d. h. ähnliche Wörter auf Deutsch, Wortbildung, Zusammenhang. Drei der Wörter sind als Beispiele gegeben.

Words I can recognize without using my dictionary	How I know these words in this text	Word class in text	Definition	German
bendy (line 3)	word formation – verb "to bend" made into an adjective by adding -y	adjective	flexible	*biegsam*
pedestrians (line 5)				
cycling (line 7)	word formation – cycle → *gerund*	verb (present progressive form of *to cycle*)	to ride a bicycle	*Rad fahren*
brake (line 8)	from context: accident	verb	to make sth go slower	*bremsen*
swerve (line 8)				
nasty (line 9)				

D Ein Wörterbuch benutzen

→ Vokabeln lernen, S. 220

Ein Wörterbuch ist ein hilfreiches Werkzeug. Es hilft Ihnen, einen Text zu verstehen und Ihr Vokabular zu erweitern. Unabhängig von der Art des Wörterbuchs, das Sie nutzen – zwei- oder einsprachig –, ist Folgendes zu beachten:

- Stellen Sie sicher, dass Ihr Wörterbuch aktuell ist. Sprachen entwickeln sich sehr schnell, also sehen Sie im Impressum nach, ob es sich um eine „überarbeitete Auflage" (*updated version*) handelt.
- Lassen Sie bei Online-Wörterbüchern Vorsicht walten. Wörter haben in verschiedenen Zusammenhängen verschiedene Bedeutungen und Computer sind nicht schlau genug, um zu erfassen, welchen Zusammenhang Sie brauchen.
- Wählen Sie nicht die erstbeste Bedeutung aus, sondern lesen Sie alle Definitionen und überprüfen Sie sie ein zweites Mal, indem Sie die neu gefundenen Wörter nachschlagen.

Skills files

- Stellen Sie sicher, dass Sie nach der richtigen Wortart suchen (Verb, Nomen, Adjektiv, Adverb).
- Vergewissern Sie sich, den Aufbau einer Seite eines Wörterbuchs verstanden zu haben. Ganz oben auf jeder Seite eines Wörterbuchs sehen Sie das erste Wort bzw. den ersten Satz sowie das letzte Wort bzw. den letzten Satz, das/der auf dieser Seite ausgeführt wird. Solange Sie das Alphabet beherrschen, werden Ihnen diese zwei Wörter helfen, das gesuchte Wort schnell zu finden.

Bevor Sie mit Ihrem Wörterbuch zu arbeiten beginnen:
- Lesen Sie die Inhaltsübersicht, um herauszufinden, was Ihr Wörterbuch neben Definitionen noch alles zu bieten hat. Lesen Sie die Nutzungshinweise sorgfältig durch – sie sind wichtig.
- Sehen Sie sich die Liste der Abkürzungen und Symbole sowie die Legende zur Verbbildung an und stellen Sie sicher, dass Sie deren Bedeutungen verstehen.
- Vergewissern Sie sich, dass Sie über Grundkenntnisse der Grammatiktermini verfügen. Wenn Sie die Bedeutung eines Adverbs nicht kennen, wird es Ihnen kaum helfen, ein Adverb nachzuschlagen.

Nutzen Sie ein Wörterbuch, um:
- **mit einem Text zu arbeiten.** Wenn Sie nach Anwendung aller Ihrer Fertigkeiten unbekannte Wörter immer noch nicht verstehen, schlagen Sie sie nach.
- **Ihr Vokabular zu erweitern.** Wenn Sie ein Ihnen unbekanntes Wort nachschlagen, nehmen Sie sich die Zeit, auch verwandte Wörter nachzuschlagen und eine Liste mit Wortfamilien anzulegen.
- *Idioms*/Redensarten zu erlernen. In einer Redensart wird ein Wort in einem feststehenden Satz verwendet und ist seiner eigentlichen Bedeutung nur entfernt ähnlich, z. B.: „to get the wrong end of the stick". Wenn Sie wissen, was „the wrong end" und „stick" bedeuten, verstehen Sie möglicherweise immer noch nicht den vollständigen Satz (etwas in den falschen Hals bekommen).

Übung 3 (Fertigkeit 1D)

A Sie üben jetzt, Wörter in Ihrem zweisprachigen Wörterbuch zu finden.

1. You have been asked to mediate the following information to a tourist travelling in Germany. Use your bilingual dictionary to find the correct English expressions for the German word *Zug*.

> *Als Tourist in Deutschland reist man am bequemsten per Zug[1]. Im Zug[2] und in Bahnhöfen ist das Rauchen verboten. Falls Sie also Raucher sind, so denken Sie daran, dass schon ein einziger Zug[3] von einer Zigarette zu Problemen führen kann. Außerdem ist es ein typischer Zug[4] vieler Mitreisender, sich bei so etwas schnell zu beschweren. Und: Achten Sie darauf, im Zug[5] nicht in einem Zug[6] zu sitzen, sonst kriegen Sie einen steifen Hals!*

2. Now look up words in the text that you do not know and write them down. → Vokabeln lernen, S. 220

B Sie lernen nun Ihr einsprachiges Wörterbuch kennen und üben den Umgang mit ihm, indem Sie zwei Wörter des ersten Absatzes des Textes *Pedestrians are the great menace to cyclists*, S. 215, nachschlagen.

Rezeption: Leseverstehen

1 Read the dictionary entries and match the numbered sections to the definitions below.

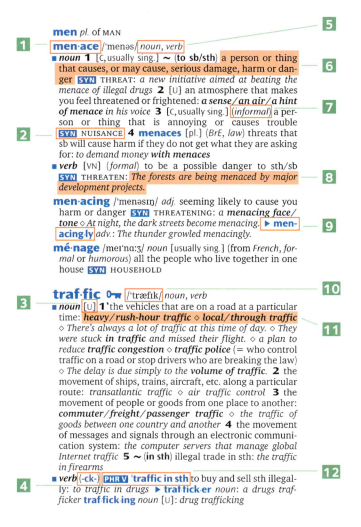

A Collocations: words that are often used with the headword
B Definition: meaning of the word, usually with an example sentence
C Derivatives: words from the same word family
D Example sentence
E Forms: unusual plurals, participles or gerunds
F Grammatical information
G Headword: correct spelling and hyphenation (*Silbentrennung*)
H Phrasal verbs or idioms
I Pronunciation: sound of word (*Aussprache*); stress (*Betonung*)
J Register: formal, informal, slang, etc.
K Synonyms: words of similar meaning
L Word class: noun, verb, adjective, etc.

2 Answer these questions using the two dictionary entries.

1 What is a synonym for "menace" as it is used in the text?
2 Which three collocations are given for "menace"?
3 What is a synonym for the verb form of "menace"?
4 What are the adjective and adverb forms of "menace"?
5 Which two word classes (parts of speech) can "traffic" be?
6 How many collocations using the word "traffic" can you find in the dictionary entry? Here are three collocations to get you started: *heavy/rush-hour traffic*; *to be stuck in traffic*
7 What else can you use the noun "traffic" to talk about apart from road vehicles and the transport of people or goods?
8 List the nouns that go with the verb phrase "to traffic in sth".

3 Practise using a dictionary by looking up three words in the text that you still need to know.

Skills files

E Vokabeln lernen → Ein Wörterbuch benutzen, S. 217

Das richtige Erlernen und Benutzen von Wörtern einer Fremdsprache macht Spaß, ist aber zeitaufwendig. Es gibt viele Arten, Vokabeln zu lernen. Sie können dies mithilfe von *Focus on Success* tun und diese Art des Lernens mit englischen Lese- und Hörverständnisübungen außerhalb des Unterrichts ergänzen. Es gibt natürlich auch eine Vielzahl von Onlineprogrammen und -spielen, um Vokabeln zu lernen, doch sie sind nicht so effektiv wie die Lernmethoden, die Sie sich selbst erarbeiten.

Listen und Zettel

- **Vokabellisten (nicht nur in einem Buch)**
  Vokabellisten, die in einem Notizbuch eingetragen werden, stellen einen leichten Weg dar, neue Wörter während des Unterrichts festzuhalten. Zuhause können Sie weitere Listen erstellen, z. B. von Lebensmitteln, die im Kühlschrank aufbewahrt werden, oder Sie schreiben Ihre Einkaufsliste auf Englisch oder Sie listen die Kleidungsstücke in Ihrem Kleiderschrank auf, nach Art, Farbe und Material sortiert.

- **Lernkarten**
  Schreiben Sie die Wörter, die Sie gern lernen möchten, auf Karteikarten. Schreiben Sie das englische Wort auf die eine Seite und die Übersetzung auf die andere. Fügen Sie eine Definition bzw. einen Beispielsatz auf Englisch unter die deutsche Übersetzung hinzu.

- **Klebezettel**
  Schreiben Sie die Bezeichnung eines Gegenstandes auf einen Notizzettel und kleben Sie ihn an den Gegenstand. Sie können nach Belieben Adjektive hinzufügen, z. B. *pretty picture, dirty laundry*.

Wortgitter und Wortgruppen

Während Ihrer Arbeit mit *Focus on Success* füllen Sie viele Wortgitter mit Wortfamilien aus. In den meisten Fällen werden Sie aufgefordert, ein Wortgitter mit unterschiedlichen Wortarten zu vervollständigen.

Noun	Verb	Adjective
enjoyment	enjoy	enjoyable
entertainment	entertain	entertaining

Wenn Sie sich auf eine Prüfung vorbereiten, können Sie Ihre Wortfamiliengitter um weitere Informationen verändern und ergänzen, z. B. indem Sie Sätze hinzufügen, in denen die Wörter im Kontext benutzt werden.

Word	Part of speech	Opposite	Synonym	Word in context
large	adjective	small	big	My mum comes from a large family. She has six sisters.
producer	noun	destroyer	manufacturer	Japan is a major producer of cars.

Verknüpfungen herstellen

- **Wortgabeln**

    Wortgabeln eignen sich gut zum Erlernen von Adjektiven und Verben.

delicious			find	
quick			have	
home-made	meal		make	friends
lovely			meet	
tasty			visit	

- **Mindmaps**

    Sie können Mindmaps zum Sammeln und Verknüpfen von Vokabeln wie auch von Ideen benutzen, um sich für eine Präsentation vorzubereiten oder einen Aufsatz und andere Schriftsätze zu planen. Der Vorteil von Mindmaps ist, dass Sie sie in jede beliebige Richtung ergänzen und erweitern können. Heben Sie bestimmte Aspekte farblich hervor. Wenn Sie eine Mindmap erstellen, vergleichen Sie Ihre mit der eines Mitstreiters / einer Mitstreiterin, der/die dasselbe Thema dargestellt hat. Es ist wahrscheinlich, dass Sie beide weitere Wörter zu Ihren Mindmaps hinzufügen können.

Gute Gewohnheiten entwickeln

- Lernen Sie Ihre Vokabeln regelmäßig und lernen Sie nie zu viel auf einmal. 20 Minuten jeden Tag sind besser als zwei Stunden pro Woche.
- Entscheiden Sie, wie häufig Sie wiederholen. Der Morgen vor der Prüfung ist nicht der effektivste Zeitpunkt. Wenn Sie Vokabeln regelmäßig das ganze Jahr hindurch wiederholen, brauchen Sie kurz vor der Prüfung nicht in Panik zu geraten.
- Ebenso wichtig ist, wo Sie lernen. Sie brauchen einen bequemen Ort mit ausreichend Licht. Es hilft auch, nicht von anderen Personen bzw. Lärm abgelenkt zu werden.
- Zu guter Letzt gehen Sie mit Ihren Lernhilfen sorgsam und ordentlich um.

F Scannen nach Einzelinformationen im Text (*reading for information / scanning*)

Beim Überfliegen eines Textes geht es um das schnelle Finden von bestimmten Informationen. In Texten wie Stellenanzeigen oder Infobroschüren müssen Sie bestimmte Informationen schnell herausfinden. Sie müssen den Text nicht in aller Tiefe lesen, doch Sie müssen sich den gesamten Text ansehen. Hierzu wenden Sie folgende Strategien an:

- Lesen Sie die Aufgaben und Fragen sorgfältig durch und stellen Sie sicher, dass Sie verstehen, was zu tun ist.
- Lesen Sie den Text schnell durch und halten Sie an, wenn Sie ein Schlüsselwort gefunden haben. Informationen zu Fragen zu Eigennamen, Zahlen, Ziffern und Geldbeträgen sollten relativ leicht zu finden sein. (Halten Sie nach Großbuchstaben, Prozentzeichen, Währungsangaben, usw. Ausschau.) Wenn Sie ein Schlüsselwort gefunden haben, lesen Sie um es herum, um die Frage zu beantworten.
- Wenn Sie ein Wort oder eine Redewendung nicht verstehen, halten Sie sich nicht damit auf. Überfliegen Sie den Text weiter, bis Sie am Ende angelangt sind. Sollte sich herausstellen, dass Sie das Wort benötigen, können Sie sich später noch darum kümmern.

Normalerweise werden die Fragen zum Text in der Reihenfolge gestellt, in der die Informationen im Text zu finden sind. In einer Prüfung können Sie den Text markieren bzw. sich die benötigten Details notieren, sobald Sie die Informationen finden, die Sie suchen.

Skills files

Wenn Sie gefragt werden, Wh-Fragen zum Text zu beantworten, denken Sie daran, dass:

Who nach Menschen fragt. Suchen Sie Informationen über die Hauptperson des Textes.
Where nach einem Ort fragt.
When nach einer Zeit fragt. Suchen Sie nach Wochentagen, Daten oder Uhrzeiten.
What nach Objekten und Ereignissen fragt. Suchen Sie nach Informationen darüber oder Vorschlägen, warum etwas passiert (ist).
Why nach einem Grund fragt. Suchen Sie nach Erklärungen, warum etwas passiert (ist).
How nach einer Methode fragt. Suchen Sie Beschreibungen, wie etwas gemacht wird.

→ Fragen zum Text beantworten, S. 228

Übung 4 (Fertigkeit 1F)

Scannen Sie den Text *South Africa for families* unten und finden Sie die Antworten zu den Fragen heraus. Sagen Sie, wie Sie die Antworten so schnell gefunden haben.

1. What holiday destination is being advertised?
2. What is the best way to see the countryside?
3. How many lodges and how many guest houses can holidaymakers choose from?
4. How much does a holiday for a family of four cost?

South Africa for families

South Africa is the perfect destination for a family holiday. The time difference from the UK is only one to two hours so children quickly settle in after the flight.

5 Many national parks are malaria free so you needn't worry about going out to watch the wildlife. Our park lodges run children's programmes.

A hire car is perfect for getting around South Africa as you can come and go as you please so you can
10 plan around your family's needs. Our guest house staff can give you lots of ideas about things to do so you can discover something new every day. You can choose from 8 lodges and 5 guest houses.

Here are just three of our many exciting activities:

15 ▶ The Garden Route offers many adventurous excursions and places of interest.
▶ Enjoy whale watching on South Africa's Whale Coast.
▶ You can't travel to South Africa and not go on a safari and the game viewing possibilities in the Kruger National Park are amazing.

An 18-day trip for a family of four can cost as little as €2,000 per person.

20 We believe that once you have experienced our beautiful country, you will never want to go home. See you soon in South Africa!

(206 words)

Cape Town, with its beautiful scenery and beaches

G Gründliches Lesen (*reading for detail / close reading*)

Gründliches Lesen bedeutet, einen Text Satz für Satz zu lesen. Hierzu gibt es folgende Strategien:

- Lesen Sie die Aufgabenstellung und die Fragen aufmerksam durch und stellen Sie sicher, dass Sie verstehen, was der Prüfer / die Prüferin von Ihnen will.
- Überfliegen Sie den Text, um einen Überblick über den Inhalt zu bekommen, und notieren Sie sich die wichtigsten Punkte. Lassen Sie diesen Schritt nicht aus. Er wird Ihnen später beim Beantworten der Fragen Zeit sparen.
- Suchen Sie Schlüsselwörter, die Ihnen helfen, die Frage(n) zu beantworten. Werden Sie z. B. nach der Meinung des Autors / der Autorin gefragt, suchen Sie nach Wörtern wie *think*, *believe*, *opinion*, usw.; das hilft Ihnen, dem Gedankengang des Autors / der Autorin zu folgen.
- Lesen Sie nun den Text Satz für Satz und beantworten Sie die Fragen.
- Wenn Sie fertig sind, lesen Sie sich Ihre Antworten durch und vergleichen Sie sie mit dem Text.

Übung 5 (Fertigkeit 1G)

Sagen Sie, ob die Aussagen unten in Bezug auf den Text *South Africa for families*, S. 222, richtig oder falsch sind.

Bitte notieren Sie sich jedes Mal den Grund für Ihre Wahl von richtig oder falsch. Die ersten zwei Aussagen sind für Sie bereits zugeordnet worden.

1. South Africa is a good place to take a family holiday. *true*
   BEISPIEL   Headline: SA for familes; text: *"a perfect destination for a family holiday"*
2. The time difference between South Africa and Britain is 5 hours. *false*
   BEISPIEL   *"time difference from the UK one to two hours"*
3. There is absolutely no risk of catching malaria in any of the national parks.
4. There are special activities for children who visit the parks.
5. You can get ideas for day trips at the tourist information office.
6. The highlight of the holiday is a safari.
7. The author of the text is sure that you will love his country.

H Sich während des Lesens Notizen machen

Sich während des Lesens Notizen zu machen ist sinnvoll. So können Sie sich die Informationen für später besser merken.

- Stellen Sie immer sicher, dass Sie den Text verstanden haben, bevor Sie sich Notizen machen. → Grobverständnis, S. 214
- Versehen Sie Ihren Notizzettel mit der Textüberschrift und der Quellenangabe. Die Quellenangabe ist wichtig, wenn Sie in Ihrem Aufsatz u. ä. zitieren wollen. Auch kann es vorkommen, dass Sie zu einem späteren Zeitpunkt auf den Originaltext zurückgreifen wollen.
- Sehen Sie sich den Text genau an und suchen Sie sich die wichtigsten Unterthemen heraus, die Sie als Überschriften benutzen können. Die Unterteilung des Textes in Absätze wird Ihnen dabei helfen. Verteilen Sie diese Überschriften großzügig über das Blatt und lassen Sie unter jeder Überschrift Platz für Notizen.
- Ihre Notizen bestehen aus Schlüsselwörtern, i. d. R. Nomen, Verben und Adjektiven. Konzentrieren Sie sich auf diese Wortarten.

Skills files

- Halten Sie nach Signalen Ausschau, z. B. Wiederholungen, Wörter, die etwas unterstreichen, oder an die Leser direkt gestellte Fragen. Dies ist ein Anhaltspunkt, was der Autor / die Autorin als wichtig erachtet.
- Sind Sie hiermit fertig, überprüfen Sie, ob Sie alle Informationen haben, die Sie benötigen. Sie können durchaus über den gesamten Text verstreut sein.
- Denken Sie immer daran, sich nur Notizen zu machen. Verschwenden Sie keine Zeit mit dem Abschreiben ganzer Textabschnitte, lassen Sie unnötige Wörter wie Pronomen und Artikel weg und verwenden Sie Abkürzungen und Symbole.

Zeichen	
=	the same as
≠	not the same as
+, &	and

Abkürzungen	
e.g.	for example
km	kilometre
w., w/o	with, without
etc.	and so on

Wortverkürzungen	
govt	government
impt	important
kids	children

Übung 6 (Fertigkeit 1H)

Stellen Sie sich vor, Sie wurden gebeten, einen Kommentar über Paparazzi zu schreiben; Sie beziehen sich hierbei auf den Text *Paparazzi – not always the celebrity's best friend*. Lesen Sie den Text und stellen Sie sicher, dass Sie verstehen, worum es geht. Anschließend schreiben Sie sich die Notizen ab und vervollständigen sie mithilfe der o. g. Tipps.

Paparazzi – not always the celebrity's best friend (Focus on Success, 2015)

benefits of paparazzi
- keep celebrities in the news
- fame and fortune for celebrities
- give the public information about stars

downsides of paparazzi
- invasion of privacy

PAPARAZZI – NOT ALWAYS THE CELEBRITY'S BEST FRIEND

A lot of people say that celebrities need the paparazzi to keep their faces in the news. You could say that is the only benefit of paparazzi. The downsides of
5 the relationship between paparazzi and celebrities are many.

The paparazzi go to extremes to get their photos. Some of them earn thousands for a good shot of a star. If the star has
10 problems, then the photo might bring a million.

Despite the laws about invasion of privacy, the paparazzi continually ignore them to get photos of celebrities. They stalk them while they are walking in a public place 15 and they follow them with their cars. In some cases, the paparazzi put celebrities in danger. How often have we heard stories on the news about celebrities having car accidents as a result of being 20 chased by paparazzi?

Film star Halle Berry was involved in a road accident involving the paparazzi a few years ago when a paparazzi followed her and drove into her car. The crash caused 25 Halle Berry to hit a wall. The shock of the accident was bad enough but, at the time, the star was pregnant and she could have lost her baby. When she got out of her car, the paparazzi ran away. Halle Berry could have lost her baby, but they didn't stay to help or to check if everything was all right. Apart from the fact that the law says you have to stay around after you've caused an accident, don't these paparazzi have any feelings?

In another case involving a star, Tori Spelling, the American actress and author, was followed by paparazzi when she was driving her two children to school. Again, the car chase ended in an accident. This time, the paparazzi did not flee the scene. Instead, he stood beside the car and took photos.

Tori Spelling and her children survived the crash but some celebrities do not survive. The most famous paparazzi chase that ended in a crash was the one in which Princess Diana was killed. Although there was evidence that the driver of the car Diana was travelling in had been drinking, popular speculation is that the paparazzi caused the crash.

Whether they caused the crash or not, the behaviour of the paparazzi was typical – some left the scene while others took photos of the wrecked car. None of them tried to help the driver or any of the passengers. If that wasn't bad enough, three of the paparazzi took photographs of Diana as she was dying. How much of an invasion of privacy is it when someone takes a photo of you when you are dying?

An incident like this should never be repeated. Taking pictures after a crash in order to make money from them should result in the photographer being banned from taking photos for life.

What is to be done about the other problems? Would making invasion of privacy laws tougher discourage paparazzi from stalking celebrities? Should it be against the law to follow and take pictures of a parent taking children to school? Fame and fortune are fuelled by paparazzi photos.

As long as celebrities need and enjoy the attention, there will be paparazzi and as long as we, the public, are interested in what our favourite stars are doing, we need the paparazzi, too. (552 words)

2 REZEPTION: HÖRVERSTEHEN

A Vor dem Hören (Voraussage des Inhalts / Vorbereitung)

Sich auf die Hörübung vorzubereiten, verstärkt das Hörverständnis. Nutzen Sie hierzu alle Informationen, die sich auf der Seite befinden. Bevor Sie zuhören:

- Sehen Sie sich alle Fotos bzw. Illustrationen auf der Seite genau an. Sie liefern Ihnen Hinweise über den Ort der Aufzeichnung.
- Lesen Sie alle Ihnen zur Verfügung gestellten Hintergrundinformationen, z. B. eine Einleitung, die die Situation beschreibt und Auskunft darüber gibt, wie viele Personen Sie hören werden.
- Lesen Sie die Aufgabenstellung sorgfältig durch. Denken Sie daran, dass die Fragen, die Sie beantworten müssen, häufig der Reihenfolge entsprechen, in der die Informationen auf der Aufzeichnung vorkommen.
- Denken Sie nach, welche Wörter und Formulierungen Sie vielleicht hören werden und schreiben Sie sie auf.
- Schreiben Sie jede Ihnen vorgegebene Tabelle ab. Füllen Sie sie auf Englisch bereits vor der Hörübung soweit wie möglich aus und vervollständigen Sie sie während des Hörens.

Skills files

B Während des ersten Hörens (Grobverständnis / listening for gist)

Ein Grobverständnis zu erhalten bedeutet, eine Ahnung zu bekommen, worum es in der Aufzeichnung geht. Während des ersten Hörens brauchen Sie nicht jedes Wort zu verstehen. Entwickeln Sie für das Hören möglichst folgende Fertigkeiten:

- Übergehen Sie Wörter, die Sie nicht verstehen.
- Konzentrieren Sie sich auf Schlüsselwörter.
- Machen Sie sich Notizen. Verwenden Sie Abkürzungen. Schreiben Sie so viel wie möglich auf, während Sie zuhören.

Ordnen Sie Ihre Notizen sofort nach dem Ende der Hörübung. Sie können sie später möglicherweise nicht mehr lesen.

Bemühen Sie sich, alle Fragen zu beantworten. Wenn Sie einen Teil der Informationen nicht verstanden haben, raten Sie, ausgehend von dem, was Sie verstanden haben.

Übung 1 (Fertigkeiten 2A und 2B)

10.30 Good morning, fans!

Gerry Davis interviews today's celebrities

In today's interview, Gerry talks to fitness celebrity Tina Michaelson while she takes a break from signing copies of her latest book for teenagers, **Do Sports and Learn Skills for Life!** in a London bookstore. During the interview, Tina explains how participating in sport teaches you skills that will help you your whole life long.

You read the announcement about the interview with Tina Michaelson and are interested in finding out more.

Listen to the interview and answer these questions in your own words.

1. What skill helps a team to win?
2. How does Gerry refer to this skill?
3. How can doing sport help you gain trust?
4. How long can sports relationships last?
5. What is the myth about students and sport?
6. What life skill can students use to prove that it is possible to be a good student and play sport?

A Sehen Sie sich das o.g. Beispiel einer Hörübung an. Sehen Sie sich das Foto genau an und lesen Sie die Programmanzeige. Lesen Sie sich die Aufgabenstellung und Fragen durch. Beantworten Sie die Fragen nicht. Dies tun Sie später. Wenn Sie sich sicher sind, alles verstanden zu haben, wählen Sie das beste Ende aus, um die folgenden Sätze zu vervollständigen.

Rezeption: Hörverstehen

1 The recording is of …
   a a private conversation.
   b a talk.
   c an interview.

2 The recording takes place …
   a at a celebrity fitness club.
   b in a bookstore.
   c on a school sports field.

3 The speakers are a
   a reporter and a fitness celebrity.
   b reporter and a fitness fan.
   c group of teenagers and a fitness celebrity.

4 The topic is …
   a skills to improve your sports perfomance.
   b developing useful skills through doing sport.
   c sports you can do all your life.

5 Three expressions I might hear are:
   a staying healthy, sport competitions, animal companions
   b life-long learning, learning to drive, nutrition
   c building relationships, team work, trusting others

B Schreiben Sie sich die zwei u.s. Sätze ab und vervollständigen Sie sie. Anschließend hören Sie die Aufzeichnung und überprüfen, ob Ihre Vorhersagen richtig waren.

I am going to listen to ___¹ with ___² about ___³
I expect to hear something about ___⁴

Hörtext → Webcode: FOSSKT1

C Während des zweiten Hörens (stichpunktartige Notizen machen)

Es ist schwierig, während des Zuhörens Notizen zu machen, weil die Aufzeichnung weiterläuft, während Sie schreiben. Daher verpassen Sie möglicherweise wichtige Informationen. Bleiben Sie ruhig! Sie haben sich bereits beim ersten Hören ein Grobverständnis angeeignet und notiert, was Sie verstehen konnten. Beim zweiten Hören versuchen Sie, sich so viel wie möglich an das zu erinnern, was Sie beim ersten Mal gehört haben. Wenn Sie es sich zur Gewohnheit machen, bei jedem Hören Stichpunkte aufzuschreiben, haben Sie bald den Bogen heraus.

Bevor Sie zuhören:
- Notieren Sie – wenn Sie die Zeit haben – Rubriken in Ihr Heft und schreiben Sie die Aufgabenstellung ganz oben auf Ihr Blatt. Wenn Sie die Anzahl der Sprecher/innen kennen, legen Sie eine Tabelle mit deren Namen an. Wenn Sie die Namen der Sprecher/innen nicht kennen, schreiben Sie ‚Sprecher/in 1', ‚Sprecher/in 2', usw.

Während Sie zuhören:
- Bleiben Sie bei der Aufgabenstellung und notieren Sie sich relevante Schlüsselwörter.
- Seien Sie aufmerksam und notieren Sie Ausdrücke, die die Gedanken strukturieren, z. B: *in my view, however, on the other hand*.
- Nutzen Sie Abkürzungen, um Zeit zu sparen. → Abkürzungen, S. 224

Nach dem Ende der Hörübung:
- Ordnen Sie Ihre Notizen frühestmöglich. Wenn Sie sich hierfür zu lang Zeit lassen, können Sie sie später möglicherweise nicht mehr deuten.

Wenn Sie in einer Prüfung Fragen zu einer Hörübung beantworten müssen:
- Formulieren Sie mithilfe Ihrer Stichpunkte die wichtigsten Punkte aus.
- Versuchen Sie, wenn Ihnen gewisse Details entgangen sind, die Antworten zu erraten, ausgehend von dem, was Sie verstanden haben.

Skills files

Übung 2 (Fertigkeit 2C)

Sie hören die Aufnahme ein zweites Mal und erledigen die Aufgabe von S. 226. Hier sind die Fragen nochmal:

1 What skill helps a team to win?
2 How does Gerry refer to this skill?
3 How can doing sport help you gain trust?
4 How long can sports relationships last?
5 What is the myth about students and sport?
6 What life skill can students use to prove that it is possible to be a good student and play sport?

> Hörtext → Webcode: FOSSKT1

1 Übertragen Sie die Tabelle in Ihr Heft und füllen Sie sie während des Hörens aus.

Questions	Tina	Gerry
1 skill for winning teams		
2 another way to describe the skill		
3 gaining trust through sport		
4 sports relationship can last …		
5 myth – students and sport		
6 skill to prove can be good student and play sport		

2 Jetzt ordnen Sie Ihre Notizen und verwenden Sie sie zum Beantworten der Fragen.

3 PRODUKTION: SCHREIBEN

A Fragen zum Text beantworten

Fragen zum Inhalt zu stellen ist eine beliebte Art herauszufinden, ob Sie einen Text verstanden haben. Bevor Sie zu schreiben beginnen:

- Stellen Sie sicher, dass Sie den Text verstehen. → Gründliches Lesen, S. 223
- Lesen Sie die Fragen sorgfältig durch.
- Fragen Sie sich: Was will der Lehrer / die Lehrerin bzw. der Prüfer / die Prüferin wissen?
- Schreiben Sie Ihre Stichpunkte auf Schmierpapier, wenn Sie Fragen aus Ihrem Buch beantworten. → Sich während des Lesens Notizen machen, S. 223
- Markieren Sie die wichtigen Textstellen während einer Prüfung bzw. einer Klassenarbeit in Ihrem Unterricht, indem Sie für verschiedene Fragen verschiedenfarbige Stifte verwenden.

Wh-Fragen beantworten → Scannen nach Einzelinformationen im Text, S. 221

Wenn Sie Wh-Fragen beantworten, denken Sie daran, dass:

- Wh-Fragen nicht einfach mit „ja" oder „nein" beantwortet werden können. Sie müssen diese Fragen jeweils kurz und sachlich beantworten.
- Wenn sich eine Wh-Frage auf eine bestimmte Handlung bezieht, Sie dasselbe Verb in Ihrer Antwort verwenden sollten.
  Where does Roger live? He lives in Berlin.

Produktion: Schreiben

- Wenn in den Fragen allgemeine Verben wie *do* und *go* verwendet werden, Sie in Ihrer Antwort ein anderes, präzisierendes Verb wählen.
  Where did Mary go? She flew to New York.
  Why did she do it? She wanted to visit a friend who lives there.
- Antworten auf Fragen, die mit *why* beginnen, häufig *because* enthalten.
  Why is Mary working so hard? Because she needs to finish the project soon.
- Sie für *Why*-Fragen auch den Imperativ verwenden (*to …*) können. In diesem Fall wird vorausgesetzt, dass der Halbsatz mit *because* in der Antwort enthalten ist.
  Why does Roger go to the gym? To get in shape. = Because he wants to get in shape.

B Einen Text zusammenfassen

Einen Text zusammenzufassen bedeutet, ihn auf seine wesentlichen Informationen zu reduzieren. Sie werden möglicherweise gefragt, einen Text zusammenzufassen, um zu zeigen, dass Sie ihn verstanden haben. Bevor Sie beginnen:

- Stellen Sie sicher, dass Sie den Text verstehen. → Rezeption: Leseverstehen, S. 214
- Lesen Sie die Anweisungen aufmerksam durch und vergewissern Sie sich, dass Sie wissen, welche Informationen aus dem Text für den Leser / die Leserin wichtig sind. Sie können dies tun, indem Sie sich *Wh*-Fragen stellen. → Scannen nach Einzelinformationen im Text, S. 221
- Machen Sie sich auf Schmierpapier stichpunktartige Notizen.
  → Sich während des Lesens Notizen machen, S. 223

Nun beginnen Sie, Ihre Zusammenfassung zu schreiben.

- Beschreiben Sie in ein oder zwei einleitenden Sätzen, wovon der Text handelt.
- Lassen Sie alles Unnötige weg. Dies schließt Beispiele, ausführliche Listen, Namen, usw. ein.
- Verwenden Sie, soweit es geht, Ihre eigenen Worte. Verwenden Sie Synonyme für Wörter aus dem Text, z. B. *think – believe*, und formulieren Sie um, z. B. *recently – in recent years*.
- Versuchen Sie, Zitate in die indirekte Rede umzuwandeln, z. B. *The author states that …*
  → Grammar files: Indirect speech, S. 266
- Verlinken Sie Ideen und lassen Sie sie in der Reihenfolge, in der sie im Text erscheinen.
- Erinnern Sie sich! Sie sollten in einer Zusammenfassung eines Textes nicht Ihre eigene Meinung äußern.

Wenn Sie fertig sind, überprüfen Sie Ihre Rechtschreibung und Grammatik.

Übung 1 (Fertigkeiten 3A und 3B)

A Read the first paragraph of the text *Cyberbullying at Wiston* and answer the following questions.

1. Where did three teenagers from Wiston Vocational College have to appear yesterday?
2. Why were they there?
3. Who was their target?
4. How did they hurt her?
5. How did the police learn what had happened?
6. What were the consequences for the three teenagers?

B **Summarize the complete text.**

Skills files

CYBERBULLYING AT WISTON

A group of three teenagers from Wiston Vocational College appeared at a juvenile court yesterday accused of using Facebook to be cruel to another student. The three teens, two boys and a girl, all aged 18, created a fake Facebook profile for another girl in their class and made it look like she wanted to live out her sexual fantasies on social media and in person. The girl's parents complained to the police and the three teenagers were quickly found. They were charged with causing their target emotional distress. All three were fined £1,000 and sentenced to do 30 days of voluntary work in a hospital. They were also banned from using Facebook, Twitter and other social media for six months.

According to the police, the group created a Facebook profile for Claire F, also 18-years old, three months ago. They manipulated real photos of Claire to make them look as if they were selfies which she herself had taken in a bedroom. The group also posted her mobile phone number.

Then they used the fake profile to pretend to be Claire and send sexual comments to other students. The mother of one of the pupils who received a sexual message reported the incident to the head of the college. She contacted Claire's parents. Before then, they knew nothing about the problem.

When they found out, Claire's parents were shocked. "Claire is a popular girl. She has always had a lot of friends and was involved in all kinds of after-school clubs," her father said. "Some weeks ago, though, she cut herself off from her social life and stopped going to her clubs," he

One of the accused waiting to return to court

went on. "She became isolated and my wife and I could see that she was unhappy. As we found out later, this change in Claire's behaviour started a few days after the fake Facebook account was set up," he said.

The charges against the three teenagers state that they created the fake profile to cause trouble for Claire. Her lawyer said in court that Claire had not only suffered emotional distress, she had also wanted to do a work placement in a company who had rejected her application because of the fake profile.

The judge said: "Growing up is not always easy and many teenagers feel unhappy. Some are so unhappy and are therefore very cruel to other people. Sadly, cyberbullying is on the rise," she went on. "I would like to see schools doing more to educate pupils and make it clear to them how much damage they can do to their peers by behaving in this way."

Claire's mother said, "I am glad that the court put such a high fine on the three kids. I think that is the only way you can discourage this. Make the bullies pay for the damage they have done." (472 words)

Produktion: Schreiben

C Mindmaps zum Inhalt eines Aufsatzes erstellen

Wenn Sie einen Aufsatz schreiben sollen, ist es sinnvoll, Ihre Ideen in Form einer Mindmap festzuhalten und hierbei auf den Inhalt statt auf das Vokabular zu achten.

→ *Vokabeln lernen, S. 220*

Hier ist der Anfang einer Mindmap gemacht, passend zur u. s. Aufgabe. Sehen Sie, wie die drei Unterpunkte *benefits, dangers, questions* genutzt werden, um Argumente zu sammeln und Fragen aufzulisten, die im Aufsatz abgedeckt werden sollen.

TASK: Describe / Comment on the benefits and the dangers of using social media.

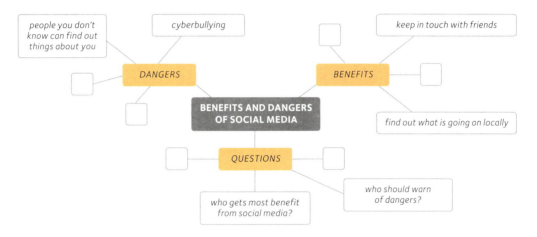

D Einen Text sinnvoll gliedern   → *Language for writing*, hintere Umschlagsklappe

Wenn Sie etwas schriftlich verfassen, müssen Sie Ihren Text klar und logisch strukturieren, damit der Leser / die Leserin den roten Faden nicht verliert. Hierfür können Sie die Sprachelemente der hinteren Umschlagsklappe dieses Buches nutzen. Hier sind einige Beispiele, wie man mithilfe dieser Elemente einen Aufsatz strukturieren kann. Weitere finden Sie online mithilfe dieses Webcodes.

Phrases → **Webcode: FOSSKP1**

Argumente gliedern	*In the text, "Cyberbullying at Wiston", we saw how three pupils used social media to hurt another pupil.* **First**, *they …* **Secondly/Then**, *they …*
Eine Begründung anführen	**Due to / Because of / As a result of** *this behaviour, Claire became isolated. She …*
Aspekte ergänzen	**In addition, / Moreover**, *the girl didn't get a job she wanted.*
Einen Gegensatz ausdrücken	**Although/While** *examples like these illustrate the dangers, social media has its benefits, too. Being active on social media can …*
Beispiele anführen	*Stephen Sutton,* **for example**, *who was diagnosed with terminal cancer aged 15, used social media …*
	→ *Using the internet to help others, S. 43*
Ein Fazit ziehen	**To sum up / To conclude**, *social media has its good and its bad sides.* **On the one hand**, *…* **On the other hand**, *…*

Skills files

Übung 2 (Fertigkeiten 3C und 3D)

A Verwenden Sie die Informationen aus Ihrem Kursbuch und Ihre eigenen Ideen, um die Mindmap in der o.g. Erklärung der Fertigkeit 3C zu vervollständigen.

B Schreiben Sie die Überschriften des Abschnitts D ab und sammeln Sie Ideen für Sätze, die Sie verwenden können, um über die Vorteile und Gefahren von sozialen Medien zu schreiben.

E Umgang mit Operatoren

Im Verlauf Ihrer Arbeit mit Ihrem Buch bzw. in einer Prüfung müssen Sie möglicherweise ein Schriftstück entsprechend besonderer Anweisungen (Operatoren) verfassen.

- Wenn Sie sich beim Schreiben auf den Text beziehen sollen, überfliegen Sie diesen, um sich einen Überblick über den Inhalt zu verschaffen. → Grobverständnis, S. 214
- Lesen Sie sich die Aufgabenstellung durch. Diese beinhaltet eine der Anweisungen aus der u. s. Tabellen. Es ist wichtig, dass Sie genau verstehen, was Sie tun sollen.
- Sammeln Sie Ideen, bevor Sie mit dem Schreiben beginnen. → Mindmaps erstellen, S. 231
- Stellen Sie sicher, dass Sie nicht dieselben Blickpunkte in unterschiedlichen Aufgaben wiederholen. Markieren Sie Textstellen für unterschiedliche Aufgaben mit unterschiedlichen Farben.
- Strukturieren Sie Ihre Antworten klar und logisch. → Einen Text sinnvoll gliedern, S. 231
- Verwenden Sie stets Ihre eigenen Worte, wenn Sie sich auf den Text beziehen. Suchen Sie Synonyme (z. B. *say – state*) sowie Möglichkeiten, Sätze in anderen Worten auszudrücken (z. B. *to a great extent – greatly*).

Übung 3 (Fertigkeit 3E)

Sehen Sie sich die Tabelle genau an und vergewissern Sie sich, dass Sie alle Anweisungen verstanden haben. Notieren Sie sich auf Deutsch:

1 wie viele Anweisungen aufgeführt sind.
2 zu welchen Überschriften die Anweisungen gehören.
3 wenn Sie Fakten, Gegenstände oder Zeichen finden sollen, die zeigen, dass etwas wahr ist.
4 wenn Sie objektiv von etwas die Vor- und Nachteile so darlegen sollen, wie sie im Text erscheinen.
5 wenn Sie Ihr eigenes Wissen einfließen lassen sollen, um die tiefere Bedeutung bzw. Botschaft eines Textes oder Witzes zu erklären.
6 wenn Sie beide Seiten einer Angelegenheit abwägen, und die Für und Wider anführen wollen.

Anweisungen, die sich auf den Inhalt beziehen

In den folgenden Anweisungen lenken Sie Ihre Aufmerksamkeit auf die Hauptgedanken des Autors / der Autorin.

Anweisung	Deutsch	Was Sie tun müssen
Summarize → Einen Text zusammenfassen, S. 229	*zusammenfassen*	Schreiben Sie die wichtigsten Textinhalte kurz und prägnant auf, und verwenden Sie hierzu Ihre eigenen Worte. Lassen Sie Ihre eigene Meinung in Form von Beispielen weg.

Produktion: Schreiben

Outline	*darstellen*	Beschreiben Sie die wichtigsten Tatsachen und teilen Sie den Entwurf nach den wichtigsten Unterpunkten auf.
Point out	*aufzeigen*	Beziehen Sie sich auf bestimmte wesentliche Textinhalte, um deren Wichtigkeit aufzuzeigen.
Say what the text is about	*sagen, worum es im Text geht*	Skizzieren Sie in eigenen Worten kurz den Inhalt. Dies ist kürzer und weniger detailliert als eine Zusammenfassung.

Die folgenden Anweisungen werden häufig verwendet, um zu überprüfen, ob Sie den Text richtig verstanden haben.

Anweisung	Deutsch	Was Sie tun müssen
Describe	*beschreiben*	Geben Sie über eine Person oder Situation bzw. einen Gegenstand Details wieder. Sie sollten viele Adjektive benutzen.
Define	*bestimmen, umreißen, definieren*	Beschreiben Sie eine Situation, ein Problem, die Bedeutung eines Begriffs, usw. sehr genau.
Say / State / Explain why … or **State the reasons for …**	*angeben / sagen / erklären, warum* oder *die Gründe angeben für …*	Erklären Sie, warum jemand etwas tat bzw. warum etwas geschah.
Find evidence in the text to show …	*Belege im Text finden für …*	Suchen Sie nach Tatsachen, die zeigen, dass etwas wahr ist.

Anweisungen, um Standpunkte aus dem Text zu vergleichen und zu analysieren

→ Einen Aufsatz oder eine Stellungnahme schreiben, S. 234

Die folgenden, häufig benutzten Anweisungen müssen Sie sehr gründlich beantworten. Bevor Sie mit dem Schreiben beginnen, sollten Sie eine Tabelle mit zwei Spalten anlegen, um einzelne Aspekte zu vergleichen.

Anweisung	Deutsch	Was Sie tun müssen
Compare	*vergleichen*	Heben Sie die Unterschiede und Ähnlichkeiten zwischen zwei Sachen/Konzepten/usw. hervor.
Contrast	*gegenüberstellen*	Heben Sie die Unterschiede zwischen zwei Sachen/Konzepten/usw. hervor.
Point out	*beschreiben*	Stellen Sie objektiv die Vor- und Nachteile von etwas dar, wie sie im Text aufgeführt werden.

Entsprechend der folgenden Anweisungen erklären Sie die im Text ausgeführten Ansichten, lesen aber auch ‚zwischen den Zeilen' und erklären implizierte Bedeutungen. Stellen Sie sicher, dass Sie Ihre Antworten und die Struktur Ihres Aufsatzes gut planen.

Anweisung	Deutsch	Was Sie tun müssen
Analyse	*analysieren*	Beschreiben und erklären Sie bestimmte Aspekte detailliert.
Describe and explain	*beschreiben und erklären*	
Examine	*untersuchen*	

Skills files

Anweisung, den Text zu interpretieren und eine Aussage zu kommentieren bzw. zu diskutieren
→ Einen Aufsatz oder eine Stellungnahme schreiben, S. 234

Entsprechend der folgenden Anweisung erklären und bewerten/evaluieren Sie sowohl die genannten als auch die implizierten Bedeutungen.

Anweisung	Deutsch	Was Sie tun müssen
Interpret	*interpretieren*	Erklären Sie die tiefere Bedeutung bzw. ‚Botschaft' einer Aussage bzw. eines Konzepts, usw. Verwenden Sie eigenes Hintergrundwissen und äußern Sie persönliche Ansichten.

Entsprechend der folgenden Anweisungen sollen Sie Ihre eigene Meinung darlegen. Wenn Sie schreiben, vertreten Sie Ihre Ansichten, doch erwähnen Sie auch Gegenargumente, um zu zeigen, dass Sie wissen, wovon Sie sprechen.

Anweisung	Deutsch	Was Sie tun müssen
Assess	*beurteilen*	Fällen Sie nach reiflicher Überlegung ein Urteil über etwas und liefern Sie Nachweise, die Ihre Meinung stützen.
Evaluate	*einschätzen, bewerten*	
Comment on	*Stellung nehmen zu*	

Entsprechend der folgenden Anweisungen sollen Sie objektiv sein. Denken Sie daran, Ihre Gedanken zunächst zu ordnen, und berücksichtigen Sie beide Seiten.

Anweisung	Deutsch	Was Sie tun müssen
Discuss	*erörtern*	Wägen Sie beide Seiten einer Sache ab und benennen Sie Für und Wider.

Übung 4 (Fertigkeit 3E)

Answer the questions about the text, *Cyberbullying at Wiston* on page 230, in your own words.

1 Describe what happened to Claire.
2 Find evidence in the text to show how Claire was affected by the bullying.

F Einen Aufsatz oder eine Stellungnahme schreiben

Einen längeren Text in einer Englischprüfung zu schreiben, stellt Ihr Sprachverständnis und Ihre Schaffenskraft auf die Probe. Wenn Sie aufgefordert sind, einen Aufsatz zu schreiben, müssen Sie eine objektive Haltung zu dem Thema einnehmen. Um dies zu erreichen, müssen Sie Argumente sammeln, die die in der Aufgabenstellung enthaltene These stützen und widerlegen. Wenn Sie „kommentieren" bzw. „diskutieren" sollen, wird erwartet, dass Sie Ihre Meinung zum Thema äußern. Hier ist es wichtig, dass Sie zur Untermauerung Ihrer Meinung Beispiele angeben.
→ Umgang mit Operatoren, S. 232

Bevor Sie mit dem Schreiben beginnen:
- Lesen Sie die Einleitung zu den Aufgaben mehrmals durch und stellen Sie sicher, dass Sie ganz genau verstehen, worüber Sie schreiben sollen.
- Achten Sie auf den genauen Wortlaut der Anweisungen. Suchen Sie nach Schlüsselwörtern in der Aufgabenstellung, die Ihnen sagt, was zu tun ist, z. B.: *identify, analyse, comment* usw.

Sobald Sie sicher sind, alles verstanden zu haben, nehmen Sie ein Blatt Schmierpapier und:

- Schreiben Sie eine Aussage auf, die sich auf die Frage bezieht, und arbeiten Sie die von Ihnen gewünschte Hauptaussage Ihres Texts heraus. Verwenden Sie für diese Aussage eine neutrale Ausdrucksweise. Schreiben Sie: *"Using social media can be beneficial or it can lead to problems."* Vermeiden Sie eine emotionale Schreibweise, wie z. B. diese: *"Everybody knows that some people use social media to be nice and others use it to be nasty."*
- Notieren Sie Schlüsselwörter, Ausdrücke bzw. kurze Sätze, um Fakten zu veranschaulichen. Wenn Sie alles aufgeschrieben haben, lesen Sie sich Ihre Notizen durch und streichen Sie jene Ideen, die Ihre Hauptaussage nicht stützen.
- Arbeiten Sie die gemeinsamen Elemente Ihrer Stichpunkte heraus und listen Sie sie auf. Aus dieser Liste entsteht die Kernaussage des jeweiligen Absatzes im Hauptteil Ihres Aufsatzes.
- Ordnen Sie Ihre Punkte nach ihrer Wichtigkeit. Beginnen Sie mit dem unwichtigsten Punkt im ersten Absatz Ihres Hauptteils und schließen Sie mit dem stärksten Argument in Ihrem letzten Absatz des Hauptteils.

Zu guter Letzt verwenden Sie Ihre Notizen für einen Entwurf. Denken Sie daran, dass jedes längere Schriftstück eines Anfangs (Einleitung), eines Mittelteils (Hauptteil) und eines Endes (Abschluss) bedarf.

→ Mindmaps zum Inhalt eines Aufsatzes erstellen, S. 231
→ Einen Text sinnvoll gliedern, S. 231

Einleitung	Stellen Sie das Thema vor und legen Sie dar, wie Sie es angehen wollen.
Hauptteil	Verwenden Sie für jedes Argument einen Absatz. Sie können erst alle Argumente dafür und dann alle Argumente dagegen darlegen. Verwenden Sie Bindeglieder wie: *However, … That said, …* , um klarzustellen, dass Sie im folgenden Absatz eine gegenteilige Meinung darlegen. Verwenden Sie Ausdrücke wie: *In my opinion, My feeling is that …* , usw., wenn Sie Ihre Meinung äußern.
Abschluss	Wiederholen Sie Ihre Einleitung. Sagen Sie, ob Sie eine der zwei Seiten befürworten.

Das Schreiben Ihres Aufsatzes:
- Um den schwierigen Moment des Anfangs zu überwinden, können Sie als erste Tat den Wortlaut der Aufgabenstellung aufschreiben. Vergessen Sie nicht, nach Fertigstellung Ihres Aufsatzes diesen ersten Satz mit Ihren eigenen Worten umzuschreiben!
- Beginnen Sie für jedes neue Argument einen neuen Absatz und arbeiten Sie Ihre Argumentationslinie stets mithilfe von strukturschaffenden Ausdrücken klar heraus.

→ *Language for writing*, hintere Umschlagsklappe

- Bleiben Sie durchgehend fokussiert. Achten Sie darauf, dass jeder Absatz Ihres Aufsatzes zu Ihrer Hauptaussage passt.

Wenn Sie mit dem Schreiben fertig sind:
- Überprüfen Sie Ihre Rechtschreibung, Grammatik und Zeichensetzung sowie Ihren Satzbau.
- Lesen Sie sich das, was Sie geschrieben haben, genau durch und verbessern Sie den Aufsatz dort, wo es der Lesefluss erfordert.

Versuchen Sie in einer Prüfung, rechtzeitig mit dem Schreiben aufzuhören, um genau das tun zu können. Fünf bis zehn Minuten sollten hierfür ausreichend sein.

Skills files

Übung 5 (Fertigkeit 3F)

A **Read the following writing tasks and find key words which tell you what to cover in your text. Say which key words helped you decide.** → Umgang mit Operatoren, S. 232

1 *Newspapers and magazines that publish paparazzi photos of celebrities can cause a lot of pain and misery. Describe the situation of celebrities, giving examples for and against this theory.*
2 *Reality shows that humiliate their candidates should be banned. Discuss this idea.*
3 *Groups of teenagers who are not intending to shop should be banned from shopping malls. Point out the main arguments for and against such a course of action.*

B **Make notes on one of the tasks and produce an outline for your comment/essay.**

4 PRODUKTION: BILDER UND CARTOONS BESCHREIBEN UND ANALYSIEREN

A Ein Bild beschreiben und deuten

Bevor Sie mit dem Schreiben beginnen, nehmen Sie Schmierpapier zur Hand, sehen sich das Bild genau an und machen sich Notizen zu den folgenden Fragen:

- Wer oder was spielt in dem Bild die Hauptrolle?
- Steht ein Element im Mittelpunkt? Warum?
- Schafft das Bild eine besondere Atmosphäre, z. B. von Gefahr, Glück?
- Was ist die „Botschaft" des Bildes?

Als Daumenregel sollte Ihre Antwort etwa zu ⅔ aus einer Bildbeschreibung und zu ⅓ aus einer Interpretation bestehen. Sagen Sie, welche Wirkung das Bild auf den Betrachter / die Betrachterin hat. Hilfreiche Redewendungen für eine Bildbeschreibung finden Sie mit Hilfe dieses Webcodes.

Phrases → **Webcode: FOSSKP2**

Übung 1 (Fertigkeit 4A)

Sehen Sie sich das Bild genau an und vervollständigen Sie die Notizen mit Wörtern aus dem Kasten.

clouds ▪ dangers ▪ having fun ▪ imagine ▪ no swimming ▪ sign ▪ unconcerned ▪ viewer

Main parts: three people ▭¹ in the sea. Blue skies with a few ▭² on the horizon. Sign shows that ▭³ is allowed here.
Focus: on the ▭⁴.
Atmosphere: relaxed, holiday atmosphere; no indication of any immediate ▭⁵.
Message: the people are ▭⁶ by the sign – they could have difficulties but the ▭⁷ can only ▭⁸ what these might be.

B Einen Cartoon beschreiben und deuten

Die o. g. Vorschläge zur Vorbereitung auf eine Bildbeschreibung eignen sich auch zur Vorbereitung auf die Beschreibung eines Cartoons. Denken Sie jedoch immer daran, dass ein/e Cartoonist/in auf etwas Besonderes hinweisen will. Die drei wichtigsten Techniken hierfür sind:

- Karikaturen, also ein oder mehrere körperliche Merkmale übertrieben darstellen.

Produktion: Bilder und Cartoons beschreiben und analysieren

- Symbole, d. h. ein bekanntes Bild verwenden, um eine Idee zu transportieren, z. B. die Freiheitsstatue, um die USA zu verkörpern.
- Bildunterschriften bzw. Sprechblasen, die die Botschaft in wenigen Worten zusammenfassen bzw. den Charakteren als Aussage zugedacht sind.

Bevor Sie über den Cartoon zu schreiben beginnen, stellen Sie sich folgende Fragen:

- Wie sind die Sachen/Personen/Charaktere gezeichnet? Sind die Personen als Karikaturen dargestellt? Stellen sie einen bestimmten „Personentyp" dar?
- Sind Symbole vorhanden? Wenn ja, was repräsentieren sie?
- Sind in der Zeichnung Nummern, Daten oder leicht erkennbare Orte zu sehen? Wenn ja, welche Funktion erfüllen sie? Was teilen sie uns mit?
- Was ist der Standpunkt des Cartoonisten / der Cartoonistin zum ausgewählten Thema?
- Welche Botschaft transportiert der Cartoon? Wie wird diese Botschaft vermittelt?

Sehen Sie sich alles auf dem Cartoon genau an und beschreiben Sie ihn ausführlich; verwenden Sie hier die Verlaufsform der Gegenwart, um auszudrücken, was die Personen tun. Denken Sie daran, dass Sie, wenn Sie die Botschaft des Cartoons nicht verstehen, sagen können, dass es *unclear* oder *ambiguous* ist. Hilfreiche Redewendungen für eine Bildbeschreibung finden Sie mit Hilfe dieses Webcodes.

Phrases → Webcode: FOSSKP2

C Ein Bild bzw. Cartoon mit einem Text vergleichen

Wenn Sie ein Bild bzw. Cartoon mit einem Text vergleichen sollen, lesen Sie den Text sorgfältig durch und sagen Sie, ob er die Botschaft der betreffenden Abbildung aufgreift oder nicht. Begründen Sie Ihre Antwort, z. B. *The image supports the text in the following way: first, … , then, … . Although the picture/cartoon shows … the text says that … .*

Übung 2 (Fertigkeiten 4B und 4C)

A Sehen Sie sich den Cartoon genau an und wählen Sie die richtige Antwort aus, um die Beschreibung zu vervollständigen.

The cartoon shows a group of middle-aged people who could be (*business people / parents*)¹. They are sitting at a round table in a (*school / meeting room*).² A sign on the table indicates that the people are talking about how to persuade people to (*eat/shop*)³ more. The man with the glasses appears to be (*making a point to / disagreeing with*)⁴ his two companions. It is likely that he is the person saying the words (*above/under*)⁵ the cartoon. According to these words, the man believes that kids are (*less/more*)⁶ likely to believe advertising messages than adults. The message of the cartoon is (*ambiguous/clear*)⁷. The cartoonist believes that people who work in the advertising industry are (*cynical/concerned*)⁸ about consumers.

"It won't bother us if we're not allowed to aim our ads at the kids. The adults are easier to fool anyway."

Skills files

B Lesen Sie den u. s. Text und wählen Sie das beste Satzende aus, um den Vergleich zwischen dem Text und der Cartoonbotschaft zu vervollständigen.

> According to a recent study, advertising aimed at young people is an important factor in deciding how kids spend their money. Young people between the ages of 13 and 17 appear to be most influenced by advertising. The study discovered that this age group is more influenced by advertising messages than adults are. As an indication that this may be true, the study discovered that requests by kids and young people for advertised products decrease as they get older.
> A spokesperson for the study said: "Consumers tend to become more critical about their purchases and less susceptible to advertising as they grow up."

1 Both the cartoon and the text describe how
   a all age groups react to advertising.
   b to persuade people to buy goods.
   c young people compare to adults when it comes to viewing advertising.
2 The speaker in the cartoon appears to believe that, when it comes to advertising,
   a adults have better judgement than kids.
   b everyone is convinced by the messages the industry puts out.
   c kids are more critical than adults.
3 The text,
   a however, gives a completely different view of the subject.
   b on the one hand, agrees with the cartoon.
   c on the other hand, suggests that no-one is convinced by advertising.
4 According to the text, as kids grow up, they
   a are less accepting of advertising messages.
   b ask their parents for more.
   c spend more money on consumer goods.
5 If we are to believe the text, the advertising executive portrayed in the cartoon is
   a analysing his target groups correctly.
   b incorrect in his analysis of his target groups.
   c taking a risk by not advertising to kids.

5 PRODUKTION: SCHAUBILDER UND STATISTIKEN BESCHREIBEN UND ANALYSIEREN

Diagramme und Kurvenbilder werden verwendet, um Informationen visuell darzustellen.

TYPES OF DIAGRAMS

Table

	Germany	UK
2010	568	261
2015	822	98

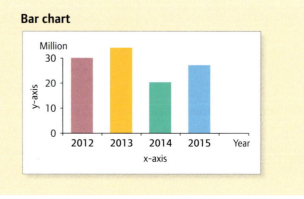

Bar chart

Produktion: Schaubilder und Statistiken beschreiben und analysieren

Pie chart

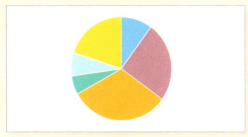

Graph, line graph

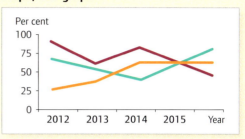

Bevor Sie mit dem Schreiben beginnen, nehmen Sie Schmierpapier zur Hand, sehen sich die Abbildung genau an und machen sich zu folgenden Fragen Notizen:

- Was sagt die Überschrift aus? Welche Beschriftung liegt vor?
- Welche Zahlen und Einheiten werden verwendet, um die Daten darzustellen?
- Wenn ein Balkendiagramm / eine Kurve vorliegt, wofür steht die x-Achse? Wofür die y-Achse?
- Welche Muster können Sie in den Daten erkennen?
- Welche Schlüsse können Sie aus diesen Mustern ziehen?
- Wie verhält sich die Abbildung zu Dingen, die Sie bereits wissen, z. B. zu einem Text, den Sie kürzlich gelesen haben, oder zu Informationen aus der Einleitung zur Aufgabenstellung?

Um Ihre Beschreibung und Analyse der Abbildung zu ordnen, nutzen Sie Ihre Notizen folgendermaßen:

▪ eine Einleitung zum Diagramm bzw. Kurvenbild (Überschrift)	*The diagram / graph shows / refers to …*
▪ ein Überblick dessen, was es darstellt	*The figures in the table show …* *The x-axis shows … , the y-axis shows …*
▪ eine ausführliche Beschreibung der Informationen	*The graph shows a huge increase …*
▪ die Beziehung zwischen den Kategorien	*Car X has twice as much … as Car Y.*
▪ eine Auswertung des Diagramms bzw. Kurvenbilds	*The figures indicate that …*

Hilfreiche Redewendungen, Schaubilder zu beschreiben, finden Sie mit Hilfe dieses Webcodes.

Phrases → Webcode: FOSSKP3

Übung 1 (Fertigkeit 5)

Vervollständigen Sie die Beschreibung und Analyse des Diagramms auf Seite 240 mit Wörtern aus dem Kasten.

> compared to ▪ constant increase ▪ fluctuate ▪ huge increase ▪
> remained more or less constant ▪ rise ▪ shows ▪ small dip ▪
> the number of devices in millions ▪ the year

Skills files

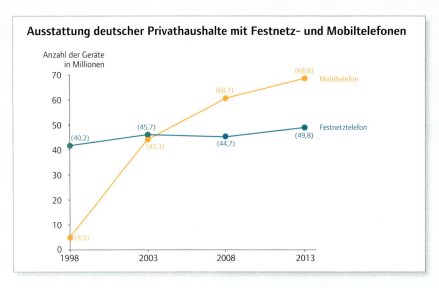

The line graph ▭¹ the development in the numbers of landlines and mobile phones in German private households from 1998 to 2013. The x-axis shows ▭² and the y-axis shows ▭³. In 1998, there were only 4.5 million mobiles in German households ▭⁴ 40.2 million landlines. During the next 15 years, the numbers of landlines ▭⁵ (all in all an increase of less than 20%), whereas the number of mobile phones showed a ▭⁶. By 2013, there were just 49.8 million landlines compared to 68.8 million mobiles. In the case of mobile phones, we see ▭⁷ in numbers over the years, whereas the numbers of landlines ▭⁸, showing a rise in total numbers during the years 1998 to 2003. This is followed by a ▭⁹ in total numbers between 2003 and 2008 and a further ▭¹⁰ to 49.8 million in 2013.

6 SCHRIFTLICHE MEDIATION

Mediation ist das Übertragen wesentlicher Textelemente von einer Sprache in eine andere. Mediation ist nicht mit dem Wort „Übersetzung" austauschbar. Sie sollen nur den Sinn des Textes übertragen und bestimmte Informationen wiedergeben.

A Vorbereitung

- Lesen Sie sich die Anweisungen sorgfältig durch. Vergewissern Sie sich, dass Sie wissen:
  - warum die Informationen in einer anderen Sprache wiedergegeben werden, z. B. weil Ihr Kollegium über Entwicklungen Ihres Tätigkeitsfeldes informiert werden sollen.
  - für wen die Mediation gedacht ist, z. B. für andere Schüler/innen, Ihr/e Chef/in.
  - welches Medium Sie nutzen sollen, z. B. eine E-Mail, eine Informationsbroschüre.
- Lesen Sie den Text zügig, um den groben Sinn zu erfassen. Verschwenden Sie keine Zeit mit einzelnen Wörtern bzw. Wörtern, die Sie nicht verstehen. → Grobverständnis, S. 214
- Lesen Sie die Anweisungen noch einmal, dann gehen Sie den Text ein weiteres Mal durch und suchen nach Textpassagen, die jene Informationen enthalten, die Sie zur Lösung der Aufgabe benötigen. In einer Prüfung können Sie die betreffenden Stellen unterstreichen oder farblich hervorheben. Folgende Textstellen können als unwesentlich betrachtet werden: Wiederholungen (oft eingeleitet durch *in other words*, *to put it another way*) und Anekdoten und Exkurse (*by the way*, *incidentally*).

B Einen Mediationstext schreiben

Schreiben Sie die wichtigsten Punkte des Textes in klarem, einfachem Deutsch auf. Halten Sie sich an das, was im Originaltext gesagt wurde. Wenn Sie damit fertig sind:

- Lesen Sie Ihren Text Korrektur, d. h. überprüfen Sie die Rechtschreibung und Grammatik.
- Lesen Sie sich Ihren Text durch und stellen Sie sicher, dass der Inhalt des Originals klar und verständlich übertragen wurde.
- Überprüfen Sie, dass Sie nur solche Informationen übernommen haben, die für die Aufgabe relevant sind.
- Überprüfen Sie, dass Sie für die Zielgruppe Ihres Textes angemessen formuliert haben.
- Überprüfen Sie, dass Sie die Mediation in dem nötigen Medium übermittelt haben.

Übung (Fertigkeit 6)

A Lesen Sie sich die Anweisungen sorgfältig durch und machen sich Notizen zur Situation und der Aufgabenstellung.

> **Situation:** Sie machen ein Praktikum in einem Jugendzentrum vor Ort. Das Zentrum bietet für seine freiwilligen Helfer/innen regelmäßig Weiterbildungen an. Die nächste Weiterbildung befasst sich mit der wachsenden Anzahl von Kindern in Europa, die in Patchwork-Familien aufwachsen. Diese Weiterbildung wird auch die finanzielle Lage der Familien beleuchten.
>
> **Aufgabe:** Ihr Chef / Ihre Chefin lässt Sie den Text *Changing face of the British family* lesen und die Situation im Vereinigten Königreich beschreiben. Er/Sie möchte, dass Sie ein Flugblatt erstellen, welches die wichtigsten Informationen darüber enthält, warum Stieffamilien in ihrer Anzahl zunehmen; dieses Flugblatt möchte er/sie während der Weiterbildung verteilen.

B Lesen Sie nun den Text und machen sich auf Englisch zu den Punkten Notizen, die Sie für Ihre Mediation benötigen.

C Jetzt können Sie Ihren Text verfassen. Vermitteln Sie die wesentlichen Punkte auf Deutsch und behalten hierbei die Zielgruppe im Auge, die Ihre Mediation lesen wird. Berücksichtigen Sie auch das Medium, das Sie benutzen sollen.

Changing face of the British family: One in three now has a step-child
Nearly two million children live in a two-parent family, study reveals

Parents increasingly regard serial relationships as normal behaviour

Nearly a third of all couples bringing up children have a child from an earlier relationship in their family, a report said yesterday.

The rapidly growing number of step-families means that nearly two million children live in a two-parent family – but with one parent who is not their own.

The army of step-children has appeared as their parents increasingly come to regard serial relationships, not one committed marriage, as normal behaviour.

A report said that the majority of parents have had at least one partnership in the past that they regarded as long-term. New details of how the shape of families has been twisted by the decline of lifelong marriage and the rise of temporary cohabitation were revealed in a study of 20,000 people carried out for an insurance company. The findings of the Family Finances report produced for Aviva were released in advance of the latest national divorce figures, published by the Office for National Statistics today.

Skills files

These are expected to show that couples who do marry rather than just live together are increasingly likely to stay together. Sarah Poulter of Aviva said: 'This research shows that there is no "normal" family any more. What was seen as the traditional model is becoming more and more diverse.
'It is now quite usual for a child to have three parents, and to live in a family that includes step-parents, half-brothers and half-sisters.'
The polling found that almost half of all adults who live with a spouse or partner or with children – 49 per cent – have had at least one past relationship which they regarded as committed, either a marriage or a cohabitation. One in six have had two past relationships they thought were permanent, and one in 20 has had three or more. The result is that 30 per cent of present two-parent families include a child from a former relationship.

The report said only one in three of these step-families gets any sort of financial help from the parent of the step-child. A third of these get only occasional payments – while only a quarter of parents whose children live with other families provide regular payments.
The analysis suggests a third of step-families that do get financial help actually rely on the payments to get by.
It also found that one in eight adults who have been through a separation postponed the break-up because they could not afford to find anywhere else to live.
Latest official figures say that there are around 5.7 million families with children under the age of 16, or under 18 and still in school. In just over two thirds of these – around four million – the parents are married. (442 words)

From: *www.dailymail.co.uk*

7 ÜBERSETZEN

Einen Text zu übersetzen verlangt Sorgfalt und Geduld. Im Gegensatz zur Mediation ist für eine Übersetzung jedes Wort des Originaltextes wichtig. Ihre Aufgabe als Übersetzer/in ist es, den Sinn des Textes mit deutschen Entsprechungen zu reproduzieren.

Merken Sie sich folgende Regeln:
- Übersetzer/innen haben keine eigene „Stimme". Selbst wenn Sie mit der Aussage nicht einverstanden sind, dürfen Sie weder den Text an sich noch den Ton verändern.
- Von Ihnen werden weder Bewertungen noch Meinungsäußerungen erwartet.
- Streben Sie keine wortgetreue Übersetzung an, denn das ist unmöglich. Stattdessen konzentrieren Sie sich beim Lesen auf Informationsblöcke, die Sie dann als Ganzes übersetzen.

Bevor Sie mit dem Schreiben beginnen:
- Lesen Sie die Überschrift sowie den gesamten Text, um einen Überblick zu bekommen.
  → Grobverständnis, S. 214
- Lesen Sie den Text noch einmal, doch dieses Mal achten Sie auf Einzelheiten. Machen Sie sich beim Lesen Notizen.
  → Gründliches Lesen, S. 223
  → Sich während des Lesens Notizen machen, S. 223
- Schreiben Sie sich Wörter und Strukturen auf, die Sie nicht verstehen.
- Wenden Sie Ihre Fertigkeiten zur Worterkennung an, um sich die Bedeutung von unbekannten Wörtern und Satzstrukturen zu erarbeiten. Verwenden Sie Ihr Wörterbuch nur, wenn es nicht anders geht.
  → Mit unbekannten Wörtern umgehen, S. 216
  → Ein Wörterbuch benutzen, S. 217

Übersetzen

Ihre Übersetzung verfassen

Wenn Sie den Text verstanden haben, können Sie mit dem Erstellen Ihrer deutschen Fassung beginnen. Schreiben Sie Ihren ersten Entwurf ‚doppelzeilig' – so haben Sie Platz für Korrekturen.

Wenn Sie mit Ihrer Übersetzung fertig sind:
- Vergleichen Sie Ihren Text und das Original Satz für Satz, um sicherzustellen, dass Sie nichts ausgelassen haben.
- Lesen Sie Ihren Text durch und vergewissern Sie sich, dass er klar und verständlich ist.
- Überprüfen Sie Ihre Rechtschreibung und Grammatik. Lassen Sie insbesondere bei den Verben und den nachfolgend genannten Problembereichen Vorsicht walten.

Tipps – Grammatik, Stil und Vokabular

Jeder Text enthält unterschiedlich knifflige Aspekte, über die Sie nachdenken müssen. Seien Sie bei den folgenden Bereichen besonders sorgfältig.

- **Knifflige grammatische Strukturen**
    - Partizipialkonstruktionen → S. 268
    - Konstruktionen mit Gerundium → S. 262
    - Passivkonstruktionen → S. 261
    - Relativsätze ohne Relativpronomen → S. 269
    - Adverbien → S. 270
    - Komparative und Superlative → S. 271
    - Verben in der Verlaufsform → S. 249–254

- **Wortstellung**
    - Verwenden Sie im Englischen stets die Reihenfolge S–V–O (*subject – verb – object*).
    - Denken Sie daran: Wenn ein deutscher Satz z. B. mit einem Adverb beginnt, wird das Verb versetzt, auf Englisch jedoch bleibt die Reihenfolge S–V–O erhalten.

- **Die Form eines Wortes ändern**
    - BEISPIELE: *There is a need to …* → Es ist notwendig, zu …
      (englisch: Nomen → deutsch: Adjektiv)
      She used to work in France. → Früher arbeitete sie in Frankreich.
      (englisch: Verbkonstruktion → deutsch: Adverb)

- **Partikeln und Ausdrücke**
    - BEISPIEL: *since* = seit (*He has been working since 6 am.*)
      = da, weil (*Since he didn't have his phone with him, he couldn't call her.*)

- **Falsche Freunde**
    - BEISPIEL: *actual* = tatsächlich / *topical, current* = aktuell

- **Häufig verwechselte Wörter**
    - BEISPIEL: *advice/advise*
      He gave me some advice. Rat(schlag)
      He advised me to see a doctor. beraten

8 PRÄSENTIEREN

Im Verlauf Ihres Schuljahres könnten Sie aufgefordert werden, eine Präsentation vorzubereiten und zu geben. Die Fertigkeit des Präsentierens können Sie in der Schule üben; das gibt Ihnen jene Sicherheit, die Sie brauchen, um eine Präsentation auf der Arbeit zu geben. An der Schule fallen Präsentationen im Allgemeinen in eine von zwei Kategorien: eine informative, objektive

Skills files

Präsentation, die auf Tatsachen beruht, und eine subjektive Präsentation, in der Sie Ihre eigene Meinung zu einem strittigen Thema vertreten.

A Vorbereitung

- Sammeln Sie möglichst viele Informationen und Ideen zu dem Thema, indem Sie im Internet und in Büchern recherchieren, mit Experten/Expertinnen sprechen, ein Brainstorming machen, usw.
- Wählen Sie jene Ideen aus, die Ihr Thema am sinnvollsten widerspiegeln, und machen Sie sich Notizen.
- Verwenden Sie Ihre Notizen, um Ihre Ideen in logische Einheiten einzuteilen.
- Ordnen Sie diese Einheiten so, dass ein roter Faden klar erkennbar ist.
- Stellen Sie Ihre Präsentation zusammen und benutzen Sie hierzu eine der u. s. Gliederungen.

Um eine informative Präsentation zu planen, z. B. *Local opportunities for work experience*.

- **Einleitung:** Das Benennen Ihres Themas und eine kurze Erläuterung über den Aufbau Ihrer Präsentation (ca. 15 % Ihrer Präsentation)
- **Entwicklung:** Beweise, die Ihre Vorstellungen belegen (ca. 75 %)
- **Schluss:** Wiederholung Ihrer Ideen und eine knappe Zusammenfassung der wichtigsten Fakten und Zahlen (ca. 10 %)

Um eine Präsentation zu einem umstrittenen Thema zu planen, z. B. *Hash should be legalized*

- **Einleitung:** Objektiver Lösungsvorschlag zu einem strittigen Problem. Äußern Sie Ihre eigene Meinung noch nicht. (ca. 10 % Ihrer Präsentation)
- **Entwicklung 1:** Argumente für den Vorschlag (*pros*) (ca. 40 %)
- **Entwicklung 2:** Argumente gegen den Vorschlag (*cons*) (ca. 40 %)
(Wie auch immer Sie persönlich zu dem Vorschlag stehen, streben Sie ein ausgewogenes Verhältnis zwischen Ihren *pros* und *cons* an.)
- **Schluss:** Ihre Meinung mit einer kurzen Angabe von Gründen. (ca. 10 %)

- Wenn Sie das geschrieben haben, was Sie sagen wollten, lesen Sie Ihre Präsentation durch. Suchen Sie nach Stellen, wo Sie etwas kürzen oder löschen können. Fragen Sie sich immer wieder: Kann ich das noch kürzer, präziser ausdrücken?
- Erstellen Sie sich nun Stichwortkarten als Erinnerungshilfe für die wichtigsten Informationen. Schreiben Sie auf Karteikarten; schreiben Sie deutlich und in Großbuchstaben und niemals ganze Sätze – Sie benötigen nur Stichwörter.
- Es hilft, Ihre Präsentation als Trockenübung zu geben, besonders vor einem Publikum.

Übung 1 (Fertigkeit 8A)

A Entscheiden Sie, welche der folgenden Themen Sie zu einer Meinungsäußerung veranlassen, weil sie für Sie strittig sind.

1. Fitness studios in our area: numbers, prices and facilities
2. The state – not the children – should look after the elderly
3. The rise of global warming from the early 1960s to the present day
4. Using animals in medical research helps people

B Wählen Sie eines der strittigen Themen aus. Sammeln Sie fünf Argumente für und gegen den Vorschlag.

C Halten Sie Ihre Meinung zu dem von Ihnen ausgewählten Vorschlag schriftlich fest. Fassen Sie Ihre Gründe kurz zusammen.

B Das Verwenden von Folien und Handouts während einer Präsentation

Folien können bei Schaubildern sinnvoll, aber als Teil Ihrer Präsentation auch hinderlich sein. Aus diesem Grund fragen Sie sich bitte vor dem Erstellen von Folien, ob sie notwendig sind. Wenn ja:

- Beschränken Sie die Textmenge auf ein Minimum und stellen Sie sicher, dass die Rechtschreibung stimmt.
- Vergewissern Sie sich, dass Kurvenbilder und andere Abbildungen groß genug sind, um von den Zuhörern/Zuhörerinnen erkannt zu werden.

Handouts sind Unterlagen, die Ihre Präsentation unterstützen. Ein Teil dieser Unterlagen enthält ggf. die von Ihnen verwendeten Folien; andere Handouts ergänzen bzw. erweitern die Informationen, die Sie präsentiert haben. Sie sollten prägnante Informationen oder/und Illustrationen enthalten und ordentlich getippt bzw. gedruckt sein. Sie sollten nicht Ihre Präsentation in einer Kurzfassung enthalten.

C Eine Präsentation halten

- Beginnen Sie mit einer Begrüßung Ihrer Zuhörer/Zuhörerinnen und stellen Sie anschließend sich und Ihr Thema vor. Versuchen Sie, das Interesse und die Aufmerksamkeit Ihrer Zuhörerschaft von Anfang an zu wecken. Sagen Sie, wie lang Sie über etwas reden werden, z. B.: *"In the next 10 minutes, I will share my ideas about …"*
- Teilen Sie Ihrem Hörerkreis mit, wie Sie Ihre Präsentation unterteilt haben bzw. wie viele Punkte Sie abdecken wollen, z. B.: *"I've divided my talk into three sections: first … second …"*
- Setzen Sie für Ihre Zuhörer/Zuhörerinnen während der Präsentation Signale, damit diese wissen, was als Nächstes kommt. So helfen Sie ihnen, Ihrer Kernaussage leichter zu folgen. Sie sollten auch klar vermitteln, wie ein Teil Ihrer Präsentation mit dem nächsten zusammenhängt; dies tun Sie mittels Hinweisen. Lassen Sie sie wissen, wo Sie sind. Nützliche Redewendungen finden Sie online mit diesem Webcode.

    Phrases → Webcode: FOSSKP4
- Nachdem Sie das Ende Ihrer Präsentation eingeläutet haben, fassen Sie sich kurz und kommen Sie zum Ende. Ermutigen Sie Ihre Zuhörer/Zuhörerinnen, Fragen zu stellen.

Übung 2 (Fertigkeit 8C)

Hören Sie zu, wie jemand eine Präsentation beginnt und beendet. Machen Sie sich Notizen und nehmen Sie hierzu die u. s. Überschriften zu Hilfe.

Hörtext → Webcode: FOSSKT2

Das Publikum begrüßen	Sich selbst vorstellen	Den Aufbau der Präsentation beschreiben	Über Fragen und Handouts informieren	Die Präsentation beenden

Skills files

D Körpersprache

- Nehmen Sie Augenkontakt auf.
- Sehen Sie in die Zuhörerschaft und lächeln Sie.
- Stehen Sie nicht steif da und verschränken Sie Ihre Arme nicht vor Ihrem Körper.
- Lesen Sie Ihre Präsentation nicht vor. Schreiben Sie nieder, was Sie sagen wollen, dann lernen Sie es, und dann sagen Sie es.

Übung 3 (Fertigkeiten 8 A bis D)

Choose one of the topics below and follow the instructions. If you have the chance, ask your teacher if you can give the presentation in class as extra practice.

- Wählen Sie ein Thema aus und nutzen Sie die Informationen aus dieser Lektion, um sich inhaltlich vorzubereiten.
  Topic 1: How to give a good presentation
  Topic 2: The theory and practice of skills as described in Focus on Success
- Erstellen Sie Folien und Handreichungen, wenn Sie sicher sind, dass Sie sie benötigen.
- Wenn Sie die Möglichkeit haben, bitten Sie Ihren Lehrer/Ihre Lehrerin, die Präsentation als zusätzliche Übung vor der Klasse halten zu dürfen und bitten Sie ihn/sie oder Ihre Mitschüler/innen (*peer correction*) um Rückmeldungen.

9 INTERAKTION

Sie werden möglicherweise im Unterricht bzw. als Teil einer Prüfung aufgefordert, an einer Diskussion bzw. einem Rollenspiel mitzuwirken. Beide dieser Aufgaben schließen einen Austausch mit anderen Menschen ein. Folgen Sie den u.s. allgemeinen Tipps.

Tipps für einen guten Austausch

- Verinnerlichen Sie die Ausdrücke auf der hinteren Umschlaginnenseite und verwenden Sie sie im Unterricht, sooft Sie können. → *Language for discussion*, hintere Umschlagsklappe
- Halten Sie sich an das Thema.
- Bleiben Sie locker und denken Sie, bevor Sie sprechen.
- Bleiben Sie immer höflich und geben Sie anderen die Möglichkeit zu reden. Hören Sie aktiv zu und gehen Sie auf die anderen Teilnehmer/innen ein. Nehmen Sie Augenkontakt auf und zeigen Sie Interesse, Überraschung, usw. Stellen Sie Fragen.
- Hören Sie aufmerksam zu, was die anderen sagen.
- Werten Sie andere niemals ab. Wenn ein/e andere/r Teilnehmer/in Probleme zu haben scheint, helfen Sie ihm/ihr, indem Sie in Worte fassen, was (Sie glauben, was) er/sie ausdrücken möchte, z. B.:
  So, you mean that … I think I understand what you're getting at. It's as if …

An Diskussionen teilnehmen

In einer Diskussion sollten Sie Ihre Meinung zum Ausdruck bringen.
- Lesen Sie die Anweisungen sorgfältig durch und entscheiden Sie, was Sie sagen möchten.
- Machen Sie sich Notizen und schreiben Sie einige Schlüsselwörter bzw. -ausdrücke auf Englisch auf.

Interaktion

- Versuchen Sie vorauszusehen, was die anderen Teilnehmer/innen sagen könnten. Überlegen Sie sich, wie Sie hierzu reagieren würden, und fügen Sie Ihren Notizen englische Ausdrücke der Zustimmung bzw. Widerrede hinzu.

Ein Rollenspiel gestalten
Ein Rollenspiel gibt die Situation und Rollen vor, die Sie spielen und erkunden.
- Lesen Sie Ihre Rollenkarte sorgfältig durch. Ihre Rollenkarte sagt Ihnen, wer Sie sind und was Sie sagen sollen. Selbst wenn Sie nicht mit dem einverstanden sind, was Ihre Figur sagt bzw. wie sie sich benimmt, „denken" Sie sich in diese Rolle hinein.
- Machen Sie sich Notizen zu den Argumenten, die Ihre Figur sagen könnte, um ihren Standpunkt zu vertreten.

Übung 1 (Fertigkeit 9)

Role play

Situation: You are going to play the role of one of four people involved in a podium discussion about free apps which are used by electronic companies to advertise and persuade teenagers to buy other apps and online games.

A Arbeiten Sie in Vierergruppen und entscheiden Sie, wer welche Rolle übernimmt. Machen Sie sich Notizen zu dem, was Sie sagen möchten, und beginnen Sie dann das Rollenspiel.

Ray Dawson: advertising analyst
You know what you are talking about and are used to people listening to you.
You believe that these apps will help companies make money.
Nobody is being forced to play these games.

Jane Jones: online marketing manager for an electronic company
You are keen to promote your company's games and think people will have a lot of fun with them. The company is not marketing the apps as educational games; they are marketed solely as games for fun.

Michael/a Griffin: a teenager
You have a lot of experience with online games. Your older brother plays online games, too. You used to spend a lot of time playing them, but you play less now as you have to concentrate on your school subjects.
You know some pupils who are addicted to games, but most of your friends are sensible and don't spend all day online.

Sam Dawson: the parent of two teenagers, aged 12 and 13
You are concerned about the effect these free apps will have on young people. You would like to see this type of advertising banned.
Your children have smart phones and electronic equipment like all their friends.
You worry that your children's school work will suffer if they spend too much time playing games.

B Wenn Sie fertig sind, bleiben Sie in Ihren Gruppen und sprechen Sie über die Übung. Tauschen Sie sich über folgende Punkte aus:
- Konnte jede/r Teilnehmer/in seine/ihre Ansichten klar vermitteln?
- Waren alle höflich?
- Hörten alle einander zu?

Skills files

10 PRÜFUNGSSTRATEGIEN

Alles, was Sie während Ihres Schuljahres gelernt haben, wird Ihnen zu guten Prüfungsergebnissen verhelfen. Seit dem Beginn Ihres Englischkurses haben Sie dieselbe Art von Aufgaben gelöst, die Sie in der Prüfung bekommen, einschließlich Lesen, Schreiben und sich beim Reden abwechseln. Das Durcharbeiten der *Building skills boxes* der jeweiligen Units sowie dieses *Skills*-Anhangs hat Ihnen die Strategien vermittelt, die Sie für einen Test bzw. eine Prüfung benötigen.

Die folgenden Tipps helfen Ihnen, in jedem Test bzw. in jeder Prüfung Ihr Bestes zu geben:

A Die schriftliche Prüfung

- Lesen Sie sich alle Fragen sorgfältig durch und stellen Sie sicher, dass Sie wissen, was zu tun ist.
- Entscheiden Sie, bei welchen Aufgaben Sie sich besonders sicher sind, dass Sie sie lösen können, und welche die meisten Punkte bringen. Gehen Sie diese Aufgaben zuerst an.
- In Bezug auf textbezogene Fragen fragen Sie sich: Welche Textstelle/n benötige ich zur Beantwortung der Frage?
- In Bezug auf Fragen zum Hörverständnis fragen Sie sich: Worauf muss ich achten?
- In Bezug auf schriftliche Aufgaben fragen Sie sich: Welche Art von Text muss ich schreiben? Dann machen Sie sich Notizen und ordnen Sie Ihren Text, bevor Sie die Endfassung schreiben. Zum Schluss überprüfen Sie Rechtschreibung und Grammatik.
- Wenn Sie mit den Prüfungsaufgaben fertig sind und bevor Sie Ihre Aufgaben abgeben, überprüfen Sie, dass Sie alle Anweisungen und jede Aufgabe ordentlich erfüllt haben. Vergewissern Sie sich, keine Frage ausgelassen zu haben.

B Die mündliche Prüfung

- Lesen Sie die Aufgabenstellung durch und legen Sie Ihre Argumentationslinie fest.
- Sofern es erlaubt ist, machen Sie sich Notizen zu dem, was Sie sagen möchten, und zwar bevor Sie zu reden beginnen (Stichpunkte reichen aus).
- Denken Sie an die idiomatischen Ausdrücke, die Sie gelernt haben, sowie die Strategie, sich abzuwechseln.
- Versuchen Sie, die Argumente vorauszuahnen, die der andere Teilnehmer / die anderen Teilnehmerinnen verwenden könnte. Versuchen Sie, Ihre Reaktion auf diese Argumente vorauszuahnen, und verwenden Sie hierfür Ausdrücke der Zustimmung, Widerrede, usw.
- Wenn Sie plötzlich einen Gedächtnisausfall haben und sich an kein einziges Wort erinnern können, umschreiben Sie, was Sie sagen möchten. Reden Sie weiter!

Wenden Sie diese Tipps bei nächster Gelegenheit an, z. B. bei einem Klassentest oder einer gestellten Prüfung. Die Rückmeldungen, die Sie auf Ihre Darbietung von Ihrer Klasse bekommen, zeigt Ihnen, in welchen Bereichen Sie sich noch verbessern können.

Grammar files

Diese *Grammar files* führen Sie durch die wichtigsten Elemente der englischen Grammatik und erklären die Formen und den Gebrauch der Strukturen. Sie können die hier angebotenen Übungen nutzen, um zu üben und Ihre Kenntnisse zu vertiefen. Die Lösungen dazu finden Sie auf www.cornelsen.de/webcodes. Geben Sie einfach den Webcode FOSGRLO im Webcode-Suchfeld ein.

Lösungen → Webcode: FOSGRLO

SIMPLE PRESENT ▪ PRESENT PROGRESSIVE

Form

	Simple present	Present progressive
Aussage	I/you/we/they **play** he/she/it **plays**	I **am playing** you/we/they **are playing** he/she/it **is playing**
Verneinung	I/you/we/they **don't play** he/she/it **doesn't play**	I'**m not playing** you/we/they **aren't playing** he/she/it **isn't playing**
Frage + Kurzantwort	Do I/you/we/they **play**? ▪ Yes, I/you/we/they **do**. ▪ No, I/you/we/they **don't**. Does he/she/it **play**? ▪ Yes, he/she/it **does**. ▪ No, he/she/it **doesn't**.	**Am** I **playing**? ▪ Yes, I **am**. ▪ No, I'**m not**. **Are** you/we/they **playing**? ▪ Yes, you/we/they **are**. ▪ No, you/we/they **aren't**. **Is** he/she/it **playing**? ▪ Yes, he/she/it **is**. ▪ No, he/she/it **isn't**.

Simple present
- In der dritten Person Singular (z. B. nach *he, Sandra, the coffee*) hängt man *s* an das Verb an bzw. *es*, wenn das Verb auf einen Zischlaut (z. B. *ch*) endet.
- Frage und Verneinung bildet man mit *do/don't* und *does/doesn't*. In Sätzen mit *does/doesn't* hat das Verb kein *(e)s*.

Present progressive
- Wenn das Verb auf *e* endet, fällt das *e* vor *ing* weg: *hope – hoping*.
- Bei einem einsilbigen Verb, das auf einen einzelnen Vokal + einzelnen Konsonanten endet, verdoppelt man den Konsonanten: *stop – sto**pp**ing, plan – pla**nn**ing*.

Gebrauch

Simple present	Present progressive
I **come** from Germany.	Wait for me! I'**m coming**.
I **don't eat** much chocolate.	It's hot today and I'**m eating** an ice-cream.
This train **doesn't stop** in Hexford.	Why **is** the train **stopping** on the bridge today?
Germany sometimes **plays** against England.	Today Germany **is playing** against Ireland.
Moni is a designer. She **designs** clothes.	At the moment she **is designing** a new style of jeans.

249

Grammar files

- Mit dem **simple present** beschreibt man einen Normalzustand und was eigentlich immer so ist – regelmäßige Vorgänge, Gewohnheiten und was zum Tagesablauf gehört, was man beruflich und in der Freizeit macht.
- Mit dem **present progressive** beschreibt man ein momentanes Geschehen, einen Einzelvorgang, der gerade im Verlauf begriffen ist.
- Das **present progressive** verwendet man auch für eine vorübergehende Tätigkeit, die mit Unterbrechungen über eine gewisse Zeit ausgeübt wird, eine vorübergehende Situation im Leben: *This week I'm helping my friend to repair his moped.*
- Das **simple present** und das **present progressive** verwendet man häufig mit den folgenden typischen Zeitangaben:

Simple present	Present progressive
- always, often, usually, sometimes, never - every morning/day/year - at … o'clock, in the morning, at lunchtime, after school - on Monday(s), at the weekend, in June, in the summer	- now, at the moment, just - today, this week, this month, this summer

Was sonst noch wichtig ist

- Das **simple present** verwendet man auch, um etwas zu erzählen – eine Filmhandlung, eine Story, einen Witz oder den Inhalt einer Sendung oder eines Textes:
  *The film tells the story of Julian Timbo and how he **becomes** a great star.*
  *In today's programme Kelly Green **talks** about her career.*

- ⚠ Bestimmte Verben kann man nur im **simple present** verwenden.

  have, need, want, like, love, hate, prefer, know, think, remember, understand, believe, realize, seem, mean, belong to

- Wenn *have* aber eine Tätigkeit beschreibt, kann es auch im **present progressive** stehen.

have = „haben, besitzen"	*have* beschreibt eine Tätigkeit
Sorry, I **have** no time.	I'**m having** lunch / a cup of tea.
Stars **have** a lot of money.	We'**re having** a great time/party.

- Das **present progressive** verwendet man auch für zukünftige Vorhaben, wenn Vorkehrungen oder Abmachungen bereits getroffen wurden oder jemand eine bestimmte Zeiteinteilung für sich vorgenommen hat:
  *I'**m meeting** Sam this evening. We'**re going** to the cinema.*
  *Susan **is flying** to London next week.*

1 Complete the sentences with simple present forms of the verbs in brackets.

EXAMPLES: A (you/know) ▬¹ Emma Gordon?   → A Do you know Emma Gordon?
          B No, ▬². I (not know) ▬³ her.   → B No, I don't. I don't know her.

1 A (you/speak) ▬¹ English?
   B Yes, ▬². But I (not use) ▬³ it very often.

**Simple present • Present progressive
Simple past • Past progressive**

2 **A** (your friend Mike / have) ▬¹ a car?
   B No, ▬². But he (have) ▬³ a motorbike.
3 **A** (English people / watch) ▬¹ German films?
   B No, ▬². They (not watch) ▬³ many non-British or non-American films.
4 **A** (your coffee / taste) ▬¹ good?
   B Yes, ▬². It (taste) ▬³ bitter, I like that.

2 Complete the sentences with present progressive forms of the verbs in brackets.

1 **A** What (you/do) ▬¹ at the moment? (you/work) ▬²?
   B No, ▬³. I (check) ▬⁴ my Facebook page.
2 **A** What language (that woman / speak) ▬¹? (she/speak) ▬² Spanish?
   B No, ▬³. She (speak) ▬⁴ Portuguese.
3 **A** Sorry, (I/phone) ▬¹ in the middle of your meal?
   B No, ▬². We (not eat) ▬³ at the moment.
4 **A** (Dennis/come) ▬¹ with us to the Swimarena this afternoon?
   B Yes, ▬². He (come) ▬³ on his moped.

3 Complete the sentences with the correct simple present or present progressive forms of the verbs in brackets.

1 I (try out) ▬¹ a new provider. I (think) ▬² it's better than my old one.
2 Where (you/come) ▬ from? Are you Canadian?
3 What (Manuela/do) ▬ ? Is she a radio journalist too?
4 What (Manuela/do) ▬¹ today? (she/interview) ▬² Kelly Green?
5 Tunisia is a hot country. It (not rain) ▬ much.
6 Oh no! It (rain) ▬ . We can forget our barbecue.

SIMPLE PAST ■ PAST PROGRESSIVE

Form

	Simple past	Past progressive
Aussage	I/you/he/she/it/we/they **played**	I/he/she/it **was playing** you/we/they **were playing**
Verneinung	I/you/he/she/it/we/they **didn't play**	I/he/she/it **wasn't playing** you/we/they **weren't playing**
Frage + Kurzantwort	**Did** I/you/he/she/it/we/they **play**? ■ Yes, I / … **did**. / ■ No, I / … **didn't**.	**Was** I/he/she/it **playing**? ■ Yes, I/he/she/it **was**. ■ No, I/he/she/it **wasn't**. **Were** you/we/they **playing**? ■ Yes, you/we/they **were**. ■ No, you/we/they **weren't**.

Simple past

- Wenn ein regelmäßiges Verb auf *e* endet, hängt man nur *d* an (hope – hoped).
- Bei einem einsilbigen Verb, das auf einen einzelnen Vokal + einzelnen Konsonanten endet, verdoppelt man den Konsonanten: *stop – sto**pp**ed, plan – pla**nn**ed*.
- ❗ Unregelmäßige Verben haben eigene Formen – s. Liste auf S. 349.

Grammar files

- Frage und Verneinung bildet man in allen Personen mit *did/didn't*. Das Verb steht dann in der Grundform und hat keine *(e)d* -Endung.

Gebrauch

Simple past
Last year I **was** in London on my birthday.
I **didn't see** my boyfriend last week.
Why **did** the computer **crash**?

Past progressive
I **was staying** with an English family.
He **was doing** a work placement project.
Nobody **was using** it.

- Mit dem **simple past** beschreibt man etwas, das in der Vergangenheit zu einem bestimmten Zeitpunkt oder in einem bestimmten Zeitraum geschehen ist.
- Mit dem **past progressive** beschreibt man etwas, das in der Vergangenheit zu einem bestimmten Zeitpunkt gerade im Gange war. Das kann auch eine vorübergehende Tätigkeit sein, die mit Unterbrechungen über eine gewisse Zeit ausgeübt wurde.

Was sonst noch wichtig ist

- Mit dem **past progressive** beschreibt man einen länger andauernden Vorgang, der durch ein Ereignis von kurzer Dauer unterbrochen wird. Dieses kurze Ereignis steht im **simple past**.
    *I **was checking** my newsfeed <u>when</u> an SMS from Julie **arrived**.*
    *We **were walking** home <u>when</u> Martina **passed** us on her moped.*

- ❗ Bestimmte Verben kann man nicht im **past progressive**, sondern nur im **simple past** verwenden.

    need, want, like, love, hate, prefer, know, think, remember, understand, believe, realize, seem, mean, belong to

---

1 Complete the sentences with simple past forms of the verbs in brackets.

1. **A** (you/make) ▬¹ a pizza at the weekend?
   B No, I (not do) ▬². I (buy) ▬³ one.
2. **A** When (you/speak) ▬¹ to your friend in England last?
   B I (skype) ▬² with her last weekend.
3. **A** (your brother/go) ▬¹ to Zurich by plane?
   B No, he (not do) ▬². He (not fly) ▬³. He (go) ▬⁴ by car. He (drive) ▬⁵ there.
4. **A** Why (you/not come) ▬¹ to Amy's party last weekend?
   B I (not feel) ▬² good. I (spend) ▬³ the whole day in bed.

2 Complete the sentences with past progressive forms of the verbs in brackets.

1. **A** You were on the phone. Who (you/speak) ▬¹ to? (you/talk) ▬² to that Susie again?
   B No, I (not talk) ▬³ to another girl. I (check) ▬⁴ something with my mum.
2. **A** Where (you/sit) ▬¹ at the concert?
   B I (not sit) ▬². I (stand) ▬³ because there weren't any seats left.
3. **A** What (Mark/do) ▬¹ out in the cold?
   B He (wait) ▬² for his brother.
4. **A** (you/ have) ▬¹ a good time when I saw you?
   B No, I was really bored. Nothing (happen) ▬².

Present perfect • Present perfect progressive

3 In each sentence there is one simple past and one past progressive form. Complete the sentences with the correct forms of the verbs in brackets.

1. I (answer) ▬¹ the last question in the test when the teacher (tell) ▬² us to stop.
2. Where (you/go) ▬¹ when I (see) ▬² you yesterday?
3. At 8.30 yesterday evening? I (be) ▬¹ at home, I (play) ▬² a computer game.
4. My friends and I (just leave) ▬¹ when it (start) ▬² to rain.
5. It (not rain) ▬¹ when I (get) ▬² on the bus.
6. It was a cold day. Samira (not want) ▬¹ a cold drink so she (drink) ▬² coffee.

PRESENT PERFECT ▪ PRESENT PERFECT PROGRESSIVE

Form

	Present perfect	Present perfect progressive
Aussage	I/you/we/they **have played** he/she/it **has played**	I/you/we/they **have been playing** he/she/it **has been playing**
Verneinung	I/you/we/they **haven't played** he/she/it **hasn't played**	I/you/we/they **haven't been playing** he/she/it **hasn't been playing**
Frage + Kurzantwort	**Have** I/you/we/they **played**? ▪ Yes, I/you/we/they **have**. ▪ No, I/you/we/they **haven't**. **Has** he/she/it **played**? ▪ Yes, he/she/it **has**. ▪ No, he/she/it **hasn't**.	**Have** I/you/we/they **been playing**? ▪ Yes, I/you/we/they **have**. ▪ No, I/you/we/they **haven't**. **Has** he/she/it **been playing**? ▪ Yes, he/she/it **has**. ▪ No, he/she/it **hasn't**.

Present perfect

- Bei regelmäßigen Verben hat das Partizip die gleiche Form wie im **simple past**. Es gelten die gleichen Schreibbesonderheiten (s. S. 251).
- ❗ Das Partizip unregelmäßiger Verben hat eine eigene Form – s. Liste auf S. 349. Es ist manchmal identisch mit dem **simple past**, manchmal aber nicht.

Gebrauch

Present perfect	Present perfect progressive
We**'ve finished** the test.	We**'ve been working** non-stop.
I **haven't had** this phone long.	I**'ve been using** my friend's phone.
Has the rain **stopped**?	How long **has** it **been raining**?

- Mit dem **present perfect** sagt man, dass etwas geschehen ist.
- Mit dem **present perfect progressive** sagt man, dass etwas eine Zeit lang bis jetzt angedauert hat.
- Beim **present perfect** steht oft ein Ergebnis im Vordergrund, während beim **present perfect progressive** das Andauern betont wird.
- ❗ Bestimmte Verben kann man nicht im **progressive** verwenden.

> need, want, like, love, hate, prefer, know, think, remember, understand, believe, realize, seem, mean, belong to

Grammar files

Was sonst noch wichtig ist

- ❗ Wenn etwas in der Vergangenheit angefangen hat und bis jetzt andauert, verwendet man das **present perfect (progressive)** – nicht, wie im Deutschen, eine Gegenwartsform.
  I've lived / I've been living here for five years. (I live here for …)
  We've sat / We've been sitting here since half past one / since it started to rain.
  (We sit here since …)

- *For* + Zeitraum (*five years, a few days*) – Antwort auf die Frage „wie lange?"
  Since + Zeitpunkt (*2012, Sunday*) – Antwort auf die Frage „seit wann?"
  I haven't seen Jenny for a few days. Is she ill?
  I haven't seen her since Sunday / since we played tennis together.

1 Complete the sentences with present perfect forms of the verbs in brackets.

1. I (see) ▬¹ the new movie. (you/see) ▬² it?
2. Susanne (make) ▬ copies for everyone.
3. My visa (not arrive) ▬¹. (yours/arrive) ▬²?
4. We (not meet) ▬¹ before. But I (hear) ▬² a lot about you.
5. (you/have) ▬¹ lunch? I (not eat) ▬².

2 Complete the sentences with present perfect progressive forms of the verbs in brackets.

1. I (wait) ▬¹ a long time. I (play) ▬² a computer game to help pass the time.
2. They (talk) ▬¹ all evening. They (discuss) ▬² the new project.
3. How long (you/work) ▬ on your presentation?
4. How long (it/snow) ▬ ?
5. We (not chat) ▬¹, we (work) ▬² hard!

3 Decide whether you should use *for* or *since* with the following expressions.

1 eighteen months	3 Tuesday morning	5 two seconds	7 2009
2 a year and a half	4 last January	6 ages	8 Christmas

4 Correct these sentences. Use the present perfect.

1. ~~I live here for six years.~~
2. ~~We know each other for a long time.~~
3. ~~Marina is ill all this week.~~
4. ~~We have this computer for years.~~
5. ~~How long are you a member of this club?~~

SIMPLE PAST ▪ PRESENT PERFECT

Gebrauch

Present perfect	Simple past
I **have been** to London.	I **went** there *last year*.
We**'ve had** rain today. We**'ve** *just* **had** a shower.	*Yesterday* it **rained** all afternoon.
Have you **seen** this film *before*?	I **saw** it *last month* with Jack.
Has Mark **phoned** *yet*? – Yes, he **has**.	*When* **did** he **phone**? – He **called** *half an hour ago*.

Simple past · Present perfect

- Mit dem **present perfect** sagt man, dass etwas – irgendwann – in der Zeit bis jetzt geschehen ist, wann ist entweder unwichtig oder unbekannt. Man stellt nur fest, **dass** etwas geschehen ist. Wird der Zeitpunkt genannt, darf man das **present perfect nicht** verwenden.
- Das **simple past** wird verwendet, wenn etwas in der Vergangenheit zu einem bestimmten Zeitpunkt oder in einem bestimmten Zeitraum geschehen ist und dieser Zeitpunkt/Zeitraum genannt wird.

Was sonst noch wichtig ist

- Das **present perfect** und **simple past** verwendet man mit typischen Zeitangaben.

Present perfect	Simple past
ein unbestimmter Zeitpunkt in der ganzen Zeit bis jetzt	ein bestimmter Zeitpunkt oder Zeitraum der abgeschlossenen Vergangenheit
already, (not) yet, before, so far, ever, never, just	yesterday, last week/month/year, … ago, when? what time? in 2013, on 13 October, in February

- Vor allem im amerikanischen Englisch werden *already*, *(not) yet*, *ever*, *never* und *just* auch mit dem **simple past** verwendet.
- Wenn man etwas erzählt, verwendet man manchmal beide Zeitformen im gleichen Zusammenhang. Zuerst berichtet man mit dem **present perfect** die „nackte" Neuigkeit, anschließend nennt man weitere Einzelheiten (einschl. des Zeitpunkts) mit dem **simple past**.
  *Ron **has broken** his leg. He **had** an accident on his moped **yesterday on his way home**.*
  *I**'ve heard** from Maria. She **sent** me an SMS **10 minutes ago**.*
- Auch wenn kein Zeitpunkt genannt wird, muss man das **simple past** verwenden, wenn etwas zu einem ganz bestimmten Zeitpunkt geschehen sein muss.
  *The team **didn't win** any medals at the London Olympics.*
  [Die Olympiade in London fand zu einem bestimmten Zeitpunkt der Vergangenheit statt.]
- Das **present perfect** verwendet man oft, wenn etwas Auswirkungen auf die Gegenwart hat.
  *I**'ve been** to London. (= Ich kenne London.)*
  *They**'ve put** the prices up 20%. (= Es ist zu teuer geworden. Diese Preise will ich nicht zahlen.)*

1 **Make dialogues as in the example.**

    EXAMPLES: **A** (you/ever/watch) ▬¹ an international football match live?
                    B Yes, I ▬². I (see) ▬³ Germany against Denmark last year.
                    A Have you ever watched an international football match live?
                    B Yes, I have. I saw Germany against Denmark last year.

1 **A** (you/ever/meet) ▬¹ a celebrity?
    B No, I ▬². But I (see) ▬³ a B-list celebrity in Berlin last month.
2 **A** (you/make) ▬¹ notes for the summary task yet?
    B No, I ▬². But I (read) ▬³ the text again last night.
3 **A** (you/ever/have) ▬¹ an accident?
    B No, I ▬². But my brother (break) ▬³ his leg on a skiing trip in January.
4 **A** (you/buy) ▬¹ your new bike yet?
    B Yes, I ▬². I (find) ▬³ a great offer on the internet.

Grammar files

2 Complete the sentences with the correct verb form: present perfect or simple past.
1. Last year I (take) ▬ a trip to Ireland.
2. I (be) ▬ there twice now.
3. I (make) ▬ good friends when I was there. We chat nearly every week.
4. Last time I (fly) ▬ with a new airline.
5. Flying (become) ▬ very cheap over the years.
6. The first time I (go) ▬¹ to Ireland it (cost) ▬² a lot of money.

PAST PERFECT ▪ SIMPLE PAST

Form des past perfect

Aussage	I/you/we/they/he/she/it **had played**
Verneinung	I/you/we/they/he/she/it **hadn't played**
Frage + Kurzantwort	**Had** I/you/we/they/he/she/it **played**? ▪ Yes, I/you/we/they/he/she/it **had**. ▪ No, I/you/we/they/he/she/it **hadn't**.

- Das **past perfect** bildet man in allen Personen gleich, mit *had* + Partizip Perfekt.

Gebrauch des past perfect

I got to the station two minutes late and the train **had** already **left**.
At four o'clock in the afternoon I still **hadn't eaten** anything.

- Mit dem **past perfect** sagt man, dass etwas zu einem Zeitpunkt in der Vergangenheit bereits geschehen und abgeschlossen war.

Unterschied zum simple past

- Wenn man z. B. eine Geschichte erzählt und es zwei oder mehr Geschehnisse gab, die miteinander in einem Zusammenhang standen, verwendet man das **simple past**.
*The plane **landed**, we **got off**, **collected** our bags and **went** to the car park.*

- Wenn es wichtig ist, auszudrücken, dass sich ein Geschehen vor einem anderen ereignet hatte, verwendet man für das zeitlich erste Geschehen das **past perfect**.
*I **wanted** to phone my girlfriend, but **couldn't** find my phone. I'**d left** it on the plane!*

- Nach *after*, *before*, *until* und *as soon as* kann entweder das **simple past** oder das **past perfect** stehen.
*After I **arrived** / **had arrived** home, I called the airline.*

- ❗ *'d* kann für *had*, aber auch für *would* stehen.
*At my grandma's 70th birthday there was loads to eat. After two platefuls I'**d (I had)** eaten enough but my boyfriend said, "I'**d (I would)** like some more, please."*

Past perfect · Simple past
Will future · Going to future

1 Which happened first, A or B?

	A	B
1	We went out	after it had stopped raining.
2	I was short of cash	because I had spent so much on presents.
3	Jack had already arrived	when I got there.
4	The policewoman explained to me	what had happened.
5	There I was at the bank	and I had left my wallet at home.

2 In each sentence there is one verb in the simple past and one in the past perfect. Complete the sentences with the correct forms.

1. The road (be) ▭¹ blocked. There (be) ▭² an accident.
2. We (not drive) ▭¹ far, when a warning light (come) ▭² on.
3. I (run) ▭¹, but the flight (close) ▭².
4. I (not remember) ▭¹ the man, although I (meet) ▭² him the year before.
5. Meg (invite) ▭¹ Tony to her party, but he (already make) ▭² other plans.

WILL FUTURE · GOING TO FUTURE

Form

	will	going to
Aussage	I/you/we/they/he/she/it **will play**	I **am going to play** you/we/they **are going to play** he/she/it **is going to play**
Verneinung	I/you/we/they/he/she/it **won't play**	I'**m not going to play** you/we/they **aren't going to play** he/she/it **isn't going to play**
Frage + Kurzantwort	**Will** I/you/we/they/he/she/it **play**? ▪ Yes, I/you/we/they/he/she/it **will**. ▪ No I/you/we/they/he/she/it **won't**.	**Am/Are/Is** … **going to play**? ▪ Yes, … **am/are/is**. ▪ No, … am **not/aren't/isn't**.

- Die Verneinung von *will* heißt *won't*. *Won't* ist die Kurzform von *will not*. Die Kurzform von *will* ist *'ll*.

Gebrauch

will	going to
We **will know** the result of the casting show soon.	I've decided. I'm never **going to take part** in a casting show.
I'**ll** perhaps/probably **be** late home tonight.	All the class **is going to meet** up at Jogi's.
I think / am sure you'**ll get** the job.	Who **is going to drive** you to the interview?

- Es gibt keine wirklich feste Regel, wann *will* und wann *going to* verwendet wird. In manchen Kontexten sind sie austauschbar. Als Faustregel gilt:
  - wenn man eine Vorhersage ausdrückt, verwendet man *will*;
  - wenn man eine Absicht, einen Plan oder ein Vorhaben ausdrückt, verwendet man *going to*.
- Nach Ausdrücken wie *I think, I promise, I hope, I'm sure, I expect* wird häufig *will* verwendet. *Going to* ist aber oft auch möglich.

Grammar files

Was sonst noch wichtig ist

- Um einen spontanen Entschluss (oft ein Angebot) auszudrücken, verwendet man *will*. Eine Gegenwartsform ist nicht möglich:
  *That bag looks heavy. Let me help you. I**'ll carry** it for you.* [Nicht: *I carry it for you.*]
  *Tea or coffee for you? – Oh I **won't have** anything to drink, thanks.* [Nicht: *I don't have …*]

- Beachten Sie den Unterschied zwischen einem spontanen und einem vorüberlegten Entschluss:
  *Someone is at the door. – OK, I**'ll see** who it is.* [spontan]
  *Susie has bought cinema tickets for this evening. We**'re going to see** a new movie.* [vorüberlegt]

- *Going to* verwendet man auch für Vorhersagen, wenn man aufgrund von eindeutigen Vorzeichen sagen kann, dass etwas mit Bestimmtheit eintreten wird:
  *Look at that car! It's far too fast. Oh no! It**'s going to crash**. There**'s going to be** an accident.*

- Mit *going to* macht man auch Vorhersagen aufgrund von persönlichen Annahmen. Man ist überzeugt, dass etwas mit Bestimmtheit eintreten wird:
  *Oil **is going to become** more and more expensive.*
  *When the exam results come out, some of us **are going to be** disappointed.*

- Man kann auch das **present progressive** für zukünftige Vorhaben verwenden, wenn Vorkehrungen oder Abmachungen bereits getroffen wurden oder jemand eine bestimmte Zeiteinteilung für sich vorgenommen hat:
  *I**'m meeting** Sam this evening. We**'re going** to the cinema.*
  *Susan **is flying** to London next week.*

1 Complete the sentences with *will/won't*.

1 Holidays on the moon (not happen) ▬ in my lifetime.
2 Sorry, but there (not be) ▬ enough time for a visit to Disneyland.
3 Why (there / not be) ▬ enough time?
4 When (we / find out) ▬ what the cost is going to be?
5 Next year is our anniversary. This school (be) ▬ 25 years old.

2 Complete the sentences with *going to*.

1 We've got so many interesting things planned. The project week (be) ▬ a big success.
2 I (ask) ▬ Tom if he can help me with this maths homework.
3 (the police officer / arrest) ▬ that man?
4 We don't need a hotel. We (stay) ▬ with friends.
5 This is a really difficult task. It (not be) ▬ easy.

3 Complete the translation.

1 Du musst uns nicht fahren. Wir nehmen ein Taxi.   You don't have to drive us. We ▬ a taxi.
2 Ich helfe Ihnen mit Ihrer Tasche.   I ▬ you with your bag.
3 Ich hole dir ein Pflaster.   I ▬ you a plaster.
4 Wir nehmen eine große Pizza und zwei Cola bitte.   We ▬ a pizza and two colas, please.
5 Lass mal, ich bezahle.   Leave it to me, I ▬ .

Modal verbs

MODAL VERBS

Verben und ihre Bedeutung

can	Keith **can** come any time.	*können*
may	I'm not sure, but we **may** be late.	*werden/können (vielleicht)*
might	Don **might** have €50 he can lend us.	*könnte(n) (vielleicht)*
must	We **must** warn Mark.	*müssen*
should	They **should** be more careful.	*sollte(n)*
ought to	I **ought to** phone my mum.	*sollte(n)*
be allowed to	**Are** we **allowed to** take photos?	*dürfen*

can, could, was/were able to

Gegenwart	I **can** see you.
Vergangenheit	
▪ generelle Fähigkeit	I **could** swim at the age of six.
▪ bestimmte Einzelsituation	I **was able to** catch the last bus.

- Nur *was/were able to* ist möglich, wenn man sagt, was jemandem in einer Einzelsituation in der Vergangenheit gelang. In Fragen und verneinten Sätzen kann man aber auch *could(n't)* verwenden:
  Were you able to see / Could you see who was driving?
  There were so many people in the room. I wasn't able to move / couldn't move.

- Nur Formen von *be able to* sind im **present perfect** möglich:
  I haven't been able to contact Martina yet.

- Man kann entweder *can* oder *will be able to* verwenden, wenn man über die Zukunft spricht.
  Shaun can come / will be able to come this evening.
  I haven't got the money with me now, but I can pay / will be able to pay you tomorrow.

must, mustn't, needn't, don't/doesn't have to, had to

Gegenwart		
▪ Aussage	We **must** meet more often.	*wir müssen*
▪ Verneinung	I **mustn't** forget Julia's birthday.	*ich darf nicht*
	You **don't have to** wait for me.	*du musst nicht*
	You **needn't** wait for me.	*du musst/brauchst nicht*
▪ Frage	How many tests **do** you **have to** do?	*müssen Sie?*
Vergangenheit		
▪ Aussage	I **had to** work late yesterday evening.	*ich musste*
▪ Verneinung	Nina **didn't have to** read her text aloud.	*Nina musste nicht*
▪ Frage	How much extra **did** you **have to** pay?	*musstet ihr?*

- ❗ *mustn't* ist ein Verbot und entspricht „nicht dürfen". „nicht müssen" drückt man mit *don't/doesn't have to* aus.
- Fragen und verneinte Sätze mit *have to* bildet man mit dem Hilfsverb *do*.

Grammar files

Was sonst noch wichtig ist
- *can* drückt aus, dass etwas generell möglich ist:
  *It **can** be very wet in November.*

- *can* kann man nicht verwenden, wenn man ausdrücken will, dass etwas möglicherweise der Fall ist:
  *We **may** / **might** / **could** be late. It depends on the traffic.* [Nicht: ~~We can be late.~~]

- *can't* und *couldn't* kann man nicht verwenden, wenn man ausdrücken will, dass etwas möglicherweise nicht der Fall ist:
  *The weather's awful. The flight **may** / **might not** go today.* [Nicht: ~~The flight can't / couldn't go.~~]

1 Decide if the underlined verb is correct. Correct the incorrect sentences.
1. I'm sorry, I <u>can't</u> help you today.
2. I can forgive him now. But a couple of months ago I <u>couldn't</u>.
3. I had to hurry, but I <u>could</u> get the train.
4. It was foggy and the plane <u>couldn't</u> land.
5. I <u>could</u> speak to the teacher before the test.
6. I <u>haven't been able to</u> reach him. Perhaps he is on holiday.

2 Decide if A or B is right.
1. I **A** mustn't / **B** don't have to forget to pay for the concert tickets.
2. You **A** mustn't / **B** don't have to come if you don't want to.
3. When was your flight? **A** Must you / **B** Did you have to get up very early?
4. You **A** mustn't / **B** needn't forget your passport.
5. We **A** needn't / **B** mustn't check in till 40 minutes before the flight.
6. He **A** mustn't / **B** needn't park there. That's the teachers' car park.

3 Decide which of the sentences are not correct.
1. **A** The problem may have something to do with the battery.
   B The problem might have something to do with the battery.
   C The problem could have something to do with the battery.

2. **A** The train may be late this morning.
   B The train can be late this morning.
   C The train might be late this morning.

3. **A** Sue could be trying to skype me. I'll switch the computer on.
   B Sue can be trying to skype me. I'll switch the computer on.
   C Sue might be trying to skype me. I'll switch the computer on.

4. **A** Ask Jerry. He can know.
   B Ask Jerry. He could know.
   C Ask Jerry. He might know.

THE PASSIVE

Form

	Aktiv	Passiv
Simple present	I **stop** you/we/they **stop** he/she/it **stops**	I **am stopped** you/we/they **are stopped** he/she/it **is stopped**
Simple past	I/he/she/it **stopped** you/we/they **stopped**	I/he/she/it **was stopped** you/we/they **were stopped**
Present perfect	I/you/we/they **have stopped** he/she/it **has stopped**	I/you/we/they **have been stopped** he/she/it **has been stopped**
Past perfect	I/you/we/they/he/she/it **had stopped**	I/you/we/they/he/she/it **had been stopped**
Futur mit *will*	I/you/we/they/he/she/it **will stop**	I/you/we/they/he/she/it **will be stopped**

- *be* + Partizip (z. B. *be stopped*) ist der Passivinfinitiv. Diese Form verwendet man nach *will* und *going to* und auch nach Modalverben wie *can, must, might, could*:
  *This law **must be stopped**.*

Gebrauch

Aktiv	Passiv
People **speak** English in South Africa.	English **is spoken** in South Africa.
Someone **stole** my phone.	My phone **was stolen**.
My mum **drove** us to the airport.	We **were driven** to the airport **by** my mum.
Police **fired** shots to control the protesters.	Shots **were fired**.

- In einem Aktivsatz sagen wir, was jemand aktiv tut. In einem Passivsatz sagen wir, was getan wird.
- Das Passiv wird verwendet, wenn es unwichtig/unbekannt ist, von wem etwas getan wird.
- In den meisten Passivsätzen wird die Person nicht genannt. Wenn sie doch genannt wird, fügt man sie mit *by* an (nicht *from!*):
  *In the film the policeman was played **by** Tom Hanks.* [Nicht: ~~from Tom Hanks~~]

- Das Passiv wird viel in Medienberichten und technischen Beschreibungen verwendet, weil es neutraler klingt:
  *The President **will be welcomed** to Britain by the Prime Minister.*
  *The machine **can be operated** in energy-saving mode.*

- Manchmal verwenden Politiker/innen, Journalist/innen und Autor/innen bewusst das Passiv, um sich von dem zu distanzieren, was sie erzählen, um „offizieller" zu wirken:
  *Hard-working families in this country tell me that too much **is being paid** to the unemployed.*

Was sonst noch wichtig ist

- Die Passivform von den **progressive tenses** wird mit *being* + Partizip gebildet:
  *A new hotel **is being built**.*
  *At the flea market all sorts of things **were being bought** and **sold**.*

Grammar files

- In einem Passivsatz wird das Objekt eines Aktivsatzes zum Subjekt:

Subjekt	Verb	Objekt
People in Italy	eat	more fruit.
More fruit	is eaten.	

- Im Gegensatz zum Deutschen kann im Englischen auch ein indirektes Objekt zum Subjekt eines Passivsatzes werden:

Subjekt	Verb	indirektes Objekt	direktes Objekt
Journalists	asked	the President	a lot of questions.
The President	was asked		a lot of questions.

Zu den Verben, bei denen dieses Satzmuster möglich ist, zählen:

ask, buy, give, offer, pay, promise, sell, send, show, tell

1 Complete the sentences with passive forms of the verbs in brackets. Be careful of the tenses.

1 When we got to the house, it was clear that we (not expect) ▬ .
2 The hotel (sell) ▬ to a Russian company last January.
3 Whenever someone enters the building at night, the alarm (activate) ▬ by the CCTV system.
4 The windows (not clean) ▬ very often. The window cleaner comes twice a year.
5 Mr Thomas's talk will last 20 minutes. Questions (can ask) ▬ at the end.
6 All windows (must close) ▬ at the end of the day.
7 I warn you: if anything like this happens again, the police (inform) ▬ .
8 The text is perfect now. All the mistakes (correct) ▬ .

2 Say the same thing in the passive.

EXAMPLES: They quickly introduced new technology.   New technology was quickly introduced.
Nobody gave me an invitation.   I wasn't given an invitation.

1 Someone has stolen my mobile phone!   My mobile phone ▬ !
2 They paid him €500.   He ▬ .
3 Make sure that someone writes all this down.   Make sure that all this ▬ .
4 Has anyone asked you to help?   ▬ you ▬ to help?
5 Somebody showed me how to operate the new system.   I ▬ how to operate the new system.
6 They've offered Tony the position.   Tony ▬ .

VERB + INFINITIVE ▪ VERB + GERUND

Gebrauch

Verb + Infinitiv	Verb + Gerundium (*ing*-Form)
I **wanted to** meet up with Mike and **managed to** organise it.	I **suggest** go**ing** by train.
We **can't afford** to wait much longer.	Sandra **avoided** talking to Matthew at the party.

Verb + infinitive · Verb + gerund

Viele Verben, u. a. folgende:		Wenige Verben, v. a. folgende:	
afford (*sich leisten*)	hope (*hoffen*)	avoid (*vermeiden*)	(not) mind (*etwas/*
choose (*wählen*)	learn (*lernen*)	dislike (*ungern tun*)	*nichts dagegen haben*)
decide (*sich entscheiden*)	manage (*es schaffen*)	enjoy (*gern tun*)	miss (*vermissen*)
	offer (*anbieten*)	finish (*zu Ende bringen*)	practise (*üben*)
demand (*verlangen*)	plan (*planen*)	give up (*aufgeben*)	recommend (*empfehlen*)
encourage (*ermuntern*)	promise (*versprechen*)	imagine (*sich vorstellen*)	risk (*riskieren*)
	refuse (*sich weigern*)	involve (*mit sich bringen*)	suggest (*vorschlagen*)
expect (*erwarten*)	seem (*scheinen*)		
hesitate (*zögern*)	threaten (*drohen*)		

Was sonst noch wichtig ist

- Auf bestimmte Verben kann ohne Bedeutungsunterschied ein Infinitiv oder eine *ing*-Form folgen: *like, love, hate, prefer, continue*.

- Einige Verben haben aber unterschiedliche Bedeutungen, je nachdem ob ein Gerundium oder ein Infinitiv folgt:
  z. B. *remember to do sth* = daran denken, etwas zu tun
  (*Please remember to learn your vocabulary.*)
  remember doing sth = sich erinnern, etwas getan zu haben
  (*I remember learning about gerunds at school.*)
  stop to do sth = anhalten, um etw (Anderes) zu tun
  (*Shall we stop to buy some food at this supermarket?*)
  stop doing sth = aufhören, etwas zu tun
  (*I've stopped eating chocolate because it's unhealthy.*)

- ❗ Beachten Sie: *like* + Infinitiv oder *ing*-Form, *dislike* nur + *ing*-Form, **would** *like/love/hate/prefer* nur + Infinitiv.

- Verben, die auf eine Präposition folgen, stehen als Gerundium.
  *Jane is responsible **for sending** all our letters.*
  *I decided **against going** to the party.*

- Eine *ing*-Form kann auch Subjekt in einem Satz sein:
  Travelling can be hard.

- Die *ing*-Form kann auch ein eigenes Objekt haben:
  Travelling long distances can be hard.

1 Complete the sentences with the infinitive or gerund of the verb in brackets.

1 After half an hour I gave up (wait) ▬ .
2 I refuse (give) ▬ this matter anymore of my time!
3 I don't mind (show) ▬ you around.
4 They threatened (call) ▬ the police.
5 We must avoid (make) ▬ the same mistake again.
6 I'd like (stay) ▬ at home.
7 Why did you give up (walk) ▬ to school?
8 Rachel seems (need) ▬ some help.

263

Grammar files

IF SENTENCES

Einleitung

In einem *if*-Satz wird gesagt, was unter bestimmten Voraussetzungen geschehen wird, geschehen würde oder geschehen wäre. Solche Sätze bestehen aus zwei Teilen. Der *if*-Teil nennt die Bedingung, der andere Teil nennt die Folge:

Bedingung	Folge
If the police find out, *Wenn die Polizei es herausbekommt,*	he'll be in trouble. *wird er Ärger bekommen.* [Das wird geschehen]
If I won a lot of money, *Wenn ich viel Geld gewinnen würde,*	I would buy a fast car. *würde ich mir ein schnelles Auto kaufen.* [Das würde geschehen]
If you had asked me, *Wenn du mich gefragt hättest,*	I would have helped you. *hätte ich dir geholfen.* [Das wäre geschehen]

Form

	If-Teil	Hauptsatz
Typ 1	**Simple present** If you **work** hard,	***will* future** you**'ll earn** a lot of money.
Typ 2	**Simple past** If I **wanted** an easy life,	***would* + Infinitive** I**'d marry** someone rich.
Typ 3	**Past perfect** If we **had taken** a taxi,	***would* + *have* + Past participle** we **wouldn't have missed** the flight.

- Anstelle von *will* kann auch ein Modalverb wie *can*, *might* oder *should* im Hauptsatz stehen.
  *If you work hard, you **can** earn a lot of money.*
  Anstelle von *would* kann ein Modalverb wie *could*, *might* oder *should* stehen.
  *If I wanted to earn more money, I **could** find a second job.*
- ❗ *would* steht nie im *if*-Teil!
- *would* kann zu *'d* verkürzt werden. *'d* ist aber auch die Kurzform von *had*:
  *I**'d** have left (= I **would** have left) home earlier if I**'d** checked (= **had** checked) the times.*
- Wenn der *if*-Teil am Satzanfang steht, wird er meist mit einem Komma vom Hauptsatz getrennt. Der Hauptsatz kann auch zuerst stehen. Dann verwendet man meist kein Komma.
  If it rains today, I'll go shopping. ABER *I'll go shopping if it rains today.*
- Die Unterschiede zwischen den drei Typen hängen davon ab, wie wahrscheinlich es ist, dass die Bedingung erfüllt wird.

Gebrauch

Typ 1	Es ist gut möglich oder wahrscheinlich, dass die Bedingung erfüllt wird. *If it rains, we'll get wet.*
Typ 2	Es ist unmöglich oder unwahrscheinlich, dass die Bedingung erfüllt wird. *If I was five years old, I'd be in kindergarten.* [Ich bin aber nicht fünf Jahre alt, also ist die Bedingung unmöglich.] *If I became famous, I'd have a lot of money.* [Es ist aber unwahrscheinlich, dass ich berühmt werde.]

If sentences

Typ 3	Es ist völlig unmöglich und absolut ausgeschlossen, dass die Bedingung erfüllt wird. *If Brad Pitt had been born a girl, would he have become famous?* [Er ist aber nicht als Mädchen geboren worden. Die Bedingung war nie Wirklichkeit und kann niemals erfüllt werden.]

- Sowohl mit Typ 2 als auch mit Typ 3 wird über etwas spekuliert:

Typ 2: was wäre, wenn …	Typ 3: was wäre gewesen, wenn …

- In Typ 2 steht das **simple past**. Es wird aber nicht über die Vergangenheit gesprochen.
- In Typ 3 wird über die Vergangenheit gesprochen.

1 In each sentence one verb is in the simple present, one verb in the future with *will*. Complete the sentences with the correct forms of the verbs in brackets.

  1 If the packet (arrive) ―¹ by Friday, that (be) ―² OK.
  2 If Manni (say) ―¹ that again, I (explode) ―²!
  3 She (not understand) ―¹ you if you (not speak) ―² more slowly.
  4 What (you/do) ―¹ if they (not offer) ―² you the job?
  5 If we (not take) ―¹ a break soon, I (die) ―² of hunger.
  6 If they (invite) ―¹ you, (you/go) ―²?

2 Complete the translation. All the sentences are type 2 conditional sentences.

  1 Wenn ich Zeit hätte, würde ich Ihnen helfen.
    If I ―¹ time, I ―² you.
  2 Wenn ich Max besser kennen würde, wüsste ich, wie ich ihm helfen könnte.
    If I ―¹ Max better, I ―² how to help him.
  3 Wenn du Francesca fragen würdest, was würde sie sagen?
    If you ―¹ Francesca, what ―²?
  4 Was würde passieren, wenn wir einfach nichts tun würden?
    What ―¹ if we simply ―² nothing?
  5 Es wäre besser, wenn Sie später noch einmal anrufen könnten.
    It ―¹ better if you ―² again later.
  6 Was tätest du, wenn die andere Firma mehr Geld bieten würde?
    What ―¹ if the other firm ―² more money?

3 Say the same thing with a conditional sentence type 3.

  EXAMPLE: I didn't know about the meeting so I didn't come.
  If I had known about the meeting, I would have come.

  1 Jenny didn't hear about the job so she didn't apply.   If Jenny ―
  2 They didn't have enough money so they didn't buy any souvenirs. If they ―
  3 I didn't have my mobile with me so I didn't call you.   If I ―

  EXAMPLE: Jack had to work on Saturday. That's why he didn't come swimming with us.
  If Jack hadn't had to work on Saturday, he would have come swimming with us.

  4 I had my mobile with me. That's why I took photos.   If I ―
  5 I stopped to talk to Martin. That's why I was late.   If I ―
  6 They drove too fast. That's why they had an accident.   If they ―

Grammar files

INDIRECT SPEECH

Zeitverschiebung

Direkte Rede: Gegenwartsform von Vollverb oder Hilfsverb	Indirekte Rede: Vergangenheitsform von Vollverb oder Hilfsverb
- **Simple present:** "I **know**." "Mark **doesn't** know."	- **Simple past:** She said (that) she **knew**. She said (that) Mark **didn't** know.
- **Present progressive:** "Ann **is** working."	- **Past progressive:** He said (that) Ann **was** working.
- **Present perfect:** "We **have** eaten."	- **Past perfect:** They said (that) they **had** eaten.

- Wenn wir wörtliche Rede indirekt wiedergeben, gibt es eine Zeitverschiebung beim Verb. Im Englischen heißt diese Zeitverschiebung *backshifting*. Die Verbform wird um eine Stufe „nach hinten verschoben". Diese Verschiebung hat nichts mit der Zeit an sich zu tun, sondern drückt einen Perspektivenwechsel aus.
- Vergangenheitsformen von Voll- oder Hilfsverben bleiben in der indirekten Rede unverändert. Sie sind ja bereits „verschoben":
  "I met Tom in town." → *Susie said she met Tom in town.*
  "We had already eaten." → *They said they had already eaten.*
  Eine **simple past**-Form kann aber wahlweise in eine **past perfect**-Form „verschoben" werden.
- *can* und *will* werden zu *could* und *would* „verschoben"; *could*, *might* und *should* bleiben unverändert:
  "I can come." → *I said I could come.*
  "You will soon find out." → *I said they would soon find out.*

Fragen, Bitten und Befehle

Fragen	
"Is it raining?"	She asked **if**/**whether** it is/was raining.
"Do you speak French?"	They asked me **if**/**whether** I speak/spoke French.
"Where is Tom?"	They wanted to know where Tom is/was.
Bitten	
"Can you help me, please?"	He **asked** me **to** help.
"Please don't tell my dad."	She **asked** me **not to** tell her dad.
Befehle	
"Sit down."	She **told** me **to** sit down.
"Don't talk."	He **told** us **not to** talk.

- Wenn man eine wörtliche Frage umformuliert, in der *do/does/did* stand, erscheint *do/does/did* in der indirekten Rede nicht:
  *"**Does** Tom know?"* → *Susie wanted to know if/whether Tom **knows**/**knew**.*
  *"**Did** you win?"* → *He asked me if/whether we **won**.*

Indirect speech

Was sonst noch wichtig ist

- Wenn mit einem Verb im **simple present** berichtet wird (hier unterstrichen), bleibt die Zeitform der direkten Rede grundsätzlich erhalten:

Direkte Rede	Indirekte Rede
"I **buy** a lot online."	Martina <u>says</u> (that) she **buys** a lot online.
"What **is** your address?"	They <u>want to know</u> what our address **is**.

- Auch wenn mit einem Verb im **simple past** berichtet wird, ist eine Zeitverschiebung nicht immer zwingend. Entscheidend ist, ob der Zeitraum vorbei ist, in dem die Aussage ursprünglich Gültigkeit hatte:
Vor einem Fußballspiel sagt ein Trainer: *"We **will** win."*
Nach Beendigung des Spiels wird berichtet: *The trainer **said** his team would win.*

Wenn das Berichtete immer oder immer noch gültig ist, muss keine Zeitverschiebung erfolgen:
Eine Physiklehrerin erzählt: *"Water **freezes** at zero."*
Es wird später berichtet: *She told us that water **freezes** at zero.*

Ann verspricht: *"When I meet Martin, I **will** ask him."*
Solange Ann Martin nicht getroffen hat, kann berichtet werden: *Ann said she **will** ask Martin.*

- Weil Zeitverschiebung mit Perspektivenwechsel zu tun hat, wird sie oft bewusst gewählt, wenn man sich von dem, was man berichtet, distanzieren und zeigen will, dass man dessen Wahrheitsgehalt nicht garantiert:
Ein Minister verspricht: *"We **won't** increase taxes."*
Eine Zeitung berichtet: *The minister said the government **wouldn't** increase taxes.*

---

1 Complete the second sentence as in the example. Use backshifting.

EXAMPLE: "They won't agree." (They will accept the offer.)
→ But you said they would accept the offer.

1. "We can't get into the system." (We have the password.)   But you said ▬
2. "I'm afraid I don't have time." (I'll discuss this with you today.)   But you said ▬ with me ▬
3. "I'm not going to the class meeting." (I don't want to miss it.)   But you said ▬
4. "I'm too tired." (I'll go to the gym with you.)   But you said ▬ with me.
5. "I don't know where to go." (I know the way.)   But you said you ▬
6. "I believe Michael." (He is lying.)   But you said ▬

2 Complete the second sentence as in the example. Use backshifting.

EXAMPLE: "Did anyone call while I was away?"
→ Tony wanted to know if anyone had called while he was away.

1. "Do you know the address?" → Penny asked me if I ▬
2. "Please don't park there." → They asked me ▬
3. "Who drives that red car?" → Someone wanted to know ▬
4. "What did you do with all those spare copies?" → He wanted to know ▬
5. "Who used the room last?" → He demanded to know ▬
6. "Please wait outside." → They asked ▬

Grammar files

PARTICIPLES

Form und Gebrauch

	Present participle (+*ing*)	Past participle (+ *ed*)
Nach *when, while, after, before*	**When/While/After/Before** surf**ing** the internet, I found some useful addresses.	
Anstelle eines Satzglieds mit *and* + Verb	The man helped us **and showed** us where to go. → The man helped us **showing** us where to go.	
Anstelle eines Relativsatzes mit Verb	Verb in der Gegenwart: Hydroponic farming is a new method **which is getting** a lot of attention. → Hydroponic farming is a new method **getting** a lot of attention.	Verb in der Vergangenheit oder im Passiv: Morton was the man **who people saw / who was seen** near the building. → Morton was the man **seen** near the building.

Was sonst noch wichtig ist

- Sätze mit Partizipien werden vor allem in der Schriftsprache verwendet. Mündlich sind sie auch möglich, klingen aber zeitweise gestelzt. In der gesprochenen Sprache verwendet man vorzugsweise Sätze mit Subjekt und Verb.

PRONOUNS AND POSSESSIVE ADJECTIVES

Form und Gebrauch

Subject pronouns		Object pronouns	Possessive adjectives
Wer?		*Wen? Wem?*	*Wessen?*
ich	I	me	my
du, Sie	you	you	your
er/sie/es	he/she/it	him/her/it	his/her/its
wir	we	us	our
ihr, Sie	you	you	your
sie	they	them	their

- Zwischen ‚mich' und ‚mir', ‚ihn' und ‚ihm', usw. macht man im Englischen keinen Unterschied. Es gibt jeweils nur eine Form.
- Die besitzanzeigenden Begleiter (*my, your, usw.*) verändern ihre Form nicht.

1 Which is the right word?

Mo and Jo are in a holiday hotel.
- **Mo** *She / They*[1] is by the pool again.
- **Jo** Who?
- **Mo** Lil Martin, that sports celebrity. Can't you see *her / she*[2]?

Participles • Pronouns and possessive adjectives
Relative clauses

Jo Is *she / they*[3] with *he / him*[4]? *Her / Their*[5] playboy.
Mo He isn't *her / their*[6] playboy. He's *her / she*[7] trainer. *They / Them*[8] are in *her / their*[9] usual place. *He's / His*[10] nice.
Jo I'm not interested in *they / them*[11]. Celebrities! Stop looking. This is *our / us*[12] holiday.
Mo I think *they're / their*[13] cool. Not like you. *Your / You're*[14] not cool. Why are *we / us*[15] still together? Look at *we / us*[16]. The non-cool pair of the year.

2 Complete the sentences with the correct translation of *sie/Sie*.

1 *Wer ist sie? Ist sie unsere neue Lehrerin?* — Who is ▬ ? Is ▬ our new teacher?
2 *Deine Schwester ist nett. Ich mag sie.* — Your sister is nice. I like ▬ .
3 *Sind Sie Kanadier?* — Are ▬ Canadian?
4 *Toni und Wally sind aus Memphis, sie sind Jazzmusiker.* — Toni and Wally are from Memphis, ▬ are jazz musicians.
5 *Schön, Sie wiederzusehen.* — Nice to see ▬ again.
6 *Meine Freundin lebt in London, ich besuche sie oft dort.* — My girlfriend lives in London, I often visit ▬ there.

RELATIVE CLAUSES

Form und Gebrauch

A 'grade A' student is someone **who/that** is very good.

Stress is something **which/that** can affect people of all ages.

- Mit einem Relativsatz bestimmt man Personen oder Sachen näher.
- Relativsätze, die Personen genauer bestimmen, werden durch *who* oder *that* eingeleitet.
- Relativsätze, die Sachen genauer bestimmen, werden durch *which* oder *that* eingeleitet.

Was sonst noch wichtig ist

- In den Beispielsätzen oben ist das Relativpronomen *who/which/that* Subjekt des Relativsatzes. Danach folgt direkt das Verb.

- Ein Relativpronomen kann auch Objekt sein. Dann steht zwischen dem Relativpronomen und dem Verb ein anderes Pronomen oder ein Ausdruck mit einem Nomen (hier unterstrichen). Dieses Pronomen bzw. dieser Ausdruck ist Subjekt des Relativsatzes:
  *Sue is online a lot. Mike is a guy (**who/that**) she met online.*
  *Teen Times is a magazine (**which/that**) my friend Duke buys.*

  Wenn *who/which/that* Objekt ist, kann man es weglassen.

- *Who/which/that* kann Objekt eines Verbs sein, wie in den Beispielen eben, oder Objekt einer Präposition (z. B. *to, with, about, for, of*). Auch hier kann das Relativpronomen weggelassen werden. Die Präposition steht dabei meist am Satzende:
  *Mrs Waters was the name of the teacher (**who/that**) Carrie spoke to.*
  *Here's the web address (**which/that**) I was talking about.*

269

Grammar files

1 Decide if you can leave out the relative pronoun.

1 The person who wrote this handbook has done a very good job.
2 The youth hostel that we stayed in was not in the centre of the city.
3 The computer which I like best is too expensive.
4 I think there's someone over there who I've met before.
5 Anyone who wants to come with me, please let me know by Thursday afternoon.
6 What am I going to do now with all the copies that I made?

2 Correct the sentences – if there is a mistake.

EXAMPLES: *The text who you looked at yesterday has been changed. The text which/that …*
I know someone who knows the manager. [The sentence is correct.]

1 Who is the person who can best help me?
2 I know someone has a lot of experience.
3 The hotel we stayed in was called The Angler.
4 I've just had an email from the people who we met at that concert.
5 The person that signs the letter may not be the person wrote it.
6 What's the address of that firm that built that new hotel?

ADJECTIVES ■ ADVERBS OF MANNER

Form und Gebrauch

Adjektiv	Adverb der Art und Weise
1. Ann is a **careful** driver. Ann ist eine vorsichtige Autofahrerin.	3. She drives **carefully**. Sie fährt vorsichtig.
2. Ann/She is **careful**. Ann ist vorsichtig.	4. She is **especially** careful in fog. Sie ist besonders vorsichtig bei Nebel.
	5. She doesn't drive **very** fast. Sie fährt nicht besonders schnell.
	6. She's **really** disciplined. Sie ist wirklich diszipliniert.

- Das fett gedruckte Wort ist ein Adjektiv oder Adverb. Das unterstrichene Wort ist das Bezugswort – das, worüber das Adjektiv/Adverb etwas aussagt.
- Ein Adjektiv beschreibt, wie jemand oder etwas ist. Es bezieht sich auf ein Nomen (z. B. *Ann*) oder Pronomen (z. B. *she*). Es steht vor einem Nomen (Satz 1) oder nach dem Verb *be* (Satz 2).
- Ein Adverb beschreibt oft, wie jemand etwas tut (z. B. *carefully*), und bezieht sich auf ein Verb (Satz 3).
- Ein Adverb kann aber auch ein anderes Wort verstärken oder abschwächen (z. B. *extremely*, *very*, *really*). Es bezieht sich dann auf ein Adjektiv (Satz 4), auf ein anderes Adverb (Satz 5) oder ein Partizip (Satz 6).

Was sonst noch wichtig ist

- Mit Adverbien der Art und Weise sagt man, wie etwas geschieht oder getan wird. Meist werden sie gebildet, indem man *ly* an das entsprechende Adjektiv anhängt:
*Mark is **quick**. He works **quickly**.*

Adjectives · Adverbs of manner
Comparison of adjectives and adverbs

- Beachten Sie diese Schreibbesonderheiten bei der Endung *ly*:

Adjektiv auf Konsonant + *y*: *y* wird zu *i*	The test is easy. I can do it eas**ily**.
Adjektiv auf *le*: *le* fällt weg	The weather is terrible. It's terri**bly** cold.
Adjektiv auf *ic*: *al* wird eingefügt	It's automatic. It changes automati**cally**.

- ❗ Das zu *good* gehörige Adverb heißt *well*:
  *Tanja is a good tennis player. She plays **well**.* [Nicht: ~~She plays good.~~]

- ❗ Einige wenige Adverbien der Art und Weise haben die gleiche Form wie das Adjektiv: *early, late, fast, hard*.

- Nach bestimmten Verben verwendet man kein Adverb der Art und Weise, sondern ein Adjektiv.

| Verben, die einen Zustand beschreiben | *seem, become, remain* |
| Verben, die eine Eigenschaft von etwas beschreiben. Man kann die Eigenschaft mit einem der fünf Sinne wahrnehmen. | *look* (nur in der Bedeutung „aussehen"), *sound* (sich anhören), *feel* (sich fühlen, sich anfühlen), *taste* (schmecken), *smell* (riechen) |

1 Complete the dialogues with the adjective or adverb form of the words in brackets.

1 Please be ▬ . (careful)
2 Drive ▬ . (careful)
3 I like the idea. It sounds ▬ . (good)
4 You look ▬ . (nervous)
5 Why are you ▬ ? (nervous)
6 You play the piano very ▬ . (good)
7 My boss answered ▬ , 'I have no time for that now.' (angry)
8 Everything was so ▬ organized. (beautiful)

2 Say the same with the word in brackets.

EXAMPLE: She has a soft voice. (speak) → *She speaks softly.*

1 His question was not very polite. (ask) → He didn't ask ▬
2 Your German is very good. (speak German) → You ▬
3 She had a happy smile. (smile) → She ▬
4 It was a strange feeling. (feel) → I ▬
5 Maureen is a fast runner. (run) → Maureen ▬
6 We don't have regular meetings. (meet) → We ▬
7 Our guests were unexpected. (come) → Our guests ▬
8 Stuntmen and women have a dangerous life. (live) → They ▬

COMPARISON OF ADJECTIVES AND ADVERBS

Form

	Komparativ (1. Steigerungsstufe)	Superlativ (2. Steigerungsstufe)
Einsilbige Adjektive: *er/est* anhängen	Which brand is **cheaper**?	Which is **cheapest**?
Zweisilbige Adjektive auf Konsonanten + *y*: *y* wird zu *i*, *er/est* anhängen	Question 2 is **easier**.	Which is the **easiest** question?

Grammar files

Mehrsilbige Adjektive: more/most voranstellen	My job is **more interesting**.	Who has the **most interesting** job?
Adverbien formgleich mit Adjektiv: er/est anhängen	John drives **faster**.	Who drives **fastest**?
Adverbien auf ly: more/most voranstellen	Who works **most carefully**?	Who works **most carefully**?

- Wichtige Adjektive und Adverbien haben Sonderformen:

good/well	better	best
bad(ly)	worse	worst

- Zu den Adverbien, die mit dem entsprechenden Adjektiv formgleich sind, zählen: *early, late, fast, hard, long*
- Schreibbesonderheiten:
    - Adjektiv auf *e*: nur *r/st* anhängen (*nice – nicer – nicest*)
    - Adjektiv auf Einzelvokal + Einzelkonsonanten: Konsonanten verdoppeln (*big – bigger – biggest*).

Gebrauch

Gleichsetzung: *as ... as*	I'm **as old as** Jenny. („so alt wie")
	I work **as hard as** everybody else. („so hart wie")
Ungleichsetzung: *er/more ... than*	I'm **older than** Martina. („älter als")
	I work **more carefully than** Thomas. („sorgfältiger als")

- Nicht *as*, sondern *than* entspricht dem deutschen „als":
  „Ich bin älter **als** du" = I am older **than** you. (Nicht: ~~I am older as you.~~)

Was sonst noch wichtig ist

- Nach *as* und *than* steht ein Pronomen in der Objektform:
  Jürgen is as old as **me**. Tanja's younger brother is taller than **her**.

1 Make comparisons with the words in brackets.

    EXAMPLE: In the summer I have a (long) longer working day than in the winter.

1. This is one of the (complicated) ▬¹ systems I have ever had to use.
2. In a foreign language, reading is normally (easy) ▬¹ ▬² listening.
3. The old handbook was much (thin) ▬¹ ▬² this one.
4. I feel (bad) ▬¹ ▬² yesterday.
5. The tickets aren't (cheap) ▬¹ ▬² last year. They're (expensive) ▬³.

2 Complete the sentences with the comparative or superlative form of the adverb.

1. You have to work (hard) ▬ .
2. The new member of the team is doing (good) ▬ now that he's had some training.
3. Four companies suggested solutions, but the German company solved the problem (efficient) ▬ .
4. My club is playing (bad) ▬ than at any time this season.
5. The changes are happening (gradual) ▬ than we expected.

POSITION OF ADVERBS OF TIME

Einleitung

- Wir unterscheiden zwischen Adverbien (ein Wort) und adverbialen Bestimmungen (mehr als ein Wort).
  *Ron **always** works hard.* [Adverb]
  *He works (1) **every day** (2) **from nine to six**.* [zwei adverbiale Bestimmungen]

- Grundsätzlich gibt es drei mögliche Stellungen für Adverbien und adverbiale Bestimmungen in einem englischen Satz.

Satzanfang	**Usually** I don't work on a Sunday.
Satzmitte	I don't **usually** work on a Sunday.
Satzende	I don't work on a Sunday **usually**.

- Viele Adverbien und adverbiale Bestimmungen können am Satzanfang oder -ende stehen. Dieser Sprachgebrauch unterscheidet sich wenig vom deutschen. Wichtige Unterschiede gibt es bei der Stellung in der Satzmitte.
- In der Satzmitte stehen Adverbien der Häufigkeit (*always, usually, normally, regularly, often, sometimes, never*) sowie kurze Adverbien wie *ever, just, now, soon, still, already*.
- Nicht in der Satzmitte, sondern am Satzende stehen *yesterday, today, again* sowie adverbiale Bestimmungen. Dazu gehören z. B. Bestimmungen mit *every, last, ago*, Uhr- und Tageszeiten:
  *I went swimming **today**.* [Nicht: *I went today swimming.*]
  *They flew to Canada **last year**.* [Nicht: *They flew last year to Canada.*]

Gebrauch

Stellung in der Satzmitte

Vor einem Verb im **simple present** oder **simple past**	I **never** smoke. He **quickly** said goodbye.
Hinter einem Hilfsverb	We don't **normally** drive. She has **never** asked.
Hinter einer Form des Verbs *be*	Anna is **always** happy. You weren't **often** here.

- In den Beispielen ist das Adverb **fett** gedruckt, das Verb/Hilfsverb unterstrichen.

Was sonst noch wichtig ist

- ❗ Ein Adverb oder eine adverbiale Bestimmung kann nicht zwischen einem Verb und seinem Objekt stehen!
  *We **always** take the bus.* [Nicht: *We take always the bus.*]
  *Stan watches TV **in the evening**.* [Nicht: *Stan watches in the evening TV.*]

Which position is right for the adverb / adverbial: A or B?

1. We **A** are **B** well prepared. (always)
2. I don't **A** drink **B** tea. (often)
3. We **A** make **B** mistakes. (never)
4. We **A** have **B** made a mistake. (never)
5. I've **A** seen this film **B**. (several times)
6. We've been **A** to San Francisco **B**. (once before)
7. This **A** happens to me **B**. (always)
8. The test doesn't **A** take **B** long. (usually)

273

Grammar files

COUNTABLE AND UNCOUNTABLE NOUNS

Einleitung
Nicht zählbare Nomen haben keine Mehrzahlform und man kann weder *a/an* noch eine Zahl davorsetzen:

| zählbar | *one book, two books, three books, etc.* |
| nicht zählbar | *weather, money, traffic, etc.* [Nicht: a weather, two moneys, three traffics] |

Gebrauch

- Bestimmte Nomen sind im Deutschen zählbar, im Englischen aber nicht.

advice	*Rat, Ratschlag, Ratschläge*	housework	*Hausarbeit, Hausarbeiten*
bread	*Brot*	information	*Information, Informationen*
damage	*Schaden, Schäden*	knowledge	*Wissen, Kenntnisse*
equipment	*Ausrüstung, Geräte*	paper	*Papier, Zettel*
furniture	*Möbel*	progress	*Fortschritt, Fortschritte*
hair	*Haar, Haare*	proof	*Beweis, Beweise*
help	*Hilfe, Hilfen, Hilfestellungen*	toast	*Toast*
homework	*Hausaufgabe, Hausaufgaben*	work	*Arbeit, Arbeiten*

- Nicht zählbare Nomen verwendet man mit *this/that* und *much*. Das Verb nach einem nicht zählbaren Nomen steht immer im Singular:
  This information *is interesting.* (Diese Information ist / Diese Informationen sind interessant.)
  How **much homework** *is there today?* (Wie viele Hausaufgaben sind heute auf?)

- Mit Ausdrücken wie *a piece of* oder *a bit of* kann man Ersatzsingular- und Pluralformen bilden:
  Can I have **a piece of paper**, *please?* (einen Zettel)
  They gave me **two** *useful* **bits of information**. (zwei nützliche Informationen)

QUANTIFIERS

Gebrauch von *some* und *any*

Aussage	I need **some** more time. Show me **some** photos.
Verneinung	I do**n't** want **any** tea, thanks. There were**n't any** interesting films.
Frage	Is there **any** butter? Does their letter give **any** details?
Bitte oder Angebot	Can I have **some** ketchup, please? Would you like **some** help?

Gebrauch von *much, many, little, a little, few, a few*

Nicht zählbar	Plural
I don't have **much** money.	Are there **many** good shops?
There is **little** time. *(wenig)*	There were **few** tourists. *(wenige)*
I need **a little** help. *(etwas, ein wenig)*	Can you give me **a few** tips? *(ein paar, einige)*

Unit word list

Dieses Wörterverzeichnis enthält alle Wörter aus **Focus on Success – 5th edition: Ausgabe Wirtschaft** in der Reihenfolge ihres Erscheinens. Nicht aufgeführt sind die Wörter aus der *Basic word list* sowie internationale Wörter wie *hotel, email* usw.
Wörter, die in den Hörverständnistexten vorkommen, sind mit einem CD-Symbol gekennzeichnet.

AE = American English	*sth* = something	*etw* = etwas	*jds* = jemandes
BE = British English	*adj* = adjective	*jd* = jemand	*Adj* = Adjektiv
pl = plural	*adv* = adverb	*jdm* = jemandem	*Adv* = Adverb
sb = somebody		*jdn* = jemanden	*coll* = colloquial

UNIT 1

page 6

cult [kʌlt]		Kult
celebrity [sə'lebrəti]		Prominente/r, Prominenz
neighbour ['neɪbə]		Nachbar/in
to sort [sɔːt]		sortieren, einordnen
to rank sb/sth [ræŋk]		jdn/etw einstufen, jdn/etw (ein-)ordnen
order ['ɔːdə]		Reihenfolge
popularity [ˌpɒpju'lærəti]		Beliebtheit, Popularität
to deserve [dɪ'zɜːv]		verdienen
status ['steɪtəs]		Status, Stellung
to define [dɪ'faɪn]		definieren
to study sth ['stʌdi]		etw genau betrachten
headline ['hedlaɪn]		Schlagzeile, Überschrift
to make sth up [ˌmeɪk 'ʌp]		etw erfinden, sich etw ausdenken
store [stɔː]		Geschäft, Laden
midnight ['mɪdnaɪt]		Mitternacht
shopper ['ʃɒpə]		Käufer/in, Kunde/Kundin
legend ['ledʒənd]		Legende
face-lift ['feɪslɪft]		Facelifting, Gesichtsstraffung
jewellery ['dʒuːəlri]		Schmuck

page 7

to get sth right [ˌget 'raɪt]		etw richtig machen, etw gut hinbekommen
statement ['steɪtmənt]		Aussage, Feststellung, Behauptung
gig [gɪg]		(Rock-, Pop-, Jazz-)Konzert
to queue [kjuː]		sich (in einer Warteschlange) anstellen
charity ['tʃærəti]		Benefiz-, Wohltätigkeit(s)-
to tour [tʊə]		auf Tour gehen
bracket ['brækɪt]		Klammer
to appear [ə'pɪə]		auftreten, erscheinen
to break sth up [ˌbreɪk 'ʌp]		etw zertrümmern, etw demolieren
to hit the headlines [ˌhɪt ðə 'hedlaɪnz]		in die Schlagzeilen kommen, Schlagzeilen machen
to collect (sth on sb) [kə'lekt]		(etw über jdn) sammeln
fortune ['fɔːtʃuːn]		Vermögen
autograph ['ɔːtəgrɑːf]		Autogramm
formula ['fɔːmjələ]		Formel
race [reɪs]		Rennen

page 8

skill [skɪl]		Fähigkeit, Fertigkeit
to predict [prɪ'dɪkt]		voraussagen, vorhersagen
use [juːs]		Gebrauch, Nutzen
to make use of sth [ˌmeɪk 'juːs əv]		von etw Gebrauch machen, etw nutzen
clue [kluː]		Hinweis, Anhaltspunkt
to go with sth [ˌgəʊ 'wɪð]		zu etw gehören
caption ['kæpʃn]		Bildunterschrift
further ['fɜːðə]		weitere/r/s *Adj*, weiter *Adv*
like [laɪk]		wie
good looking [ˌgʊd 'lʊkɪŋ]		gutaussehend, attraktiv
talented ['tæləntɪd]		begabt, talentiert
to be scared [bi 'skeəd]		Angst haben
onto ['ɒntə]		auf
stage [steɪdʒ]		Bühne
huge [hjuːdʒ]		riesig, Riesen-
audience ['ɔːdiəns]		Publikum
member of the audience [ˌmembər əv ði 'ɔːdiəns]		Zuschauer/in
to feel uncomfortable [ˌfiːl ʌn'kʌmftəbl]		sich unbehaglich fühlen
judge [dʒʌdʒ]		Richter/in, Juror/in
spot [spɒt]		Platz, Stelle
change [tʃeɪndʒ]		Wandel, Verwandlung
to take place [ˌteɪk 'pleɪs]		stattfinden
to perform [pə'fɔːm]		singen, spielen, auftreten
to wave sth [weɪv]		etw schwenken, mit etw wedeln
magical ['mædʒɪkl]		magisch, traumhaft
cheers *pl* [tʃɪəz]		Jubel, Applaus
to wash over sb/sth [ˌwɒʃ 'əʊvə]		jdn überkommen, etw überschwemmen
life-changing ['laɪf ˌtʃeɪndʒɪŋ]		lebensverändernd
to hold sb back [ˌhəʊld 'bæk]		jdn bremsen
to move on [ˌmuːv 'ɒn]		weiterkommen, weitergehen
level ['levl]		Stufe, Niveau, Ebene
competition [ˌkɒmpə'tɪʃn]		Wettbewerb, Wettkampf
to finish second [ˌfɪnɪʃ 'sekənd]		Zweite/r werden
to sign [saɪn]		unterschreiben
contract ['kɒntrækt]		Vertrag
record company ['rekɔːd ˌkʌmpəni]		Plattenfirma
to release [rɪ'liːs]		veröffentlichen
follow-up ['fɒləʊ ʌp]		Folge-, Nachfolger
career [kə'rɪə]		Karriere, Laufbahn

page 9

to compare [kəm'peə]		vergleichen
to shake [ʃeɪk]		zittern
dirty ['dɜːti]		schmutzig
to criticize ['krɪtɪsaɪz]		kritisieren
show [ʃəʊ]		(TV-, Radio-)Sendung
to take part in sth [ˌteɪk 'pɑːt ɪn]		an etw teilnehmen
to make sb up [ˌmeɪk 'ʌp]		jdn schminken

275

Unit word list

script [skrɪpt] — Drehbuch
to **practise** ['præktɪs] — üben, trainieren
to **look forward to sth** [ˌlʊk 'fɔːwəd tə] — sich auf etw freuen

page 10
on one's own [ɒn wʌnz 'əʊn] — allein
background ['bækgraʊnd] — Hintergrund
to **be related to sth** [bi rɪ'leɪtɪd tə] — mit etw in Zusammenhang stehen
fame [feɪm] — Ruhm
childhood sweetheart [ˌtʃaɪldhʊd 'swiːthɑːt] — Jugendliebe
to **split (up)** [splɪt] — (Paar:) sich trennen
current ['kʌrənt] — aktuell
achievement [ə'tʃiːvmənt] — Errungenschaft, Leistung
to **inspire** [ɪn'spaɪə] — inspirieren, anregen
challenge ['tʃælɪndʒ] — Herausforderung, (große) Aufgabe
relationship [rɪ'leɪʃnʃɪp] — Beziehung, Verhältnis
tabloid press ['tæblɔɪd pres] — Boulevardpresse

page 11
expression [ɪk'spreʃn] — Ausdruck
to **cry one's eyes out** [ˌkraɪ wʌnz 'aɪz aʊt] — wie ein Schlosshund heulen
close [kləʊs] — nah, dicht, eng
to **fulfil** [fʊl'fɪl] — erfüllen
pleasure ['pleʒə] — Vergnügen
My pleasure. [ˌmaɪ 'pleʒə] — Gern geschehen.
to **prove** [pruːv] — beweisen
to **design** [dɪ'zaɪn] — entwerfen, gestalten
scene [siːn] — Szene
ordinary ['ɔːdnri] — normal, gewöhnlich
pretty ['prɪti] — ziemlich
attention [ə'tenʃn] — Aufmerksamkeit, Beachtung
on the other hand [ɒn ði 'ʌðə hænd] — andererseits
public ['pʌblɪk] — öffentlich
platform ['plætfɔːm] — Podium
to **talk sth over** [ˌtɔːk 'əʊvə] — etw besprechen
to **accept** [ək'sept] — akzeptieren, gutheißen
to **concentrate on sth** ['kɒnsntreɪt ɒn] — sich auf etw konzentrieren
to **support** [sə'pɔːt] — unterstützen
openness ['əʊpənnəs] — Offenheit
step [step] — Schritt
label ['leɪbl] — (Mode-)Firma, Marke
to **admire** [əd'maɪə] — bewundern
to **focus on sth** ['fəʊkəs ɒn] — sich auf etw konzentrieren
role-play ['rəʊl pleɪ] — Rollenspiel
to **role-play** ['rəʊl pleɪ] — mit verteilten Rollen spielen
area ['eəriə] — Gebiet, Bereich, Feld
to **thank** [θæŋk] — danken
footballer ['fʊtbɔːlə] — Fußballer/in
to **congratulate sb on sth** [kən'grætʃuleɪt] — jdm zu etw gratulieren
support [sə'pɔːt] — Unterstützung, Hilfe
to **face sth** [feɪs] — sich einer Sache stellen
to **train** [treɪn] — trainieren

UNIT 2

page 12
participant [pɑː'tɪsɪpənt] — Teilnehmer/in
spectator [spek'teɪtə] — Zuschauer/in
survey ['sɜːveɪ] — Umfrage
according to [ə'kɔːdɪŋ tə] — entsprechend, nach, gemäß

keep-fit [ˌkiːp'fɪt] — Fitness(-)
aerobics [eə'rəʊbɪks] — Aerobic
to **be keen on sth** [bi 'kiːn ɒn] — auf etw versessen sein

page 13
to **ring the doorbell** [ˌrɪŋ ðə 'dɔːbel] — (an der Tür) klingeln, läuten
stadium ['steɪdiəm] — Stadion
chess [tʃes] — Schach
chess set ['tʃes set] — Schachspiel (Figuren + Brett)
swimming pool ['swɪmɪŋ puːl] — Schwimmbad
racing car ['reɪsɪŋ kɑː] — Rennwagen
rules pl **of the game** [ˌruːlz əv ðə 'geɪm] — Spielregeln
since [sɪns] — seit
gym [dʒɪm] — Fitness-Studio
changing room ['tʃeɪndʒɪŋ ruːm] — Umkleidekabine, Umkleide
cold [kəʊld] — Erkältung
national team [ˌnæʃnəl 'tiːm] — Nationalmannschaft
personality [ˌpɜːsə'næləti] — Persönlichkeit
involved in sth [ɪn'vɒlvd ɪn] — an etw beteiligt, bei etw engagiert
to **lose** [luːz] — verlieren
interest (in sth) ['ɪntrəst] — Interesse (an etw)
to **look up to sb** [ˌlʊk 'ʌp tə] — zu jdm aufsehen, jdn bewundern
champion ['tʃæmpiən] — Meister/in
to **overcome** [ˌəʊvə'kʌm] — überwinden
disability [ˌdɪsə'bɪləti] — Behinderung
swimmer ['swɪmə] — Schwimmer/in
medal ['medl] — Medaille

page 14
ending ['endɪŋ] — Schluss, Ende
illegal [ɪ'liːgl] — verboten, illegal
substance ['sʌbstəns] — Substanz, Stoff
to **improve** [ɪm'pruːv] — (sich) verbessern, (sich) steigern
performance [pə'fɔːməns] — Leistung, Abschneiden
injury ['ɪndʒəri] — Verletzung
to **occur** [ə'kɜː] — vorfallen, geschehen
paragraph ['pærəgrɑːf] — (Text:) Absatz
professional [prə'feʃnl] — professionell, Profi-
to **record** [rɪ'kɔːd] — aufzeichnen
decade ['dekeɪd] — Jahrzehnt
throughout the decades [θruːˌaʊt ðə 'dekeɪdz] — durch/über die Jahrzehnte
improvement in sth [ɪm'pruːvmənt ɪn] — Verbesserung bei etw
material [mə'tɪəriəl] — Material, Werkstoff
to **come fourth** [ˌkʌm 'fɔːθ] — Vierte/r werden
to **compete** [kəm'piːt] — (bei einem Wettbewerb) antreten
junior ['dʒuːniə] — Junioren-
national ['næʃnəl] — Landes-, national
triathlon [traɪ'æθlən] — Triathlon
cyclist ['saɪklɪst] — Radfahrer/in
racing cyclist ['reɪsɪŋ saɪklɪst] — Radrennfahrer/in
to **announce** [ə'naʊns] — verkünden, ankündigen
retirement [rɪ'taɪəmənt] — Rücktritt, Rückzug
competitive [kəm'petətɪv] — wettkampfmäßig
agency ['eɪdʒənsi] — Agentur

sample ['sɑːmpl]	Probe
to charge sb with sth [tʃɑːdʒ]	jdn einer Sache beschuldigen, jdn einer Sache anklagen
organization [ˌɔːɡənaɪˈzeɪʃn]	Organisation
according to [əˈkɔːdɪŋ tə]	laut, zufolge
Olympic [əˈlɪmpɪk]	olympisch
committee [kəˈmɪti]	Komitee
study [ˈstʌdi]	Untersuchung, Studie
historical [hɪˈstɒrɪkl]	historisch
evolution [ˌiːvəˈluːʃn]	Entwicklung
phenomenon [fəˈnɒmɪnən]	Phänomen, Erscheinung
century [ˈsentʃəri]	Jahrhundert
to refer to sb/sth [rɪˈfɜː tə]	jdn/etw erwähnen, sich auf jdn/etw beziehen
mixture [ˈmɪkstʃə]	Mischung
cocaine [kəʊˈkeɪn]	Kokain
caffeine [ˈkæfiːn]	Koffein
strychnine [ˈstrɪknaɪn]	Strychnin
nitroglycerine [ˌnaɪtrəʊˈɡlɪsəriːn]	Nitroglycerin
to stimulate [ˈstɪmjuleɪt]	anregen, stimulieren
breathing [ˈbriːðɪŋ]	Atmung
to suffer sth [ˈsʌfə]	an etw leiden, etw erleiden
hallucination [həˌluːsɪˈneɪʃn]	Halluzination, Wahnvorstellung
to refuse [rɪˈfjuːz]	sich weigern
to chase sb [tʃeɪs]	jdn verfolgen, jdn jagen
to bat an eyelid [ˌbæt ən ˈaɪlɪd]	mit der Wimper zucken
to enter a competition [ˌentər ə kɒmpəˈtɪʃn]	an einem Wettkampf/Wettbewerb teilnehmen
guy [ɡaɪ]	Typ, Kerl
corrupt [kəˈrʌpt]	korrupt
to cycle on [ˌsaɪkl ˈɒn]	weiterradeln

page 15

to summarize [ˈsʌməraɪz]	zusammenfassen
notebook [ˈnəʊtbʊk]	Heft, Notizbuch
heading [ˈhedɪŋ]	Rubrik, Überschrift
reference (to sth) [ˈrefərəns]	Verweis (auf etw)
aspect [ˈæspekt]	Gesichtspunkt, Aspekt
sub-heading [ˌsʌb ˈhedɪŋ]	Teilrubrik, Zwischenüberschrift
to scan [skæn]	(Text) überfliegen
repetition [ˌrepəˈtɪʃn]	Wiederholung
connection [kəˈnekʃn]	Verbindung
legal [ˈliːɡl]	erlaubt, legal
to structure [ˈstrʌktʃə]	strukturieren
to appear [əˈpɪə]	scheinen
in general [ɪn ˈdʒenrəl]	im Allgemeinen, generell
to sum up [ˌsʌm ˈʌp]	zusammenfassen

page 16

to highlight [ˈhaɪlaɪt]	hervorheben
to join [dʒɔɪn]	beitreten, eintreten, mitmachen
at all [ət ˈɔːl]	überhaupt
to replace [rɪˈpleɪs]	ersetzen, austauschen
instructor [ɪnˈstrʌktə]	Lehrer/in
to trip [trɪp]	stolpern
to fit [fɪt]	passen
muscle [ˈmʌsl]	Muskel
to ache [eɪk]	schmerzen, wehtun
session [ˈseʃn]	Sitzung
to suggest [səˈdʒest]	vorschlagen
to take sb along [ˌteɪk əˈlɒŋ]	jdn mitnehmen
craze [kreɪz]	Modewelle, Trend
workout [ˈwɜːkaʊt]	(Fitness-)Training
called [kɔːld]	namens
tape [teɪp]	(Ton-)Band
instead of [ɪnˈsted əv]	anstatt
to cancel [ˈkænsl]	absagen, stornieren
to improvise [ˈɪmprəvaɪz]	improvisieren
to name [neɪm]	nennen, benennen
it wasn't long before … [ɪt wɒznt ˌlɒŋ bɪˈfɔː]	es dauerte nicht lange, bis …
worldwide [ˈwɜːldwaɪd]	weltweit

page 17

overweight [ˌəʊvəˈweɪt]	übergewichtig
slim [slɪm]	schlank
cardiovascular [ˌkɑːdiəʊˈvæskjələ]	Herz-Kreislauf-
metabolism [məˈtæbəlɪzəm]	Stoffwechsel
calorie [ˈkæləri]	Kalorie
to measure [ˈmeʒə]	messen
blood vessel [ˈblʌd vesl]	Blutgefäß
joy [dʒɔɪ]	Freude
excitement [ɪkˈsaɪtmənt]	Begeisterung
musical [ˈmjuːzɪkl]	musikalisch, Musik-
process [ˈprəʊses]	Ablauf, Vorgang, Prozess
to change sth into sth [ˈtʃeɪndʒ ɪntə]	etw in etw umwandeln
growth [ɡrəʊθ]	Wachstum
speaker [ˈspiːkə]	Sprecher/in
to panic [ˈpænɪk]	in Panik geraten
to get the hang of it [ˌɡet ðə ˈhæŋ əv ɪt]	den richtigen Dreh finden
mainly [ˈmeɪnli]	hauptsächlich
atmosphere [ˈætməsfɪə]	Stimmung, Atmosphäre
to join in [ˌdʒɔɪn ˈɪn]	mitmachen
to stand up [ˌstænd ˈʌp]	aufstehen, sich hinstellen
school leaving party [ˈskuːl liːvɪŋ pɑːti]	Schulabgangsfeier
benefit [ˈbenɪfɪt]	Nutzen, Vorteil, Pluspunkt
to strengthen [ˈstreŋθn]	kräftigen, stärken
lung [lʌŋ]	Lunge
to increase sth [ɪnˈkriːs]	etw steigern
to reduce [rɪˈdjuːs]	senken, reduzieren, verringern
to boost [buːst]	ankurbeln
to burn [bɜːn]	(sich) verbrennen
to lose weight [ˌluːz ˈweɪt]	abnehmen
last but not least [ˌlɑːst bʌt nɒt ˈliːst]	zu guter Letzt, nicht zuletzt
to feel low [ˌfiːl ˈləʊ]	schlecht gelaunt sein, deprimiert sein
worried [ˈwʌrid]	besorgt, beunruhigt
care [keə]	Sorge
to talk sb through sth [ˈtɔːk θruː]	jdm etw der Reihe nach erklären
warm-up [ˈwɔːm ʌp]	Aufwärmen
cool down [ˌkuːl ˈdaʊn]	Abkühlen
dance routine [ˈdɑːns ruːtiːn]	Tanzschritte
move [muːv]	Schritt, Bewegung
to shake sth [ʃeɪk]	etw schütteln, mit etw wackeln
hip [hɪp]	Hüfte
touch [tʌtʃ]	Berührung
to get sb hooked [ˌɡet ˈhʊkt]	jdn anfixen
to give sth a try [ˌɡɪv ə ˈtraɪ]	etw ausprobieren
unhealthy [ʌnˈhelθi]	nicht gesund
All the best, [ˌɔːl ðə ˈbest]	Mit besten Grüßen, Alles Gute

Unit word list

UNIT 3

page 18

brand	[brænd]	Marke
power	['paʊə]	Macht, Stärke, Kraft
fashionable	['fæʃnəbl]	modisch
gap	[gæp]	Lücke
to come down to sth	[ˌkʌm 'daʊn tə]	auf etw hinauslaufen, auf etw ankommen
emotional	[ɪ'məʊʃənl]	gefühlsmäßig, emotional
thinking	['θɪŋkɪŋ]	Denken
to go for sth	['gəʊ fə]	etw nehmen, etw gut finden

page 19

consumer	[kən'sjuːmə]	Verbraucher/in, Konsument/in
choice	[tʃɔɪs]	Wahl, Entscheidung
availability	[əˌveɪlə'bɪləti]	Verfügbarkeit
affordable	[ə'fɔːdəbl]	erschwinglich
though	[ðəʊ]	aber, dagegen, allerdings
packaging	['pækɪdʒɪŋ]	Verpackung
to affect	[ə'fekt]	beeinflussen, sich auswirken auf
background	['bækgraʊnd]	Herkunft
sportswear	['spɔːtsweə]	Sportkleidung
to advertise sth	['ædvətaɪz]	etw bewerben, für etw werben
goods pl	[gʊdz]	Waren, Güter
to suggest	[sə'dʒest]	unterstellen, suggerieren
athlete	['æθliːt]	Sportler/in, Athlet/in
over-achiever	[ˌəʊvərə'tʃiːvə]	Überflieger
to achieve sth	[ə'tʃiːv]	etw erreichen, etw leisten
to display	[dɪ'spleɪ]	zeigen
value	['væljuː]	Wert
belief	[bɪ'liːf]	Überzeugung
depending on	[dɪ'pendɪŋ ɒn]	je nach(dem)
to persuade	[pə'sweɪd]	überzeugen, überreden
including	[ɪn'kluːdɪŋ]	einschließlich
to pack	[pæk]	verpacken
to identify with sb/sth	[aɪ'dentɪfaɪ wɪð]	sich mit jdm/etw identifizieren
to grow up	[ˌgrəʊ 'ʌp]	aufwachsen

page 20

sold out	[ˌsəʊld 'aʊt]	ausverkauft
to rewrite	[ˌriː'raɪt]	umformulieren, neu schreiben
allowance	[ə'laʊəns]	Taschengeld
actually	['æktʃuəli]	in der Tat, eigentlich, wirklich
similarity	[ˌsɪmə'lærəti]	Ähnlichkeit
discount	['dɪskaʊnt]	Rabatt, Nachlass
discount label	['dɪskaʊnt leɪbl]	Billigmarke
sweater	['swetə]	Pullover
preference	['prefrəns]	Vorliebe
to celebrate	['selɪbreɪt]	feiern
athletic	[æθ'letɪk]	sportlich, athletisch
challenging	['tʃælɪndʒɪŋ]	anspruchsvoll, fordernd

page 21

comparison	[kəm'pærɪsn]	Steigerung (von Adjektiven)
crowded	['kraʊdɪd]	voll (mit Leuten), überfüllt
tasty	['teɪsti]	schmackhaft, lecker
competitive	[kəm'petətɪv]	konkurrenzfähig, (Preise:) günstig
to collect sth	[kə'lekt]	etw abholen
to sponsor	['spɒnsə]	(finanziell) unterstützen, sponsern
run	[rʌn]	Lauf
it's not long before	[ɪts nɒt ˌlɒŋ 'bɪfɔː]	es dauert nicht lange, bis
to pick sb/sth up	[ˌpɪk 'ʌp]	jdn/etw abholen
stripe	[straɪp]	Streifen
(it's a) pity	['pɪti]	schade
you guys	[juː 'gaɪz]	ihr
gear	[gɪə]	Ausrüstung, Kleidung
Thank goodness!	[ˌθæŋk 'gʊdnəs]	Gott sei Dank!
fee	[fiː]	Gebühr
entrance fee	['entrəns fiː]	Teilnahmegebühr
still	[stɪl]	(immer) noch, dennoch
to matter	['mætə]	wichtig sein, darauf ankommen
to feel comfortable	[ˌfiːl 'kʌmftəbl]	sich wohlfühlen
affordability	[əˌfɔːdə'bɪləti]	Erschwinglichkeit, Bezahlbarkeit
to interrupt	[ˌɪntə'rʌpt]	unterbrechen, ins Wort fallen
to pretend	[prɪ'tend]	vorgeben; so tun, als ob
sweatshop	['swetʃɒp]	Ausbeutungsbetrieb
amateur	['æmətə]	Amateur(-), Hobby-
professional	[prə'feʃənl]	Profi
to meet up	[ˌmiːt 'ʌp]	sich treffen
to cheer for sb	['tʃɪə fə]	jdn anfeuern, jdm zujubeln
even though	['iːvn ðəʊ]	selbst wenn, obwohl
sports gear	['spɔːts gɪə]	Sportkleidung, Sportausrüstung

page 22

flap	[flæp]	Umschlagklappe
cover	['kʌvə]	(Buch-)Umschlag, Einband
logical(ly)	['lɒdʒɪkl]	logisch
debate	[dɪ'beɪt]	Diskussion, Debatte
to make sure	[ˌmeɪk 'ʃʊə]	sicherstellen; dafür sorgen, dass
whenever	[wen'evə]	jedes Mal, wenn; wann (auch) immer
to pay attention to sth	[ˌpeɪ ə'tenʃn tə]	auf etw achten
to give an opinion	[ˌgɪv ən ə'pɪnɪən]	eine Meinung äußern
to give a reason	[ˌgɪv ə 'riːzn]	eine Begründung anführen
to disagree with sth	[ˌdɪsə'griː wɪð]	einer Sache nicht zustimmen, gegen etw sein, etw ablehnen
to keep sth safe	[ˌkiːp 'seɪf]	etw aufbewahren
on the one hand	[ɒn ðə 'wʌn hænd]	einerseits
in fact	[ɪn 'fækt]	um genau zu sein, eigentlich
to take sth into account	[ˌteɪk ɪntu ə'kaʊnt]	etw in Betracht ziehen, etw berücksichtigen
on the whole	[ɒn ðə 'həʊl]	im Großen und Ganzen

page 23

victim	['vɪktɪm]	Opfer
either ... or	[ˌaɪðə 'ɔː]	entweder ... oder
(the) latest	['leɪtɪst]	der/die/das allerneueste/n
to suit sb	[suːt]	(Kleidung:) jdm stehen
to walk along sth	[wɔːk]	etw (Straße etc.) entlanggehen
high street	['haɪ striːt]	Hauptgeschäftsstraße, Einkaufsstraße

glossy	['glɒsi]		Hochglanz-
toned	[təʊnd]		straff, durchtrainiert
cover	['kʌvə]		Titelseite
fingernail	['fɪŋgəneɪl]		Fingernagel
to squeeze oneself into sth	['skwiːz ɪntə]		sich in etw hineinzwängen
skinny	['skɪni]		hauteng
copy	['kɒpi]		Nachahmung, Imitat
watch	[wɒtʃ]		Armbanduhr
up to	['ʌp tə]		bis
to admit	[əd'mɪt]		zugeben, (ein)gestehen
stuff	[stʌf]		Zeug, Sache(n)
to bet	[bet]		wetten
for what it's worth	[fə wɒt ɪts 'wɜːθ]		meiner (bescheidenen) Meinung nach
to stick to sth	['stɪk tə]		bei etw bleiben, sich an etw halten
item (of clothing)	['aɪtəm]		Kleidungsstück
to suit sb/sth	[suːt]		zu jdm/etw passen
no matter ...	[ˌnəʊ 'mætə]		ganz egal, ...
to draw attention to sb/sth	[ˌdrɔː ə'tenʃn tə]		Aufmerksamkeit auf jdn/ etw ziehen
acne	['ækni]		Akne
Yuck!	[jʌk]		Igitt! Bäh!
as far as I'm concerned	[əz ˌfɑːr əz ˌaɪm kən'sɜːnd]		was mich betrifft
tight	[taɪt]		knapp, eng
to stare at sb	['steər ət]		jdn anstarren
matter	['mætə]		Angelegenheit, Sache
unique	[juː'niːk]		einzigartig
to copy	['kɒpi]		nachahmen, imitieren
to experiment	[ɪk'sperɪmənt]		experimentieren
particular	[pə'tɪkjələ]		bestimmt, speziell
secret	['siːkrɪt]		Geheimnis
to overdo it	[ˌəʊvə'duː ɪt]		es übertreiben
all at once	[ˌɔːl ət 'wʌns]		auf einmal
I'm afraid	[aɪm ə'freɪd]		leider
criticism (of sb/sth)	['krɪtɪsɪzəm]		Kritik (an jdm/etw)
fake	[feɪk]		Fälschung, Imitation
collection	[kə'lekʃn]		Sammlung

page 24

bullet point	['bʊlɪt pɔɪnt]		Stichpunkt
preparation (for sth)	[ˌprepə'reɪʃn]		Vorbereitung (auf etw)
waste of time	[ˌweɪst əf 'taɪm]		Zeitverschwendung
to keep up with sb/sth	[ˌkiːp 'ʌp wɪð]		mit jdm/etw Schritt halten
to influence	['ɪnfluəns]		beeinflussen

UNIT 4

page 25

leisure	['leʒə]		Freizeit, Muße
to surf the internet	[ˌsɜːf ði 'ɪntənet]		im Internet surfen
to mind sth	[maɪnd]		etw gegen etw haben
to hang out	[ˌhæŋ 'aʊt]		rumhängen, sich rumtreiben
lack	[læk]		Mangel
area	['eəriə]		Gegend, Region
riding	['raɪdɪŋ]		Reiten
to save up	[ˌseɪv 'ʌp]		sparen

page 26

instead	[ɪn'sted]		stattdessen
to interpret	[ɪn'tɜːprɪt]		interpretieren
instructions pl	[ɪn'strʌkʃnz]		Anleitung, Anweisung(en)
drawing	['drɔːɪŋ]		Zeichnung
speech bubble	['spiːtʃ bʌbl]		Sprechblase
to relate to sth	[rɪ'leɪt tə]		sich auf etw beziehen
to get sth	[get]		etw verstehen, etw kapieren
joke	[dʒəʊk]		Witz
to study sth	['stʌdi]		sich etw genau ansehen
cartoonist	[kɑː'tuːnɪst]		Karikaturist/in
to draw	[drɔː]		zeichnen
to make a point	[ˌmeɪk ə 'pɔɪnt]		ein Argument vortragen, etw sagen wollen
human being	[ˌhjuːmən 'biːɪŋ]		Mensch, menschliches Wesen

page 27

among	[ə'mʌŋ]		unter, inmitten, zwischen
curfew	['kɜːfjuː]		Sperrstunde
unless	[ən'les]		es sei denn, außer wenn
to put an end to sth	[ˌpʊt ən 'end tə]		mit etw Schluss machen, einen Schlussstrich unter etw ziehen
at least	[ət 'liːst]		zumindest, mindestens
to accompany	[ə'kʌmpəni]		begleiten
legal guardian	[ˌliːgl 'gɑːdiən]		Vormund, Erziehungsberechtigte/r
to approach sb	[ə'prəʊtʃ]		an jdn herantreten
to provide	[prə'vaɪd]		zur Verfügung stellen
ID	[ˌaɪ 'diː]		Personalausweis
to object to sth	[əb'dʒekt tə]		etw ablehnen, gegen etw Einwände haben
spokesman	['spəʊksmən]		Sprecher
to argue	['ɑːgjuː]		argumentieren, geltend machen
retailer	['riːteɪlə]		Einzelhändler/in
to back	[bæk]		unterstützen
incident	['ɪnsɪdənt]		Vorfall, Zwischenfall
complaint	[kəm'pleɪnt]		Beschwerde, Klage, Reklamation
bid	[bɪd]		Versuch
to maintain sth	[meɪn'teɪn]		etw aufrechterhalten
to estimate	['estɪmeɪt]		schätzen
to state	[steɪt]		darlegen, festlegen
appropriate(ly)	[ə'prəʊpriət]		angemessen, passend
...-oriented	['ɔːrientɪd]		...orientiert
adequate(ly)	['ædɪkwət]		ausreichend, angemessen
to cover	['kʌvə]		bedecken
visible	['vɪzəbl]		sichtbar
undergarments pl	['ʌndəgɑːmənts]		Unterwäsche
permitted	[pə'mɪtɪd]		erlaubt, gestattet
measure	['meʒə]		Maßnahme
to divide	[dɪ'vaɪd]		teilen
intent	[ɪn'tent]		Absicht
to loiter	['lɔɪtə]		herumlungern
initiative	[ɪ'nɪʃətɪv]		Aktion, Initiative
to escort sb	[ɪ'skɔːt]		jdn begleiten, jdn eskortieren
exemption	[ɪg'zempʃn]		Ausnahme, Befreiung
to boast sth	[bəʊst]		etw aufweisen (können)
to abridge	[ə'brɪdʒ]		(Text) kürzen
to adapt	[ə'dæpt]		(Text) bearbeiten

page 28

mediation	[ˌmiːdi'eɪʃn]		Vermittlung
written	['rɪtn]		schriftlich
sense	[sens]		Sinn
to be aimed at sb	[bi 'eɪmd ət]		sich an jdn richten

Unit word list

to **paraphrase** [ˈpærəfreɪz]	umschreiben, paraphrasieren	**Cheers!** [tʃɪəz]	Tschüs! Mach's gut! Danke!
sort [sɔːt]	Art, Sorte	**insight** [ˈɪnsaɪt]	Einblick
to **re-read** [ˌriːˈriːd]	erneut lesen	to **run** [rʌn]	(Unternehmen) führen, betreiben
colleague [ˈkɒliːg]	Kollege/Kollegin	**at first hand** [ət ˌfɜːst ˈhænd]	aus erster Hand, hautnah
to **mess around** [ˌmes əˈraʊnd]	herumalbern, herumgammeln	**contact details** pl [ˈkɒntækt diːteɪlz]	Kontaktdaten
to **cause** [kɔːz]	verursachen	to **mention** [ˈmenʃn]	erwähnen
to **be on sale** [bi ɒn ˈseɪl]	angeboten werden, zum Verkauf stehen	**job advertisement** [ˈdʒɒb ədvɜːtɪsmənt]	Stellenanzeige, Stellenausschreibung
to **move house** [ˌmuːv ˈhaʊs]	umziehen	to **let sb know sth** [ˌlet ˈnəʊ]	jdm etw mitteilen
to **lift** [lɪft]	heben	**at the latest** [ət ðə ˈleɪtɪst]	spätestens
to **complain** [kəmˈpleɪn]	sich beschweren, sich beklagen	**Yours sincerely** [ˌjɔːz sɪnˈsɪəli]	(Brief:) Mit freundlichen Grüßen

page 29

social skills pl [ˌsəʊʃl ˈskɪlz]	Sozialkompetenz	**page 32**	
to **exchange** [ɪksˈtʃeɪndʒ]	austauschen	to **contrast** [kənˈtrɑːst]	gegenüberstellen, vergleichen
moans pl [məʊnz]	Gejammer, Genörgel	**abbreviation** [əˌbriːviˈeɪʃn]	Abkürzung
sex [seks]	Geschlecht	**chatty** [ˈtʃæti]	mitteilsam, geschwätzig
the opposite sex [ði ˌɒpəzɪt ˈseks]	das andere Geschlecht	**etiquette** [ˈetɪket]	Etikette, Regeln
to **text** [tekst]	eine SMS schicken, simsen	**subject line** [ˈsʌbdʒɪkt laɪn]	(Brief:) Betreffzeile
peer [pɪə]	Gleichaltrige/r, Altersgenosse	to **get into the habit of doing sth** [ˌget ɪntə ðə ˈhæbɪt əv]	sich angewöhnen, etw zu tun
to **interact** [ˌɪntərˈækt]	interagieren, aufeinander eingehen	to **type sth in** [ˌtaɪp ˈɪn]	etw eintippen
site [saɪt]	Website	**capital letter** [ˌkæpɪtl ˈletə]	Großbuchstabe
to **get together** [ˌget təˈgeðə]	sich treffen	**spelling** [ˈspelɪŋ]	Rechtschreibung
apart from [əˈpɑːt frəm]	abgesehen von, außer	**application** [ˌæplɪˈkeɪʃn]	Bewerbung
to **look after sb** [lʊk ˈɑːftə]	sich um jdn kümmern	to **submit** [səbˈmɪt]	einreichen, vorlegen, zusenden
siblings pl [ˈsɪblɪŋz]	Geschwister	to **take sth further** [ˌteɪk ˈfɜːðə]	etw (weiter) verfolgen
nearby adv [ˈnɪəbaɪ]	in der Nähe	to **confirm** [kənˈfɜːm]	bestätigen
opportunity [ˌɒpəˈtjuːnəti]	Gelegenheit, Möglichkeit, Chance	to **be available** [bi əˈveɪləbl]	(Telefon:) zu sprechen sein
to **socialize** [ˈsəʊʃəlaɪz]	sich treffen, unter Leute gehen	**set-up** [ˈsetʌp]	Aufbau
to **be pleased** [bi ˈpliːzd]	sich freuen	**page 33**	
to **keep in touch** [ˌkiːp ɪn ˈtʌtʃ]	in Verbindung bleiben	to **separate** [ˈsepəreɪt]	trennen, loslösen
face to face [ˌfeɪs tə ˈfeɪs]	persönlich	to **soften** [ˈsɒfn]	mildern, abmildern
ability [əˈbɪləti]	Fähigkeit, Befähigung	**surname** [ˈsɜːneɪm]	Nachname
especially [ɪˈspeʃəli]	besonders, insbesondere	**proper name** [ˌprɒpə ˈneɪm]	Eigenname
page 30		**line** [laɪn]	Leitung
to **come round** [ˌkʌm ˈraʊnd]	vorbeikommen	**digit** [ˈdɪdʒɪt]	Ziffer
all right by me [ˌɔːl ˌraɪt baɪ ˈmiː]	in Ordnung für mich	**separately** [ˈseprətli]	einzeln
there's little point in doing sth [ðeəz ˌlɪtl pɔɪnt ɪn ˈduːɪŋ]	es hat wenig Sinn, etw zu tun	to **spell** [spel]	buchstabieren
		to **put sb through** [ˌpʊt ˈθruː]	(Telefon:) jdn durchstellen, jdn verbinden
		to **leave a message** [ˌliːv ə ˈmesɪdʒ]	eine Nachricht hinterlassen

JOB SKILLS 1

page 31

vocational college [vəʊˌkeɪʃənl ˈkɒlɪdʒ]	Fachoberschule, Berufskolleg	**page 34**	
work experience [ˈwɜːk ɪkspɪəriəns]	Praktikum	**as things turn out** [əz ˌθɪŋz tɜːn ˈaʊt]	wie sich herausstellt
writer [ˈraɪtə]	Verfasser/in	**appointment** [əˈpɔɪntmənt]	Termin, Verabredung
suggestion [səˈdʒestʃən]	Vorschlag	to **bother sb** [ˈbɒðə]	jdn belästigen, jdn stören
to **apply for a job** [əˌplaɪ fər ə ˈdʒɒb]	sich auf eine Stelle bewerben	**luck** [lʌk]	Glück
trainee [treɪˈniː]	Auszubildende/r	to **be unavailable** [bi ˌʌnəˈveɪləbl]	(Telefon:) nicht zu sprechen sein
native language [ˌneɪtɪv ˈlæŋgwɪdʒ]	Muttersprache	to **have a chat** [həv ə ˈtʃæt]	sich unterhalten, miteinander plaudern
secretary [ˈsekrətri]	Sekretär/in	**leaflet** [ˈliːflət]	Broschüre, Merkblatt
hostel [ˈhɒstl]	Herberge, Wohnheim	**definitely** [ˈdefɪnətli]	absolut, ganz sicher
sometime [ˈsʌmtaɪm]	irgendwann	to **hold the line** [ˌhəʊld ðə ˈlaɪn]	am Apparat bleiben
		likely [ˈlaɪkli]	wahrscheinlich
		caller [ˈkɔːlə]	Anrufer/in
		to **carry out** [ˌkæri ˈaʊt]	durchführen, ausführen

to respond to sth	[rɪˈspɒnd tə]	auf etw reagieren, auf etw antworten
to take a message	[ˌteɪk ə ˈmesɪdʒ]	etw ausrichten, eine Nachricht notieren
to read sth back	[ˌriːd ˈbæk]	etw (zur Kontrolle) vorlesen
to enquire about sth	[ɪnˈkwaɪər əbaʊt]	sich nach etw erkundigen
department	[dɪˈpɑːtmənt]	Abteilung
accounts	[əˈkaʊnts]	Buchhaltung
to hold on	[ˌhəʊld ˈɒn]	warten
engaged	[ɪnˈgeɪdʒd]	(Telefon:) besetzt

UNIT 5

page 35

virtual	[ˈvɜːtʃuəl]	virtuell
role	[rəʊl]	Rolle
poster	[ˈpəʊstə]	Plakat
gallery	[ˈgæləri]	Galerie
gallery walk	[ˈgæləri wɔːk]	Galerierundgang
to put sth up	[ˌpʊt ˈʌp]	etw (Bild etc.) aufhängen
per	[pə]	pro

page 36

to skim	[skɪm]	(Text) überfliegen
to underline	[ˌʌndəˈlaɪn]	unterstreichen
bold	[bəʊld]	fett(gedruckt)
type	[taɪp]	Schrift, Type
italics pl	[ɪˈtælɪks]	Kursivschrift
lonely	[ˈləʊnli]	einsam
habit	[ˈhæbɪt]	Gewohnheit
Briton	[ˈbrɪtn]	Brite/Britin
average	[ˈævərɪdʒ]	Durchschnitt
poll	[pəʊl]	Umfrage
to suggest	[səˈdʒest]	darauf hindeuten, nahelegen
third	[θɜːd]	Drittel
quarter	[ˈkwɔːtə]	Viertel
usage	[ˈjuːsɪdʒ]	Nutzung
to exceed	[ɪkˈsiːd]	übersteigen
to base on sth	[ˈbeɪs ɒn]	auf etw basieren
to carry out	[ˌkæri ˈaʊt]	durchführen, ausführen
primary	[ˈpraɪməri]	Haupt-, hauptsächlich
reader	[ˈriːdə]	Dozent/in
psychology	[saɪˈkɒlədʒi]	Psychologie
to tend to do sth	[ˈtend tə]	dazu neigen, etw zu tun
largely	[ˈlɑːdʒli]	weitgehend, überwiegend
dependent on sth	[dɪˈpendənt ɒn]	von etw abhängig
all the time	[ˌɔːl ðə ˈtaɪm]	ständig, die ganze Zeit
to cut sb off from sth	[ˌkʌt ˈɒf frəm]	jdn von etw abschneiden
several	[ˈsevrəl]	mehrere
left out of sth	[ˌleft ˈaʊt əv]	von etw ausgeschlossen
to isolate	[ˈaɪsəleɪt]	absondern, isolieren

page 37

at the expense of sth	[ət ði ɪkˈspens əv]	auf Kosten von etw
regardless of sth	[rɪˈgɑːdləs əv]	ungeachtet einer Sache
update	[ˈʌpdeɪt]	Aktualisierung
to engage with sb	[ɪnˈgeɪdʒ wɪð]	auf jdn zugehen
channel	[ˈtʃænl]	Kanal
to listen in	[ˌlɪsn ˈɪn]	mithören
presence	[ˈprezns]	Anwesenheit, Präsenz
amount	[əˈmaʊnt]	Betrag
sum	[sʌm]	Summe
representative	[ˌreprɪˈzentətɪv]	repräsentativ
to get involved with sb	[ˌget ɪnˈvɒlvd wɪð]	mit jdm zu tun haben
account	[əˈkaʊnt]	Konto
to be called	[bi ˈkɔːld]	heißen
unfit	[ʌnˈfɪt]	nicht fit
to spell	[spel]	buchstabieren, (richtig) schreiben
handwriting	[ˈhændraɪtɪŋ]	Handschrift
thumb	[θʌm]	Daumen
childhood	[ˈtʃaɪldhʊd]	Kindheit
to hand sth in	[ˌhænd ˈɪn]	etw abgeben
suggestion	[səˈdʒestʃən]	Vorschlag
to take a vote	[ˌteɪk ə ˈvəʊt]	abstimmen

page 38

entry	[ˈentri]	(Blog:) Beitrag, Meldung
importance	[ɪmˈpɔːtns]	Bedeutung, Wichtigkeit
anecdote	[ˈænɪkdəʊt]	Anekdote
call for help	[ˌkɔːl fə ˈhelp]	Hilferuf
wall	[wɔːl]	Wand, Pinnwand
conclusion	[kənˈkluːʒn]	Schlussfolgerung, Schluss
helpline	[ˈhelplaɪn]	Hotline, Sorgentelefon
to suffer from sth	[ˈsʌfə frəm]	unter etw leiden
solution	[səˈluːʃn]	Lösung
counsellor	[ˈkaʊnsələ]	Berater/in
to take a call	[ˌteɪk ə ˈkɔːl]	einen Anruf entgegennehmen, ans Telefon gehen
to go viral	[ˌgəʊ ˈvaɪrəl]	sich (im Internet) rasend schnell verbreiten
to laugh at sb	[ˈlɑːf ət]	über jdn lachen, jdn auslachen
to point at sb/sth	[ˈpɔɪnt ət]	auf jdn/etw zeigen
desperate	[ˈdespərət]	verzweifelt
fully	[ˈfʊli]	vollkommen, völlig
cruel	[kruːəl]	grausam, gemein
to trust	[trʌst]	vertrauen
appointment	[əˈpɔɪntmənt]	Termin
talk	[tɔːk]	Gerede
advice	[ədˈvaɪs]	(guter) Rat, Ratschläge
to see sb	[siː]	zu jdm gehen
practical	[ˈpræktɪkl]	zweckmäßig, praktisch (umsetzbar)
to delete	[dɪˈliːt]	löschen, tilgen
to advise sb	[ədˈvaɪz]	jdn beraten, jdm etw raten
to contact sb	[ˈkɒntækt]	sich mit jdm in Verbindung setzen

page 39

to block	[blɒk]	sperren
to deactivate	[ˌdiːˈæktɪveɪt]	stilllegen, deaktivieren
legal action	[ˌliːgl ˈækʃn]	rechtliche Schritte
to take legal action	[teɪk ˌliːgl ˈækʃn]	rechtliche Schritte unternehmen
setting	[ˈsetɪŋ]	Einstellung
to bother sb	[ˈbɒðə]	jdn belästigen
right-hand	[ˈraɪt hænd]	rechte/r/s, auf der rechten Seite
screen	[skriːn]	Bildschirm
to reactivate	[ˌriːˈæktɪveɪt]	wieder in Betrieb nehmen, reaktivieren
at any time	[ət ˌeni ˈtaɪm]	jederzeit
to log in	[ˌlɒg ˈɪn]	sich einloggen
to log out	[ˌlɒg ˈaʊt]	sich ausloggen
deletion	[dɪˈliːʃn]	Löschung, Tilgung
epitaph	[ˈepɪtɑːf]	Grabinschrift

Unit word list

to **hire sb** [ˈhaɪə]	jdn beauftragen, jdn engagieren	to **deal with sth** [ˈdiːl wɪð]	mit etw zurechtkommen, mit etw umgehen
lawyer [ˈlɔːjə]	Anwalt/Anwältin	to **look sth up** [ˌlʊk ˈʌp]	etw (Vokabel etc.) nachschlagen
specialist lawyer [ˌspeʃəlɪst ˈlɔːjə]	Fachanwalt/-anwältin	**context** [ˈkɒntekst]	Zusammenhang, Kontext
service [ˈsɜːvɪs]	Dienst, Dienstleistung	**uninvited** [ˌʌnɪnˈvaɪtɪd]	un(ein)geladen
provider [prəˈvaɪdə]	Anbieter	**noise** [nɔɪz]	Lärm
thousand [ˈθaʊznd]	tausend, Tausend	**next door** [ˌnekst ˈdɔː]	nebenan
		to **end up** [ˌend ˈʌp]	landen

page 40

unwanted [ˌʌnˈwɒntɪd]	unerwünscht		
schoolboy [ˈskuːlbɔɪ]	Schuljunge		

page 42

drunken [ˈdrʌŋkən]	betrunken	**text message** [ˈtekst mesɪdʒ]	SMS
crasher [ˈkræʃə]	ungeladener Gast	to **upload** [ˌʌpˈləʊd]	hochladen
to **trash sth** [træʃ]	etw demolieren		
pound [paʊnd]	Pfund		

page 43

reveller [ˈrevələ]	Feiernde/r	**mess** [mes]	Chaos
to **gatecrash** [ˈgeɪtkræʃ]	uneingeladen erscheinen	to **expand** [ɪkˈspænd]	erweitern
damage [ˈdæmɪdʒ]	Schaden	to **act out** [ˌækt ˈaʊt]	spielen, vorspielen
vomit [ˈvɒmɪt]	Erbrochenes	**horrified** [ˈhɒrɪfaɪd]	entsetzt
terraced BE [ˈterəst]	Reihenhaus-	**invite** [ˈɪnvaɪt]	Einladung
property [ˈprɒpəti]	Immobilie(n), Anwesen	to **wash** [wɒʃ]	abwaschen, abwischen
riot [ˈraɪət]	Aufstand, Aufruhr	to **apologize** [əˈpɒlədʒaɪz]	sich entschuldigen
riot police [ˈraɪət pəliːs]	Bereitschaftspolizei	**behaviour** [bɪˈheɪvjə]	Benehmen, Verhalten
to **break up** [ˌbreɪk ˈʌp]	(Menschenmenge) zerstreuen	**cancer** [ˈkænsə]	Krebs (Krankheit)
trouble [ˈtrʌbl]	Ärger, Problem(e)	**fundraiser** [ˈfʌndreɪzə]	Spendensammler/in
danger [ˈdeɪndʒə]	Gefahr	to **raise money** [ˌreɪz ˈmʌni]	Geld beschaffen
details pl [ˈdiːteɪlz]	Angaben	**plight** [plaɪt]	Notlage
to **realize** [ˈrɪəlaɪz]	wissen, erkennen, klar sein	to **spread** [spred]	sich verbreiten
invitation [ˌɪnvɪˈteɪʃn]	Einladung	to **diagnose sb with sth** [ˈdaɪəgnəʊz wɪð]	etw (Krankheit) bei jdm feststellen/diagnostizieren
to **throw** [θrəʊ]	werfen	**terminal** [ˈtɜːmɪnl]	im Endstadium, tödlich
to **throw a party** [ˌθrəʊ ə ˈpɑːti]	eine Party geben/schmeißen	**rather than** [ˈrɑːðə ðən]	anstatt
privacy [ˈprɪvəsi]	Privatsphäre	to **dwell on sth** [ˈdwel ɒn]	sich mit etw aufhalten
absolutely [ˈæbsəluːtli]	absolut	**misfortune** [ˌmɪsˈfɔːtʃuːn]	Unglück, Missgeschick
essential [ɪˈsenʃl]	wesentlich, unerlässlich	to **draw up** [ˌdrɔː ˈʌp]	(Text) verfassen, abfassen
to **make sb aware of sth** [ˌmeɪk əˈweər əv]	jdn über etw informieren, jdn auf etw hinweisen	**bucket** [ˈbʌkɪt]	Eimer
poisoning [ˈpɔɪzənɪŋ]	Vergiftung	**bucket list** [ˈbʌkɪt lɪst]	Liste der Dinge, die man tun möchte, bevor man stirbt.
laughing gas [ˈlɑːfɪŋ gæs]	Lachgas	**skydive** [ˈskaɪdaɪv]	Fallschirmsprung
canister [ˈkænɪstə]	Dose, Büchse	**drums** pl [drʌmz]	Schlagzeug
to **toss** [tɒs]	werfen	**final** [ˈfaɪnl]	Finale
living room [ˈlɪvɪŋ ruːm]	Wohnzimmer	**initially** [ɪˈnɪʃəli]	anfangs, anfänglich
carpet [ˈkɑːpɪt]	Teppich(boden)	to **set out to do sth** [ˌset ˈaʊt tə]	sich vornehmen, etw tun
to **clean up** [ˌkliːn ˈʌp]	aufräumen, saubermachen	**fundraising** [ˈfʌndreɪzɪŋ]	Spendensammeln, Geldbeschaffung
to **damage** [ˈdæmɪdʒ]	beschädigen	**campaign** [kæmˈpeɪn]	Aktion, Kampagne
skylight [ˈskaɪlaɪt]	Oberlicht, Dachfenster	to **attract** [əˈtrækt]	anlocken, anziehen
bouncer [ˈbaʊnsə]	Türsteher/in	to **attract attention** [əˌtrækt əˈtenʃn]	Aufmerksamkeit erregen
in advance [ɪn ədˈvɑːns]	im Voraus	**inspirational** [ˌɪnspɪˈreɪʃnəl]	anregend, inspirierend
unable [ʌnˈeɪbl]	nicht in der Lage, unfähig	to **benefit** [ˈbenɪfɪt]	nutzen, Nutzen bringen, profitieren
to **cope (with sth)** [ˈkəʊp wɪð]	etw bewältigen, mit etw klarkommen, mit etw fertig werden	to **research sth** [rɪˈsɜːtʃ]	etw recherchieren, Nachforschungen über etw anstellen
to **turn up** [ˌtɜːn ˈʌp]	auftauchen	**findings** pl [ˈfaɪndɪŋz]	Ergebnisse
shocked [ʃɒkt]	schockiert		

page 44

to **drop sb off** [ˌdrɒp ˈɒf]	jdn (wohin)bringen	to **prefer** [prɪˈfɜː]	vorziehen, bevorzugen
aged [eɪdʒd]	im Alter von	**physical** [ˈfɪzɪkəl]	physisch, materiell, körperlich (im Gegensatz zu virtuell)
to **wreck** [rek]	demolieren		
chaos [ˈkeɪɒs]	Chaos		
to **do sb harm** [du ˈhɑːm]	jdm etwas (an)tun	**increasingly** [ɪnˈkriːsɪŋli]	zunehmend
apparently [əˈpærəntli]	anscheinend	**stressful** [ˈstresfəl]	stressig
reputation [ˌrepjuˈteɪʃn]	Ansehen, Ruf	**free time** [friː ˈtaɪm]	Freizeit
to **shoot up** [ˌʃuːt ˈʌp]	rasant ansteigen	**ecommerce** [ˈiːkɒmɜːs]	Internet-Handel
		to **step in** [ˌstep ˈɪn]	hier: ins Spiel kommen

page 41

immediately [ɪˈmiːdiətli]	unverzüglich, unmittelbar, sofort
to **get drunk** [ˌget ˈdrʌŋk]	sich betrinken

282

customer	[ˈkʌstəmə]	Kunde/Kundin	digital signage [ˌdɪdʒɪtl ˈsaɪnɪdʒ]	digitale Außenwerbung
search engine	[ˈsɜːtʃ endʒɪn]	Suchmaschine	ad, advert, advertisement [æd, ˈædvɜːt, ədˈvɜːtɪsmənt]	Anzeige, Werbung
once	[wʌns]	sobald		
kind	[kaɪnd]	Art	viral ad	[ˌvaɪrəl ˈæd]	Internet-Werbespot
to indicate	[ˈɪndɪkeɪt]	zeigen, hinweisen	element	[ˈelɪmənt]	Baustein, Element
social group	[ˌsəʊʃəl ˈɡruːp]	soziale Gruppe, soziale Gemeinschaft	ambition	[æmˈbɪʃn]	Ziel, Ehrgeiz
			excitement	[ɪkˈsaɪtmənt]	Spannung, Aufregung
to fall into sth	[ˈfɔːl ɪntuː]	unter etw fallen, zu etw gehören	horror	[ˈhɒrə]	Schrecken
			tragedy	[ˈtrædʒədi]	Tragödie
purchasing power [ˈpɜːtʃəsɪŋ paʊə]		Kaufkraft	humour	[ˈhjuːmə]	Humor
			mystery	[ˈmɪstri]	Rätsel, Rätselhaftigkeit
to save time	[ˌseɪv ˈtaɪm]	Zeit sparen	provocation	[ˌprɒvəˈkeɪʃn]	Provokation
straight away	[streɪt əˈweɪ]	sofort	reward	[rɪˈwɔːd]	Belohnung, Lohn
approach	[əˈprəʊtʃ]	Vorgehen, Herangehensweise	to contain	[kənˈteɪn]	enthalten
to save sth	[seɪv]	etw ersparen	**page 46**		
frustration	[frʌˈstreɪʃən]	Enttäuschung, Frust	giant	[ˈdʒaɪənt]	riesig, riesenhaft
to roam	[rəʊm]	durchstreifen	note	[nəʊt]	Ton, Note
aisle	[aɪəl]	Gang	likely	[ˈlaɪkli]	wahrscheinlich
to discover	[dɪˈskʌvə]	entdecken	to be likely to do sth	[bi ˈlaɪkli tə]	etw wahrscheinlich tun (werden)
item	[ˈaɪtəm]	Punkt, Gegenstand			
to mean to do sth	[ˌmiːn tə ˈduː]	gedenken, etw zu tun	to skip sth	[skɪp]	etw auslassen, etw überspringen
to purchase	[ˈpɜːtʃəs]	kaufen			
currently	[ˈkʌrəntli]	zurzeit, derzeit	escalator	[ˈeskəleɪtə]	Rolltreppe
in stock	[ˌɪn ˈstɒk]	vorrätig, auf Lager	in favor of doing sth AE [ɪn ˈfeɪvər əv]		um (stattdessen) etw zu tun
to compete with sb	[kəmˈpiːt wɪð]	mit jdm im Wettbewerb stehen, konkurrieren	to compose	[kəmˈpəʊz]	komponieren
			subway AE	[ˈsʌbweɪ]	U-Bahn
player	[ˈpleɪə]	hier: Firma, Wettbewerber	to view sth	[vjuː]	(sich) etw ansehen
stationary	[ˈsteɪʃənəri]	ortsansässig, fest	concept	[ˈkɒnsept]	Idee, Gedanke, Konzept
capacity	[kəˈpæsəti]	Kapazität, Leistungsvermögen	to create	[kriˈeɪt]	(er)schaffen, entwerfen, kreieren
to reach sth	[riːtʃ]	etw erreichen, an etw herankommen	ad(vertising) agency	[ˈæd eɪdʒənsi]	Werbeagentur
client base	[ˈklaɪənt beɪs]	Kundenstamm	goal	[ɡəʊl]	Ziel, Absicht
range	[reɪndʒ]	Sortiment, Bandbreite	do-good	[ˈduː ɡʊd]	weltverbessernd
to increase	[ɪnˈkriːs]	erhöhen, vergrößern	to promote sth	[prəˈməʊt]	für etw werben, etw bewerben
efficiency	[əˈfɪʃəntsi]	Effizienz, Leistungsfähigkeit			
to capitalize on sth [ˈkæpɪtəlaɪz ɒn]		aus etw Nutzen ziehen	environmental(ly) [ɪnˌvaɪrənˈmentl]		umweltmäßig, Umwelt-
close	[kləʊs]	nah	environmentally friendly [ɪnˌvaɪrənˌmentəli ˈfrendli]		umweltfreundlich
trade	[treɪd]	Handel			
to summarize	[ˈsʌməraɪz]	zusammenfassen	competitive	[kəmˈpetətɪv]	umkämpft, wettbewerbsintensiv
to conduct	[ˈkɒndʌkt]	hier: durchführen			
participant	[pɑːˈtɪsɪpənt]	Teilnehmer/in	eco-	[ˈiːkəʊ]	Öko-
to name	[neɪm]	benennen	traditional	[trəˈdɪʃənl]	herkömmlich
to rate	[reɪt]	beurteilen, bewerten	effective	[ɪˈfektɪv]	wirksam, effektiv
according to priority [əˌkɔːdɪŋ tə praɪˈɒrəti]		gemäß der Priorität	competition	[ˌkɒmpəˈtɪʃn]	Konkurrenz, Konkurrenzkampf
graph	[ɡrɑːf]	Diagramm, Graphik	sound	[saʊnd]	solide, untadelig
similarity	[ˌsɪməˈlærəti]	Ähnlichkeit, Gemeinsamkeit	fierce	[fɪəs]	heftig, erbittert
instead of	[ɪnˈsted əv]	(an)statt	approach	[əˈprəʊtʃ]	Ansatz, Herangehensweise
low	[ləʊ]	niedrig	deputy manager	[ˌdepjəti ˈmænɪdʒə]	stellvertretende/r Geschäftsführer/in
deal	[diːl]	Geschäft			
no need to do sth	[nəʊ ˌniːd tə ˈduː]	nicht nötig, etw zu tun	commuter	[kəˈmjuːtə]	Pendler/in
			to choose sth over sth [ˈtʃuːz əʊvə]		etw einer anderen Sache vorziehen
wide	[waɪd]	groß, umfangreich			
variety	[vəˈraɪəti]	Vielfalt, Auswahl	to increase	[ɪnˈkriːs]	steigen, zunehmen
to compare	[kəmˈpeə]	vergleichen	phase	[feɪz]	Phase
to research sth	[rɪˈsɜːtʃ]	recherchieren nach etw	release	[rɪˈliːs]	Veröffentlichung
strength	[streŋθ]	Stärke	to enter sth	[ˈentə]	an etw teilnehmen
			contest	[ˈkɒntest]	Wettbewerb
UNIT 6			to submit sth	[səbˈmɪt]	etw einreichen, etw einsenden
page 45					
advertising	[ˈædvətaɪzɪŋ]	Werbung	submission	[səbˈmɪʃn]	Einsendung
billboard	[ˈbɪlbɔːd]	Reklametafel, Plakatwand			

Unit word list

thoughtful [ˈθɔːtfl]	wohlüberlegt, gut durchdacht
game machine [ˈgeɪm məʃiːn]	Videospielgerät, Spielautomat
to turn sb/sth into sb/sth [ˈtɜːn ɪntə]	jdn/etw zu jdm/etw machen
can [kæn]	Dose
to encourage sb to do sth [ɪnˈkʌrɪdʒ]	jdn ermuntern, etw zu tun
to invent [ɪnˈvent]	erfinden
bottle bank [ˈbɒtl bæŋk]	Glascontainer
arcade [ɑːˈkeɪd]	Spielautomat
amusement arcade [əˈmjuːzmənt ɑːkeɪd]	Spielhalle
noise [nɔɪz]	Geräusch
passer-by [ˈpɑːsə baɪ]	Passant/in
conventional [kənˈvenʃənl]	konventionell, herkömmlich

page 47

deep [diːp]	tief
rubbish [ˈrʌbɪʃ]	Müll, Abfall
rubbish bin [ˈrʌbɪʃ bɪn]	Mülltonne
crash [kræʃ]	Schlag, Krach
to step [step]	treten
to be fun [bi ˈfʌn]	Spaß machen
to protect [prəˈtekt]	schützen
metal [ˈmetl]	Metall
government [ˈgʌvənmənt]	Regierung, öffentliche Verwaltung
ground [graʊnd]	(Erd-)Boden

page 48

in addition [ɪn əˈdɪʃn]	außerdem, darüber hinaus
for this reason [fə ðɪs ˈriːzn]	aus diesem Grund
to give a presentation [gɪv ə ˌpreznˈteɪʃn]	ein Referat halten
slide [slaɪd]	Dia, (Overhead-)Folie
to take turns [ˌteɪk ˈtɜːnz]	sich abwechseln
to number [ˈnʌmbə]	nummerieren
hand-held [ˈhænd held]	in der Hand gehalten
quick reference [ˌkwɪk ˈrefərəns]	schnelles Nachschlagen
to form [fɔːm]	bilden
invention [ɪnˈvenʃn]	Erfindung
public transport [ˌpʌblɪk ˈtrænspɔːt]	öffentliche Verkehrsmittel
ticket inspector [ˈtɪkɪt ɪnspektə]	Fahrkartenkontrolleur/in
to fine sb [faɪn]	jdn mit einer Geldbuße belegen
to stamp [stæmp]	stempeln, abstempeln
lottery [ˈlɒtəri]	Lotterie, Verlosung
instant(ly) [ˈɪnstənt]	sofortig, augenblicklich
salary [ˈsæləri]	Gehalt
speed [spiːd]	Geschwindigkeit
speed camera [ˈspiːd kæmərə]	Geschwindigkeitsüberwachungskamera, Radarfalle
speed limit [ˈspiːd lɪmɪt]	Geschwindigkeitsbegrenzung
to reward [rɪˈwɔːd]	belohnen
fine [faɪn]	Geldbuße
traffic lights pl [ˈtræfɪk laɪts]	Ampel
motorist BE [ˈməʊtərɪst]	Autofahrer/in
to jump red lights [ˌdʒʌmp red ˈlaɪts]	bei Rot über eine Ampel fahren
driving licence [ˈdraɪvɪŋ laɪsns]	Führerschein
knowledge [ˈnɒlɪdʒ]	Wissen, Kenntnis(se)
visuals pl [ˈvɪʒuəlz]	visuelle Hilfsmittel
OHP transparency [ˌəʊ eɪtʃ ˈpiː trænspærənsi]	Overheadfolie
introductions pl [ˌɪntrəˈdʌkʃnz]	Vorstellen
to hand over [ˌhænd ˈəʊvə]	übergeben
in conclusion [ɪn kənˈkluːʒn]	abschließend, zum Schluss
to be pleased to do sth [bi ˈpliːzd tə]	etw gern tun

page 49

giant [ˈdʒaɪənt]	Riese
to make the difference [ˌmeɪk ðə ˈdɪfrəns]	entscheidend sein, den entscheidenden Unterschied ausmachen
to start out [ˌstɑːt ˈaʊt]	(zunächst) anfangen
office clerk [ˈɒfɪs klɑːk]	Büroangestellte/r
soap [səʊp]	Seife
dope [dəʊp]	Depp
managing director [ˌmænɪdʒɪŋ dəˈrektə]	Geschäftsführer/in
in-tray [ˈɪn treɪ]	Posteingang(skorb)
to fire sb [faɪə]	jdn feuern
to hire sb [ˈhaɪə]	jdn einstellen
I've never looked back. [aɪv ˌnevə lʊkt ˈbæk]	Ich habe es nie bereut.
to set up [ˌset ˈʌp]	(Unternehmen) gründen
manufacturer [ˌmænjuˈfæktʃərə]	Hersteller/in, Produzent/in
to know sth inside out [ˌnəʊ ˌɪnsaɪd ˈaʊt]	etw in- und auswendig kennen
to stand out [ˌstænd ˈaʊt]	auffallen, herausstechen
research [rɪˈsɜːtʃ]	Recherche, Nachforschungen, Untersuchungen
to colour [ˈkʌlə]	färben
hair care [ˈheəkeə]	Haarpflege
secret [ˈsiːkrɪt]	heimlich, geheim
fascinating [ˈfæsɪneɪtɪŋ]	faszinierend
caller [ˈkɔːlə]	Anrufer/in
to legalize [ˈliːgəlaɪz]	legalisieren
lying [ˈlaɪɪŋ]	Lügen
seriously [ˈsɪəriəsli]	im Ernst
to cook a meal [ˌkʊk ə ˈmiːl]	eine Mahlzeit zubereiten, ein Essen kochen
to paint [peɪnt]	malen
trash [træʃ]	Müll
beetle [ˈbiːtl]	Käfer
bare [beə]	kahl, nackt
college [ˈkɒlɪdʒ]	Fachhochschule
promotion [prəˈməʊʃn]	Werbung
broke [brəʊk]	kaputt
niche [nɪtʃ]	Nische
targeted [ˈtɑːgɪtɪd]	gezielt, ins Visier genommen
blanket [ˈblæŋkɪt]	pauschal, umfassend
to be designed to do sth [bi dɪˈzaɪnd tə]	dazu gedacht sein, etw zu tun; darauf ausgelegt sein, etw zu tun
maximum [ˈmæksɪməm]	maximal, Höchst-
to be supposed to do sth [bi səˈpəʊzd tə]	etw tun sollen
to ship [ʃɪp]	verschicken
to bottle [ˈbɒtl]	in Flaschen abfüllen
vending machine [ˈvendɪŋ məʃiːn]	(Verkaufs-)Automat
to donate [dəʊˈneɪt]	spenden
vacation AE [vəˈkeɪʃn]	Urlaub
to join [dʒɔɪn]	mitmachen, (Radio etc.:) in einer Sendung sein, (Telefon:) (mit jdm) sprechen

washing powder ['wɒʃɪŋ paʊdə]	Waschpulver	to feel sth [fiːl]	etw anfassen, etw ertasten
sales pl [seɪlz]	Verkauf, Verkäufe, Absatz, Vertrieb	mouse [maʊs]	Maus
factor ['fæktə]	Faktor	to survive [sə'vaɪv]	überleben
life-cycle ['laɪf saɪkl]	Lebensdauer, Lebenszyklus	to rebuild [ˌriː'bɪld]	umbauen, erneuern
maximum ['mæksɪməm]	Höchstwert	series ['sɪəriːz]	Reihe, Serie
car wash ['kɑː wɒʃ]	Autowaschanlage		
hairdressing salon ['heədresɪŋ sælɒn]	Friseursalon		
electrician [ɪˌlek'trɪʃn]	Elektriker/in		
perfume ['pɜːfjuːm]	Parfüm		
sports car ['spɔːts kɑː]	Sportwagen		

page 50

to intend [ɪn'tend]	beabsichtigen		
arrangement [ə'reɪndʒmənt]	Abmachung, Vereinbarung, Vorbereitung, Regelung		
salesman ['seɪlzmən]	Verkäufer, Vertreter		
deal [diːl]	Geschäft, Abschluss		
profit ['prɒfɪt]	Gewinn, Profit		
Head Office [ˌhed 'ɒfɪs]	Zentrale, Direktion, Hauptverwaltung		
Human Resources (HR) [ˌhjuːmən rɪ'sɔːsɪz]	Personal(abteilung)		
luck [lʌk]	Glück		
limited ['lɪmɪtɪd]	begrenzt, beschränkt		
publisher ['pʌblɪʃə]	Verleger/in		
straight [streɪt]	direkt, gleich		
to phone in [ˌfəʊn 'ɪn]	(in einer Sendung) anrufen		
to get bored [ˌget 'bɔːd]	sich langweilen		
to launch [lɔːntʃ]	(Produkt) auf den Markt bringen, einführen		

page 52

to continue to do sth [kən'tɪnjuː tə]	etw weiterhin tun
graph [grɑːf]	Diagramm, Kurve
chart [tʃɑːt]	Diagramm, Tabelle
bar chart [ˈbɑː tʃɑːt]	Säulendiagramm
figure ['fɪgə]	Zahl, Ziffer
statistics [stə'tɪstɪks]	Statistik(en)
visual ['vɪʒuəl]	visuell
change [tʃeɪndʒ]	Veränderung
spending ['spendɪŋ]	Ausgaben, Aufwendungen
billion ['bɪliən]	Milliarde
per cent [pə'sent]	Prozent
note [nəʊt]	Hinweis
directory [də'rektəri]	Telefonbuch
source [sɔːs]	Quelle

page 53

axis ['æksɪs]	Achse
line chart ['laɪn tʃɑːt]	Liniendiagramm
upwards ['ʌpwədz]	steigend
downwards ['daʊnwədz]	fallend
percentage [pə'sentɪdʒ]	Prozentsatz, Anteil
point [pɔɪnt]	Komma (bei Dezimalzahlen)
target group ['tɑːgɪt gruːp]	Zielgruppe
branded goods pl [ˌbrændɪd 'gʊdz]	Markenware, Markenartikel
writer ['raɪtə]	Autor/in, Schriftsteller/in

page 51

commercial [kə'mɜːʃl]	(Werbe-)Spot
to pick sth out [ˌpɪk 'aʊt]	etw heraussuchen
to read sth closely [ˌriːd 'kləʊsli]	etw genau (durch)lesen
to come across sth [ˌkʌm ə'krɒs]	auf etw stoßen
visionary ['vɪʒənri]	Visionär/in
genius ['dʒiːniəs]	Genie
to brand a product [ˌbrænd ə 'prɒdʌkt]	ein Markenprodukt schaffen
household name ['haʊshəʊld neɪm]	bekannter Name, Begriff
sunny ['sʌni]	sonnig
threatening ['θretnɪŋ]	bedrohlich
scary ['skeəri]	unheimlich, beängstigend
to come up with sth [ˌkʌm 'ʌp wɪð]	sich etw ausdenken, sich etw einfallen lassen
likeable ['laɪkəbl]	sympathisch
to be about to do sth [bi ə'baʊt tə]	im Begriff sein, etw zu tun; gerade dabei sein, etw zu tun
to target sb ['tɑːgɪt]	jdn ins Visier nehmen, auf jdn abzielen
strategy ['strætədʒi]	Strategie
high-end [ˌhaɪ 'end]	hochklassig, hochwertig
everyday ['evrideɪ]	alltäglich, Alltags-
constant ['kɒnstənt]	ständig, andauernd
function ['fʌŋkʃn]	Funktion
powerful ['paʊəfl]	stark, mächtig, kräftig
manual ['mænjuəl]	Bedienungsanleitung
jargon ['dʒɑːgən]	Fachsprache, Jargon
entrepreneur [ˌɒntrəprə'nɜː]	Unternehmer/in
accessible [ək'sesəbl]	zugänglich, erreichbar, offen

page 54

to divide [dɪ'vaɪd]	unterteilen, einteilen
stage [steɪdʒ]	Stufe, Phase
according to [ə'kɔːdɪŋ tə]	entsprechend, gemäß
sales pl [seɪəlz]	Erträge, Umsatz
profit ['prɒfɪt]	Profit, Gewinn
during ['dʒʊərɪŋ]	während
lifetime ['laɪftaɪm]	Lebensdauer
initial creation [ɪˌnɪʃəl kri'eɪʃən]	Erschaffung
development [dɪ'veləpmənt]	Entwicklung
decline [dɪ'klaɪn]	Verfall, Niedergang
to fail [feɪl]	scheitern
certain ['sɜːtən]	gewiss
continually [kən'tɪnjuəli]	dauernd, fortwährend
growth stage ['grəʊθ steɪdʒ]	Entwicklungsstadium, Wachstumsphase
to complete [kəm'pliːt]	beenden, abschließen
introductory phase [ˌɪntrə'dʌktəri feɪz]	Einführungsphase, Werbephase
to bring onto the market [brɪŋ ˌɒntu ðə 'mɑːkɪt]	auf den Markt bringen
potential [pə'tenʃəl]	potenziell, möglich
supplier [sə'plaɪə]	Lieferant
to make aware [ˌmeɪk ə'weə]	bewusst machen, in Kenntnis setzen
as [æz]	da, weil
distribution [ˌdɪstrɪ'bjuːʃən]	Verteilung, Verbreitung
accepted [ək'septəd]	akzeptiert, angenommen
to face competition [ˌfeɪs ˌkɒmpə'tɪʃən]	sich dem Wettbewerb stellen
to ensure [ɪn'ʃɔː]	sicherstellen, gewährleisten
to stay relevant to sb [ˌsteɪ 'reləvənt tə]	wichtig, von Bedeutung bleiben

285

Unit word list

maturity stage [məˈtʃʊərəti steɪdʒ]	Reifephase	
peak [piːk]	Gipfel, Spitze	
to decline [dɪˈklaɪn]	sinken, fallen, zurückgehen	
generally [ˈdʒenərəli]	im Allgemeinen, üblicherweise	
to adapt to sth [əˈdæpt tə]	sich an etw anpassen	
to modify [ˈmɒdɪfaɪ]	verändern	
target market [ˈtɑːgɪt mɑːkɪt]	Zielmarkt, Kundenzielgruppe	
to market sth [ˈmɑːkɪt]	etw vermarkten	
due to [ˈdjuː tə]	aufgrund von	
decrease [ˌdiːˈkriːs]	Abnahme, Rückgang	
gradually [ˈgrædʒuəli]	allmählich	
to initiate [ɪˈnɪʃieɪt]	einleiten, beginnen	
advancement [ədˈvɑːnsmənt]	Fortschritt, Weiterentwicklung	
increase [ɪnˈkriːs]	Anstieg	
competition [ˌkɒmpəˈtɪʃən]	Wettbewerb	
taste [teɪst]	Geschmack	
to be faced with sth [bi ˈfeɪst wɪð]	mit etw konfrontiert sein	
to drop [drɒp]	fallenlassen	
to maintain [ˌmeɪnˈteɪn]	behalten	
to harvest [ˈhɑːvɪst]	(ab)ernten	
to eliminate [ɪˈlɪmɪneɪt]	aussondern, beseitigen	
entirely [ɪnˈtaɪəli]	völlig, ganz	
to involve [ɪnˈvɒlv]	beinhalten, einschließen	
to launch [lɔːntʃ]	auf den Markt bringen	
to require [rɪˈkwaɪə]	erfordern	
cost [kɒst]	Kosten	
cost reduction [ˌkɒst rɪˈdʌkʃən]	Kostensenkung	
revenue [ˈrevənjuː]	Einnahme, Ertrag	
pace [peɪs]	Geschwindigkeit, Tempo	

UNIT 7
page 55

beyond [bɪˈjɒnd]	darüber hinaus
Hinduism [ˈhɪnduːɪzəm]	Hinduismus
Catholicism [kəˈθɒləsɪzəm]	Katholizismus, der katholische Glaube
Judaism [ˈdʒuːdeɪɪzəm]	Judaismus, Judentum
extended [ɪkˈstendɪd]	erweitert
extended family [ɪkˌstendɪd ˈfæməli]	Großfamilie
immediate [ɪˈmiːdiət]	unmittelbar
peer group [ˈpɪə gruːp]	Altersgruppe, Bezugsgruppe, Umfeld
role model [ˈrəʊl mɒdl]	Vorbild
chore [tʃɔː]	(lästige Routine-)Aufgabe

page 56

safely [ˈseɪfli]	mit Gewissheit
twin [twɪn]	Zwilling
to spoil [spɔɪl]	(Kind) verwöhnen
to turn to sb [ˈtɜːn tə]	sich an jdn wenden
day-to-day [ˌdeɪ tə ˈdeɪ]	tagtäglich
chat [tʃæt]	Unterhaltung, Schwätzchen
to go under [ˌgəʊ ˈʌndə]	Pleite gehen
financial [faɪˈnænʃl]	finanziell, Finanz-
to get sb through [ˌget ˈθruː]	jdn durchbringen; jdm helfen, etw zu überstehen
these days [ˌðiːz ˈdeɪz]	zurzeit
freedom [ˈfriːdəm]	Freiheit
root [ruːt]	Wurzel
what's more [ˌwɒts ˈmɔː]	zudem

to set an example [ˌset ən ɪgˈzɑːmpl]	ein Beispiel setzen, mit gutem Beispiel vorangehen
to have a hard time [həv ə ˌhɑːd ˈtaɪm]	es schwer haben
to be caught [bi ˈkɔːt]	festsitzen, in der Klemme sitzen

page 57

to gossip [ˈgɒsɪp]	tratschen, schwatzen
to borrow sth [ˈbɒrəʊ]	sich etw ausleihen
noisy [ˈnɔɪzi]	laut, lärmend
nuclear [ˈnjuːkliə]	Kern-
various [ˈveəriəs]	verschieden, mehrere, allerlei
to be involved in sth [bi ɪnˈvɒlvd ɪn]	sich an etw beteiligen, bei etw mitmachen
drama [ˈdrɑːmə]	Schauspiel
whatever [wɒtˈevə]	was auch immer
at the end of the day [ət ði end əv ðə ˈdeɪ]	letzten Endes, unterm Strich
cheerful [ˈtʃɪəfl]	fröhlich
tea BE [tiː]	Zwischenmahlzeit am Nachmittag, Abendessen
to be a pain (in the neck) [bi ə ˈpeɪn]	jdm auf die Nerven gehen
to mind one's own business [ˌmaɪnd wʌnz əʊn ˈbɪznəs]	sich um seinen eigenen Kram kümmern
tension [ˈtenʃn]	Spannung
laugh [lɑːf]	Lachen, Gelächter
hill [hɪl]	Berg, Anhöhe, Hügel
grass [grɑːs]	Rasen, Gras
independent [ˌɪndɪˈpendənt]	unabhängig
unnecessary [ʌnˈnesəsəri]	überflüssig, unnötig
abbreviation [əˌbriːviˈeɪʃn]	Abkürzung
needs pl [niːdz]	Bedürfnisse, Bedarf

page 58

lifestyle [ˈlaɪfstaɪl]	Lebensweise, Lebensführung
to tidy up [ˌtaɪdi ˈʌp]	aufräumen
housework [ˈhaʊswɜːk]	Hausarbeit
to do (the/some) ironing [duː ˈaɪənɪŋ]	bügeln
paperwork [ˈpeɪpəwɜːk]	Büroarbeit, Schreibarbeit
feature [ˈfiːtʃə]	Hintergrundbericht, Reportage
talent [ˈtælənt]	Begabung, Talent

page 59

drama club [ˈdrɑːmə klʌb]	Schauspiel-AG
to feel embarrassed [ˌfiːl ɪmˈbærəst]	sich genieren, sich schämen
to raise sth [reɪz]	etw (Thema etc.) ansprechen
to respond (to sth) [rɪˈspɒnd]	(auf etw) reagieren, (auf etw) antworten
sympathetic(ally) [ˌsɪmpəˈθetɪk]	einfühlsam
to point sth out [ˌpɔɪnt ˈaʊt]	auf etw hinweisen
informal [ɪnˈfɔːml]	informell, locker
contracted [kənˈtræktɪd]	zusammengezogen
shy [ʃaɪ]	schüchtern
saying [ˈseɪɪŋ]	Sprichwort, Redensart

page 60

grade AE [greɪd]	Note
grade A student [ˌgreɪd ˈeɪ stjuːdnt]	Einserschüler/in

ridiculous(ly) [rɪˈdɪkjələs]	lächerlich, unglaublich	first of all [ˌfɜːst əv ˈɔːl]	zuallererst
to make it [ˈmeɪk ɪt]	es schaffen	I suppose [aɪ səˈpəʊz]	wohl
to start on sb [stɑːt]	jdn angreifen, jdn kritisieren	shared house [ˌʃeəd ˈhaʊs]	Wohngemeinschaft
to hoover [ˈhuːvə]	staubsaugen	to check sth out [ˌtʃek ˈaʊt]	sich etw ansehen
load [ləʊd]	Ladung	comfortable [ˈkʌmftəbl]	angenehm
washing [ˈwɒʃɪŋ]	Wäsche	to get sth wrong [ˌget ˈrɒŋ]	bei etw einen Fehler machen, etw falsch machen
plus [plʌs]	außerdem		
nosey [ˈnəʊzi]	(auf unangenehme Weise) neugierig	monthly [ˈmʌnθli]	monatlich
receipt [rɪˈsiːt]	Quittung	budget [ˈbʌdʒɪt]	Etat, Haushalt, Budget
by the way [baɪ ðə ˈweɪ]	übrigens, nebenbei erwähnt	heating [ˈhiːtɪŋ]	Heizung
part-time [ˌpɑːtˈtaɪm]	Teilzeit-	bill [bɪl]	Rechnung
to ban sb from doing sth [ˈbæn frəm]	jdm verbieten, etw zu tun	on time [ɒn ˈtaɪm]	pünktlich
		credit rating [ˈkredɪt reɪtɪŋ]	(Bewertung/Einstufung der) Bonität, Kreditwürdigkeit
to feel left out [fiːl ˌleft ˈaʊt]	sich ausgeschlossen fühlen	disaster [dɪˈzɑːstə]	Katastrophe
to turn into sth [ˈtɜːn ɪntə]	zu etw werden	to lend sb sth [lend]	jdm etw leihen
to take sth [teɪk]	etw ertragen	it doesn't matter [ɪt dʌznt ˈmætə]	es ist egal
to drive sb away [ˌdraɪv əˈweɪ]	jdn vertreiben	by oneself [baɪ wʌnˈself]	allein
to cut a long story short [tə kʌt ə lɒŋ ˌstɔːri ˈʃɔːt]	lange Rede, kurzer Sinn	strong advice [ˌstrɒŋ ədˈvaɪs]	dringender Rat
benefits pl [ˈbenɪfɪts]	Sozialleistungen	washing up [ˌwɒʃɪŋ ˈʌp]	Geschirrspülen
Department for Work and Pensions [dɪˌpɑːtmənt fə ˌwɜːk ən ˈpenʃnz]	brit. Arbeits- und Sozialministerium	and so on [ənd ˈsəʊ ɒn]	und so weiter
		(French) fries pl AE [fraɪz]	Pommes frites
to manage [ˈmænɪdʒ]	verwalten, regeln	to go wrong [ˌgəʊ ˈrɒŋ]	schieflaufen
welfare [ˈwelfeə]	Sozialfürsorge, Sozialhilfe	to get angry [ˌget ˈæŋgri]	sich ärgern
benefits office [ˈbenɪfɪts ɒfɪs]	Sozialamt	to get upset [ˌget ʌpˈset]	sich aufregen
		thought [θɔːt]	Gedanke
to drop [drɒp]	fallen, (Noten:) schlechter werden	boomerang [ˈbuːməræŋ]	Bumerang
		to rescue [ˈreskjuː]	retten, bergen
properly [ˈprɒpəli]	richtig, ordentlich, korrekt	**page 63**	
in order to [ɪn ˈɔːdə tə]	um … zu	usefulness [ˈjuːsfəlnəs]	Nutzen, Zweckmäßigkeit
to find sb sth [faɪnd]	jdm etw besorgen	to sniff sth [snɪf]	an etw riechen
brief(ly) [briːf]	kurz, knapp	duvet cover [ˈduːveɪ kʌvə]	Bettdeckenbezug
page 61		raw [rɔː]	roh
idiomatic [ˌɪdiəˈmætɪk]	idiomatisch, redensartlich	chips pl BE [tʃɪps]	Pommes frites
weekday [ˈwiːkdeɪ]	Werktag, Wochentag	nutrient [ˈnjuːtriənt]	Nährstoff
suitable [ˈsuːtəbl]	passend	to be up to sth [bi ˈʌp tə]	etw vorhaben
as necessary [əz ˈnesəsəri]	nötigenfalls	on a need-to-know basis [ɒn ə ˌniːd tə ˈnəʊ beɪsɪs]	im (unumgänglichen) Bedarfsfall
to get on [ˌget ˈɒn]	vorwärtskommen, zurechtkommen		
		alive [əˈlaɪv]	lebendig, am Leben
to get over sth [ˌget ˈəʊvə]	über etw hinwegkommen, etw verkraften	sink [sɪŋk]	Spüle
		page 64	
tiny [ˈtaɪni]	winzig	to be about to do sth [bi əˌbaʊt tə ˈduː]	gleich etw tun werden
stage [steɪdʒ]	Phase, Abschnitt		
move [muːv]	Schritt, Umzug	common [ˈkɒmən]	üblich, bekannt
page 62		tool [tuːl]	Werkzeug, Instrument
mind [maɪnd]	Gedanken	to categorize [ˈkætɪgəraɪz]	einstufen, kategorisieren, klassifizieren
to go from bad to worse [gəʊ frəm ˌbæd tə ˈwɜːs]	immer schlimmer werden		
		segmentation [ˌsegmenˈteɪʃən]	Aufteilung, Zerlegung
ahead [əˈhed]	voraus, vorausliegend		
to step off [ˌstep ˈɒf]	aussteigen	use [juːs]	Gebrauch, Verwendung
to blow [bləʊ]	wehen, blasen	persona [pəˈsəʊnə]	Rolle
steadily [ˈstedɪli]	ununterbrochen	marketer [ˈmɑːkɪtə]	Vermarkter
to pull sth tight [ˌpʊl ˈtaɪt]	etw straff ziehen	to carry out [ˌkæri ˈaʊt]	durchführen
lane [leɪn]	Weg, Gasse	research [rɪˈsɜːtʃ]	Untersuchung, Recherche
towards sth [təˈwɔːdz]	zu etw hin, auf etw zu	to find out about sth [ˌfaɪnd ˈaʊt əbaʊt]	über etw mehr erfahren
to return to sth [rɪˈtɜːn tə]	sich wieder einer Sache zuwenden		
		life goal [ˈlaɪf gəʊl]	Lebensziel
youth [juːθ]	Jugend	belief [bɪˈliːf]	Überzeugung, Meinung
to fall behind [ˌfɔːl bɪˈhaɪnd]	zurückfallen, in Rückstand geraten	attitude [ˈætɪtjuːd]	Haltung
		towards [təˈwɔːdz]	gegenüber
false start [ˌfɔːls ˈstɑːt]	Fehlstart	data [ˈdeɪtə]	Daten
experienced [ɪkˈspɪəriənst]	erfahren	to create [kriˈeɪt]	schaffen
efficient(ly) [ɪˈfɪʃnt]	effizient	to represent [ˌrepriˈzent]	repräsentieren
		characteristic [ˌkærəktəˈrɪstɪk]	Eigenschaft

287

Unit word list

profile [ˈprəʊfaɪəl]	Profil	clerical [ˈklerɪkl]	Büro-
nurse [nɜːs]	Krankenschwester	numerical [njuːˈmerɪkl]	Zahl-, zahlenmäßig
volunteer [ˌvɒlənˈtɪə]	freiwillige/r Helfer/in, Ehrenamtliche/r	instruction [ɪnˈstrʌkʃn]	Anweisung
disadvantaged [ˌdɪsədˈvɑːntɪdʒd]	benachteiligt	accountant [əˈkaʊntənt]	Buchhalter/in
homework [ˈhəʊmwɜːk]	Hausaufgaben	administrator [ədˈmɪnɪstreɪtə]	Verwalter/in
in his/her early 20s [ɪn hɪz ˌɜːli ˈtwentiz]	Anfang zwanzig	intuitional [ˌɪntjuˈɪʃnəl]	intuitiv
chain [tʃeɪn]	Kette	unstructured [ʌnˈstrʌktʃəd]	unstrukturiert
ambitious [æmˈbɪʃəs]	ehrgeizig	imagination [ɪˌmædʒɪˈneɪʃn]	Phantasie, Vorstellungskraft
to train [treɪn]	sich ausbilden lassen	creativity [ˌkriːeɪˈtɪvəti]	schöpferische Begabung, Kreativität
social life [ˈsəʊʃəl laɪf]	Sozialleben	journalist [ˈdʒɜːnəlɪst]	Journalist/in
usually [ˈjuːʒuəli]	normalerweise	architect [ˈɑːkɪtekt]	Architekt/in
to look after sb [ˌlʊk ˈɑːftə]	auf jdn aufpassen	designer [dɪˈzaɪnə]	Gestalter/in, Designer/in, Konstrukteur/in
education [ˌedjuˈkeɪʃn]	Erziehung, Bildung	dancer [ˈdɑːnsə]	Tänzer/in
later [ˈleɪtə]	später	organizational [ˌɔːgənaɪˈzeɪʃənl]	organisatorisch
broad [brɔːd]	breit, ausgedehnt	economic [ˌiːkəˈnɒmɪk]	wirtschaftlich
term [tɜːm]	hier: Ausmaß	gain [geɪn]	Gewinn, Vorteil
based on [ˈbeɪst ɒn]	basierend auf	politician [ˌpɒləˈtɪʃn]	Politiker/in
extensive [ɪkˈstentsɪv]	umfangreich	to enlighten [ɪnˈlaɪtn]	aufklären
demographics pl [ˌdeməˈgræfɪks]	die Demographie	caring [ˈkeərɪŋ]	fürsorglich
gender [ˈdʒendə]	Geschlecht	to be skilled with sth [bi ˈskɪld wɪð]	mit etw gut umgehen können
race [reɪs]	Rasse	social worker [ˈsəʊʃl wɜːkə]	Sozialarbeiter/in
occupation [ˌɒkjuˈpeɪʃən]	Beruf, Arbeit, Tätigkeit	nurse [nɜːs]	Krankenpfleger/-schwester
social class [ˈsəʊʃəl klɑːs]	soziale Schicht	priest [priːst]	Priester/in, Geistliche/r
breakfast cereals [ˈbrekfəst sɪərɪəls]	Frühstücksflocken	company car [ˈkʌmpəni kɑː]	Firmenwagen
whole grain [həʊl greɪn]	Vollkorn	flexible [ˈfleksəbl]	flexibel
organically produced [ɔːˌgænɪkəli prəˈdjuːst]	auf der Basis biologisch angebauter Produkte	working hours pl [ˌwɜːkɪŋ ˈaʊəz]	Arbeitszeiten
character trait [ˈkærəktə treɪt]	Charaktereigenschaften	pay [peɪ]	Bezahlung, Lohn
market segment [ˈmɑːkɪt segmənt]	Marktsegment	promotion [prəˈməʊʃn]	Beförderung, (beruflicher) Aufstieg
		promotion prospects pl [prəˈməʊʃn prɒspekts]	Aufstiegschancen
to belong to sth [biˈlɒŋ tə]	zu etw gehören	working conditions pl [ˌwɜːkɪŋ kənˈdɪʃnz]	Arbeitsbedingungen
to put sth up [ˌpʊt ˈʌp]	etw aufhängen, aufstellen	job security [ˌdʒɒb sɪˈkjʊərəti]	Arbeitsplatzsicherheit

UNIT 8
page 65

realistic [ˌriːəˈlɪstɪk]	realistisch	insurance [ɪnˈʃʊərəns]	Versicherung
doer [ˈduːə]	Macher/in	medical insurance [ˌmedɪkl ɪnˈʃʊərəns]	Krankenversicherung
investigative [ɪnˈvestɪgətɪv]	erforschend, Untersuchungs-	category [ˈkætəgəri]	Kategorie
thinker [ˈθɪŋkə]	Denker/in	involved [ɪnˈvɒlvd]	dazugehörig
organizer [ˈɔːgənaɪzə]	Organisator/in	to design [dɪˈzaɪn]	konstruieren, planen
artistic [ɑːˈtɪstɪk]	künstlerisch	construction worker [kənˈstrʌkʃn wɜːkə]	Bauarbeiter/in
creator [kriˈeɪtə]	Schöpfer/in	ideal [aɪˈdiːəl]	ideal
enterprising [ˈentəpraɪzɪŋ]	geschäftstüchtig, risikofreudig	baker [ˈbeɪkə]	Bäcker/in
persuader [pəˈsweɪdə]	jd, der andere überzeugt und mitreißt	satisfying [ˈsætɪsfaɪɪŋ]	befriedigend
		rewarding [rɪˈwɔːdɪŋ]	lohnend, erfüllend
helper [ˈhelpə]	Helfer/in		

page 66

mechanical [mɪˈkænɪkl]	mechanisch	job advertisement [ˌdʒɒb ədˈvɜːtɪsmənt]	Stellenanzeige, -ausschreibung
mechanic [mɪˈkænɪk]	Mechaniker/in	work experience [ˈwɜːk ɪkspɪərɪəns]	Praktikum
carpenter [ˈkɑːpəntə]	Zimmerer/in, Schreiner/in	temporary [ˈtemprəri]	vorübergehend, befristet
engineer [ˌendʒɪˈnɪə]	Ingenieur/in	recruitment [rɪˈkruːtmənt]	Personalbeschaffung
police officer [pəˈliːs ɒfɪsə]	Polizist/in	job title [ˈdʒɒb taɪtl]	Stellenbezeichnung
to observe [əbˈzɜːv]	beobachten	full-time [ˌfʊl ˈtaɪm]	Vollzeit-
to investigate [ɪnˈvestɪgeɪt]	ermitteln, untersuchen	requirement [rɪˈkwaɪəmənt]	Voraussetzung, Bedingung, Anforderung
to evaluate [ɪˈvæljueɪt]	bewerten, beurteilen	board and lodging [ˌbɔːd ənd ˈlɒdʒɪŋ]	Kost und Logis
to solve [sɒlv]	lösen	return airfare [rɪˌtɜːn ˈeəfeə]	Kosten für Hin- und Rückflug
psychologist [saɪˈkɒlədʒɪst]	Psychologe/Psychologin		
management consultant [ˌmænɪdʒmənt kənˈsʌltənt]	Unternehmensberater/in		
programmer [ˈprəʊgræmə]	Programmierer/in		

to **apply (for a job)** [ə'plaɪ]	sich (um/auf eine Stelle) bewerben	**terms** pl [tɜːmz]	Bedingungen, Konditionen
CV (curriculum vitae) [ˌsiː 'viː, kəˌrɪkjələm 'viːtaɪ]	Lebenslauf	**owner** ['əʊnə]	Besitzer/in
		medical ['medɪkl]	medizinisch
cover letter ['kʌvə letə]	Anschreiben, Begleitschreiben	**secretary** ['sekrətri]	Sekretär/in
		bank clerk ['bæŋk klɑːk]	Bankangestellte/r
internship ['ɪntɜːnʃɪp]	Praktikum	**elsewhere** [ˌels'weə]	woanders, anderswo
charity ['tʃærəti]	Wohltätigkeitsorganisation	to **supply** [sə'plaɪ]	liefern, bieten
to **set sth up** [ˌset 'ʌp]	etw einrichten	**sustainable** [sə'steɪnəbl]	nachhaltig
community [kə'mjuːnəti]	Gemeinde, Gemeinschaft	**treatment** ['triːtmənt]	Behandlung
to **staff** [stɑːf]	(mit Personal) besetzen		
highly motivated [ˌhaɪli 'məʊtɪveɪtɪd]	hochmotiviert	**page 68**	
		qualification [ˌkwɒlɪfɪ'keɪʃn]	Abschluss, Qualifikation
intern ['ɪntɜːn]	Praktikant/in		
to **volunteer to do sth** [ˌvɒlən'tɪə tə]	sich bereit erklären, etw zu tun	**typing** ['taɪpɪŋ]	Schreibmaschinenschreiben
		standard ['stændəd]	Niveau
management ['mænɪdʒmənt]	Führung, Management	**surgery** ['sɜːdʒəri]	(Arzt-)Praxis
		pleasant ['pleznt]	angenehm
administration [ədˌmɪnɪ'streɪʃn]	Verwaltung	**as regards ...** [əz rɪ'gɑːdz]	was ... betrifft
		band [bænd]	Gehaltsstufe, Gehaltsklasse
fully ['fʊli]	vollständig	**pay scale** ['peɪ skeɪl]	Lohntarif, Lohntabelle
fully equipped [ˌfʊli ɪ'kwɪpt]	vollausgestattet	**secure** [sɪ'kjʊə]	sicher
location [ləʊ'keɪʃn]	Standort, Ort	**shortage** ['ʃɔːtɪdʒ]	Mangel
to **insure** [ɪn'ʃʊə]	versichern	**staff** [stɑːf]	Personal, Belegschaft, Mitarbeiter/innen
accommodation [əˌkɒmə'deɪʃn]	Unterkunft		
homestay accommodation ['həʊmsteɪ əkɒmədeɪʃn]	Unterbringung bei Gasteltern	**satisfaction** [ˌsætɪs'fækʃn]	Zufriedenheit
		profession [prə'feʃn]	Beruf
travel expenses pl ['trævl ɪkspensɪz]	Reisekosten, Fahrtkosten	**caring profession** ['keərɪŋ prəfeʃn]	Pflegeberuf
		maths [mæθs]	Mathe(matik) (Schulfach)
registered ['redʒɪstəd]	eingetragen, (staatlich) anerkannt	**trainee** [treɪ'niː]	Auszubildende/r
		cashier [kæ'ʃɪə]	Kassierer/in
post [pəʊst]	Stelle, Posten	to **cash a cheque** [ˌkæʃ ə 'tʃek]	einen Scheck einlösen
to **advertise a job** [ˌædvətaɪz ə 'dʒɒb]	eine Stelle ausschreiben		
		payment ['peɪmənt]	Zahlung
technician [tek'nɪʃn]	Techniker/in	**microwave** ['maɪkrəweɪv]	Mikrowelle
allowance [ə'laʊəns]	Aufwandsentschädigung	**entry level pay** [ˌentri levl 'peɪ]	Einstiegsgehalt, Anfangsgehalt
asap (as soon as possible) [ˌeɪ es eɪ 'piː]	baldmöglichst		
		customer services advisor [ˌkʌstəmə 'sɜːvɪsɪz ədvaɪzə]	Kundenberater/in
duration [dju'reɪʃn]	Dauer		
to **be responsible for sth** [bi rɪ'spɒnsəbl fə]	für etw zuständig/verantwortlich sein	**apprenticeship** [ə'prentɪʃɪp]	Ausbildung, Lehre
		qualified ['kwɒlɪfaɪd]	mit Abschluss, qualifiziert
set [set]	Kulisse	**crisis** ['kraɪsɪs]	Krise
lighting ['laɪtɪŋ]	Beleuchtung, Licht	**careers advisor** [kə'rɪəz ədvaɪzə]	Berufsberater/in
prop [prɒp]	Requisite		
maintenance ['meɪntənəns]	Wartung, Instandhaltung	**entry level** ['entri levl]	Einstieg, Anfang
equipment [ɪ'kwɪpmənt]	Ausrüstung, Geräte	**a word of warning** [ə ˌwɜːd əv 'wɔːnɪŋ]	Hinweis, Warnung
candidate ['kændɪdət]	Bewerber/in		
electrical [ɪ'lektrɪkl]	elektrisch, Elektro-	**ambitious** [æm'bɪʃəs]	ehrgeizig
DIY (do-it-yourself) [ˌdiː aɪ 'waɪ]	Heimwerker-, Heimwerken	**plate** [pleɪt]	Teller
		to **offer sb sth on a plate** [ˌɒfər ɒn ə 'pleɪt]	jdm etw auf dem Silbertablett servieren
shift [ʃɪft]	Schicht		
equal opportunities pl [ˌiːkwəl ɒpə'tjuːnətiz]	Chancengleichheit	**yearly** ['jɪəli]	jährlich, Jahres-
		income ['ɪnkʌm]	Einkommen
employer [ɪm'plɔɪə]	Arbeitgeber/in	**irregular** [ɪ'regjələ]	unregelmäßig
		salesperson ['seɪlzpɜːsn]	Vertreter/in, Verkäufer/in
page 67		to **work hard** [ˌwɜːk 'hɑːd]	hart arbeiten, fleißig sein
equivalent [ɪ'kwɪvələnt]	Entsprechung		
to **administer** [əd'mɪnɪstə]	verwalten	**page 69**	
to **accommodate** [ə'kɒmədeɪt]	unterbringen	**workplace** ['wɜːkpleɪs]	Arbeitsplatz
		to **mind sth** [maɪnd]	auf etw achten
to **maintain** [meɪn'teɪn]	warten, instand halten	to **grab sth** [græb]	sich etw schnappen
equality [ɪ'kwɒləti]	Gleichheit	**wheely** ['wiːli]	auf Rollen
voluntary ['vɒləntri]	freiwillig	**filing cabinet** ['faɪlɪŋ kæbɪnət]	Aktenschrank
administrative [əd'mɪnɪstrətɪv]	Verwaltungs-		
		to **make for sth** ['meɪk fə]	sich auf den Weg nach etw machen
technological [ˌteknə'lɒdʒɪkl]	technologisch		
		to **be on the increase** [bi ɒn ði 'ɪŋkriːs]	auf dem Vormarsch sein, zunehmen

Unit word list

driving force	[ˌdraɪvɪŋ 'fɔːs]	treibende Kraft
ever-improving	[ˌevər ɪm'pruːvɪŋ]	stetig besser werdend
electronics *pl*	[ˌɪlek'trɒnɪks]	Elektronik
employee	[ɪm'plɔiiː]	Angestellte/r, Beschäftigte/r
workforce	['wɜːkfɔːs]	Belegschaft
increase	['ɪŋkriːs]	Zunahme, Steigerung
to cause sb to do sth	[kɔːz]	jdn dazu veranlassen, etw zu tun
to rethink	[ˌriː'θɪŋk]	überdenken
corporate	['kɔːpərət]	Unternehmens-, von Unternehmen
infrastructure	['ɪnfrəstrʌktʃə]	Infrastruktur
manufacturing	[ˌmænju'fæktʃərɪŋ]	Fertigung
to require	[rɪ'kwaɪə]	erfordern, benötigen
mobile	['məʊbaɪl]	mobil
pad	[pæd]	(Notiz-)Block; Bude
by default	[baɪ dɪ'fɔːlt]	automatisch
therefore	['ðeəfɔː]	daher, deshalb, demzufolge
meeting room	['miːtɪŋ ruːm]	Sitzungsraum, Besprechungsraum
to plug in(to)	[ˌplʌg 'ɪn]	anschließen, einstecken
to counteract sth	[ˌkaʊntər'ækt]	einer Sache entgegenwirken
loneliness	['ləʊnlinəs]	Einsamkeit
homing	['həʊmɪŋ]	Heimfindeverhalten (z. B. von Brieftauben)
instinct	['ɪnstɪŋkt]	Instinkt
to acknowledge	[ək'nɒlɪdʒ]	anerkennen, zugeben
allotted	[ə'lɒtɪd]	zugewiesen
car park	['kɑː pɑːk]	Parkplatz, -haus, -garage
to tend to do sth	['tend tə]	dazu neigen, etw zu tun
spot	[spɒt]	Platz, Ort, Fleck, Punkt
gradual	['grædʒuəl]	schrittweise, allmählich
development	[dɪ'veləpmənt]	Entwicklung
to address	[ə'dres]	(Problem etc.) ansprechen, angehen, thematisieren
concern	[kən'sɜːn]	Sorge, Befürchtung
wide-ranging	['waɪd reɪndʒɪŋ]	breit gefächert
cultural	['kʌltʃərəl]	kulturell, kulturbezogen
practice	['præktɪs]	Praxis, Ausübung, Verfahren, Ablauf, Praktik
informality	[ˌɪnfɔː'mæləti]	Formlosigkeit, Ungezwungenheit
norm	[nɔːm]	Norm
senior	['siːniə]	leitend
legal department	[ˌliːgl dɪ'pɑːtmənt]	juristische Abteilung
finance	['faɪnæns]	Finanz(-)
majority	[mə'dʒɒrəti]	Mehrheit
to be territorial	[bi ˌterə'tɔːriəl]	sein Revier verteidigen
open-plan office	[ˌəʊpən plæn 'ɒfɪs]	Großraumbüro
to personalize	['pɜːsnəlaɪz]	individuell gestalten
barrier	['bæriə]	Hürde
to cross	[krɒs]	überqueren, überwinden
to judge	[dʒʌdʒ]	beurteilen
in time	[ɪn 'taɪm]	rechtzeitig

page 70

to drop in	[ˌdrɒp 'ɪn]	vorbeikommen, hereinschauen
to gravitate to sth	['grævɪteɪt tə]	von etw angezogen werden
continuity	[ˌkɒntɪn'juːəti]	Kontinuität, Fortdauer
belonging	[bɪ'lɒŋɪŋ]	Zugehörigkeit
to shake sth off	[ˌʃeɪk 'ɒf]	etw abschütteln
totally	['təʊtəli]	voll und ganz
suit	[suːt]	Anzug
tie	[taɪ]	Krawatte
to dress down	[ˌdres 'daʊn]	sich leger kleiden
sector	['sektə]	Sektor, Bereich
global(ly)	['gləʊbl]	weltweit, global
to downsize	['daʊnsaɪz]	verkleinern, gesundschrumpfen
prestigious	[pre'stɪdʒəs]	repräsentativ, prestigeträchtig
rapid(ly)	['ræpɪd]	rasch, schnell
centrally heated	[ˌsentrəli 'hiːtɪd]	zentralbeheizt
moveable	['muːvəbl]	beweglich, mobil
fixed	[fɪkst]	fest, festgelegt, fest installiert
routine	[ruː'tiːn]	(fester) Ablauf, Routine

page 71

to store	[stɔː]	aufbewahren, lagern
file	[faɪl]	Akte, Ordner
office block	['ɒfɪs blɒk]	Bürogebäude
sudden	['sʌdn]	plötzlich
to employ sb	[ɪm'plɔɪ]	jdn beschäftigen, jdn einstellen
casual	['kæʒuəl]	leger, zwanglos
to mediate	['miːdieɪt]	vermitteln
technique	[tek'niːk]	Methode, Technik
gist	[dʒɪst]	das Wesentliche
to take a seat	[ˌteɪk ə 'siːt]	Platz nehmen
premises *pl*	['premɪsɪz]	Geschäftsräume
permanent	['pɜːmənənt]	dauerhaft
Must rush.	[ˌmʌst 'rʌʃ]	Ich muss weg.
to get back to sb	[ˌget 'bæk tə]	sich bei jdm (zurück)melden

page 72

finance director	[ˌfaɪnæns də'rektə]	kaufmännische/r Leiter/in
market share	[ˌmɑːkɪt 'ʃeə]	Marktanteil
competitor	[kəm'petɪtə]	Konkurrent/in, Konkurrenz
to break down	[ˌbreɪk 'daʊn]	zusammenbrechen
strike	[straɪk]	Streik
to go on strike	[ˌgəʊ ɒn 'straɪk]	streiken
receptionist	[rɪ'sepʃənɪst]	Empfangsmitarbeiter/in
job rotation	['dʒɒb rəʊteɪʃn]	Arbeitsplatzrotation, (innerbetrieblicher) Arbeitsplatzwechsel
to stand in for sb	[ˌstænd 'ɪn fə]	jdn vertreten
to retrain	[ˌriː'treɪn]	umschulen

page 73

to draw	[drɔː]	ziehen
to split	[splɪt]	(sich) aufteilen
separate	['seprət]	getrennt, separat
to conduct sth	[kən'dʌkt]	etw durchführen
to ensure	[ɪn'ʃʊə]	sicherstellen; dafür sorgen, dass
to conclude	[kən'kluːd]	schließen, beenden

page 74

business leader	['bɪznəs liːdə]	erfolgreich Wirtschaftende/r
founder	['faʊndə]	Gründer/in

company founder ['kʌmpəni faʊndə]	Geschäftsgründer/in	
female ['fi:meɪl]	Frau, weiblich	
male [meɪl]	Mann, männlich	
conclusion [kən'klu:ʒən]	Schlussfolgerung	
to draw a conclusion [ˌdrɔ: ə kən'klu:ʒən]	eine Schlussfolgerung ziehen	
ratio ['reɪʃiəʊ]	Verhältnis	
tertiary education [ˌtɜ:ʃəri ˌedju'keɪʃən]	Hochschulausbildung	
among [ə'mʌŋ]	darunter, davon	
legislator ['ledʒɪsleɪtə]	Gesetzgeber	
senior official [ˌsi:niə ə'fɪʃəl]	höherer Beamter/höhere Beamtin	
source [sɔ:s]	Quelle	
enrolled [ɪn'rəʊl]	eingeschrieben, immatrikuliert	
quota ['kwəʊtə]	Quote	
female quota ['fi:meɪl kwəʊtə]	Frauenquote	
to employ [ɪm'plɔɪ]	anstellen, beschäftigen	
aim [eɪm]	Ziel	
professional [prə'feʃnl]	Berufs-	
leadership ['li:dəʃɪp]	Führung, Leitung	
government ['gʌvənmənt]	Regierung	
ceiling ['si:lɪŋ]	Decke	
to assure [ə'ʃɔ:]	sicherstellen, gewährleisten	
equal ['i:kwəl]	gleich	
pay [peɪ]	Lohn	
dominated by ['dɒmɪneɪtɪd baɪ]	beherrscht von	
middle-aged [ˌmɪdəl 'eɪdʒd]	mittleren Alters	
regulation [ˌregju'leɪʃən]	Regulierung	
from the outside [ˌfrɒm ði ˌaʊt'saɪd]	von außen	
corporate ['kɔ:pərət]	unternehmerisch	
to vote on sth ['vəʊt ɒn]	über etw abstimmen	

JOB SKILLS 2

page 75

office assistant [ˌɒfɪs ə'sɪstənt]	Bürokaufmann/-frau	
duty ['dju:ti]	Aufgabe, Pflicht, Arbeit	
located in [ləʊ'keɪtɪd ɪn]	in (… gelegen)	
accurate ['ækjərət]	genau	
to be willing to do sth [bi 'wɪlɪŋ tə]	bereit sein, etw zu tun	
a must [ə 'mʌst]	ein Muss	
plc [ˌpi: el 'si:]	AG	
business studies ['bɪznəs stʌdiz]	Betriebswirtschaft	
to seek [si:k]	suchen	
to update [ˌʌp'deɪt]	aktualisieren	
spreadsheet ['spredʃi:t]	Tabellenkalkulation	
to be equivalent to sth [bi ɪ'kwɪvələnt tə]	einer Sache entsprechen	
native speaker [ˌneɪtɪv 'spi:kə]	Muttersprachler/in	
fluent ['flu:ənt]	(Sprache:) fließend	
oral ['ɔ:rəl]	mündlich	
intermediate [ˌɪntə'mi:diət]	mittlere/r/s (Niveau)	
pressure ['preʃə]	Druck	
reference ['refərəns]	Referenz, Zeugnis	
referee [ˌrefə'ri:]	Referenzgeber/in	
on request [ɒn rɪ'kwest]	auf Wunsch, auf Verlangen	

page 76

body ['bɒdi]	(Brief:) Hauptteil	
complimentary close [ˌkɒmplɪˌmentri 'kləʊz]	(Brief:) Schlussformel	
enclosure (encl.) [ɪn'kləʊʒə]	(Brief:) Anlage	
inside address [ˌɪnsaɪd ə'dres]	Empfängeranschrift	
salutation [ˌsælju'teɪʃn]	(Brief:) Anrede	
signature ['sɪgnətʃə]	Unterschrift	
writer's address [ˌraɪtəz ə'dres]	Absenderanschrift	
attn. (= attention) [ə'tenʃn]	(Brief:) zu Händen	
ref. (= reference) ['refərəns]	(Brief:) Zeichen	
copy ['kɒpi]	Ausgabe	
currently ['kʌrəntli]	zurzeit	
to be keen to do sth [bɪ 'ki:n tə]	etw unbedingt tun wollen	
English-speaking ['ɪŋglɪʃ spi:kɪŋ]	englischsprachig	
in addition to sth [ɪn ə'dɪʃn tə]	zusätzlich zu etw	
to be an asset to sb [bi ən 'æset tə]	für jdn eine Bereicherung sein	
to appreciate [ə'pri:ʃieɪt]	zu schätzen wissen, schätzen	
to grant sb sth [grɑ:nt]	jdm etw gewähren	
interview ['ɪntəvju:]	Vorstellungsgespräch	

page 77

section ['sekʃn]	Abschnitt	
applicant ['æplɪkənt]	Bewerber/in	
to compile [kəm'paɪl]	erstellen, zusammenstellen	
educational [ˌedʒu'keɪʃənl]	schulisch, Bildungs-	
correction [kə'rekʃn]	Korrekturlesen, Korrektur	
to pin [pɪn]	(mit einer Nadel) befestigen, anbringen	

page 78

to interview sb ['ɪntəvju:]	mit jdm ein Vorstellungsgespräch führen	
strength [streŋθ]	Stärke	
weakness ['wi:knəs]	Schwäche	
to report to sb [rɪ'pɔ:t tə]	jdm unterstellt sein	
surprised [sə'praɪzd]	erstaunt, überrascht	
superior [su:'pɪəriə]	Vorgesetzte/r	
to invite sb to do sth [ɪn'vaɪt tə]	jdn auffordern, etw zu tun	
Speaking. ['spi:kɪŋ]	(Telefon:) Am Apparat.	
to go backpacking [ˌgəʊ 'bækpækɪŋ]	auf Rucksacktour gehen	
to gain [geɪn]	erwerben	
to take responsibility [teɪk rɪˌspɒnsə'bɪləti]	Verantwortung übernehmen	
right away [ˌraɪt ə'weɪ]	sofort	
careless ['keələs]	nachlässig	
to attend sth [ə'tend]	an etw teilnehmen	
reservation [ˌrezə'veɪʃn]	Reservierung	
assessment [ə'sesmənt]	Beurteilung, Einstufung	
to send sth out [ˌsend 'aʊt]	etw verschicken	
interviewer ['ɪntəvju:ə]	Person, die ein Vorstellungsgespräch führt	
responsibility [rɪˌspɒnsə'bɪləti]	Aufgabe, Zuständigkeit	

UNIT 9

page 79

multiculturalism [ˌmʌlti'kʌltʃərəlɪzm]	Multikulturalität, Multikulturismus, kulturelle Vielfalt	
festival ['festɪvl]	Fest, Festtag, Festival	
to light [laɪt]	(Kerze etc.) anzünden	

Unit word list

to **march** [mɑːtʃ]	marschieren
candle [ˈkændl]	Kerze
dragon [ˈdrægən]	Drachen
lantern [ˈlæntən]	Laterne
pipe band [ˈpaɪp bænd]	Dudelsackkapelle
New Year [ˌnjuː ˈjɪə]	Neujahr
lion [ˈlaɪən]	Löwe
display [dɪˈspleɪ]	Vorführung
parade [pəˈreɪd]	Parade
march [mɑːtʃ]	Marsch
ceilidh [ˈkeɪlɪ]	geselliges Beisammensein mit Musik und Tanz (schottischer Brauch)
midsummer [ˌmɪdˈsʌmə]	Mittsommer, Sommersonnenwende
cuisine [kwɪˈziːn]	Küche, Kochkunst
craft [krɑːft]	Handwerk

page 80

refugee [ˌrefjuˈdʒiː]	Flüchtling
coast [kəʊst]	Küste
to **separate** [ˈsepəreɪt]	trennen, abspalten
violent [ˈvaɪələnt]	heftig
given name [ˈɡɪvn neɪm]	Vorname
soldier [ˈsəʊldʒə]	Soldat/in
to **kick sth down** [ˌkɪk ˈdaʊn]	etw eintreten
to **wave sth around** [ˌweɪv əˈraʊnd]	mit etw herumfuchteln
rifle [ˈraɪfl]	Gewehr
to **drag** [dræɡ]	zerren
to **force** [fɔːs]	zwingen
facing sth [ˈfeɪsɪŋ]	gegen etw, mit dem Gesicht zu etw
to **be in command** [bi ˌɪn kəˈmɑːnd]	das Kommando führen, die Befehle geben, das Sagen haben
inch [ɪntʃ]	Zoll (= 2,54 cm)
to **shudder** [ˈʃʌdə]	erschaudern, zittern
fear [fɪə]	Angst
to **tremble** [ˈtrembl]	beben, zittern
to **look on** [ˌlʊk ˈɒn]	zusehen
terrified [ˈterɪfaɪd]	entsetzt
to **shoot** [ʃuːt]	schießen
bullet [ˈbʊlɪt]	(Gewehr-)Kugel
to **scream** [skriːm]	schreien
peace [piːs]	Frieden
to **raise sth** [reɪz]	etw anheben, etw hochheben
to **point sth at sb** [ˈpɔɪnt ət]	etw auf jdn richten, mit etw auf jdn zielen
traitor [ˈtreɪtə]	Verräter/in
enemy [ˈenəmi]	Feind/in
forehead [ˈfɔːhed]	Stirn
mongrel [ˈmɒŋɡrəl]	Mischling, Bastard
to **drop one's voice** [ˌdrɒp wʌnz ˈvɔɪs]	die Stimme senken
equally [ˈiːkwəli]	gleichermaßen, genauso
safety [ˈseɪfti]	Sicherheit
authority [ɔːˈθɒrəti]	Behörde
welcoming [ˈwelkəmɪŋ]	gastfreundlich

page 81

evil [ˈiːvl]	böse, schlecht
border [ˈbɔːdə]	Grenze
body [ˈbɒdi]	Leichnam
law [lɔː]	Justiz
kind [kaɪnd]	freundlich, gütig, nett
to **arrest** [əˈrest]	verhaften
detention centre [dɪˈtenʃn sentə]	Auffanglager, Haftanstalt
homeless [ˈhəʊmləs]	obdachlos
unpleasant [ʌnˈpleznt]	unangenehm, unschön
court [kɔːt]	Gericht(shof)
basket [ˈbɑːskɪt]	Korb
amount [əˈmaʊnt]	Menge
tinned [tɪnd]	in Dosen, Dosen-
checkout [ˈtʃekaʊt]	Kasse
counter [ˈkaʊntə]	Schalter, Theke
to **drop one's eyes** [ˌdrɒp wʌnz ˈaɪz]	den Blick senken
deal [diːl]	Abmachung, Geschäft
wallet [ˈwɒlɪt]	Brieftasche, (Herren-)Portemonnaie
voucher [ˈvaʊtʃə]	Gutschein
asylum seeker [əˈsaɪləm siːkə]	Asylbewerber/in
change [tʃeɪndʒ]	Wechselgeld
queue [kjuː]	Warteschlange
courtroom [ˈkɔːtruːm]	Gerichtssaal
to **humiliate** [hjuːˈmɪlieɪt]	demütigen, erniedrigen
meanwhile [ˈmiːnwaɪl]	inzwischen, unterdessen
to **file** [faɪl]	feilen
nail [neɪl]	Nagel
to **comb** [kəʊm]	kämmen
exhibition [ˌeksɪˈbɪʃn]	Ausstellung
humiliation [hjuːˌmɪliˈeɪʃn]	Demütigung, Erniedrigung
proud [praʊd]	stolz
penny [ˈpeni]	Pfennig, Penny
to **reduce sb to sth** [rɪˈdjuːs]	jdn zu etw bringen
to **amount to sth** [əˈmaʊnt tə]	auf etw hinauslaufen
to **live off aid** [lɪv ˌɒf ˈeɪd]	von Sozialhilfe leben
to **wonder** [ˈwʌndə]	sich fragen
mathematician [ˌmæθəməˈtɪʃn]	Mathematiker/in
promising [ˈprɒmɪsɪŋ]	vielversprechend
airline [ˈeəlaɪn]	Fluglinie
silent(ly) [ˈsaɪlənt]	still, schweigend
to **shake one's head** [ˌʃeɪk wʌnz ˈhed]	den Kopf schütteln
in disgust [ɪn dɪsˈɡʌst]	angewidert
to **shuffle** [ˈʃʌfl]	schlurfen
line [laɪn]	Reihe
down the line [ˌdaʊn ðə ˈlaɪn]	weiter
death [deθ]	Tod

page 82

understanding [ˌʌndəˈstændɪŋ]	Verständnis
to **make a point to sb** [ˌmeɪk ə ˈpɔɪnt tə]	jdm etw zu verstehen geben
to **recognize** [ˈrekəɡnaɪz]	(wieder)erkennen
to **jump the queue** [ˌdʒʌmp ðə ˈkjuː]	sich vordrängeln
to **wait for one's turn** [ˌweɪt fə wʌnz ˈtɜːn]	warten, bis man an der Reihe ist
to **face sb** [feɪs]	jdn konfrontieren
goal [ɡəʊl]	(Ballspiel:) Tor
to **behave** [bɪˈheɪv]	sich benehmen, sich verhalten

page 83

earnings pl [ˈɜːnɪŋz]	Einkünfte, Verdienst
reduction [rɪˈdʌkʃn]	Verringerung, Senkung
pride [praɪd]	Stolz

on top of [ɒn 'tɒp əv]	auf	
cupboard ['kʌbəd]	Schrank	
health and safety [ˌhelθ ənd 'seɪfti]	Arbeitsschutz	
cure [kjʊə]	Heilung, Therapie	
cost of living [ˌkɒst əv 'lɪvɪŋ]	Lebenshaltungskosten	
great-grandfather [ˌgreɪt 'grænfɑːðə]	Urgroßvater	
to take pride in sth [ˌteɪk 'praɪd ɪn]	auf etw Wert legen, sich mit etw Mühe geben	
excellent ['eksələnt]	ausgezeichnet, hervorragend	
to land [lænd]	landen	

page 84

purpose ['pɜːpəs]	Absicht, Zweck
What now for …? [ˌwɒt 'naʊ fə]	Wie steht es um …?
policy ['pɒləsi]	Politik, Kurs, Konzept
harmony ['hɑːməni]	Harmonie
to have the guts to do sth [həv ðə 'gʌts tə]	den Mumm haben, etw zu tun
law [lɔː]	Gesetz
to pass a law [ˌpɑːs ə 'lɔː]	ein Gesetz verabschieden
to reject [rɪ'dʒekt]	ablehnen, zurückweisen
to deport [dɪ'pɔːt]	abschieben
violent ['vaɪələnt]	gewalttätig
gang [gæŋ]	Bande
Muslim ['mʊzlɪm]	muslimisch, Moslem
to take over [ˌteɪk 'əʊvə]	die Macht übernehmen
to save oneself sth [seɪv]	sich etw ersparen
to calm down [ˌkɑːm 'daʊn]	sich beruhigen
not … either [nɒt 'aɪðə]	auch nicht
minority [maɪ'nɒrəti]	Minderheit
moderate ['mɒdərət]	gemäßigt, maßvoll
MP (Member of Parliament) [ˌem 'piː]	Parlamentsabgeordnete/r
wave [weɪv]	Welle
descendant [dɪ'sendənt]	Nachfahre, Nachkomme
contribution [ˌkɒntrɪ'bjuːʃn]	Beitrag
to make a contribution [ˌmeɪk ə ˌkɒntrɪ'bjuːʃn]	einen Beitrag leisten
to be a two-way street [bi ə ˌtuː weɪ 'striːt]	auf Gegenseitigkeit beruhen
vibrant ['vaɪbrənt]	dynamisch, voller Leben
peaceful ['piːsfl]	friedlich
varied ['veərid]	vielfältig, abwechslungsreich
to hide (away) [haɪd]	sich verstecken, sich verbergen
to put sth down to sth [ˌpʊt 'daʊn tə]	etw einer Sache zuschreiben
ethnic ['eθnɪk]	ethnisch, Volks-
to integrate ['ɪntɪgreɪt]	(sich) integrieren
He has a (good) point. [hi: ˌhæz ə 'pɔɪnt]	Da ist etwas dran. Da hat er recht.
migrant ['maɪgrənt]	Migrant/in
racial ['reɪʃl]	rassisch, Rassen-

page 85

lively ['laɪvli]	lebendig, lebhaft, rege
population [ˌpɒpju'leɪʃn]	Bevölkerung
struggle ['strʌgl]	Kampf
engine ['endʒɪn]	Motor

page 86

shipyard ['ʃɪpjɑːd]	Werft
to fall in love with sb/sth [ˌfɔːl ɪn 'lʌv wɪð]	sich in jdn/etw verlieben
to emigrate ['emɪgreɪt]	auswandern
to build sth up [ˌbɪld 'ʌp]	etw aufbauen
deportation [ˌdiːpɔː'teɪʃn]	Abschiebung
to escape from sth [ɪ'skeɪp frəm]	einer Sache entkommen
port [pɔːt]	Hafen, Hafenstadt
parliament ['pɑːləmənt]	Parlament
to retire [rɪ'taɪə]	in den Ruhestand gehen, in Rente gehen
unemployment [ˌʌnɪm'plɔɪmənt]	Arbeitslosigkeit
to claim unemployment benefits [ˌkleɪm ʌnɪm'plɔɪmənt benɪfɪts]	Arbeitslosengeld beziehen
housing ['haʊzɪŋ]	Wohnungsbau, Wohnungen
approximately (approx.) [ə'prɒksɪmətli]	zirka (ca.)
presenter [prɪ'zentə]	Moderator/in
agricultural [ˌægrɪ'kʌltʃərəl]	landwirtschaftlich, Landwirtschafts-
free movement [ˌfriː 'muːvmənt]	Freizügigkeit
rural ['rʊərəl]	ländlich
uncontrolled [ˌʌnkən'trəʊld]	ungeregelt, unkontrolliert
incomer ['ɪnkʌmə]	Zuzügler, Ankömmling
issue ['ɪʃuː]	Streitpunkt, Frage, Problem, Thema
the other way round [ði ˌʌðə weɪ 'raʊnd]	umgekehrt
war [wɔː]	Krieg
replacement [rɪ'pleɪsmənt]	Ersatz, Ersetzung, Austausch
unemployment rate [ˌʌnɪm'plɔɪmənt reɪt]	Arbeitslosenquote
pressure ['preʃə]	Druck

page 87

course of action [ˌkɔːs əv 'ækʃn]	Vorgehen, Maßnahmen
sir [sɜː]	mein Herr
jacket ['dʒækɪt]	Jacke, Jackett
to deal with sth ['diːl wɪð]	mit etw zu tun haben
label ['leɪbl]	Beschriftung, Bezeichnung
explanation [ˌeksplə'neɪʃn]	Erläuterung, Erklärung
to select [sɪ'lekt]	auswählen
to contrast [kən'trɑːst]	gegenüberstellen, vergleichen
to take sb in [ˌteɪk 'ɪn]	jdn aufnehmen
host [həʊst]	Gastgeber
approximate [ə'prɒksɪmət]	ungefähr, angenähert
similarly ['sɪmələli]	in ähnlicher Weise, genauso, ebenso

page 88

gesture ['dʒestʃə]	Geste, Gestik, Handbewegung
to take time [ˌteɪk 'taɪm]	Zeit benötigen, dauern
patient ['peɪʃənt]	geduldig
to pick [pɪk]	wählen, aussuchen
intercultural [ˌɪntə'kʌltʃərəl]	interkulturell
competence ['kɒmpɪtəns]	Fähigkeit, Können, Kompetenz
to merge [mɜːdʒ]	sich zusammenschließen, fusionieren
to set up [set 'ʌp]	gründen, aufbauen, errichten
branch [brɑːntʃ]	Zweigstelle, Filiale
abroad [ə'brɔːd]	im Ausland

293

Unit word list

to **acquire** sth [əˈkwaɪə]	sich etw aneignen, etw erwerben
courtesy [ˈkɜːtəsi]	Höflichkeit, Entgegenkommen
code [kəʊd]	Norm
to **address** sb [əˈdres]	jdn ansprechen
to **introduce** sb [ˌɪntrəˈdjuːs]	jdn vorstellen
to **shake hands** [ˌʃeɪk ˈhændz]	sich die Hand geben
usual [ˈjuːʒuəl]	gewöhnlich, normal
setting [ˈsetɪŋ]	Situation
cheek [tʃiːk]	Wange
to **bow** [baʊ]	sich verbeugen
personal space [ˌpɜːsənəl ˈspeɪs]	Privatsphäre
to **be comfortable** [bi ˈkʌmftəbl]	sich wohlfühlen
touching [ˈtʌtʃɪŋ]	Berühren
closeness [ˈkləʊsnəs]	Nähe
with regard to [wɪð rɪˈɡɑːd tə]	in Bezug auf
eye contact [ˈaɪ kɒntækt]	Augenkontakt
to **value** [ˈvæljuː]	werten
honest [ˈɒnɪst]	ehrlich
trustworthy [ˈtrʌstwɜːði]	vertrauenswürdig, zuverlässig
dominance [ˈdɒmɪnəns]	Dominanz, Überheblichkeit
to **notice** [ˈnəʊtɪs]	bemerken, wahrnehmen, beachten
disagreement [ˌdɪsəˈɡriːmənt]	Uneinigkeit, Meinungsverschiedenheit
to **come across as** [kʌm əˈkrɒs]	auf andere wirken
rude [ruːd]	unhöflich, grob
to **soften** [ˈsɒfn]	mildern, weichmachen
harsh [hɑːʃ]	scharf, harsch
a couple of [ə ˈkʌpl əv]	einige
to **confuse** [kənˈfjuːz]	irritieren, verwirren
not at all [ˌnɒt ət ˈɔːl]	überhaupt nicht
prepared [prɪˈpeəd]	vorbereitet
plenty of [ˈplenti əv]	viel
to **concern** [kənˈsɜːn]	betreffen
right-hand drive [ˌraɪthænd ˈdraɪv]	rechtsgesteuert
pitfall [ˈpɪtfɔːl]	Fallstrick, Fallgrube
innocent [ˈɪnəsnt]	unschuldig
meaning [ˈmiːnɪŋ]	Bedeutung
offensive [əˈfensɪv]	anstößig, beleidigend
advisable [ədˈvaɪzəbl]	ratsam
to **avoid** [əˈvɔɪd]	vermeiden, verhindern
astonished [əˈstɒnɪʃd]	erstaunt, überrascht, verwundert
self-evident [ˌself ˈevɪdənt]	selbstverständlich
recently [ˈriːsntli]	vor Kurzem, neulich
shaving razor [ˈʃeɪvɪŋ reɪzə]	Rasiermesser
sharp [ʃɑːp]	scharf
slang word [ˈslæŋ wɜːd]	umgangssprachliches Wort
buttocks pl [ˈbʌtəks]	das Gesäß, der Hintern
as a result [əz ə rɪˈzʌlt]	infolgedessen, als Folge davon
imagery [ˈɪmɪdʒəri]	Symbolik
equally [ˈiːkwəli]	gleichermaßen
to **package** [ˈpækɪdʒ]	verpacken, präsentieren
common [ˈkɒmən]	verbreitet, üblich
to **say the least** [ˌseɪ ðə liːst]	gelinde gesagt
careful(ly) [ˈkeəfəl]	vorsichtig, sorgfältig
to **portray** [pɔːˈtreɪ]	darstellen, schildern
tricky [ˈtrɪki]	kompliziert, heikel
to **associate** [əˈsəʊʃieɪt]	in Verbindung bringen, assoziieren
dominant [ˈdɒmɪnənt]	marktbeherrschend
shade [ʃeɪd]	Farbton, Nuance
vending machine [ˈvendɪŋ məʃiːn]	Getränkeautomat
light adj [laɪt]	hell
particular [pəˈtɪkjʊlə]	besondere/r/s, spezifisch
to **symbolize** [ˈsɪmbəlaɪz]	symbolisieren
unfortunate [ʌnˈfɔːtʃənət]	unglücklich
safe(ly) [seɪf]	sicher
topic [ˈtɒpɪk]	Thema
way [weɪ]	Art und Weise
association [əˌsəʊsiˈeɪʃən]	Assoziation
ethical [ˈeθɪkəl]	moralisch vertretbar, ethisch, dem Berufsethos entsprechend
to **outline** [ˈaʊtlaɪn]	skizzieren, grob beschreiben
to **be aware of sth** [bi əˈweər əv]	sich einer Sache bewusst sein, etw kennen

UNIT 10

page 89

clothing bank [ˈkləʊðɪŋ bæŋk]	Altkleidersammelbehälter
beggar [ˈbeɡə]	Bettler/in
to **beg for sth** [ˈbeɡ fə]	um etw betteln
donation [dəʊˈneɪʃn]	Spende

page 90

poverty [ˈpɒvəti]	Armut
producer [prəˈdjuːsə]	Produzent/in
Not on our watch. [nɒt ɒn ˈaʊə wɒtʃ]	Nicht mit uns!
mission [ˈmɪʃn]	Auftrag, Mission
atrocities pl [əˈtrɒsətiz]	Gräueltaten
to **invite sb to do sth** [ɪnˈvaɪt]	jdn auffordern, etw zu tun
to **lobby sb** [ˈlɒbi]	auf jdn Einfluss nehmen
donor [ˈdəʊnə]	Spender/in
schooling [ˈskuːlɪŋ]	Schulbesuch, Schulbildung
benefactor [ˈbenɪfæktə]	Wohltäter/in
sponsorship [ˈspɒnsəʃɪp]	Förderung
accountancy [əˈkaʊntənsi]	Buchhaltung, Rechnungswesen
tear [tɪə]	Träne
loan [ləʊn]	Darlehen, Kredit
foundation [faʊnˈdeɪʃn]	Stiftung
to **feed** [fiːd]	ernähren, mit Nahrung versorgen
life saving [ˈlaɪf seɪvɪŋ]	lebensrettend
medicine [ˈmedsn]	Arznei(mittel), Medizin
handout [ˈhændaʊt]	Almosen
ongoing [ˈɒnɡəʊɪŋ]	laufend
to **empower sb to do sth** [ɪmˈpaʊə]	jdn befähigen, etw zu tun
self-sustainable [ˌself səˈsteɪnəbl]	selbsttragend, lebensfähig
to **enable** [ɪˈneɪbl]	befähigen
to **make a difference** [ˌmeɪk ə ˈdɪfrəns]	etw bewirken
valuable [ˈvæljuəbl]	wertvoll
along the way [əˌlɒŋ ðə ˈweɪ]	dabei, währenddessen
to **value** [ˈvæljuː]	wertschätzen, schätzen
from all walks of life [frəm ˌɔːl wɔːks əv ˈlaɪf]	aus allen Gesellschaftsschichten, aus allen Lebensbereichen

currently ['kʌrəntli]	zurzeit
to **trouble sb** ['trʌbl]	jdn bekümmern, jdm Schwierigkeiten bereiten
Salvation Army [sæl,veɪʃn 'ɑːmi]	Heilsarmee
toddler ['tɒdlə]	Kleinkind
day centre ['deɪ sentə]	Tagesstätte für Senioren
companionship [kəm'pænjənʃɪp]	Gemeinschaft, Gesellschaft

page 91

homelessness ['həʊmləsnəs]	Obdachlosigkeit
psychological [,saɪkə'lɒdʒɪkl]	psychologisch
armed [ɑːmd]	bewaffnet
home country [,həʊm 'kʌntri]	Heimatland
in the long term [ɪn ðə 'lɒŋ tɜːm]	langfristig
in the short term [ɪn ðə ,ʃɔːt 'tɜːm]	kurzfristig
horrific [hə'rɪfɪk]	schrecklich, entsetzlich
act [ækt]	Handlung, Tat
to **finance** ['faɪnæns]	finanzieren
(the) good [ɡʊd]	Wohl

page 92

giving ['ɡɪvɪŋ]	Spenden
level ['levl]	Grad, Höhe
gross domestic product (GDP) [,ɡrəʊs də,mestɪk 'prɒdʌkt]	Bruttosozialprodukt
tax [tæks]	Steuer
to **give to charity** [,ɡɪv tə 'tʃærəti]	(für wohltätige Zwecke) spenden
good cause [ɡʊd 'kɔːz]	guter Zweck
disabled [dɪs'eɪbld]	behindert
surgery ['sɜːdʒəri]	Operation
in need [ɪn 'niːd]	bedürftig, in Not
regardless of sth [rɪ'ɡɑːdləs əv]	ungeachtet einer Sache
religious [rɪ'lɪdʒəs]	religiös
funding ['fʌndɪŋ]	Finanzierung, Geldmittel
to **feel sorry for sb** [,fiːl 'sɒri fə]	jd tut einem leid
responsibility [rɪ,spɒnsə'bɪləti]	Verantwortung, Zuständigkeit
to **fund** [fʌnd]	finanzieren
charitable ['tʃærətəbl]	wohltätig, gemeinnützig
line graph ['laɪn ɡrɑːf]	Liniendiagramm
striking ['straɪkɪŋ]	auffallend, auffällig, hervorstechend
progression [prə'ɡreʃn]	Entwicklung, Steigerung
to **rank sixth** [ræŋk 'sɪksθ]	den sechsten Platz einnehmen
times [taɪmz]	mal

page 93

attitude ['ætɪtjuːd]	Einstellung, Haltung
walk [wɔːk]	Spaziergang, Rundgang
gardening ['ɡɑːdnɪŋ]	Gartenarbeit
target ['tɑːɡɪt]	Ziel
pen friend ['pen frend]	Brieffreund/in

page 94

orphan ['ɔːfn]	Waise
orphanage ['ɔːfənɪdʒ]	Waisenhaus
Boxing Day ['bɒksɪŋ deɪ]	2. Weihnachtstag
to **strike** [straɪk]	treffen
fishing village ['fɪʃɪŋ vɪlɪdʒ]	Fischerdorf
to **be asleep** [bi ə'sliːp]	schlafen
scream [skriːm]	Schrei
to **smash** [smæʃ]	zertrümmern, zerstören
to **sweep away** [,swiːp ə'weɪ]	fortschwemmen, erfassen, wegreißen
whilst [waɪlst]	während
despite [dɪ'spaɪt]	trotz
blow [bləʊ]	Schlag
to **escape sth narrowly** [ɪ,skeɪp 'nærəʊli]	einer Sache knapp entkommen
to **hitch-hike** ['hɪtʃ haɪk]	per Anhalter fahren, trampen
embassy ['embəsi]	Botschaft
to **rejoin sb** [rɪ'dʒɔɪn]	jdn wieder treffen
to **adopt sb** [ə'dɒpt]	jdn adoptieren
ultimately ['ʌltɪmətli]	letztlich, letztendlich
strength [streŋθ]	Stärke, Kraft
humanitarian [hjuː,mænɪ'teəriən]	humanitär
a great deal [ə ,ɡreɪt 'diːl]	eine erhebliche Menge
to **hand sth out** [,hænd 'aʊt]	etw verteilen, etw ausgeben
confidence ['kɒnfɪdəns]	Selbstvertrauen, Zuversicht
to **knock sb off sth** [,nɒk 'ɒf]	jdn von etw herunterstoßen
to **be worse off** [bi ,wɜːs 'ɒf]	schlechter dran sein
independence [,ɪndɪ'pendəns]	Unabhängigkeit
movement ['muːvmənt]	Bewegung
enterprise ['entəpraɪz]	Unternehmen
to **found** [faʊnd]	gründen
commitment to sth [kə'mɪtmənt tə]	Engagement für etw, Einsatz für etw
portion ['pɔːʃn]	Teil
sole [səʊl]	alleinig
essentials pl [ɪ'senʃlz]	lebensnotwendige Güter
shelter ['ʃeltə]	Unterkunft, Tierheim
nutrition [njuː'trɪʃn]	Nahrung, Ernährung
medication [,medɪ'keɪʃn]	Arzneimittel
impact ['ɪmpækt]	Einfluss, Auswirkung
to **make an impact** [,meɪk ən 'ɪmpækt]	etw bewirken, etw verändern
opening ['əʊpnɪŋ]	Eröffnung
memory of sb ['meməri]	Gedenken an jdn
to **mark** [mɑːk]	(Jahrestag etc.) begehen
anniversary [,ænɪ'vɜːsəri]	Jahrestag

page 95

to **destroy** [dɪ'strɔɪ]	zerstören
force [fɔːs]	Gewalt, Kraft
ride [raɪd]	Fahrt
unpaid [,ʌn'peɪd]	unbezahlt
intention [ɪn'tenʃn]	Absicht
flood [flʌd]	Überschwemmung
fatality [fə'tæləti]	Todesfall, Todesopfer
NGO (non-governmental organization) [,en dʒiː 'əʊ]	Nichtregierungsorganisation
citizen ['sɪtɪzn]	Bürger/in
to **put in work** [pʊt ,ɪn 'wɜːk]	Arbeit leisten

page 96

occupation [,ɒkju'peɪʃn]	Beruf, Tätigkeit, Beschäftigung
contribution [,kɒntrɪ'bjuːʃn]	(finanzielle) Zuwendung, Spende
madam ['mædəm]	gnädige Frau
banker ['bæŋkə]	Bankkaufmann/-frau
earthquake ['ɜːθkweɪk]	Erdbeben

Unit word list

to **have spare cash** [həv ˌspeə ˈkæʃ]		Geld übrig haben
to **run** [rʌn]		(Unternehmen etc.) führen, betreiben
to **transfer** [trænsˈfɜː]		(Geld) überweisen
so far [ˌsəʊ ˈfɑː]		bislang
medical student [ˌmedɪkl ˈstjuːdnt]		Medizinstudent/in
walk-in medical centre [ˌwɔːk ɪn ˈmedɪkl sentə]		Ambulanz

page 97

saleswoman [ˈseɪlzwʊmən]		Verkäuferin
myth [mɪθ]		Mythos, Märchen
aid [eɪd]		Hilfe
disease [dɪˈziːz]		Krankheit
misunderstanding [ˌmɪsʌndəˈstændɪŋ]		Missverständnis
developing country [dɪˌveləpɪŋ ˈkʌntri]		Entwicklungsland
to **treat** [triːt]		behandeln
corrupt [kəˈrʌpt]		korrupt, bestechlich
official [əˈfɪʃl]		Beamte/r, Funktionär/in
concrete [ˈkɒŋkriːt]		konkret
mosquito net [məsˈkiːtəʊ net]		Moskitonetz
farming [ˈfɑːmɪŋ]		Landwirtschaft
health care [ˈhelθ keə]		Gesundheitswesen, medizinische Versorgung
preventable [prɪˈventəbl]		vermeidbar
proverb [ˈprɒvɜːb]		Sprichwort
for a lifetime [fər ə ˈlaɪftaɪm]		ein Leben lang

page 98

to **agree (on sth)** [əˈgriː]		(etw) zustimmen, übereinstimmen
single [ˈsɪŋgl]		alleinstehend
to **get closed** [get ˈkləʊzd]		geschlossen werden
pastry [ˈpeɪstri]		Gebäck
office worker [ˈɒfɪs wɜːkə]		Büroangestellte/r
ingredients [ɪnˈgriːdiənts]		Zutaten
additional(ly) [əˈdɪʃənl]		zusätzlich
to **keep accounts** [ˌkiːp əˈkaʊnts]		Buchführung machen
micro loan [ˈmaɪkrəʊ ləʊn]		Kleinstkredit
the realities [riˈælətiz]		die tatsächlichen Gegebenheiten
stark(ly) [stɑːk]		unangenehm, erbarmungslos
apparent [əˈpærənt]		offensichtlich, sichtbar
chief executive [ˌtʃiːf ɪgˈzekjətɪv]		Hauptgeschäftsführer/in, Firmenchef/in
assistance [əˈsɪstəns]		Hilfe, Unterstützung
pioneer [ˌpaɪəˈnɪə]		Vorreiter/in, Wegbereiter/in
microfinance [ˌmaɪkrəʊˈfaɪnæns]		Kleinstfinanzierung
otherwise [ˈʌðəwaɪz]		anderenfalls, sonst
access to sth [ˈækses tə]		Zugriff auf etw, Zugang zu etw
capital [ˈkæpɪtl]		Kapital
proper [ˈprɒpə]		richtig
poverty line [ˈpɒvəti laɪn]		Armutsgrenze
cosmetics pl [kɒzˈmetɪks]		Kosmetik
to **sell sth door to door** [sel ˌdɔː tə ˈdɔː]		etw per Haustürgeschäft verkaufen
law school [ˈlɔː skuːl]		juristische Fakultät, Jurastudium
grocery store [ˈgrəʊsəri stɔː]		Lebensmittelladen

client [ˈklaɪənt]		Kunde/Kundin
cleaning products [ˈkliːnɪŋ prɒdʌkts]		Putzmittel
nearby adj [ˌnɪəˈbaɪ]		nahe (gelegen)
proceeds pl [ˈprəʊsiːdz]		Erlös, Ertrag
neighbourhood [ˈneɪbəhʊd]		Nachbarschaft
critic [ˈkrɪtɪk]		Kritiker/in
on a small scale [ɒn ə ˌsmɔːl ˈskeɪl]		in kleinem Umfang
underlying adj [ˌʌndəˈlaɪɪŋ]		eigentlich, grundlegend
hardly adv [ˈhɑːdli]		kaum
academic study [ˌækəˌdemɪk ˈstʌdi]		wissenschaftliche Studie
in recent years [ɪn ˈriːsnt jɪəz]		in den letzten Jahren
evidence [ˈevɪdəns]		Beweise, Beweismittel
as a whole [əz ə ˈhəʊl]		im Ganzen
exception [ɪkˈsepʃn]		Ausnahme
citrus [ˈsɪtrəs]		Zitrusfrucht
every six month [ˌevri sɪks ˈmʌnθ]		alle sechs Monate
soil [sɔɪl]		Erde, Boden, Erdreich
fertiliser BE [ˈfɜːtəlaɪzə]		Dünger
labour [ˈleɪbə]		Arbeitskräfte
insecticide [ɪnˈsektɪsaɪd]		Insektengift
to **take out a loan** [teɪk ˌaʊt ə ˈləʊn]		einen Kredit abschließen
to **refuse sth** [rɪˈfjuːz]		etw verweigern
non-profit [ˌnɒnˈprɒfɪt]		gemeinnützig
to **pitch sth** [pɪtʃ]		etw anpreisen

UNIT 11

page 99

reach [riːtʃ]		Reichweite
bread roll [ˈbred rəʊl]		Brötchen
cardboard [ˈkɑːdbɔːd]		Pappe
supply chain [səˈplaɪ tʃeɪn]		Lieferkette
item [ˈaɪtəm]		Artikel, Gegenstand
to **manufacture** [ˌmænjuˈfæktʃə]		fertigen, herstellen
raw product [ˌrɔː ˈprɒdʌkt]		Ausgangsprodukt, Roherzeugnis
to **originate from** [əˈrɪdʒɪneɪt frəm]		kommen aus
within [wɪˈðɪn]		innerhalb, binnen
to **grow** [grəʊ]		(Pflanze) anbauen
to **import** [ɪmˈpɔːt]		importieren, einführen
wheat [wiːt]		Weizen
lettuce [ˈletɪs]		Kopfsalat

page 100

globalization [ˌgləʊbəlaɪˈzeɪʃn]		Globalisierung
case study [ˈkeɪs stʌdi]		Fallstudie
growth [grəʊθ]		Wachstum, Zunahme
influence [ˈɪnfluəns]		Einfluss
to **spread** [spred]		sich ausbreiten, sich verbreiten
trader [ˈtreɪdə]		Händler/in
trading [ˈtreɪdɪŋ]		Handel
cooperative [kəʊˈɒpərətɪv]		Genossenschaft
to **transform** [trænsˈfɔːm]		(völlig) verändern
to **raise sth** [reɪz]		etw steigern, etw erhöhen
to **switch to sth** [ˈswɪtʃ tə]		auf etw umstellen
organic [ɔːˈgænɪk]		biologisch, Bio-
buyer [ˈbaɪə]		Einkäufer/in
facilities pl [fəˈsɪlətiz]		Anlage(n), Einrichtungen

to **process** [prəʊˈses]	verarbeiten
finished product [ˌfɪnɪʃt ˈprɒdʌkt]	Endprodukt
clinic [ˈklɪnɪk]	Klinik
secondary school [ˈsekəndri skuːl]	weiterführende Schule
textile [ˈtekstaɪl]	Textil-
back [bæk]	Rücken
to **care about sth** [ˈkeər əbaʊt]	sich um etw kümmern
to **injure** [ˈɪndʒə]	verletzen
to **collapse** [kəˈlæps]	einstürzen
order [ˈɔːdə]	Auftrag, Bestellung
to **fill an order** [ˌfɪl ən ˈɔːdə]	einen Auftrag ausführen
union [ˈjuːniən]	Gewerkschaft
to **take action** [ˌteɪk ˈækʃn]	handeln
offshore [ˌɒfˈʃɔː]	im/ins Ausland
folks pl [fəʊks]	Leute
carpentry [ˈkɑːpəntri]	Schreinerei
depressed [dɪˈprest]	(Wirtschaft:) flau, am Boden
to **re-skill** [ˌriːˈskɪl]	umschulen
computer-aided [kəmˈpjuːtər eɪdɪd]	computergestützt
automated [ˈɔːtəmeɪtɪd]	automatisiert
to **expand** [ɪkˈspænd]	expandieren, ausweiten
electronic [ˌɪlekˈtrɒnɪk]	elektronisch, Elektronik-
component [kəmˈpəʊnənt]	Bauteil
to **turn out** [ˌtɜːn ˈaʊt]	sich herausstellen
co-worker [ˈkəʊwɜːkə]	Kollege/Kollegin
to **go inland** [gəʊ ˈɪnlænd]	ins Landesinnere gehen
employment [ɪmˈplɔɪmənt]	Anstellung, Arbeit
people [ˈpiːpl]	Volk

page 101

to **mention** [ˈmenʃn]	erwähnen, nennen
to **change for the better** [ˌtʃeɪndʒ fə ðə ˈbetə]	sich zum Besseren verändern
point of view [ˌpɔɪnt əv ˈvjuː]	Perspektive, Blickwinkel, Standpunkt
to **farm** [fɑːm]	(Land) bewirtschaften
to **govern** [ˈgʌvn]	regieren, verwalten, führen
agreement [əˈgriːmənt]	Vereinbarung, Absprache
to **construct** [kənˈstrʌkt]	bauen, errichten, konstruieren
transformation [ˌtrænzfəˈmeɪʃn]	(grundlegende) Veränderung, Umwandlung
expansion [ɪkˈspænʃn]	Ausweitung, Expansion
to **look a mess** [ˌlʊk ə ˈmes]	fürchterlich aussehen
democracy [dɪˈmɒkrəsi]	Demokratie

page 102

petrol [ˈpetrəl]	Benzin
petrol-driven [ˈpetrəl drɪvn]	benzingetrieben
mass production [ˌmæs prəˈdʌkʃn]	Massenproduktion
personal transport [ˌpɜːsənl ˈtrænspɔːt]	Individualverkehr
to **export** [ɪkˈspɔːt]	ausführen, exportieren
link [lɪŋk]	Verbindung, Verknüpfung, Beziehung
plant [plɑːnt]	Fabrik, Werk, Anlage
to **link** [lɪŋk]	verbinden, verknüpfen
aircraft [ˈeəkrɑːft]	Flugzeug
maker [ˈmeɪkə]	Hersteller, Erbauer
shared [ʃeəd]	gemeinsam
to **test** [test]	erproben, testen
even so [ˈiːvn səʊ]	dennoch, allerdings

page 103

order [ˈɔːdə]	Bestellung
particularly [pəˈtɪkjələli]	besonders
related [rɪˈleɪtɪd]	zugehörig
to **consist of sth** [kənˈsɪst əv]	aus etw bestehen
ironic [aɪˈrɒnɪk]	ironisch
to **remind sb (of sth)** [rɪˈmaɪnd]	jdn (an etw) erinnern
secondly [ˈsekəndli]	zweitens
collapse [kəˈlæps]	Einsturz
sharp [ʃɑːp]	scharf
attack [əˈtæk]	Attacke, Angriff
care [keə]	Sorge, Fürsorge, Sorgfalt

page 104

to **re-shore** [ˌriːˈʃɔː]	(Industrie) wieder im Inland ansiedeln, wieder ins Inland verlagern
head [hed]	Leiter/in, Chef/in
industrialized [ɪnˈdʌstriəlaɪzd]	industrialisiert
low-cost [ˌləʊˈkɒst]	billig, kostengünstig
to **undercut** [ˌʌndəˈkʌt]	unterbieten
section [ˈsekʃn]	Bereich, Teil
industrial [ɪnˈdʌstriəl]	Industrie-
wasteland [ˈweɪstlənd]	Brachland
wage [weɪdʒ]	Lohn
floor care [ˈflɔː keə]	Bodenpflege
slight [slaɪt]	leicht, gering
overheads pl [ˈəʊvəhedz]	Fixkosten, Betriebskosten
rent [rent]	Miete
labour [ˈleɪbə]	Arbeit

page 105

demand [dɪˈmɑːnd]	Nachfrage
to **meet a demand** [ˌmiːt ə dɪˈmɑːnd]	eine Nachfrage befriedigen
delay [dɪˈleɪ]	Verzögerung
stock [stɒk]	(Lager-)Bestand, Vorrat
breakage [ˈbreɪkɪdʒ]	Bruchschaden
faulty [ˈfɔːlti]	defekt, fehlerhaft
balance [ˈbæləns]	Bilanz, Saldo
water heater [ˈwɔːtə hiːtə]	Warmwasserbereiter, Boiler
cash machine [ˈkæʃ məʃiːn]	Geldautomat
rate [reɪt]	Tempo, Quote, Rate, Anteil
loss [lɒs]	Verlust
to **slow** [sləʊ]	sich verlangsamen, sich abschwächen
to **balance** [ˈbæləns]	ausgleichen
roughly [ˈrʌfli]	ungefähr

page 106

development [dɪˈveləpmənt]	(Immobilie:) Erschließung, Bau
to **hyphenate** [ˈhaɪfəneɪt]	mit einem Bindestrich schreiben
to **decrease** [dɪˈkriːs]	abnehmen, zurückgehen
sharp(ly) [ʃɑːp]	stark
steady [ˈstedi]	kontinuierlich, stabil
slightly [ˈslaɪtli]	geringfügig, leicht
climb [klaɪm]	Anstieg
fall [fɔːl]	Absturz, Rückgang
declin [dɪˈklaɪn]	Rückgang
to **remain** [rɪˈmeɪn]	bleiben

page 107

sales director [ˈseɪlz dərektə]	Verkaufsleiter/in, Vertriebsleiter/in

297

Unit word list

to **identify** [aɪˈdentɪfaɪ]	erkennen, bestimmen, identifizieren	to **be left for dead** [bi ˌleft fə ˈded]	als tot zurückgelassen werden
recession [rɪˈseʃn]	Rezession	**emergency** [ɪˈmɜːdʒənsi]	Notfall, Not-
flat [flæt]	(Umsatz etc.:) konstant, unverändert; (Hierarchie:) flach	to **recover fully** [rɪˌkʌvə ˈfʊli]	wieder völlig gesund werden
to **face sth** [feɪs]	mit etw konfrontiert werden, sich einer Sache gegenübersehen	**page 110**	
		to **make room** [meɪk ˈruːm]	Platz machen
to **fight back** [ˌfaɪt ˈbæk]	sich wehren, sich zurückkämpfen	to **pass sth on** [ˌpɑːs ˈɒn]	etw weitergeben, etw weiterreichen
optimistic [ˌɒptɪˈmɪstɪk]	optimistisch	**degree** [dɪˈɡriː]	Abschluss
running [ˈrʌnɪŋ]	in Folge	to **juggle** [ˈdʒʌɡl]	miteinander vereinbaren, jonglieren
to **cut costs** [kʌt ˈkɒsts]	Kosten senken	**casual job** [ˌkæʒuəl ˈdʒɒb]	Nebenjob
to **go out of business** [ɡəʊ ˌaʊt əv ˈbɪznəs]	das Geschäft aufgeben, Pleite gehen	to **self-fund** [ˌself ˈfʌnd]	selbst finanzieren
partly [ˈpɑːtli]	teils, teilweise	**congressman** [ˈkɒŋɡresmən]	Kongressabgeordneter
operation [ˌɒpəˈreɪʃn]	Betrieb, Geschäftstätigkeit	**retail** [ˈriːteɪl]	Einzelhandel(s-)
bottom line [ˌbɒtəm ˈlaɪn]	das, worauf es (unterm Strich) ankommt	to **make sb redundant** [ˌmeɪk rɪˈdʌndənt]	jdn (betriebsbedingt) entlassen
to **last** [lɑːst]	dauern, andauern, so bleiben	**previous** [ˈpriːviəs]	vorherig, früher
		to **land sth** [lænd]	etw an Land ziehen
page 108		**middle management** [ˌmɪdl ˈmænɪdʒmənt]	mittlere Führungsebene
ethnicity [eθˈnɪsəti]	Volkszugehörigkeit, Ethnizität	**skilled** [skɪld]	qualifiziert, erfahren
aligned with [əˈlaɪnd]	verbunden mit, ausgerichtet auf	to **be sick of sth** [bi ˈsɪk əv]	von etw die Nase voll haben
to **practice** [ˈpræktɪs]	(Religion:) ausüben	**rather** [ˈrɑːðə]	eher, lieber
Christian [ˈkrɪstʃən]	Christ/in	**endless** [ˈendləs]	endlos, fortwährend
Buddhist [ˈbʊdɪst]	Buddhist/in	to **terminate** [ˈtɜːmɪneɪt]	beenden
literacy [ˈlɪtərəsi]	Alphabetisierung, die Lese- und Schreibfähigkeit	**full-time** [ˌfʊl ˈtaɪm]	Vollzeit-
		nannying [ˈnæniɪŋ]	Kinderbetreuung
literate [ˈlɪtərət]	alphabetisiert, des Lesens und Schreibens mächtig	**out-of-state** [ˌaʊt əv ˈsteɪt]	in einem anderen Bundesstaat
illiterate [ɪˈlɪtərət]	Analphabet/in sein	**applicant** [ˈæplɪkənt]	Bewerber/in
graduate [ˈɡrædʒuət]	Absolvent/in	**pay packet** [ˈpeɪ pækɪt]	Lohntüte, Gehalt
shelter [ˈʃeltə]	Obdach	**minimum wage** [ˌmɪnɪməm ˈweɪdʒ]	Mindestlohn
starvation [stɑːˈveɪʃn]	Verhungern	**editor** [ˈedɪtə]	Herausgeber/in
undernourished [ˌʌndəˈnʌrɪʃt]	unterernährt	to **take a chance on sb** [ˌteɪk ə ˈtʃɑːns ɒn]	es mit jdm versuchen, jdm eine Chance geben
drinking water [ˈdrɪŋkɪŋ wɔːtə]	Trinkwasser	to **state** [steɪt]	erklären, feststellen
housing [ˈhaʊzɪŋ]	Unterkunft	**ought to** [ˈɔːt tə]	sollen
switchboard [ˈswɪtʃbɔːd]	Klapptafel	**contributor** [kənˈtrɪbjuːtə]	Autor/in (von Zeitschriftenartikeln)
world event [ˈwɜːld ɪvent]	Weltgeschehen	**entry-level** [ˈentri levl]	Einstiegs-
anonymous(ly) [əˈnɒnɪməs]	anonym	to **be rigged against sb** [bi ˈrɪɡd əɡenst]	jdn (systematisch) benachteiligen, gegen jdn arbeiten
to **seek** [siːk]	suchen		
asylum [əˈsaɪləm]	Asyl	**stream** [striːm]	Strom
to **flee (sth)** [fliː]	flüchten (vor etw)	to **be unique to sth** [bi juˈniːk tə]	etw ausschließlich betreffen
to **improve** [ɪmˈpruːv]	verbessern	**lazy** [ˈleɪzi]	faul
burden [ˈbɜːdn]	Last, Belastung, Bürde	to **mooch off sth** [ˌmuːtʃ ˈɒf]	von etw schmarotzen
		hopeless [ˈhəʊpləs]	hoffnungslos

UNIT 12

page 109

changing [ˈtʃeɪndʒɪŋ]	im Wandel	**page 111**	
jobless [ˈdʒɒbləs]	arbeitslos	**dole** [dəʊl]	Arbeitslosengeld
elderly [ˈeldəli]	ältere/r/s	**dole bludger** [ˈdəʊl blʌdʒə]	Sozialschmarotzer
the elderly [ði ˈeldəli]	Senioren	**useless** [ˈjuːsləs]	nutzlos
pension [ˈpenʃn]	Rente, Pension	**unexpected(ly)** [ˌʌnɪkˈspektɪd]	unerwartet
pensioner [ˈpenʃənə]	Rentner/in	**afterwards** [ˈɑːftəwədz]	danach, darauf
to **recover** [rɪˈkʌvə]	sich erholen	**publication** [ˌpʌblɪˈkeɪʃn]	Veröffentlichung
joblessness [ˈdʒɒbləsnəs]	Arbeitslosigkeit	**edition** [ɪˈdɪʃn]	Ausgabe
millennial [mɪˈleniəl]	Jahrtausend-	to **outline** [ˈaʊtlaɪn]	skizzieren, grob beschreiben
to **campaign** [kæmˈpeɪn]	kämpfen		
her native Pakistan [hə ˌneɪtɪv pækɪˈstɑːn]	ihr Geburtsland Pakistan	**page 112**	
		journalism [ˈdʒɜːnəlɪzəm]	Journalismus
to **shoot sb** [ʃuːt]	jdn erschießen	**assistance** [əˈsɪstəns]	Hilfe, Unterstützung

graduation [ˌgrædʒuˈeɪʃn]	(Schul-/Universitäts-) Abschluss	wedding [ˈwedɪŋ]	Hochzeit
interviewee [ˌɪntəvjuːˈiː]	Person, mit der ein Vorstellungsgespräch geführt wird	affluent [ˈæfluənt]	wohlhabend
		construction company [kənˈstrʌkʃn kʌmpəni]	Baufirma
shipbuilding [ˈʃɪpbɪldɪŋ]	Schiffbau	to stop sb from doing sth [stɒp]	jdn daran hindern, etw zu tun
to meet a deadline [ˌmiːt ə ˈdedlaɪn]	eine Frist / einen Termin einhalten	to carry on [ˌkæri ˈɒn]	weitermachen
		tiring [ˈtaɪərɪŋ]	anstrengend
page 113		warehouse [ˈweəhaʊs]	Lager
to play the piano [ˌpleɪ ðə piˈænəʊ]	Klavier spielen	forklift (truck) [ˈfɔːklɪft]	Gabelstapler
harbour [ˈhɑːbə]	Hafen	**page 117**	
to edit [ˈedɪt]	(Text) redigieren, bearbeiten	fuel [ˈfjuːəl]	Brennstoff, Treibstoff
original material [əˌrɪdʒənl məˈtɪəriəl]	eigene Beiträge	sadly [ˈsædli]	leider
		there's no escape from the fact that [ðeəz nəʊ ɪˌskeɪp frəm ðə ˈfækt ðət]	man kann nicht außer Acht lassen, dass; man muss der Tatsache ins Auge sehen, dass
to confirm [kənˈfɜːm]	bestätigen		
page 114			
retirement [rɪˈtaɪəmənt]	Ruhestand, Rente	allowance [əˈlaʊəns]	Zuschuss
to age [eɪdʒ]	altern	per annum [pər ˈænəm]	pro Jahr
resource [rɪˈsɔːs]	Ressource	to support [səˈpɔːt]	(Argument) untermauern, stützen
senior citizen [ˌsiːniə ˈsɪtɪzn]	Senior/in, ältere/r Mitbürger/in		
		moreover [mɔːrˈəʊvə]	überdies
to be still going strong [bi ˌstɪl gəʊɪŋ ˈstrɒŋ]	gut dabei sein, immer noch in Form sein	furthermore [ˌfɜːðəˈmɔː]	darüber hinaus
		for instance [fərˈɪnstəns]	zum Beispiel
startling [ˈstɑːtlɪŋ]	alarmierend, erschreckend, erstaunlich	**page 118**	
		exploitation [ˌeksplɔɪˈteɪʃn]	Ausbeutung
scrapheap [ˈskræphiːp]	Schrotthaufen	CEO (Chief Executive Officer) [ˌsiː iː ˈəʊ]	Vorstandsvorsitzende/r
to retire sb [rɪˈtaɪə]	jdn in den Ruhestand versetzen		
		booming [ˈbuːmɪŋ]	blühend, florierend
social engineering [ˌsəʊʃl ˌendʒɪˈnɪərɪŋ]	Änderung gesellschaftlicher Strukturen, angewandte Sozialwissenschaft	to challenge [ˈtʃælɪndʒ]	(heraus-)fordern
		capable of [ˈkeɪpəbl əv]	fähig zu
		menial (job) [ˈmiːniəl]	(Tätigkeit:) niedrig, untergeordnet
to be past it [bi ˈpɑːst ɪt]	die besten Jahre hinter sich haben, jenseits von Gut und Böse sein		
		to partake in sth [pɑːˈteɪk ɪn]	an etw teilhaben
mental(ly) [ˈmentl]	geistig	training [ˈtreɪnɪŋ]	Schulung
to ignore [ɪgˈnɔː]	nicht beachten, ignorieren	throughout their time [θruːˌaʊt ðeə ˈtaɪm]	ihre ganze Zeit lang
reliability [rɪˌlaɪəˈbɪləti]	Zuverlässigkeit, Verlässlichkeit		
		to afford sth [əˈfɔːd]	sich etw leisten
wish [wɪʃ]	Wunsch	healthcare [ˈhelθkeə]	Gesundheitspflege
to act as sth [ˈækt əz]	als etw fungieren	expenses pl [ɪkˈspensɪz]	Ausgaben
adviser [ədˈvaɪzə]	Berater/in	potential [pəˈtenʃl]	Potenzial, Leistungsvermögen
lifetime [ˈlaɪftaɪm]	(ganzes) Leben		
to guide [gaɪd]	führen	to hurt [hɜːt]	verletzen
heart-warming [ˈhɑːt wɔːmɪŋ]	herzerwärmend	to leave [liːv]	fortgehen
		tangible [ˈtændʒəbl]	fühlbar, greifbar, konkret
to team up with sb [ˌtiːm ˈʌp wɪð]	mit jdm zusammenarbeiten, sich mit jdm zusammentun	to take advantage of sb [ˌteɪk ədˈvɑːntɪdʒ əv]	jdn missbrauchen, ausnutzen
home for the elderly [ˌhəʊm fə ði ˈeldəli]	Altenheim	to report [rɪˈpɔːt]	berichten, melden, anzeigen
		authorities pl [ɔːˈθɒrətiz]	Leitung, oberste Dienststelle
native speaker [ˌneɪtɪv ˈspiːkə]	Muttersprachler/in	to network [ˈnetwɜːk]	netzwerken, sich verbinden
retirement home [rɪˈtaɪəmənt həʊm]	Altersheim	in terms of [ɪn ˈtɜːmz əv]	in Bezug auf
		to receive [rɪˈsiːv]	erhalten
page 115		condition [kənˈdɪʃn]	Bedingung, Kondition
ancient [ˈeɪnʃənt]	alt, historisch, antik	to get lost [get ˈlɒst]	verlorengehen
gay [geɪ]	schwul, lesbisch	standard of living [ˌstændəd əv ˈlɪvɪŋ]	Lebensstandard
equal society [ˌiːkwəl səˈsaɪəti]	gerechte Gesellschaft		
		in charge [ɪn ˈtʃɑːdʒ]	leitend, verantwortlich
page 116		however ... [haʊˈevə]	wie ... auch immer, sowenig ... auch
to work sth out [ˌwɜːk ˈaʊt]	etw herausfinden		
closely related [ˌkləʊsli rɪˈleɪtɪd]	eng verwandt	future [ˈfjuːtʃə]	zukünftig
		employer [ɪmˈplɔɪə]	Arbeitgeber/in
to make sense [ˌmeɪk ˈsens]	Sinn ergeben, sinnvoll sein	to stay in touch [ˌsteɪ ɪn ˈtʌtʃ]	in Verbindung bleiben
characteristic [ˌkærəktəˈrɪstɪk]	Merkmal, charakteristische Eigenschaft	recommendation [ˌrekəmenˈdeɪʃn]	Empfehlung

Unit word list

JOB SKILLS 3
page 119

to **give directions** [ˌgɪv dəˈrekʃnz]	den Weg beschreiben
booking [ˈbʊkɪŋ]	Buchung
reservation [ˌrezəˈveɪʃn]	Reservierung
to **be located in** [bi ləʊˈkeɪtɪd ɪn]	sich in … befinden, in … liegen
directions pl [dəˈrekʃnz]	Wegbeschreibung
to **turn right/left** [ˌtɜːn ˈraɪt, ˈleft]	rechts/links abbiegen
café [ˈkæfeɪ]	Café
within walking distance [wɪðɪn ˈwɔːkɪŋ dɪstəns]	in Laufweite
straight ahead [ˌstreɪt əˈhed]	geradeaus
to **keep to the right/left** [ˌkiːp tə ˈraɪt, ˈleft]	sich rechts/links halten

page 120

storeroom [ˈstɔːruːm]	Lagerraum
marvellous [ˈmɑːvələs]	toll, phantastisch
corridor [ˈkɒrɪdɔː]	Flur, Gang
impressed [ɪmˈprest]	beeindruckt
to **find one's way around** [faɪnd wʌnz ˌweɪ əˈraʊnd]	sich zurechtfinden
photocopier [ˈfəʊtəʊkɒpiə]	Fotokopiergerät
office supplies pl [ˈɒfɪs səplaɪz]	Büromaterial
Research and Development (R&D) [rɪˌsɜːtʃ ən dɪˈveləpmənt]	Forschung(s-) und Entwicklung(sabteilung)
quality control [ˈkwɒləti kəntrəʊl]	Qualitätskontrolle
reception [rɪˈsepʃn]	Empfang
remaining [rɪˈmeɪnɪŋ]	übrig, verbleibend
blank [blæŋk]	leer, frei
memory [ˈmeməri]	Gedächtnis
emergency exit [ɪˈmɜːdʒənsi eksɪt]	Notausgang, Fluchtweg
emergency exit plan [ɪˌmɜːdʒənsi ˈeksɪt plæn]	Fluchtwegplan
to **exhibit** [ɪgˈzɪbɪt]	ausstellen
trade fair [ˈtreɪd feə]	Handelsmesse, Fachmesse
non-smoking [ˌnɒnˈsməʊkɪŋ]	Nichtraucher-
as requested [əz rɪˈkwestɪd]	wie gewünscht
Best wishes [ˌbest ˈwɪʃɪz]	(Brief:) Mit den besten Wünschen

page 121

to **be due** [bi ˈdjuː]	(Flugzeug etc.:) planmäßig ankommen
confirmation [ˌkɒnfəˈmeɪʃn]	Bestätigung
to **let sb know sth** [ˌlet ˈnəʊ]	jdm etw mitteilen, jdm etw sagen
(business) contact [ˈkɒntækt]	Ansprechpartner/in, Geschäftspartner/in
Regards [rɪˈgɑːdz]	(Brief:) Viele Grüße
to **reserve** [rɪˈzɜːv]	reservieren
ranking [ˈræŋkɪŋ]	Rangfolge
seating [ˈsiːtɪŋ]	Bestuhlung
wheelchair [ˈwiːltʃeə]	Rollstuhl
projector [prəˈdʒektə]	Beamer
screen [skriːn]	Leinwand
selection [sɪˈlekʃn]	Auswahl
non-alcoholic [ˌnɒn ælkəˈhɒlɪk]	alkoholfrei
vegetarian [ˌvedʒəˈteərɪən]	vegetarisch
to **exceed** [ɪkˈsiːd]	überschreiten
wheelchair access [ˈwiːltʃeər ækses]	behindertengerechter Zugang
throughout [θruːˈaʊt]	überall, in ganz …
disabled facilities pl [dɪsˌeɪbld fəˈsɪlətiz]	behindertengerechte Toiletten
equipped with [ɪˈkwɪpt wɪð]	ausgestattet mit
stationery [ˈsteɪʃənri]	Schreibpapier, Schreibwaren
dietary [ˈdaɪətri]	Ernährungs-
to **cater for sth** [ˈkeɪtə fə]	auf etw eingehen
to **stay overnight** [ˌsteɪ əʊvəˈnaɪt]	übernachten
reasonable [ˈriːznəbl]	vernünftig
to **mix and match** [ˌmɪks ən ˈmætʃ]	individuell zusammenstellen
marker [ˈmɑːkə]	Filzstift
to **cater** [ˈkeɪtə]	Speisen und Getränke liefern
buffet lunch [ˈbʊfeɪ lʌntʃ]	Lunchbuffet
rental price [ˈrentl praɪs]	Mietpreis

UNIT 13
page 123

priority [praɪˈɒrəti]	Priorität, Vorrang
data protection [ˌdeɪtə prəˈtekʃn]	Datenschutz
waste [weɪst]	Müll
dependence [dɪˈpendəns]	Abhängigkeit
extremism [ɪkˈstriːmɪzm]	Extremismus
identity [aɪˈdentəti]	Identität
theft [θeft]	Diebstahl
radicalization [ˌrædɪkəlaɪˈzeɪʃn]	Radikalisierung
surveillance [sɜːˈveɪləns]	Überwachung
terrorist [ˈterərɪst]	Terrorist/in, Terror-
attack [əˈtæk]	Anschlag, Attentat

page 124

finishing line [ˈfɪnɪʃɪŋ laɪn]	Ziellinie
pressure cooker [ˈpreʃə kʊkə]	Schnellkochtopf
bomb [bɒm]	Bombe
to **explode** [ɪkˈspləʊd]	explodieren
suspect [ˈsʌspekt]	Verdächtige/r
firefight [ˈfaɪəfaɪt]	Schusswechsel
manhunt [ˈmænhʌnt]	Verbrecherjagd
to **shut down** [ˌʃʌt ˈdaʊn]	schließen
resident [ˈrezɪdənt]	Anwohner/in, Bewohner/in
urban [ˈɜːbən]	städtisch, Stadt-
desert [ˈdezət]	Wüste
back yard [ˌbæk ˈjɑːd]	Hinterhof
to **state** [steɪt]	aussagen
to **bomb sth** [bɒm]	einen Bombenanschlag auf etw verüben
to **claim** [kleɪm]	behaupten
to **radicalize** [ˈrædɪkəlaɪz]	radikalisieren
to **engage in sth** [ɪnˈgeɪdʒ ɪn]	aktiv werden
violence [ˈvaɪələns]	Gewalt
multiple [ˈmʌltɪpl]	mehrere, vielfach
to **dominate** [ˈdɒmɪneɪt]	beherrschen, dominieren
battlefield [ˈbætlfiːld]	Schlachtfeld
century [ˈsentʃəri]	Jahrhundert
commander [kəˈmɑːndə]	Kommandant/in, Anführer/in
modernity [məˈdɜːnəti]	Moderne
mobility [məʊˈbɪləti]	Mobilität

to **originate from sth** [əˈrɪdʒɪneɪt frəm]	von etw ausgehen, aus etw kommen	to **be in favour of sth** [bɪ ɪn ˈfeɪvər əv]	für etw sein
weapon [ˈwepən]	Waffe	**man of the cloth** [ˌmæn əv ðə ˈklɒθ]	Geistlicher
destructive [dɪˈstrʌktɪv]	zerstörerisch	**prayer** [preə]	Gebet
to **plague** [pleɪg]	plagen, heimsuchen	**prayer vigil** [ˈpreə vɪdʒɪl]	Gebetswache
tactic [ˈtæktɪk]	Taktik	to **pray** [preɪ]	beten
essentially [ɪˈsenʃəli]	im Wesentlichen	to **join together** [ˌdʒɔɪn təˈgeðə]	sich zusammenschließen
law enforcement [ˈlɔː ɪnfɔːsmənt]	Gesetzesvollzug, Innere Sicherheit, Exekutive		
criminal justice [ˌkrɪmɪnl ˈdʒʌstɪs]	Strafjustiz	**page 127**	
arsenal [ˈɑːsnəl]	Instrumentarium, Waffenlager	to **prevent** [prɪˈvent]	verhindern, verhüten
		thorough(ly) [ˈθʌrə]	gründlich, sorgfältig
law enforcement agency [ˈlɔː ɪnfɔːsmənt eɪdʒənsi]	Strafverfolgungsbehörde, Exekutivorgan	to **put** [pʊt]	formulieren, sagen, in Worte fassen
extension [ɪkˈstenʃn]	Erweiterung, Ausbau	**security service** [sɪˈkjʊərəti sɜːvɪs]	Geheimdienst
to **root sth out** [ˌruːt ˈaʊt]	etw beseitigen, etw ausmerzen	**sensitive** [ˈsensətɪv]	sensibel, (Information:) vertraulich
mass media pl [ˌmæs ˈmiːdiə]	Massenmedien	**internal** [ɪnˈtɜːnl]	inländisch, Inlands-
cable news [ˈkeɪbl njuːz]	TV-Nachrichtensender	to **post** [pəʊst]	(Brief:) einwerfen, schicken
responsible [rɪˈspɒnsəbl]	verantwortungsvoll	**police force** [pəˈliːs fɔːs]	Polizei
breathless(ly) [ˈbreθləs]	atemlos	**precaution** [prɪˈkɔːʃn]	Vorkehrung, Sicherheitsmaßnahme
to **await** [əˈweɪt]	erwarten, abwarten	to **be willing to do sth** [bɪ ˈwɪlɪŋ tə]	bereit sein, etw zu tun
page 125			
bomber [ˈbɒmə]	Bombenattentäter/in	**page 128**	
explosive device [ɪkˌspləʊsɪv dɪˈvaɪs]	Sprengsatz	to **defend** [dɪˈfend]	verteidigen
to **sensationalize sth** [senˈseɪʃənəlaɪz]	reißerisch über etw berichten	to **let oneself in for sth** [ˌlet wʌnˈself ˈɪn fə]	sich auf etw einlassen
suicide [ˈsuːɪsaɪd]	Selbstmord	to **harm sb** [hɑːm]	jdm schaden
suicide bomber [ˌsuːɪsaɪd ˈbɒmə]	Selbstmordattentäter/in	**self-defence** [ˌself dɪˈfens]	Selbstverteidigung
devastating [ˈdevəsteɪtɪŋ]	verheerend	**specialist** [ˈspeʃəlɪst]	Spezial-, Fach-
attacker [əˈtækə]	Attentäter/in	**request** [rɪˈkwest]	Bitte, Wunsch, Anfrage
explosive [ɪkˈspləʊsɪv]	Sprengstoff	to **instruct sb to do sth** [ɪnˈstrʌkt]	jdn beauftragen, etw zu tun
cross [krɒs]	Kreuz	to **install** [ɪnˈstɔːl]	installieren
guilty [ˈgɪlti]	schuldig	**undetectable** [ˌʌndɪˈtektəbl]	nicht erkennbar, nicht nachweisbar
police station [pəˈliːs steɪʃn]	Polizeiwache	**spyware** [ˈspaɪweə]	Spionagesoftware
page 126		to **transmit** [trænsˈmɪt]	übertragen, übermitteln, senden
to **have one's say** [hæv wʌnz ˈseɪ]	seine Meinung äußern, zu Wort kommen	to **track sb** [træk]	jds Spur verfolgen
threat [θret]	Bedrohung	to **log** [lɒg]	aufzeichnen, protokollieren
to **be under threat** [bɪ ˌʌndə ˈθret]	bedroht werden	**school-age** [ˈskuːl eɪdʒ]	im Schulalter
army [ˈɑːmi]	Armee	to **intercept** [ˌɪntəˈsept]	abfangen, abhören
officer [ˈɒfɪsə]	Offizier/in	to **be mistaken** [bɪ mɪˈsteɪkən]	sich irren
to **get you nowhere** [ˌget jə ˈnəʊweə]	zu nichts führen, nichts bringen	**keystroke** [ˈkiːstrəʊk]	Tastenanschlag, Herunterdrücken einer Taste
conflict zone [ˈkɒnflɪkt zəʊn]	Krisenregion, Konfliktzone	**handy** [ˈhændi]	praktisch
host [həʊst]	(Radio-/TV-)Moderator/in	to **input** [ˈɪnpʊt]	eingeben
law and order [ˌlɔː ənd ˈɔːdə]	Recht und Ordnung	**access code** [ˈækses kəʊd]	Zugangscode
security forces pl [sɪˈkjʊərəti fɔːsɪz]	Sicherheitskräfte	**page 129**	
armed forces pl [ˌɑːmd ˈfɔːsɪz]	Streitkräfte	**silent** [ˈsaɪlənt]	stumm
massive(ly) [ˈmæsɪv]	massiv	**microphone** [ˈmaɪkrəfəʊn]	Mikrofon
to **border with sth** [ˈbɔːdə wɪð]	an etw grenzen	to **go unnoticed** [ˌgəʊ ʌnˈnəʊtɪst]	unbemerkt bleiben
to **supply sb with sth** [səˈplaɪ]	jdn mit etw versorgen, jdn mit etw beliefern	to **switch to sth** [ˈswɪtʃ tə]	auf etw umschalten
westerner [ˈwestənə]	Mensch aus der westlichen Welt	**delivery** [dɪˈlɪvəri]	Lieferung
		van [væn]	Lieferwagen
to **arm sb** [ɑːm]	jdn bewaffnen	**lawnmower** [ˈlɔːnməʊə]	Rasenmäher
pacifist [ˈpæsɪfɪst]	Pazifist/in	to **knock sth off** [ˌnɒk ˈɒf]	etw abschlagen
		mirror [ˈmɪrə]	Spiegel
		to **stick sth on** [ˌstɪk ˈɒn]	etw befestigen
		washing machine [ˈwɒʃɪŋ məʃiːn]	Waschmaschine

Unit word list

to **be priced at …** [bi ˈpraɪst ət] … kosten
purchase [ˈpɜːtʃəs] Kauf
to **save** [seɪv] (Daten) sichern
embarrassing [ɪmˈbærəsɪŋ] peinlich, unangenehm
to **prompt sb to do sth** [prɒmpt] jdn veranlassen, etw zu tun
to **withdraw** [wɪðˈdrɔː] (Geld) abheben
untraceable [ˌʌnˈtreɪsəbl] nicht ausfindig zu machen
to **be sick and tired of sth** [bi ˌsɪk ən ˈtaɪəd əv] die Nase von etw gestrichen voll haben
straightaway [ˌstreɪtəˈweɪ] sofort, sogleich
nasty [ˈnɑːsti] gemein, hässlich, böse
to **beg sb to do sth** [beg] jdn anflehen, etw zu tun
to **concede** [kənˈsiːd] eingestehen, einräumen
utter [ˈʌtə] völlig, vollkommen
defeat [dɪˈfiːt] Niederlage
obtainable [əbˈteɪnəbl] erhältlich
suspicious [səˈspɪʃəs] misstrauisch
spouse [spaʊz] Ehegatte
to **spy on sb** [ˈspaɪ ɒn] jdn ausspionieren
the small print [ðə ˈsmɔːl prɪnt] das Kleingedruckte
tormentor [tɔːˈmentə] Peiniger
encrypted [ɪnˈkrɪptɪd] verschlüsselt
in person [ɪn ˈpɜːsn] persönlich

page 130

means of transport [ˌmiːnz əv ˈtrænspɔːt] Verkehrsmittel
to **obtain sth** [əbˈteɪn] etw erhalten, an etw gelangen
to **launch an attack** [ˌlɔːntʃ ən əˈtæk] einen Angriff starten
consequence [ˈkɒnsɪkwəns] Folge, Konsequenz
to **cancel** [ˈkænsl] abbrechen
cybercrime [ˈsaɪbəkraɪm] Cyberkriminalität
bank robbery [ˈbæŋk rɒbəri] Banküberfall, Bankraub
to **rob a bank** [ˌrɒb ə ˈbæŋk] eine Bank überfallen, eine Bank ausrauben
to **hijack** [ˈhaɪdʒæk] kapern

page 131

extract [ˈekstrækt] Auszug, Ausschnitt
novel [ˈnɒvl] Roman
term [tɜːm] Begriff
to **publish** [ˈpʌblɪʃ] veröffentlichen
fictional [ˈfɪkʃənl] fiktiv
totalitarian [ˌtəʊtəlɪˈteəriən] totalitär
to **gaze** [geɪz] starren, blicken
to **contrive** [kənˈtraɪv] bewerkstelligen
beneath [bɪˈniːθ] unterhalb, unter
telescreen [ˈteliskriːn] Televisor
whisper [ˈwɪspə] Flüstern
field of vision [ˌfiːld əv ˈvɪʒn] Sichtfeld
plaque [plɑːk] Platte, Tafel
to **command** [kəˈmɑːnd] beherrschen
to **plug in on sth** [ˌplʌg ˈɪn ɒn] sich in etw einschalten
wire [ˈwaɪə] Draht
guesswork [ˈgeswɜːk] Mutmaßung, Spekulation
at any rate [ət eni ˈreɪt] auf jeden Fall
assumption [əˈsʌmpʃn] Annahme
to **overhear** [ˌəʊvəˈhɪə] belauschen, aufschnappen
darkness [ˈdɑːknəs] Dunkelheit
movement [ˈmuːvmənt] Bewegung
to **scrutinize** [ˈskruːtənaɪz] genau ansehen, überprüfen
parallel [ˈpærəlel] Parallele

page 132

CCTV (closed-circuit television) [ˌsiː siː tiː ˈviː] Videoüberwachung
CCTV camera [ˌsiː siː tiː ˈviː kæmərə] Überwachungskamera
to **be located** [bi ləʊˈkeɪtɪd] sich befinden
to **disclose** [dɪsˈkləʊz] offenlegen
campaigner [kæmˈpeɪnə] Aktivist/in
care home [ˈkeə həʊm] Pflegeheim
scheme [skiːm] Plan, Programm
invaluable [ɪnˈvæljuəbl] unschätzbar, unbezahlbar
crime detection [ˈkraɪm dɪtekʃn] Aufdecken von Straftaten
evidence [ˈevɪdəns] Beweise, Beweismittel
murder [ˈmɜːdə] Mord
footage [ˈfʊtɪdʒ] Film-/Bildmaterial
to **be a stark reminder** [bi ə ˌstɑːk rɪˈmaɪndə] etw jäh vor Augen führen, etw überdeutlich machen
potential(ly) [pəˈtenʃl] potenziell
to **monitor** [ˈmɒnɪtə] überwachen
to **recognize** [ˈrekəgnaɪz] anerkennen, begreifen
democratic [ˌdeməˈkrætɪk] demokratisch
to **threaten** [ˈθretn] bedrohen

page 134

to **differ** [ˈdɪfə] sich unterscheiden, abweichen
high-flyer [ˌhaɪ ˈflaɪə] Überflieger/in, Erfolgsmensch
to **burn out** [ˌbɜːn ˈaʊt] bis zur Erschöpfung arbeiten
to **take hold of sth** [teɪk ˈhəʊld əv] ergreifen, sich annehmen
wasteful [ˈweɪstfl] verheerend, verschwenderisch
corporate culture [ˈkɔːpərət kʌltʃə] Unternehmenskultur
to **eradicate** [ɪˈrædɪkeɪt] ausrotten, ausmerzen
catalyst [ˈkætəlɪst] Auslöser, Beschleuniger
inability [ˌɪnəˈbɪləti] Unfähigkeit
addictive [əˈdɪktɪv] abhängig machend
overwhelming [ˌəʊvəˈwelmɪŋ] überwältigend
exhaustion [ɪgˈzɔːstʃən] Erschöpfung
condition [kənˈdɪʃn] Zustand
to **result in** [rɪˈzʌltɪn] führen zu
disillusionment [ˌdɪsɪˈluːʒnmənt] Ernüchterung, hier etwa: Antriebslosigkeit
dysfunctional [dɪsˈfʌŋkʃənl] dysfunktional, abträglich
leader [ˈliːdə] Leiter/in, Führungsperson
to **tackle** [ˈtækl] bewältigen, in Angriff nehmen
to **take a step back** [ˌteɪk ə step ˈbæk] einen Schritt zurücktreten
annual(ly) [ˈænjuəl] jährlich
work pattern [ˈwɜːk pætn] Arbeitsprofil, Tätigkeit
lateral [ˈlætərəl] seitlich
lateral development [ˌlætərəl dɪˈveləpmənt] (Personalentwicklung:) neue Verantwortungsbereiche, breitgefächerte Kompetenzen
to **combat** [ˈkɒmbæt] bekämpfen
repetitive [rɪˈpetətɪv] (sich) wiederholend
routine [ruːˈtiːn] regelmäßig, laufend
mentor meeting [ˌmentə ˈmiːtɪŋ] Gespräch mit dem/der Vorgesetzten, Mitarbeitergespräch
summer hours [ˈsʌmə aʊəz] Sommerarbeitszeit
study leave [ˈstʌdi liːv] Fortbildungsurlaub

healthy ['helθi]	gesund	
exercise ['eksəsaɪz]	Bewegung, Sport	
highly ['haɪli]	sehr, äußerst	
to discount [dɪs'kaʊnt]	Rabatt gewähren	
membership ['membəʃɪp]	Mitgliedschaft	
to provide sth [prə'vaɪd]	für etw sorgen	
to insist on [ɪn'sɪst ɒn]	bestehen auf	
to stamp sth out [ˌstæmp 'aʊt]	etw ausmerzen	
need [niːd]	Notwendigkeit, Bedürfnis	
workload ['wɜːkləʊd]	Arbeitspensum	
to handle sth ['hændl]	bewältigen, erledigen	
honestly ['ɒnəstli]	ernsthaft	
expectation [ˌekspek'teɪʃn]	Erwartung	
disappointment [ˌdɪsə'pɔɪntmənt]	Enttäuschung	
to get rid of sth [ˌget 'rɪd əv]	etw loswerden	
schedule ['ʃedjuːl]	Zeitplan, Einteilung	
sideways ['saɪdweɪz]	seitlich, seitwärts	
tiredness ['taɪədnəs]	Müdigkeit	
mental ['mentl]	psychisch	
price tag ['praɪs tæg]	Preisschild	
attached [ə'tætʃt]	angeheftet, beigefügt	

UNIT 14

page 135

solar ['səʊlə]	Sonnen-, Solar-
biomass ['baɪəʊmæs]	Biomasse
fossil fuel ['fɒsl fjuːəl]	fossiler Brennstoff
geothermal power [dʒiːəʊˌθɜːml paʊə]	Erdwärme
hydro-electric power [ˌhaɪdrəʊ ɪˌlektrɪk 'paʊə]	Wasserkraft
methane ['miːθeɪn]	Methan
nuclear power [ˌnjuːkliə 'paʊə]	Kernkraft
solar power [ˌsəʊlə 'paʊə]	Sonnenenergie
tidal power [ˌtaɪdl 'paʊə]	Gezeitenkraft
wind power ['wɪnd paʊə]	Windkraft
renewable [rɪ'njuːəbl]	erneuerbar
breakdown ['breɪkdaʊn]	Zusammenbruch
to make sth up [ˌmeɪk 'ʌp]	etw ausmachen

page 136

climate ['klaɪmət]	Klima
climate change ['klaɪmət tʃeɪndʒ]	Klimawandel
angry ['æŋgri]	aufgebracht, ungehalten
man-made ['mæn meɪd]	künstlich, menschlichen Ursprungs
cause [kɔːz]	Ursache
global warming [ˌgləʊbl 'wɔːmɪŋ]	Erderwärmung
advocate ['ædvəkət]	Befürworter/in
scientist ['saɪəntɪst]	(Natur-)Wissenschaftler/in
denier [dɪ'naɪə]	Leugner/in
carbon dioxide [ˌkɑːbən daɪ'ɒksaɪd]	Kohlendioxid
carbon dioxide level [ˌkɑːbən daɪ'ɒksaɪd levl]	Kohlendioxidkonzentration, -gehalt
previously ['priːviəsli]	zuvor, vorher
variability [ˌveərɪə'bɪləti]	Schwankung, Unbeständigkeit
degree [dɪ'griː]	Grad
to try sb [traɪ]	jdn vor Gericht stellen
high crime [ˌhaɪ 'kraɪm]	Schwerverbrechen

humanity [hjuː'mænəti]	Menschheit, Menschlichkeit
coal [kəʊl]	Kohle
coal-fired ['kəʊl faɪəd]	kohlegetrieben
power plant ['paʊə plɑːnt]	Kraftwerk
to be to blame [bi tə 'bleɪm]	Schuld sein
to quote [kwəʊt]	zitieren
news anchor ['njuːz æŋkə]	Nachrichtensprecher/in
large-scale ['lɑːdʒ skeɪl]	in großem Umfang/Ausmaß
greenhouse gas [ˌgriːnhaʊs 'gæs]	Treibhausgas
to reflect [rɪ'flekt]	reflektieren
to escape [ɪ'skeɪp]	entweichen
temperature ['temprətʃə]	Temperatur

page 137

atmospheric [ˌætməs'ferɪk]	atmosphärisch, in der Atmosphäre
to pass [pɑːs]	überschreiten
beyond [bɪ'jɒnd]	jenseits, über
major ['meɪdʒə]	bedeutend, wichtig, groß
disastrous [dɪ'zɑːstrəs]	katastrophal, verheerend
unstoppable [ˌʌn'stɒpəbl]	unaufhaltsam
cyclone ['saɪkləʊn]	Wirbelsturm, Zyklon, Sturmtief
to warm [wɔːm]	sich erwärmen
ocean ['əʊʃn]	Ozean, Weltmeer
ice sheet ['aɪs ʃiːt]	Eisdecke
to melt [melt]	schmelzen, abschmelzen
sea level ['siː levl]	Meeresspiegel
island ['aɪlənd]	Insel
coastal ['kəʊstl]	Küsten-
to drown [draʊn]	ertrinken, im Meer versinken
worrying ['wʌriɪŋ]	besorgniserregend
emission [ɪ'mɪʃn]	Ausstoß, Emission
panel ['pænl]	Gremium, Ausschuss
to prepare [prɪ'peə]	(Bericht etc.) erstellen, verfassen
as long as [əz 'lɒŋ əz]	solange
co-author [ˌkəʊ 'ɔːθə]	Mitautor/in, Mitverfasser/in
economics [ˌiːkə'nɒmɪks]	Ökonomie, Wirtschaft(swissenschaft)
urgently ['ɜːdʒəntli]	dringend, nachdrücklich
carbon ['kɑːbən]	Kohlenstoff
investment [ɪn'vestmənt]	Investition
existing [ɪg'zɪstɪŋ]	bestehend, vorhanden
to commute [kə'mjuːt]	(zur Arbeit) pendeln
to pollute [pə'luːt]	(die Umwelt) verschmutzen
in turn [ɪn 'tɜːn]	wiederum
quality of life [ˌkwɒləti əv 'laɪf]	Lebensqualität
to limit ['lɪmɪt]	begrenzen, einschränken
at the same time [ət ðə ˌseɪm 'taɪm]	gleichzeitig
to encourage [ɪn'kʌrɪdʒ]	fördern
largely ['lɑːdʒli]	größtenteils, überwiegend
sceptic ['skeptɪk]	Skeptiker/in
flooding ['flʌdɪŋ]	Überschwemmung
to call for sth ['kɔːl fə]	zu etw aufrufen

page 138

oil [ɔɪl]	Öl
natural gas [ˌnætʃrəl 'gæs]	Erdgas
to power ['paʊə]	antreiben, mit Energie versorgen
by contrast [baɪ 'kɒntrɑːst]	im Gegensatz dazu, dagegen
to flood [flʌd]	überschwemmen

303

Unit word list

page 139

Head of Science [ˌhed əf ˈsaɪəns]		Fachbereichsleiter/in Naturwissenschaft
sixth-form college [ˈsɪksθ fɔːm kɒlɪdʒ]		Oberstufenzentrum, Studienkolleg
grateful [ˈɡreɪtfl]		dankbar
to specialize in sth [ˈspeʃəlaɪz ɪn]		sich auf etw spezialisieren
research [rɪˈsɜːtʃ]		Forschung
plain [pleɪn]		schlicht
freely [ˈfriːli]		ungehindert, nach Belieben
unlike [ˌʌnˈlaɪk]		anders als
power station [ˈpaʊə steɪʃn]		Kraftwerk, Elektrizitätswerk
ton [tʌn]		Tonne
pollution [pəˈluːʃn]		Umweltverschmutzung

page 140

conference [ˈkɒnfərəns]		Konferenz
journey [ˈdʒɜːni]		Reise, Fahrt
sb's take on sth [ˈteɪk ɒn]		jds Einschätzung von etw
controversial [ˌkɒntrəˈvɜːʃl]		umstritten
hydraulic [haɪˈdrɔːlɪk]		hydraulisch
to fracture [ˈfræktʃə]		brechen, aufbrechen
shale [ʃeɪl]		Schiefer
rock [rɒk]		Fels, Gestein
to inquire [ɪnˈkwaɪə]		nachfragen, sich erkundigen
to drill [drɪl]		bohren
to pump [pʌmp]		pumpen
crack [kræk]		Spalte
surface [ˈsɜːfɪs]		Oberfläche
well [wel]		Bohrloch
enthusiastic(ally) [ɪnˌθjuːziˈæstɪk]		begeistert
requirement [rɪˈkwaɪəmənt]		Bedarf
to rely on sth [rɪˈlaɪ ɒn]		sich auf etw verlassen, auf etw angewiesen sein
to light up [ˌlaɪt ˈʌp]		leuchten, aufleuchten
one by one [ˌwʌn baɪ ˈwʌn]		der Reihe nach
tunnel [ˈtʌnl]		Tunnel
nuclear power station [ˌnjuːkliə ˈpaʊə steɪʃn]		Kernkraftwerk
nuclear plant [ˌnjuːkliə ˈplɑːnt]		Kernkraftwerk
to close down [ˌkləʊz ˈdaʊn]		stilllegen
working life [ˌwɜːkɪŋ ˈlaɪf]		Betriebsdauer
barrage [ˈbærɑːʒ]		Staumauer

page 141

subsidy [ˈsʌbsədi]		Subvention
corrosion [kəˈrəʊʒn]		Korrosion, Zersetzung
cost-effective [ˌkɒst ɪˈfektɪv]		rentabel
close to [ˈkləʊs tə]		nahe bei, in der Nähe von
onshore [ˌɒnˈʃɔː]		an Land
to become annoyed [ˌbɪkʌm əˈnɔɪd]		sich ärgern, sich aufregen
wind farm [ˈwɪnd fɑːm]		Windpark
offshore [ˌɒfˈʃɔː]		auf See
to invest [ɪnˈvest]		investieren
by chance [baɪ ˈtʃɑːns]		zufällig

page 142

to opt for sth [ˈɒpt fə]		sich für etw entscheiden
to corrode [kəˈrəʊd]		korrodieren, zersetzen
vehicle [ˈviːəkl]		Fahrzeug
to turn sth on [ˌtɜːn ˈɒn]		etw an-/einschalten
structure [ˈstrʌktʃə]		Bauwerk, Konstruktion
press conference [ˈpres kɒnfərəns]		Pressekonferenz
editor [ˈedɪtə]		Redakteur/in
commercial [kəˈmɜːʃl]		gewerblich, kommerziell
planning permission [ˈplænɪŋ pəmɪʃn]		Baugenehmigung

page 143

electricity bill [ɪˌlekˈtrɪsəti bɪl]		Stromrechnung
to beg [beɡ]		flehen, eindringlich bitten
council [ˈkaʊnsl]		(Stadt-, Gemeinde-)Rat
application [ˌæplɪˈkeɪʃn]		Antrag
farmland [ˈfɑːmlænd]		Ackerland, landwirtschaftliche Nutzfläche
drilling [ˈdrɪlɪŋ]		Bohrung(en)
drilling rig [ˈdrɪlɪŋ rɪɡ]		Bohrturm
waste water [ˌweɪst ˈwɔːtə]		Abwasser
worries pl [ˈwʌriz]		Bedenken
councillor [ˈkaʊnsələ]		Ratsmitglied
to leak [liːk]		sickern, entweichen
groundwater [ˈɡraʊndwɔːtə]		Grundwasser
supplies pl [səˈplaɪz]		Vorräte, Vorkommen
tap [tæp]		Wasserhahn
on fire [ɒn ˈfaɪə]		in Flammen
concrete [ˈkɒŋkriːt]		Beton
steel [stiːl]		Stahl
well casing [ˈwel keɪsɪŋ]		Bohrlochverrohrung, Bohrlochwandung
regulation [ˌreɡjuˈleɪʃn]		Vorschrift
in return [ɪn rɪˈtɜːn]		im Gegenzug, als Ausgleich
to be required to do sth [bi rɪˈkwaɪəd tə]		etw tun müssen; verpflichtet sein, etw zu tun
community benefits pl [kəˈmjuːnəti benɪfɪts]		Zahlungen an die Gemeinde
earnings pl [ˈɜːnɪŋz]		Einnahmen, Gewinn
golf course [ˈɡɒlf kɔːs]		Golfplatz
to treat [triːt]		(Abwasser) klären
to weigh [weɪ]		abwägen
to calm [kɑːm]		beruhigen
in principle [ɪn ˈprɪnsəpl]		prinzipiell, grundsätzlich

page 144

appliance [əˈplaɪəns]		Haushaltsgerät
scrap [skræp]		Schrott
proportion [prəˈpɔːʃn]		Anteil
broken [ˈbrəʊkən]		kaputt, defekt
to fit sth with sth [fɪt]		etw mit etw ausstatten
tracking device [ˈtrækɪŋ dɪvaɪs]		Ortungsgerät
trace [treɪs]		Spur
estimate [ˈestɪmət]		Schätzung
loudspeaker [ˌlaʊdˈspiːkə]		Lautsprecher
fridge [frɪdʒ]		Kühlschrank
poisonous [ˈpɔɪzənəs]		giftig
arsenic [ˈɑːsnɪk]		Arsen
lead [led]		Blei
mercury [ˈmɜːkjəri]		Quecksilber
to forbid [fəˈbɪd]		verbieten, untersagen
to dump [dʌmp]		(Müll) (wild) abladen
toxic [ˈtɒksɪk]		giftig, Gift-
nationwide [ˈneɪʃnwaɪd]		landesweit
remaining [rɪˈmeɪnɪŋ]		übrig, verbleibend
to ship [ʃɪp]		versenden, verschiffen
to profit [ˈprɒfɪt]		profitieren
battery pack [ˈbætəri pæk]		Akku
interval [ˈɪntəvl]		(zeitlicher) Abstand
to unload [ˌʌnˈləʊd]		entladen
alarm [əˈlɑːm]		Alarmsignal
collection [kəˈlekʃn]		Abholung

to shine light on sth	[ˌʃaɪn 'laɪt ɒn]	Licht auf etw werfen
shadowy	['ʃædəʊi]	zwielichtig
customs pl	['kʌstəmz]	Zoll
powerless	['paʊələs]	machtlos, unfähig
stop	[stɒp]	Station
dubious	['djuːbiəs]	zweifelhaft
dealer	['diːlə]	Händler/in
exporter	[ɪk'spɔːtə]	Exporteur/in
wait	[weɪt]	Warten, Wartezeit
capital	['kæpɪtl]	Hauptstadt
out in the open	[ˌaʊt ɪn ði 'əʊpən]	im Freien
to pile	[paɪl]	stapeln
mud	[mʌd]	Schlamm
umbrella	[ʌm'brelə]	Regenschirm
clearance sale	['klɪərəns seɪl]	Räumungsverkauf
farther	['fɑːðə]	weiter
mark	[mɑːk]	Markierung, Zeichen
to shake sth	[ʃeɪk]	an etw rütteln
to activate	['æktɪveɪt]	aktivieren
dump	[dʌmp]	Müllhalde

page 145

hub	[hʌb]	Drehkreuz, (Verkehrs-)Knoten
forwarding agency	['fɔːwədɪŋ eɪdʒənsi]	Spedition
shipping company	['ʃɪpɪŋ kʌmpəni]	Transportunternehmen, Spediteur, Reederei
middleman	['mɪdlmən]	Zwischenhändler
value chain	['væljuː tʃeɪn]	Wertschöpfungskette
to break sth apart	[ˌbreɪk ə'pɑːt]	etw auseinandernehmen
to set fire to sth	[ˌset 'faɪə tə]	etw anzünden
insulating foam	['ɪnsjuleɪtɪŋ fəʊm]	Isolierschaum
cable	['keɪbl]	Kabel
coating	['kəʊtɪŋ]	Ummantelung, (Kabel-)Mantel
copper	['kɒpə]	Kupfer
district	['dɪstrɪkt]	Bezirk
breeding ground	['briːdɪŋ graʊnd]	Brutplatz
migratory bird	[ˌmaɪɡrətri 'bɜːd]	Zugvogel
graveyard	['ɡreɪvjɑːd]	Friedhof
to poison	['pɔɪzn]	vergiften
to gut	[ɡʌt]	ausweiden, ausschlachten
worthless (to sb)	['wɜːθləs]	wertlos (für jdn)
scrapyard	['skræpjɑːd]	Schrottplatz
mystery	['mɪstri]	Rätsel, Geheimnis

page 146

environment	[ɪn'vaɪrənmənt]	Umwelt, Umfeld
degrowth	[diːɡrəʊθ]	Wachstumsrücknahme
consumption	[kən'sʌmpʃn]	Verbrauch, Konsum
proponent	[prə'pəʊnənt]	Befürworter/in
overconsumption	[ˌəʊvəkən'sʌmpʃn]	zu hoher Verbrauch, übertriebener Konsum
mainstream	['meɪnstriːm]	etabliert
economist	[ɪ'kɒnəmɪst]	Wirtschaftswissenschaftler/in
forward	['fɔːwəd]	vorwärts, nach vorn, voran
progress	['prəʊɡres]	Fortschritt(e)
continuously	[kən'tɪnjuəsli]	fortlaufend
to earn	[ɜːn]	verdienen
to spend	[spend]	(Geld:) ausgeben
humanity	[hjuː'mænəti]	Menschheit
to live on sth	['lɪv ɒn]	sich von etw ernähren, von etw leben
ecological overshoot	[iːkəˌlɒdʒɪkl ˌəʊvə'ʃuːt]	ökologischer Überschuss
to keep doing sth	[ˌkiːp 'duːɪŋ]	weiterhin etw tun
one day	[wʌn 'deɪ]	eines Tages
to run out	[rʌn 'aʊt]	zu Ende gehen, sich erschöpfen
meat	[miːt]	Fleisch
to cut down	[kʌt 'daʊn]	(Wald:) abholzen
ecosystem	['iːkəʊsɪstəm]	Ökosystem
ecological footprint	[iːkəˌlɒdʒɪkl 'fʊtprɪnt]	ökologischer Fußabdruck
to demonstrate	['demənstreɪt]	zeigen
attempt	[ə'tempt]	Versuch
to sustain	[sə'steɪn]	ertragen, erleiden, aushalten
to consume	[kən'sjuːm]	verbrauchen, konsumieren
excess	[ɪk'ses]	Überschuss
to accomplish	[ə'kʌmplɪʃ]	erreichen, vollbringen
urban garden	[ˌɜːbən 'ɡɑːdn]	Stadtgarten
sharing economy	[ˌʃeərɪŋ ɪ'kɒnəmi]	Ökonomie des Teilens
possession	[pə'zeʃən]	Besitz(tum)
to remove	[rɪ'muːv]	entfernen
to mend	[mend]	reparieren, flicken, ausbessern
gadget	['ɡædʒɪt]	Gerät
to convince	[kən'vɪns]	überzeugen
to embrace sth	[ɪm'breɪs]	etw annehmen, begrüßen
sufficiency	[sə'fɪʃnsi]	Hinlänglichkeit, hinreichende Menge und Qualität
to scale down	[ˌskeɪl 'daʊn]	reduzieren, senken
to be prepared to do	[bi prɪ'peəd]	bereit sein, zu tun

UNIT 15

page 147

cactus	['kæktəs]	Kaktus
drought	[draʊt]	Dürre
over-exploitation	[ˌəʊvər eksplɔɪ'teɪʃn]	Raubbau, übermäßiger Abbau
stork	[stɔːk]	Storch
famine	['fæmɪn]	Hungersnot

page 148

to be equivalent to sth	[bi ɪ'kwɪvələnt tə]	einer Sache entsprechen
crop	[krɒp]	Nutzpflanze, Feldfrucht
pastureland	['pɑːstʃəlænd]	Weideland
to hit	[hɪt]	erreichen
crop production	['krɒp prədʌkʃn]	Pflanzenproduktion, pflanzliche Erzeugung
to demand	[dɪ'mɑːnd]	nachfragen, verlangen
rich	[rɪtʃ]	(Nahrung) gehaltvoll, reichhaltig
to succeed	[sək'siːd]	erfolgreich sein, Erfolg haben
diet	['daɪət]	Ernährung, Kost
vital	['vaɪtl]	lebensnotwendig, unerlässlich

Unit word list

to **clear** [klɪə]	räumen, roden	to **become extinct** [bɪˌkʌm ɪkˈstɪŋkt]	aussterben
prairie [ˈpreəri]	Prärie	to **breed** [briːd]	züchten
forest [ˈfɒrɪst]	Wald	**pre-historic** [ˌpriːhɪˈstɒrɪk]	prähistorisch
ice-free [ˈaɪs friː]	eisfrei	**selective** [sɪˈlektɪv]	selektiv
agriculture [ˈægrɪkʌltʃə]	Landwirtschaft	**breeding** [ˈbriːdɪŋ]	Zucht, Züchtung
species [ˈspiːʃiːz]	(Biologie:) Art	**feature** [ˈfiːtʃə]	Merkmal, Eigenschaft
to **store** [stɔː]	speichern	to **aim at sth** [ˈeɪm ət]	etw anstreben
catastrophe [kəˈtæstrəfi]	Katastrophe	**wool** [wʊl]	Wolle
square mile [ˈskweə maɪl]	Quadratmeile	**sheep** [ʃiːp]	Schaf
ice-covered [ˈaɪs kʌvəd]	eisbedeckt	**resistance** [rɪˈzɪstəns]	Widerstandsfähigkeit, Resistenz
undeveloped [ˌʌndɪˈveləpt]	(Land:) unbebaut	**herd** [hɜːd]	Herde
cropland [ˈkrɒplænd]	Ackerland	**crop** [krɒp]	Ernte
to **plant** [plɑːnt]	pflanzen, anpflanzen	to **modify** [ˈmɒdɪfaɪ]	modifizieren
page 149		**genetic** [dʒəˈnetɪk]	genetisch
share [ʃeə]	Anteil	**seed** [siːd]	Samen, Saatgut
fresh water [ˌfreʃ ˈwɔːtə]	Süßwasser	**laboratory** [ləˈbɒrətri]	Labor
lake [leɪk]	(Binnen-)See	**by laboratory design** [baɪ ləˌbɒrətri dɪˈzaɪn]	im Labor geplant
wetland [ˈwetlənd]	Feuchtgebiet, Sumpfgebiet	**herbicide** [ˈhɜːbɪsaɪd]	Unkrautvernichtungsmittel
acre [ˈeɪkə]	Morgen (ca. 4047 qm)	**spray** [spreɪ]	Spritzmittel
variety [vəˈraɪəti]	(Pflanzen-)Sorte	**weed** [wiːd]	Unkraut
greatly [ˈgreɪtli]	erheblich	**pollen** [ˈpɒlən]	Blütenstaub, Pollen
farm chemicals pl [ˈfɑːm kemɪklz]	Landwirtschaftschemikalien	to **fertilize** [ˈfɜːtəlaɪz]	befruchten
polluting [pəˈluːtɪŋ]	umweltschädlich	**in no time** [ɪn ˈnəʊ taɪm]	im Nu
fertilizer [ˈfɜːtəlaɪzə]	Dünger, Düngemittel	**resistant to sth** [rɪˈzɪstənt tə]	resistent gegen etw
precious [ˈpreʃəs]	kostbar	**chemical control** (of pests) [ˌkemɪkl kənˈtrəʊl]	Schädlingsbekämpfung(smittel)
irrigation [ˌɪrɪˈgeɪʃn]	Bewässerung	**downside** [ˈdaʊnsaɪd]	Nachteil
biofuel [ˌbaɪəʊˈfjuːəl]	Biokraftstoff	**hydroponics** [ˌhaɪdrəʊˈpɒnɪks]	Hydrokultur
grain [greɪn]	Getreide		
to **cut** [kʌt]	reduzieren, einschränken	**page 153**	
use-by date [ˈjuːs baɪ deɪt]	Haltbarkeitsdatum	**thick** [θɪk]	dick, stark
cooperation [kəʊˌɒpəˈreɪʃn]	Zusammenarbeit, Zusammenwirken	to **absorb** [əbˈsɔːb]	aufnehmen, absorbieren
		flow [fləʊ]	Strom, Fluss
page 150		to **take off** [ˌteɪk ˈɒf]	(Flugzeug:) abheben, starten
destruction [dɪˈstrʌkʃn]	Zerstörung	**passenger** [ˈpæsɪndʒə]	Passagier
equals [ˈiːkwəlz]	gleich	to **take off** [ˌteɪk ˈɒf]	(Produkt:) gut anlaufen, gut ankommen
midday [ˌmɪdˈdeɪ]	Mittag	to **take up space** [ˌteɪk ʌp ˈspeɪs]	Platz einnehmen
to **multiply** [ˈmʌltɪplaɪ]	multiplizieren	**vertical(ly)** [ˈvɜːtɪkl]	senkrecht, vertikal
junior [ˈdʒuːniə]	Jung-, Nachwuchs-	to **float** [fləʊt]	(auf dem Wasser) treiben
dawn [dɔːn]	Morgendämmerung		
garment [ˈgɑːmənt]	Kleidungsstück	**page 154**	
		to **trick sb into doing sth** [trɪk]	jdn (mit einer List) dazu bringen, etw zu tun
page 151		to **take sth on** [ˌteɪk ˈɒn]	(Aufgabe) übernehmen
graphic [ˈgræfɪk]	Grafik	to **take sb on** [ˌteɪk ˈɒn]	es mit jdm aufnehmen, gegen jdn antreten
to **join sth** [dʒɔɪn]	etw (miteinander) verbinden	to **hunt** [hʌnt]	jagen
divorce [dɪˈvɔːs]	Scheidung	**protein** [ˈprəʊtiːn]	Eiweiß, Protein
to **work sth out** [ˌwɜːk ˈaʊt]	etw ausrechnen	**fishing** [ˈfɪʃɪŋ]	Fischerei, Befischung
utility bills pl [juːˈtɪləti bɪlz]	Rechnungen für Versorgungsleistungen	to **maintain stocks** [meɪnˌteɪn ˈstɒks]	den Bestand erhalten
food pantry AE [ˈfuːd pæntri]	Tafel, karitative Essensausgabe	**population** [ˌpɒpjuˈleɪʃn]	(Biologie:) Population
parcel [ˈpɑːsl]	Paket	to **crash** [kræʃ]	abstürzen, zusammenbrechen
to **take the point** [ˌteɪk ðə ˈpɔɪnt]	den Standpunkt verstehen	**severe** [sɪˈvɪə]	ernst, schwer
		diamond-shaped [ˈdaɪəmənd ʃeɪpt]	rautenförmig
page 152		**cage** [keɪdʒ]	Käfig
GM (genetically modified) [ˌdʒiː ˈem]	genmanipuliert	**unpolluted** [ˌʌnpəˈluːtɪd]	unverschmutzt
to **fear** [fɪə]	fürchten		
selection [sɪˈlekʃn]	Auslese, Selektion		
to **adapt (to sth)** [əˈdæpt]	sich (an etw) anpassen		
adaptation [ˌædæpˈteɪʃn]	Anpassung, Anpassungsleistung		
gene [dʒiːn]	Gen		
to **pass sth to sb** [ˈpɑːs tə]	jdm etw weiterreichen		
to **reproduce** [ˌriːprəˈdjuːs]	sich fortpflanzen		

page 155

dome	[dəʊm]	Kuppel
horizontal(ly)	[ˌhɒrɪˈzɒntl]	waagrecht, horizontal
turn	[tɜːn]	Runde, Umdrehung
running cost	[ˈrʌnɪŋ kɒst]	Betriebskosten
frame	[freɪm]	Rahmen
container	[kənˈteɪnə]	Behälter
shelf, shelves	[ʃelf, ʃelfvz]	Regal, Regale
surprisingly	[səˈpraɪzɪŋli]	erstaunlicherweise
light bulb	[ˈlaɪt bʌlb]	Glühbirne
hectare	[ˈhekteə]	Hektar
to fail	[feɪl]	ausfallen
food security	[ˈfuːd sɪkjʊərəti]	Ernährungssicherung
proposal	[prəˈpəʊzl]	Vorschlag
redevelopment	[ˌriːdɪˈveləpmənt]	Sanierung
splendid	[ˈsplendɪd]	prächtig
turbine	[ˈtɜːbaɪn]	Turbine
hall	[hɔːl]	Saal, Halle
Grade 1 building	[ˌgreɪd ˈwʌn bɪldɪŋ]	denkmalgeschütztes Gebäude
to pull down	[ˌpʊl ˈdaʊn]	(Gebäude) abreißen
to redevelop	[ˌriːdɪˈveləp]	sanieren
committee	[kəˈmɪti]	Ausschuss, Kommission, Komitee
chairperson	[ˈtʃeəpɜːsn]	Vorsitzende/r

page 156

scale	[skeɪl]	Ausmaß, Umfang
to depend on sth	[dɪˈpend ɒn]	von etw abhängen, auf etw angewiesen sein
cassava	[kəˈsɑːvə]	Maniok, Kassava
pest	[pest]	Schädling
diversity	[daɪˈvɜːsəti]	Vielfalt
to deter	[dɪˈtɜː]	abschrecken, abhalten
to certify	[ˈsɜːtɪfaɪ]	zertifizieren
credit	[ˈkredɪt]	Verdienst
undergraduate	[ˌʌndəˈgrædʒuət]	Student/in (vor dem ersten akad. Grad)
to lurch	[lɜːtʃ]	schlingern, taumeln
steep	[stiːp]	steil
rutted	[ˈrʌtɪd]	zerfurcht, ausgefahren
pickup	[ˈpɪkʌp]	Pritschenwagen
to green	[griːn]	begrünen
to drift	[drɪft]	wehen
slope	[sləʊp]	Hang
forested	[ˈfɒrɪstɪd]	bewaldet
brick	[brɪk]	Ziegel
partially	[ˈpɑːʃəli]	teilweise
to plaster	[ˈplɑːstə]	verputzen
corrugated metal	[ˌkɒrəgeɪtɪd ˈmetl]	Wellblech
short-sleeved	[ˌʃɔːt ˈsliːvd]	kurzärmlig
blouse	[blaʊz]	Bluse
wraparound skirt	[ˌræpəraʊnd ˈskɜːt]	Wickelrock
porch	[pɔːtʃ]	Veranda
to raise	[reɪz]	(Pflanzen) anbauen
passion fruit	[ˈpæʃn fruːt]	Passionsfrucht
spinach	[ˈspɪnɪtʃ]	Spinat
leafy vegetable	[ˌliːfi ˈvedʒtəbl]	Blattgemüse
backup	[ˈbækʌp]	Ersatz, Reserve
strategic(ally)	[strəˈtiːdʒɪk]	strategisch
row	[rəʊ]	Reihe
sunflower	[ˈsʌnflaʊə]	Sonnenblume
whitefly	[ˈwaɪtflaɪ]	Mottenschildlaus

compost	[ˈkɒmpɒst]	Kompost
runoff	[ˈrʌnɒf]	Abfluss, abfließendes Wasser
to contaminate	[kənˈtæmɪneɪt]	verunreinigen, kontaminieren
stream	[striːm]	Bach, Fließgewässer
life-altering	[ˈlaɪf ɔːltərɪŋ]	lebensverändernd
liberation	[lɪbəˈreɪʃn]	Befreiung
debt	[det]	Schulden
crippling	[ˈkrɪplɪŋ]	lähmend, mörderisch
expense	[ɪkˈspens]	Kosten, Aufwand
per capita income	[pə ˌkæpɪtə ˈɪnkʌm]	Pro-Kopf-Einkommen

page 157

skeptical AE	[ˈskeptɪkl]	skeptisch
to be aware of sth	[bi əˈweər ɒv]	sich einer Sache bewusst sein, etw kennen
sweeping views pl	[ˌswiːpɪŋ ˈvjuːz]	atemberaubende Ausblicke, umwerfende Sicht
to cultivate	[ˈkʌltɪveɪt]	bewirtschaften
terraced	[ˈterəst]	terrassiert
scarred	[skɑːd]	vernarbt, gezeichnet
to erode	[ɪˈrəʊd]	erodieren
terrace	[ˈterəs]	Terrasse
to retain	[rɪˈteɪn]	zurückhalten, behalten, bewahren

page 158

origin	[ˈɒrɪdʒɪn]	Herkunft
to settle	[ˈsetl]	sich niederlassen
pull factor	[ˈpʊl fæktə]	etwa: Anreizwirkung, Anziehungsgrund
fertile	[ˈfɜːtaɪl]	fruchtbar
wealth	[welθ]	Wohlstand
political security	[pəˌlɪtɪkl sɪˈkjʊərəti]	politische Stabilität/Sicherheit
natural disaster	[ˌnætʃrəl dɪˈzɑːstə]	Naturkatastrophe
supply	[səˈplaɪ]	Versorgung, Vorrat
vast	[vɑːst]	enorm, riesig
media coverage	[ˈmiːdiə kʌvərɪdʒ]	Berichterstattung
to make up	[ˌmeɪk ˈʌp]	ausmachen, bilden
to be at risk of/from sth	[bi ət ˈrɪsk ɒv]	gefährdet sein durch etw, bedroht sein von etw
civilian	[səˈvɪliən]	Zivilist/in
frequent	[ˈfriːkwənt]	ständig, regelmäßig
total	[ˈtəʊtl]	Gesamt-
constitution	[ˌkɒnstɪˈtjuːʃn]	Verfassung
court system	[ˈkɔːt sɪstəm]	Gerichtsbarkeit
election	[ɪˈlekʃn]	Wahl
to hold elections	[ˌhəʊld ɪˈlekʃns]	eine Wahl abhalten
elite	[eɪˈliːt]	Elite
to be subject to sth	[bi ˈsʌbdʒɪkt tə]	etw unterliegen
forced labour	[ˌfɔːst ˈleɪbə]	Zwangsarbeit
to lead (to)	[liːd]	führen (zu)
prison	[ˈprɪzn]	Gefängnis
hunger	[ˈhʌŋgə]	Hunger
killing	[ˈkɪlɪŋ]	das Töten
to contribute	[kənˈtrɪbjuːt]	beitragen
insurgency	[ɪnˈsɜːdʒənsi]	Aufstand
affected	[əˈfektɪd]	betroffen
fighting	[ˈfaɪtɪŋ]	Kampf
root cause	[ˈruːt kɔːz]	Grundursache
suffering	[ˈsʌfərɪŋ]	Leiden

307

Unit word list

drought [draʊt]		Dürre
crop [krɒp]		Getreide
to leave [liːv]		zurücklassen, hinterlassen
displaced [dɪsˈpleɪsd]		vertrieben
case [keɪs]		Fall
massacre [ˈmæsəkə]		Massaker
to visualize [ˈvɪʒuəlaɪz]		verbildlichen
push factor [ˈpʊʃ fæktə]		*etwa:* Vertreibungsursache

UNIT 16
page 159

compass [ˈkʌmpəs]	Kompass
contraceptive [ˌkɒntrəˈseptɪv]	Verhütungsmittel
internal combustion engine [ɪnˌtɜːnl kəmˈbʌstʃən endʒɪn]	Verbrennungsmotor
printing press [ˈprɪntɪŋ pres]	Druckerpresse
refrigeration [rɪˌfrɪdʒəˈreɪʃn]	Kühlung, Kälteerzeugung
wheel [wiːl]	Rad

page 160

spread [spred]	Verbreitung, Ausbreitung
to type in [ˌtaɪp ˈɪn]	eintippen
to hit [hɪt]	(Taste) drücken
transaction [trænˈzækʃn]	(Geschäfts-)Vorgang, Transaktion
additional(ly) [əˈdɪʃənl]	zusätzlich
to fail [feɪl]	versagen
dramatic(ally) [drəˈmætɪk]	dramatisch
colonial power [kəˌləʊniəl ˈpaʊə]	Kolonialmacht
to lay cables [ˌleɪ ˈkeɪblz]	Kabel verlegen
landline [ˈlændlaɪn]	Festnetz(-)
highway *AE* [ˈhaɪweɪ]	Autobahn
textbook [ˈtekstbʊk]	Lehrbuch
jungle [ˈdʒʌŋgl]	Dschungel
savannah [səˈvænə]	Savanne
button [ˈbʌtn]	Knopf, Button
merchant [ˈmɜːtʃənt]	Händler/in
to access sth [ˈækses]	auf etw zugreifen
harvest [ˈhɑːvɪst]	Ernte
veterinarian [ˌvetərɪˈneərɪən]	Tierarzt/-ärztin, Veterinär/in
substitute [ˈsʌbstɪtjuːt]	Ersatz
to keep watch over sb [ˌkiːp ˈwɒtʃ əʊvə]	über jdn wachen, jdn beobachten
to be in power [bi ɪn ˈpaʊə]	an der Macht sein
cutting-edge [ˌkʌtɪŋ ˈedʒ]	Spitzen-, auf dem neusten Stand
limitation [ˌlɪmɪˈteɪʃn]	Einschränkung
obstacle [ˈɒbstəkl]	Hindernis
enabled [ɪˈneɪbld]	fähig
to coax sth out of sth [kəʊks]	etw aus etw herausholen
trajectory [trəˈdʒektəri]	Flugbahn, Weg
breed [briːd]	Rasse
calving [ˈkɑːvɪŋ]	Kalben
feed [fiːd]	Futter
fertility cycle [fəˈtɪləti saɪkl]	Fruchtbarkeitszyklus
to practise [ˈpræktɪs]	praktizieren
remote [rɪˈməʊt]	entlegen
diagnosis, diagnoses [ˌdaɪəgˈnəʊsɪs, ˌdaɪəgˈnəʊsiːs]	Diagnose, Diagnosen

page 161

epidemic [ˌepɪˈdemɪk]	Epidemie, Seuche
influential [ˌɪnfluˈenʃl]	einflussreich
consulting firm [kənˈsʌltɪŋ fɜːm]	Beratungsfirma
satisfied [ˈsætɪsfaɪd]	zufrieden(gestellt)
ranking [ˈræŋkɪŋ]	Rangliste
governance [ˈgʌvnəns]	Regierungshandeln
leadership [ˈliːdəʃɪp]	Führung
to award sth to sb [əˈwɔːd]	jdm etw verleihen, jdm etw zuerkennen
commendable [kəˈmendəbl]	vorbildlich
in a row [ɪn ə ˈrəʊ]	nacheinander
worthy of sth [ˈwɜːði əv]	einer Sache würdig
primarily [praɪˈmerəli]	vorrangig, hauptsächlich
civil society [ˌsɪvl səˈsaɪəti]	Bürgergesellschaft
border customs officer [ˌbɔːdə ˈkʌstəmz ɒfɪsə]	(Grenz-)Zollbeamte/beamtin
to extort [ɪkˈstɔːt]	erpressen, abnötigen
to pressure [ˈpreʃə]	unter Druck setzen
tribe [traɪb]	Stamm
to overcome [ˌəʊvəˈkʌm]	bewältigen, überwinden
isolated [ˈaɪsəleɪtɪd]	abgeschottet, abgeschieden, isoliert
to sow [səʊ]	säen
discord [ˈdɪskɔːd]	Zwietracht
commerce [ˈkɒmɜːs]	Handel
mid-century [ˌmɪd ˈsentʃəri]	Jahrhundertmitte
IT developer [ˌaɪ ˈtiː dɪˈveləpə]	IT-Entwickler/in

page 162

addition [əˈdɪʃn]	Hinzufügung
convention [kənˈvenʃn]	Übereinkunft, Gepflogenheit, Konvention
to speak up [ˌspiːk ˈʌp]	lauter sprechen
to answer the phone [ˌɑːnsə ðə ˈfəʊn]	ans Telefon gehen

page 163

case [keɪs]	Koffer
trainers *pl* [ˈtreɪnəz]	Turnschuhe
for ages [fər ˈeɪdʒɪz]	ewig, eine Ewigkeit
library [ˈlaɪbrəri]	Bibliothek, Bücherei
at one time [ət ˌwʌn ˈtaɪm]	gleichzeitig
comprehensive school [kɒmprɪˈhensɪv skuːl]	Gesamtschule
to confiscate [ˈkɒnfɪskeɪt]	beschlagnahmen, konfiszieren

page 164

artificial intelligence [ˌɑːtɪˌfɪʃl ɪnˈtelɪdʒəns]	künstliche Intelligenz
aim [eɪm]	Absicht, Ziel, Zweck
scary [ˈskeəri]	gruselig, schaurig
tempting [ˈtemptɪŋ]	verlockend
to dismiss sth as sth [dɪsˈmɪs]	etw als etw abtun
notion [ˈnəʊʃn]	Vorstellung, Auffassung
to point to sth [ˈpɔɪnt tə]	auf etw hindeuten
driverless [ˈdraɪvələs]	führerlos
civilization [ˌsɪvəlaɪˈzeɪʃn]	Zivilisation
to magnify [ˈmægnɪfaɪ]	vergrößern, verstärken
eradication [ɪˌrædɪˈkeɪʃn]	Ausrottung
military [ˈmɪlətri]	Militär
autonomous [ɔːˈtɒnəməs]	autonom
superhuman [ˌsuːpəˈhjuːmən]	übermenschlich
to outsmart [ˌaʊtˈsmɑːt]	überlisten, austricksen

308

to manipulate [məˈnɪpjuleɪt]	manipulieren	special committee [ˌspeʃl kəˈmɪti]	Sonderausschuss
institute [ˈɪnstɪtjuːt]	Institut	representative [ˌreprɪˈzentətɪv]	Repräsentant/in, Abgeordnete/r
vastness [ˈvɑːstnəs]	unermessliche Weite	pressures pl [ˈpreʃəz]	Belastungen
universe [ˈjuːnɪvɜːs]	Universum	robot [ˈrəʊbɒt]	Roboter
The best is yet to come. [ðə ˌbest ɪs jet tə ˈkʌm]	Das Beste kommt noch. Die besten Zeiten stehen uns noch bevor.	domestic [dəˈmestɪk]	heimisch, Inlands-
meaningful [ˈmiːnɪŋfl]	wichtig, bedeutend, sinnstiftend	to declare [dɪˈkleə]	verkünden

page 168

robotics [rəʊˈbɒtɪks]	Robotertechnik
dishwasher [ˈdɪʃwɒʃə]	Spülmaschine
to load the dishwasher [ˌləʊd ðə ˈdɪʃwɒʃə]	die Spülmaschine einräumen
to unveil [ˌʌnˈveɪl]	enthüllen, vorstellen
to manipulate [məˈnɪpjuleɪt]	handhaben, bedienen
unfamiliar [ˌʌnfəˈmɪliə]	unbekannt, ungewohnt
humanlike [ˈhjuːmənlaɪk]	menschenähnlich
grasp [grɑːsp]	Griff
outing [ˈaʊtɪŋ]	Ausflug, Ausfahrt
depth [depθ]	(räumliche) Tiefe
wrist [rɪst]	Handgelenk
to calculate [ˈkælkjuleɪt]	berechnen
to grasp [grɑːsp]	greifen, ergreifen
novel [ˈnɒvl]	neu, neuartig
robotic [rəʊˈbɒtɪk]	Roboter-
obstruction [əbˈstrʌkʃn]	Hindernis
to go for sth [ˈgəʊ fə]	etw wählen, etw wagen
collaborator [kəˈlæbəreɪtə]	Mitarbeiter/in
ambitious [æmˈbɪʃəs]	ehrgeizig
a bunch of [əˈbʌntʃ əv]	eine Menge
to scatter [ˈskætə]	verteilen, verstreuen
set [set]	Menge
to figure out [ˌfɪgər ˈaʊt]	herausfinden
to assign sb sth [əˈsaɪn]	jdm etw zuweisen, jdn mit etw beauftragen
duty [ˈdjuːti]	Aufgabe, Pflicht
necessity [nəˈsesəti]	Notwendigkeit
manipulative [məˈnɪpjələtɪv]	manipulativ
faculty [ˈfæklti]	Fähigkeit
cutlery [ˈkʌtləri]	Besteck
fiddly [ˈfɪdli]	knifflig, fummelig
symmetrical [sɪˈmetrɪkl]	symmetrisch
to represent [ˌreprɪˈzent]	vertreten, repräsentieren
airborne drone [ˌeəbɔːn ˈdrəʊn]	Flugdrohne
novelty [ˈnɒvlti]	Neues, Neuartiges
to perform sth [pəˈfɔːm]	etw ausführen, etw durchführen
alongside [əˌlɒŋˈsaɪd]	neben
uncertainty [ʌnˈsɜːtnti]	Ungewissheit

page 169

unstructured [ʌnˈstrʌktʃəd]	unstrukturiert
discipline [ˈdɪsəplɪn]	Disziplin
mechanical engineering [mɪˌkænɪkl ˌendʒɪˈnɪərɪŋ]	Maschinenbau
electrical engineering [ɪˌlektrɪkl ˌendʒɪˈnɪərɪŋ]	Elektrotechnik
unexpected [ˌʌnɪkˈspektɪd]	unerwartet
setback [ˈsetbæk]	Rückschlag
to complicate [ˈkɒmplɪkeɪt]	komplizieren
pinkie [ˈpɪŋki]	kleiner Finger
to approach sth [əˈprəʊtʃ]	sich einer Sache nähern
to be keen to do sth [bi ˈkiːn tə]	etw unbedingt tun wollen
to transfer [trænsˈfɜː]	übergeben, weitergeben
bi-manual [ˌbaɪˈmænjuəl]	beidhändig

page 165

outcome [ˈaʊtkʌm]	Ergebnis, Resultat
superior [suːˈpɪəriə]	überlegen
alien [ˈeɪliən]	außerirdisch
to devote [dɪˈvəʊt]	widmen
industrialist [ɪnˈdʌstriəlɪst]	Industrielle/r
general [ˈdʒenrəl]	General
to reap the benefits [ˌriːp ðə ˈbenɪfɪts]	die Früchte ernten, die Vorteile nutzen

page 166

to enjoy oneself [ɪnˈdʒɔɪ wʌnself]	sich (gut) amüsieren
vase [vɑːz]	Vase
missing [ˈmɪsɪŋ]	vermisst
test drive [ˈtest draɪv]	Testfahrt
road testing [ˈrəʊd testɪŋ]	Fahrversuche, Fahrerprobung, Straßentests
test track [ˈtest træk]	Teststrecke
to perform [pəˈfɔːm]	(leistungsmäßig) abschneiden
failure [ˈfeɪljə]	Ausfall, Defekt
(car) crash [kræʃ]	Autounfall
human error [ˌhjuːmən ˈerə]	menschliches Versagen
property damage [ˈprɒpəti dæmɪdʒ]	Sachschaden, Sachschäden
association [əˌsəʊsiˈeɪʃn]	Verband, Vereinigung
freeway AE [ˈfriːweɪ]	Autobahn
smooth(ly) [smuːð]	reibungslos
to speed up [ˌspiːd ˈʌp]	beschleunigen
to slow down [ˌsləʊ ˈdaʊn]	bremsen
tailback [ˈteɪlbæk]	Rückstau
gallon [ˈgælən]	Gallone (= 3,78 l in den USA)
service station [ˈsɜːvɪs steɪʃn]	Tankstelle

page 167

to suffer from sth [ˈsʌfə frəm]	unter etw zu leiden haben
in-car entertainment [ˌɪn kɑːr entəˈteɪnmənt]	Unterhaltungselektronik im Auto
operator [ˈɒpəreɪtə]	Betreiber/in
city planner [ˈsɪti plænə]	Stadtplaner/in
emergency service [ɪˈmɜːdʒənsi sɜːvɪs]	Notfalldienst
accident and emergency department (A&E) [ˌæksɪdənt ənd ɪˈmɜːdʒənsi dɪpɑːtmənt]	Notaufnahme
legislature [ˈledʒɪsleɪtʃə]	Gesetzgebung

309

Unit word list

to **lack** sth [læk]	etw nicht haben	**reception** [rɪˈsepʃn]	Empfang
sense of touch [ˌsens əf ˈtʌtʃ]	Tastsinn	**handout** [ˈhændaʊt]	Arbeitsblatt
tactile sensing [ˌtæktaɪl ˈsensɪŋ]	Tastempfinden	**refreshment** [rɪˈfreʃmənt]	Erfrischung
sufficient [səˈfɪʃnt]	ausreichend, hinreichend	**name tag** [ˈneɪm tæg]	Namensschild
to **operate** [ˈɒpəreɪt]	tätig sein	**place card** [ˈpleɪs kɑːd]	Platzkarte, Tischkarte
enthusiastic about sth [ɪnˌθjuːziˈæstɪk əbaʊt]	von etw begeistert	to **leak** [liːk]	auslaufen
acronym [ˈækrənɪm]	Akronym, Abkürzung	to **dry out** [ˌdraɪ ˈaʊt]	austrocknen
homage [ˈhɒmɪdʒ]	Huldigung, Hommage	**pad** [pæd]	Notizblock
flaxen-haired [ˌflæksn ˈheəd]	strohblond, flachsblond	to **type** sth **up** [ˌtaɪp ˈʌp]	etw (am Computer) formulieren, etw ausarbeiten
to **chuckle** [ˈtʃʌkl]	kichern, schmunzeln	**agenda** [əˈdʒendə]	Tagesordnung
unpredictable [ˌʌnprɪˈdɪktəbl]	launenhaft, unkalkulierbar	**on** sb's **behalf** [ɒn bɪˈhɑːf]	in jds Namen
		item [ˈaɪtəm]	Tagesordnungspunkt

page 170

sensor [ˈsensə]	Sensor		
to **locate** sb/sth [ləʊˈkeɪt]	jdn/etw finden		
occupied [ˈɒkjupaɪd]	besetzt		
map [mæp]	Karte		
unoccupied [ˌʌnˈɒkjupaɪd]	unbesetzt		
to **explore** [ɪkˈsplɔː]	erkunden, erforschen		
internet of things (IoT) [ˌɪntənet əv ˈθɪŋz]	das Internet der Dinge		
real-time [ˌriːəl ˈtaɪm]	Echtzeit-		
to **move** [muːv]	bewegen		
ad hoc [ˌæd ˈhɒk]	sofort, spontan		
interaction [ˌɪntərˈækʃən]	Einwirkung, Interaktion, Zusammenspiel		
welcome [ˈwelkəm]	willkommen, gewollt		
motion sensor [ˈməʊʃn sensə]	Bewegungssensor		
to **sense** [sens]	erkennen, bemerken		
to **kick out** [ˌkɪk ˈaʊt]	rausschmeißen		
space [speɪs]	Raum, Platz		
spaceship [ˈspeɪsʃɪp]	Raumschiff		
light-hearted [ˌlaɪt ˈhɑːtɪd]	scherzhaft, zwanglos		
sinister [ˈsɪnɪstə]	unheimlich		
to **breed** [briːd]	ausbrüten		
resentment [rɪˈzentmənt]	Ärger, Missgunst		
clash [klæʃ]	Konflikt, Streit		
to **generate** [ˈdʒenəreɪt]	generieren		
cloud [klaʊd]	Wolke, Datenwolke		
record [ˈrekɔːd]	Aufzeichnung		
convenience [kənˈviːniəns]	Komfort, Bequemlichkeit		
to **add up** [ˌæd ˈʌp]	(sich) addieren		
disadvantage [ˌdɪsədˈvɑːntɪdʒ]	Nachteil		
invasive [ɪnˈveɪsɪv]	in die Privatsphäre eingreifend		
viewpoint [ˈvjuːpɔɪnt]	Standpunkt		

JOB SKILLS 4

page 171

email exchange [ˈiːmeɪl ɪksˌtʃeɪndʒ]	E-Mail-Korrespondenz
initial [ɪˈnɪʃl]	erste/r/s
to **attend** sth [əˈtend]	an etw teilnehmen
member of staff [ˌmembər əv ˈstɑːf]	Mitarbeiter/in
to **get to know** sb [ˌget tə ˈnəʊ]	jdn kennenlernen
in good time [ɪn ˌgʊd ˈtaɪm]	rechtzeitig

page 172

projector [prəˈdʒektə]	Beamer

page 173

break [breɪk]	Pause
gossip [ˈgɒsɪp]	Klatsch, Tratsch
taboo [təˈbuː]	Tabu
chilly [ˈtʃɪli]	kühl
section [ˈsekʃn]	Abteilung
to **get down to business** [get ˌdaʊn tə ˈbɪznəs]	zur Sache kommen

page 174

millennium [mɪˈleniəm]	Jahrtausend
talk [tɔːk]	Vortrag
to **customize** [ˈkʌstəmaɪz]	auf den Kundenbedarf zuschneiden
to **near** [nɪə]	sich nähern
focus [ˈfəʊkəs]	Schwerpunkt
to **distribute** [dɪˈstrɪbjuːt]	verteilen, austeilen
to **conclude** [kənˈkluːd]	abschließend
bit [bɪt]	Teil

BUSINESS TOPIC 1

page 175

personalized [ˈpɜːsənəlaɪzd]	personalisiert
to **suit** [suːt]	passen für/zu
personalization [ˌpɜːsənəlaɪˈzeɪʃən]	Personalisierung
to **aim to do** sth [eɪm]	bemüht sein, etw zu tun
customer experience [ˈkʌstəmə ɪkˈspɪəriəns]	Kundenerlebnis
to **give preference to** sth [ˌgɪv ˈprefərəns]	etw den Vorzug geben
to **build a relationship** [ˌbɪld ə rɪˈleɪʃənʃɪp]	eine Beziehung herstellen
key [kiː]	Schlüssel-
improvement [ɪmˈpruːvmənt]	Verbesserung
loyalty [ˈlɔɪəlti]	Treue
likely [ˈlaɪkli]	wahrscheinlich
to **continue to do** sth [kənˈtɪnjuː]	weiterhin etw tun
view [vjuː]	Ansicht, Bild
to **provide** [prəˈvaɪd]	bereitstellen, liefern
invasion [ɪnˈveɪʒən]	Eindringen
impression [ɪmˈpreʃən]	Eindruck
to **invade** [ɪnˈveɪd]	eindringen
notably [ˈnəʊtəbli]	besonders
retailer [ˈriːteɪlə]	Händler
to **examine** [ɪgˈzæmɪn]	untersuchen
related [rɪˈleɪtɪd]	ähnlich
to **recommend** [ˌrekəˈmend]	empfehlen
comparable [ˈkɒmpərəbəl]	vergleichbar
especially [ɪˈspeʃəli]	besonders
therefore [ˈðeəfɔː]	deshalb
special offer [ˌspeʃl ˈɒfə]	Sonderangebot

upcoming [ˈʌpkʌmɪŋ]	bevorstehend, anstehend	identification [aɪˌdentɪfɪˈkeɪʃn]	Ausweis
tempted [ˈtemptɪd]	versucht	to apply [əˈplaɪ]	*(Make-up:)* auftragen
bargain [ˈbɑːgɪn]	Sonderangebot, Schnäppchen	inappropriate [ˌɪnəˈprəʊpriət]	unangemessen
advanced [ədˈvɑːnst]	fortgeschritten	to extend sth to sb [ɪkˈstend]	jdm etw anbieten
real time [ˌrɪəl ˈtaɪm]	Echtzeit	to get in touch with sb [ˌget ɪn ˈtʌtʃ]	sich an jdn wenden, *hier:* anrufen
ability [əˈbɪləti]	Fähigkeit, Möglichkeit	recording [rɪˈkɔːdɪŋ]	Aufzeichnung
to present sb with sth [prɪˈzent wɪð]	jdm etw präsentieren	to delete [dɪˈliːt]	löschen
additional [əˈdɪʃənəl]	zusätzlich	details *pl* [ˈdiːteɪlz]	(persönliche) Angaben
		skin [skɪn]	Haut
page 176		allowed [əˈlaʊd]	erlaubt, gestattet
moreover [mɔːrˈəʊvə]	darüber hinaus	to draw the line [ˌdrɔː ðə ˈlaɪn]	die Grenze ziehen
to run an advert [ˌrʌn ən ˈædvɜːt]	eine Anzeige schalten	when it comes to [ˌwen ɪt ˈkʌmz tə]	was etw betrifft
amount [əˈmaʊnt]	Menge	to cross a line [ˌkrɒs ə ˈlaɪn]	eine rote Linie überschreiten
audience [ˈɔːdiəns]	Publikum	customer satisfaction [ˌkʌstəmə ˌsætɪsˈfækʃən]	Kundenzufriedenheit
responsible [rɪˈspɒnsəbəl]	verantwortungsvoll	to deliver [dɪˈlɪvə]	liefern
manner [ˈmænə]	Art, Weise	savings *pl* [ˈseɪvɪŋz]	Einsparung, Ersparnis
core [kɔː]	Kern, Herzstück	coupon [ˈkuːpɒn]	Gutschein
purpose [ˈpɜːpəs]	Absicht, Zweck		
limit [ˈlɪmɪt]	Grenze	**BUSINESS TOPIC 2**	
annoying [əˈnɔɪɪŋ]	lästig, ärgerlich	**page 178**	
creepy [ˈkriːpi]	gruselig	built-in [ˌbɪlt ˈɪn]	eingebaut, installiert
uncomfortable [ʌnˈkʌmftəbəl]	unangenehm, unbehaglich	obsolescence [ˌɒbsəˈlesəns]	Veralterung, Überalterung
to reveal [rɪˈviːəl]	verraten, offenbaren, deutlich machen	distinct [dɪˈstɪŋkt]	unterschiedlich
		to expect [ɪkˈspekt]	erwarten
one-off [ˌwʌn ˈɒf]	einmalig	slim [slɪm]	dünn
follow-up [ˈfɒləʊ ʌp]	Folge-, Anschluss-	previous [ˈpriːviəs]	vorangehend, vorherig
to irritate [ˈɪrɪteɪt]	ärgern, irritieren	stylish [ˈstaɪlɪʃ]	modisch
to be about sth [ˌbi əˈbaʊt]	um etw gehen	less [les]	weniger
to monitor [ˈmɒnɪtə]	überwachen	sleek [sliːk]	geschmeidig, schnittig, glatt
to question sth [ˈkwestʃən]	etw prüfen	probably [ˈprɒbəbli]	wahrscheinlich
first and foremost [ˌfɜːst ən ˈfɔːməʊst]	vor allem, in erster Linie	to last [lɑːst]	(vor-)halten, dauern
to sum up [ˌsʌm ˈʌp]	zusammenfassen	various [ˈveəriəs]	mehrere
individualized [ˌɪndɪˈvɪdʒuəlaɪzd]	individualisiert, zugeschnitten	to unscrew [ˌʌnˈskruː]	herausschrauben, aufschrauben
loss of [ˈlɒs əv]	Verlust an	far [fɑː]	weitaus, viel
privacy [ˈprɪvəsi]	Datenschutz, Privatsphäre	cheap [ˈtʃiːp]	preiswert
degree [dɪˈgriː]	Grad	survey sheet [ˈsɜːveɪ ʃiːt]	Fragebogen
to spy on sb [ˈspaɪ ɒn]	jdn ausspionieren	classmate [ˈklɑːsmeɪt]	Klassenkamerad/in
unknown [ˌʌnˈnəʊn]	unbekannt	to note down [nəʊt ˈdaʊn]	aufschreiben
granddaughter [ˈgrændɔːtə]	Enkelin	rarely [ˈreəli]	selten
		even though [ˌiːvən ˈðəʊ]	obwohl
page 177		ever [ˈevə]	jemals
recording [rɪˈkɔːdɪŋ]	Aufnahme	to break [breɪk]	kaputtgehen
manager [ˈmænɪdʒə]	Geschäftsführer/in	lifespan [ˈlaɪfspæn]	Lebensdauer, Laufzeit
to seem [siːm]	scheinen, den Anschein haben	to transform [trænsˈfɔːm]	umwandeln
hairstyle [ˈheəstaɪl]	Frisur	findings *pl* [ˈfaɪndɪŋz]	Ergebnisse
voucher [ˈvaʊtʃə]	Gutschein	**page 179**	
beauty treatment [ˈbjuːti triːtmənt]	kosmetische Behandlung	in favour of [ɪn ˈfeɪvər əv]	zugunsten
regular [ˈregjələ]	regelmäßig	costly [ˈkɒstli]	teuer
to presume [prɪˈzjuːm]	annehmen, mutmaßen	to undercut [ˌʌndəˈkʌt]	unterbieten, untergraben
to book [bʊk]	buchen	in fact [ɪn ˈfækt]	tatsächlich, eigentlich
contact form [ˈkɒntækt fɔːm]	Kontaktformular	device [dɪˈvaɪs]	Gerät
appointment [əˈpɔɪntmənt]	Termin, Verabredung	to emerge [ɪˈmɜːdʒ]	auftauchen, herauskommen
worthwhile [ˌwɜːθˈwaɪl]	wertvoll	repair shop [rɪˈpeə ʃɒp]	Werkstatt
to wear [weə]	tragen	to mend [mend]	reparieren
occasionally [əˈkeɪʒənəli]	manchmal, gelegentlich	available [əˈveɪləbəl]	verfügbar
self-confident [ˌself ˈkɒnfɪdənt]	selbstbewusst	screw [skruː]	Schraube
to be in doubt [bi ˌɪn ˈdaʊt]	Zweifel haben	nowadays [ˈnaʊədeɪz]	heutzutage

311

Unit word list

compatible [kəmˈpætəbəl]	kompatibel, passend	paint [peɪnt]	Malerei, Anstrich
average [ˈævərɪdʒ]	durchschnittlich	captive [ˈkæptɪv]	gefangen
loo [luː]	Toilette	surrounded by [səˈraʊndɪd baɪ]	umgeben von
fragile [ˈfrædʒaɪl]	zerbrechlich		
drop [drɒp]	Tropfen	digital native [ˌdɪdʒɪtl ˈneɪtɪv]	jemand, der mit Computern und dem Internet aufgewachsen ist
to lead sb to do sth [liːd]	jdn dazu bringen, etw zu tun		
risk [rɪsk]	Risiko, Gefahr	to provoke a reaction [prəˌvəʊk ə riˈækʃn]	eine Reaktion provozieren
to stand up [ˌstænd ˈʌp]	sich erheben, sich widersetzen	fairly adv [ˈfeəli]	ziemlich
to lose out [ˌluːz ˈaʊt]	schlecht wegkommen	viral (marketing) [ˈvaɪrəl]	virales Marketing
abandoned [əˈbændənd]	aufgegeben, liegengelassen	to spend time doing sth [ˌspend ˈtaɪm]	mit etw Zeit verbringen
cupboard [ˈkʌbəd]	Schrank	subconscious [ˌsʌbˈkɒnʃəs]	unterbewusst
eventually [ɪˈventʃuəli]	schlussendlich, schließlich	memorable [ˈmemərəbl]	einprägsam, unvergesslich
screen [skriːn]	Bildschirm	to stick [stɪk]	kleben, heften, klemmen
to meet the needs [ˌmiːt ðə ˈniːdz]	die Bedürfnisse befriedigen	permission [pəˈmɪʃn]	Erlaubnis, Genehmigung
		actual [ˈæktʃuəl]	tatsächlich
page 180		establishment [ɪˈstæblɪʃmənt]	Establishment, gesellschaftliche Ordnung
removable [rɪˈmuːvəbəl]	austauschbar		
rental [ˈrentəl]	Miete	saturated [ˈsætʃəreɪtɪd]	gesättigt
package [ˈpækɪdʒ]	Paket	escape [ɪˈskeɪp]	Entrinnen, Entkommen
durable [ˈdjʊərəbəl]	haltbar, langlebig	sphere [sfɪə]	Sphäre
in operation [ɪn ˌɒpəˈreɪʃn]	in Betrieb	intrusive [ɪnˈtruːsɪv]	aufdringlich
economic model [ˌiːkəˈnɒmɪk ˈmɒdəl]	Geschäftsmodell	to backfire coll [ˈbækfaɪə]	nach hinten losgehen
to develop [dɪˈveləp]	(sich) entwickeln, entstehen	**page 183**	
reluctant [rɪˈlʌktənt]	abgeneigt, zögernd	finally [ˈfaɪnəli]	letztendlich
age [eɪdʒ]	Zeitalter	advertiser [ˈædvətaɪzə]	Werber/in
obsessed [əbˈsest]	besessen	the Tube [ðə ˈtjuːb]	(Londoner) U-Bahn
unwillingness [ʌnˈwɪlɪŋnəs]	Widerwillen	to enjoy sth [ɪnˈdʒɔɪ]	sich an etw erfreuen
		literally [ˈlɪtərəli]	buchstäblich, im wahrsten Sinne des Wortes
## BUSINESS TOPIC 3			
page 181		platform [ˈplætfɔːm]	Bahnsteig
saturation from [sætʃəˈreɪʃn frəm]	Sättigung von	ticket machine [ˈtɪkɪt məʃiːn]	Fahrkartenautomat
marketing campaign [ˌmɑːkɪtɪŋ kæmˈpeɪn]	Marketingkampagne	to reflect [rɪˈflekt]	spiegeln, wiedergeben
		crew [kruː]	Team, Mannschaft
trade magazine [ˈtreɪd mægəziːn]	Fachzeitschrift, Handelsmagazin	to be more of … [bi ˈmɔːr əv]	eher … sein
specialized in [ˈspeʃəlaɪzd ɪn]	spezialisiert auf	puppy [ˈpʌpi]	Hundewelpe
unusual [ʌnˈjuːʒʊəl]	ungewöhnlich	to surround sb/sth [səˈraʊnd]	jdn/etw umgeben
buzz [bʌz]	Summen, Dröhnen, Gerücht	racism [ˈreɪsɪzəm]	Rassismus
to create a buzz for something [kriˌeɪt ə ˈbʌz fə]	Begeisterung für etwas erzeugen	To be honest, … [tə bi ˈɒnɪst]	Ehrlich gesagt, …
private sphere [ˈpraɪvət sfɪə]	Privatsphäre	luckily [ˈlʌkɪli]	glücklicherweise
exciting [ɪkˈsaɪtɪŋ]	aufregend	collective [kəˈlektɪv]	Gemeinschaft, Verband
warfare [ˈwɔːfeə]	Krieg; Kriegsführung	amusing [əˈmjuːzɪŋ]	lustig, amüsant
military force [ˌmɪlətri ˈfɔːs]	Militärkampf	way more [ˌweɪ ˈmɔː]	weitaus
inexpensive [ˌɪnɪkˈspensɪv]	preiswert	to raise awareness [ˌreɪz əˈweənəs]	Bewusstsein schärfen, Aufmerksamkeit erzielen
to ambush sb [ˈæmbʊʃ]	jdn aus dem Hinterhalt überfallen	neglected [nɪˈglektɪd]	vernachlässigt, verwahrlost
to attack [əˈtæk]	angreifen	underground [ˈʌndəgraʊnd]	U-Bahn
to capture [ˈkæptʃə]	gefangen nehmen	don't get me started with … coll [dəʊnt get mi ˈstɑːtɪd wɪθ]	komm mir nicht mit …
to take sb prisoner [ˌteɪk ˈprɪznə]	jdn gefangen nehmen		
unaware [ˌʌnəˈweə]	in Unkenntnis, unwissend	bother [ˈbɒðə]	Ärger
medium-sized [ˈmiːdiəm saɪzd]	mittelgroß	to penetrate [ˈpenɪtreɪt]	eindringen, einsickern
		bombarded [bɒmˈbɑːdɪd]	bombardiert, überhäuft
page 182		exposed [ɪkˈspəʊzd]	ausgesetzt
junk mail [ˈdʒʌŋk meɪl]	Reklamesendung, Spam	basically [ˈbeɪsɪkli]	im Grunde
opposite [ˈɒpəzɪt]	Gegenteil		
to grab sb's attention [ˌgræb əˈtenʃn]	jds Aufmerksamkeit auf sich ziehen	## BUSINESS TOPIC 4	
		page 184	
to project [prəˈdʒekt]	projizieren	business leadership [ˌbɪznəs ˈliːdəʃɪp]	Geschäftsführung
		collaborative [kəˈlæbərətɪv]	gemeinschaftlich, behilflich

with that in mind [wɪð ˌðæt ɪn ˈmaɪnd]	vor diesem Hintergrund	
size [saɪz]	Maß, Format, Größe	
one size fits all [wʌn ˌsaɪz fɪts ˈɔːl]	Einheitsgröße	
C.E.O = Chief Executive Officer [ˌsiː iː ˈəʊ]	Vorstandsvorsitzende/r	
tall [tɔːl]	groß	
hierarchical [ˌhaɪəˈrɑːkɪkl]	hierarchisch	
top [tɒp]	höchste/r/s, oberste/r/s	
level [ˈlevl]	Ebene	
to filter [ˈfɪltə]	durchlaufen, filtern	
in contrast [ɪn ˈkɒntrɑːst]	hingegen, dagegen	
autonomy [ɔːˈtɒnəmi]	Unabhängigkeit, Eigenständigkeit	
to sound [saʊnd]	klingen, sich anhören	
boring [ˈbɔːrɪŋ]	langweilig	
like-minded [ˌlaɪk ˈmaɪndɪd]	gleichgesinnt	
to make sth happen [ˌmeɪk ˈhæpən]	etw in die Tat umsetzen, realisieren	
layer [ˈleɪə]	Ebene, Schicht	
to iron out [ˌaɪən ˈaʊt]	ausbügeln, glattbügeln	
synonymous [sɪˈnɒnɪməs]	gleichbedeutend	
home to sth/sb [ˈhəʊm tə]	Heimat/Basis von etw/jdm	
to try out [ˌtraɪ ˈaʊt]	ausprobieren	
collegial [kəˈliːdʒɪəl]	kollegial	
to prioritize [praɪˈɒrətaɪz]	Schwerpunkte setzen, priorisieren	
overview [ˈəʊvəvjuː]	Überblick	

page 185

to adopt [əˈdɒpt]	übernehmen
to be vocal [bi ˈvəʊkl]	sich lautstark äußern
former [ˈfɔːmə]	früher
trouble-makers [ˈtrʌblmeɪkəz]	Störenfried, Unruhestifter/in
susceptible to sth [səˈseptəbl tə]	empfänglich für etw
to bully [ˈbʊli]	schikanieren, große Reden schwingen
in places [ɪn ˈpleɪsɪz]	stellenweise
to fit in [ˌfɪt ˈɪn]	hineinpassen
self-motivated [ˌself ˈməʊtɪveɪtɪd]	eigenmotiviert
to be driven to do sth [bi ˈdrɪvn]	den Antrieb/Willen haben, etw zu tun
excluded [ɪkˈskluːdɪd]	ausgeschlossen
supposedly [səˈpəʊzɪdli]	angeblich, vermeintlich
power structure [ˈpaʊə strʌktʃə]	Machtgefüge
disorganized [dɪsˈɔːɡənaɪzd]	chaotisch, durcheinander
to run smoothly [rʌn ˈsmuːðli]	reibungslos laufen

page 186

autocratic [ˌɔːtəˈkrætɪk]	autokratisch
closely [ˈkləʊsli]	genau, eingehend
majority vote [məˈdʒɒrəti vəʊt]	Mehrheitsbeschluss
empowered [ɪmˈpaʊəd]	gestärkt
laisser-faire [ˌleseɪ ˈfeə]	(Wirtschaft:) liberal
guidance [ˈɡaɪdəns]	Führung
unsure [ˌʌnˈʃʊə]	unsicher
to set priorities [set praɪˈɒrətiz]	Prioritäten setzen
to meet deadlines [miːt ˈdedlaɪnz]	Fristen/Termine einhalten
to correspond [ˌkɒrɪˈspɒnd]	entsprechen, gleichen
to act out [ˌækt ˈaʊt]	vorführen
to guess [ɡes]	(er-)raten

BUSINESS TOPIC 5
page 187

merger [ˈmɜːdʒə]	Verschmelzung, Fusionierung
partnership [ˈpɑːtnəʃɪp]	Partnerschaft, Handelsgesellschaft
shortly [ˈʃɔːtli]	bald, gleich, in kurzer Zeit
to arise [əˈraɪz]	aufkommen, sich ergeben
to tie [taɪ]	verbinden, verknüpfen
to untie [ʌnˈtaɪ]	aufknoten, aufschnüren
knot [nɒt]	Knoten
to tie a knot [taɪ ə ˈnɒt]	einen Knoten machen
profitable [ˈprɒfɪtəbl]	lohnend, rentabel, gewinnbringend
expertise [ˌekspəˈtiːz]	Fachwissen
client pool [ˈklaɪənt puːl]	Kundenstamm
headquarters [ˌhedˈkwɔːtəz]	die Zentrale, der Hauptsitz
well-known [ˌwelˈnəʊn]	bekannt
unsuccessful [ˌʌnsəkˈsesfl]	misslungen, erfolglos
dominance [ˈdɒmɪnəns]	(Wirtsch.:) Marktherrschaft
marriage [ˈmærɪdʒ]	Ehe
unhappy [ʌnˈhæpi]	unglücklich
diverse [daɪˈvɜːs]	unterschiedlich
economical [ˌiːkəˈnɒmɪkl]	wirtschaftlich, billig
lower-end [ˌləʊər ˈend]	einfach, (Wirtsch.:) weniger kaufkräftig
exclusive [ɪkˈskluːsɪv]	exklusiv, einzigartig
whereby [weəˈbaɪ]	wodurch
to take seriously [teɪk ˈsɪəriəsli]	Ernst nehmen
to impose [ɪmˈpəʊz]	einführen, aufbürden
to make fun of sth [meɪk ˈfʌn əv]	sich über etw lustig machen
incompatible [ˌɪnkəmˈpætəbl]	unvereinbar, inkompatibel
unimportant [ˌʌnɪmˈpɔːtənt]	unwichtig, unerheblich
nonetheless [ˌnʌnðəˈles]	trotzdem, nichtsdestotrotz
to be used to sth [bi ˈjuːst tə]	gewohnt sein an etw
whereas [ˌweərˈæz]	während
clothing [ˈkləʊðɪŋ]	Kleidung

page 188

old-fashioned [ˌəʊldˈfæʃnd]	altmodisch
to assess [əˈses]	beurteilen, festsetzen
to scrap [skræp]	aussondern, ausrangieren
hurdle [ˈhɜːdl]	Hürde, Hindernis
cup [kʌp]	Becher
reusable [ˌriːˈjuːzəbl]	wiederverwendbar
mug [mʌɡ]	Becher
insignificant [ˌɪnsɪɡˈnɪfɪkənt]	unwichtig, unbedeutend
transparency [trænsˈpærənsi]	Transparenz
to give sb the chance to do sth [ɡɪv ðə ˈtʃɑːns]	die Gelegenheit geben, etw zu tun
chief human resources officer [ˌtʃiːf ˌhjuːmən rɪˈsɔːsɪz ɒfɪsə]	Leiter/in der Personalabteilung
anxious [ˈæŋkʃəs]	ängstlich, besorgt
handbook [ˈhændbʊk]	Betriebshandbuch, Leitfaden
to range [reɪndʒ]	reichen, sich bewegen, sich erstrecken

Unit word list

dress code ['dres kəʊd]	Kleiderordnung	
beforehand [bɪ'fɔːhænd]	zuvor, im Voraus, vorher	
insecure [ˌɪnsɪ'kjʊə]	unsicher	
to instigate sth ['ɪnstɪgeɪt]	etw anregen, initiieren	
buddy ['bʌdi]	Kamerad, Kumpel	
on a personal level [ɒn ə ˌpɜːsənl 'levl]	persönlich, auf persönlicher Ebene	
to bond [bɒnd]	(sich) binden	
stabilization [ˌsteɪbəlaɪ'zeɪʃn]	Stabilisierung	
unsolved [ˌʌn'sɒlvd]	ungelöst	
united [ju'naɪtɪd]	vereint, verbunden	
to leave behind [ˌliːv bɪ'haɪnd]	zurücklassen, hinterlassen	
effort ['efət]	Anstrengung, Mühe	
to pay off [ˌpeɪ 'ɒf]	sich auszahlen	

page 189

to reassure sb [ˌriːə'ʃʊə]	jdn beruhigen, jdm Mut machen	
to comment on sth ['kɒment ɒn]	etw erläutern, kommentieren	
to experience [ɪk'spɪəriəns]	erleben, erfahren	
standoffish [ˌstænd'ɒfɪʃ]	reserviert, distanziert	
to brush sth off [ˌbrʌʃ 'ɒf]	etw ignorieren	
well-meaning [ˌwel 'miːnɪŋ]	wohlgemeint	
occasion [ə'keɪʒn]	Gelegenheit	
to proceed [prə'siːd]	fortschreiten	
since [sɪns]	da, weil	
disrespectful [ˌdɪsrɪ'spektfl]	respektlos	
proven ['pruːvn]	erwiesen	
offended [ə'fendɪd]	beleidigt, verletzt	

BUSINESS TOPIC 6
page 190

social responsibility [ˌsəʊʃl rɪspɒnsə'bɪləti]	soziale/gesellschaftliche Verantwortung	
CSR = corporate social responsibility [siː ˌes ɑː, ˌkɔːpərət ˌsəʊʃl rɪˌspɒnsə'bɪləti]	soziale/gesellschaftliche Verantwortung von Unternehmen	
code of conduct [ˌkəʊd əv 'kɒndʌkt]	Verhaltenskodex	
guideline ['gaɪdlaɪn]	Richtlinie, Leitlinie	
to form part of sth [fɔːm 'pɑːt əv]	Teil von etw sein	
business ethics ['bɪznəs eθɪks]	Geschäftsethik	
to spot [spɒt]	erkennen, entdecken	
to apply to sb/sth [ə'plaɪ tə]	für jdn/etw gelten	
shareholder ['ʃeəhəʊldə]	Aktionär/in, Gesellschafter/in	
they have come to expect [ðeɪ həv ˌkʌm tu ɪk'spekt]	sie erwarten inzwischen	
to stock [stɒk]	auf Lager haben	
locally sourced [ˌləʊkəli 'sɔːst]	aus der Region, regional	
fair trade [ˌfeə 'treɪd]	aus fairem Handel, fair gehandelt	
developing world [dɪˌveləpɪŋ 'wɜːld]	Dritte Welt, Entwicklungsländer	
fairly adj ['feəli]	fair, gerecht	
philanthropy [fɪ'lænθrəpi]	Menschenliebe, Nächstenliebe	
social licence [ˌsəʊʃl 'laɪsns]	soziale Akzeptanz	
approval [ə'pruːvl]	Zustimmung, Anerkennung	
thus [ðʌs]	dadurch, somit	
job market ['dʒɒb mɑːkɪt]	Arbeitsmarkt	
with respect to [wɪð rɪ'spekt tə]	in Bezug auf	

page 191

mutual(ly) ['mjuːtʃuəl]	beiderseitig, gegenseitig	
beneficial [ˌbenɪ'fɪʃl]	nützlich, nutzbringend	
in the light of [ɪn ðə 'laɪt əv]	im Lichte von	
Creating Shared Value (CSV) [kriˌeɪtɪŋ ˌʃeəd 'væljuː, siː es viː]	Schaffung von gemeinsamem Mehrwert	
nutritious [nju'trɪʃəs]	nahrhaft	
professional development [prəˌfeʃnl dɪ'veləpmənt]	berufliches Fortkommen	
contentment [kən'tentmənt]	Zufriedenheit	
to manifest itself in sth ['mænɪfest ɪtself ɪn]	sich in etw äußern	
entire [ɪn'taɪə]	ganze/r/s	
factory floor ['fæktəri flɔː]	Fabrikhalle	
end customer ['end kʌstəmə]	Endkunde/-kundin	
to self-regulate [ˌself 'regjuleɪt]	sich selbst regulieren	
to discourage [dɪs'kʌrɪdʒ]	abschrecken, abhalten, demotivieren	
harmful to sb ['hɑːmfl tə]	(gesundheits-)schädlich für jdn	
such as ['sʌtʃ əz]	wie zum Beispiel	
tobacco [tə'bækəʊ]	Tabak	
junk food ['dʒʌŋk fuːd]	ungesundes Fertigessen	
risk management [rɪsk 'mænɪdʒmənt]	Risikomanagement	
to undo [ʌn'duː]	zunichtemachen, zerstören	
regulatory body [regjuˌleɪtəri 'bɒdi]	Aufsichtsbehörde, Kontrollorgan	
long-lasting [ˌlɒŋ 'lɑːstɪŋ]	dauerhaft, langlebig	

page 192

publically ['pʌblɪkli]	öffentlich	
to accuse [ə'kjuːz]	anklagen, beschuldigen	
unethical [ʌn'eθɪkl]	skrupellos, unrecht, unmoralisch	
human rights [ˌhjuːmən 'raɪts]	Menschenrechte	
corporate governance [ˌkɔːpərət 'gʌvnəns]	Unternehmensführung	
accountability [əˌkaʊntə'bɪləti]	Verantwortung, Verantwortlichkeit	
labour practices pl ['leɪbə præktɪsəz]	Arbeitsmethoden	
media ['miːdiə]	medial	
convincing [kən'vɪnsɪŋ]	überzeugend	
beneficiary [ˌbenɪ'fɪʃəri]	Nutznießer/in	
idealistic [ˌaɪdiə'lɪstɪk]	idealistisch	
conscience ['kɒnʃəns]	Gewissen	
clear conscience [ˌklɪə 'kɒnʃəns]	reines Gewissen	
to combine [kəm'baɪn]	kombinieren, verbinden	
capitalism ['kæpɪtəlɪzəm]	Kapitalismus	
to cultivate ['kʌltɪveɪt]	kultivieren	

BUSINESS TOPIC 7
page 193

to move around [ˌmuːv ə'raʊnd]	herumlaufen, umherbewegen	
to push [pʊʃ]	(Möbel:) schieben	
to line up [ˌlaɪn 'ʌp]	in eine Linie stellen, aufreihen	
to keep within reach [ˌkiːp wɪðɪn 'riːtʃ]	in Reichweite behalten	

314

to **label** [ˈleɪbl]	beschriften	
continent [ˈkɒntɪnənt]	Kontinent	
sheet [ʃiːt]	Blatt	
world map [ˌwɜːld ˈmæp]	Weltkarte	
percent [pəˈsent]	Prozent	
representation [ˌreprɪzenˈteɪʃn]	Vertretung, Repräsentanz	
GDP = gross domestic product [dʒiː diː ˈpiː, ˌgrɒs dəˌmestɪk ˈprɒdʌkt]	Bruttoinlandsprodukt (BIP)	
to **seat sb** [siːt]	jdn setzen	
left *adj* [left]	übrig	
total [ˈtəʊtl]	Gesamtmenge	

page 194

spread [spred]	verbreitet
overpopulation [ˌəʊvəpɒpjuˈleɪʃn]	Überbevölkerung
depleting resources [dɪˌpliːtɪŋ rɪˈsɔːsɪz]	schwindende Ressourcen
persecution [ˌpɜːsɪˈkjuːʃn]	Verfolgung
influx [ˈɪnflʌks]	Zustrom
shelter [ˈʃeltə]	Schutz, Obdach
desperation [ˌdespəˈreɪʃn]	Verzweiflung
hopelessness [ˈhəʊpləsnəs]	Aussichtslosigkeit
distribution [ˌdɪstrɪˈbjuːʃn]	Verteilung
divide between rich and poor [dɪˌvaɪd bɪˌtwiːn ˌrɪtʃ ən ˈpɔː]	die Kluft zwischen Reich und Arm
to **re-home sb** [ˌriː ˈhəʊm]	jdn unterbringen, jdm eine Wohnung verschaffen
to **repay** [rɪˈpeɪ]	zurückzahlen
economic adviser [iːkəˌnɒmɪk ədˈvaɪzə]	Wirtschaftsberater/in
European Commission [ˌjʊərəpiːən kəˈmɪʃn]	Europäische Kommission
midst [mɪdst]	die Mitte
both … and … [bəʊθ ənd]	sowohl … als auch …
voting public [ˌvəʊtɪŋ ˈpʌblɪk]	Wählerschaft
concerned [kənˈsɜːnd]	besorgt
to **take a toll on sb/sth** [teɪk ə ˈtəʊl ɒn]	jdn/etw stark strapazieren
skill level [ˈskɪl levl]	Könnensstufe, Fähigkeitsstufe
innovator [ˈɪnəveɪtə]	Erfinder/in, Umgestalter/in
taxpayer [ˈtækspeɪə]	Steuerzahler/in
investor [ɪnˈvestə]	Investor/in, Kapitalanleger/in
enterprise [ˈentəpraɪz]	Unternehmungsgeist
politically [pəˈlɪtɪkli]	politisch
stable [ˈsteɪbl]	stabil
output [ˈaʊtpʊt]	Leistung, Produktion
dull [dʌl]	langweilig, uninteressant, öde
local [ˈləʊkl]	der/die Einheimische
to **spurn** [spɜːn]	abweisen

page 195

workforce [ˈwɜːkfɔːs]	berufstätige Bevölkerung
birth rate [ˈbɜːθ reɪt]	Geburtenrate
economic growth [iːkəˌnɒmɪk ˈgrəʊθ]	Wirtschaftswachstum
policymaker [ˈpɒləsimeɪkə]	politische/r Entscheidungsträger/in
practitioner [prækˈtɪʃənə]	Praktiker/in
upfront [ʌpˈfrʌnt]	im Voraus, Vorausklug, sinnvoll
wise [waɪz]	klug, sinnvoll
to **yield** [jiːld]	einbringen, ergeben
substantial [səbˈstænʃl]	wesentlich, erheblich
dividend [ˈdɪvɪdend]	Gewinnanteil, Dividende
twice [twaɪs]	zweimal
unlikely [ʌnˈlaɪkli]	unwahrscheinlich
well-developed [ˌwel dɪˈveləpt]	gut entwickelt

BUSINESS TOPIC 8

page 196

in ten year's time [ɪn ˌten ˌjɪəz ˈtaɪm]	in zehn Jahren
space [speɪs]	Weltraum
to **open up** [ˌəʊpən ˈʌp]	eröffnen, erschließen
path [pɑːθ]	Weg, Pfad, Laufbahn
not yet [nɒt ˈjet]	noch nicht
to **be ready for sth** [bi ˈredi fə]	bereit sein für etw
demand [dɪˈmɑːnd]	Anforderung
tour guide [ˈtʊə gaɪd]	Reiseführer/in
to **become reality** [bɪˈkʌm riˈæləti]	wahr werden
spacecraft [ˈspeɪskrɑːft]	Raumschiff, Raumfahrzeug
weightlessness [ˈweɪtləsnəs]	Schwerelosigkeit
advance [ədˈvɑːns]	Fortschritt
medical science [ˌmedɪkl ˈsaɪəns]	Medizin
bio-engineering [ˌbaɪəʊ endʒɪˈnɪərɪŋ]	Biotechnik
to **prolong** [prəˈlɒŋ]	verlängern
organ [ˈɔːgən]	Organ
customized [ˈkʌstəmaɪzd]	individuell angepasst, zugeschnitten
body part [ˈbɒdi pɑːt]	Körperteil
illness [ˈɪlnəs]	Krankheit
personalized [ˈpɜːsənəlaɪzd]	individuell gestaltet, personalisiert
for fashion reasons [fə ˈfæʃn riːznz]	aus modischen Gründen
Ethical Technology Advocate [ˌeθɪkl tekˈnɒlədʒi ˈædvəkət]	Beauftragte/r für Technikethik
office task [ˈɒfɪs tɑːsk]	Büroarbeit
manual labour [ˌmænjuəl ˈleɪbə]	Handarbeit
customer service [ˌkʌstəmə ˈsɜːvɪs]	Kundendienst

page 197

communicator [kəˈmjuːnɪkeɪtə]	Kommunikator/in
interface [ˈɪntəfeɪs]	Schnittstelle, Verbindung
sophisticated [səˈfɪstɪkeɪtɪd]	technisch ausgefeilt, weiterentwickelt
critically [ˈkrɪtɪkli]	kritisch; *hier:* sehr, äußerst
to **set guidelines** [ˌset ˈgaɪdlaɪnz]	Regeln, Richtlinien aufstellen
strict [strɪkt]	streng
content [ˈkɒntent]	Inhalt
curator [kjʊəˈreɪtə]	Pfleger/in, Verwalter/in
by the year 2020 [baɪ ðə ˈjɪə]	bis zum Jahr 2020
software-brain interfaces [ˌsɒftweə ˌbreɪn ˈɪntəfeɪs]	computergesteuerte Schnittstellen
neuroscientist [ˌnjʊərəʊˈsaɪəntɪst]	Hirnforscher/in
storage capacity [ˈstɔːrɪdʒ kəˈpæsəti]	Lagerkapazität

Unit word list

orbit [ˈɔːbɪt]	Umlaufbahn	
physical work [ˌfɪzɪkl ˈwɜːk]	körperliche Arbeit	
amazing [əˈmeɪzɪŋ]	unglaublich, fantastisch	
painful [ˈpeɪnfl]	schmerzend	
not anymore [nɒt eniˈmɔː]	nicht mehr	
manual task [ˌmænjuəl ˈtɑːsk]	Handarbeit, händische Arbeit	
entry-level [ˈentri levl]	Einstiegs-	

page 198

advertised [ˈædvətaɪzd]	(Job:) ausgeschrieben
job opening [ˈdʒɒb əʊpnɪŋ]	offene Stelle, Stellenangebot
silent observer [ˌsaɪlənt əbˈzɜːvə]	stiller Beobachter
to memorize [ˈmeməraɪz]	einprägen, auswendig lernen
to keep in mind [ˌkiːp ɪn ˈmaɪnd]	an etw denken, sich an etw erinnern
confident [ˈkɒnfɪdənt]	selbstsicher, souverän
body language [ˈbɒdi læŋgwɪdʒ]	Körpersprache
clear [klɪə]	verständlich, klar
relevant [ˈreləvənt]	maßgeblich, sachbezogen
to project [prəˈdʒekt]	übertragen, zeigen

BUSINESS TOPIC 9
page 199

based [beɪst]	ansässig
to shape [ʃeɪp]	formen, gestalten, entwickeln
to insult [ɪnˈsʌlt]	beleidigen, beschimpfen
competition [ˌkɒmpəˈtɪʃn]	die Konkurrenz
to mock sb [mɒk]	jdn verspotten, verhöhnen
incompetent [ɪnˈkɒmpɪtənt]	unfähig, nicht kompetent
carpooling [ˈkɑːpuːlɪŋ]	das Bilden einer Fahrgemeinschaft
at the push of a button [ət ðə ˈpʊʃ əv ə bʌtn]	auf Knopfdruck
extremely [ɪkˈstriːmli]	äußerst
whose [huːz]	dessen
implementation [ˌɪmplɪmenˈteɪʃn]	Umsetzung, Durchführung
mirror image [ˈmɪrər ɪmɪdʒ]	Spiegelbild
ruthless [ˈruːθləs]	schonungslos, skrupellos
overly [ˈəʊvəli]	übermäßig
anyway [ˈeniweɪ]	trotzdem
transportation [ˌtrænspɔːˈteɪʃn]	Transport
furious [ˈfjʊəriəs]	wütend, erbost
to violate (the law) [ˈvaɪəleɪt]	(das Gesetz) brechen, verletzen
court order [ˈkɔːt ɔːdə]	Gerichtsbeschluss, Gerichtsentscheidung
along with [əˈlɒŋ wɪð]	zusammen mit
myriad [ˈmɪriəd]	Myriade, Unzahl
in the wake of sth [ɪn ðə ˈweɪk əv]	im Gefolge von etw
breathtaking [ˈbreθteɪkɪŋ]	atemberaubend
amazed [əˈmeɪzd]	verblüfft, überrascht
condensed [kənˈdenst]	verdichtet, zusammengefasst, kondensiert
algorithm [ˈælgərɪðəm]	Algorithmus
on the stock [ɒn ðə ˈstɒk]	an der Börse
craziness [ˈkreɪzinəs]	Verrücktheit
dozens of [ˈdʌznz əv]	Dutzende an/von
drone [drəʊn]	Drohne
be it for … [ˈbi ɪt fə]	sei es für …

the holy grail [ðə ˌhəʊli ˈgreɪl]	der Heilige Gral
to overtake [ˌəʊvəˈteɪk]	überholen
to misunderstand [ˌmɪsʌndəˈstænd]	missverstehen
nor conj [nɔː]	auch nicht
intelligence service [ɪnˈtelɪdʒəns sɜːvɪs]	Nachrichtendienst
as to sth [ˈæz tə]	was etw betrifft
to witness sth [ˈwɪtnəs]	etw miterleben, Zeuge einer Sache sein
societal [səˈsaɪətl]	gesellschaftlich
to alter [ˈɔːltə]	verändern

page 200

to determine [dɪˈtɜːmɪn]	bestimmen
to capture [ˈkæptʃə]	(Markt:) erobern
mankind [mænˈkaɪnd]	Menschheit
interference [ˌɪntəˈfɪərəns]	Störung, Beeinflussung
external [ɪkˈstɜːnl]	außen, extern, äußerlich
to stand in the way [ˌstænd ɪn ðə ˈweɪ]	im Weg stehen
this much is certain [ðɪs ˌmʌtʃ ɪz ˈsɜːtn]	so viel ist gewiss
framework [ˈfreɪmwɜːk]	Rahmen
to wish to do sth [ˌwɪʃ tə ˈduː]	sich wünschen, etw zu tun; etw tun wollen
to suggest [səˈdʒest]	behaupten, andeuten
to trade [treɪd]	handeln
to rule [ruːl]	regieren
considerable [kənˈsɪdərəbl]	beträchtlich, beachtlich
funds pl [fʌndz]	das Geld, die Mittel
protection [prəˈtekʃn]	Schutz
hard [hɑːd]	schwer, schwierig
piece of advice [piːs əv ədˈvaɪs]	Rat, Ratschlag
property [ˈprɒpəti]	Eigentum, Besitz
to lock away [lɒk əˈweɪ]	wegschließen, einschließen
securely [sɪˈkjʊəli]	sicher
it's worth … [ɪts ˈwɜːθ]	es lohnt sich, …
customer account [ˌkʌstəmər əˈkaʊnt]	Kundenkonto
in case of [ɪn ˈkeɪs əv]	im Fall von
relating to [rɪˈleɪtɪŋ tə]	bezüglich, im Zusammenhang mit
accidentally [ˌæksɪˈdentəli]	versehentlich, unbeabsichtigt
reliable [rɪˈlaɪəbl]	sicher, verlässlich, glaubwürdig
to hack into sth [ˈhæk ɪntə]	in etw eindringen
to keep up-to-date [kiːp ˌʌp tə ˈdeɪt]	aktualisieren
self-employed [ˌself ɪmˈplɔɪd]	freiberuflich, selbständig

page 201

record [ˈrekɔːd]	Nachweis, Beleg
to trace [treɪs]	verfolgen, feststellen, aufspüren
outside [ˌaʊtˈsaɪd]	betriebsfremd, außerhalb
wireless [ˈwaɪələs]	drahtlos
to fall victim to sb/sth [ˌfɔːl ˈvɪktɪm tə]	jdm/etw zum Opfer fallen
to encounter sth [ɪnˈkaʊntə]	etw ausgesetzt sein, mit etw in Berührung kommen
to surprise [səˈpraɪz]	überraschen

316

BUSINESS TOPIC 10
page 202

chemicals	[ˈkemɪklz]	Chemikalien
pharmaceutical	[ˌfɑːməˈsuːtɪkl]	pharmazeutisch, Pharma-
chemical	[ˈkemɪkl]	chemisch, Chemie-
best known for	[best nəʊn fə]	am besten/meisten bekannt für
to bid	[bɪd]	ein Angebot machen, bieten
to take over	[ˌteɪk ˈəʊvə]	(Firma:) übernehmen
worth	[wɜːθ]	wert
monopoly	[məˈnɒpəli]	alleiniges Handelsrecht, Monopolstellung
pesticide	[ˈpestɪsaɪd]	Pflanzenschutzmittel, Pestizid
takeover	[ˈteɪkəʊvə]	Übernahme
two-thirds	[tuː ˈθɜːdz]	zwei Drittel
amongst	[əˈmʌŋst]	zwischen, unter
regulator	[ˈregjuleɪtə]	Behörde
farmer	[ˈfɑːmə]	Bauer, Bäuerin; Landwirt/in
however	[haʊˈevə]	hingegen, jedoch, allerdings
opposition	[ˌɒpəˈzɪʃn]	Widerstand, Gegenwehr
to run for sth	[ˈrʌn fə]	für etw kandidieren
presidential nomination	[prezɪˌdenʃl nɒmɪˈneɪʃn]	Präsidentschaftsnominierung
to block	[blɒk]	blockieren
multinational	[ˌmʌltiˈnæʃnəl]	multinational
corporation	[ˌkɔːpəˈreɪʃn]	Unternehmen
main	[meɪn]	Haupt-
a handful	[ə ˈhændfʊl]	eine Handvoll
vulnerable to sth	[ˈvʌlnərəbl tə]	verletzbar, gefährdet durch etw
leaving	[ˈliːvɪŋ]	Verlassen
complication	[ˌkɒmplɪˈkeɪʃn]	Komplikation
controversy	[ˈkɒntrəvɜːsi]	Streit, Diskussion
notable	[ˈnəʊtəbl]	bemerkenswert
potent	[ˈpəʊtnt]	stark, hochwirksam
to provoke	[prəˈvəʊk]	auslösen, verursachen
long-term	[ˌlɒŋˈtɜːm]	langfristig, Langzeit-
widespread	[ˈwaɪdspred]	weit verbreitet
mistrust	[ˌmɪsˈtrʌst]	Misstrauen
to ban	[bæn]	verbieten
to discourage	[dɪsˈkʌrɪdʒ]	unterbinden, zu verhindern suchen
environmentalist	[ɪnˌvaɪrənˈmentəlɪst]	Umweltschützer/in
to force	[fɔːs]	drängen
off the market	[ˌɒf ðə ˈmɑːkɪt]	aus dem Markt
known	[nəʊn]	bekannt
outcry	[ˈaʊtkraɪ]	Entrüstung, Aufschrei
labelling	[ˈleɪblɪŋ]	Beschriftung, Kennzeichnung

page 203

elementary	[ˌelɪˈmentri]	elementar, grundlegend
to decrease sth	[dɪˈkriːs]	etw mindern, reduzieren
to take control of sb/sth	[teɪk kənˈtrəʊl əv]	die Kontrolle über jdn/etw erlangen
to overlook	[ˌəʊvəˈlʊk]	übersehen
to perceive	[pəˈsiːv]	wahrnehmen

page 204

Federal Trade Commission (FTC)	[ˌfedərəl ˈtreɪd kəmɪʃn, ef tiː siː]	etwa: Bundeskartellamt in den USA

supporter	[səˈpɔːtə]	Unterstützer/in
supportive	[səˈpɔːtɪv]	unterstützend
opposing	[əˈpəʊzɪŋ]	gegnerisch
interest group	[ˈɪntrəst gruːp]	Interessengruppe
to moderate	[ˈmɒdəreɪt]	moderieren
to draft	[drɑːft]	entwerfen
opponent	[əˈpəʊnənt]	Gegner
opposite adj	[ˈɒpəzɪt]	entgegengesetzt
party	[ˈpɑːti]	Partei
to turn off topic	[ˌtɜːn ɒf ˈtɒpɪk]	vom Thema abkommen
final adj	[ˈfaɪnl]	letzte/r/s
to weigh up	[ˌweɪ ˈʌp]	abwägen
famine	[ˈfæmɪn]	Hungersnot
food security	[ˈfuːd sɪkjʊərəti]	Ernährungssicherung
irreversible consequences	[ɪrɪˌvɜːsəbl ˈkɒnsɪkwənsɪz]	unumkehrbare Konsequenzen
to modify sth	[ˈmɒdɪfaɪ]	etw modifizieren, verändern
medical research	[ˌmedɪkl rɪˈsɜːtʃ]	medizinische Forschung
gene therapy	[ˈdʒiːn θerəpi]	Gentherapie

BUSINESS TOPIC 11
page 205

to rise	[raɪz]	ansteigen
to diminish	[dɪˈmɪnɪʃ]	abnehmen, schwinden
to be concerned with sth	[bi kənˈsɜːnd wɪð]	mit etw befasst sein
fund	[fʌnd]	Fond
awareness	[əˈweənəs]	Bewusstsein, Aufmerksamkeit
to sustain	[səˈsteɪn]	fortsetzen
small-scale	[ˌsmɔːl ˈskeɪl]	in kleinem Maßstab
to surface	[ˈsɜːfɪs]	zutage treten
to keep animals	[ˌkiːp ˈænɪmlz]	Tiere halten
dweller	[ˈdwelə]	Bewohner/in
bee	[biː]	Biene
to supply	[səˈplaɪ]	ausrüsten
coop	[kuːp]	Hühnerstall
aquaponics	[ˌækwəˈpɒnɪks]	Kombination aus Aquakultur (Aufzucht von Fischen) und Hydroponik (Hydrokultur)
beekeeping	[ˈbiːkiːpɪŋ]	Imkerei, Bienenhaltung
edible	[ˈedəbl]	essbar
shore	[ʃɔː]	Ufer, Küste
landscape	[ˈlændskeɪp]	Landschaft
rooftop	[ˈruːftɒp]	Hausdach
backyards	[ˌbækˈjɑːdz]	Hinterhof, Garten hinter dem Haus
playground	[ˈpleɪgraʊnd]	Spielplatz
well off	[ˌwel ˈɒf]	wohlhabend, vermögend
social housing	[ˌsəʊʃl ˈhaʊzɪŋ]	sozialer Wohnungsbau

page 206

indoor	[ˈɪndɔː]	innen-
allotment	[əˈlɒtmənt]	Schrebergarten, Kleingarten, Parzelle
polytunnel	[ˈpɒlɪtʌnl]	Folienzelt
participation	[pɑːˌtɪsɪˈpeɪʃn]	Teilnahme
mental health	[ˌmentl ˈhelθ]	psychisches Wohl
mental health patient	[ˌmentl ˈhelθ peɪʃnt]	psychisch Kranke/r

Unit word list

well-being ['wel biːɪŋ]		Wohlbefinden
monolingual [ˌmɒnəˈlɪŋgwəl]		einsprachig

page 207
slice [slaɪs]		Scheibe
pork [pɔːk]		Schwein
to **guarantee** [ˌgærənˈtiː]		garantieren, sicherstellen
chicken breast [ˈtʃɪkɪn brest]		Hühnerbrust

BUSINESS TOPIC 12
page 208
in time [ɪn ˈtaɪm]		mit der Zeit
naïve [naɪˈiːv]		naiv, blauäugig
wearable [ˈweərəbl]		tragbar
strongly [ˈstrɒŋli]		stark
to **evolve** [ɪˈvɒlv]		sich entwickeln
out of date [ˌaʊt əv ˈdeɪt]		überholt, veraltet
radical(ly) [ˈrædɪkl]		völlig, drastisch, radikal
home automation [ˌhəʊm ɔːtəˈmeɪʃn]		Haustechnik, Haushaltsautomatisierung
energy-saving [ˈenədʒi seɪvɪŋ]		das Energiesparen
pocket [ˈpɒkɪt]		Tasche
lock [lɒk]		Schloss
energy-efficient [ˌenədʒi ɪˈfɪʃnt]		energiesparend
seamlessly [ˈsiːmləsli]		nahtlos, reibungslos

page 209
energetic [ˌenəˈdʒetɪk]		energiegeladen, aktiv
sleep [sliːp]		Schlaf
to **enjoy** [ɪnˈdʒɔɪ]		genießen
set *adj* [set]		bestimmt
optimization [ˌɒptɪmaɪˈzeɪʃn]		Optimierung
to **look out for sth** [ˌlʊk ˈaʊt fə]		auf etw achten
rest [rest]		Ruhe, Erholung
mattress [ˈmætrəs]		Matratze
tracker [ˈtrækə]		*hier etwa:* Überwachungsgerät
pattern [ˈpætn]		Muster
to **establish** [ɪˈstæblɪʃ]		einführen, etablieren
place an order [ˌpleɪs ən ˈɔːdə]		einen Auftrag erteilen
even [ˈiːvn]		überhaupt
biometric [ˌbaɪəʊˈmetrɪk]		biometrisch
to **swipe** [swaɪp]		*(Finger:)* rüberziehen, wischen
to **take sth on board** [ˌteɪk ɒn ˈbɔːd]		etw bedenken
to **implement** [ˈɪmplɪmənt]		realisieren, verwirklichen
paperless [ˈpeɪpələs]		papierlos
damaging [ˈdæmɪdʒɪŋ]		schädigend, umweltbelastend

page 210
sketch [sketʃ]		Skizze
vote [vəʊt]		Abstimmung

A–Z word list

Dieses Wörterverzeichnis enthält alle Wörter aus **Focus on Success – 5th edition: Ausgabe Wirtschaft** in alphabetischer Reihenfolge. Nicht aufgeführt sind die Wörter aus der *Basic word list* sowie internationale Wörter wie *hotel*, *email* usw.

Wörter, die in den Hörverständnistexten vorkommen, sind mit einem *T* hinter der Seitenzahl gekennzeichnet.

A

abandoned *179* aufgegeben, liegengelassen
abbreviation *32* Abkürzung
ability *29* Fähigkeit, Befähigung, Möglichkeit
about, to **be ~ sth** *176* um etw gehen
to **be ~ to do sth** *51* im Begriff sein, etw zu tun; gerade dabei sein, etw zu tun
to **abridge** *27* (Text) kürzen
abroad *88T* im Ausland
absolutely *40* absolut
to **absorb** *153* aufnehmen, absorbieren
academic study *98* wissenschaftliche Studie
across, to **come ~ as** *88T* auf andere wirken; to **come ~ sth** *51* auf etw stoßen
to **accept** *11T* akzeptieren, gutheißen
accepted *54* akzeptiert, angenommen
access code *128* Zugangscode
to **access sth** *160* auf etw zugreifen
access to sth *98* Zugriff auf etw, Zugang zu etw
accessible *51* zugänglich, erreichbar, offen
accident, ~ **and emergency department (A&E)** *167* Notaufnahme
accidentally *200T* versehentlich, unbeabsichtigt
to **accommodate** *67* unterbringen
accommodation *66* Unterkunft; **homestay ~** *66* Unterbringung bei Gasteltern
to **accompany** *27* begleiten
to **accomplish** *146* erreichen, vollbringen
according to *12* entsprechend, nach, gemäß; *14* laut, zufolge; **~ priority** *44* gemäß der Priorität
account *37* Konto; to **take sth into ~** *22* etw in Betracht ziehen, etw berücksichtigen
accountability *192* Verantwortung, Verantwortlichkeit
accountancy *90* Buchhaltung, Rechnungswesen
accountant *65* Buchhalter/in
accounts *pl 34* Buchhaltung; to **keep ~** *98* Buchführung machen
accurate *75* genau
to **accuse** *192* anklagen, beschuldigen
to **ache** *16* schmerzen, wehtun
to **achieve sth** *19* etw erreichen, etw leisten

achievement *10* Errungenschaft, Leistung
to **acknowledge** *69* anerkennen, zugeben
acne *23* Akne
to **acquire sth** *88T* sich etw aneignen, etw erwerben
acre *149* Morgen (ca. 4047 qm)
acronym *169* Akronym, Abkürzung
to **act**, **~ as sth** *114* als etw fungieren; **~ out** *43* spielen, vorspielen; *186* vorführen
act *91* Handlung, Tat
action, to **take ~** *100* handeln; **legal ~** *39* rechtliche Schritte; to **take ~** *100* handeln; to **take legal ~** *39* rechtliche Schritte unternehmen; **course of ~** *87* Vorgehen, Maßnahmen
to **activate** *144* aktivieren
actual *182* tatsächlich
actually *20* in der Tat, eigentlich, wirklich
ad hoc *170* sofort, spontan
ad(vertising) agency *46* Werbeagentur
ad *45* Anzeige, Werbung
to **adapt** *27* (Text:) bearbeiten; **~ to sth** *54* sich an etw anpassen
adaptation *152* Anpassung, Anpassungsleistung
to **add up** *170* (sich) addieren
addictive *134* abhängig machend
addition *162* Hinzufügung; **in ~** *48* außerdem, darüber hinaus; **in ~ to sth** *76* zusätzlich zu etw
additional(ly) *98* zusätzlich
to **address** *69* (Problem etc.) ansprechen, angehen, thematisieren; **~ sb** *88T* jdn ansprechen
adequate(ly) *27* ausreichend, angemessen
to **administer** *67* verwalten
administration *66* Verwaltung
administrative *67* Verwaltungs-
administrator *65* Verwalter/in
to **admire** *11* bewundern
to **admit** *23* zugeben, (ein)gestehen
to **adopt** *185* übernehmen
to **adopt sb** *94* jdn adoptieren
advance *196* Fortschritt; **in ~** *40* im Voraus
advanced *175* fortgeschritten
advancement *54* Fortschritt, Weiterentwicklung

advantage, to **take ~ of sb** *118* jdn missbrauchen, ausnutzen
advert *45* Anzeige, Werbung; to **run an ~** *176* eine Anzeige schalten
to **advertise**, **~ sth** *19* etw bewerben, für etw werben; **~ a job** *66* eine Stelle ausschreiben
advertiser *183T* Werber/in
advertising *45* Werbung
advertisement *45* Anzeige, Werbung; **job ~** *31* Stellenanzeige
advice *38T* (guter) Rat, Ratschläge; **piece of ~** *200T* Rat, Ratschlag; **strong ~** *62T* dringender Rat
advisable *88T* ratsam
to **advise sb** *38* jdn beraten, jdm etw raten
adviser *114* Berater/in
advocate *136* Befürworter/in
aerobics *pl 12* Aerobic
to **affect** *19* beeinflussen, sich auswirken auf
affected *158* betroffen
affluent *116* wohlhabend
to **afford sth** *118* sich etw leisten
affordability *21T* Erschwinglichkeit, Bezahlbarkeit
affordable *19* erschwinglich
afraid, I'm ~ *23* leider
afterwards *111* danach, darauf
age *180* Zeitalter; **age, for ~s** *163* ewig, eine Ewigkeit; **school-age** *128* im Schulalter
to **age** *114* altern
aged *40* im Alter von
agency *14* Agentur; **ad(vertising) ~** *46* Werbeagentur; **forwarding ~** *145* Spedition; **law enforcement ~** *124* Strafverfolgungsbehörde, Exekutivorgan
agenda *172* Tagesordnung
to **agree (on sth)** *98* (etw) zustimmen, übereinstimmen
agreement *101* Vereinbarung, Absprache
agricultural *86T* landwirtschaftlich, Landwirtschafts-
agriculture *148* Landwirtschaft
ahead *62* voraus, vorausliegend
aid *97* Hilfe
aim *74* Ziel; *164* Absicht, Zweck
aimed, to **be ~ at sb** *28* sich an jdn richten
to **aim**, **~ at sth** *152* etw anstreben; **~ to do sth** *175* bemüht sein, etw zu tun

A–Z word list

airborne drone *168* Flugdrohne
aircraft *102* Flugzeug
airline *81* Fluglinie
aisle *44* Gang
alarm *144* Alarmsignal
algorithm *199* Algorithmus
alien *165* außerirdisch
aligned with *108* verbunden mit, ausgerichtet auf
alive *63* lebendig, am Leben
all, ~ at once *23* auf einmal; **~ right by me** *30* für mich in Ordnung; **A~ the best,** *17* Mit besten Grüßen, Alles Gute; **~ the time** *36* ständig, die ganze Zeit; **first of ~** *62T* zuallererst, zunächst
allotment *206* Schrebergarten, Kleingarten, Parzelle
allotted *69* zugewiesen
allowance *20* Taschengeld; *66* Aufwandsentschädigung; *117T* Zuschuss
allowed *177* erlaubt, gestattet
along, ~ the way *90* dabei, währenddessen; **~ with** *199* zusammen mit
alongside *168* neben
to **alter** *199* verändern
amateur *21T* Amateur(-), Hobby-
amazed *199* verblüfft, überrascht
amazing *197* unglaublich, fantastisch
ambition *45* Ziel, Ehrgeiz
ambitious *64* ehrgeizig
to **ambush sb** *181* jdn aus dem Hinterhalt überfallen
among *27* unter, inmitten, zwischen; *74* darunter, davon
amongst *202* zwischen, unter
amount *37* Betrag; *81* Menge
to **amount to sth** *81* auf etw hinauslaufen
amusement arcade *46* Spielhalle
amusing *183* lustig, amüsant
anchor, news ~ *136* Nachrichtensprecher/in
ancient *115* alt, historisch, antik
and so on *62T* und so weiter
anecdote *38* Anekdote
angry *136* aufgebracht, ungehalten; to **get ~** *62T* sich ärgern
anniversary *94* Jahrestag
to **announce** *14* verkünden, ankündigen
annoying *176* lästig, ärgerlich
annual(ly) *134* jährlich
annum, per ~ *117T* pro Jahr
anonymous(ly) *108* anonym
to **answer the phone** *162* ans Telefon gehen
anxious *188* ängstlich, besorgt
anyway *199* trotzdem
apart from *29* abgesehen von, außer
to **apologize** *43* sich entschuldigen
apparent *98* offensichtlich, sichtbar
apparently *40* anscheinend
to **appear** *7* auftreten, erscheinen; *15* scheinen
appliance *144* Haushaltsgerät
applicant *77* Bewerber/in

application *32* Bewerbung; *143T* Antrag
to **apply** *177T* *(Make-up:)* auftragen
to **apply, ~ for a job** *31* sich (um/auf eine Stelle) bewerben; **~ to sb/sth** *190* für jdn/etw gelten
appointment *34T* Termin, Verabredung
to **appreciate** *76* zu schätzen wissen, schätzen
apprenticeship *68T* Ausbildung, Lehre
approach *44* Ansatz, Herangehensweise, Vorgehen
to **approach, ~ sb** *27* an jdn herantreten; **~ sth** *169* sich einer Sache nähern
appropriate(ly) *27* angemessen, passend
approval *190* Zustimmung, Anerkennung
approximate *87* ungefähr, angenähert
approximately (approx.) *86* zirka (ca.)
aquaponics *205* Kombination aus Aquakultur (Aufzucht von Fischen) und Hydroponik (Hydrokultur)
arcade *46* Spielautomat
architect *65* Architekt/in
area *11* Gebiet, Bereich, Feld; *25* Gegend, Region
to **argue** *27* argumentieren, geltend machen
to **arise** *187* aufkommen, sich ergeben
to **arm sb** *126T* jdn bewaffnen
armed *91* bewaffnet; **~ forces** pl *126T* Streitkräfte
army *126* Armee
arrangement *50* Abmachung, Vereinbarung, Vorbereitung, Regelung
to **arrest** *81* verhaften
arsenal *124* Instrumentarium, Waffenlager
arsenic *144* Arsen
artificial intelligence *164* künstliche Intelligenz
artistic *65* künstlerisch
as *54* da, weil; **~ a result** *88T* infolgedessen, als Folge davon; **~ a whole** *98* im Ganzen; **~ far as I'm concerned** *23* was mich betrifft; *78T* von mir aus; **~ long as** *137* solange; **~ necessary** *61* nötigenfalls; **~ regards … ** *68T* was … betrifft; **~ requested** *120* wie gewünscht; **~ things turn out** *34T* wie sich herausstellt; **~ to sth** *199* was etw betrifft
asap (as soon as possible) *66* baldmöglichst
asleep, to be ~ *94* schlafen
aspect *15* Gesichtspunkt, Aspekt
to **assess** *188* beurteilen, festsetzen
assessment *78T* Beurteilung, Einstufung
asset *76* Vermögen; to **be an ~ to sb** *76* für jdn eine Bereicherung sein
to **assign sb sth** *168* jdm etw zuweisen, jdn mit etw beauftragen
assistance *98* Hilfe, Unterstützung
to **associate** *88T* in Verbindung bringen, assoziieren

association *88* Assoziation; *166T* Verband, Vereinigung
assumption *131* Annahme
to **assure** *74* sicherstellen, gewährleisten
astonished *88T* erstaunt, überrascht, verwundert
asylum *108* Asyl; **~ seeker** *81* Asylbewerber/in
at, ~ all *16* überhaupt; **~ any rate** *131* auf jeden Fall; **~ any time** *39* jederzeit; **~ first hand** *31* aus erster Hand, hautnah; **~ least** *27* zumindest, mindestens; **~ one time** *163* gleichzeitig; **~ the end of the day** *57* letzten Endes, unterm Strich; **~ the expense of sth** *37* auf Kosten von etw; **~ the latest** *31* spätestens; **~ the push of a button** *199* auf Knopfdruck; **~ the same time** *137* gleichzeitig
athlete *19* Sportler/in, Athlet/in
athletic *20* sportlich, athletisch
atmosphere *17T* Stimmung, Atmosphäre
atmospheric *137* atmosphärisch, in der Atmosphäre
atrocities pl *90* Gräueltaten
attached *134* angeheftet, beigefügt
to **attack** *181* angreifen
attack *103* Attacke, Angriff; *123* Anschlag, Attentat; to **launch an ~** *130* einen Angriff starten
attacker *125* Attentäter/in
attempt *146* Versuch
to **attend sth** *78T* an etw teilnehmen
attention *11T* Aufmerksamkeit, Beachtung; to **attrack ~** *43* Aufmerksamkeit erregen; to **draw ~ to sb/sth** *23* Aufmerksamkeit auf jdn/etw ziehen; to **grab sb's ~** *182* jds Aufmerksamkeit auf sich ziehen; to **pay ~ to sth** *22* auf etw achten
attitude *64* Haltung; *93* Einstellung
attn. (= attention) *76* *(Brief:)* zu Händen
to **attract** *43* anlocken, anziehen; **~ attention** *43* Aufmerksamkeit erregen
audience *8* Publikum
authorities pl *118* Leitung, oberste Dienststelle
authority *80* Behörde
autocratic *186* autokratisch
autograph *7* Autogramm
automated *100* automatisiert
autonomous *164* autonom
autonomy *184* Unabhängigkeit, Eigenständigkeit
availability *19* Verfügbarkeit
available *179* verfügbar; to **be ~** *32* *(Telefon:)* zu sprechen sein
average *179* durchschnittlich
average *36* Durchschnitt
to **avoid** *88T* vermeiden, verhindern
to **await** *124* erwarten, abwarten
to **award sth to sb** *161* jdm etw verleihen, jdm etw zuerkennen

aware, to be ~ of sth *88* sich einer Sache bewusst sein, etw kennen; **to make ~** *54* bewusst machen, in Kenntnis setzen; **to make sb ~ of sth** *40* jdn über etw informieren, jdn auf etw hinweisen
awareness *205* Bewusstsein, Aufmerksamkeit; **to raise ~** *183* Bewusstsein schärfen, Aufmerksamkeit erzielen
axis *53* Achse

B

to back *27* unterstützen
back *100* Rücken; **~ yard** *124* Hinterhof
to backfire *coll 182* nach hinten losgehen
background *10* Hintergrund; *19* Herkunft
backpacking, to go ~ *78T* auf Rucksacktour gehen
backup *156* Ersatz, Reserve
backyards *205* Hinterhof, Garten hinter dem Haus
bad, to go from ~ to worse *62* immer schlimmer werden
baker *65* Bäcker/in
balance *105* Bilanz, Saldo
to balance *105* ausgleichen
to ban *202* verbieten; **to ~ sb from doing sth** *60* jdm verbieten, etw zu tun
band *68T* Gehaltsstufe, Gehaltsklasse
bank, ~ clerk *67* Bankangestellte/r; **~ robbery** *130* Banküberfall, Bankraub
banker *96T* Bankkaufmann/-frau
bar chart *52* Säulendiagramm
bare *49T* kahl, nackt
bargain *175* Sonderangebot, Schnäppchen
barrage *140* Staumauer
barrier *69* Hürde
to base on sth *36* auf etw basieren
based *199* ansässig; **~ on** *64* basierend auf
basically *183* im Grunde
basket *81* Korb
to bat an eyelid *14* mit der Wimper zucken
battery pack *144* Akku
battlefield *124* Schlachtfeld
to be, be it for ... *199* sei es für ...; **~ up to sth** *63* etw vorhaben
beauty treatment *177T* kosmetische Behandlung
to become, to ~ annoyed *141* sich ärgern, sich aufregen; **to ~ extinct** *152* aussterben; **to ~ reality** *196* wahr werden
bee *205* Biene
beekeeping *205* Imkerei, Bienenhaltung
beetle *49T* Käfer
beforehand *188* zuvor, im Voraus, vorher

to beg *143* flehen, eindringlich bitten; **~ for sth** *89* um etw betteln; **~ sb to do sth** *129* jdn anflehen, etw zu tun
beggar *89* Bettler/in
behalf, on sb's ~ *172* in jds Namen
to behave *82* sich benehmen, sich verhalten
behaviour *43* Benehmen, Verhalten
belief *19* Überzeugung; *64* Meinung
to belong to sth *64* zu etw gehören
belonging *70* Zugehörigkeit
beneath *131* unterhalb, unter
benefactor *90* Wohltäter/in
beneficial *191* nützlich, nutzbringend
beneficiary *192* Nutznießer/in
benefit *17T* Nutzen, Vorteil, Pluspunkt
to benefit *43* nutzen, Nutzen bringen, profitieren
benefits *pl 60* Sozialleistungen; **~ office** *60* Sozialamt; **community ~** *pl 143T* Zahlungen an die Gemeinde; **to claim unemployment ~** *86* Arbeitslosengeld beziehen; **to reap the ~** *165* die Früchte ernten, die Vorteile nutzen;
best, ~ known for *202* am besten/meisten bekannt für; **B~ wishes** *120* (*Brief:*) Mit den besten Wünschen; **The ~ is yet to come.** *164* Das Beste kommt noch. Die besten Zeiten stehen uns noch bevor.
to bet *23* wetten
beyond *55* darüber hinaus; *137* jenseits, über
to bid *202* ein Angebot machen, bieten
bid *27* Versuch
bill *62T* Rechnung
billboard *45* Reklametafel, Plakatwand
billion *52* Milliarde
bi-manual *169* beidhändig
bio-engineering *196* Biotechnik
biofuel *149* Biokraftstoff
biomass *135* Biomasse
biometric *209* biometrisch
bird, migratory **~** *145* Zugvogel
birth rate *195* Geburtenrate
bit *174* Teil
to blame, to be to ~ *136* Schuld sein
blank *120* leer, frei
blanket *49T* pauschal, umfassend
to block *39* sperren; *202* blockieren
blood vessel *17* Blutgefäß
blouse *156* Bluse
to blow *62* wehen, blasen
blow *94* Schlag
board, ~ and lodging *66* Kost und Logis; **to take sth on ~** *209* etw bedenken
to boast sth *27* etw aufweisen (können)
body *76* (*Brief:*) Hauptteil; *81* Leichnam; **~ language** *198* Körpersprache; **~ part** *196* Körperteil
bold *36* fett(gedruckt)
bomb *124* Bombe
to bomb sth *124* einen Bombenanschlag auf etw verüben

bombarded *183* bombardiert, überhäuft
bomber *125* Bombenattentäter/in
to bond *188* (sich) binden
to book *177T* buchen
booking *119* Buchung
boomerang *62T* Bumerang
booming *118* blühend, florierend
to boost *17T* ankurbeln
border *81* Grenze; **~ customs officer** *161* (Grenz-)Zollbeamter/-beamtin
to border with sth *126T* an etw grenzen
boring *184* langweilig
to borrow sth *57* sich etw ausleihen
both ... and ... *194* sowohl ... als auch ...
bother *183* Ärger
to bother sb *34T* jdn belästigen, jdn stören
to bottle *49T* in Flaschen abfüllen
bottle bank *46* Glascontainer
bottom line *107T* das, worauf es (unterm Strich) ankommt
bored, to get ~ *50* sich langweilen
bouncer *40* Türsteher/in
to bow *88T* sich verbeugen
Boxing Day *94* 2. Weihnachtstag
bracket *7* Klammer
branch *88T* Zweigstelle, Filiale
to brand a product *51* ein Markenprodukt schaffen
branded goods *pl 53* Markenware, Markenartikel
bread roll *99* Brötchen
break *173* Pause
to break *178* kaputtgehen; **~ down** *72* zusammenbrechen; **~ sth apart** *145* etw auseinandernehmen; **~ sth up** *7* etw zertrümmern, etw demolieren; **~ up** *40* (Menschenmenge) zerstreuen
breakage *105* Bruchschaden
breakdown *135* Zusammenbruch
breakfast cereals *64* Frühstücksflocken
breathing *14* Atmung
breathless(ly) *124* atemlos
breathtaking *199* atemberaubend
to breed *152* züchten; *170* ausbrüten
breed *160* Rasse
breeding *152* Zucht, Züchtung; **~ ground** *145* Brutplatz
brick *156* Ziegel
brief(ly) *60* kurz, knapp
to bring onto the market *54* auf den Markt bringen
Briton *36* Brite/Britin
broad *64* breit, ausgedehnt
broke *49T* kaputt
broken *144* kaputt, defekt
to brush sth off *189* etw ignorieren
bucket *43* Eimer
bucket list *43* Liste der Dinge, die man tun möchte, bevor man stirbt
Buddhist *108* Buddhist/in
buddy *188* Kamerad, Kumpel

321

A–Z word list

budget *62T* Etat, Haushalt, Budget
buffet lunch *122* Lunchbuffet
to **build**, ~ **a relationship** *175* eine Beziehung herstellen; ~ **sth up** *86* etw aufbauen
built-in *178* eingebaut, installiert
bullet *80* (Gewehr-)Kugel; ~ **point** *24* Stichpunkt
to **bully** *185* schikanieren, große Reden schwingen
bunch, a ~ of *168* eine Menge
burden *108* Last, Belastung, Bürde
to **burn** *17T* (sich) verbrennen; to ~ **out** *134* bis zur Erschöpfung arbeiten
business, ~ ethics *190* Geschäftsethik; ~ **leader** *74* erfolgreich Wirtschaftende/r; ~ **leadership** *184* Geschäftsführung; ~ **studies** *75* Betriebswirtschaft; to **go out of ~** *107T* das Geschäft aufgeben, Pleite gehen; to **get down to ~** *173* zur Sache kommen; to **mind one's own ~** *57* sich um seinen eigenen Kram kümmern
buttocks *pl 88T* das Gesäß, der Hintern
button *160* Knopf, Button; **at the push of a ~** *199* auf Knopfdruck
buyer *100* Einkäufer/in
buzz *181* Summen, Dröhnen, Gerücht; to **create a ~ for something** *181* Begeisterung für etwas erzeugen
by, ~ chance *141* zufällig; ~ **contrast** *138* im Gegensatz dazu, dagegen; ~ **default** *69* automatisch; ~ **laboratory design** *152* im Labor geplant; ~ **oneself** *62T* allein; ~ **the way** *60* übrigens, nebenbei erwähnt; ~ **the year 2020** *197* bis zum Jahr 2020

C

CEO = Chief Executive Officer *184* Vorstandsvorsitzende/r
cable *145* Kabel; ~ **news** *124* TV-Nachrichtensender
cactus *147* Kaktus
caffeine *14* Koffein
cage *154* Käfig
to **calculate** *168* berechnen
call, ~ for help *38* Hilferuf; to **take a ~** *38T* einen Anruf entgegennehmen, ans Telefon gehen
to **call, ~ for sth** *137* zu etw aufrufen
called *16* namens; to **be ~** *37* heißen
caller *34* Anrufer/in
to **calm** *143* beruhigen; ~ **down** *84* sich beruhigen
calorie *17* Kalorie
calving *160* Kalben
camera, CCTV ~ *132* Überwachungskamera; **speed ~** *48* Geschwindigkeitsüberwachungskamera, Radarfalle
campaign *43* Aktion, Kampagne
to **campaign** *109* kämpfen
campaigner *132* Aktivist/in

can *46* Dose
to **cancel** *16* absagen, stornieren; *130* abbrechen
cancer *43* Krebs (Krankheit)
candidate *66* Bewerber/in
candle *79* Kerze
canister *40* Dose, Büchse
capable of *118* fähig zu
capacity *44* Kapazität, Leistungsvermögen
capital *98* Kapital; *144* Hauptstadt
capitalism *192* Kapitalismus
to **capitalize on sth** *44* aus etw Nutzen ziehen
caption *8* Bildunterschrift
captive *182* gefangen
to **capture** *181* gefangen nehmen; *200* (Markt:) erobern
car, ~ park *69* Parkplatz, -haus, -garage; ~ **wash** *49* Autowaschanlage; **in-~ entertainment** *167* Unterhaltungselektronik im Auto; **racing ~** *13* Rennwagen; **sports ~** *49* Sportwagen
carbon *137* Kohlenstoff
carbon dioxide *136* Kohlendioxid; ~ **level** *136* Kohlendioxidkonzentration, -gehalt
cardboard *99* Pappe
cardiovascular *17* Herz-Kreislauf-
care *17T* Sorge; *103* Fürsorge, Sorgfalt; ~ **home** *132* Pflegeheim; **health ~** *97* Gesundheitswesen, medizinische Versorgung; *118* Gesundheitspflege
to **care about sth** *100* sich um etw kümmern
career *8* Karriere, Laufbahn
careers advisor *68* Berufsberater/in
careful(ly) *88T* vorsichtig, sorgfältig
careless *78T* nachlässig
caring *65* fürsorglich; ~ **profession** *68T* Pflegeberuf
carpenter *65* Zimmerer/in, Schreiner/in
carpentry *100* Schreinerei
carpet *40* Teppich(boden)
carpooling *199* das Bilden einer Fahrgemeinschaft
to **carry, ~ on** *116* weitermachen; ~ **out** *34* durchführen, ausführen
cartoonist *26* Karikaturist/in
case *158* Fall; *163* Koffer; ~ **study** *100* Fallstudie; **in ~ of** *200T* im Fall von
to **cash a cheque** *68T* einen Scheck einlösen
cash, ~ machine *105* Geldautomat; to **have spare ~** *96T* Geld übrig haben
cashier *68T* Kassierer/in
cassava *156* Maniok, Kassava
casual *71* leger, zwanglos; ~ **job** *110* Nebenjob
catalyst *134* Auslöser, Beschleuniger
catastrophe *148* Katastrophe
to **catch, to be caught** *56* festsitzen, in der Klemme sitzen
to **categorize** *64* einstufen, kategorisieren, klassifizieren

category *65* Kategorie
to **cater** *122* Speisen und Getränke liefern; ~ **for sth** *122* auf etw eingehen
Catholicism *55* Katholizismus, der katholische Glaube
cause *136* Ursache
to **cause** *28* verursachen; ~ **sb to do sth** *69* jdn dazu veranlassen, etw zu tun
CCTV (closed-circuit television) *132* Videoüberwachung; ~ **camera** *132* Überwachungskamera
ceilidh *79* geselliges Beisammensein mit Musik und Tanz (schottischer Brauch)
ceiling *74* Decke
to **celebrate** *20* feiern
celebrity *6* Prominente/r, Prominenz
centrally heated *70* zentralbeheizt
century *14* Jahrhundert
CEO (Chief Executive Officer) *118* Vorstandsvorsitzende/r
certain *54* gewiss
to **certify** *156* zertifizieren
chain *64* Kette
chairperson *155* Vorsitzende/r
to **challenge** *118* (heraus-)fordern
challenge *10* Herausforderung, (große) Aufgabe
challenging *20* anspruchsvoll, fordernd
champion *13* Meister/in
chance, by ~ *141* zufällig; to **take a ~ on sb** *110* es mit jdm versuchen, jdm eine Chance geben
change *8* Wandel, Verwandlung; *52* Veränderung; *81* Wechselgeld
to **change, ~ for the better** *101* sich zum Besseren verändern; ~ **sth into sth** *17* etw in etw umwandeln
changing *109* im Wandel
changing room *13* Umkleidekabine, Umkleide
channel *37* Kanal
chaos *40* Chaos
character trait *64* Charaktereigenschaften
characteristic *64* Eigenschaft; *116* Merkmal
to **charge sb with sth** *14* jdn einer Sache beschuldigen, jdn einer Sache anklagen
charge, in ~ *118* leitend, verantwortlich
charitable *92* wohltätig, gemeinnützig
charity *7* Benefiz-, Wohltätigkeit(s-); *66* Wohltätigkeitsorganisation; to **give sth to ~** *92* (für wohltätige Zwecke) spenden
chart *52* Diagramm, Tabelle; **bar ~** *52* Säulendiagramm; **line ~** *53* Liniendiagramm
to **chase sb** *14* jdn verfolgen, jdn jagen
chat *56* Unterhaltung, Schwätzchen; to **have a ~** *34T* sich unterhalten, miteinander plaudern
chatty *32* mitteilsam, geschwätzig

cheap *178* preiswert
to **check**, ~ **sth out** *62T* sich etw ansehen
checkout *81* Kasse
cheek *88T* Wange
to **cheer for sb** *21T* jdn anfeuern, jdm zujubeln
cheerful *57* fröhlich
cheers *pl 8* Jubel, Applaus; C~! *31* Tschüs! Mach's gut! Danke!
chemical *202* chemisch, Chemie-; ~ **control (of pests)** *152* Schädlingsbekämpfung(smittel)
chemicals *202* Chemikalien
cheque, to cash a ~ *68T* einen Scheck einlösen
chess *13* Schach; ~ **set** *13* Schachspiel (Figuren + Brett)
chicken breast *207* Hühnerbrust
chief, ~ **executive** *98* Hauptgeschäftsführer/in, Firmenchef/in; ~ **human resources officer** *188* Leiter/in der Personalabteilung
childhood *37* Kindheit; ~ **sweetheart** *10* Jugendliebe
chilly *173* kühl
chips *pl BE 63* Pommes frites
choice *19* Wahl, Entscheidung
to **choose,** ~ **sth over sth** *46* etw einer anderen Sache vorziehen
chore *55* (lästige Routine-)Aufgabe
Christian *108* Christ/in; *126* christlich
to **chuckle** *169* kichern, schmunzeln
citizen *95* Bürger/in
citrus *98* Zitrusfrucht
city planner *167* Stadtplaner/in
civil society *161* Bürgergesellschaft
civilian *158* Zivilist/in
civilization *164* Zivilisation
to **claim** *124* behaupten; ~ **unemployment benefits** *86* Arbeitslosengeld beziehen
clash *170* Konflikt, Streit
classmate *178* Klassenkamerad/in
to **clean up** *40* aufräumen, saubermachen
cleaning products *98* Putzmittel
to **clear** *148* räumen, roden
clear *198* verständlich, klar; ~ **conscience** *192* reines Gewissen
clearance sale *144* Räumungsverkauf
clerical *65* Büro-
clerk, bank ~ *67* Bankangestellte/r
client *98* Kunde/Kundin; ~ **base** *44* Kundenstamm; ~ **pool** *187* Kundenstamm
climate *136* Klima; ~ **change** *136* Klimawandel
climb *106* Anstieg
clinic *100* Klinik
close *11* nah, dicht, eng; ~ **to** *141* nahe bei, in der Nähe von
to **close down** *140* stilllegen
closely *186* genau, eingehend; ~ **related** *116* eng verwandt
closeness *88T* Nähe
clothing *187* Kleidung; ~ **bank** *89* Altkleidersammelbehälter

cloud *170* Wolke, Datenwolke
clue *8* Hinweis, Anhaltspunkt
coal *136* Kohle; ~-**fired** *136* kohlegetrieben
coast *80* Küste
coastal *137* Küsten-
coating *145* Ummantelung, (Kabel-)Mantel
co-author *137* Mitautor/in, Mitverfasser/in
to **coax sth out of sth** *160* etw aus etw herausholen
cocaine *14* Kokain
code *88T* Norm; ~ **of conduct** *190* Verhaltenskodex
cold *13* Erkältung
collaborative *184* gemeinschaftlich, behilflich
collaborator *168* Mitarbeiter/in
to **collapse** *100* einstürzen
collapse *103* Einsturz
colleague *28* Kollege/Kollegin
to **collect,** ~ **sth on sb** *7* (etw über jdn sammeln; ~ **sth** *21* etw abholen
collection *23* Sammlung; *144* Abholung
collective *183* Gemeinschaft, Verband
college *49T* Fachhochschule
collegial *184* kollegial
colonial power *160* Kolonialmacht
to **colour** *49T* färben
to **comb** *81* kämmen
to **combat** *134* bekämpfen
to **combine** *192* kombinieren, verbinden
to **come,** ~ **across as** *88T* auf andere wirken; ~ **across sth** *51* auf etw stoßen; ~ **down to sth** *18* auf etw hinauslaufen, auf etw ankommen; ~ **fourth** *14* Vierte/r werden; ~ **round** *30* vorbeikommen; ~ **up with sth** *51* sich etw ausdenken, sich etw einfallen lassen; **The best is yet to ~.** *164* Das Beste kommt noch. Die besten Zeiten stehen uns noch bevor.
comfortable *62T* angenehm; to **be ~** *88T* sich wohlfühlen
to **command** *131* beherrschen
command *80* Kommando, Befehl; to **be in ~** *80* das Kommando führen, die Befehle geben, das Sagen haben
commander *124* Kommandant/in, Anführer/in
commendable *161* vorbildlich
to **comment on sth** *189* etw erläutern, kommentieren
commerce *161* Handel
commercial *51* (Werbe-)Spot
commercial *142* gewerblich, kommerziell
commitment to sth *94* Engagement für etw, Einsatz für etw
committee *14* Komitee; *155* Ausschuss, Kommission
common *64* üblich, bekannt; *88T* verbreitet
communicator *197* Kommunikator/in

community *66* Gemeinde, Gemeinschaft; ~ **benefits** *pl 143T* Zahlungen an die Gemeinde
to **commute** *137* (zur Arbeit) pendeln
commuter *46* Pendler/in
companionship *90* Gemeinschaft, Gesellschaft
company, ~ **car** *65* Firmenwagen; ~ **founder** *74* Geschäftsgründer/in
comparable *175* vergleichbar
to **compare** *9* vergleichen
comparison *21* Steigerung (von Adjektiven)
compass *159* Kompass
compatible *179* kompatibel, passend
to **compete** *14* (bei einem Wettbewerb) antreten; ~ **with sb** *44* mit jdm im Wettbewerb stehen, konkurrieren
competence *88T* Fähigkeit, Können, Kompetenz
competition *8* Wettkampf; *46* Konkurrenz, Konkurrenzkampf; *54* Wettbewerb
competitive *14* wettkampfmäßig; *21* konkurrenzfähig, (Preise:) günstig; *46* umkämpft, wettbewerbsintensiv
competitor *72* Konkurrent/in, Konkurrenz
to **compile** *77* erstellen, zusammenstellen
to **complain** *28* sich beschweren, sich beklagen
complaint *27* Beschwerde, Klage, Reklamation
to **complete** *54* beenden, abschließen
completion *164* Ausführung, Erledigung (einer Aufgabe)
to **complicate** *169* komplizieren
complication *202* Komplikation
complimentary close *76* (Brief:) Schlussformel
component *100* Bauteil
to **compose** *46* komponieren
compost *156* Kompost
comprehensive school *163* Gesamtschule
computer-aided *100* computergestützt
to **concede** *129* eingestehen, einräumen
to **concentrate on sth** *11T* sich auf etw konzentrieren
concept *46* Idee, Gedanke, Konzept
to **concern** *88T* betreffen; to **be ~ed with sth** *205* mit etw befasst sein
concern *69* Sorge, Befürchtung
concerned *194* besorgt
to **conclude** *73* schließen, beenden; *174* abschließen
conclusion *38* Schluss *74* Schlussfolgerung; to **draw a ~** *74* eine Schlussfolgerung ziehen; **in ~** *48* abschließend, zum Schluss
concrete *97* konkret
concrete *143T* Beton
condensed *199* verdichtet, zusammengefasst, kondensiert

A–Z word list

condition *118* Bedingung, Kondition; *134* Zustand
to **conduct** *44* hier: durchführen
conference *140* Konferenz
confidence *94* Selbstvertrauen, Zuversicht
confident *198* selbstsicher, souverän; **self-~** *177T* selbstbewusst
to **confirm** *32* bestätigen
confirmation *121* Bestätigung
to **confiscate** *163* beschlagnahmen, konfiszieren
conflict zone *126* Krisenregion, Konfliktzone
to **confuse** *88T* irritieren, verwirren
to **congratulate sb on sth** *11* jdm zu etw gratulieren
congressman *110* Kongressabgeordneter
connection *15* Verbindung
contrast, by ~ *138* im Gegensatz dazu, dagegen; **in ~** *184* hingegen, dagegen
conscience *192* Gewissen; **clear ~** *192* reines Gewissen
consequence *130* Folge, Konsequenz; **irreversible ~s** *204* unumkehrbare Konsequenzen
considerable *200T* beträchtlich, beachtlich
to **consist of sth** *103* aus etw bestehen
constant *51* ständig, andauernd
constitution *158* Verfassung
to **construct** *101* bauen, errichten, konstruieren
construction, ~ company *116* Baufirma; **~ worker** *65* Bauarbeiter/in
consulting firm *161* Beratungsfirma
to **consume** *146* verbrauchen, konsumieren
consumer *19* Verbraucher/in, Konsument/in
consumption *146* Verbrauch, Konsum
contact, ~ details *pl 31* Kontaktdaten; **~ form** *177T* Kontaktformular; **business ~** *121* Ansprechpartner/in, Geschäftspartner/in
to **contact sb** *38* sich mit jdm in Verbindung setzen
to **contain** *45* enthalten
container *155T* Behälter
to **contaminate** *156* verunreinigen, kontaminieren
content *197* Inhalt
contentment *191* Zufriedenheit
contest *46* Wettbewerb
context *41* Zusammenhang, Kontext
continent *193* Kontinent
continually *54* dauernd, fortwährend
to **continue to do sth** *52* etw weiterhin tun
continuity *70* Kontinuität, Fortdauer
continuously *146* fortlaufend
contraceptive *159* Verhütungsmittel
contract *8* Vertrag
contracted *59* zusammengezogen

to **contrast** *32* gegenüberstellen, vergleichen
to **contribute** *158* beitragen
contribution *84* Beitrag; *96* (finanzielle) Zuwendung, Spende; to **make a ~** *84* einen Beitrag leisten
contributor *110* Autor/in (von Zeitschriftenartikeln)
to **contrive** *131* bewerkstelligen
controversial *140* umstritten
controversy *202* Streit, Diskussion
convenience *170* Komfort, Bequemlichkeit
convention *162* Übereinkunft, Gepflogenheit, Konvention
conventional *46* konventionell, herkömmlich
to **convince** *146* überzeugen
convincing *192* überzeugend
to **cook a meal** *49T* eine Mahlzeit zubereiten, ein Essen kochen
cool down *17T* Abkühlen
coop *205* Hühnerstall
cooperation *149* Zusammenarbeit, Zusammenwirken
cooperative *100* Genossenschaft
to **cope (with sth)** *40* etw bewältigen, mit etw klarkommen, mit etw fertig werden
copper *145* Kupfer
copy *23* Nachahmung, Imitat; *76* Ausgabe
to **copy** *23* nachahmen, imitieren
core *176* Kern, Herzstück
corporate *69* Unternehmens-, von Unternehmen; *74* unternehmerisch; **~ culture** *134* Unternehmenskultur; **~ governance** *192* Unternehmensführung
corporation *202* Unternehmen
correction *77* Korrekturlesen, Korrektur
to **correspond** *186* entsprechen, gleichen
corridor *120T* Flur, Gang
to **corrode** *142* korrodieren, zersetzen
corrosion *141* Korrosion, Zersetzung
corrugated metal *156* Wellblech
corrupt *14* korrupt, bestechlich
cosmetics *pl 98* Kosmetik
cost *54* Kosten; **~ of living** *83* Lebenshaltungskosten; **~ reduction** *54* Kostensenkung; **~ effective** *141* rentabel; to **cut ~s** *107T* Kosten senken; **low-~** *104* billig, kostengünstig; **running ~s** *155* Betriebskosten
costly *179* teuer
council *143T* (Stadt-, Gemeinde-)Rat
councillor *143T* Ratsmitglied
counsellor *38T* Berater/in
counter *81* Schalter, Theke
to **counteract sth** *69* einer Sache entgegenwirken
couple, a ~ of *88T* einige
coupon *177* Gutschein
course *164* Weg, Vorgehensweise; **~ of action** *87* Vorgehen, Maßnahmen

court *81* Gericht(shof); **~ order** *199* Gerichtsbeschluss, Gerichtsentscheidung; **~ system** *158* Gerichtsbarkeit
courtesy *88T* Höflichkeit, Entgegenkommen
courtroom *81* Gerichtssaal
cover *22* (Buch-)Umschlag, Einband; *23* Titelseite; **~ letter** *66* Anschreiben, Begleitschreiben
to **cover** *27* bedecken
co-worker *100* Kollege/Kollegin
crack *140* Spalte
craft *79* Handwerk
crash *47* Schlag, Krach; **car ~** *166T* Autounfall
to **crash** *154* abstürzen, zusammenbrechen
crasher *40* ungeladener Gast
craze *16* Modewelle, Trend
craziness *199* Verrücktheit
to **create** *46* (er)schaffen, entwerfen, kreieren; **~ a buzz for something** *181* Begeisterung für etwas erzeugen
Creating Shared Value (CSV) *191* Schaffung von gemeinsamem Mehrwert
creativity *65* schöpferische Begabung, Kreativität
creator *65* Schöpfer/in
credit *156* Verdienst; **~ rating** *62T* (Bewertung/Einstufung der) Bonität, Kreditwürdigkeit
creepy *176* gruselig
crew *183T* Team, Mannschaft
crime, ~ detection *132* Aufdecken von Straftaten; **high ~** *136* Schwerverbrechen
criminal justice *124* Strafjustiz
crippling *156* lähmend, mörderisch
crisis *68T* Krise
critic *98* Kritiker/in
critically *197* kritisch; hier: sehr, äußerst
criticism (of sb/sth) *23* Kritik (an jdm/etw)
to **criticize** *9* kritisieren
crop *148* Nutzpflanze, Feldfrucht; *152* Ernte; *158* Getreide; **~ production** *148* Pflanzenproduktion, pflanzliche Erzeugung
cropland *148* Ackerland
to **cross** *69* überqueren, überwinden; **~ a line** *177* eine rote Linie überschreiten
cross *125* Kreuz
crossroads *164* Scheideweg
crowded *21* voll (mit Leuten), überfüllt
cruel *38T* grausam, gemein
to **cry one's eyes out** *11* wie ein Schlosshund heulen
CSR = corporate social responsibility *190* soziale/gesellschaftliche Verantwortung von Unternehmen
cuisine *79* Küche, Kochkunst
cult *6* Kult
to **cultivate** *157* bewirtschaften; *192* kultivieren

cultural 69 kulturell, kulturbezogen
cup 188 Becher
cupboard 83 Schrank
curator 197 Pfleger/in, Verwalter/in
cure 83 Heilung, Therapie
curfew 27 Sperrstunde
current 10 aktuell
currently 44 zurzeit, derzeit
customer 44 Kunde/Kundin; ~ **account** 200T Kundenkonto; ~ **experience** 175 Kundenerlebnis; ~ **satisfaction** 177 Kundenzufriedenheit; ~ **service** 196 Kundendienst; ~ **services advisor** 68T Kundenberater/in
to **customize** 174 auf den Kundenbedarf zuschneiden
customized 196 individuell angepasst, zugeschnitten
customs pl 144 Zoll
to **cut** 149 reduzieren, einschränken; ~ **a long story short** 60 lange Rede, kurzer Sinn; ~ **costs** 107T Kosten senken; ~ **down** 146 (Wald) abholzen; ~ **sb off from sth** 36 jdn von etw abschneiden
cutlery 168 Besteck
cutting-edge 160 Spitzen-, auf dem neusten Stand
CV (curriculum vitae) 66 Lebenslauf
cybercrime 130 Cyberkriminalität
to **cycle on** 14 weiterradeln
cycle, changing-~ 49 Lebensdauer, Lebenszyklus; **fertility** ~ 160 Fruchtbarkeitszyklus
cyclist 14 Radfahrer/in
cyclone 137 Wirbelsturm, Zyklon, Sturmtief

D

damage 40 Schaden; **property** ~ 166T Sachschaden, Sachschäden
to **damage** 40 beschädigen
damaging 209 schädigend, umweltbelastend
dance routine 17T Tanzschritte
dancer 65 Tänzer/in
danger 40 Gefahr
darkness 131 Dunkelheit
data 64 Daten; ~ **protection** 123 Datenschutz
dawn 150 Morgendämmerung
day, ~ **centre** 90 Tagesstätte für Senioren; ~ **-to-day** 56 tagtäglich; **at the of the** ~ 57 letzten Endes, unterm Strich
to **deactivate** 39 stilllegen, deaktivieren
dead, **to be left for** ~ 109 als tot zurückgelassen werden
deadline, **to meet a** ~ 112 eine Frist / einen Termin einhalten
deal 44 Geschäft, Abschluss; 81 Abmachung; **a great** ~ 94 eine erhebliche Menge

to **deal with sth** 41 mit etw zurechtkommen, mit etw umgehen; 87 mit etw zu tun haben
dealer 144 Händler/in
death 81 Tod
debate 22 Diskussion, Debatte
debt 156 Schulden
decade 14 Jahrzehnt
to **declare** 167 verkünden
decline 54 Verfall, Niedergang; ~ 106 Rückgang
to **decline** 54 sinken, fallen, zurückgehen
decrease 54 Abnahme, Rückgang
to **decrease** 106 abnehmen, zurückgehen; ~ **sth** 203 etw mindern, reduzieren
deep 47 tief
default 69 Voreinstellung; **by** ~ 69 automatisch
defeat 129 Niederlage
defence, self-~ 128 Selbstverteidigung
to **defend** 128 verteidigen
to **define** 6 definieren
definitely 34T absolut, ganz sicher
degree 110 Abschluss; 136 Grad
degrowth 146 Wachstumsrücknahme
delay 105 Verzögerung
to **delete** 38T löschen, tilgen
deletion 39 Löschung, Tilgung
to **deliver** 177 liefern
delivery 129 Lieferung
demand 105 Nachfrage; 196 Anforderung; **meet a** ~ 105 eine Nachfrage befriedigen
to **demand** 148 nachfragen, verlangen
democracy 101 Demokratie
democratic 132 demokratisch
demographic pl 64 die Demographie
to **demonstrate** 146 zeigen
denier 136 Leugner/in
department, **D~ for Work and Pensions** 60 brit. Arbeits- und Sozialministerium; **legal** ~ 69 juristische Abteilung
to **depend on sth** 156 von etw abhängen, auf etw angewiesen sein
dependence 123 Abhängigkeit
dependent on sth 36 von etw abhängig
depending on 19 je nach(dem)
depleting resources 194 schwindende Ressourcen
to **deport** 84 abschieben
deportation 86 Abschiebung
depressed 100 (Wirtschaft:) flau, am Boden
depth 168 (räumliche) Tiefe
deputy manager 46 stellvertretende/r Geschäftsführer/in
descendant 84 Nachfahre, Nachkomme
desert 124 Wüste
to **deserve** 6 verdienen
to **design** 11T entwerfen, gestalten; 65 konstruieren, planen; **to be designed to do sth** 49T dazu gedacht

sein, etw zu tun; darauf ausgelegt sein, etw zu tun
design, **by laboratory** ~ 152 im Labor geplant
designer 65 Gestalter/in, Designer/in, Konstrukteur/in
desperate 38T verzweifelt
desperation 194 Verzweiflung
despite 94 trotz
to **destroy** 95 zerstören
destruction 150 Zerstörung
destructive 124 zerstörerisch
details pl 40 Angaben; 177 persönliche Angaben
detention centre 81 Auffanglager, Haftanstalt
to **deter** 156 abschrecken, abhalten
to **determine** 200 bestimmen
devastating 125 verheerend
to **develop** 180 (sich) entwickeln, entstehen
developing, ~ **country** 97 Entwicklungsland; ~ **world** 190 Dritte Welt, Entwicklungsländer
development 54 Entwicklung; 106 (Immobilie:) Erschließung, Bau
device 179 Gerät
to **devote** 165 widmen
to **diagnose sb with sth** 43 etw (z. B. Krankheit) bei jdm feststellen/diagnostizieren
diagnosis, diagnoses 160 Diagnose, Diagnosen
diamond-shaped 154 rautenförmig
diet 148 Ernährung, Kost
dietary 122 Ernährungs-
to **differ** 134 sich unterscheiden, abweichen
difference, **to make a** ~ 90 etw bewirken; **to make the** ~ 49T entscheidend sein, den entscheidenden Unterschied ausmachen
digit 33 Ziffer
digital, ~ **native** 182 jemand, der mit Computern und dem Internet aufgewachsen ist; ~ **signage** 45 digitale Außenwerbung
to **diminish** 205 abnehmen, schwinden
directions pl 119 Wegbeschreibung; **to give** ~ 119 den Weg beschreiben
directory 52 Telefonbuch
dirty 9 schmutzig
disability 13 Behinderung
disabled 92 behindert; ~ **facilities** pl 122 behindertengerechte Toiletten
disadvantage 170 Nachteil
disadvantaged 64 benachteiligt
to **disagree with sth** 22 einer Sache nicht zustimmen, gegen etw sein, etw ablehnen
disagreement 88T Uneinigkeit, Meinungsverschiedenheit
disappointment 134 Enttäuschung
disaster 62T Katastrophe; **natural** ~ 158 Naturkatastrophe
disastrous 137 katastrophal, verheerend
discipline 169 Disziplin

A–Z word list

to **disclose** 132 offenlegen
discord 161 Zwietracht
to **discount** 134 Rabatt gewähren
discount 20 Rabatt, Nachlass; **~ label** 20 Billigmarke
to **discourage** 191 abschrecken, abhalten, demotivieren; 202 unterbinden, zu verhindern suchen
to **discover** 44 entdecken
disease 97 Krankheit
disgust, in ~ 81 angewidert
dishwasher 168 Spülmaschine
disillusionment 134 Ernüchterung, *hier etwa:* Antriebslosigkeit
to **dismiss sth as sth** 164 etw als etw abtun
disorganized 185 chaotisch, durcheinander
displaced 158 vertrieben
to **display** 19 zeigen
display 79 Vorführung
disrespectful 189 respektlos
distinct 178 unterschiedlich
to **distribute** 174 verteilen, austeilen
distribution 54 Verteilung, Verbreitung
district 145 Bezirk
diverse 187 unterschiedlich
diversity 156 Vielfalt
to **divide** 27 teilen; 54 unterteilen, einteilen; **~ between rich and poor** 194 die Kluft zwischen Reich und Arm
dividend 195 Gewinnanteil, Dividende
divorce 151 Scheidung
DIY (do-it-yourself) 66 Heimwerker-, Heimwerken
doer 65 Macher/in
do-good 46 weltverbessernd
dole 111 Arbeitslosengeld; **~ bludger** 111 Sozialschmarotzer
dome 155 Kuppel
domestic 167 heimisch, Inlands-
dominance 88T Dominanz, Überheblichkeit; 187 *(Wirtschaft:)* Marktherrschaft
dominant 88T marktbeherrschend
to **dominate** 124 beherrschen, dominieren
dominated by 74 beherrscht von
to **donate** 49T spenden
donation 89 Spende
donor 90 Spender/in
don't get me started with ... *coll* 183 komm mir nicht mit ...
door, to sell sth ~ to ~ 98 etw per Haustürgeschäft verkaufen; **next ~** 41 nebenan
dope 49T Depp
doubt 177T Zweifel; **to be in ~** 177T Zweifel haben
down the line 81 weiter
downside 152 Nachteil
to **downsize** 70 verkleinern, gesundschrumpfen
downwards 53 fallend
dozens of 199 Dutzende an/von
to **draft** 204 entwerfen
to **drag** 80 zerren

dragon 79 Drachen
drama 57 Schauspiel; **~ club** 59 Schauspiel-AG
dramatic(ally) 160 dramatisch
to **draw** 26 zeichnen; 73 ziehen; **~ a conclusion** 74 eine Schlussfolgerung ziehen; **~ attention to sb/sth** 23 Aufmerksamkeit auf jdn/etw ziehen; **~ the line** 177 die Grenze ziehen; **~ up** 43 *(Text)* verfassen, abfassen
drawing 26 Zeichnung
dress code 188 Kleiderordnung
to **dress down** 70 sich leger kleiden
to **drift** 156 wehen
to **drill** 140 bohren
drilling 143T Bohrung(en); **~ rig** 143T Bohrturm
drinking water 108 Trinkwasser
to **drive, ~ sb away** 60 jdn vertreiben; **to be driven to do sth** 185 den Antrieb/Willen haben, etw zu tun; **petrol-~** 102 benzingetrieben
driverless 76 führerlos
driving, ~ force 69 treibende Kraft; **~ licence** 48 Führerschein
drone 199 Drohne
to **drop** 54 fallenlassen; 60 fallen, *(Noten:)* schlechter werden; **~ in** 70 vorbeikommen, hereinschauen; **~ one's eyes** 81 den Blick senken; **~ one's voice** 80 die Stimme senken; **~ sb off** 40 jdn (wohin)bringen
drop 179 Tropfen
drought 147 Dürre
to **drown** 137 ertrinken, im Meer versinken
drums *pl* 43 Schlagzeug
drunken 40 betrunken
to **dry out** 172 austrocknen
dubious 144 zweifelhaft
due, ~ to 54 aufgrund von; **to be ~** 121T *(Flugzeug etc.:)* planmäßig ankommen
dull 194 langweilig, uninteressant, öde
to **dump** 144 *(Müll)* (wild) abladen
dump 144 Müllhalde
durable 180 haltbar, langlebig
duration 66 Dauer
during 54 während
duty 75 Aufgabe, Pflicht, Arbeit
duvet cover 63 Bettdeckenbezug
to **dwell on sth** 43 sich mit etw aufhalten
dweller 205 Bewohner/in
dysfunctional 134 dysfunktional, abträglich

E

early, in his/her ~ 20s 64 Anfang zwanzig
to **earn** 146 verdienen
earnings *pl* 83 Einkünfte, Verdienst; 143T Einnahmen, Gewinn
earthquake 96T Erdbeben
eco- 46 Öko-

ecological, ~ footprint 146 ökologischer Fußabdruck; **~ overshoot** 146 ökologischer Überschuss
ecommerce 44 Internet-Handel
economic 65 wirtschaftlich; **~ adviser** 194 Wirtschaftsberater/in; **~ growth** 195 Wirtschaftswachstum; **~ model** 180 Geschäftsmodell
economical 187 wirtschaftlich, billig
economics 137 Ökonomie, Wirtschaft(swissenschaft)
economist 146 Wirtschaftswissenschaftler/in
ecosystem 146 Ökosystem
edible 205 essbar
to **edit** 113 *(Text)* redigieren, bearbeiten
edition 111 Ausgabe
editor 110 Herausgeber/in; **~** 142 Redakteur/in
education 64 Erziehung, Bildung
educational 77 schulisch, Bildungs-
effective 46 wirksam, effektiv; **cost ~** 141 rentabel
efficiency 44 Effizienz, Leistungsfähigkeit
efficient(ly) 62T effizient
effort 188 Anstrengung, Mühe
either 164 eine/r/s (von beiden)
either ... or 23 entweder ... oder
elderly 109 ältere Menschen, Senioren; **home for the ~** 114 Altenheim
elderly 115 ältere/s/r
election 158 Wahl; **to hold ~s** 158 eine Wahl abhalten
electrical 66 elektrisch, Elektro-; **~ engineering** 169 Elektrotechnik
electrician 49 Elektriker/in
electricity bill 143 Stromrechnung
electronic 100 elektronisch, Elektronik-
electronics *pl* 69 Elektronik
element 45 Baustein, Element
elementary 203 elementar, grundlegend
to **eliminate** 54 aussondern, beseitigen
elite 158 Elite
elsewhere 67 woanders, anderswo
email exchange 171 E-Mail-Korrespondenz
embarrassed, to feel ~ 59 sich genieren, sich schämen
embarrassing 129 peinlich, unangenehm
embassy 94 Botschaft
to **embrace sth** 146 etw annehmen, begrüßen
to **emerge** 179 auftauchen, herauskommen
emergency 109 Notfall, Not-; **~ exit** 120 Notausgang, Fluchtweg; **~ exit plan** 120 Fluchtwegplan; **~ service** 167 Notfalldienst
to **emigrate** 86 auswandern
emission 137 Ausstoß, Emission
emotional 18 gefühlsmäßig, emotional

to **employ sb** *71* jdn beschäftigen, jdn einstellen
employed, self-~ *200* freiberuflich, selbständig;
employee *69* Angestellte/r, Beschäftigte/r
employer *66* Arbeitgeber/in
employment *100* Anstellung, Arbeit
to **empower sb to do sth** *90* jdn befähigen, etw zu tun
empowered *186* gestärkt
to **enable** *90* befähigen
enabled *160* fähig
enclosure (encl.) *76* (Brief:) Anlage
to **encounter sth** *201* etw ausgesetzt sein, mit etw in Berührung kommen
to **encourage** *137* fördern; **~ sb to do sth** *46* jdn ermuntern, etw zu tun
encrypted *129* verschlüsselt
end, at the ~of the day *57* letzten Endes, unterm Strich; **~ customer** *191* Endkunde/Endkundin; **high-~** *51* hochklassig, hochwertig; to **put an ~ to sth** *27* mit etw Schluss machen, einen Schlussstrich unter etw ziehen
to **end up** *41* landen
ending *14* Schluss, Ende
endless *110* endlos, fortwährend
enemy *80* Feind/in
energetic *209* energiegeladen, aktiv
energy, ~-efficient *208* energiesparend; **~-saving** *208* das Energiesparen
enforcement, law ~ *124* Gesetzesvollzug, Innere Sicherheit, Exekutive; **law ~ agency** *124* Strafverfolgungsbehörde, Exekutivorgan
to **engage, ~ in sth** *124* aktiv werden; **~ with sb** *37* auf jdn zugehen
engaged *34* (Telefon:) besetzt
engine *85* Motor
engineer *65* Ingenieur/in
engineering, mechanical ~ *169* Maschinenbau; **social ~** *114* Änderung gesellschaftlicher Strukturen, angewandte Sozialwissenschaft
to **enjoy** *209* genießen; **~ oneself** *166* sich (gut) amüsieren; **~ sth** *183T* sich an etw erfreuen
to **enlighten** *65* aufklären
to **enquire about sth** *34* sich nach etw erkundigen
enrolled *74* eingeschrieben, immatrikuliert
to **ensure** *54* sicherstellen, gewährleisten, dafür sorgen, dass
to **enter sth** *46* an etw teilnehmen; **~ a competition** *14* an einem Wettkampf/Wettbewerb teilnehmen
enterprise *94* Unternehmen; *194* Unternehmungsgeist
enterprising *65* geschäftstüchtig, risikofreudig
enthusiastic *140* begeistert; **~ about sth** *169* von etw begeistert
entire *191* ganze/r/s
entirely *54* vollständig, völlig, ganz
entrance fee *21T* Teilnahmegebühr

entrepreneur *51* Unternehmer/in
entry *38* (Blog:) Beitrag, Meldung
entry-level *68* Einstieg, Anfang; *110* Einstiegs-; **~ pay** *68T* Einstiegsgehalt, Anfangsgehalt
environment *146* Umwelt, Umfeld
environmental(ly) *46* umweltmäßig **~ly friendly** *46* umweltfreundlich
environmentalist *202* Umweltschützer/in
epidemic *161* Epidemie, Seuche
epitaph *39* Grabinschrift
equal *74* gleich; **~ opportunities** *pl* *66* Chancengleichheit; **~ society** *115* gerechte Gesellschaft
equality *67* Gleichheit
equally *80* gleichermaßen, genauso
equals *150* gleich
equipment *66* Ausrüstung, Geräte
equipped with *122* ausgestattet mit
equivalent *67* Entsprechung
equivalent, to be ~ to sth *75* einer Sache entsprechen
to **eradicate** *134* ausrotten, ausmerzen
eradication *164* Ausrottung
to **erode** *157* erodieren
escalator *46* Rolltreppe
escape *182* Entrinnen, Entkommen; **there's no ~ from the fact that** *117T* man kann nicht außer Acht lassen, dass; man muss der Tatsache ins Auge sehen, dass
to **escape** *136* entweichen; **~ from sth** *86* einer Sache entkommen; **~ sth narrowly** *94* einer Sache knapp entkommen
to **escort sb** *27* jdn begleiten, jdn eskortieren
especially *29* besonders, insbesondere
essential *40* wesentlich, unerlässlich
essentially *124* im Wesentlichen
essentials *pl 94* lebensnotwendige Güter
to **establish** *209* einführen, etablieren
establishment *182* Establishment, gesellschaftliche Ordnung
to **estimate** *27* schätzen
estimate *144* Schätzung
ethical *88* moralisch vertretbar, ethisch, dem Berufsethos entsprechend; **E~ Technology Advocate** *196* Beauftragte/r für Technikethik
ethnic *84* ethnisch, Volks-
ethnicity *108* Volkszugehörigkeit, Ethnizität
etiquette *32* Etikette, Regeln
European Commission *194* Europäische Kommission
to **evaluate** *65* bewerten, beurteilen
even *209* überhaupt; **~ so** *102* dennoch, allerdings; **~ though** *21T* selbst wenn, obwohl
eventually *179* schlussendlich, schließlich
ever *178* jemals; **~-improving** *69* stetig besser werdend
every six month *98* alle sechs Monate
everyday *51* alltäglich, Alltags-

evidence *98* Beweise, Beweismittel
evident, self-~ *88T* selbstverständlich
evil *81* böse, schlecht
evolution *14* Entwicklung
to **evolve** *208* sich entwickeln
to **examine** *175* untersuchen
example, to set an ~ *56* ein Beispiel setzen, mit gutem Beispiel vorangehen
to **exceed** *36* übersteigen; *121* überschreiten
excellent *83* ausgezeichnet, hervorragend
exception *98* Ausnahme
excess *146* Überschuss
to **exchange** *29* austauschen
excitement *17* Begeisterung; *45* Spannung, Aufregung
exciting *181* aufregend
excluded *185* ausgeschlossen
exclusive *187* exklusiv, einzigartig
exemption *27* Ausnahme, Befreiung
exercise *134* Bewegung, Sport
exhaustion *134* Erschöpfung
to **exhibit** *120* ausstellen
exhibition *81* Ausstellung
existing *137* bestehend, vorhanden
to **expand** *43* erweitern; *100* expandieren, ausweiten
expansion *101* Ausweitung, Expansion
to **expect** *178* erwarten
expectation *134* Erwartung
expense *156* Kosten, Aufwand; **at the ~ of sth** *37* auf Kosten von etw
expenses *pl 118* Ausgaben
to **experience** *189* erleben, erfahren
experienced *62T* erfahren
to **experiment** *23* experimentieren
expertise *187* Fachwissen
explanation *87* Erläuterung, Erklärung
to **explode** *124* explodieren
exploitation *118* Ausbeutung; Abbau (von Rohstoffen); **over-~** *147* Raubbau, übermäßiger Abbau
to **explore** *170* erkunden, erforschen
explosive *125* Sprengstoff; **~ device** *125* Sprengsatz
to **export** *102* ausführen, exportieren
exporter *144* Exporteur/in
exposed *183* ausgesetzt
expression *11* Ausdruck
to **extend sth to sb** *177T* jdm etw anbieten
extended *55* erweitert; **~ family** *55* Großfamilie
extension *124* Erweiterung, Ausbau
extensive *64* umfangreich
external *200* außen, extern, äußerlich
extinction *164* Vernichtung, Ausrottung, Aussterben
to **extort** *161* erpressen, abnötigen
extract *131* Auszug, Ausschnitt
extremely *199* äußerst
extremism *123* Extremismus
eye, ~ contact *88T* Augenkontakt; to **drop one's ~s** *81* den Blick senken; to **cry one's ~s out** *11* wie ein Schlosshund heulen

A–Z word list

eyelid, to bat an ~ *14* mit der Wimper zucken

F

to face, ~ competition *54* sich dem Wettbewerb stellen; **~ sb** *82* jdn konfrontieren; **~ sth** *11* sich einer Sache stellen; mit etw konfrontiert werden; **to be faced with sth** *54* mit etw konfrontiert sein
face, ~ to face *29* persönlich; **~-lift** *6* Facelifting, Gesichtsstraffung
facilities *pl 100* Anlage(n), Einrichtungen
facing sth *80* gegen etw, mit dem Gesicht zu etw
fact, in ~ *22* tatsächlich, eigentlich, um genau zu sein
factor *49* Faktor; **pull ~** *158 etwa:* Anreizwirkung, Anziehungsgrund; **push ~** *158 etwa:* Vertreibungsursache
factory floor *191* Fabrikhalle
faculty *168* Fähigkeit
to fail *54* scheitern; *155T* ausfallen; *160* versagen
failure *166T* Ausfall, Defekt
fair trade *190* aus fairem Handel, fair gehandelt
fairly *adj 190* fair, gerecht; *adv 182* ziemlich
fake *23* Fälschung, Imitation
fall *106* Absturz, Rückgang
to fall, ~ behind *62* zurückfallen, in Rückstand geraten; **~ in love with sb/sth** *86* sich in jdn/etw verlieben; **~ into sth** *44* unter etw fallen, zu etw gehören; **~ victim to sb/sth** *201* jdm/etw zum Opfer fallen
false start *62* Fehlstart
fame *10* Ruhm
famine *147* Hungersnot
far *178* weitaus, viel
to farm *101* *(Land)* bewirtschaften
farm chemicals *pl 149* Landwirtschaftschemikalien
farmer *202* Bauer, Bäuerin; Landwirt/in
farming *97* Landwirtschaft
farmland *143T* Ackerland, landwirtschaftliche Nutzfläche
farther *144* weiter
fascinating *49T* faszinierend
fashion, for ~ reasons *196* aus modischen Gründen
fashionable *18* modisch
fatality *95* Todesfall, Todesopfer
faulty *105* defekt, fehlerhaft
favor, in ~ of doing sth *AE 46* um (stattdessen) etw zu tun
favour, to be in ~ of sth *126T* für etw sein; **in ~ of** *179* zugunsten
fear *80* Angst
to fear *152* fürchten
feature *58* Hintergrundbericht, Reportage; *152* Merkmal, Eigenschaft

Federal Trade Commission (FTC) *204 etwa:* Bundeskartellamt in den USA
fee *21T* Gebühr
to feed *90* ernähren, mit Nahrung versorgen
feed *160* Futter
to feel, ~ comfortable *21T* sich wohlfühlen; **~ embarrassed** *59* sich genieren, sich schämen; **~ left out** *60* sich ausgeschlossen fühlen; **~ low** *17T* schlecht gelaunt sein, deprimiert sein; **~ sorry for sb** *92* jd tut einem leid; **~ sth** *51* etw anfassen, etw ertasten; **~ uncomfortable** *8* sich unbehaglich fühlen
female *74* Frau, weiblich; **~ quota** *74* Frauenquote
fertile *158* fruchtbar
fertiliser *BE 98* Dünger
fertility cycle *160* Fruchtbarkeitszyklus
to fertilize *152* befruchten
fertilizer *149* Dünger, Düngemittel
festival *79* Fest, Festtag, Festival
fictional *131* fiktiv
fiddly *168* knifflig, fummelig
field of vision *131* Sichtfeld
fierce *46* heftig, erbittert
to fight back *107T* sich wehren, sich zurückkämpfen
fighting *158* Kampf
figure *52* Zahl, Ziffer
to figure out *168* herausfinden
file *71* Akte, Ordner
to file *81* feilen
filing cabinet *69* Aktenschrank
to fill an order *100* einen Auftrag ausführen
to filter *184* durchlaufen, filtern
final *43* Finale
final *adj 204* letzte/r/s
finally *183T* letztendlich
finance *69* Finanz(-); **~ director** *72* kaufmännische/r Leiter/in
to finance *91* finanzieren
financial *56* finanziell, Finanz-
to find, ~ one's way around *120T* sich zurechtfinden; **~ out about sth** *64* über etw mehr erfahren; **~ sb sth** *60* jdm etw besorgen
findings *pl 43* Ergebnisse
fine *48* Geldbuße
to fine sb *48* jdn mit einer Geldbuße belegen
fingernail *23* Fingernagel
to finish, ~ second *8* Zweite/r werden
finished product *100* Endprodukt
finishing line *124* Ziellinie
to fire sb *49T* jdn feuern
fire, on ~ *143T* in Flammen; **to set ~ to sth** *145* etw anzünden
firefight *124* Schusswechsel
first, ~ and foremost *176* vor allem, in erster Linie; **~ of all** *62T* zuallererst; **at ~ hand** *31* aus erster Hand, hautnah

fishing *154* Fischerei, Befischung; **~ village** *94* Fischerdorf
to fit *16* passen; **~ in** *185* hineinpassen; **~ sth with sth** *144* etw mit etw ausstatten
fixed *70* fest, festgelegt, fest installiert
flap *22* Umschlagklappe
flat *107T* *(Umsatz etc.:)* konstant, unverändert; *(Hierarchie:)* flach
flaxen-haired *169* strohblond, flachsblond
to flee (sth) *108* flüchten (vor etw)
flexible *65* flexibel
to float *153* (auf dem Wasser) treiben
flood *95* Überschwemmung
to flood *138* überschwemmen
flooding *137* Überschwemmung
floor care *104* Bodenpflege
flow *153* Strom, Fluss
fluent *75* *(Sprache:)* fließend
flyer, high-~ *134* Überflieger/in, Erfolgsmensch
focus *174* Schwerpunkt
to focus on sth *11* sich auf etw konzentrieren
folks *pl 100* Leute
follow-up *8* Folge-, Nachfolger, Anschluss-
food, ~ pantry *AE 151* Tafel, karitative Essensausgabe; **~ security** *155T* Ernährungssicherung
footage *132* Film-/Bildmaterial
footballer *11* Fußballer/in
footprint, ecological ~ *146* ökologischer Fußabdruck
to forbid *144* verbieten, untersagen
to force *80* zwingen; *202* drängen
force *95* Gewalt, Kraft; **driving ~** *69* treibende Kraft; **police ~** *127* Polizei
forced labour *158* Zwangsarbeit
forehead *80* Stirn
forest *148* Wald
forested *156* bewaldet
forklift (truck) *116* Gabelstapler
to form *48* bilden; **~ part of sth** *190* Teil von etw sein
former *185* früher
formula *7* Formel
fortune *7* Vermögen
forward *146* vorwärts, nach vorn, voran; **to look ~ to sth** *9* sich auf etw freuen
to forward sth *145* etw (ver)schicken
forwarding agency *145* Spedition
fossil fuel *135* fossiler Brennstoff
to found *94* gründen
foundation *90* Stiftung
founder *74* Gründer/in; **company ~** *74* Geschäftsgründer/in
to fracture *140* brechen, aufbrechen
fragile *179* zerbrechlich
frame *155* Rahmen
framework *200* Rahmen
free, ~ movement *86T* Freizügigkeit; **~ time** *44* Freizeit
freedom *56* Freiheit
freely *139* ungehindert, nach Belieben

freeway *AE* 166T Autobahn
French fries *pl AE* 62T Pommes frites
frequent 158 ständig, regelmäßig
fresh water 149 Süßwasser
fridge 144 Kühlschrank
from the outside 74 von außen
frustration 44 Enttäuschung, Frust
fuel 117 Brennstoff, Treibstoff
to **fulfil** 11 erfüllen
full-time 66 Vollzeit-
fully 38T vollkommen, völlig, vollständig; ~ **equipped** 66 vollausgestattet
fun, to be ~ 47 Spaß machen; to **make ~ of sth** 187 sich über etw lustig machen
to **function** 160 fungieren, funktionieren
fund 205 Fond
to **fund** 92 finanzieren; to **self-~** 110 selbst finanzieren
funding 92 Finanzierung, Geldmittel
fundraiser 43 Spendensammler/in
fundraising 43 Spendensammeln, Geldbeschaffung
funds *pl* 200T das Geld, die Mittel
furious 199 wütend, erbost
further 8 weitere/r/s *Adj*; weiter *Adv*; to **take sth ~** 32 etw (weiter) verfolgen
furthermore 117 darüber hinaus
future 118 zukünftig

G

gadget 146 Gerät
gain 65 Gewinn, Vorteil
to **gain** 78T erwerben
gallery 35 Galerie; ~ **walk** 35 Galerierundgang
gallon 166T Gallone (= 3,78 l in den USA)
game machine 46 Videospielgerät, Spielautomat
gang 84 Bande
gap 18 Lücke
gardening 93 Gartenarbeit
garment 150 Kleidungsstück
gas, greenhouse ~ 136 Treibhausgas; **laughing ~** 40 Lachgas, **natural ~** 138 Erdgas
to **gatecrash** 40 uneingeladen erscheinen
to **gather** 164 sammeln, zusammentragen
gay 115 schwul, lesbisch
to **gaze** 131 starren, blicken
GDP = gross domestic product 193 Bruttoinlandsprodukt (BIP)
gear 21T Ausrüstung, Kleidung
gender 64 Geschlecht
gene 152 Gen; ~ **therapy** 204 Gentherapie
general 165 General
general, in ~ 15 im Allgemeinen, generell
generally 54 im Allgemeinen, üblicherweise

to **generate** 170 generieren
genetic 152 genetisch; ~ **mutation** 202 Genmutation
genius 51 Genie
geothermal power 135 Erdwärme
gesture 88 Geste, Gestik, Handbewegung
to **get, ~ angry** 62T sich ärgern; ~ **back to sb** 71T sich bei jdm (zurück)melden; ~ **bored** 50 sich langweilen; ~ **closed** 98 geschlossen werden; ~ **down to business** 173 zur Sache kommen; ~ **drunk** 41 sich betrinken; ~ **in touch with sb** 177T sich an jdn wenden, *hier:* anrufen; ~ **into the habit of doing sth** 32 sich angewöhnen, etw zu tun; ~ **involved with sb** 37 mit jdm zu tun haben; ~ **lost** 118 verlorengehen; ~ **on** 61 vorwärtskommen, zurechtkommen; ~ **over sth** 61 über etw hinwegkommen, etw verkraften; ~ **rid of sth** 134 etw loswerden; ~ **sb hooked** 17T jdn anfixen; ~ **sb through** 56 jdn durchbringen; jdm helfen, etw zu überstehen; ~ **sth** 26 etw verstehen, etw kapieren; ~ **sth right** 7 etw richtig machen, etw gut hinbekommen; ~ **sth wrong** 62T bei etw einen Fehler machen, etw falsch machen; ~ **the hang of it** 17 den richtigen Dreh finden; ~ **to know sb** 171 jdn kennen lernen; ~ **together** 29 sich treffen; ~ **upset** 62T sich aufregen; ~ **you nowhere** 126 zu nichts führen, nichts bringen
giant 46 riesig, riesenhaft
giant 49T Riese
gig 7 (Rock-, Pop-, Jazz-)Konzert
gist 71 das Wesentliche
to **give, ~ a presentation** 48 ein Referat halten; ~ **a reason** 22 eine Begründung anführen; ~ **an opinion** 22 eine Meinung äußern; ~ **directions** 119 den Weg beschreiben; ~ **preference to sth** 175 etw den Vorzug geben; ~ **sth a try** 17T etw ausprobieren; ~ **sb the chance to do sth** 188 jdm die Gelegenheit geben, etw zu tun; ~ **to charity** 92 (für wohltätige Zwecke) spenden
given name 80 Vorname
giving 92 Spenden
global(ly) 70 weltweit, global; ~ **warming** 136 Erderwärmung
globalization 100 Globalisierung
glossy 23 Hochglanz-
GM (genetically modified) 152 genmanipuliert
to **go, ~ for sth** 18 etw nehmen, etw gut finden; 168 etw wählen, etw wagen; ~ **from bad to worse** 62 immer schlimmer werden; ~ **inland** 100 ins Landesinnere gehen; ~ **on strike** 72 streiken; ~ **out of business** 107T das Geschäft aufgeben, Pleite gehen; ~ **under** 56 Pleite gehen; ~ **unnoticed** 129 unbemerkt bleiben; ~ **viral** 38T sich (im Internet) rasend schnell verbreiten; ~ **with sth** 8 zu etw gehören; ~ **wrong** 62T schieflaufen
goal 46 Ziel, Absicht; 82 (Ballspiel:) Tor
golf course 143T Golfplatz
good, ~ cause 92 guter Zweck; ~ **looking** 8 gutaussehend, attraktiv
good, the ~ 91 Wohl
goods *pl* 19 Waren, Güter
to **gossip** 57 tratschen, schwatzen
gossip 173 Klatsch, Tratsch
to **govern** 101 regieren, verwalten, führen
governance 161 Regierungshandeln
government 47 Regierung, öffentliche Verwaltung
to **grab, ~ sth** 69 sich etw schnappen; ~ **sb's attention** 182 jds Aufmerksamkeit auf sich ziehen
grade *AE* 60 Note; **G~ 1 building** 155 denkmalgeschütztes Gebäude; ~ **A student** 60 Einserschüler/in
gradual(ly) 54 allmählich
graduate 108 Absolvent/in
graduation 112 (Schul-/Universitäts-)Abschluss
grain 149 Getreide
granddaughter 176 Enkelin
to **grant sb sth** 76 jdm etw gewähren
graph 44 Diagramm, Graphik, Kurve; **line ~** 92 Liniendiagramm
graphic 151 Grafik
grasp 168 Griff
to **grasp** 168 greifen, ergreifen
grass 57 Rasen, Gras
grateful 139 dankbar
graveyard 145 Friedhof
to **gravitate to sth** 70 von etw angezogen werden
great-grandfather 83 Urgroßvater
greatly 149 erheblich
to **green** 156 begrünen
greenhouse gas 136 Treibhausgas
grocery store 98 Lebensmittelladen
gross domestic product (GDP) 92 Bruttosozialprodukt
ground 47 (Erd-)Boden
groundwater 143T Grundwasser
to **grow** 99 (Pflanze) anbauen; ~ **up** 19 aufwachsen
growth 17 Wachstum, Zunahme; ~ **stage** 54 Entwicklungsstadium, Wachstumsphase
to **guarantee** 207 garantieren, sicherstellen
guardian, legal ~ 27 Vormund, Erziehungsberechtigte/r
to **guess** 186 (er-)raten
guesswork 131 Mutmaßung, Spekulation
guidance 186 Führung
to **guide** 114 führen
guideline 190 Richtlinie, Leitlinie; to **set ~s** 197 Regeln, Richtlinien aufstellen
guilty 125 schuldig

329

A–Z word list

to **gut** *145* ausweiden, ausschlachten
guts *pl*, to **have the ~ to do sth** *84* den Mumm haben, etw zu tun
guy *14* Typ, Kerl
gym *13* Fitness-Studio

H

habit *36* Gewohnheit; to **get into the ~ of doing sth** *32* sich angewöhnen, etw zu tun
to **hack into sth** *200T* in etw eindringen
hair care *49T* Haarpflege
hairdressing salon *49* Friseursalon
hairstyle *177T* Frisur
hall *155* Saal, Halle
hallucination *14* Halluzination, Wahnvorstellung
hand, at first ~ *31* aus erster Hand, hautnah; **on the one ~** *22* einerseits; **on the other ~** *11T* andererseits; to **shake ~s** *88T* sich die Hand geben;
to **hand, ~ over** *48* übergeben; **~ sth in** *37* etw abgeben; **~ sth out** *94* etw verteilen, etw ausgeben
handbook *188* Betriebshandbuch, Leitfaden
handful, a ~ *202* eine Handvoll
hand-held *48* in der Hand gehalten
to **handle sth** *134* bewältigen, erledigen
handout *90* Almosen; *172* Arbeitsblatt
handwriting *37* Handschrift
handy *128* praktisch
to **hang out** *25* rumhängen, sich rumtreiben
hang, to **get the ~ of it** *17* den richtigen Dreh finden
harbour *113* Hafen
hard *200T* schwer, schwierig
hardly *adv 98* kaum
to **harm sb** *128* jdm schaden
harm, to **do sb ~** *40* jdm etwas (an)tun
harmful to sb *191* (gesundheits-) schädlich für jdn
harmony *84* Harmonie
harsh *88T* scharf, harsch
to **harvest** *54* (ab)ernten
harvest *160* Ernte
to **have, ~ a chat** *34T* sich unterhalten, miteinander plaudern; **~ a hard time** *56* es schwer haben; **~ one's say** *126* seine Meinung äußern, zu Wort kommen; **~ spare cash** *96T* Geld übrig haben; **~ the guts to do sth** *84* den Mumm haben, etw zu tun; **He has a (good) point.** *84* Da ist etwas dran. Da hat er recht.
head *104* Leiter/in, Chef/in; **H~ of Science** *139* Fachbereichsleiter/in Naturwissenschaft; **~ Office** *50* Zentrale, Direktion, Hauptverwaltung; to **shake one's ~** *81* den Kopf schütteln
heading *15* Rubrik, Überschrift

headline *6* Schlagzeile, Überschrift; to **hit the ~s** *7* in die Schlagzeilen kommen, Schlagzeilen machen
headquarters *187* die Zentrale, der Hauptsitz
health *190* Gesundheit; **~ and safety** *83* Arbeitsschutz; **~ care** *97* Gesundheitswesen, medizinische Versorgung; *118* Gesundheitspflege
healthy *134* gesund
heart-warming *114* herzerwärmend
heating *62T* Heizung
hectare *155T* Hektar
helper *65* Helfer/in
helpline *38* Hotline, Sorgentelefon
herbicide *152* Unkrautvernichtungsmittel
herd *152* Herde
to **hide (away)** *84* sich verstecken, sich verbergen
hierarchical *184* hierarchisch
high, ~ crime *136* Schwerverbrechen; **~ street** *23* Hauptgeschäftsstraße, Einkaufsstraße; **~-end** *51* hochklassig, hochwertig; **~-flyer** *134* Überflieger/in, Erfolgsmensch
to **highlight** *16* hervorheben
highly *134* sehr, äußerst; **~ motivated** *66* hochmotiviert
highway *AE 160* Autobahn
to **hijack** *130* kapern
hill *57* Berg, Anhöhe, Hügel
Hinduism *55* Hinduismus
hip *17T* Hüfte
to **hire sb** *39* jdn beauftragen, jdn engagieren; *49T* jdn einstellen
historical *14* historisch
to **hit** *148* erreichen; *160* (Taste) drücken; **~ the headlines** *7* in die Schlagzeilen kommen, Schlagzeilen machen
to **hitch-hike** *94* per Anhalter fahren, trampen
to **hold, ~ elections** *158* eine Wahl abhalten; **~ on** *34* warten; **~ sb back** *8* jdn bremsen; **~ the line** *34T* am Apparat bleiben
hold, to **take ~ of sth** *134* ergreifen, sich annehmen
homage *169* Huldigung, Hommage
home, ~ automation *208* Haustechnik, Haushaltsautomatisierung; **~ country** *91* Heimatland; **~ for the elderly** *114* Altenheim; **~ to sth/sb** *184* Heimat/Basis von etw/jdm; **care ~** *132* Pflegeheim; **retirement ~** *114* Altersheim
homeless *81* obdachlos
homelessness *91* Obdachlosigkeit
homestay accommodation *66* Unterbringung bei Gasteltern
homework *64* Hausaufgaben
homing *69* Heimfindeverhalten (z. B. von Brieftauben)
honest *88T* ehrlich; **To be ~, …** *183T* Ehrlich gesagt, …
honestly *134* ernsthaft
hooked, to **get ~ sb** *17T* jdn anfixen

to **hoover** *60* staubsaugen
hopeless *110* hoffnungslos
hopelessness *194* Aussichtslosigkeit
horizontal(ly) *155* waagrecht, horizontal
horrific *91* schrecklich, entsetzlich
horrified *43* entsetzt
horror *45* Schrecken
host *87* Gastgeber; *126T* (Radio-/TV-)Moderator/in
hostel *31* Herberge, Wohnheim
house, to **move ~** *28* umziehen
household name *51* bekannter Name, Begriff
housework *58* Hausarbeit
housing *86* Wohnungsbau, Wohnungen; *108* Unterkunft; **social ~** *205* sozialer Wohnungsbau;
however … *118* wie … auch immer, sowenig … auch; *202* hingegen, jedoch, allerdings
hub *145* Drehkreuz, (Verkehrs-)Knoten
huge *8* riesig, Riesen-
human, ~ being *26* Mensch, menschliches Wesen; **~ error** *166T* menschliches Versagen; **H~ Resources (HR)** *50* Personal(abteilung); **~ rights** *192* Menschenrechte
humanitarian *94* humanitär
humanity *136* Menschheit, Menschlichkeit
humanlike *168* menschenähnlich
to **humiliate** *81* demütigen, erniedrigen
humiliation *81* Demütigung, Erniedrigung
humour *45* Humor
hunger *158* Hunger
to **hunt** *154* jagen
hurdle *188* Hürde, Hindernis
to **hurt** *118* verletzen
hydraulic *140* hydraulisch
hydro-electric power *135* Wasserkraft
hydroponics *152* Hydrokultur(-)
to **hyphenate** *106* mit einem Bindestrich schreiben

I

I suppose *62T* wohl
I'm afraid *23* leider
I've never looked back. *49T* Ich habe es nie bereut.
ice, ~ sheet *137* Eisdecke; **~-covered** *148* eisbedeckt; **~-free** *148* eisfrei
ID *27* Personalausweis
ideal *65* ideal
idealistic *192* idealistisch
identification *177T* Ausweis
to **identify** *107* erkennen, bestimmen, identifizieren; **~ with sb/sth** *19* sich mit jdm/etw identifizieren
identity *123* Identität
idiomatic *61* idiomatisch, redensartlich
to **ignore** *114* nicht beachten, ignorieren
illegal *14* verboten, illegal
illiterate *108* Analphabet/in sein

illness 196 Krankheit
imagery 88T Symbolik
imagination 65 Phantasie, Vorstellungskraft
immediate(ly) 41 unverzüglich, unmittelbar, sofort
impact 94 Einfluss, Auswirkung; to **make an ~** 94 etw bewirken, etw verändern
to **implement** 209 realisieren, verwirklichen
implementation 199 Umsetzung, Durchführung
to **import** 99 importieren, einführen
importance 38 Bedeutung, Wichtigkeit
to **impose** 187 einführen, aufbürden
impressed 120T beeindruckt
impression 175 Eindruck
to **improve** 14 (sich) verbessern, (sich) steigern
improvement 175 Verbesserung; **~ in sth** 14 Verbesserung bei etw
to **improvise** 16 improvisieren
inability 134 Unfähigkeit
inappropriate 177T unangemessen
in-car entertainment 167 Unterhaltungselektronik im Auto
inch 80 Zoll (= 2,54 cm)
incident 27 Vorfall, Zwischenfall
including 19 einschließlich
income 68 Einkommen
incomer 86T Zuzügler, Ankömmling
incompatible 187 unvereinbar, inkompatibel
incompetent 199 unfähig, nicht kompetent
to **increase** 44 erhöhen, vergrößern; 46 steigen, zunehmen; **~ sth** 17T etw steigern
increase 54 Anstieg; 69 Zunahme, Steigerung; to **be on the ~** 69 auf dem Vormarsch sein, zunehmen
increasingly 44 zunehmend
independence 94 Unabhängigkeit
independent 57 unabhängig
to **indicate** 44 zeigen, hinweisen
individual 134 der/die Einzelne
individualized 176 individualisiert, zugeschnitten
indoor 206 innen-
industrial 104 Industrie-
industrialist 165 Industrielle/r
industrialized 104 industrialisiert
inexpensive 181 preiswert
to **influence** 24 beeinflussen
influence 100 Einfluss
influential 161 einflussreich
influx 194 Zustrom
informal 59 informell, locker
informality 69 Formlosigkeit, Ungezwungenheit
infrastructure 69 Infrastruktur
ingredients 98 Zutaten
initial 171 erste/r/s; **~ creation** 54 Erschaffung
initially 43 anfangs, anfänglich
to **initiate** 54 einleiten, beginnen
initiative 27 Aktion, Initiative

to **injure** 100 verletzen
injury 14 Verletzung
inland, to **go ~** 100 ins Landesinnere gehen
innocent 88T unschuldig
innovator 194 Erfinder/in, Umgestalter/in
to **input** 128 eingeben
to **inquire** 140 nachfragen, sich erkundigen
insecticide 98 Insektengift
insecure 188 unsicher
inside, **~ address** 76 Empfängeranschrift
insight 31 Einblick
insignificant 188 unwichtig, unbedeutend
to **insist on** 134 bestehen auf
inspirational 43 anregend, inspirierend
to **inspire** 10 inspirieren, anregen
to **install** 128 installieren
instant(ly) 48 sofortig, augenblicklich
instead 26 stattdessen; **~of** 16 (an)statt
to **instigate sth** 188 etw anregen, initiieren
instinct 69 Instinkt
institute 164 Institut
to **instruct sb to do sth** 128 jdn beauftragen, etw zu tun
instructions pl 26 Anleitung, Anweisung
instructor 16 Lehrer/in
insulating foam 145 Isolierschaum
to **insult** 199 beleidigen, beschimpfen
insurance 65 Versicherung; **medical ~** 65 Krankenversicherung
to **insure** 66 versichern
insurgency 158 Aufstand
to **integrate** 84 (sich) integrieren
intelligence service 199 Nachrichtendienst
to **intend** 50 beabsichtigen
intent 27 Absicht
intention 95 Absicht
to **interact** 29 interagieren, aufeinander eingehen
interaction 170 Einwirkung, Interaktion, Zusammenspiel
to **intercept** 128 abfangen, abhören
intercultural 88T interkulturell
interest (in sth) 13 Interesse (an etw); **~ group** 204 Interessengruppe
interface 197 Schnittstelle, Verbindung
interference 200 Störung, Beeinflussung
intermediate 75 mittlere/r/s (Niveau)
intern 66 Praktikant/in
internal 127 inländisch, Inlands-; **~ combustion engine** 159 Verbrennungsmotor
internet of things (IoT) 170 das Internet der Dinge
internship 66 Praktikum
to **interpret** 26 interpretieren
to **interrupt** 21T unterbrechen, ins Wort fallen

interval 144 (zeitlicher) Abstand
interview 76 Vorstellungsgespräch
to **interview sb** 78 mit jdm ein Vorstellungsgespräch führen
interviewee 112 Person, mit der ein Vorstellungsgespräch geführt wird
interviewer 78 Person, die ein Vorstellungsgespräch führt
in-tray 49T Posteingang(skorb)
to **introduce sb** 88T jdn vorstellen
introductions pl 48 Vorstellen
introductory phase 54 Einführungsphase, Werbephase
intrusive 182 aufdringlich
intuitional 65 intuitiv
to **invade** 175 eindringen
invaluable 132 unschätzbar, unbezahlbar
invasion 175 Eindringen
invasive 170 in die Privatsphäre eingreifend
to **invent** 46 erfinden
invention 48 Erfindung
to **invest** 141 investieren
to **investigate** 65 ermitteln, untersuchen
investigative 65 erforschend, Untersuchungs-
investment 137 Investition
investor 194 Investor/in, Kapitalanleger/in
invitation 40 Einladung
invite 43 Einladung
to **invite sb to do sth** 78 jdn auffordern, etw zu tun
to **involve** 54 beinhalten, einschließen
involved 65 dazugehörig; **~ in sth** 13 an etw beteiligt, bei etw engagiert; to **get ~ with sb** 37 mit jdm zu tun haben
to **iron out** 184 ausbügeln, glattbügeln
ironing, to **do (the/some) ~** 58 bügeln
ironic 103 ironisch
irregular 68 unregelmäßig
irreversible consequences 204 unumkehrbare Konsequenzen
irrigation 149 Bewässerung
to **irritate** 176 ärgern, irritieren
island 137 Insel
to **isolate** 36 absondern, isolieren
isolated 161 abgeschottet, abgeschieden, isoliert
issue 86T Streitpunkt, Frage, Problem, Thema
IT developer 161 IT-Entwickler/in
it doesn't matter 62T es ist egal
it wasn't long before … 16 es dauerte nicht lange, bis …
it's not long before 21 es dauert nicht lange, bis
italics pl 36 Kursivschrift
item 44 Punkt, Gegenstand; 99 Artikel; 172 Tagesordnungspunkt; **~ (of clothing)** 23 Kleidungsstück
it's worth … 200T es lohnt sich, …

331

A–Z word list

J

jacket *87T* Jacke, Jackett
jargon *51* Fachsprache, Jargon
jewellery *6* Schmuck
job, ~ advertisement *31* Stellenanzeige, -ausschreibung; **~ market** *190* Arbeitsmarkt; **~ opening** *198* offene Stelle, Stellenangebot; **~ rotation** *72* Arbeitsplatzrotation, (innerbetrieblicher) Arbeitsplatzwechsel; **~ title** *66* Stellenbezeichnung
jobless *109* arbeitslos
joblessness *109* Arbeitslosigkeit
to **join,** *16* beitreten, eintreten, mitmachen; *49T (Radio etc.:)* in einer Sendung sein, *(Telefon:)* (mit jdm) sprechen; **~ sth** *151* etw (miteinander) verbinden; **~ together** *126T* sich zusammenschließen
joke *26* Witz
journalism *112* Journalismus
journalist *65* Journalist/in
journey *140* Reise, Fahrt
joy *17* Freude
Judaism *55* Judaismus, Judentum
judge *8* Richter/in, Juror/in
to **judge** *69* beurteilen
to **juggle** *110* miteinander vereinbaren, jonglieren
to **jump, ~ red lights** *48* bei Rot über eine Ampel fahren; **~ the queue** *82* sich vordrängeln
jungle *160* Dschungel
junior *14* Junioren-; *150* Jung-, Nachwuchs-
junk, ~ food *191* ungesundes Fertigessen; **~ mail** *182* Reklamesendung, Spam

K

keen, to **be ~ on sth** *12* auf etw versessen sein; to **be ~ to do sth** *76* etw unbedingt tun wollen
to **keep, ~ accounts** *98* Buchführung machen; **~ animals** *205* Tiere halten; **~ doing sth** *146* weiterhin etw tun; **~ in mind** *198* an etw denken, sich an etw erinnern; **~ in touch** *29* in Verbindung bleiben; **~ sth safe** *22* etw aufbewahren; **~ to the right/left** *119* sich rechts/links halten; **~ up with sb/sth** *24* mit jdm/etw Schritt halten; **~ up-to-date** *200T* aktualisieren; **~ watch over sb** *160* über jdn wachen, jdn beobachten; **~ within reach** *193* in Reichweite behalten
keep-fit *12* Fitness(-)
key *175* Schlüssel-
keystroke *128* Tastenanschlag, Herunterdrücken einer Taste
to **kick, ~ out** *170* rausschmeißen; **~ sth down** *80* etw eintreten
killing *158* das Töten
kind *44* Art
kind *81* freundlich, gütig, nett

to **knock, ~ sb off sth** *94* jdn von etw herunterstoßen; **~ sth off** *129* etw abschlagen
knot *187* Knoten; to **tie a ~** *187* einen Knoten machen
to **know, ~ sth inside out** *49T* etw in- und auswendig kennen; to **get ~ sb** *171* jdn kennen lernen
knowledge *48* Wissen, Kenntnis(se)
known *202* bekannt

L

to **label** *193* beschriften
label *11* (Mode-)Firma, Marke; *87* Beschriftung, Bezeichnung
labelling *202* Beschriftung, Kennzeichnung
laboratory *152* Labor; **by ~ design** *152* im Labor geplant
labour *98* Arbeitskräfte; *104* Arbeit; **forced ~** *158* Zwangsarbeit; **~ practices** *pl 192* Arbeitsmethoden
lack *25* Mangel
to **lack sth** *169* etw nicht haben
laisser-faire *186* (Wirtschaft:) liberal
lake *149* (Binnen-)See
to **land** *83* landen; **~ sth** *110* etw an Land ziehen
landline *160* Festnetz(-)
landscape *205* Landschaft
lane *62* Weg, Gasse
lantern *79* Laterne
largely *36* weitgehend, überwiegend, größtenteils
large-scale *136* in großem Umfang/Ausmaß
to **last** *107T* dauern, andauern, so bleiben, (vor-)halten
last but not least *17T* zu guter Letzt, nicht zuletzt
later *64* später
lateral *134* seitlich
lateral development *134* (Personalentwicklung:) neue Verantwortungsbereiche, breitgefächerte Kompetenzen
latest, the ~ *23* der/die/das allerneueste/n
laugh *57* Lachen, Gelächter
to **laugh at sb** *38T* über jdn lachen, jdn auslachen
laughing gas *40* Lachgas
to **launch** *50* (Produkt) auf den Markt bringen, einführen; **~ an attack** *130* einen Angriff starten
law *81* Justiz; *84* Gesetz; **~ and order** *126T* Recht und Ordnung; **~ enforcement** *124* Gesetzesvollzug, Innere Sicherheit, Exekutive; **~ enforcement agency** *124* Strafverfolgungsbehörde, Exekutivorgan; **~ school** *98* juristische Fakultät, Jurastudium; to **pass a ~** *84* ein Gesetz verabschieden
lawnmower *129* Rasenmäher
lawyer *39* Anwalt/Anwältin; **specialist ~** *39* Fachanwalt/-anwältin

to **lay cables** *160* Kabel verlegen
layer *184* Ebene, Schicht
lazy *110* faul
lead *144* Blei
to **lead (to)** *158* führen (zu); **~ sb to do sth** *179* jdn dazu bringen, etw zu tun
leader *134* Leiter/in, Führungsperson
leadership *74* Führung, Leitung
leaflet *34T* Broschüre, Merkblatt
leafy vegetable *156* Blattgemüse
to **leak** *143T* sickern, entweichen; *172* auslaufen
to **leave** *118* fortgehen; *158* zurücklassen, hinterlassen; **~ a message** *33* eine Nachricht hinterlassen; **~ behind** *188* zurücklassen, hinterlassen
leaving *202* Verlassen
left *adj 193* übrig; **~ out of sth** *36* von etw ausgeschlossen
legal, ~ action *39* rechtliche Schritte; **~ department** *69* juristische Abteilung; **~ guardian** *27* Vormund, Erziehungsberechtigte/r
to **legalize** *49T* legalisieren
legend *6* Legende
legislator *74* Gesetzgeber
legislature *167* Gesetzgebung
leisure *25* Freizeit, Muße
to **lend sb sth** *62T* jdm etw leihen
less *178* weniger
to **let, ~ oneself in for sth** *128* sich auf etw einlassen; **~ sb know sth** *31* jdm etw mitteilen;
letter *32* Buchstabe; *43* Brief; **cover ~** *66* Anschreiben, Begleitschreiben
lettuce *99* Kopfsalat
level *8* Stufe, Niveau, Ebene; *92* Grad, Höhe; **on a personal ~** *188* persönlich, auf persönlicher Ebene
liberation *156* Befreiung
library *163* Bibliothek, Bücherei
licence, driving ~ *48* Führerschein; **social ~** *190* soziale Akzeptanz
life, ~ goal *64* Lebensziel; **~ saving** *90* lebensrettend; **~-altering** *156* lebensverändernd; **~-changing** *8* lebensverändernd; **~-cycle** *49* Lebensdauer, Lebenszyklus
lifespan *178* Lebensdauer, Laufzeit
lifestyle *58* Lebensweise, Lebensführung
lifetime *54* Lebensdauer; *114* (ganzes) Leben; **for a ~** *97* ein Leben lang
to **lift** *28* heben
to **light** *79* (Kerze etc.) anzünden
light *adj 88T* hell
light, ~ bulb *155T* Glühbirne; **in the ~ of** *191* im Lichte von; to **jump red ~s** *48* bei Rot über eine Ampel fahren; to **shine ~ on sth** *144* Licht auf etw werfen
to **light up** *140* leuchten, aufleuchten
light-hearted *170* scherzhaft, zwanglos
lighting *66* Beleuchtung, Licht
like *8* wie
likeable *51* sympathisch

likely *34* wahrscheinlich; **to be ~ to do sth** *46* etw wahrscheinlich tun (werden)
like-minded *184* gleichgesinnt
limit *176* Grenze; **speed ~** *48* Geschwindigkeitsbegrenzung
to limit *137* begrenzen, einschränken
limitation *160* Einschränkung
limited *50* begrenzt, beschränkt
line *81* Reihe; **to draw the ~** *177* die Grenze ziehen; **~ chart** *53* Liniendiagramm; **~ graph** *92* Liniendiagramm; **down the ~** *81* weiter; **subject ~** *32* (Brief:) Betreffzeile; **to cross a ~** *177* eine rote Linie überschreiten; **to hold the ~** *34T* am Apparat bleiben; **poverty ~** *98* Armutsgrenze
to line up *193* in eine Linie stellen, aufreihen
link *102* Verbindung, Verknüpfung, Beziehung
to link *102* verbinden, verknüpfen
lion *79* Löwe
to listen in *37* mithören
literacy *108* Alphabetisierung, die Lese- und Schreibfähigkeit
literally *183T* buchstäblich, im wahrsten Sinne des Wortes
literate *108* alphabetisiert, des Lesens und Schreibens mächtig
to live, ~ off aid *81* von Sozialhilfe leben; **~ on sth** *146* sich von etw ernähren, von etw leben
lively *85* lebendig, lebhaft, rege
livestock *152* Vieh
living, ~ room *40* Wohnzimmer
load *60* Ladung
to load the dishwasher *168* die Spülmaschine einräumen
loan *90* Darlehen, Kredit; **to take out a ~** *98* einen Kredit abschließen
to lobby sb *90* auf jdn Einfluss nehmen
local *194* der/die Einheimische
locally sourced *190* aus der Region, regional
to locate sb/sth *170* jdn/etw finden
located in *75* in (… gelegen)
location *66* Standort, Ort
lock *208* Schloss
to lock away *200T* wegschließen, einschließen
to log *128* aufzeichnen, protokollieren; **~ in** *39* sich einloggen; **~ out** *39* sich ausloggen
logical(ly) *22* logisch
to loiter *27* herumlungern
loneliness *69* Einsamkeit
lonely *36* einsam
long, ~-lasting *191* dauerhaft, langlebig; **~-term** *202* langfristig, Langzeittoilette
loo *127* Toilette
to look, ~ a mess *101* fürchterlich aussehen; **~ after sb** *29* sich um jdn kümmern; *64* auf jdn aufpassen; **~ forward to sth** *9* sich auf etw freuen; **~ on** *80* zusehen; **~ out for sth** *209* auf etw achten; **~ sth up** *41* etw (Vokabel etc.) nachschlagen; **~ up to sb** *13* zu jdm aufsehen, jdn bewundern
to lose, *13* verlieren; **~ out** *179* schlecht wegkommen; **~ weight** *17T* abnehmen
loss (of) *105* Verlust (an)
lottery *48* Lotterie, Verlosung
loudspeaker *144* Lautsprecher
low *44* niedrig; **~-cost** *104* billig, kostengünstig
lower-end *187* einfach, *(Wirtschaft:)* weniger kaufkräftig
loyalty *175* Treue
luck *34T* Glück
luckily *183T* glücklicherweise
lung *17T* Lunge
to lurch *156* schlingern, taumeln
lying *49T* Lügen

M

machine, ~ cash *105* Geldautomat; **game ~** *46* Videospielgerät, Spielautomat; **ticket ~** *183T* Fahrkartenautomat; **vending ~** *49T* (Verkaufs-) Automat; Getränkeautomat; **washing ~** *129* Waschmaschine
madam *96T* gnädige Frau
magical *8* magisch, traumhaft
to magnify *164* vergrößern, verstärken
main *202* Haupt-
mainly *17T* hauptsächlich
mainstream *146* etabliert
to maintain *54* behalten; *67* warten, instand halten; **~ sth** *27* etw aufrecht erhalten; **~ stocks** *154* den Bestand erhalten
maintenance *66* Wartung, Instandhaltung
major *137* bedeutend, wichtig, groß
majority *69* Mehrheit; **vote** *186* Mehrheitsbeschluss
to make, ~ a contribution *84* einen Beitrag leisten; **~ a difference** *90* etw bewirken; **~ a point** *26* ein Argument vortragen, etw sagen wollen; **~ a point to sb** *82* jdm etw zu verstehen geben; **~ an impact** *94* etw bewirken, etw verändern; **~ aware** *54* bewusst machen, in Kenntnis setzen; **~ for sth** *69* sich auf den Weg nach etw machen; **~ fun of sth** *187* sich über etw lustig machen; **~ it** *60* es schaffen; **~ room** *110* Platz machen; **~ sb aware of sth** *40* jdn über etw informieren, jdn auf etw hinweisen; **~ sb redundant** *110* jdn (betriebsbedingt) entlassen; **~ sb up** *9* jdn schminken; **~ sense** *116* Sinn ergeben, sinnvoll sein; **~ sth happen** *184* etw in die Tat umsetzen, realisieren; **~ sth up** *6* etw erfinden, sich etw ausdenken; *135* etw ausmachen; **~ sure** *22* sicherstellen; dafür sorgen, dass; **~ the difference** *49T* entscheidend sein, den entscheidenden Unterschied ausmachen; **~ up** *158* ausmachen, bilden;
~ use of sth *8* von etw Gebrauch machen, etw nutzen
maker *102* Hersteller, Erbauer
male *74* Mann, männlich
man of the cloth *126T* Geistlicher
to manage *60* verwalten, regeln
management *66* Führung, Management; **~ consultant** *65* Unternehmensberater/in
manager *177T* Geschäftsführer/in; **deputy ~** *46* stellvertretende/r Geschäftsführer/in
managing director *49T* Geschäftsführer/in
manhunt *124* Verbrecherjagd
to manifest itself in sth *191* sich in etw äußern
to manipulate *164* manipulieren; *168* handhaben, bedienen
manipulative *168* manipulativ
mankind *200* Menschheit
man-made *136* künstlich, menschlichen Ursprungs
manner *176* Art, Weise
manual *51* Bedienungsanleitung
manual, ~ labour *196* Handarbeit; **~ task** *197* Handarbeit, händische Arbeit
to manufacture *99* fertigen, herstellen
manufacturer *49T* Hersteller/in, Produzent/in
manufacturing *69* Fertigung
map *170* Karte
to march *79* marschieren
march *79* Marsch
to mark *94* (Jahrestag etc.) begehen
mark *144* Markierung, Zeichen
marker *122* Filzstift
market, ~ segment *64* Marktsegment; **~ share** *72* Marktanteil; **to bring onto the ~** *54* auf den Markt bringen; **job ~** *190* Arbeitsmarkt
to market sth *54* etw vermarkten
marketer *64* Vermarkter
marketing campaign *181* Marketingkampagne
marriage *187* Ehe
marvellous *120T* toll, phantastisch
mass, ~ media *pl 124* Massenmedien; **~ production** *102* Massenproduktion
massacre *158* Massaker
massive(ly) *126T* massiv
material *14* Material, Werkstoff
mathematician *81* Mathematiker/in
maths *68T* Mathe(matik) (Schulfach)
to matter *21T* wichtig sein, darauf ankommen
matter *23* Angelegenheit, Sache; **no ~ …** *23* ganz egal, …
mattress *209* Matratze
maturity stage *54* Reifephase
maximum *49T* maximal, Höchst-, *66* höchstens
maximum *49* Höchstwert
to mean to do sth *44* gedenken, etw zu tun
meaning *88T* Bedeutung

A–Z word list

meaningful *164* wichtig, bedeutend, sinnstiftend
means of transport *130* Verkehrsmittel
meanwhile *81* inzwischen, unterdessen
to **measure** *17* messen
measure *27* Maßnahme
meat *146* Fleisch
mechanic *65* Mechaniker/in
mechanical *65* mechanisch; ~ **engineering** *169* Maschinenbau
medal *13* Medaille
media *192* medial
media, ~ **coverage** *158* Berichterstattung; **mass** ~ *pl 124* Massenmedien
to **mediate** *71* vermitteln
mediation *28* Vermittlung
medical *67* medizinisch; ~ **insurance** *65* Krankenversicherung; ~ **research** *204* medizinische Forschung; ~ **science** *196* Medizin; ~ **student** *96T* Medizinstudent/in
medication *94* Arzneimittel
medicine *90* Arznei(mittel), Medizin
medium-sized *181* mittelgroß
to **meet,** ~ **a deadline** *112* eine Frist / einen Termin einhalten; ~ **a demand** *105* eine Nachfrage befriedigen; ~ **the needs** *179* die Bedürfnisse befriedigen; ~ **up** *21T* sich treffen
meeting room *69* Sitzungsraum, Besprechungsraum
to **melt** *137* schmelzen, abschmelzen
member, ~ **of staff** *171* Mitarbeiter/in ~ **of the audience** *8* Zuschauer/in
membership *134* Mitgliedschaft
memorable *182* einprägsam, unvergesslich
to **memorize** *198* einprägen, auswendig lernen
memory, ~ **of sb** *94* Gedenken an jdn
to **mend** *146* reparieren, flicken, ausbessern
menial (job) *118* (Tätigkeit:) niedrig, untergeordnet
mental *134* psychisch; ~ **health** *206* psychisches Wohl; ~ **health patient** *206* psychisch Kranke/r
mental(ly) *114* geistig
to **mention** *31* erwähnen; *101* nennen
mentor meeting *134* Gespräch mit dem/der Vorgesetzten, Mitarbeitergespräch
merchant *160* Händler/in
mercury *144* Quecksilber
to **merge** *88T* sich zusammenschließen, fusionieren
merger *187* Verschmelzung, Fusionierung
mess *43* Chaos; **to look a** ~ *101* fürchterlich aussehen
to **mess around** *28* herumalbern, herumgammeln
message, to leave a ~ *33* eine Nachricht hinterlassen
metabolism *17* Stoffwechsel
metal *47* Metall

methane *135* Methan
micro loan *98* Kleinstkredit
microfinance *98* Kleinstfinanzierung
microphone *129* Mikrofon
microwave *68T* Mikrowelle
mid-century *161* Jahrhundertmitte
midday *150* Mittag
middle management *110* mittlere Führungsebene
middle-aged *74* mittleren Alters
middleman *145* Zwischenhändler
midnight *6* Mitternacht
midst *194* die Mitte
midsummer *79* Mittsommer, Sommersonnenwende
migrant *84* Migrant/in
migratory bird *145* Zugvogel
military *164* Militär
military force *181* Militärkampf
millennial *109* Jahrtausend-
millennium *174* Jahrtausend
mind *62* Gedanken; to **keep in** ~ *198* an etw denken, sich an etw erinnern
to **mind,** ~ **one's own business** *57* sich um seinen eigenen Kram kümmern; ~ **sth** *25* etw gegen etw haben; ~ **sth** *69* auf etw achten
minimum wage *110* Mindestlohn
minority *84* Minderheit
mirror *129* Spiegel; ~ **image** *199* Spiegelbild
misfortune *43* Unglück, Missgeschick
missing *166* vermisst
mission *90* Auftrag, Mission
to **mistake sth** *128* etw verkennen; to **be mistaken** *128* sich irren
mistrust *202* Misstrauen
to **misunderstand** *199* missverstehen
misunderstanding *97* Missverständnis
to **mix and match** *122* individuell zusammenstellen
mixture *14* Mischung
moans *pl 29* Gejammer, Genörgel
mobile *69* mobil
mobility *124* Mobilität
to **mock sb** *199* jdn verspotten, verhöhnen
to **moderate** *204* moderieren
moderate *84* gemäßigt, maßvoll
modernity *124* Moderne
to **modify** *54* verändern; *152* modifizieren
to **modify sth** *204* etw modifizieren, verändern
money, to raise ~ *43* Geld beschaffen
mongrel *80* Mischling, Bastard
to **monitor** *132* überwachen
monolingual *206* einsprachig
monopoly *202* alleiniges Handelsrecht, Monopolstellung
monthly *62T* monatlich
to **mooch off sth** *110* von etw schmarotzen
more, to be ~ **of …** *183T* eher … sein
moreover *117* überdies, darüber hinaus
mosquito net *97* Moskitonetz

motion sensor *170* Bewegungssensor
motivated, highly ~ *66* hochmotiviert; **self-**~ *185* eigenmotiviert
motorist *BE 48* Autofahrer/in
mouse *51* Maus
to **move** *170* bewegen
move *17T* Schritt, Bewegung; *61* Umzug
to **move,** ~ **around** *193* herumlaufen, umherbewegen; ~ **house** *28* umziehen; ~ **on** *8* weiterkommen, weitergehen
moveable *70* beweglich, mobil
movement *94* Bewegung
MP (Member of Parliament) *84* Parlamentsabgeordnete/r
mud *144* Schlamm
mug *188* Becher
multiculturalism *79* Multikulturalität, Multikulturismus, kulturelle Vielfalt
multinational *202* multinational
multiple *124* mehrere, vielfach
to **multiply** *150* multiplizieren
murder *132* Mord
muscle *16* Muskel
musical *17* musikalisch, Musik-
Muslim *84* muslimisch, Moslem
must *75* Muss
Must rush. *71T* Ich muss weg.
mutual(ly) *191* beiderseitig, gegenseitig
My pleasure. *11T* Gern geschehen.
myriad *199* Myriade, Unzahl
mystery *45* Rätsel, Rätselhaftigkeit; *145* Geheimnis
myth *97* Mythos, Märchen

N

nail *81* Nagel
naïve *208* naiv, blauäugig
to **name** *16* nennen, benennen
name tag *172* Namensschild
nannying *110* Kinderbetreuung
nasty *129* gemein, hässlich, böse
national *14* Landes-, national; ~ **team** *13* Nationalmannschaft
nationwide *144* landesweit
native, ~ **language** *31* Muttersprache; ~ **speaker** *75* Muttersprachler/in
natural, ~ **disaster** *158* Naturkatastrophe; ~ **gas** *138* Erdgas
to **near** *174* sich nähern
nearby *adv 29* in der Nähe; *adj 98* nahe (gelegen)
necessity *168* Notwendigkeit
need *134* Notwendigkeit, Bedürfnis; ~**s** *pl 57* Bedürfnisse, Bedarf; **in** ~ *92* bedürftig, in Not; to **meet the** ~**s** *179* die Bedürfnisse befriedigen; **no** ~ **to do sth** *44* nicht nötig, etw zu tun
to **need, on a** ~**-to-know basis** *63* im (unumgänglichen) Bedarfsfall
neglected *183* vernachlässigt, verwahrlost
neighbour *6* Nachbar/in

334

neighbourhood *98* Nachbarschaft
network *29* Netz, Netzwerk
neuroscientist *197* Hirnforscher/in
New Year *79* Neujahr
news, ~ anchor *136* Nachrichtensprecher/in
next door *41* nebenan
NGO (non-governmental organization) *95* Nichtregierungsorganisation
niche *49T* Nische
nitroglycerine *14* Nitroglycerin
no, ~ matter … *23* ganz egal, …; **~ need to do sth** *44* nicht nötig, etw zu tun
noise *41* Lärm; *46* Geräusch
noisy *57* laut, lärmend
non, ~-alcoholic *121* alkoholfrei; **~-profit** *98* gemeinnützig; **~-smoking** *120* Nichtraucher-
nonetheless *187* trotzdem, nichtsdestotrotz
nor *conj* *199* auch nicht
norm *69* Norm
nosey *60* (auf unangenehme Weise) neugierig
not, ~ … either *84* auch nicht; **~ anymore** *197* nicht mehr; **~ at all** *88T* überhaupt nicht; **N~ on our watch.** *90* Nicht mit uns! **~ yet** *196* noch nicht
notable *202* bemerkenswert
notably *175* besonders
note *46* Ton, Note; *52* Hinweis
to **note down** *178* aufschreiben
notebook *15* Heft, Notizbuch
to **notice** *88T* bemerken, wahrnehmen, beachten
notion *164* Vorstellung, Auffassung
novel *131* Roman
novel *168* neu, neuartig
novelty *168* Neues, Neuartiges
nowadays *179* heutzutage
nowhere, to get you ~ *126* zu nichts führen, nichts bringen
nuclear *57* Kern-; **~ plant** *140* Kernkraftwerk; **~ power** *135* Kernkraft; **~ power station** *140* Kernkraftwerk
to **number** *48* nummerieren
numerical *65* Zahl-, zahlenmäßig
nurse *64* Krankenpfleger/-schwester
nutrient *63* Nährstoff
nutrition *94* Nahrung, Ernährung
nutritious *191* nahrhaft

O

to **object to sth** *27* etw ablehnen, gegen etw Einwände haben
to **observe** *65* beobachten
obsessed *180* besessen
obsolescence *178* Veralterung, Überalterung
obstacle *160* Hindernis
obstruction *168* Hindernis
to **obtain sth** *130* etw erhalten, an etw gelangen
obtainable *129* erhältlich

occasion *189* Gelegenheit
occasionally *177T* manchmal, gelegentlich
occupation *64* Beruf, Arbeit, Tätigkeit, Beschäftigung
occupied *170* besetzt
to **occur** *14* vorfallen, geschehen
ocean *137* Ozean, Weltmeer
off the market *202* aus dem Markt
offended *189* beleidigt, verletzt
offensive *88T* anstößig, beleidigend
to **offer, ~ sb sth on a plate** *68* jdm etw auf dem Silbertablett servieren
office, ~ assistant *75* Bürokaufmann/-frau; **~ block** *71* Bürogebäude; **~ clerk** *49T* Büroangestellte/r; **~ supplies** *pl* *120T* Büromaterial; **~ task** *196* Büroarbeit; **~ worker** *98* Büroangestellte/r
officer *126* Offizier/in
official *97* Beamte/r, Funktionär/in
offshore *100* im/ins Ausland; *141* auf See
OHP transparency *48* Overheadfolie
oil *138* Öl
old-fashioned *188* altmodisch
Olympic *14* olympisch
once *44* sobald; **all at ~** *23* auf einmal
one, ~ by one *140* der Reihe nach; **~ day** *146* eines Tages; **~ size fits all** *184* Einheitsgröße; **~-off** *176* einmalig
ongoing *90* laufend
onshore *141* an Land
onto *8* auf
to **open up** *196* eröffnen, erschließen
opening *94* Eröffnung; **job ~** *198* offene Stelle, Stellenangebot
openness *11T* Offenheit
open-plan office *69* Großraumbüro
open, out in the ~ *144* im Freien
to **operate** *169* tätig sein
operation *107T* Betrieb, Geschäftstätigkeit; **in ~** *180* in Betrieb
operator *167* Betreiber/in
opponent *204* Gegner
opportunity *29* Gelegenheit, Möglichkeit, Chance
opposing *204* gegnerisch
opposite *182* Gegenteil
opposite *adj* *204* entgegengesetzt; **the ~ sex** *29* das andere Geschlecht
opposition *202* Widerstand, Gegenwehr
to **opt for sth** *142* sich für etw entscheiden
optimistic *107T* optimistisch
optimization *209* Optimierung
oral *75* mündlich
orbit *197* Umlaufbahn
order *6* Reihenfolge; *100* Auftrag, Bestellung; **court ~** *199* Gerichtsbeschluss, Gerichtsentscheidung; **to fill an ~** *100* einen Auftrag ausführen; **in ~ to** *60* um … zu; **law and ~** *126T* Recht und Ordnung
ordinary *11T* normal, gewöhnlich

organ *196* Organ
organic *100* biologisch, Bio-
organically produced *64* auf der Basis biologisch angebauter Produkte
organization *14* Organisation
organizational *65* organisatorisch
organizer *65* Organisator/in
…-oriented *27* …orientiert
origin *158* Herkunft
original material *113* eigene Beiträge
to **originate from sth** *99* aus etw kommen; *124* von etw ausgehen
orphan *94* Waise
orphanage *94* Waisenhaus
other, the ~ way round *86T* umgekehrt
otherwise *98* anderenfalls, sonst
ought to *110* sollen
out in the open *144* im Freien
outcome *165* Ergebnis, Resultat
outcry *202* Entrüstung, Aufschrei
outing *168* Ausflug, Ausfahrt
to **outline** *88* skizzieren, grob beschreiben
out, ~ of date *208* überholt, veraltet; **~-of-state** *110* in einem anderen Bundesstaat
output *194* Leistung, Produktion
outside *201* betriebsfremd, außerhalb; **from the ~** *74* von außen
to **outsmart** *164* überlisten, austricksen
over-achiever *19* Überflieger
to **overcome** *13* überwinden, bewältigen
overconsumption *146* zu hoher Verbrauch, übertriebener Konsum
to **overdo it** *23* es übertreiben
over-exploitation *147* Raubbau, übermäßiger Abbau
overheads *pl* *104* Fixkosten, Betriebskosten
to **overhear** *131* belauschen, aufschnappen
to **overlook** *203* übersehen
overly *199* übermäßig
overpopulation *194* Überbevölkerung
overshoot, ecological ~ *146* ökologischer Überschuss
to **overtake** *199* überholen
overview *184* Überblick
overweight *17* übergewichtig
overwhelming *134* überwältigend
own, on one's ~ *10* allein
owner *67* Besitzer/in

P

pace *54* Geschwindigkeit, Tempo
pacifist *126T* Pazifist/in
to **pack** *19* verpacken
package *180* Paket
to **package** *88T* verpacken, präsentieren
packaging *19* Verpackung
packet, pay ~ *110* Lohntüte, Gehalt
pad *69* (Notiz-)Block; Bude

A–Z word list

pain, to be a ~ (in the neck) *57* jdm auf die Nerven gehen
painful *197* schmerzend
paint *182* Malerei, Anstrich
to paint *49T* malen
panel *137* Gremium, Ausschuss
to panic *17* in Panik greaten
pantry *151* Speisekammer; **food ~** AE *151* Tafel, karitative Essensausgabe
paperless *209* papierlos
paperwork *58* Büroarbeit, Schreibarbeit
parade *79* Parade
paragraph *14* (Text:) Absatz
parallel *131* Parallele
to paraphrase *28* umschreiben, paraphrasieren
parcel *151* Paket
parliament *86* Parlament
to partake in sth *118* an etw teilhaben
partially *156* teilweise
participant *12* Teilnehmer/in
participation *206* Teilnahme
particular *23* bestimmt, speziell; *88T* besondere/r/s, spezifisch
particularly *103* besonders
partly *107T* teils, teilweise
partnership *187* Partnerschaft, Handelsgesellschaft
party *204* Partei
to pass *137* überschreiten; **to ~ a law** *84* ein Gesetz verabschieden; **to ~ sth on** *110* etw weitergeben, etw weiterreichen; **to ~ sth to sb** *152* jdm etw weiterreichen
passenger *153* Passagier
passer-by *46* Passant/in
passion fruit *156* Passionsfrucht
past, to be ~ it *114* die besten Jahre hinter sich haben, jenseits von Gut und Böse sein
pastry *98* Gebäck
pastureland *148* Weideland
path *196* Weg, Pfad, Laufbahn
patient *88* geduldig
pattern *209* Muster
pay *65* Bezahlung, Lohn
to pay, ~ attention to sth *22* auf etw achten; **~ off** *188* sich auszahlen
pay, ~ packet *110* Lohntüte, Gehalt; **~ scale** *68T* Lohntarif, Lohntabelle
payment *68T* Zahlung
peace *80* Frieden
peaceful *84* friedlich
peak *54* Gipfel, Spitze
peer *29* Gleichaltrige/r, Altersgenosse; **~ group** *55* Altersgruppe, Bezugsgruppe, Umfeld
pen friend *93* Brieffreund/in
to penetrate *183* eindringen, einsickern
penny *81* Pfennig, Penny
pension *109* Rente, Pension
pensioner *109* Rentner/in
people *100* Volk

per *35* pro; **~ annum** *117T* pro Jahr; **~ capita income** *156* Pro-Kopf-Einkommen; **~ cent** *52* Prozent
to perceive *203* wahrnehmen
percent *193* Prozent
percentage *53* Prozentsatz, Anteil
to perform *8* singen, spielen, auftreten; **~** *166T* (leistungsmäßig) abschneiden; **~ sth** *168* etw ausführen, etw durchführen
performance *14* Leistung, Abschneiden
perfume *49* Parfüm
permission *182* Erlaubnis, Genehmigung; **~ permission** *142* Baugenehmigung
permitted *27* erlaubt, gestattet
persecution *194* Verfolgung
person, in ~ *129* persönlich
persona *64* Rolle
personal, ~ space *88T* Privatsphäre; **~ transport** *102* Individualverkehr
personalization *175* Personalisierung
to personalize *69* individuell gestalten
personality *13* Persönlichkeit
personalized *175* individuell gestaltet, personalisiert
to persuade *19* überzeugen, überreden
persuader *65* jd, der andere überzeugt und mitreißt
pest *156* Schädling
pesticide *202* Pflanzenschutzmittel, Pestizid
petrol *102* Benzin; **~-driven** *102* benzingetrieben
pharmaceutical *202* pharmazeutisch, Pharma-
phase *46* Phase
phenomenon *14* Phänomen, Erscheinung
philanthropy *190* Menschenliebe, Nächstenliebe
to phone in *50* (in einer Sendung) anrufen
phone, to answer the ~ *162* ans Telefon gehen
photocopier *120T* Fotokopiergerät
physical *44* physisch, materiell, körperlich (im Gegensatz zu virtuell); **~ work** *197* körperliche Arbeit
to pick *88T* wählen, aussuchen; **~ sb/sth up** *21T* jdn/etw abholen; **~ sth out** *51* etw heraussuchen
pickup *156* Pritschenwagen
piece of advice *200T* Rat, Ratschlag
to pile *144* stapeln
to pin *77* (mit einer Nadel) befestigen, anbringen
pinkie *169* kleiner Finger
pioneer *98* Vorreiter/in, Wegbereiter/in
pipe band *79* Dudelsackkapelle
to pitch sth *98* etw anpreisen
pitfall *88T* Fallstrick, Fallgrube
pity, it's a ~ *21T* schade
place, in ~s *185* stellenweise; **~ card** *172* Platzkarte, Tischkarte

to place an order *209* einen Auftrag erteilen
to plague *124* plagen, heimsuchen
plain *139* schlicht
planning permission *142* Baugenehmigung
plant *102* Fabrik, Werk, Anlage; **nuclear ~** *140* Kernkraftwerk; **power ~** *136* Kraftwerk
to plant *148* pflanzen, anpflanzen
plaque *131* Platte, Tafel
to plaster *156* verputzen
plate *68* Teller; **to offer sb sth on a ~** *68* jdm etw auf dem Silbertablett servieren
platform *11T* Podium; *183T* Bahnsteig
to play the piano *113* Klavier spielen
player *44* hier: Firma, Wettbewerber
playground *205* Spielplatz
plc *75* AG
pleasant *68T* angenehm
pleased, to be ~ *29* sich freuen
pleasure *11T* Vergnügen; **My ~.** *11T* Gern geschehen.
plenty of *88T* viel
plight *43* Notlage
to plug, ~ in(to) *69* anschließen, einstecken; **~ in on sth** *131* sich in etw einschalten
plus *60* außerdem
pocket *208* Tasche
point *53* (vor Dezimalstellen) Komma; *84* Argument; **~ of view** *101* Perspektive, Blickwinkel, Standpunkt; **there's little ~ in doing sth** *30* es hat wenig Sinn, etw zu tun; **He has a (good) ~.** *84* Da ist etwas dran. Da hat er recht.; **to make a ~** *26* ein Argument vortragen, etw sagen wollen; **to make a ~ to sb** *82* jdm etw zu verstehen geben; **to take the ~** *151* den Standpunkt verstehen
to point, ~ at sb/sth *38T* auf jdn/etw zeigen; **~ sth at sb** *80* etw auf jdn richten, mit etw auf jdn zielen; **~ sth out** *59* auf etw hinweisen; **~ to sth** *164* auf etw hindeuten
to poison *145* vergiften
poisoning *40* Vergiftung
poisonous *144* giftig
police, ~ force *127* Polizei; **~ officer** *65* Polizist/in; **~ station** *125* Polizeiwache
policy *84* Politik, Kurs, Konzept
policymaker *195* politische/r Entscheidungsträger/in
political security *158* politische Stabilität/Sicherheit
politically *194* politisch
politician *65* Politiker/in
poll *36* Umfrage
pollen *152* Blütenstaub, Pollen
to pollute *137* (die Umwelt) verschmutzen
polluting *149* umweltschädlich
pollution *139* Umweltverschmutzung
polytunnel *206* Folienzelt

popularity *6* Beliebtheit, Popularität
population *85* Bevölkerung; *154* (Biologie:) Population
porch *156* Veranda
pork *207* Schwein
port *86* Hafen, Hafenstadt
portion *94* Teil
to **portray** *88T* darstellen, schildern
possession *146* Besitz(tum)
to **post** *127* (Brief:) einwerfen, schicken
post *66* Stelle, Posten
poster *35* Plakat
potent *202* stark, hochwirksam
potential *118* Potenzial, Leistungsvermögen
potential(ly) *54* potenziell, möglich
pound *40* Pfund
poverty *90* Armut; ~ **line** *98* Armutsgrenze
to **power** *138* antreiben, mit Energie versorgen
power *18* Macht, Stärke, Kraft; ~ **plant** *136* Kraftwerk; ~ **station** *139* Kraftwerk, Elektrizitätswerk; ~ **structure** *185* Machtgefüge; to **be in** ~ *160* an der Macht sein; **nuclear** ~ *135* Kernkraft; **solar** ~ *135* Sonnenenergie
powerful *51* stark, mächtig, kräftig
powerless *144* machtlos, unfähig
practical *38T* zweckmäßig, praktisch (umsetzbar)
practice *69* Praxis, Ausübung, Verfahren, Ablauf, Praktik
to **practise** *9* üben, trainieren; *108* (Religion:) ausüben; *160* praktizieren
practitioner *195* Praktiker/in
prairie *148* Prärie
to **pray** *126T* beten
prayer *126T* Gebet; ~ **vigil** *126T* Gebetswache
precaution *127* Vorkehrung, Sicherheitsmaßnahme
precious *149* kostbar
to **predict** *8* voraussagen, vorhersagen
to **prefer** *44* vorziehen, bevorzugen
preference *20* Vorliebe; to **give** ~ **to sth** *175* etw den Vorzug geben;
pre-historic *152* prähistorisch
premises *pl 71T* Geschäftsräume
preparation (for sth) *24* Vorbereitung (auf etw)
to **prepare** *137* (Bericht etc.) erstellen, verfassen
prepared *88T* vorbereitet; to **be ~ to do** *146* bereit sein, zu tun
presence *37* Anwesenheit, Präsenz
to **present**, ~ **sb with sth** *175* jdm etw präsentieren
presentation, to give a ~ *48* ein Referat halten
presenter *86T* Moderator/in
presidential nomination *202* Präsidentschaftsnominierung

press, ~ **conference** *142* Pressekonferenz; **printing** ~ *159* Druckerpresse; **tabloid** ~ *10* Boulevardpresse
pressure *75* Druck; ~ **cooker** *124* Schnellkochtopf
to **pressure** *161* unter Druck setzen
pressures *pl 167* Belastungen
prestigious *70* repräsentativ, prestigeträchtig
to **presume** *177T* annehmen, mutmaßen
to **pretend** *21T* vorgeben; so tun, als ob
pretty *11T* ziemlich
to **prevent** *127* verhindern, verhüten
preventable *97* vermeidbar
previous *110* vorherig, früher; *178* vorangehend
previously *136* zuvor, vorher
price tag *134* Preisschild
priced, to be ~ at ... *129* ... kosten
pride *83* Stolz; to **take ~ in sth** *83* auf etw Wert legen, sich mit etw Mühe geben
priest *65* Priester/in, Geistliche/r
primary *36* Haupt-, hauptsächlich
primarily *161* vorrangig, hauptsächlich
principle, in ~ *143* prinzipiell, grundsätzlich
print, the small ~ *129* das Kleingedruckte
printing press *159* Druckerpresse
to **prioritize** *184* Schwerpunkte setzen, priorisieren
priority *123* Priorität, Vorrang; **according to ~** *44* gemäß der Priorität; to **set priorities** *186* Prioritäten setzen
prison *158* Gefängnis
prisoner, to take sb ~ *181* jdn gefangen nehmen
privacy *40* Privatsphäre; *176* Datenschutz; ~ **sphere** *181* Privatsphäre
probably *178* wahrscheinlich
to **proceed** *189* fortschreiten
proceeds *pl 98* Erlös, Ertrag
process *17* Ablauf, Vorgang, Prozess
to **process** *100* verarbeiten
producer *90* Produzent/in
profession *68T* Beruf
professional *14* professionell, Prof(i-) *74* Berufs-; ~ **development** *191* berufliches Fortkommen
profile *64* Profil
profit *50* Gewinn, Profit; **non-** ~ *98* gemeinnützig
to **profit** *144* profitieren
profitable *187* lohnend, rentabel, gewinnbringend
programmer *65* Programmierer/in
progress *146* Fortschritt(e)
progression *92* Entwicklung, Steigerung
to **project** *182* projizieren; übertragen, zeigen
projector *121* Beamer
to **prolong** *196* verlängern
promising *81* vielversprechend

to **promote sth** *46* für etw werben, etw bewerben
promotion *49T* Werbung; *65* Beförderung, (beruflicher) Aufstieg; ~ **prospects** *pl 65* Aufstiegschancen
to **prompt sb to do sth** *129* jdn veranlassen, etw zu tun
prop *66* Requisite
proper *98* richtig; ~ **name** *33* Eigenname
properly *60* richtig, ordentlich, korrekt
property *40* Immobilie(n), Anwesen; *200T* Eigentum, Besitz; ~ **damage** *166T* Sachschaden, Sachschäden
proponent *146* Befürworter/in
proportion *144* Anteil
proposal *155* Vorschlag
to **protect** *47* schützen
protection *200T* Schutz
protein *154* Eiweiß, Protein
proud *81* stolz
to **prove** *11T* beweisen
proven *189* erwiesen
proverb *97* Sprichwort
to **provide** *27* zur Verfügung stellen; *175* bereitstellen, liefern; ~ **sth** *134* für etw sorgen
provider *39* Anbieter
provocation *45* Provokation
to **provoke** *202* auslösen, verursachen; ~ **a reaction** *182* eine Reaktion provozieren
psychological *91* psychologisch
psychologist *65* Psychologe/Psychologin
psychology *36* Psychologie
public *11T* öffentlich; ~ **transport** *48* öffentliche Verkehrsmittel
publically *192* öffentlich
publication *111* Veröffentlichung
publicly *199* öffentlich
to **publish** *131* veröffentlichen
publisher *50* Verleger/in
to **pull**, ~ **down** *155* (Gebäude) abreißen; ~ **sth tight** *62* etw straff ziehen
pull factor *158* etwa: Anreizwirkung, Anziehungsgrund
to **pump** *140* pumpen
puppy *183T* Hundewelpe
to **purchase** *44* kaufen
purchase *129* Kauf
purchasing power *44* Kaufkraft
purpose *84* Absicht, Zweck
to **push** *193* (Möbel:) schieben
push, ~ **factor** *158* etwa: Vertreibungsursache; **at the ~ of a button** *199* auf Knopfdruck
to **put** *127* formulieren, sagen, in Worte fassen; ~ **an end to sth** *27* mit etw Schluss machen, einen Schlussstrich unter etw ziehen; ~ **in work** *95* Arbeit leisten; ~ **sb through** *33* (Telefon:) jdn durchstellen, jdn verbinden; ~ **sth down** to **sth** *84* etw einer Sache zuschreiben; ~ **sth up** *64* etw aufhängen, aufstellen

337

A–Z word list

Q

qualification *68* Abschluss, Qualifikation
qualified *68T* mit Abschluss, qualifiziert
quality, ~ control *120T* Qualitätskontrolle; ~ of life *137* Lebensqualität
quarter *36* Viertel
to question sth *176* etw prüfen
to queue *7* sich (in einer Warteschlange) anstellen
queue *81* Warteschlange; to jump the ~ *82* sich vordrängeln
quick reference *48* schnelles Nachschlagen
quota *74* Quote; female ~ *74* Frauenquote
to quote *136* zitieren

R

race *7* Rennen; *64* Rasse
racial *84* rassisch, Rassen-
racing, ~ car *13* Rennwagen; ~ cyclist *14* Radrennfahrer/in
racism *183T* Rassismus
radical(ly) *208* völlig, drastisch, radikal
radicalization *123* Radikalisierung
to radicalize *124* radikalisieren
to raise *156* (Pflanzen) anbauen; *80* etw anheben, etw hochheben; *100* etw steigern, etw erhöhen; ~ awareness *183* Bewusstsein schärfen, Aufmerksamkeit erzielen; ~ money *43* Geld beschaffen; ~ sth *59* etw (Thema etc.) ansprechen
range *44* Sortiment, Bandbreite
to range *188* reichen, sich bewegen, sich erstrecken
to rank, ~ sb/sth *6* jdn/etw einstufen, jdn/etw (ein-)ordnen; ~ sixth *92* den sechsten Platz einnehmen
ranking *121* Rangfolge; *161* Rangliste
rapid(ly) *70* rasch, schnell
rarely *178* selten
to rate *44* beurteilen, bewerten
rate *105* Tempo, Quote, Rate, Anteil; at any ~ *131* auf jeden Fall
rather *110* eher, lieber; ~ than *43* anstatt
ratio *74* Verhältnis; female to male ~ *74* Verhältnis von Frauen zu Männern
raw *63* roh; ~ product *99* Ausgangsprodukt, Roherzeugnis
reach *99* Reichweite; to keep within ~ *193* in Reichweite behalten
to reach sth *44* etw erreichen, an etw herankommen
to reactivate *39* wieder in Betrieb nehmen, reaktivieren
to read, ~ sth back *34* etw (zur Kontrolle) vorlesen; ~ sth closely *51* etw genau (durch)lesen; to re-~ *28* erneut lesen
reader *36* Dozent/in

ready, to be ~ for sth *196* bereit sein für etw
real time, in ~ *175* in Echtzeit
realistic *65* realistisch
reality, the realities *98* die tatsächlichen Gegebenheiten
to realize *40* wissen, erkennen, klar sein
real-time *170* Echtzeit-
to reap the benefits *165* die Früchte ernten, die Vorteile nutzen
reason, for this ~ *48* aus diesem Grund; to give a ~ *22* eine Begründung anführen
reasonable *122* vernünftig
to reassure sb *189* jdn beruhigen, jdm Mut machen
to rebuild *51* umbauen, erneuern
receipt *60* Quittung
to receive *118* erhalten
recent, in ~ years *98* in den letzten Jahren
recently *88T* vor Kurzem, neulich
reception *120T* Empfang
receptionist *72* Empfangsmitarbeiter/in
recession *107T* Rezession
to recognize *82* (wieder)erkennen; *132* anerkennen, begreifen
to recommend *175* empfehlen
recommendation *118* Empfehlung
record *8* Schallplatte; *170* Aufzeichnung; *201* Nachweis, Beleg; ~ company *8* Plattenfirma
to record *14* aufzeichnen
recording *177* Aufnahme, Aufzeichnung
to recover *109* sich erholen; ~ fully *109* wieder völlig gesund werden
recruitment *66* Personalbeschaffung
to redevelop *155* sanieren
redevelopment *155* Sanierung
to reduce *17T* senken, reduzieren, verringern; ~ sb to sth *81* jdn zu etw bringen
reduction *83* Verringerung, Senkung; cost ~ *54* Kostensenkung
redundant, to make sb ~ *110* jdn (betriebsbedingt) entlassen
ref. (= reference) *76* (Brief:) Zeichen
to refer to sb/sth *14* jdn/etw erwähnen, sich auf jdn/etw beziehen
referee *75* Referenzgeber/in
reference *75* Referenz, Zeugnis
reference (to sth) *15* Verweis (auf etw)
to reflect *136* reflektieren; *183T* spiegeln, wiedergeben
refreshment *172* Erfrischung
refrigeration *159* Kühlung, Kälteerzeugung
refugee *80* Flüchtling
to refuse *14* sich weigern; ~ sth *98* etw verweigern
regardless of sth *37* ungeachtet einer Sache
Regards *121* (Brief:) Viele Grüße

registered *66* eingetragen, (staatlich) anerkannt
regular *177T* regelmäßig
to regulate, to self-~ *191* sich selbst regulieren
regulation *74* Regulierung; *143T* Vorschrift
regulator *202* Behörde
regulatory body *191* Aufsichtsbehörde, Kontrollorgan
to re-home sb *194* jdn unterbringen, jdm eine Wohnung verschaffen
to reject *84* ablehnen, zurückweisen
to rejoin sb *94* jdn wieder treffen
to relate to sth *26* sich auf etw beziehen
related *103* zugehörig; *175* ähnlich; to be ~ to sth *10* mit etw in Zusammenhang stehen
relating to *200T* bezüglich, im Zusammenhang mit
relationship *10* Beziehung, Verhältnis; to build a ~ *175* eine Beziehung herstellen
to release *8* veröffentlichen
release *46* Veröffentlichung
relevant *198* maßgeblich, sachbezogen
reliability *114* Zuverlässigkeit, Verlässlichkeit
reliable *200T* sicher, verlässlich, glaubwürdig
religious *92* religiös
reluctant *180* abgeneigt, zögernd
to rely on sth *140* sich auf etw verlassen, auf etw angewiesen sein
to remain *106* bleiben
remaining *120* übrig, verbleibend
to remind sb (of sth) *103* jdn (an etw) erinnern
reminder, to be a stark ~ *132* etw jäh vor Augen führen, etw überdeutlich machen
remote *160* entlegen
removable *180* austauschbar
to remove *146* entfernen
renewable *135* erneuerbar
rent *104* Miete
rental *180* Miete; ~ price *122* Mietpreis
repair shop *179* Werkstatt
to repay *194* zurückzahlen
repetition *15* Wiederholung
repetitive *134* (sich) wiederholend
to replace *16* ersetzen, austauschen
replacement *86T* Ersatz, Ersetzung, Austausch
to report *118* berichten, melden, anzeigen; ~ to sb *78* jdm unterstellt sein
to represent *64* repräsentieren; *168* vertreten
representation *193* Vertretung, Repräsentanz
representative *37* repräsentativ
representative *167* Repräsentant/in, Abgeordnete/r
to reproduce *152* sich fortpflanzen

338

reputation 40 Ansehen, Ruf
request 128 Bitte, Wunsch, Anfrage;
  on ~ 75 auf Wunsch, auf Verlangen
to **require** 54 erfordern, benötigen; to
  be required to do sth 143T etw tun
  müssen; verpflichtet sein, etw zu tun
requirement 66 Voraussetzung,
  Bedingung, Anforderung; 140 Bedarf
to **re-read** 28 erneut lesen
to **rescue** 62 retten, bergen
research 49T Recherche, Nachforschungen, Untersuchungen; 139 Forschung; **R~ and Development
  (R&D)** 120T Forschung(s-) und
  Entwicklung(sabteilung); **medical ~**
  204 medizinische Forschung
to **research sth** 43 etw recherchieren,
  Nachforschungen über etw anstellen
resentment 170 Ärger, Missgunst
reservation 78T Reservierung
to **reserve** 121 reservieren
to **re-shore** 104 (Industrie) wieder im
  Inland ansiedeln, wieder ins Inland
  verlagern
resident 124 Anwohner/in, Bewoh-
  ner/in
resistance 152 Widerstandsfähigkeit,
  Resistenz
resistant to sth 152 resistent gegen
  etw
to **re-skill** 100 umschulen
resource 114 Ressource; 146 Roh-
  stoff; **depleting ~s** 194 schwindende
  Ressourcen
to **respond to sth** 34 auf etw reagieren, auf etw antworten
responsibility 78 Aufgabe, Zuständig-
  keit; 92 Verantwortung; **social ~**
  190 soziale/gesellschaftliche Verantwortung; to **take ~** 78T Verantwortung übernehmen
responsible 124 verantwortungsvoll;
  to **be ~ for sth** 66 für etw zuständig/
  verantwortlich sein
rest 209 Ruhe, Erholung
to **result in** 134 führen zu
result, as a ~ 88T infolgedessen, als
  Folge davon
retail 110 Einzelhandel(s-)
retailer 27 (Einzel)Händler/in
to **retain** 157 zurückhalten, behalten,
  bewahren
to **rethink** 69 überdenken
to **retire** 86 in den Ruhestand gehen,
  in Rente gehen; **~ sb** 114 jdn in den
  Ruhestand versetzen
retirement 14 Rücktritt, Rückzug;
  114 Ruhestand, Rente; **~
  home** 114 Altersheim
to **retrain** 72 umschulen
return, ~ airfare 66 Kosten für Hin-
  und Rückflug; **in ~** 143T im Gegen-
  zug, als Ausgleich
to **return to sth** 62 sich wieder einer
  Sache zuwenden
reusable 188 wiederverwendbar
to **reveal** 176 verraten, offenbaren,
  deutlich machen

reveller 40 Feiernde/r
revenue 54 Einnahme, Ertrag
reward 45 Belohnung, Lohn
to **reward** 48 belohnen
rewarding 65 lohnend, erfüllend
to **rewrite** 20 umformulieren, neu
  schreiben
rich 148 (Nahrung) gehaltvoll, reich-
  haltig
rich, between ~ and poor 194 die
  Kluft zwischen Reich und Arm
rid, to get ~ of sth 134 etw loswerden
ride 95 Fahrt
ridiculous(ly) 60 lächerlich, unglaublich
riding 25 Reiten
rifle 80 Gewehr
to **rig** 110 manipulieren; to **be rigged
  against sb** 110 jdn (systematisch)
  benachteiligen, gegen jdn arbeiten
right away 78T sofort
right, ~-hand 39 rechte/r/s, auf der
  rechten Seite; **~-hand
  drive** 88T rechtsgesteuert
right, human ~s 192 Menschenrechte
to **ring the doorbell** 13 (an der Tür)
  klingeln, läuten
riot 40 Aufstand, Aufruhr; **~ police**
  40 Bereitschaftspolizei
to **rise** 205 ansteigen
risk 179 Risiko, Gefahr; **~ management** 191 Risikomanagement; to **be
  at ~ of/from sth** 158 gefährdet sein
  durch etw, bedroht sein von etw
road testing 166T Fahrversuche,
  Fahrerprobung, Straßentests
to **roam** 44 durchstreifen
to **rob a bank** 130 eine Bank überfallen, eine Bank ausrauben
robbery, bank ~ 130 Banküberfall,
  Bankraub
robot 167 Roboter
robotic 168 Roboter-
robotics 168 Robotertechnik
rock 140 Fels, Gestein
role 35 Rolle; **~ model** 55 Vorbild;
  ~-play 11 Rollenspiel
to **role-play** 11 mit verteilten Rollen
  spielen
rooftop 205 Hausdach
root 56 Wurzel; **~ cause** 158 Grund-
  ursache
to **root sth out** 124 etw beseitigen,
  etw ausmerzen
rotation, job ~ 72 Arbeitsplatzrotation, (innerbetrieblicher) Arbeitsplatzwechsel
roughly 105 ungefähr
routine 134 regelmäßig, laufend
routine 70 (fester) Ablauf, Routine
row 156 Reihe; **in a ~** 161 nachein-
  ander
rubbish 47 Müll, Abfall; **~
  bin** 47 Mülltonne
rude 88T unhöflich, grob
rules of the game 13 Spielregeln
to **rule** 200 regieren
run 21 Lauf

to **run** 31 (Unternehmen etc.) führen,
  betreiben; **~ an advert** 176 eine
  Anzeige schalten; **~ for sth** 202 für
  etw kandidieren; **~ out** 146 zu Ende
  gehen, sich erschöpfen; **~ smoothly** 185 reibungslos laufen
running 107T in Folge;
  ~ cost 155 Betriebskosten
runoff 156 Abfluss, abfließendes
  Wasser
rural 86T ländlich
ruthless 199 schonungslos, skrupellos
rutted 156 zerfurcht, ausgefahren

S

sadly 117T leider
safe(ly) 88 sicher
safely 56 mit Gewissheit
safety 80 Sicherheit; **health and ~** 83
  Arbeitsschutz
salary 48 Gehalt
sale 28 Verkauf; to **be on ~** 28 ange-
  boten werden, zum Verkauf stehen
sales pl 49 Verkauf, Verkäufe, Absatz,
  Vertrieb; 54 Erträge, Umsatz; **~ director** 107 Verkaufsleiter/in, Vertriebs-
  leiter/in
salesman 50 Verkäufer, Vertreter
salesperson 68 Vertreter/in, Verkäu-
  fer/in
saleswoman 97 Verkäuferin
salutation 76 (Brief:) Anrede
Salvation Army 90 Heilsarmee
sample 14 Probe
satisfaction 68T Zufriedenheit
satisfied 161 zufrieden(gestellt)
satisfying 65 befriedigend
saturated 182 gesättigt
saturation from 181 Sättigung von
savannah 160 Savanne
to **save** 129 (Daten) sichern; **~ oneself
  sth** 84 sich etw ersparen; **~
  sth** 44 etw ersparen; **~ time** 44 Zeit
  sparen; **~ up** 25 sparen
savings pl 177 Einsparung, Ersparnis
to **say, ~ the least** 88T gelinde gesagt
say, to have one's ~ 126 seine Meinung äußern, zu Wort kommen
saying 59 Sprichwort, Redensart
scale 156 Ausmaß, Umfang; **on a
  small ~** 98 in kleinem Umfang; **pay ~**
  68T Lohntarif, Lohntabelle
to **scale down** 146 reduzieren, senken
to **scan** 15 (Text) überfliegen
scared 8 Angst haben
scarred 157 vernarbt, gezeichnet
scary 51 unheimlich, beängsti-
  gend; 164 gruselig, schaurig
to **scatter** 168 verteilen, verstreuen
scene 11T Szene
sceptic 137 Skeptiker/in
schedule 134 Zeitplan, Einteilung
scheme 132 Plan, Programm
school, ~ leaving party 17T Schulab-
  gangsfeier; **~-age** 128 im Schulalter;

A–Z word list

secondary ~ *100* weiterführende Schule
schoolboy *40* Schuljunge
schooling *90* Schulbesuch, Schulbildung
scientist *136* (Natur-)Wissenschaftler/in
to scrap *188* aussondern, ausrangieren
scrap *144* Schrott
scrapheap *114* Schrotthaufen
scrapyard *145* Schrottplatz
to scream *80* schreien
scream *94* Schrei
screen *39* Bildschirm; *121* Leinwand
screw *179* Schraube
script *9* Drehbuch
to scrutinize *131* genau ansehen, überprüfen
sea level *137* Meeresspiegel
seamlessly *208* nahtlos, reibungslos
search engine *44* Suchmaschine
seat, to take a ~ *71T* Platz nehmen
to seat sb *193* jdn setzen
seating *121* Bestuhlung
secondary school *100* weiterführende Schule
secondly *103* zweitens
secret *23* Geheimnis
secret *49T* heimlich, geheim
secretary *31* Sekretär/in
section *77* Abschnitt; *104* Bereich, Teil; *173* Abteilung
sector *70* Sektor, Bereich
secure(ly) *68T* sicher
security, ~ forces pl *126T* Sicherheitskräfte; ~ service *127* Geheimdienst; job ~ *188* Arbeitsplatzsicherheit; political ~ *158* politische Stabilität/Sicherheit
to see sb *38T* zu jdm gehen
seed *152* Samen, Saatgut
to seek *75* suchen
to seem *177T* scheinen, den Anschein haben
segment, market ~ *64* Marktsegment
segmentation *64* Aufteilung, Zerlegung
to select *87* auswählen
selection *121* Auswahl, Selektion
selective *152* selektiv
self, ~-confident *177T* selbstbewusst; ~-defence *128* Selbstverteidigung; ~-employed *200* freiberuflich, selbständig; ~-evident *88T* selbstverständlich; ~-motivated *185* eigenmotiviert; ~-sustainable *90* selbsttragend, lebensfähig; to ~-fund *110* selbst finanzieren; to ~-regulate *191* sich selbst regulieren
to sell sth door to door *98* etw per Haustürgeschäft verkaufen
to send sth out *78T* etw verschicken
senior *69* leitend, *114* älter; ~ citizen *114* Senior/in, ältere/r Mitbürger/in; ~ official *74* höherer Beamter/höhere Beamtin
to sensationalize sth *125* reißerisch über etw berichten

to sense *170* erkennen, bemerken
sense *28* Sinn; ~ of touch *169* Tastsinn; to make ~ *116* Sinn ergeben, sinnvoll sein
sensitive *127* sensibel, (Information:) vertraulich
sensor *170* Sensor
to separate *33* trennen, loslösen; *80* abspalten
separate *73* getrennt, separat
separately *33* einzeln
series *51* Reihe, Serie
seriously *49T* im Ernst; to take ~ *187* Ernst nehmen
service station *166T* Tankstelle
session *16* Sitzung
set *66* Kulisse; ~ *168* Menge
set-up *32* Aufbau
set adj *209* bestimmt
to set, ~ an example *56* ein Beispiel setzen, mit gutem Beispiel vorangehen; ~ fire to sth *145* etw anzünden; ~ guidelines *197* Regeln, Richtlinien aufstellen; ~ out to do sth *43* sich vornehmen, etw tun; ~ priorities *186* Prioritäten setzen; ~ sth up *66* etw einrichten; ~ up *49T* (Unternehmen etc.:) gründen
setback *169* Rückschlag
setting *39* Einstellung; *88T* Situation
to settle *158* sich niederlassen
several *36* mehrere
severe *154* ernst, schwer
sex *29* Geschlecht; the opposite ~ *29* das andere Geschlecht
shade *88T* Farbton, Nuance
shadowy *144* zwielichtig
to shake *9* zittern; ~ sth *17T* etw schütteln, mit etw wackeln; *144* an etw rütteln; ~ hands *88T* sich die Hand geben; ~ one's head *81* den Kopf schütteln; ~ sth off *70* etw abschütteln
shale *140* Schiefer
to shape *199* formen, gestalten, entwickeln
share *149* Anteil; market ~ *72* Marktanteil
shared *102* gemeinsam; ~ house *62T* Wohngemeinschaft
shareholder *190* Aktionär/in, Gesellschafter/in
sharing economy *146* Ökonomie des Teilens
sharp *88T* scharf; sharp(ly) *106* stark
shaving razor *88T* Rasiermesser
sheep *152* Schaf
sheet *193* Blatt; ice ~ *137* Eisdecke
shelf, shelves *155T* Regal, Regale
shelter *94* Unterkunft, Tierheim; *108* Obdach; *194* Schutz
shift *66* Schicht
to shine light on sth *144* Licht auf etw werfen
to ship *49T* verschicken; *144* versenden, verschiffen
shipbuilding *112* Schiffbau

shipping company *145* Transportunternehmen, Spediteur, Reederei
shipyard *86* Werft
shocked *40* schockiert
to shoot *80* schießen; ~ sb *109* jdn erschießen; ~ up *40* rasant ansteigen
shopper *6* Käufer/in, Kunde/Kundin
shore *205* Ufer, Küste; to re-~ *104* (Industrie) wieder im Inland ansiedeln, wieder ins Inland verlagern
short, to cut a long story ~ *60* lange Rede, kurzer Sinn
shortage *68T* Mangel
shortly *187* bald, gleich, in kurzer Zeit
short-sleeved *156* kurzärmlig
show *9* (TV-, Radio-)Sendung
to shudder *80* erschaudern, zittern
to shuffle *81* schlurfen
to shut down *124* schließen
shy *59* schüchtern
siblings pl *29* Geschwister
sick, to be ~ of sth *110* von etw die Nase voll haben; to be ~ and tired of sth *129* die Nase von etw gestrichen voll haben
sideways *134* seitlich, seitwärts
to sign *8* unterschreiben
signature *76* Unterschrift
silent(ly) *81* still, schweigend; *129* stumm; silent observer *198* stiller Beobachter
similarity *20* Ähnlichkeit; *44* Gemeinsamkeit
similarly *87* in ähnlicher Weise, genauso, ebenso
since *13* seit; *189* da, weil
single *98* alleinstehend
sinister *170* unheimlich
sink *63* Spüle
sir *87T* mein Herr
site *29* Website
sixth-form college *139* Oberstufenzentrum, Studienkolleg
size *184* Maß, Format, Größe
skeptical AE *157* skeptisch
sketch *210* Skizze
skill *8* Fähigkeit, Fertigkeit; ~ level *194* Könnensstufe, Fähigkeitsstufe; social ~s pl *29* Sozialkompetenz
skilled *110* qualifiziert, erfahren; to be ~ with sth *65* mit etw gut umgehen können
to skim *36* (Text) überfliegen
skin *177* Haut
skinny *23* hauteng
to skip sth *46* etw auslassen, etw überspringen
skydive *43* Fallschirmsprung
skylight *40* Oberlicht, Dachfenster
slang word *88T* umgangssprachliches Wort
sleek *178* geschmeidig, schnittig, glatt
sleep *209* Schlaf
slice *207* Scheibe
slide *48* Dia, (Overhead-)Folie
slight *104* leicht, gering
slightly *106* geringfügig, leicht
slim *17* schlank; *178* dünn

slope *156* Hang
to slow *105* sich verlangsamen, sich abschwächen; ~ **down** *166T* bremsen
small, the ~ **print** *129* das Kleingedruckte
small-scale *205* in kleinem Maßstab
to smash *94* zertrümmern, zerstören
smooth(ly) *166T* reibungslos, problemlos; to **run** ~ *185* reibungslos laufen
to sniff sth *63* an etw riechen
so far *96T* bislang
soap *49T* Seife
social, ~ **class** *64* soziale Schicht; ~ **engineering** *114* Änderung gesellschaftlicher Strukturen, angewandte Sozialwissenschaft; ~ **group** *44* soziale Gruppe, soziale Gemeinschaft; ~ **housing** *205* sozialer Wohnungsbau; ~ **licence** *190* soziale Akzeptanz; ~ **life** *64* Sozialleben; ~ **responsibility** *190* soziale/gesellschaftliche Verantwortung; ~ **skills** pl *29* Sozialkompetenz; ~ **worker** *65* Sozialarbeiter/in
to socialize *29* sich treffen, unter Leute gehen
societal *199* gesellschaftlich
to soften *33* mildern, abmildern; *88T* weichmachen
software-brain interfaces *197* computergesteuerte Schnittstellen
soil *98* Erde, Boden, Erdreich
solar *135* Sonnen-, Solar-; ~ **power** *135* Sonnenenergie
sold out *20* ausverkauft
soldier *80* Soldat/in
sole *94* alleinig
solution *38T* Lösung
to solve *65* lösen
sometime *31* irgendwann
sophisticated *197* technisch ausgefeilt, weiterentwickelt
to sort *6* sortieren, einordnen
sort *28* Art, Sorte
to sound *184* klingen, sich anhören
sound *46* solide, untadelig
source *52* Quelle
to sow *161* säen
space *170* Raum, Platz; *196* Weltraum; to **take up** ~ *153* Platz einnehmen
spaceship *170* Raumschiff, Raumfahrzeug
to speak up *162* lauter sprechen
speaker *17* Sprecher/in
Speaking. *78T* (Telefon:) Am Apparat.
special, ~ **committee** *167* Sonderausschuss; ~ **offer** *175* Sonderangebot
specialist *128* Spezial-, Fach-; ~ **lawyer** *39* Fachanwalt/-anwältin
to specialize in sth *139* sich auf etw spezialisieren
specialized in *181* spezialisiert auf
species *148* (Biologie:) Art
spectator *12* Zuschauer/in
speech bubble *26* Sprechblase

speed *48* Geschwindigkeit; ~ **camera** *48* Geschwindigkeitsüberwachungskamera, Radarfalle; ~ **limit** *48* Geschwindigkeitsbegrenzung
to speed up *166T* beschleunigen
to spell *33* buchstabieren *37* (richtig) schreiben
to spend *146* (Geld:) ausgeben
to spend time doing sth *182* mit etw Zeit verbringen
spending *52* Ausgaben, Aufwendungen
sphere *182* Sphäre
spinach *156* Spinat
splendid *155* prächtig
to split *73* (sich) aufteilen; to ~ **(up)** *10* (Paar:) sich trennen
to spoil *56* (Kind:) verwöhnen
spokesman *27* Sprecher
to sponsor *21* (finanziell) unterstützen, sponsern
sponsorship *90* Förderung
sports, ~ **car** *49* Sportwagen; ~ **gear** *21* Sportkleidung, Sportausrüstung
sportswear *19* Sportkleidung
to spot *190* erkennen, entdecken
spot *8* Platz, Stelle, Ort, Fleck, Punkt
spouse *129* Ehegatte
spray *152* Spritzmittel
to spread *43* sich verbreiten, sich ausbreiten
spread *194* verbreitet
spread *160* Verbreitung, Ausbreitung
spreadsheet *75* Tabellenkalkulation
to spurn *194* abweisen
to spy on sb *129* jdn ausspionieren
spyware *128* Spionagesoftware
square mile *148* Quadratmeile
to squeeze, ~ **oneself into sth** *23* sich in etw hineinzwängen
stabilization *188* Stabilisierung
stable *194* stabil
stadium *13* Stadion
to staff *66* (mit Personal:) besetzen
staff *68T* Personal, Belegschaft, Mitarbeiter/innen
stage *8* Bühne; *54* Stufe, Phase; *61* Abschnitt; **growth** ~ *54* Entwicklungsstadium, Wachstumsphase
to stamp *48* stempeln, abstempeln; ~ **sth out** *134* etw ausmerzen
to stand, ~ **in for sb** *72* jdn vertreten; ~ **in the way** *200* im Weg stehen; ~ **out** *49T* auffallen, herausstechen
to stand up *17T* aufstehen, sich hinstellen; *179* sich erheben, sich widersetzen
standard *68T* Niveau; ~ **of living** *118* Lebensstandard
standoffish *189* reserviert, distanziert
to stare at sb *23* jdn anstarren
stark *98* unangenehm, erbarmungslos; to **be a** ~ **reminder** *132* etw jäh vor Augen führen, etw überdeutlich machen

to start, ~ **on sb** *60* jdn angreifen, jdn kritisieren; ~ **out** *49T* (zunächst) anfangen
started, don't get me ~ with … coll *183* komm mir nicht mit …
startling *114* alarmierend, erschreckend, erstaunlich
starvation *108* Verhungern
to state *27* darlegen, festlegen; *110* erklären, feststellen; *124* aussagen
statement *7* Aussage, Feststellung, Behauptung
station, ~ **radio/TV** *160* (Radio-/Fernseh-)Sender; **police** ~ *125* Polizeiwache
stationary *44* ortsansässig, fest
stationery *122* Schreibpapier, Schreibwaren
statistics *52* Statistik(en)
status *6* Status, Stellung
to stay, ~ **in touch** *118* in Verbindung bleiben; ~ **overnight** *122* übernachten; ~ **relevant to sb** *54* wichtig, von Bedeutung bleiben
steadily *62* ununterbrochen
steady *106* kontinuierlich, stabil
steel *143T* Stahl
steep *156* steil
step *11T* Schritt; to **take a** ~ **back** *134* einen Schritt zurücktreten
to step *47* treten; ~ **in** *44* hier: ins Spiel kommen; ~ **off** *62* aussteigen
to stick *182* kleben, heften, klemmen; ~ **sth on** *129* etw befestigen; ~ **to sth** *23* bei etw bleiben, sich an etw halten
still *21T* (immer) noch, dennoch
to stimulate *14* anregen, stimulieren
to stock *190* auf Lager haben
stock *105* (Lager-)Bestand, Vorrat; **in** ~ *44* vorrätig, auf Lager; **on the** ~ *199* an der Börse; to **maintain ~s** *154* den Bestand erhalten
stop *144* Station
to stop sb from doing sth *116* jdn daran hindern, etw zu tun
storage capacity *197* Lagerkapazität
store *6* Geschäft, Laden
to store *71* aufbewahren, lagern; *148* speichern
storeroom *120* Lagerraum
stork *147* Storch
story, to **cut a long** ~ **short** *60* lange Rede, kurzer Sinn
straight *50* direkt, gleich; ~ **ahead** *119* geradeaus; ~ **away** *44* sofort
straightaway *129* sofort, sogleich
strategic(ally) *156* strategisch
strategy *51* Strategie
stream *110* Strom; *156* Bach, Fließgewässer
street, to **be a two-way** ~ *84* auf Gegenseitigkeit beruhen; **high** ~ *23* Hauptgeschäftsstraße, Einkaufsstraße
strength *44* Stärke, Kraft
to strengthen *17T* kräftigen, stärken

341

A–Z word list

stressful 44 stressig
strict 197 streng
strike 72 Streik; **to go on ~** 72 streiken
to **strike** 94 treffen
striking 92 auffallend, auffällig, hervorstechend
stripe 21T Streifen
strong, ~ advice 62T dringender Rat; to **be still going ~** 114 gut dabei sein, immer noch in Form sein
strongly 208 stark
to **structure** 15 strukturieren
structure 142 Bauwerk, Konstruktion
struggle 85 Kampf
strychnine 14 Strychnin
study 14 Untersuchung, Studie; **~ leave** 134 Fortbildungsurlaub
to **study sth** 6 etw genau betrachten, sich etw genau ansehen
stuff 23 Zeug, Sache(n)
stylish 178 modisch
subconscious 182 unterbewusst
sub-heading 15 Teilrubrik, Zwischenüberschrift
subject, ~ line 32 (Brief:) Betreffzeile; to **be ~ to sth** 158 etw unterliegen
submission 46 Einsendung
to **submit (sth)** 32 (etw) einreichen, vorlegen, zusenden
subsidy 141 Subvention
substance 14 Substanz, Stoff
substantial 195 wesentlich, erheblich
substitute 160 Ersatz
subway AE 46 U-Bahn
to **succeed** 148 erfolgreich sein, Erfolg haben
such as 191 wie zum Beispiel
sudden 71 plötzlich
to **suffer from sth** 38 unter etw leiden
to **suffer sth** 14 an etw leiden, etw erleiden
suffering 158 Leiden
sufficiency 146 Hinlänglichkeit, hinreichende Menge und Qualität
sufficient 169 ausreichend, hinreichend
to **suggest** 16 vorschlagen; 19 unterstellen, suggerieren; 36 darauf hindeuten, nahelegen; 200 behaupten, andeuten
suggestion 31 Vorschlag
suicide 125 Selbstmord; **~ bomber** 125 Selbstmordattentäter/in
suit 70 Anzug
to **suit, ~ sb/sth** 23 zu jdm/etw passen; für jdn/etw passen; **~ sb** 23 (Kleidung:) jdm stehen
suitable 61 passend
sum 37 Summe
to **summarize** 15 zusammenfassen
summer hours 134 Sommerarbeitszeit
sunflower 156 Sonnenblume
sunny 51 sonnig
superhuman 164 übermenschlich
superior 78 Vorgesetzte/r
superior 165 überlegen
supplier 54 Lieferant

supplies pl 143T Vorräte, Vorkommen; **office ~** pl 120T Büromaterial
supply 158 Versorgung, Vorrat; **~ chain** 99 Lieferkette
to **supply** 67 liefern, bieten; 205 ausrüsten; **~ sb with sth** 126T jdn mit etw versorgen, jdm mit etw beliefern
to **support** 11T unterstützen; **~** 117 (Argument) untermauern, stützen
support 11 Unterstützung, Hilfe
supporter 204 Unterstützer/in
supportive 204 unterstützend
supposed, to **be ~ to do sth** 49T etw tun sollen
supposedly 185 angeblich, vermeintlich
to **surf the internet** 25 im Internet surfen
to **surface** 205 zutage treten
surface 140 Oberfläche
surgery 68T (Arzt-)Praxis; **~** 92 Operation
surname 33 Nachname
to **surprise** 201 überraschen
surprised 78 erstaunt, überrascht
surprisingly 155T erstaunlicherweise
to **surround sb/sth** 183T jdn/etw umgeben
surrounded by 182 umgeben von
surveillance 123 Überwachung
survey 12 Umfrage, Studie; **~ sheet** 178 Fragebogen
to **survive** 51 überleben
susceptible to sth 185 empfänglich für etw
suspect 124 Verdächtige/r
suspicious 129 misstrauisch
to **sustain** 146 ertragen, erleiden, aushalten; **~** 205 fortsetzen
sustainable 67 nachhaltig; **self-~** 90 selbsttragend, lebensfähig
sweater 20 Pullover
sweatshop 21T Ausbeutungsbetrieb
to **sweep away** 94 fortschwemmen, erfassen, wegreißen
sweeping views pl 157 atemberaubende Ausblicke, umwerfende Sicht
swimmer 13 Schwimmer/in
swimming pool 13 Schwimmbad
to **swipe** 209 (Finger) rüberziehen, wischen
to **switch to sth** 100 auf etw umstellen; 129 auf etw umschalten
switchboard 108 Klapptafel
to **symbolize** 88T symbolisieren
symmetrical 168 symmetrisch
sympathetic(ally) 59 einfühlsam
synonymous 184 gleichbedeutend

T

tabloid press 10 Boulevardpresse
taboo 173 Tabu
to **tackle** 134 bewältigen, in Angriff nehmen
tactic 124 Taktik
tactile sensing 169 Tastempfinden
tailback 166T Rückstau

take, sb's ~ on sth 140 jds Einschätzung von etw
to **take, ~ a call** 38T einen Anruf entgegennehmen, ans Telefon gehen; **~ a chance on sb** 110 es mit jdm versuchen, jdm eine Chance geben; **~ a message** 34 etw ausrichten, eine Nachricht notieren; **~ a seat** 71T Platz nehmen; **~ a step back** 134 einen Schritt zurücktreten; **~ a toll on sb/sth** 194 jdn/etw stark strapazieren; **~ a vote** 37 abstimmen; **~ action** 100 handeln; **~ advantage of sb** 118 jdn missbrauchen, ausnutzen; **~ control of sb/sth** 203 die Kontrolle über jdn/etw erlangen; **~ hold of sth** 134 ergreifen, sich annehmen; **~ legal action** 39 rechtliche Schritte unternehmen; **~ off** 153 (Flugzeug:) abheben, starten; 153 (Produkt:) gut anlaufen, gut ankommen; **~ out a loan** 98 einen Kredit abschließen; **~ over** 84 die Macht übernehmen; 202 (Firma:) übernehmen; **~ part in sth** 9 an etw teilnehmen ; **~ place** 8 stattfinden; **~ pride in sth** 83 auf etw Wert legen, sich mit etw Mühe geben; **~ responsibility** 78T Verantwortung übernehmen; **~ sb along** 16 jdn mitnehmen ; **~ sb in** 87 jdn aufnehmen; **~ sb on** 154 es mit jdm aufnehmen, gegen jdn antreten; **~ sb prisoner** 181 jdn gefangen nehmen; **~ seriously** 187 Ernst nehmen; **~ sth** 60 etw ertragen; **~ sth further** 32 etw (weiter) verfolgen; **~ sth into account** 22 etw in Betracht ziehen, etw berücksichtigen; **~ sth on** 154 (Aufgabe) übernehmen; **~ sth on board** 209 etw bedenken; **~ the point** 151 den Standpunkt verstehen; **~ time** 88 Zeit benötigen, dauern; **~ turns** 48 sich abwechseln; **~ up space** 153 Platz einnehmen
takeover 202 Übernahme
talent 58 Begabung, Talent
talented 8 begabt, talentiert
talk 38T Gerede; 174 Vortrag
to **talk, ~ sb through sth** 17T jdm etw der Reihe nach erklären; **~ over** 11T etw besprechen
tall 184 groß
tangible 118 fühlbar, greifbar, konkret
tap 143T Wasserhahn
tape 16 (Ton-)Band
target 93 Ziel; **~ group** 53 Zielgruppe; **~ market** 54 Zielmarkt, Kundenzielgruppe
to **target sb** 51 jdn ins Visier nehmen, auf jdn abzielen
targeted 49T gezielt, ins Visier genommen
task, office ~ 196 Büroarbeit
taste 54 Geschmack
tasty 21 schmackhaft, lecker
tax 92 Steuer
taxpayer 194 Steuerzahler/in

tea *BE 57* Zwischenmahlzeit am Nachmittag, Abendessen
to **team up with sb** *114* mit jdm zusammenarbeiten, sich mit jdm zusammentun
tear *90* Träne
technician *66* Techniker/in
technique *71* Methode, Technik
technological *67* technologisch
telescreen *131* Televisor
temperature *136* Temperatur
temporary *66* vorübergehend, befristet
tempted *175* versucht
tempting *164* verlockend
to **tend to do sth** *36* dazu neigen, etw zu tun
tension *57* Spannung
term *64 hier:* Ausmaß; *131* Begriff; **in ~s of** *118* in Bezug auf; **in the long ~** *91* langfristig; **in the short ~** *91* kurzfristig; **long-~** *202* langfristig, Langzeit-
terminal *43* im Endstadium, tödlich
to **terminate** *110* beenden
terms *pl 67* Bedingungen, Konditionen
terrace *157* Terrasse
terraced *157* terrassiert
terraced *BE 40* Reihenhaus-
terrified *80* entsetzt
territorial, to be ~ *69* sein Revier verteidigen
terrorist *123* Terrorist/in, Terror-
tertiary education *74* Hochschulausbildung
to **test** *102* erproben, testen
test, ~ drive *166T* Testfahrt; **~ track** *166T* Teststrecke
to **text** *29* eine SMS schicken, simsen
text message *42* SMS
textbook *160* Lehrbuch
textile *100* Textil-
to **thank** *11* danken
Thank goodness! *21T* Gott sei Dank!
theft *123* Diebstahl
there, ~'s little point in doing sth *30* es hat wenig Sinn, etw zu tun; **~'s no escape from the fact that** *117T* man kann nicht außer Acht lassen, dass; man muss der Tatsache ins Auge sehen, dass
therefore *69* daher, deshalb, demzufolge
these days *56* zurzeit
thick *153* dick, stark
thinker *65* Denker/in
thinking *18* Denken
third *36* Drittel
this much is certain *200* so viel ist gewiss
thorough(ly) *127* gründlich, sorgfältig
though *19* aber, dagegen, allerdings
thought *62T* Gedanke
thoughtful *46* wohlüberlegt, gut durchdacht
thousand *39* tausend, Tausend
threat *126* Bedrohung; to **be under ~** *126* bedroht werden
to **threaten** *132* bedrohen

threatening *51* bedrohlich
throughout *122* überall, in ganz …; **~ the decades** *14* durch/über die Jahrzehnte; **~ their time** *118* ihre ganze Zeit lang
to **throw** *40* werfen; **~ a party** *40* eine Party geben/schmeißen
thumb *37* Daumen
thus *190* dadurch, somit
ticket, ~ inspector *48* Fahrkartenkontrolleur/in; **~ machine** *183T* Fahrkartenautomat
tidal power *135* Gezeitenkraft
to **tidy up** *58* aufräumen
to **tie** *187* verbinden, verknüpfen; **~ a knot** *187* einen Knoten machen
tie *70* Krawatte
tight *23* knapp, eng; to **pull sth ~** *62* etw straff ziehen
time, at any ~ *39* jederzeit; **at one ~** *163* gleichzeitig; **at the same ~** *137* gleichzeitig; to **have a hard ~** *56* es schwer haben; **in good ~** *171* rechtzeitig; **in no ~** *152* im Nu; **in ~** *69* rechtzeitig; **in ~** *208* mit der Zeit; **on ~** *62T* pünktlich; **full-~** *66* Vollzeit-; **part-~** *60* Teilzeit-; to **spend ~ doing sth** *182* mit etw Zeit verbringen; to **take ~** *88* Zeit benötigen, dauern
times *92* mal
tinned *81* in Dosen, Dosen-
tiny *61* winzig
tiredness *134* Müdigkeit
tiring *116* anstrengend
To be honest, … *183T* Ehrlich gesagt, …
tobacco *191* Tabak
toddler *90* Kleinkind
toll, to take a ~ on sb/sth *194* jdn/etw stark strapazieren;
ton *139* Tonne
toned *23* straff, durchtrainiert
tool *64* Werkzeug, Instrument
top *184* höchste/r/s, oberste/r/s
top, on ~ of *83* auf
topic *88* Thema
tormentor *129* Peiniger
to **toss** *40* werfen
total *158* Gesamt-; *193* Gesamtmenge
totalitarian *131* totalitär
totally *70* voll und ganz
touch *17T* Berührung; to **get in ~ with sb** *177T* sich an jdn wenden, *hier:* anrufen; to **keep in ~** *29* in Verbindung bleiben
touching *88T* Berühren
to **tour** *7* auf Tour gehen
tour guide *196* Reiseführer/in
towards *64* gegenüber; **~ sth** *62* zu etw hin, auf etw zu
toxic *144* giftig, Gift-
to **trace** *201* verfolgen, feststellen, aufspüren
trace *144* Spur
to **track sb** *128* jds Spur verfolgen
tracker *209 hier etwa:* Überwachungsgerät

tracking device *144* Ortungsgerät
to **trade** *200* handeln
trade *44* Handel; **~ fair** *120* Handelsmesse, Fachmesse; **~ magazine** *181* Fachzeitschrift, Handelsmagazin
trader *100* Händler/in
trading *100* Handel
traditional *46* herkömmlich
traffic lights *pl 48* Ampel
tragedy *45* Tragödie
to **train** *11* trainieren; *64* sich ausbilden lassen
trainee *31* Auszubildende/r
trainers *pl 163* Turnschuhe
training *118* Schulung
traitor *80* Verräter/in
trajectory *160* Flugbahn, Weg
transaction *160* (Geschäfts-)Vorgang, Transaktion
to **transfer** *96T* (Geld) überweisen; *169* übergeben, weitergeben
to **transform** *100* (völlig) verändern; *178* umwandeln
transformation *101* (grundlegende) Veränderung, Umwandlung
to **transmit** *128* übertragen, übermitteln, senden
transparency *188* Transparenz
transportation *199* Transport
trash *49T* Müll
to **trash sth** *40* etw demolieren
travel expenses *pl 66* Reisekosten, Fahrtkosten
to **treat** *97* behandeln; *143T* (Abwasser) klären
treatment *67* Behandlung
to **tremble** *80* beben, zittern
triathlon *14* Triathlon
tribe *161* Stamm
to **trick sb into doing sth** *154* jdn (mit einer List) dazu bringen, etw zu tun
tricky *88T* kompliziert, heikel
to **trip** *16* stolpern
trouble *40* Ärger, Problem(e); **~-makers** *185* Störenfried, Unruhestifter/in
to **trouble sb** *90* jdn bekümmern, jdm Schwierigkeiten bereiten
to **trust** *38T* vertrauen
trustworthy *88T* vertrauenswürdig, zuverlässig
to **try, ~ out** *184* ausprobieren; **~ sb** *136* jdn vor Gericht stellen
try, to give sth a ~ *17T* etw ausprobieren
(the) Tube *183T* (Londoner) U-Bahn
tunnel *140* Tunnel
turbine *155* Turbine
turn *155* Runde, Umdrehung; **in ~** *137* wiederum; to **take ~s** *48* sich abwechseln
to **turn, ~ into sth** *60* zu etw werden; **~ off topic** *204* vom Thema abkommen; **~ out** *100* sich herausstellen; **~ right/left** *119* rechts/links abbiegen; **~ sb/sth into sb/sth** *46* jdn/etw zu jdm/etw machen; **~ sth on** *142* etw an-/einschalten; **~ to**

343

A–Z word list

sb *56* sich an jdn wenden; ~
up *40* auftauchen
twice *195* zweimal
twin *56* Zwilling
two-thirds *202* zwei Drittel
type *36* Schrift, Type
to **type**, ~ **(sth) in** *160* (etw) eintippen; ~ **sth up** *172* etw (am Computer) formulieren, etw ausarbeiten
typing *68T* Schreibmaschinenschreiben

U

ultimately *94* letztlich, letztendlich
umbrella *144* Regenschirm
unable *40* nicht in der Lage, unfähig
unavailable, to be ~ *34T* (Telefon:) nicht zu sprechen sein
unaware *181* in Unkenntnis, unwissend
uncertainty *168* Ungewissheit
uncomfortable *176* unangenehm, unbehaglich; to **feel** ~ *8* sich unbehaglich fühlen
uncontrolled *86T* ungeregelt, unkontrolliert
under, to go ~ *56* Pleite gehen
to **undercut** *104* unterbieten; *179* untergraben
undergarments *pl 27* Unterwäsche
undergraduate *156* Student/in (vor dem ersten akad. Grad)
underground *183* U-Bahn
to **underline** *36* unterstreichen
underlying *adj 98* eigentlich, grundlegend
undernourished *108* unterernährt
understanding *82* Verständnis
undetectable *128* nicht erkennbar, nicht nachweisbar
undeveloped *148* (Land:) unbebaut
to **undo** *191* zunichtemachen, zerstören
unemployment *86* Arbeitslosigkeit; ~ **rate** *86T* Arbeitslosenquote; to **claim** ~ **benefits** *86* Arbeitslosengeld beziehen
unethical *192* skrupellos, unrecht, unmoralisch
unexpected(ly) *111* unerwartet
unfamiliar *168* unbekannt, ungewohnt
unfit *37* nicht fit
unfortunate *88T* unglücklich
unhappy *187* unglücklich
unhealthy *17* nicht gesund
unimportant *187* unwichtig, unerheblich
uninvited *41* un(ein)geladen
union *100* Gewerkschaft
unique *23* einzigartig; to **be** ~ **to sth** *110* etw ausschließlich betreffen
united *188* vereint, verbunden
universe *164* Universum
unknown *176* unbekannt
unless *27* es sei denn, außer wenn
unlike *139* anders als
unlikely *195* unwahrscheinlich
to **unload** *144* entladen
unnecessary *57* überflüssig, unnötig
unnoticed, to go ~ *129* unbemerkt bleiben
unoccupied *170* unbesetzt
unpaid *95* unbezahlt
unpleasant *81* unangenehm, unschön
unpolluted *154* unverschmutzt
unpredictable *169* launenhaft, unkalkulierbar
to **unscrew** *178* herausschrauben, aufschrauben
unsolved *188* ungelöst
unstoppable *137* unaufhaltsam
unstructured *65* unstrukturiert
unsuccessful *187* misslungen, erfolglos
unsure *186* unsicher
to **untie** *187* aufknoten, aufschnüren
untraceable *129* nicht ausfindig zu machen
unusual *181* ungewöhnlich
to **unveil** *168* enthüllen, vorstellen
unwanted *40* unerwünscht
unwillingness *180* Widerwillen
up to *23* bis
upcoming *175* bevorstehend, anstehend
update *37* Aktualisierung
to **update** *75* aktualisieren
upfront *195* im Voraus, Voraus-
to **upload** *42* hochladen
upwards *53* steigend
urban *124* städtisch, Stadt-; ~ **garden** *146* Stadtgarten
urgently *137* dringend, nachdrücklich
usage *36* Nutzung
to **use, to be used to sth** *187* gewohnt sein an etw
use *8* Gebrauch, Nutzen, Verwendung; ~**-by date** *149* Haltbarkeitsdatum; to **make** ~ **of sth** *8* von etw Gebrauch machen, etw nutzen
usefulness *63* Nutzen, Zweckmäßigkeit
useless *111* nutzlos
usual *88T* gewöhnlich, normal
usually *64* normalerweise
utility bills *pl 151* Rechnungen für Versorgungsleistungen
utter *129* völlig, vollkommen

V

vacation *AE 49T* Urlaub
valuable *90* wertvoll
value, ~ **chain** *145* Wertschöpfungskette
to **value** *88T* werten; *90* wertschätzen, schätzen
van *129* Lieferwagen
variability *136* Schwankung, Unbeständigkeit
varied *84* vielfältig, abwechslungsreich
variety *44* Vielfalt, Auswahl; *149* (Pflanzen-)Sorte
various *57* verschieden, mehrere, allerlei
vase *166* Vase
vast *158* enorm, riesig
vastness *164* unermessliche Weite
vegetarian *121* vegetarisch
vehicle *142* Fahrzeug
vending machine *49T* (Verkaufs-)Automat; Getränkeautomat
vertical(ly) *153* senkrecht, vertikal
vessel *17* Gefäß; **blood** ~ *17* Blutgefäß
veterinarian *160* Tierarzt/-ärztin, Veterinär/in
vibrant *84* dynamisch, voller Leben
victim *23* Opfer; ~ **to sb/sth** *201* jdm/etw zum Opfer fallen
view *175* Ansicht, Bild; **point of** ~ *101* Perspektive, Blickwinkel, Standpunkt; **sweeping** ~**s** *157* atemberaubende Ausblicke, umwerfende Sicht
to **view sth** *46* (sich) etw ansehen
viewpoint *170* Standpunkt
to **violate (the law)** *199* (das Gesetz) brechen, verletzen
violence *124* Gewalt
violent *80* heftig; *84* gewalttätig
viral, ~ **marketing** *182* virales Marketing; ~ **ad** *45* Internet-Werbespot; to **go** ~ *38T* sich (im Internet) rasend schnell verbreiten
visible *27* sichtbar
visionary *51* Visionär/in
visual *52* visuell
to **visualize** *158* verbildlichen
visuals *pl 48* visuelle Hilfsmittel
vital *148* lebensnotwendig, unerlässlich
vocal, to be ~ *185* sich lautstark äußern
vocational college *31* Fachoberschule, Berufskolleg
voice, to drop one's ~ *80* die Stimme senken
voluntary *67* freiwillig
to **volunteer to do sth** *66* sich bereit erklären, etw zu tun
vomit *40* Erbrochenes
vote *210* Abstimmung; **majority** ~ *186* Mehrheitsbeschluss; to **take a** ~ *37* abstimmen
to **vote on sth** *74* über etw abstimmen
voting public *194* Wählerschaft
voucher *81* Gutschein
vulnerable to sth *202* verletzbar, gefährdet durch etw

W

wage *104* Lohn; **minimum** ~ *110* Mindestlohn
wait *144* Warten, Wartezeit
to **wait**, ~ **for one's turn** *82* warten, bis man an der Reihe ist
wake, in the ~ **of sth** *199* im Gefolge von etw
walk *93* Spaziergang, Rundgang; **from all** ~**s of life** *90* aus allen Gesell-

schaftsschichten, aus allen Lebensbereichen
to **walk along sth** *23* etw (Straße etc.) entlanggehen
walk-in medical centre *96T* Ambulanz
wall *38* Wand, Pinnwand
wallet *81* Brieftasche, (Herren-)Portemonnaie
war *86T* Krieg
warehouse *116* Lager
warfare *181* Krieg; Kriegsführung
to **warm** *137* sich erwärmen
warm-up *17T* Aufwärmen
warning, a word of ~ *68* Hinweis, Warnung
to **wash** *43* abwaschen, abwischen; **~ over sb/sth** *8* jdn überkommen, etw überschwemmen
washing *60* Wäsche, das Waschen; **~ machine** *129* Waschmaschine; **~ powder** *49* Waschpulver; **~-up** *62T* Geschirrspülen
waste *123* Müll; *176* Verschwendung; **~ of time** *24* Zeitverschwendung; **~ water** *143T* Abwasser
wasteful *134* verheerend, verschwenderisch
wasteland *104* Brachland
watch *23* Armbanduhr; **N~ on our watch.** *90* Nicht mit uns!
water heater *105* Warmwasserbereiter, Boiler
wave *84* Welle
to **wave, ~ sth** *8* etw schwenken, mit etw wedeln; **~ sth around** *80* mit etw herumfuchteln
way *88* Art und Weise; **the other ~ round** *86T* umgekehrt; **~ more** *183* weitaus; **by the ~** *60* übrigens, nebenbei erwähnt
weakness *78* Schwäche
wealth *158* Wohlstand
weapon *124* Waffe
to **wear** *177T* tragen
wearable *208* tragbar
wedding *116* Hochzeit
weed *152* Unkraut
weekday *61* Werktag, Wochentag
to **weigh (up)** *143T* abwägen
weight, to lose ~ abnehmen
weightlessness *196* Schwerelosigkeit
welcome *170* willkommen, gewollt
welcoming *80* gastfreundlich
welfare *60* Sozialfürsorge, Sozialhilfe
well *140* Bohrloch; **~ casing** *143T* Bohrlochverrohrung, Bohrlochwandung

well, ~ off *205* wohlhabend, vermögend; **~-being** *206* Wohlbefinden; **~-developed** *195* gut entwickelt; **~-known** *187* bekannt; **~-meaning** *189* wohlgemeint
westerner *126T* Mensch aus der westlichen Welt
wetland *149* Feuchtgebiet, Sumpfgebiet
what, W~ now for …? *84* Wie steht es um …? **~'s more** *56* zudem
whatever *57* was auch immer
wheat *99* Weizen
wheel *159* Rad
wheelchair *121* Rollstuhl; **~ access** *122* behindertengerechter Zugang
wheely *69* auf Rollen
when it comes to *177* was etw betrifft
whenever *22* jedes Mal, wenn; wann (auch) immer
whereas *187* während
whereby *187* wodurch
whilst *94* während
whisper *131* Flüstern
whitefly *156* Mottenschildlaus
whole, as a ~ *98* im Ganzen; **on the ~** *22* im Großen und Ganzen
whole grain *64* Vollkorn
whose *199* dessen
wide *44* groß, umfangreich; **~-ranging** *69* breit gefächert
widespread *202* weit verbreitet
willing, to be ~ to do sth *75* bereit sein, etw zu tun
wind, ~ farm *141* Windpark; **~ power** *135* Windkraft
wire *131* Draht
wireless *201* drahtlos
wise *195* klug, sinnvoll
wish *114* Wunsch
to **wish to do sth** *200* sich wünschen, etw zu tun; etw tun wollen
with, ~ regard to *88T* in Bezug auf; **~ respect to** *190* in Bezug auf; **~ that in mind** *184* vor diesem Hintergrund
to **withdraw** *129* (Geld) abheben
within *99* innerhalb, binnen; **~ walking distance** *119* in Laufweite
to **witness sth** *199* etw miterleben, Zeuge einer Sache sein
to **wonder** *81* sich fragen
wool *152* Wolle
work, ~ experience *31* Praktikum; **~ pattern** *134* Arbeitsprofil, Tätigkeit; **Department for W~ and**

Pensions *60* brit. Arbeits- und Sozialministerium; **to put in ~** *95* Arbeit leisten
to **work, ~ hard** *68* hart arbeiten, fleißig sein; **~ sth out** *116* etw herausfinden; *151* etw ausrechnen
worker, co-~ *100* Kollege/Kollegin; **construction ~** *65* Bauarbeiter/in; **office ~** *98* Büroangestellte/r; **social ~** *65* Sozialarbeiter/in
workforce *69* Belegschaft; *195* berufstätige Bevölkerung
working, ~ conditions *pl 65* Arbeitsbedingungen; **~ hours** *pl 65* Arbeitszeiten; **~ life** *140* Betriebsdauer
workload *134* Arbeitspensum
workout *16* (Fitness-)Training
workplace *69* Arbeitsplatz
world, ~ event *108* Weltgeschehen; **~ map** *193* Weltkarte
worldwide *16* weltweit
worried *17T* besorgt, beunruhigt
worries *pl 143* Bedenken
worrying *137* besorgniserregend
worse, to be ~ off *94* schlechter dran sein; **to go from bad to ~** *62* immer schlimmer werden
worth *202* wert; **for what it's ~** *23* meiner (bescheidenen) Meinung nach
worthless (to sb) *145* wertlos (für jdn)
worthwhile *177T* wertvoll
worthy of sth *161* einer Sache würdig
wraparound skirt *156* Wickelrock
to **wreck** *40* demolieren
wrist *168* Handgelenk
writer *31* Verfasser/in; *53* Autor/in, Schriftsteller/in; **~'s address** *76* Absenderanschrift
written *28* schriftlich

Y

year, by the ~ 2020 *197* bis zum Jahr 2020; **in ten ~'s time** *196* in zehn Jahren; **New Y~** *79* Neujahr
yearly *68* jährlich, Jahres-
to **yield** *195* einbringen, ergeben
you guys *21T* ihr
Yours sincerely *31* *(Brief:)* Mit freundlichen Grüßen
yourself, DIY (do-it-yourself) *66* Heimwerker-, Heimwerken
youth *62* Jugend
Yuck! *23* Igitt! Bäh!

Geographical names

Abingdon ['æbɪŋdən]	Abingdon (Stadt an der Themse in Oxfordshire)	(the) Far East [ˌfɑːr 'iːst]	der Ferne Osten
Accra ['ækrə]	Accra (Hauptstadt von Ghana)	Finland ['fɪnlənd]	Finnland
		Florida ['flɒrɪdə]	Florida
Africa ['æfrɪkə]	Afrika	France [frɑːns]	Frankreich
African ['æfrɪkən]	afrikanisch, Afrikaner/in	Germany ['dʒɜːməni]	Deutschland
America [ə'merɪkə]	Amerika	Ghana ['gɑːnə]	Ghana
American [ə'merɪkən]	amerikanisch, Amerikaner/in	Ghanaian [gɑː'neɪən]	ghanaisch, Ghanaer/in
Amsterdam ['æmstədæm]	Amsterdam	Glasgow ['glɑːsgəʊ]	Glasgow
Anglo-Irish [ˌæŋgləʊ 'aɪrɪʃ]	anglo-irisch	Goa ['gəʊə]	Goa
Antarctic [ænt'ɑːktɪk]	Antarktis, antarktisch	Great Barrier Reef [ˌgreɪt 'bæriə riːf]	Großes Barriereriff
Arab ['ærəb]	arabisch, Araber/in	Greece [griːs]	Griechenland
Arctic ['ɑːktɪk]	Arktis, arktisch	Greek [griːk]	Grieche/Griechin, griechisch
Asia ['eɪʃə]	Asien	Greenland ['griːnlənd]	Grönland
Asian ['eɪʃn]	asiatisch, Asiate/-in	Guinea ['gɪni]	Guinea
Australia [ɒ'streɪliə]	Australien	Haiti ['heɪti]	Haiti
Australian [ɒ'streɪliən]	australisch, Australier/in	Hawaii [hə'waɪi]	Hawaii
Austria ['ɒstriə]	Österreich	Heathrow [ˌhiːθ'rəʊ]	Heathrow (Flughafen westlich von London)
Austrian ['ɒstriən]	österreichisch, Österreicher/in	Highgate ['haɪgeɪt]	Highgate (Stadtteil im Norden Londons)
Bangladesh [ˌbæŋglə'deʃ]	Bangladesch	Honolulu [ˌhɒnə'luːluː]	Honolulu (Hauptstadt von Hawaii)
Bangladeshi [ˌbæŋglə'deʃi]	bangladeschisch, Bangladescher/in		
Bath [bɑːθ]	Bath (Stadt in Somerset)	Hungary ['hʌŋgəri]	Ungarn
Belgian ['beldʒən]	belgisch, Belgier/in	Iceland ['aɪslənd]	Island
Belgium ['beldʒəm]	Belgien	India ['ɪndiə]	Indien
Benin [be'niːn]	Benin	Indian ['ɪndiən]	indisch, Inder/in
Birmingham ['bɜːmɪŋəm]	Birmingham	Indian Ocean [ˌɪndiən 'əʊʃn]	Indischer Ozean
Black Forest [ˌblæk 'fɒrɪst]	Schwarzwald	Indonesia [ˌɪndəʊ'niːziə]	Indonesien
Bosnia ['bɒzniə]	Bosnien	Iran [ɪ'rɑːn]	Iran
Brazil [brə'zɪl]	Brasilien	Iranian [ɪ'reɪniən]	iranisch, Iraner/in
Brazilian [brə'zɪliən]	brasilianisch, Brasilianer/in	Iraq [ɪ'rɑːk]	Irak
Bristol ['brɪstl]	Bristol (Stadt in Südwestengland)	Ireland ['aɪələnd]	Irland
		Irish ['aɪrɪʃ]	irisch, Ire/Irin
Britain ['brɪtn]	Großbritannien	Italy ['ɪtəli]	Italien
Briton ['brɪtn]	Brite/Britin	Jamaica [dʒə'meɪkə]	Jamaika
Brittany ['brɪtəni]	Bretagne	Jamaican [dʒə'meɪkən]	jamaikanisch, Jamaikaner/in
Brixton ['brɪkstən]	Brixton (Stadtteil im Süden Londons)		
		Kenya ['kenjə]	Kenia
Brussels ['brʌslz]	Brüssel	Kenyan ['kenjən]	kenianisch, Kenianer/in
Burkina Faso [bəˌkiːnə 'fæsəʊ]	Burkina Faso	Kilimanjaro [ˌkɪlɪmən'dʒɑːrəʊ]	Kilimandscharo
California [ˌkælə'fɔːniə]	Kalifornien		
Canada ['kænədə]	Kanada	Korea [kə'rɪə]	Korea
Central America [ˌsentrəl ə'merɪkə]	Mittelamerika	Korean [kə'rɪən]	koreanisch, Koreaner/in
		Kosovo ['kɒsəvəʊ]	Kosovo
Chicago [ʃɪ'kɑːgəʊ]	Chicago	Kosovian [kə'səʊviən]	kosovarisch, Kosovare/-in
China ['tʃaɪnə]	China	Latin America [ˌlætɪn ə'merɪkə]	Lateinamerika
Chinese [tʃaɪ'niːz]	chinesisch, Chinese/-in		
Cologne [kə'ləʊn]	Köln	Latin American [ˌlætɪn ə'merɪkən]	lateinamerikanisch, Lateinamerikaner/in
Colombo [kə'lɒmbəʊ]	Colombo (Hauptstadt von Sri Lanka)		
		London ['lʌndən]	London
Columbia [kə'lʌmbiə]	Kolumbien	Malawi [mə'lɑːwi]	Malawi
Dallas ['dæləs]	Dallas	Mali ['mɑːli]	Mali
Danish ['deɪnɪʃ]	dänisch, Däne/-in	Manchester ['mæntʃɪstə]	Manchester
Denmark ['denmɑːk]	Dänemark	Massachusetts [ˌmæsə'tʃuːsɪts]	Massachusetts
Dublin ['dʌblɪn]	Dublin		
East Ham [ˌiːst 'hæm]	East Ham (Stadtteil im Osten Londons)	Miami [maɪ'æmi]	Miami
		Milan [mɪ'læn]	Mailand
Edinburgh ['edɪnbərə]	Edinburgh	(the) Netherlands ['neðələndz]	die Niederlande
Egypt ['iːdʒɪpt]	Ägypten		
England ['ɪŋglənd]	England	New York [ˌnjuː 'jɔːk]	New York
Eritrea [ˌerɪ'trɪə]	Eritrea	Niger ['naɪdʒə]	Niger
Eritrean [ˌerɪ'trɪən]	eritreisch, Eritreer/in	North America [ˌnɔːθ ə'merɪkə]	Nordamerika
Ethiopia [ˌiːθi'əʊpiə]	Äthiopien		
Ethiopian [ˌiːθi'əʊpiən]	äthiopisch, Äthiopier/in	North Sea [ˌnɔːθ 'siː]	Nordsee
Europe ['jʊərəp]	Europa	Northern Ireland [ˌnɔːðən 'aɪələnd]	Nordirland
		Oxford ['ɒksfəd]	Oxford

Oxford Circus [ˌɒksfəd ˈsɜːkəs]	Oxford Circus *(Platz und U-Bahn-Station in der Londoner Innenstadt)*	**Sri Lanka** [ˌsriː ˈlæŋkə]	Sri Lanka
Pacific Ocean [pəˌsɪfɪk ˈəʊʃn]	Pazifischer Ozean	**Staffordshire** [ˈstæfədʃə]	Staffordshire *(Grafschaft in Mittelengland)*
Pakistan [ˌpækɪˈstɑːn]	Pakistan	**Staines** [ˈsteɪnz]	Staines *(Stadt in Surrey)*
Pakistani [ˌpækɪˈstɑːni]	pakistanisch, Pakistaner/in	**sub-Saharan Africa** [sʌb səˌhɑːrən ˈæfrɪkə]	Schwarzafrika
Panama [ˈpænəmɑː]	Panama	**Sudan** [suˈdɑːn]	Sudan
(the) Philippines [ˈfɪləpiːnz]	die Philippinen	**Sudanese** [ˌsuːdəˈniːz]	sudanesisch, Sudanese/-in
Pittsburgh [ˈpɪtsbɜːg]	Pittsburgh *(Stadt in Pennsylvania)*	**Sweden** [ˈswiːdn]	Schweden
		Swede [swiːd]	Schwede/-in
Poland [ˈpəʊlənd]	Polen	**Swedish** [ˈswiːdɪʃ]	schwedisch, Schwede/-in
Polish [ˈpəʊlɪʃ]	polnisch, Pole/Polin	**Switzerland** [ˈswɪtsələnd]	Schweiz
Portugal [ˈpɔːtʃʊgl]	Portugal	**Swiss** [swɪs]	schweizerisch, Schweizer/in
Portuguese [ˌpɔːtʃuˈgiːz]	portugiesisch, Portugiese/-in	**Sydney** [ˈsɪdni]	Sydney
		Syria [ˈsɪriə]	Syrien
Red Sea [ˌred ˈsiː]	Rotes Meer	**Tanzania** [ˌtænzəˈniːə]	Tansania
River Clyde [ˌrɪvə ˈklaɪd]	der Clyde *(Fluss in Schottland)*	**Texas** [ˈteksəs]	Texas
		Tokyo [ˈtəʊkiəʊ]	Tokio
River Thames [ˌrɪvə ˈtemz]	die Themse	**Turkey** [ˈtɜːki]	Türkei
Romania [ruːˈmeɪniə]	Rumänien	**Turkish** [ˈtɜːkɪʃ]	türkisch, Türke/-in
Romanian [ruːˈmeɪniən]	rumänisch, Rumäne/-in	**Uganda** [juˈgændə]	Uganda
Russia [ˈrʌʃə]	Russland	**Ugandan** [juˈgændən]	ugandisch, Ugander/in
Russian [ˈrʌʃn]	russisch, Russe/Russin	**United Kingdom (UK)** [juˌnaɪtɪd ˈkɪŋdəm]	Vereinigtes Königreich
Scotland [ˈskɒtlənd]	Schottland		
Scot [skɒt]	Schotte/-in	**United States (USA)** [juˌnaɪtɪd ˈsteɪts]	Vereinigte Staaten
Scottish [ˈskɒtɪʃ]	schottisch, Schotte/-in	**Vancouver** [vænˈkuːvə]	Vancouver
Shanghai [ˌʃæŋˈhaɪ]	Schanghai	**Wales** [weɪlz]	Wales
Singapore [ˌsɪŋəˈpɔː]	Singapur	**Welsh** [welʃ]	walisisch, Waliser/in
South Africa [ˌsaʊθ ˈæfrɪkə]	Südafrika	**Warsaw** [ˈwɔːsɔː]	Warschau
South America [ˌsaʊθ əˈmerɪkə]	Südamerika	**Wembley** [ˈwembli]	Wembley *(Stadtteil im Nordwesten Londons)*
South Carolina [ˌsaʊθ ˌkærəˈlaɪnə]	South Carolina	**Wimbledon** [ˈwɪmbldən]	Wimbledon *(Stadtteil im Süden Londons)*
South Pole [ˌsaʊθ ˈpəʊl]	Südpol	**Winchester** [ˈwɪntʃɪstə]	Winchester *(Stadt im Süden Englands)*
Spain [speɪn]	Spanien		
Spanish [ˈspænɪʃ]	spanisch, Spanier/in	**Zambia** [ˈsæmbiə]	Sambia

Irregular verbs

be	was/were	been	sein
beat	beat	beaten	schlagen, besiegen
become	became	become	werden
begin	began	begun	anfangen, beginnen
bend	bent	bent	(sich) beugen
blow	blew	blown	wehen, blasen, ziehen
break	broke	broken	brechen
breed	bred	bred	sich vermehren, sich ausbreiten
bring	brought	brought	(mit)bringen
build	built	built	bauen
burn	burnt/burned	burnt/burned	(ver)brennen
buy	bought	bought	kaufen
catch	caught	caught	fangen, fassen, erreichen
choose	chose	chosen	(aus)wählen
come	came	come	kommen
cost	cost	cost	kosten
cut	cut	cut	schneiden
deal (with)	dealt (with)	dealt (with)	sich kümmern um, umgehen mit
dig	dug	dug	graben
do	did	done	tun, machen
draw	drew	drawn	zeichnen
dream	dreamt/dreamed	dreamt/dreamed	träumen
drink	drank	drunk	trinken
drive	drove	driven	fahren
eat	ate	eaten	essen
fall	fell	fallen	fallen
feed	fed	fed	füttern, ernähren
feel	felt	felt	(sich) fühlen, empfinden
fight	fought	fought	kämpfen
find	found	found	finden
fit	fit/fitted	fit/fitted	passen, anbringen, entsprechen
fly	flew	flown	fliegen
forbid	forbade	forbidden	verbieten
forget	forgot	forgotten	vergessen
get	got	got (*AE* gotten)	bekommen
give	gave	given	geben
go	went	gone	gehen, fahren
grow	grew	grown	wachsen
hang	hung	hung	hängen
have	had	had	haben
hear	heard	heard	hören
hide	hid	hidden	(sich) verstecken
hit	hit	hit	schlagen
hold	held	held	halten, festhalten
hurt	hurt	hurt	verletzen
keep	kept	kept	behalten
know	knew	known	kennen, wissen
lay	laid	laid	legen
lead	led	led	führen
lean	leant/leaned	leant/leaned	sich lehnen, sich beugen
learn	learnt/learned	learnt/learned	lernen
leave	left	left	abfahren, verlassen, weggehen
let	let	let	lassen
lie	lay	lain	liegen
light	lit	lit	anzünden, beleuchten
lose	lost	lost	verlieren
make	made	made	machen
mean	meant	meant	meinen, bedeuten
meet	met	met	treffen
pay	paid	paid	bezahlen
put	put	put	setzen, stellen, legen
quit	quit/quitted	quit/quitted	verlassen, aufhören
read	read	read	lesen
ride	rode	ridden	reiten, fahren
ring	rang	rung	anrufen, läuten
rise	rose	risen	(an)steigen
run	ran	run	laufen, rennen
say	said	said	sagen
see	saw	seen	sehen
seek	sought	sought	suchen
sell	sold	sold	verkaufen
send	sent	sent	senden, schicken
set	set	set	setzen, stellen
shake	shook	shaken	schütteln
shine	shone	shone	scheinen, glänzen
show	showed	shown	zeigen
shrink	shrank	shrunk	schrumpfen, zurückgehen
shut	shut	shut	schließen
sing	sang	sung	singen
sink	sank	sunk	sinken
sit	sat	sat	sitzen
sleep	slept	slept	schlafen
slide	slid	slid	(ab)rutschen, (ab)sacken
smell	smelt/smelled	smelt/smelled	riechen
speak	spoke	spoken	sprechen
spell	spelt/spelled	spelt/spelled	buchstabieren
spend	spent	spent	ausgeben, verbringen
spread	spread	spread	(sich) verbreiten
stand	stood	stood	stehen
steal	stole	stolen	stehlen
swim	swam	swum	schwimmen
take	took	taken	nehmen
teach	taught	taught	unterrichten, beibringen
tell	told	told	sagen, erzählen
think	thought	thought	denken
throw	threw	thrown	werfen
understand	understood	understood	verstehen
wake	woke	woken	aufwachen, -wecken
wear	wore	worn	tragen
win	won	won	gewinnen
write	wrote	written	schreiben

Quellenverzeichnis

Bildrechte

S. 6/1: Fotolia / Brian Jackson; **S. 6/2:** Fotolia / corepics; **S. 6/3:** Shutterstock / Augustino; **S. 6/4:** Shutterstock / conrado; **S. 6/5:** Shutterstock / Intrepix; **S. 6/6:** Fotolia / Korta; **S. 8:** Shutterstock / Featureflash; **S. 10/1:** Shutterstock / racorn; **S. 10/2:** Shutterstock / racorn; **S. 12/1:** Shutterstock / Monkey Business Images; **S. 12/2:** Shutterstock / Carme Balcells; **S. 12/3:** Shutterstock / Andresr; **S. 12/4:** Shutterstock / Monkey Business Images; **S. 12/5:** Shutterstock / wavebreakmedia; **S. 14:** FOTOFINDER / © PhotoAlto; **S. 18/1:** Shutterstock / Luciano Mortula; **S. 18/2:** Shutterstock / mikecphoto; **S. 21:** Shutterstock / Monkey Business Images; **S. 22:** Shutterstock / Monkey Business Images; **S. 23:** Shutterstock / Monkey Business Images; **S. 24:** Shutterstock / Monkey Business Images; **S. 25/1:** Shutterstock / Shane Gross; **S. 25/2:** Shutterstock / anthonymooney; **S. 25/3:** Shutterstock / auremar; **S. 25/4:** Shutterstock / M.Stasy; **S. 25/5:** Shutterstock / merzzie; **S. 25/6:** Shutterstock / Rommel Canlas; **S. 25/7:** Shutterstock / Syda Productions; **S. 26:** Cartoonstock / Marty Bucella; **S. 27:** Glow Images / Blend Images LLC; **S. 29:** Shutterstock / Blend Images LLC; **S. 30:** Isobel Williams, Berlin; **S. 31:** Shutterstock / Minerva Studio; **S. 34:** Shutterstock / Minerva Studio; **S. 35/1:** Shutterstock / Syda Productions; **S. 35/2:** Shutterstock / Robert Kneschke; **S. 35/3:** Shutterstock / Leigh J; **S. 35/4:** Shutterstock / gpointstudio; **S. 35/5:** Shutterstock / Antonio Guillem; **S. 35/6:** Shutterstock / RossHelen; **S. 35/7:** Shutterstock / Monkey Business Images; **S. 36:** Shutterstock / Photographee.eu; **S. 38/1:** Shutterstock / Photographee.eu; **S. 38/2:** Shutterstock / Agenturfotografin; **S. 40:** Shutterstock / Catherine Murray; **S. 43:** action press / SWNSaction press; **S. 44/1:** Fotolia / Dejan Jovanovic; **S. 44/2:** Statista 2015 / Apparel Magazine, PwC; **S. 45/1:** Shutterstock / Evgeny Atamanenko; **S. 45/2:** Shutterstock / Syda Productions; **S. 45/3:** Shutterstock / Thinglass; **S. 45/4:** Shutterstock / rangizzz; **S. 45/5:** Shutterstock / michaeljung; **S. 45/6:** Shutterstock / Valentina Razumova; **S. 45/7:** Fotolia / Dirima; **S. 45/8:** Fotolia / Photocreo Bednarek; **S. 45/9:** Electrolux Hausgeräte GmbH; **S. 46:** VW 2009 – DDB Stockholm; **S. 47:** VW 2009 – DDB Stockholm; **S. 51:** Mauritius Images / Alamy; **S. 54:** Fotolia / majivecka; **S. 55/1:** Shutterstock / Goodluz; **S. 55/2:** Shutterstock / Rawpixel; **S. 55/3:** Shutterstock / qvist; **S. 55/4:** Shutterstock / mato; **S. 55/5:** Shutterstock / AntonioDiaz; **S. 55/6:** Shutterstock / Goodluz; **S. 55/7:** Shutterstock / wavebreakmedia; **S. 55/8:** Shutterstock / Mark Skalny; **S. 56/1:** Shutterstock / Alena Ozerova; **S. 56/2:** Fotolia / Monkey Business; **S. 57:** glow images / Stockbroker; **S. 60:** Cornelsen / Oxford Designers & Illustrators; **S. 63/1:** Cornelsen / Oxford Designers & Illustrators; **S. 63/2:** Shutterstock / wavebreakmedia; **S. 64/1:** Shutterstock / Monkey Business Images; **S. 64/2:** Shutterstock / wavebreakmedia; **S. 65:** Cornelsen / Oxford Designers & Illustrators; **S. 67/1:** Shutterstock / Adam Gregor; **S. 67/2:** Shutterstock / racorn; **S. 67/3:** glow images / GammaA; **S. 67/4:** glow images / Fancy; **S. 69:** Shutterstock / Maslowski Marcin; **S. 70:** Shutterstock / Gemenacom; **S. 74/2:** Cartonstock / Mark Lynch; **S. 74:** Statista 2016 / Goldman Sachs, World econmic Forum, United Nations; **S. 75:** Shutterstock / Minerva Studio; **S. 79/1:** Mauritius Images / Alamy; **S. 79/2:** Fotolia / Val Thoermer; **S. 79/3:** Shutterstock / Olivier Juneau; **S. 79/4:** Photoshot / Xinhua; **S. 80/1:** Cornelsen / Oxford Designers & Illustrators; **S. 81:** Cornelsen / Oxford Designers & Illustrators; **S. 84/1:** Shutterstock / Daniel M Ernst; **S. 84/2:** Shutterstock / GSPhotography; **S. 84/3:** Shutterstock / dotshock; **S. 84/4:** Shutterstock / Nadino; **S. 86/1:** Shutterstock / Daniel M Ernst; **S. 86/2:** Shutterstock / GSPhotography; **S. 88:** Shutterstock / Lik Studio; **S. 89/1:** Shutterstock / Monkey Business Images; **S. 89/2:** Shutterstock / Panaspics; **S. 89/3:** Shutterstock / Monkey Business Images; **S. 89/4:** Shutterstock / wrangler; **S. 89/5:** glow images / Ariel Skelley/Blend Images LLC; **S. 89/6:** Shutterstock / Leremy; **S. 90/1:** Shutterstock / Leremy; **S. 90/2:** Shutterstock / Sylvie Bouchard; **S. 90/3:** Shutterstock / karelnoppe; **S. 90/4:** Shutterstock / Goodluz; **S. 90/5:** Shutterstock / bikeriderlondon; **S. 92/1:** Shutterstock / spotmatik; **S. 92/2:** Shutterstock / scigelova; **S. 92/3:** Shutterstock / Levent Konuk; **S. 92/4:** Shutterstock / bikeriderlondon; **S. 94/1:** Bulls Press / Barcroft Media; **S. 94/2:** Bulls Press / Barcroft Media; **S. 96:** Shutterstock / Andresr; **S. 98:** Shutterstock / wavebreakmedia; **S. 99:** Cornelsen / Oxford Designers & Illustrators; **S. 100/1:** Shutterstock / Sylvie Bouchard; **S. 100/2:** Shutterstock / mortalpious; **S. 100/3:** Shutterstock / Darryl Brooks; **S. 100/4:** Shutterstock / Stuart Jenner; **S. 102/1:** akg-images / akg-images; **S. 102/2:** Visum / ANDIA / VISUM; **S. 103:** Cartoonstock / Hajo de Reijger; **S. 109/1:** action press / Patrik Österberg / AOP Sweden; **S. 109/2:** Cornelsen / Oxford Designers &

Quellenverzeichnis

Illustrators; **S. 109/3:** Cornelsen / Oxford Designers & Illustrators; **S. 109/4:** Cornelsen / Oxford Designers & Illustrators; **S. 110:** Mauritius Images / Alamy; **S. 114/1:** Fotolia / Hunor Kristo; **S. 114/2:** Fotolia / Ermolaev Alexandr; **S. 117:** Shutterstock / Martina Ebel; **S. 119:** Shutterstock / Minerva Studio; **S. 123/1:** Shutterstock / arindambanerjee; **S. 123/2:** Shutterstock / Jonathan Nafzger; **S. 123/3:** Shutterstock / eldeiv; **S. 123/4:** Shutterstock / Pablo Hidalgo - Fotos593; **S. 123/5:** Shutterstock / alexmillos; **S. 123/6:** Shutterstock / withGod; **S. 123/7:** Shutterstock / Phatic-Photography; **S. 123/8:** Fotolia / Ingo Bartussek; **S. 124:** Shutterstock / fmua; **S. 126/1:** Shutterstock / Daniel M Ernst; **S. 126/2:** Shutterstock / Charlotte Purdy; **S. 126/3:** Shutterstock / racorn; **S. 126/4:** Shutterstock / Kinga; **S. 128:** Fotolia / beugdesign; **S. 131:** Photoshot / UPPA/Photoshot; **S. 132:** Shutterstock / Vasin Lee; **S. 133/1:** Shutterstock / Dubova; **S. 133/2:** Shutterstock / Dubova; **S. 134:** Statista / Gallup; **S. 135:** Cornelsen / Oxford Designers & Illustrators; **S. 138:** Topic Media; **S. 140:** Cornelsen / Oxford Designers & Illustrators; **S. 143:** Cornelsen / Oxford Designers & Illustrators; **S. 144:** Mauritius Images / Alamy; **S. 146/1:** Fotolia / doidam10; **S. 146/2:** Fotolia / alisonhancock; **S. 147/1:** Pars International / @ Clay Bennett / The Christian Science Monitor; **S. 147/2:** Cagle Cartoons / Dario Castillejos; **S. 147/3:** Cornelsen / Oxford Designers & Illustrators; **S. 148:** Cornelsen / Oxford Designers & Illustrators; **S. 151:** Shutterstock / StockCube; **S. 153:** Cornelsen / Oxford Designers & Illustrators; **S. 155/1:** action press / KYODO NEWS; **S. 155/2:** Reuters / Edgar Su; **S. 156:** Mauritius Images / Alamy; **S. 158/1:** F1 online; **S. 158/2:** Laif / Anthony Asael/Hemis.fr; **S. 159/1:** Shutterstock / beboy; **S. 159/2:** Shutterstock / Dimedrol68; **S. 159/3:** Shutterstock / Dja65; **S. 159/4:** Fotolia / areeya_ann; **S. 159/5:** Shutterstock / Somchai Som; **S. 159/6:** Shutterstock / kavione; **S. 159/7:** Shutterstock / Denis Dryashkin; **S. 159/8:** Shutterstock / catolla; **S. 159/9:** Shutterstock / Nikonaft; **S. 159/10:** Shutterstock / Mike Flippo; **S. 159/11:** Shutterstock / pzAxe; **S. 159/12:** Shutterstock / Anna Hoychuk; **S. 161:** Mauritius Images / Alamy; **S. 164:** Shutterstock / Mopic; **S. 166:** Shutterstock / Krivosheev Vitaly; **S. 168:** University of Birmingham; **S. 170:** Shutterstock / chombosan; **S. 171:** Shutterstock / Minerva Studio; **S. 175/2:** Fotolia / Maksym Yemelyanov; **S. 175/1:** Fotolia / customdesigner; **S. 177:** cartoonstock / Marty Bucella; **S. 176:** Fotolia / Feng Yu; **S. 179/1:** Fotolia / Giuseppe Porzani; **S. 179/2:** Shutterstock / wk1003mike; **S. 179/3:** Fotolia / Petra Nowack; **S. 181/1:** Mauritius images / David Colbran / Alamy; **S. 181/2:** picture-alliance / dpa; **S. 181/3:** Mauritius images / Thomas Lehne/ lotuseaters / Alamy; **S. 181/4:** picture-alliance / Wolfram Steinberg/dpa; **S. 183:** Mauritius images / Michael Kemp / Alamy; **S. 184:** Cartoonstock / Jim Sizemore; **S. 186:** Shutterstock / ASDF_MEDIA; **S. 186:** Shutterstock / Rawpixel.com; **S. 186:** Shutterstock / Diego Cervo; **S. 187:** Shutterstock / ESB Essentials; **S. 188:** Fotolia / Africa Studio; **S. 189:** Fotolia / ajr_images; **S. 190/1:** Cartoonstock / Piero Tonin; **S. 190/2:** Fotolia / CandyBox Images; **S. 191:** Fotolia / onblast; **S. 192/1:** Fotolia / tulpahn; **S. 192/2:** Fotolia / tulpahn; **S. 192/3:** Fotolia / tulpahn; **S. 194:** Fotolia / aalutcenko; **S. 195:** Shutterstock / hanohiki; **S. 196/1:** Fotolia / cosmicvue; **S. 196/2:** Shutterstock / Willyam Bradberry; **S. 198:** Shutterstock / Andrey_Popov; **S. 199/1:** Shutterstock / zimmytws; **S. 199/2:** Shutterstock / TZIDO SUN; **S. 200:** Shutterstock / Keith Bell; **S. 201:** Statista 2017 / Bitkom; **S. 202:** Shutterstock / Everett Historical; **S. 203:** Fotolia / SolisImages; **S. 205:** Fotolia / alisonhancock; **S. 206:** Fotolia / lozt; **S. 207/1:** Fotolia / Pavlo Kucherov; **S. 207/2:** Fotolia / photocrew; **S. 207/3:** Fotolia / fotomaster; **S. 207/4:** Fotolia / stockphoto mania; **S. 207/5:** Fotolia / ExQuisine; **S. 207/6:** Fotolia / creativenature.nl; **S. 207/7:** Fotolia / Natika; **S. 207/8:** Shutterstock / Coprid; **S. 207/9:** Fotolia / mates; **S. 207/10:** Fotolia / Natika; **S. 208/1:** Cartoonstock / Andrew Toos; **S. 208/2:** Cartoonstock / Jon Carter; **S. 208/3:** Cartoonstock / Tim Cordell; **S. 208/4:** Fotolia / Artur Marciniec; **S. 210:** Fotolia / WavebreakmediaMicro; **S. 212:** Cornelsen / Oxford Designers & Illustrators; **S. 213:** Cornelsen / Oxford Designers & Illustrators; **S. 215:** Shutterstock / Radu Razvan; **S. 222:** Shutterstock / michaeljung; **S. 226:** Shutterstock / bikeriderlondon; **S. 230:** Fotolia / govicinity; **S. 236:** Shutterstock / Tish1; **S. 237:** Cartoonstock / S. Haris

Textrechte
S. 27: Daily Mail Reporter, 11.05.2012; **S. 36/37:** The Independent / Pat Hurst, 10.04.2013; **S. 40:** Daily Mail / Mark Duell, 03.10.2013; **S. 43:** BBC / Sian Lloyd, 14.05.2014; **S. 46:** Los Angeles Times / Kelsey Ramos, 15.10.2009; **S. 69:** The Telegraph / Violet Johnstone, 10.10.2002; **S. 80/81:** Bloomsbury Publishing, Refugee Boy by Benjamin Zephaniah, 28.08.2001; **S. 90:** BBC / Emily Buchanan, 10.06.2011; **S. 90:** MicroLoan Foundation UK / Paul Abbott, September 2014; **S. 90:** Samaritans Volunteering Department / Elizabeth Scowcroft; September 2014; **S. 90:** The Salvation Army UK, September 2014; **S. 94:** Gandys London / Orphans for Orphans, http://www.gandyslondon.com/orphans-for-orphans; **S. 98:** The Independent / Matthew Glynn, 22.08.2015; **S. 110:** The Sydney Morning Herald / Georgia Leaker, 09.07.2013; **S. 124:** @ Jonathan R. White / Huffington Post, 21.04.2013; **S. 131:** Penguin Books London, Nineteen Eighty-Four by George Orwell, 1949; **S. 132:** The Telegraph / David Barrett, 10.07.2013; **S. 134:** The Guardian / Howard Awbery, 06.01.2015; **S. 156/157:** National Geographic / Tim Folger, Oktober 2014; **S. 160/161:** Spiegel Online / Jan Puhl, 05.12.2013; **S. 168/169:** BBC / Michael Eyre, 11.09.2014; **S. 170:** The Guardian / Claire Burke, 15.09.2016; **S. 195:** The Business Insider / Lianna Brinded, 18.05.2016; **S. 199:** Spiegel Online international / Thomas Schulz, 04.03.2015; **S. 210:** SZ Online/ Susanne Klein, 17.11.2016; **S. 215:** The Independent / James Delay, 07.08.2008; S. 241 Daily Mail Online / Steve Doughty, 06.02.2014

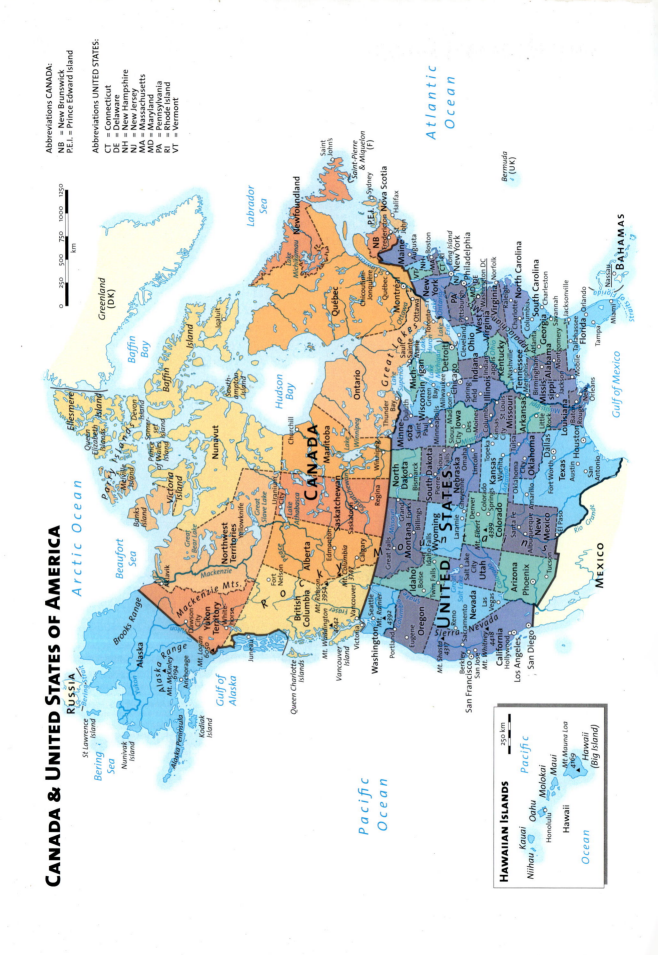